C000268728

THE SUTTON COMPANION TO

CATHEDRALS & ABBEYS

STEPHEN FRIAR

SUTTON PUBLISHING

This book was first published in 2007 by
Sutton Publishing Limited· Phoenix Mill
Thrupp · Stroud · Gloucestershire · GL5 2BU

British Library Cataloguing in Publication Data
A catalogue record for this book is available from the British Library.

ISBN 978-0-7509-3890-0

Title-page illustration: The ruins of Whitby Abbey.

'It is good to be here. Here man more purely lives, less oft doth fall, more promptly rises, walks with stricter heed, more safely rests, dies happier, is freed earlier from cleansing fires, and gains withall a brighter crown.'

St Bernard

Plaque on the north cloister wall, Hailes Abbey, Gloucestershire.

Typeset in 9/13.5pt Photina MT.
Typesetting and origination by
Sutton Publishing Limited.
Printed and bound in England.

Contents

ACKNOWLEDGEMENTS

The author acknowledges with gratitude the invaluable assistance of the following people in the preparation of this book: John Crook, Jane Entrican, Kate Friar, Clare Jackson, Judith Oppenheimer, Nick Reynolds and Catherine Watson.

The author and publisher would like to thank the following for their permission to reproduce illustrations: Mick Aston, Batsford Ltd, Birmingham Picture Library, James Bond, The British Library, CADW, John Crook, Derry Brabbs, English Heritage, John Ferguson, Forde Abbey, Tom Friar, Getty Images, Hereford Cathedral, Andrew Jamieson, Judges Postcards Ltd, Anthony Kersting, Mary Evans Picture Library, John Mennell, Monumental Brass Society, Roy Morgan, Florence Morris, National Monuments Record, Society of Antiquaries, Richard Sale, Geoffrey Wheeler and Anthony Wood.

Unless otherwise stated, all pictures are from the author's collection.

The *Companion to Cathedrals and Abbeys* is for Kate, without whose encouragement and forebearance it would not have been written.

Introduction

During the writing of this book I have often been asked which is my favourite abbey or cathedral. There is no simple answer: subjective recollection is more potent than objective analysis. First, there are those cathedrals that, when seen from a distance for the first time, have left a lasting impression: Lincoln, high on its limestone ridge, its triple towers visible for miles across the surrounding levels; Gloucester's graceful white tower commanding the Severn Vale like a beacon; mighty Durham, citadel of the Prince Bishops, dominating its lofty peninsula above the River Wear; and (more than any other) distant Ely, 'floating like a great ship at anchor' on the Fens. And then there are those places where one can almost hear time passing: at winter evensong in the shadowy recesses of Gloucester's wonderful Perpendicular presbytery; on the sublime time-worn curve of the chapter house stair at Wells; at Salisbury – the most perfect cathedral close in England and the tallest spire, shimmering in the heat-haze of a summer noon; on entering Durham's magnificent Romanesque nave and sensing the aura of St Cuthbert's saintliness which still pervades the place. And, of course, there are innumerable individual works of brilliance: among them, the matchless twelfth-century glass in the Trinity Chapel at Canterbury, the west front at Wells, the Neville Screen at Durham, Birmingham's glowing Burne-Jones windows, Ely's exquisite Octagon and the great Crécy window and cloister vault at Gloucester.

Even in this predominantly secular age, Britain's cathedrals remain potent symbols of historical continuity. Their purpose was to reveal God's majesty, to declare the supremacy of the Church and the devotion of the men who built them and financed their construction. They were intended, literally, to be awesome.

Similarly, our medieval abbeys, most of them sad remnants of a glorious past, serve to remind us of the dedication of those who strove to achieve the monastic ideal. For me, it is the Cistercians whose piety endures: not only at Fountains and Rievaulx but also at sequestered Abbey Cwmhir, deep in the green valley of the Clywedog, resting place of the last true Prince of Wales; at lonely Strata Florida, 'far from the concourse of men'; and at Hailes Abbey – my favourite place, though the heady scent of wallflowers no longer fills the ruined cloister as it did in my boyhood. All these, and many others, draw me time and again. No two cathedrals or abbeys are alike in their conception, their location, their construction or their history, and for me it this that gives them their limitless appeal.

This book has presented me with the same problem that I encountered with other volumes in the *Companion* series: that of keeping the title as concise as possible. Consequently, it does not refer to the priories, nunneries, friaries, commanderies, preceptories, colleges, hospitals, almshouses and various other religious institutions that are discussed in the pages of this book.

Regrettably, space has not allowed for detailed consideration of religious festivals, church administration, ecclesiastical legislation, parochial organisation, liturgical vestments, church plate and numerous other matters that are to be found in my *Companion to Churches*, which was revised and published in paperback in 2003.

The *Companion* is arranged alphabetically and consists of a number of primary entries (e.g. CLOISTER) from which cross-references lead on to a larger number of secondary entries (e.g. CELLARIUM, CHAPTER HOUSE, DORTER, FRATER, LAY BROTHERS, REREDORTER, SOUTH RANGE, etc.). Many of the terms encountered when visiting an abbey or cathedral are included, either as short individual entries or by cross-referencing. These include the terminology of associated subjects, such as architecture and church music, while entries on subjects such as the ANGLO-SAXON CHURCH and MONASTICISM are intended to assist in placing research in a wider historical context.

Cross-references are indicated by CAPITAL LETTERS and, where necessary, these are picked out in *italic* type in the entries to which the reader is referred.

Suggestions for further reading will be found in Appendix 1, while the addresses of organisations are listed in Appendix 2. The *Companion* is not a gazetteer; however, an Index of Places is included in Appendix 3.

Stephen Friar
Folke, Dorset

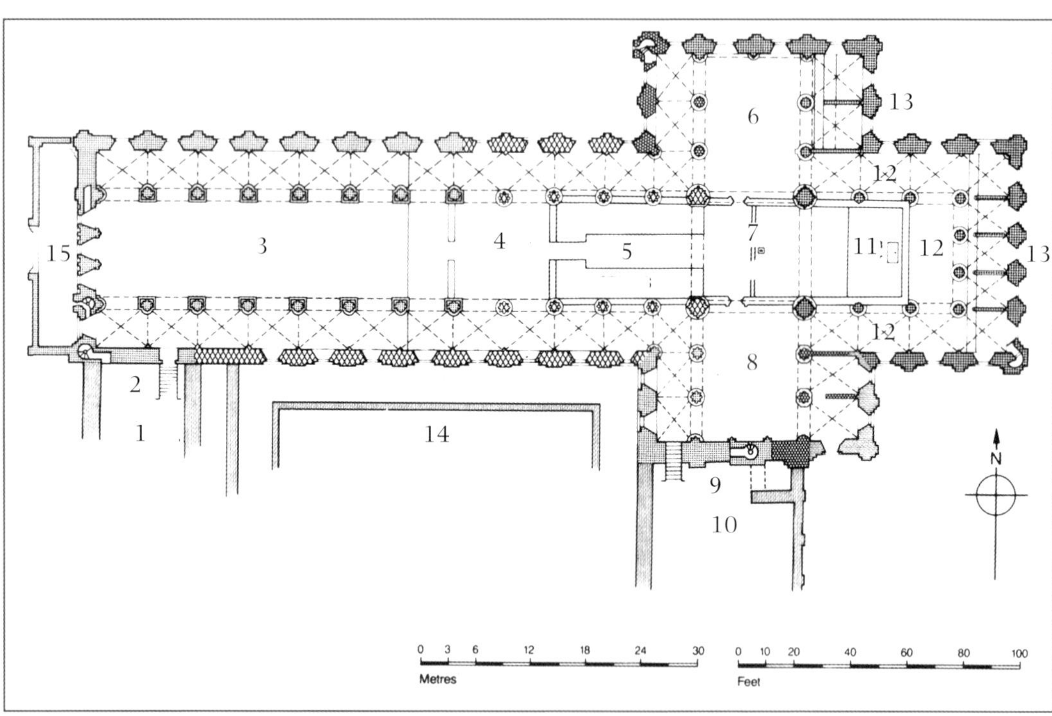

Plan of a monastic church (Byland Abbey)

1 *Lay brothers' dormitory (dorter)*
2 *Lay brothers' night stair*
3 *Lay brothers' choir*
4 *Retro-choir*
5 *Monks' choir stalls*
6 *North transept*
7 *Tower above*
8 *South transept*
9 *Night stair*
10 *Monks' dormitory (dorter)*
11 *High altar*
12 *Ambulatory*
13 *Subsidiary altars*
14 *Cloister*
15 *Galilee porch*

(National Monuments Record/English Heritage)

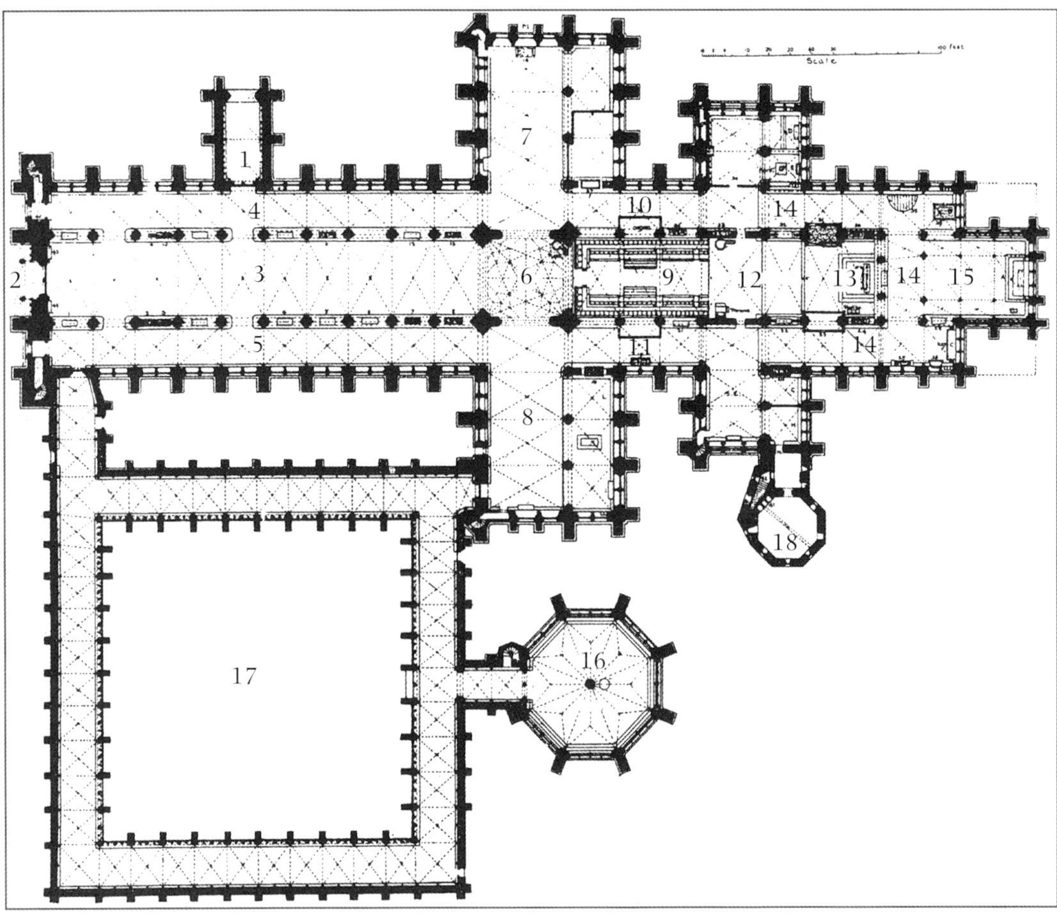

Plan of a canonical church (Salisbury Cathedral)

1 *North porch*
2 *West front*
3 *Nave*
4 *North aisle*
5 *South aisle*
6 *Crossing beneath tower*
7 *North transept*
8 *South transept*
9 *Choir*
10 *North choir aisle*
11 *South choir aisle*
12 *Presbytery*
13 *High altar*
14 *Ambulatory*
15 *Lady chapel (The Trinity Chapel)*
16 *Chapter house*
17 *Cloister*
18 *Sacristy*

(Courtesy of Geoffrey Wheeler)

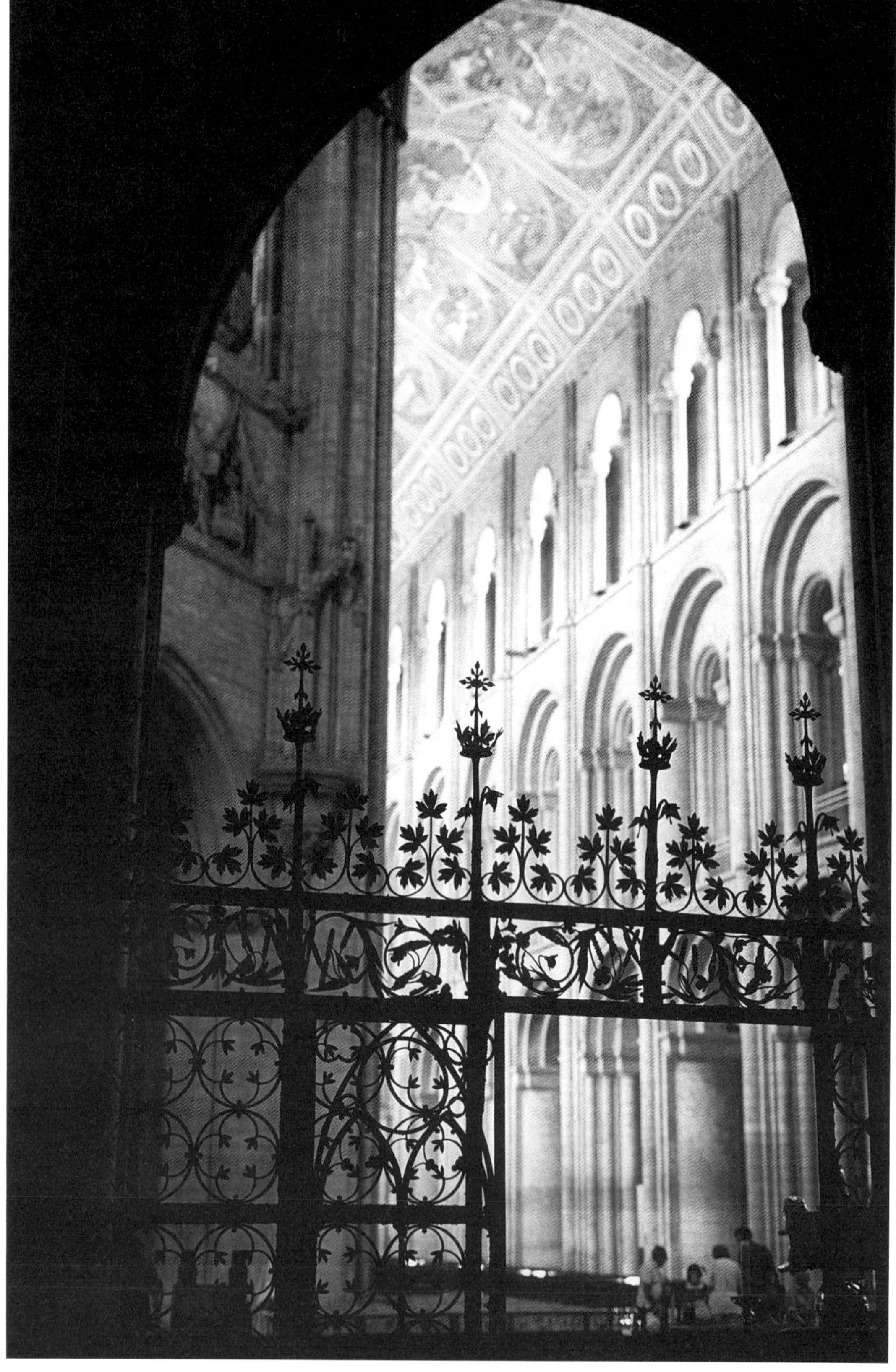

The nave at Ely Cathedral.

ABACUS The flat slab forming the upper section of a CAPITAL (*see* PIER).

ABBACY The office of an ABBOT or ABBESS. Although appointed for life, resignation was possible and deposition, although often painfully litigious, could be effected by a visiting bishop (*see* VISITATION (ECCLESIASTICAL)), by the head of the order or by papal bull. The office was absolute and a religious community was therefore entirely dependent on the whims and vagaries of its head.

ABBESS The superior of certain communities of BENEDICTINE NUNS and of orders of canonesses, especially those of the Franciscan Order (the Poor Clares, *see* MINORESS). Like abbots, abbesses had jurisdiction over the lives of their subjects, received the TITHES of appropriated churches (*see* APPROPRIATION), presented secular vicars to serve parochial churches and enjoyed the privileges of a feudal lord over the temporal estates attached to their abbeys. The Abbess of Shaftesbury, for example, held her own manorial courts and provided seven knights for the king's service. And like an abbot, an abbess bore a CROZIER as a symbol of her office.
See also ABBOT

ABBEY From the Latin *abbatia*, derived from Syriac *abba* meaning 'father', an abbey was a major monastic establishment of the Benedictine orders or certain orders of the Canons regular (*see* CANON REGULAR). An abbey was superior to a PRIORY, although in practice several priories attained religious eminence and economic prosperity which greatly exceeded that of many abbeys. Where an abbot was also a bishop, the administration of the community would be delegated to a prior and its church designated as a CATHEDRAL PRIORY: at Durham for example.

Following the DISSOLUTION OF THE MONASTERIES many abbey churches were acquired by local communities as parish churches. In most cases the CLAUSTRAL and domestic buildings were demolished, or adapted for other purposes, and where an abbey church was considered too large for the needs of a parish, it was reduced in size by removing or shortening the nave, as at Abbey Dore in Herefordshire. Fortunately, many magnificent abbey churches have survived intact: Tewkesbury in Gloucestershire, for example, Selby in Yorkshire and Sherborne in Dorset which, in 1539, was purchased by the townspeople for the sum of £337. At the same time the adjoining parish church of All Hallows was demolished and in 1560 the LADY CHAPEL was acquired by the Governors of Sherborne School, who converted it into a residence for the headmaster. There are also instances of abbey churches (now parish churches) which appear to have been reduced in size but, in fact, were never completed. Milton Abbey in Dorset, for example, was rebuilt after a disastrous fire (*totaliter inflammavit*) in 1309. But, by the time of the Dissolution of the Monasteries, only the CHOIR, CROSSING and transepts had been completed.
See also ANGLO-SAXON CHURCH, MINSTERS, MONASTIC BUILDINGS *and* PRIORY

ABBEY BUILDINGS *see* MONASTIC BUILDINGS

ABBEY TOWN *see* TOWNS

ABBOT The SUPERIOR (literally 'father') of a major religious establishment of one of the Benedictine orders or of certain orders of the Canons Regular (*see* CANON REGULAR). 'In the monastery he is considered to represent the person of Christ, seeing that he is called by His name' (Benedict: *Rule*). Normally elected for life by the monks of his abbey, his appointment was, nevertheless, subject to the consent of the secular ruler. This was not always freely given, and the pope could also interfere, especially when the appointment was to Christchurch, Canterbury which was closely associated with the Primacy of All England. An abbot exercised considerable authority in the governance of an abbatial community. His paternal supremacy was absolute: obedience was one of the essential monastic VOWS and he was to be obeyed 'as if the command had come from God'. As Christ's representative, honour was due to him without reservation or qualification. The abbot's absolute authority was restricted only by conscience and the order's RULE. Benedict required him to be a father, not a tyrant:

> An abbot who is worthy to have charge of a monastery ought always to remember by what title he is called. Let him always place mercy before judgement that he may find mercy himself; let him not be jealous or suspicious for so he will never find peace; let him strive rather to be loved than to be feared; let him be prudent in his correction, lest while he strive to scour off the rust, he break the vessel; let him acknowledge the difficult task he has undertaken – that of directing souls and adapting himself to many varied characters (*Rule*).

Many abbots were socially equal to the barons (one Cistercian abbot held the rank of earl), which status brought with it feudal responsibilities and involvement in the affairs of state (in parliament abbots far outnumbered the bishops). Consequently an abbot's monastic duties were often delegated to his deputy, the PRIOR, while a staff of OBEDIENTIARIES, bailiffs (who supervised his granges), legal advisers, clerks and chaplains was supplemented by a variety of 'upper' and 'lower' household servants. At the end of the fifteenth century, the Abbot of Glastonbury was effectively the chief executive of a vast corporation, next to Westminster the greatest monastic house in Britain, whose Somerset estates generated an annual income in excess of £3,000 – millions of pounds by today's standards. He was a hugely powerful man in his own right, accustomed to moving in the corridors of political power and providing lavish hospitality for his aristocratic guests.
See also FEUDAL SYSTEM, MITRED ABBOT *and* PRIORY

ABBOT'S LODGINGS *see* SUPERIOR'S LODGINGS

ABBOT'S TABLE Originally, an abbot would eat at the 'high table' in the monks' FRATER but, as his status in medieval society increased, he would be expected to offer lavish hospitality to his distinguished guests in his private hall (*see* SUPERIOR'S LODGINGS). As the guests were not obliged to eat as monks, the food supplied by the abbot's KITCHENS was more generous and varied and often included meat.
See also MISERICORD

ABLUTIONS (i) The washing of the chalice by the celebrant following the EUCHARIST.
See also PISCINA *and* LAVABO
(ii) The monks' toilet which usually took place in the LAVER following PRIME. The monks washed and shaved in order of seniority, the junior members of the community following the professed (*see* LAVATORIUM *and* RASURA). On Sundays and feast-days the early mass was often delayed until the washing was finished. At the same time spiritual cleansing was conducted in the CHAPTER HOUSE, where a priest would be in attendance during the ablutions to administer the sacrament of the Penance.

The Benedictine rule prescribed that 'the use of baths shall be offered to the sick as often as is necessary; to the healthy, especially the young, it shall not so readily be conceded.' Thus, while bathing was acknowledged to be therapeutic, the practice was, in most houses, considered to be an indulgence and was restricted to three or four occasions a year, often at the festal seasons of Christmas, Easter and Pentecost. Very few permanent monastic bath-houses (*balnearium*) have survived, that at Canterbury being located at some remove to the east of the CLOISTER. Recent excavations to the south of the warming house (*see* CALEFACTORIUM) at Cistercian Kirkstall Abbey revealed a small stone chamber with steps leading down to it and both inlet and outlet pipes. This may have been a monastic bath.

There is, however, documentary evidence of their use in infirmaries (*see* INFIRMARY) and HOSPITALS and considerable archaeological evidence of complex systems for the supply of water and the removal of waste (*see* DRAINS). Many ascetics immersed themselves in cold water as a DISCIPLINE, while bathing in hot water was considered to be an effective means of treating various diseases:

> A bath should by no means be refused to a body when compelled thereto by needs of ill health. Let it be taken without grumbling when ordered by a physician so that even though a brother be unwilling, what ought to be done for health may be done at the order of him who is set over you. Should he wish for one, however, when it is not advantageous then his desire is not to be gratified. Sometimes, what gives pleasure is thought to do good even though it may do harm.

Provision of large quantities of hot water was always a problem, not least for the community's CHAMBERLAIN, who was responsible for the bath-house and for the provision of bathtubs, soap and towels.

ABSENCE On occasion, it was permissible for a monk to be absent from his convent in order to attend to 'necessary business'. If the absence was for two nights or more then he would receive a solemn blessing at his departure and on his return. He would be expected to recite the canonical hours, either privately in his lodgings or at a convenient church, and where practicable he was expected to attend mass and to observe the regulations of his order.

ABSOLUTION The formal pronouncement by a priest or bishop of Christ's forgiveness of sins to the penitent. Under the influence of the Anglo-Saxon and Celtic missionary monks, the early system of public penance, exclusion and reconciliation was replaced by the secret confession of sins, followed by absolution and then penance. By the thirteenth century, penance consisted of three elements: contrition (an awareness of one's sins and a desire to abandon them), confession (a thorough admission of those sins to a confessor – *see* CONFESSION), and satisfaction (a punishment or penance to be undertaken in expiation for the sin).
See also INDULGENCE, PENANCE *and* SHRINES

ABSTINENCE The penitential or disciplinary practice of abstaining from certain kinds of food, in contradistinction to FASTING. From very early times, Christians observed a Friday abstinence in memory of Christ's Passion. In the Middle Ages, abstinence was also practised on Wednesdays in LENT, Ember Days, Rogation Days and on the vigils of certain major feasts.

ABUTMENT A mass of masonry or brickwork against which an arch abuts or from which it springs. Structurally, an abutment resists the lateral thrust of an arch and may be a pier, wall or BUTTRESS.
See also ARCH *and* VAULTING

ACADEMIC CLERK *see* CHURCH MUSIC

ACCIDIE One of the 'Seven Deadly Sins' – restlessness preventing work or prayer.

ACCUSATIONS The first 'reserved business' at a meeting of a monastic CHAPTER was the revelation of breaches of DISCIPLINE – the 'accusations'. All members of the community could speak, except novices, and accusations were usually concerned with breaches of the rules of observance, neglect of hospitality or almsgiving and breaches of the rule of silence.

ACOLYTE A person assisting a priest: specifically one who is dedicated to service at the altar (*see* MINOR ORDERS).

ACOUSTIC CHAMBERS *see* AMPLIFIERS

ADIT An entrance or approach to a building.

ADMINISTRATOR A non-member of a community, usually a layman, who was charged with the administration of the temporal affairs of a religious house. Enclosed communities were particularly dependent on lay administrators who were effectively estate managers. Administrators were also appointed to correct the business affairs of houses whose finances had become unmanageable, usually through the acquisition of debts.
See also LAY OFFICIALS

ADVOWSON The right of nomination or presentation to an ecclesiastical benefice. An advowson was held by a PATRON, who might be an individual or institution, clerical or secular, and was a form of property which might be bought, sold or given away.

AEDICULE Originally a small room or sacred shrine, the term came to be used to describe an opening framed by columns or pillars and a pediment.

AGRICULTURE *see* BARNS, GRANGE, TIMBER, VINEYARDS *and* WOOL

AISLE From the Latin *ala* meaning 'wing', an aisle is a lateral extension of a NAVE from which it is divided by an ARCADE of pillars. In larger monastic and collegiate churches, an aisle was intended to provide a processional route associated with the elaboration of the liturgy (*see* PROCESSIONS). Often the TRANSEPT was incorporated into an aisle, and the aisles themselves were sometimes extended outwards, especially in the late medieval period. This, of course, resulted in the nave windows being blocked by the roof of the enlarged aisle and, in order that sufficient natural light should be admitted to the nave, the nave walls and roof also had to be raised to accommodate a CLERESTORY.

Most non-Benedictine churches were constructed without aisles, although a single aisle was sometimes added to the north side of the nave, the presence of the CLOISTER precluding the construction of an aisle on the southern elevation, as at Bolton, Dorchester (Oxfordshire) and Lanercost.

Although the various orders of friars built their churches without naves, later urban churches were often provided with aisles in order to accommodate increasing numbers of people attracted by the friars' preaching (*see* FRIARY).

Several major churches have double aisles, providing five parallel chambers: at Chichester Cathedral, for example, where double aisles were formed out of a range of thirteenth-century subsidiary chapels. The aisles of HALL-CHURCHES are of the same height as the nave. At Leominster Priory in Herefordshire the great north 'aisle' was the nave of the former (Benedictine) monastic church.
See also AMBULATORY, MEDIEVAL ARCHITECTURE *and* RETRO-CHOIR

ALABASTER Calcium sulphate, a form of gypsum, found in certain strata of rocks in the north Midlands (notably at Chellaston in Derbyshire) and elsewhere. Alabaster was used in medieval sculpture (particularly in EFFIGIES) because of the

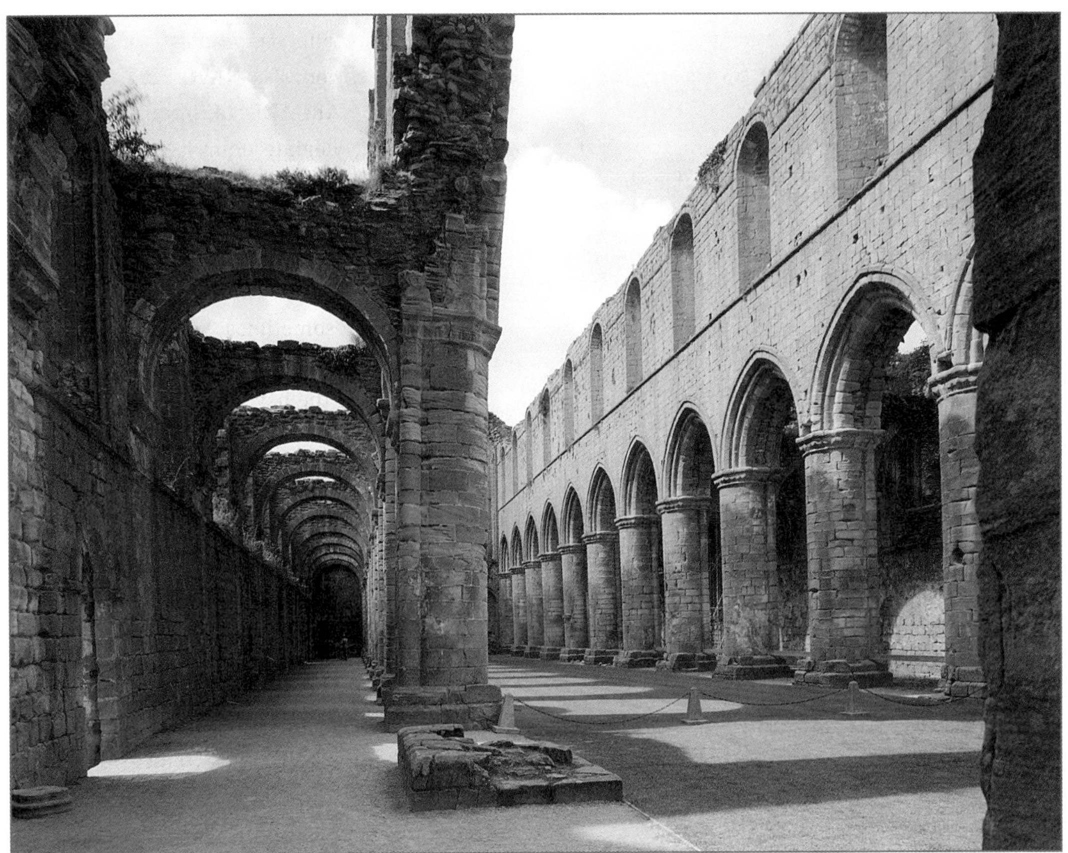

The south aisle and nave of Fountains Abbey, Yorkshire. (National Monuments Record/English Heritage)

ease and speed with which it could be carved. Dressed alabaster is exceptionally smooth to the touch and is white with occasional flecks of red, although most medieval MONUMENTS were originally coloured and sometimes gilded.
See also PURBECK MARBLE

ALBACIO Whitewash.

ALCOVE A vaulted recess or large NICHE.

ALIEN In a medieval context, one who was unable to hold or inherit titles or land.

ALIEN PRIORY A direct dependency in England of a continental religious house. There were two types of alien priory: conventual houses, in which a community followed a claustral life under a PRIOR, and (more commonly) manors, sometimes with an appropriated church, from which revenues were diverted to the mother house (*see* APPROPRIATION). Many alien priories originated in benefactions made by the followers of William I from their newly acquired English estates to monasteries at home. At one time there were over one hundred alien priories in England and, of the conventual houses, several churches have survived. Good examples are the Priory Church of St Mary and St Martin at Blyth in Nottinghamshire (from Rouen) and the Priory Church of St Mary and St Blaise at Boxgrove, Sussex (from Lessay). It is often difficult to determine the precise relationship between alien priories and parishes, particularly in those manors where there was an appropriated church, but it is known that at Ecclesfield in Yorkshire the 'custos' of the priory served the cure of the parish church. The PREMONSTRATENSIAN CANONS are known to have held some 150 appropriated parish churches, which they served as rectors and vicars.

During the Hundred Years War the alien priories were widely suspected of acting as conduits for money and intelligence and were rigorously suppressed. In some cases their personnel and resources were used for other religious purposes: for establishing chantries (*see* CHANTRY) and CHANTRY COLLEGES or for supplementing existing monastic foundations, for example. Some of the larger houses (notably those of the CLUNIACS) obtained charters of DENIZATION and became independent monasteries under English priors or dependencies of established English houses. Others were suppressed and their income used to found educational establishments: both Eton and Winchester were founded at this time. By the second quarter of the fifteenth century, alien priories had ceased to exist.
See also DAUGHTER HOUSE *and* PRIORY

ALIENATION The transfer of ownership of property rights.

ALMERY *see* CHEST CUPBOARD

ALMONER (ELEMOSINARIUS) In a religious community, one who is responsible for distributing ALMS and for providing medical and welfare services. Every religious house was under an obligation to distribute food and clothing to those in need. Sometimes money and medicine were provided and even board and lodging. A proportion of the produce of a monastery's estates and workshops was set aside for this purpose, and the KITCHENS and buttery (*see* LARDER) invariably prepared surpluses of food and drink that were transferred to the almoner's reserves. Stocks of clothing were maintained and, when a monk died, his rations were customarily given to the poor for thirty days following his death. The almoner was also a monastery's medical and welfare officer, whose duties included the supervision of the daily MAUNDY and the Great Maundy, and the education of any children resident in the almonry. To these responsibilities were added various tasks, depending on the practices of different houses, including the provision of walking sticks for infirm and aged monks and the obtaining of rods for maintaining DISCIPLINE, both in the school (if there was one – *see* ALMONRY) and within the community itself. The work was demanding and an almoner was often assisted by a sub-almoner and (in larger houses) by servants. He was also permitted to be absent from the morning offices so that he could carry out his duties. Alms-giving was always expected to be reciprocal: those in receipt of alms were reminded of their spiritual obligations and expected to offer prayers for the community.

ALMONRY (DOMUS ELEMOSINARIA) Monastic buildings always included an almonry from which ALMS were distributed. At first, alms were dispensed at a monastery's gateway but, as the services provided increased, so buildings were erected nearby for the purpose. Several almonries had infirmaries or ALMSHOUSES attached, while others supported a school (*see* CHILDREN *and* SCHOOLS). At Durham, for example, there was an INFIRMARY for the maintenance of four elderly women and lodgings for 'the children of the almonry' who were educated and maintained at the community's expense. Some almonries were singularly impressive: that at St Albans contained a 'hall, chapel, chamber, kitchens, cellar and all other buildings necessary for the scholars and their masters'. Following the DISSOLUTION OF THE MONASTERIES, the sudden withdrawal of the social and welfare services provided by the monastic almonries had an often devastating effect on a local populace. A number of former monastic churches, now adapted for parochial use, retain evidence of almonries. At Dorchester (Oxfordshire), where the almonry was combined with a GUEST

HOUSE, the *dole window* from which alms were distributed may still be seen, together with the almoner's seat.
See also BEDE-HOUSE

ALMS A donation of food, clothing or money given to the poor, to destitute wayfarers and to pilgrims. It has been estimated that one tenth of monastic income was devoted to alms-giving. No needy person who called at the gatehouse of a religious house was ever to be turned away, although there were usually appointed times for the distribution of alms. Alms could also include medical treatment, education or hospitality, and guest houses, infirmaries and hospices were often provided for that purpose (*see also* ALMONRY, BEDE-HOUSE, HOSPICE, INFIRMARY *and* ALMSHOUSES). Of course, spiritual alms, intercessory prayers for the souls of BENEFACTORS and founders and for all God's people, both living and dead, were the *raison d'être* of all religious houses.

ALMSHOUSES Medieval almshouses were established as charitable foundations by religious bodies, trade guilds and individual BENEFACTORS to care for the elderly, poor and infirm (*see also* ALMONRY). Each almshouse would have a WARDEN, master or prior and would comprise an infirmary hall and chapel, similar in plan to a monastic INFIRMARY. Known as spital houses, bede-houses or *maisons dieu*, some were devoted to the care of lepers or lazars (such as the lazar houses of the Order of St Lazarus) and these would be divided into small cells or separate cottages instead of a corporate infirmary (*see also* HOSPITALS).

The almshouse of St John the Baptist and St John the Evangelist at Sherborne, Dorset.

In the later Middle Ages many monastic and collegiate hospices became permanent homes for the poor and elderly, who observed a modified rule and were required to pray for the repose of the founder in return for board and lodging. In 1547 most were dissolved as places of worship. The Elizabethans, however, re-established many old hospitals as almshouses and, encouraged by their example, the wealthy and charitable of the seventeenth and eighteenth centuries founded new establishments, the inmates of which were carefully selected for their unquestionable virtue.

Typical of a number of medieval foundations which continue to operate today are the almshouses at Sherborne in Dorset, built in 1437 under royal licence at a cost of £80 raised (unusually) by public subscription. They were intended for 'twelve pore feeble and ympotent old men and four old women', cared for by a housewife who was required to share in the meals of the residents, presumably to ensure that they were properly fed.

ALTAR CROSS It is not known precisely when the altar cross was introduced, but it has been suggested that it may have evolved from the medieval practice of placing the head of the processional cross on the altar during the service. The cross thereby became the focal point of worship, particularly at the EUCHARIST.
See also ALTARS *and* CANDLES

ALTAR LIGHTS There is evidence to suggest that the practice of placing a candle or CANDLES on the altar dates from *c.* 1175. Before the Reformation, it was customary for a single candle to be placed on the altar or, at most, one on either side of the ALTAR CROSS. Thereafter any number was acceptable, and three (on each side) considered the most effective. The legality of this practice was contested in the nineteenth century but was confirmed in 1890. Strictly speaking, it is not correct to place anything else (such as flowers) on the altar.
See also LAMPS

ALTARS The term, with its sacrificial connotations, was adopted by the early Church to describe the Eucharist table which, at that time, was probably little more than a simple wooden table in a private house. It was also the custom to celebrate the EUCHARIST on the tombs of martyrs, which may account for the later practice of constructing altars of stone. Strictly speaking, the term 'altar' should be applied only to medieval stone altars, although it is commonly used also to describe post-Reformation communion tables.

In Britain, most Celtic and early Anglo-Saxon churches had free-standing, wooden altars. But from the first decade of the sixth century stone was used, especially where altars were erected over the interred RELICS of saints. At that time it was customary to have only one altar in a church, usually on a raised platform (*predella*) at the east end of the PRESBYTERY. The front was covered with a decorative cloth (*frontal*) or a carved and painted panel known as the *antependium* and a RETABLE may have been fitted above the back of the altar. This was a frame for a decorative panel or a shelf on which ornaments could be placed (*see also* REREDOS). Illustrations in several early medieval manuscripts suggest that altars may also have been covered by an arched roof (*ciborium*), supported at the corners by pillars.

Some altars must have been truly magnificent works of art. William of Malmesbury, writing in *c.* 1125, tells us that, on his return from Rome in AD 700, St Aldhelm brought with him

> An altar of shining white marble six feet long [1.8m], four feet deep [1.2m] and three palms thick [30cm], with a lip projecting from the stone and beautifully carved round the edge. He gave the altar to Ine [king of the West Saxons] who placed it for the service of the Mother of God in a royal villa called Briwetune [Bruton in Somerset] where it stands to this day, a living proof of the sanctity of Aldhelm.

By 1000, there was an increasing tendency to dedicate altars to specific saints and, as it was considered essential that a celebrant should face the east, space to accommodate additional altars against eastern walls was at a premium. Similarly, as more monks entered the priesthood, so additional altars were required in the great abbey churches. These private altars were usually positioned in the TRANSEPT or at the eastern end of the church which was often extended for the purpose, as at the Cistercian abbey of Dore in Herefordshire, where an eastern aisle gave access to a row of five chapels, and at Fountains and Durham, where nine altars were provided in an eastern termination (*see* CHEVET). Subsidiary altars were also to be found in the presbytery aisles, the CRYPT, on the western side of arcade piers in the nave and, for communal purposes, in a monastery's FARMERY, CHAPTER HOUSE, GUEST HOUSE and CAPELLA ANTE PORTAS.

In Cistercian houses, the nave was the LAY BROTHERS' church and they worshipped at a JESUS ALTAR set against the west side of the ROOD SCREEN. In many churches, the practice of saying private masses (attended only by the celebrant and an ACOLYTE) also resulted in the provision of subsidiary PRIVILEGED ALTARS, sometimes enclosed by a PARCLOSE (screen) and provided with a SQUINT in order that the celebrant could observe what was taking place at the HIGH ALTAR. By the fifteenth century most large churches (including monastic ones) had at least one CHANTRY CHAPEL in which a priest was engaged to recite masses for the soul of the founder and others nominated by him in his will.

Common features of medieval altars were the CELURE and the BALDACCHINO, a cloth canopy suspended above the altar, and *riddel curtains* (from the French *rideau* meaning 'curtain') which screened the altar table at the back and sides. The *riddel posts*, which were affixed to the four corners of the altar table to support the curtain, later developed into tall, slender pillars, each surmounted with the gilded figure of an angel. A PISCINA (wash-basin and drain) was always provided near an altar, and sometimes a SEDILIA (seating) and AUMBRY (cupboard).

From the early thirteenth century, the *High Altar* in the presbytery, where the priest celebrated the Sacrifice of the Mass, was concealed from the nave by a chancel screen or, in cathedrals and abbey churches, by a PULPITUM and ROOD SCREEN. But the doctrine of the Sacrifice of the Mass, and the medieval concept of the mystery of the *inner sanctum*, were rejected by the sixteenth-century reformers who brought the congregation into the CHANCEL, or moved the altar into the nave (*see* NAVE ALTAR), where the Eucharist was shared as a family at 'God's Board'. An Act of Edward VI (1547–53) required that all altar stones were to be removed and destroyed, although in many cases they were hidden by Roman Catholics in anticipation of better times. A few have been found intact and restored (though not always in their original position), the top (or *mensa*) almost invariably bearing five engraved crosses – one at each corner and another in the centre.

Elizabethan and Jacobean communion tables were usually splendidly carved in wood, with bulbous legs. The accessibility of the new communion tables caused problems, however, particularly from stray dogs, and rails to prevent profanation were widely introduced in churches from the early years of Elizabeth I's reign. These were disliked by the Puritans, but were often restored following the Restoration of 1660 and became known as communion rails.

ALURE A walk or passageway behind a PARAPET.

AMBO A raised platform in a basilica from which the scriptures were read and the LITURGY conducted. PULPITS replaced ambos after the fourteenth century.

AMBRY *see* AUMBRY

AMBULATORY A covered way for liturgical PROCESSIONS. A characteristic of Norman churches, the ambulatory is a semicircular AISLE enclosing an apsidal PRESBYTERY (*see also* CHEVET). By the mid-twelfth century, the apsidal form was less popular in England and was superseded by a square-ended eastern termination (*see* APSE). As a result, the term is also applied to the right-angled conjunction of the north and south presbytery aisles found in many larger churches. Norwich Cathedral Priory is one of the few Norman churches to have retained its original apse and ambulatory, while the twelfth-century ambulatory at Cistercian Abbey Dore, Herefordshire, has survived in what is now the parish church.

In some churches the ambulatory to the east of the High Altar was constructed to the full height of the building and is often described as a RETRO-CHOIR, especially where it has been enlarged to accommodate SHRINES. At Lincoln Cathedral, for example, the Angel Choir was built to house the translated remains of St Hugh (canonised 1220). It contains a number of tombs and CHANTRY CHAPELS, deliberately erected in close proximity to the saint's shrine (which was destroyed at the Reformation), and was provided with entrances to the north and south for the benefit of pilgrims. A similar space, between the presbytery and LADY CHAPEL at Chichester Cathedral is described in the guidebook as a retro-choir although here, as elsewhere, the space is more correctly an ambulatory. Uniquely, the magnificent apsidal CHAPTER HOUSE at Cistercian Rievaulx Abbey had an ambulatory, possibly intended to accommodate the LAY BROTHERS during sermons.

AMPLIFIERS (*also* ACOUSTIC CHAMBERS *or* RESONATORS) Earthenware vessels, usually set in the eastern face of a CHANCEL wall in order to amplify the voice of the priest during the mass. In many monastic churches acoustic chambers were intended to provide extra resonance and amplification during the singing of PLAINSONG and to make 'hauteyn speche ring out as round as dooth a belle'. Those at Fountains Abbey in Yorkshire consisted simply of rows of ceramic jars laid on their sides, but elsewhere sophisticated, drain-like series of boxes were constructed beneath choir stalls for the same purpose. The twelfth-century set of acoustic chambers at St Gregory's Priory in Canterbury, Kent is 0.9m wide (3ft) and 0.6m deep (2ft), with tiled floors and walls mortared with chalk and flint. They were built to allow the low notes of male voices to reverberate and supposedly added lustre to the sound. Acoustic chambers were clearly *de rigueur* in the Middle Ages, although it is doubtful whether they were really effective.

ANALOGIUM *see* CHAPTER HOUSE

ANATHEMA Literally, 'separated' or 'accursed'. In the early Church anathematisation was used against heretics and, from the sixth century, was distinguished from EXCOMMUNICATION, the former requiring total separation from the Church and the latter exclusion from the Sacraments.

ANCASTER STONE An easily carved, grey limestone from Wilsford Heath, Lincolnshire.

ANCHORITE (*fem.* anchoress) A religious recluse living a solitary life of silence, prayer and mortification. Unlike a HERMIT, an anchorite would be 'walled up for life' in a tiny CELL (*anchorage*). Anchorages could only be established with the consent of a bishop, who had to be satisfied that the anchorite possessed both the spiritual integrity and the material resources to survive in his strictly enclosed quarters. Finchale Priory was founded by St Godric (b. 1065) who, following a career as a freebooter and pirate, gave up the sea for life as an anchorite, first near Carlisle and then in a cave in Weardale. Having received permission from Bishop Flambard of Durham to make himself a chapel at Finchale, he survived (it is said) to the age of 105 – despite his habit of standing in a hole in the river bed so that the water came up to his neck. After his death, his tomb and chapel were incorporated into

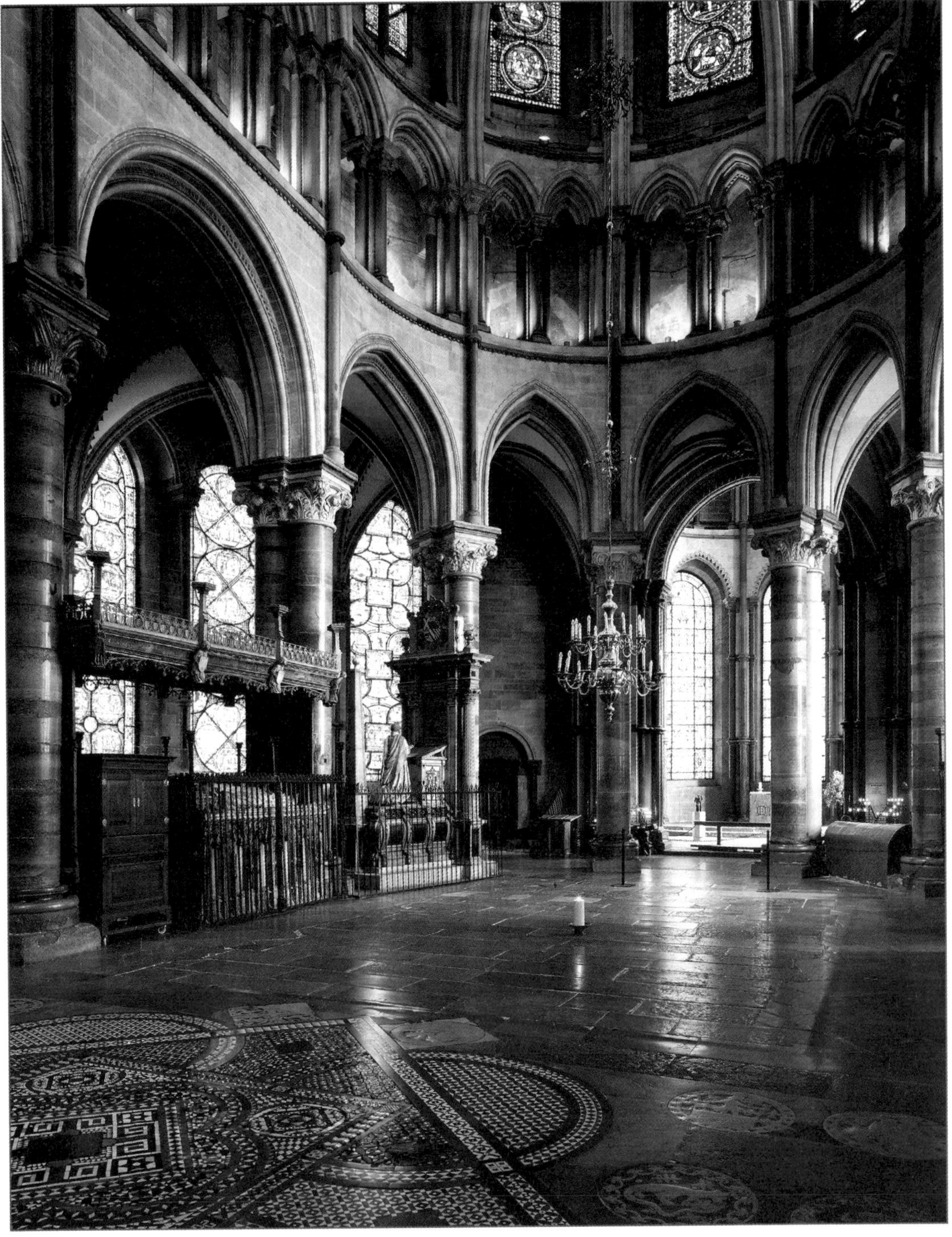

The ambulatory and Trinity Chapel at Canterbury Cathedral. (© John Crook/info@john-crook.com)

the Benedictine abbey at Finchale. Some anchorites lived by means of an endowment: the Black Prince maintained an anchorite, in the park of Restormel Castle above the Fowey river in Cornwall, who said masses for the souls of his benefactor's ancestors. Several monastic communities made provision for anchorites: at Durham, for example, an anchorite's cell, consisting of an elevated chapel between two piers, overlooked St Cuthbert's shrine.
See also COENOBITE

ANCIENT DEEDS Documents at The National Archives (formerly the Public Record Office), mostly drawn from monastic and private muniments, relating to conveyances of land, covenants, bonds, wills, etc. 'earlier in date than the end of Elizabeth I's reign' (1603).
Further information:
Descriptive Catalogue of Ancient Deeds (6 vols), HMSO.

ANGELUS BELL A bell rung to mark each stage of the *Angelus*, a devotion repeated three times daily (early morning, noon and evening) as a memorial of the Incarnation.
See also BELLS

ANGLICAN CHANT A simple type of harmonised melody used in the Anglican Church for singing unmetrical texts, principally the PSALMS and Canticles. A short melody is repeated to each verse of the text, the varying numbers of syllables in different lines being accommodated by the use of a reciting note at the opening of each line.
See also CHURCH MUSIC, PLAINSONG *and* VERSICLES

ANGLO-SAXON CHRONICLE One of the prime historical sources for the Anglo-Saxon period, the *Chronicle* purports to run from 494 to 1154, the year of Henry II's accession to the throne. Much of the earlier material is almost certainly folklore and hearsay, but from the tenth century onwards it is very reliable. There are several versions, since various monasteries kept annual records of what seemed to them to be significant events. Later chronicles, such as those of Henry of Huntingdon, Gervase of Canterbury, Ralph of Coggeshall and Roger of Howden, continued the tradition into the later medieval period.

ANGLO-SAXON CHURCH The Roman emperor Constantine's acceptance of Christianity in 312 was to have important consequences for the development of the Church in Britain. It ensured that Roman Britain was in part Christian before the end of Imperial rule (in 410) and it led to the conversion of Ireland by Roman missionaries in the fifth century and to the creation of a CELTIC CHURCH, which was to be instrumental in later Pictish and Anglo-Saxon conversions. But the Roman Christians left little archaeological evidence of their faith, other than a number of (often enigmatic) Christian symbols in the fabric of their villas, notably at Chedworth and Cirencester in Gloucestershire, Frampton and Hinton-St-Mary in Dorset and Lullingstone in Kent.

Following the withdrawal of Rome, the Church survived in the west, in Cornwall, Ireland and Wales, isolated from the mainstream of Christianity and with its own customs, liturgy and a multiplicity of indigenous 'saints'. Elsewhere, the integration of immigrants from north Germany and Scandinavia introduced a vigorous paganism, the potency of which was to affect significantly later Christian belief. The first Anglo-Saxon settlers were mercenaries who overthrew their British masters and founded their own independent states. Further settlers arrived during the fifth and sixth centuries and by the end of the seventh century three major political and military powers had emerged: Northumbria (in north-east England and the south of Scotland), Mercia (in the Midlands) and Wessex (in the south and south-west).

In 597, a papal mission of forty monks landed on the Isle of Thanet in Kent, led by Augustine (d. 604/5), who was destined to become the first archbishop of Canterbury. Sees were quickly established at Canterbury, London and Rochester and within a few months Christianity was adopted by Ethelbert (d. 616), king of Kent, whose wife, Bertha, daughter of the Frankish king Charibert, was already a Christian.

The year 597 also marked the death of Saint Columba (521–97) who, with his twelve companions, had travelled from Ireland in *c.* 563 and established a missionary base on Iona, from where they embarked on the conversion of the far north. But while Christianity had managed to survive in those areas of sub-Roman Britain where Saxon culture had not penetrated, the administration and customs of the Celtic Church in the north and west differed fundamentally from the Augustinian model in the south. Its priests operated among isolated tribal communities, often in wild and inhospitable terrain, far removed from the influence of Rome. It was of necessity a Church of scattered monasteries and itinerant missions in which the hieratic organisation of the Roman church, with its bishops and dioceses, had little relevance. In *c.* 603 Augustine attempted to reach agreement with representatives of the Celtic Church on differences in discipline and practice, but without success. By 627 Christianity had reached Northumbria, and the Celtic Aidan was sent from Iona, at the request of the Northumbrian King Oswald, to be consecrated bishop of Lindisfarne (Holy Island) in 635. It was from the efforts of Aidan and his followers that the Christianity of most of northern and midland England sprang.

The Process of Conversion

A remarkable feature of the period was the rapidity with which conversion was achieved. The conversion of a district usually began with the royal household (consequently new bishoprics were often conterminous with tribal territories) and with the founding of a missionary base (*see* MINSTERS): an early ninth-century charter to the minster at Worcester shows that it consisted of nine priests, four deacons and five clerks. Having been advised by Rome that the native population should not be alienated by the imposition of a raw Christian ideology on an already diverse and complex religious culture, the minster priests deliberately chose to preach at sites which had already acquired some local significance: at places of pagan worship or the meeting places of legislative assemblies (*gemotes*), for example. As regular itineraries were established within an ever-expanding minster territory (*parochium*), so stone crosses were erected at preaching sites and many of these have survived, often beside the churches that replaced them.

But 'conversion' was rarely universal, for while the aristocracy may have adopted Christianity as its official religion, and while in 664 Bede was able to write 'if any priest happened to come to a village, the villagers immediately gathered together and sought from him the word of life', a formidable element of paganism survived in the customs and practices of the peasantry and is evident, for example, in the uninhibited vigour of later Romanesque carving.

Throughout the first half of the seventh century, disputes concerning the observances of the Celtic and Roman traditions continued to hinder the work of the missions (*see* CELTIC CHURCH). But, following the Synod of Whitby (664) and the Councils of Hertford (673) and Hatfield (680), common agreement was reached concerning the rights and duties of clerics and monks and the governance of the Church, which was reformed on the Roman model by dividing dioceses and extending the episcopate. The Councils were presided over by Archbishop Theodore (*c.* 602–90), who was appointed to the see of Canterbury in 668 and was chiefly responsible for the organisation of the missionary territories. As a result of his highly effective administration a 'national' Church was created long before the political unification of the country.

A Reformed Church

The second migration, of Vikings from Denmark and Norway, began with sporadic incursions in the late eighth century, followed by systematic plundering and colonisation from *c.* 850. Isolated monasteries were easy and attractive targets and the brethren lived in constant fear – vividly expressed in the words of an Irish monk, written in the margin of the manuscript on which he was working :

> Fierce and wild is the wind tonight,
> It tosses the tresses of the sea to white;
> On such a night I take my ease;
> Fierce Norsmen only course the quiet seas.

The first monastery to suffer was the Celtic missionary base at Lindisfarne on the Northumbrian coast, which was plundered by Viking raiders in June 793. In common with many other remote and vulnerable communities Lindisfarne was eventually abandoned, the monks taking with them the precious relics of St Cuthbert. In 875 they made their way to Norham, where they reassembled the timber church they had transported from Lindisfarne, and then to Chester-le-Street where they settled in 883. But it was not until *c.* 995 that the monks, and the relics of St Cuthbert, found a permanent home at Durham.

The English kingdoms of East Anglia, Northumbria and Mercia were eventually subjugated, but during the tenth century the West Saxon kings retaliated and briefly created an English kingdom, theoretically unified, but in practice divided into regions approximating to the old kingdoms and ruled by powerful overlords.

The invasions of the ninth century wrought destruction and disorder in the Church, but reconstruction was begun under Alfred the Great, king of Wessex (871–99) and the mid-tenth century saw a flowering of Anglo-Saxon culture (*see* DARK AGES) and the rejuvenation of large-scale monasticism in England – a development which was to affect profoundly the subsequent nature of medieval society. Supported by the Anglo-Saxon monarchy, the Church was purged and strict Benedictine rule was imposed by Dunstan (*c.* 909–88), son of a West Saxon nobleman, Abbot of Glastonbury (940) and Archbishop of Canterbury (959) under King Edgar (959–75), with whom he worked to reform both Church and state. The twin pillar of reform was Ethelwold (*c.* 908–84), bishop of Winchester (963) and compiler of the *Regularis Concordia*, a code of monastic observance approved by the Synod of Winchester in *c.* 970. Ethelwold was a singularly powerful and influential cleric, ecclesiastically puritanical and yet an enthusiastic patron of the tenth-century artistic renaissance, and his reformed monastic houses evolved into one of the wealthiest and most powerful forces in England. Under his influence, Winchester became the political and cultural centre of Anglo-Saxon society.

In such a climate, it is hardly surprising that there should be a parallel proliferation of church building, inspired by the clergy and supported enthusiastically by landowners and magnates, which continued into the eleventh century. An inscription on a sundial at St Gregory's Minster, Kirkdale in Yorkshire records that Orm rebuilt the church at the time of Edward the Confessor (1042–65) and Tosti, the Earl of Northumberland (1055–65):

> Orm, son of Gamal, bought St Gregory's minster when it was all broken down and fallen, and he let it be made anew from the ground to Christ and St Gregory, in the days of Edward the King and Tosti the Earl, and Haward wrought me, and Brand the Priest.

Organisation

By the eleventh century, there were four types of church: headminsters, minsters, daughter churches (*chapelries*) and 'field churches' (*proprietary chapels*). *Headminsters* were the great abbeys and cathedral priories, centres of diocesan administration, culture and commerce which had grown out of the tenth-century renaissance. In those areas where the process of conversion was incomplete, the minsters (*monasteria*) continued to function as missionary centres where priests lived a communal life and from where they ventured out to preach, to celebrate the mass and to baptise converts. Ancillary to the minsters, and dependent on them, were daughter churches or *chapelries*, each served by a single priest and strategically located within the minster territory (*parochium*). Chapelries were of two types: those with a burial ground and those without, a distinction which in some cases was perpetuated even into the nineteenth century. While many chapelries were later abandoned as settlements declined, a number continued as dependent churches for several centuries. Others became parish churches or continued as subsidiary chapels within the parochial system.

From the eighth century, landowners also began building chapels on their estates. Indeed, in late Anglo-Saxon England, possession of a proprietary chapel (sometimes described as a *thane's church*) was considered to be an attribute of rank. Most were served by a priest, who may also have acted as the lord's chaplain, and the estate retained the church's tithes and other dues, while the lord exercised proprietorial rights, including the right to appoint a priest (*advowson*). Where proprietary chapels have survived as parish churches, they will often be found in close proximity to one another, especially in towns, or on the periphery of a settlement and close to a former fortified site, manor house or moated enclosure.

Within a district, the ancient pattern of minster and subsidiary chapelries may yet be discernible in surviving documents such as charters, monastic and cathedral records, court proceedings, land grants and bishops' records; in place-names (such as Yetminster, Iwerne Minster and Charminster in Dorset) and church dedications; in the delineation of ecclesiastical boundaries; and in the structure and location of the churches themselves. In many areas, former minster churches retained exclusive rights of baptism and burial, or continued to demand dues from their daughter churches even though they had attained parochial status. The former chapelries of Wayford, Seaborough and Misterton in Somerset, for example, continued until the nineteenth century to pay their dues and to bury their dead in the churchyard of the mother church at Crewkerne while, on the patronal feast-day of St Bartholomew (24 August), the parishioners of Wayford would present the key to their church at the High Altar at Crewkerne, thereby acknowledging their subsidiary status. At Bromyard in Herefordshire, late sixteenth-century records provide evidence not only of the collegiate origins of the PARISH CHURCH but also of the survival of the Anglo-Saxon *parochium*:

> the stalls in the choir were not only for the prebends there, but also for the fifteen other priests of the fifteen inferior churches thereabouts which came continuously once a year upon Whitsun Monday to help to say service in the collegiate church confessing the same to be the Mother Church.

By the Norman Conquest the influence of the 'old minsters' had been superseded by that of the subsidiary churches they had created, and the parish was emerging as the fundamental unit of ecclesiastical administration.

See also AUGUSTINIANS, CELTIC CHURCH, MEDIEVAL CHURCH, NORMANS, PRIORY *and* WALES, THE MEDIEVAL CHURCH IN

ANNIVELLAR A chantry priest who said masses for the souls of his benefactors on the anniversaries of their deaths.

ANNO DOMINI (AD) Latin, meaning 'in the year of our Lord'. The current system of dating is based on the theoretical date of the birth of Christ although this is now generally considered to have been several years earlier.

See also GREGORIAN CALENDAR *and* JULIAN CALENDAR

ANTE-CHAPEL The western end of a (usually medieval) collegiate chapel, originally separated from the CHOIR by a screen or PULPITUM.

ANTE-CHURCH An extension at the west end of a church comprising several bays of both NAVE and AISLES.
See also NARTHEX

ANTE-NAVE *see* NARTHEX

ANTEPENDIUM *see* ALTARS

ANTHEM In the LITURGY of the Church of England there is a place reserved for the anthem, the Anglicised form of the ANTIPHON derived from the Latin MOTET. The repertory of English anthems is large and contains many noble works as well as much that is banal.
See also CATHEDRAL MUSIC

ANTIPHON A piece of sacred music sung by two choirs alternately, with each choir (CANTORIS and DECANI) facing the other in the CHOIR STALLS. Also the setting of sentences, usually from the scriptures, recited before and after the psalms and Canticles in the divine office (*see* PRECES *and* VERSICLES).
See also ANGLICAN CHANT, CHURCH MUSIC *and* PLAINSONG

ANTIPHONARIUM A collection of sacred chants and the book in which they were kept. This was normally placed on a LECTERN between the CHOIR STALLS.

ANTONY THE GREAT, SAINT *see* MONASTICISM

APOPHYGE The concave curve formed where the shaft of a COLUMN joins a capital (at the upper end) or base (at the lower).

APOSTASY The renunciation of one's vocation, notably by a religious who has taken perpetual VOWS. A monk who deserted his community thereby committed a crime and a warrant for his arrest could be issued by a secular authority. When apprehended, he would be returned to his house 'to be chastened according to the rule of his order'.
See also RECRUITMENT

APPARITOR An officer of an ecclesiastical court.

APPEALS In the Middle Ages appeals (by both clergy and laity) to a judicial authority above that of a DIOCESE, were directed to the pope. From the mid-twelfth century, successive kings attempted to restrict appeals to Rome but they were not abolished until 1534, when Henry VIII made the Court of Delegates (*see* DELEGATES, COURT OF) the final arbiter in such matters.

APPORT An annual rent paid by a dependent PRIORY to a mother house (*see* CLUNIACS).

APPROPRIATION The annexation of parish TITHES and other endowments to a religious house. Where a monastery became rector it received the bulk of the revenues of the living while the parish church was served by a vicar who received a small income.
See also CARTULARY, IMPROPRIATION *and* MEDIEVAL CHURCH

APRON A shortened CASSOCK worn by bishops, deans and archdeacons.

APSE A polygonal or semicircular recess characteristic of the early basilicas of the Christian church and introduced into Anglo-Saxon architecture by missionaries from Rome at the end of the sixth century. The apse was widely used by the Normans, in both domestic and ecclesiastical buildings, but was abandoned by the Cistercians of the twelfth century in favour of the square-ended chancel or chapel. Of the two Norman apses to have survived in major English churches that at Norwich Cathedral is surmounted by a later

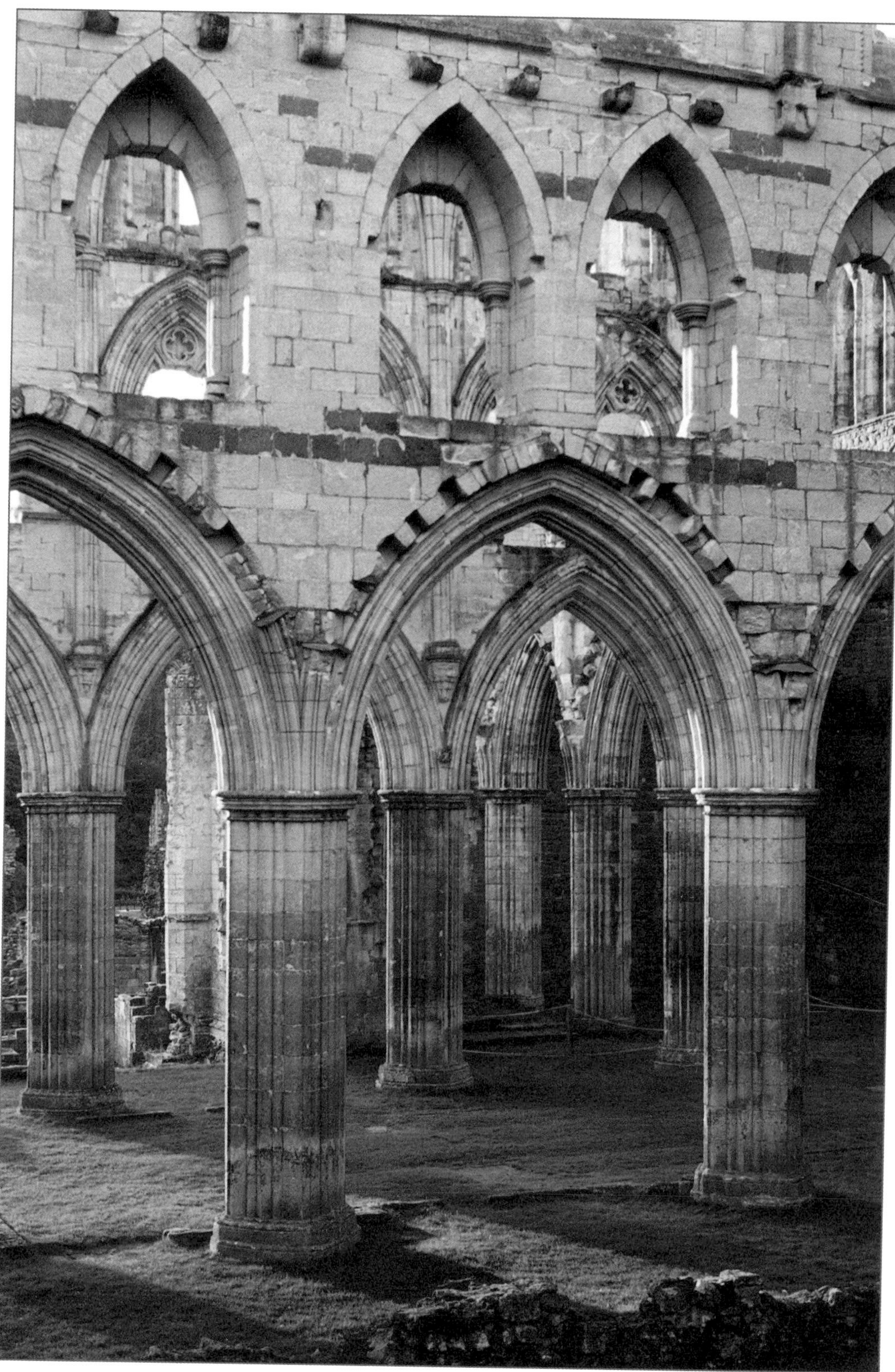

Arcades at Rievaulx Abbey, Yorkshire.

CLERESTORY and vault, while the apse at Peterborough is one of the purest Romanesque interiors in England, despite the insertion of later window tracery.

APSIDAL In the form of an APSE.

AQUAMANILE Ewer in which priests washed their hands during the mass.

ARCADE A range of arches resting on piers or columns. The term is also used to describe the arched division between the nave of a church and its aisles. A *blind arcade* is a decorative arcade attached to a wall.
See also ARCH, BAY, COLUMN, GALLERY, PIER *and* TRIFORIUM

ARCH A curved series of radiating wedge-shaped bricks or blocks of stone (*voussoirs*) so arranged above an opening that they support one another and are capable of carrying a considerable weight (*see also* LINTEL). The uppermost central block is the *keystone* and the pair of horizontal blocks from which the arch rises on either side of an opening are the *springers*. Between the springers is the notional *springing line*, which determines the geometry of the different types of arch. The walling or support on or against which an arch rests is the *abutment* and the width between abutments is termed the *span* (*see also* CAPITAL, COLUMN *and* PIER). The under-surface of an arch is the *soffit* and the height of the arch, measured between the soffit of the keystone and the centre of the springing line, is known as the *rise*.

Saxon arches were usually of the *triangular* or *mitre* type, formed by a pair of stone slabs joined in a mitre at the top. From the semicircular *classical arch* of ancient Rome derived the Romanesque arch of the early medieval period (popularly known as the 'Norman arch') which was either semicircular (with its centre on the springing line), *segmental* (with its centre below the springing line), or *stilted* (with its centre above the springing line).

The essence of Gothic architecture was the *pointed arch* (the French *arc brisé* or 'broken arch'), which originated in the Middle East and reached western Europe by the twelfth century (*see* VAULTING). Its principal forms were the tall narrow *lancet arch* associated with the Early English style of Gothic architecture; the *equilateral arch*, the radii of which were equal to the span; the *obtuse arch* with a span greater than its radius; the *ogee arch*, characteristic of the fourteenth century; and the *four-centred arch* which is commonly found in buildings dating from the late medieval and Tudor periods.

Not all arches fit neatly into these stereotypes, however. At Wimborne Minster, for example, three bays of the nave arcades have pointed arches but, with heavily incised chevron decoration, stout rounded piers and plain capitals and bases, they are clearly transitional Romanesque. A *strainer* is an arch which spans an internal space to prevent walls from leaning (the finest examples are those above the crossing at Gloucester Cathedral); *interlacing* consists of semicircular arches which interlace and overlap, especially in Romanesque blind arcading (*see* ARCADE); the *Tudor arch* is an extreme form of the late fifteenth-century four-centre arch in which the upper curves are almost flat; and the *straight arch* is a rectangular opening the lintel of which is composed of radiating voussoirs. There are, of course, numerous other variations, including the *rampant arch* in which the springing at either side of the opening is at different levels.
See also CENTERING *and* SCAFFOLDING AND CRANES

ARCHAIC WORDS *see* INSCRIPTIONS

ARCHBISHOP *see* CLERGY (CHURCH OF ENGLAND) *and* SIGNATURES (ARCHBISHOPS AND BISHOPS)

ARCHDIOCESE A DIOCESE of which the holder is *ex officio* archbishop, e.g. York.
ARCHES, COURT OF The CONSISTORY COURT of the PROVINCE of Canterbury which, at one time,

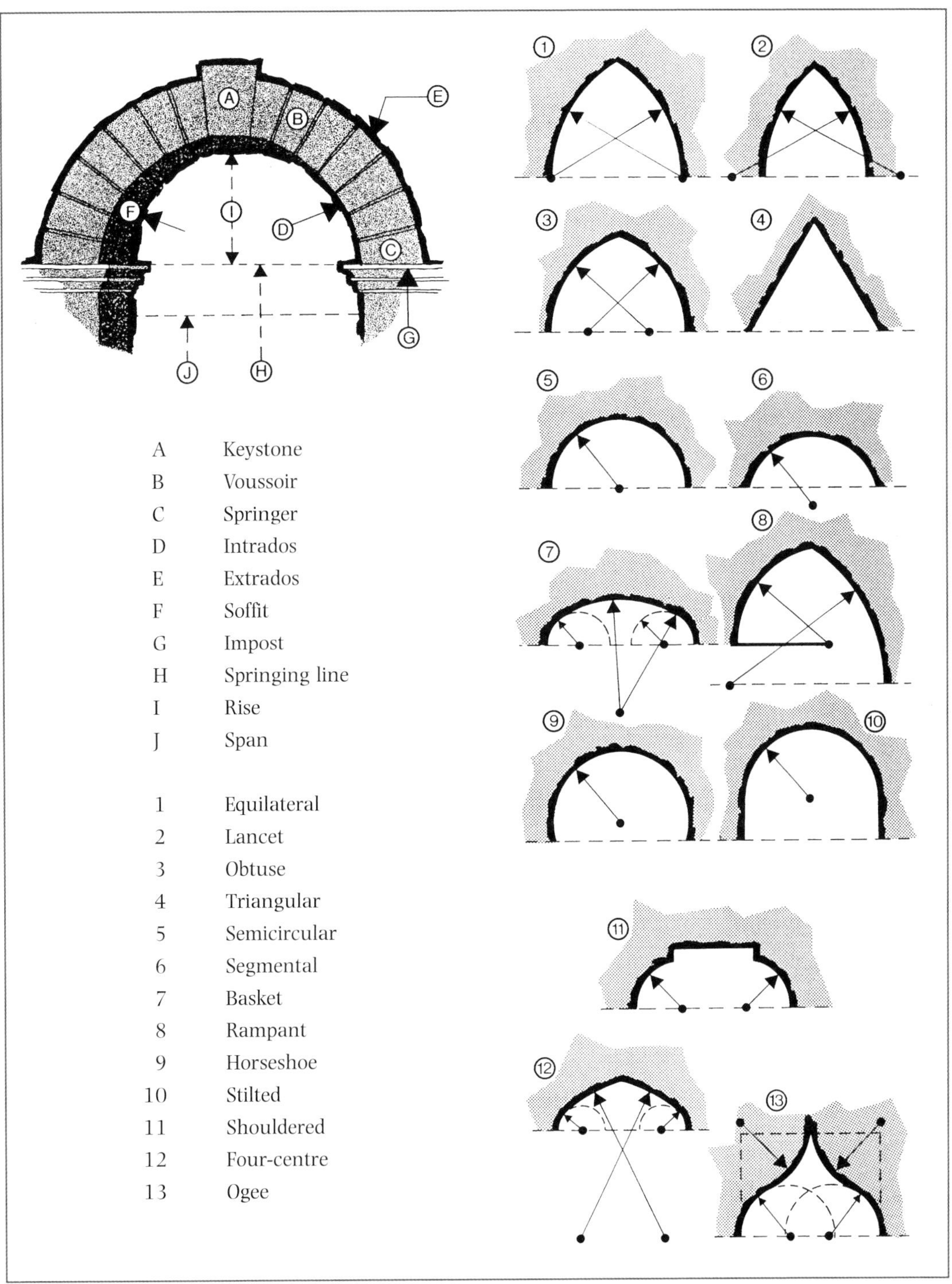

Arches. (Courtesy of John Ferguson)

met at Bow Church (the Church of St Mary-le-Bow or St Mary of the Arches) in Cheapside, London. The name derived from the stone arches of the original eleventh-century church.

ARCHITECTS *see* MASTER MASONS AND ARCHITECTS

ARCHITECTURAL ORNAMENT *see* MEDIEVAL ARCHITECTURAL ORNAMENT

ARCHITECTURE *see* MEDIEVAL ARCHITECTURE

ARCHITRAVE (i) A moulded frame round a window or door.
(ii) A horizontal beam resting on the tops of columns.

ARCHIVES As a consequence of the Parochial Registers and Records Measure of 1978, most documentary sources have been deposited where they will be expertly conserved and made accessible to the public, either in DIOCESAN REGISTRIES or in county record offices.

Diocesan records normally include BISHOPS' REGISTERS, BISHOPS' TRANSCRIPTS, records of diocesan administration, faculties (*see* FACULTY), visitation (*see* VISITATION (ECCLESIASTICAL)) and records of ecclesiastical courts (*see* COURTS (ECCLESIASTICAL)) together with wills, inventories and other probate documents. Archives from parishes which were formerly dependencies of cathedral chapters or monastic and collegiate foundations or were proprietary churches of great estates will more often be found in national repositories such as The National Archives (formerly the Public Record Office), the British Library, the Royal Commission on Historical Manuscripts, the Library of the House of Lords and the Bodleian Library, Oxford.

There are ECCLESIASTICAL LIBRARIES at various cathedrals, and the archives of St Paul's are deposited at the Guildhall Library in London. Archives relating to the Province of Canterbury are at Lambeth Palace, London (*see also* FACULTY) and those of the Province of York at the Borthwick Institute of Historical Research at the University of York.
For the addresses of these and other relevant organisations *see* APPENDIX II.
See also NATIONAL MONUMENTS RECORD *and* WELSH RECORDS

ARCHIVIST In most monastic and collegiate communities, the office of archivist was performed by the librarian (*see* ARMARIUS). He maintained the deeds, charters, licences and other records of the community, including the NECROLOGY, and it was he who drew up and preserved the documents in which were recorded the solemn vows of each professed monk.

ARMARIUM A recessed book cupboard, a book store or library. The rule of St Benedict stressed the importance of divine reading (*lectio divina*) in the life of a monastery, and time was set aside for this purpose. Most Cistercian *armoria* are in the vicinity of the CLOISTER, where the best light for reading would be found in the north alley.
See also ARMARIUS, AUMBRY *and* LIBRARIES

ARMARIUS The senior monastic official (usually the PRECENTOR) who supervised the ARMARIUM and SCRIPTORIUM. He was responsible for maintaining, binding and repairing the books in the *armarium* and was required to provide materials and tools for the scriptorium. He kept a register of borrowers, arranged for the purchase of new books and compiled weekly rosters (*tabulae*) of duties.

Books were extraordinarily valuable and required constant attention in order to protect them from the ravages of dust, damp and insects. It was often necessary to engage skilled professionals to undertake these tasks and monastic accounts containing frequent references to payments for the repair of books and the provision of new bindings. The armarius was expected to be aware of the whereabouts of every book and manuscript and was held to be personally responsible for any book that was taken out of the abbey precincts. Specific grants were allocated to the armarius for the purchasing or making of new books, while the names of donors were recorded by him so that they might be commemorated at mass and the offices. He was responsible for the provision and maintenance of service books and lectionaries and for instructing readers and singers. Temporary documents, such as rosters and lists, were usually inscribed on wax tablets that could be reused.

In the scriptorium, the armarius was responsible for ensuring that there was a constant supply of good-quality inks, colours and gold leaf for illumination (*see* MANUSCRIPT ILLUMINATION), materials on which to write (*see* PARCHMENT *and* VELLUM), and the tools for preparing the writing surface, for ruling lines and for writing, painting and burnishing (*see* INK *and* PENS).

ARMATURE A metal structure used to reinforce TRACERY, canopies, slender columns or sculptural decoration. Iron armatures were introduced into large untraceried windows to support the stained glass and these were often wrought into elaborate decorative patterns, as in the wonderful late twelfth- and early thirteenth-century windows in the Trinity Chapel at Canterbury Cathedral (*see* STAINED GLASS *and* WINDOWS).

ARMIGEROUS An *armiger* is one who is entitled to bear a coat of arms by lawful authority and is thereby armigerous.
See also HERALDRY

ARMORY (i) A system of personal identification by means of hereditary devices placed on, or associated with, a shield. Armory is generally (and erroneously) referred to as HERALDRY.
(ii) A dictionary of coats of arms listed alphabetically by surname: notably Sir Bernard Burke's *General Armory of England, Ireland, Scotland and Wales*, published in 1842 and reprinted by *Heraldry Today* in 1984.

ARMS OF OFFICE In HERALDRY, the vertical division of a shield to incorporate the arms of (e.g.) a bishopric to the dexter (the left when viewed from the front) and the personal arms of the incumbent to the sinister (the right).
See also HERALDRY (ECCLESIASTICAL)

ARMS, ROYAL *see* ROYAL ARMS

ARRIS In architecture, the sharp edge produced at the meeting of two flat or curved surfaces.

ASCETICISM The word means 'discipline' or 'training' – and was described by St Benedict as 'the more perfect way' for those who follow God. Asceticism was a system of practices intended to combat vices and develop virtues through mortification of the flesh, severe self-discipline, ABSTINENCE and austerity. Early ascetics tended to withdraw from the world, either as solitaries or in communities. In Britain, extreme asceticism was more often found in the Celtic Church than that of Rome. In the Middle Ages, ascetics sometimes joined formal religious orders such as the Cistercians or Austin Canons.

ASHLAR Smooth-faced MASONRY constructed of square-hewn FREESTONE. Also thin slabs of DRESSED STONE used for facing walls over RUBBLE.

ASPERGES (i) The ceremony of sanctification by the sprinkling of consecrated water. Following the blessing of the water, the community would process through the monastery, inviting God's blessing on its constituent parts and the activities that took place in each. The asperges would be followed by a celebration of High Mass.
(ii) The sprinkler used for that purpose, usually a perforated ball finial attached by a silver stem to a wooden handle. Asperges, and the buckets in which the HOLY WATER was carried during the service, may still be found in some cathedral treasuries. Holy water (which may contain a small quantity of salt) was similarly used for other purposes such as ceremonial cleansing, dedi-

cations, blessings and exorcisms.

ASPIRANT One who aspires to a religious vocation.

ATTACHED *see* ENGAGED

AUDITORIUM *see* PARLOUR

AUDITORY CHURCH A church designed primarily to enable the congregation to see and hear the preacher.

AUGMENTATION, COURT OF Created in 1535, the Court of Augmentation administered the lands, possessions and revenues of the dissolved religious houses and succeeded in augmenting the royal income by £32,000 a year (*see* DISSOLUTION OF THE MONASTERIES). The Court's function was transferred to the Exchequer in 1554.

AUGUSTINIANS (*also* AUSTIN *or* REGULAR CANONS) Communities of clerics who, from the mid-eleventh century in Italy and France, adopted the Rule of St Augustine of Hippo (354–430), which required strict personal poverty, celibacy and obedience (*see* RULE). Their ethos was formally approved at Lateran synods in 1059 and 1063 and by the early twelfth century members of these communities, which had spread throughout western Europe, came to be known as *Regular Canons*. Like monks, they were bound to the DIVINE OFFICE (*Opus Dei*) and led a communal life. But, unlike monks, all canons were priests, their rule was less severe and they were not confined to their houses. The Augustinian habit consisted of a black cassock, white surplice and hooded black cloak and, as a result, they came to be known as the Black Canons. They are also referred to as *Austin Canons*, this being an early English form of Augustine.

The Augustinians arrived in England at the beginning of the twelfth century and by 1200 had established 140 foundations in England and Wales. (These were to rise in number to over 200 before declining to 170 at the Dissolution of the Monasteries.) They appear to have selected ancient monastic sites for many of their houses and where there were survivors of an earlier community they sometimes joined it: at Bardsey Island in Gwynedd, for example. Each house was governed by a 'prelate', usually a prior, although there were some two dozen houses, mostly in the Midlands, which were described as ABBEYS. They appear to have had parochial responsibilities which may explain why so many Augustinian churches and dependent chapelries have survived, in whole or in part. Examples are Llanthony in Monmouthshire, Cartmel in Lancashire, Bolton and Bridlington in Yorkshire and Waltham in Essex, while the cathedrals of Bristol, Oxford, Carlisle, Portsmouth and Southwark were all Augustinian foundations (Carlisle became a CATHEDRAL PRIORY in 1133). The Augustinians were noted for their HOSPITALS, of which St Thomas and St Bartholomew's (London) were the first and, perhaps, the best known.

Independent Augustinian congregations include the PREMONSTRATENSIAN CANONS or 'White Canons', who adopted a particularly austere way of life. There were also Augustinian (Austin) Canonesses with over twenty houses in medieval England and Wales, most of which appear to have suffered from inadequate endowments. Most ranked as PRIORIES, although Burnham Canonsleigh in Buckinghamshire and Lacock in Wiltshire were abbeys.

The Augustinian Friars (usually referred to as Austin Friars or the Hermit Friars of St Augustine) were constituted from three small congregations of English hermits in *c.* 1256. They established forty priories in England and Wales and worked as mendicants within the territories (*limites*) assigned to each house. Their constitution was modelled on that of the Dominicans (*see* FRIARS) and their habit consisted of a long black gown and hood over a white cassock – hence, the Black Friars.

See also AUSTIN CANONESSES

AUMBRY *or* AMBRY A secure chest or cupboard in which altar plate, mass vessels and other sacred

items and RELICS were stored. Usually formed within a rectangular recess in a wall, in larger monastic and collegiate churches there were often several aumbries in the PRESBYTERY, some of which may have been located beneath the top (*mensa*) of the altar. The term is also used to describe cupboards with more mundane uses: those for storing towels near the monastic LAVATORIUM, for example, and 'civerys' in which the FRATER table furnishings were kept. At Norwich, eight or more such recesses in the cloister are described as 'civerys'.
See also ARMARIUM, CHEST CUPBOARD, CREDENCE, PISCINA *and* VEIL

AUMBRY LAMP A light, burned constantly in the SANCTUARY in honour of the Blessed sacrament. This may be coloured red if suspended above an altar, or white if the Sacrament is nearby (*see* LAMPS).

AUSTIN CANONESSES Nuns following the rule of St Augustine. There were more than twenty houses of Austin canonesses in medieval England and Wales. With the exception of Lacock and Burnham Canonsleigh (which were abbeys), they were ranked as priories but, for the most part, they were small and poorly endowed.
See also AUGUSTINIANS *and* NUNS AND NUNERIES

AUSTIN CANONS *and* AUSTIN FRIARS *see* AUGUSTINIANS *and* FRIARS

AVOWESS *see* BRASSES (MONUMENTAL), EFFIGIES *and* VOWESS

AXIAL TOWER A tower located above the CROSSING of a cruciform church.
See also TOWERS

B

BAKEHOUSE (PISTRINUM) A monastic bakehouse was generally located in the outer court, usually near the granary and mill. Huge quantities of bread were required in the larger monasteries, not only to feed the community (*see* FRATER), but also for HOSPITALITY and ALMS. The Benedictine rule decreed: 'Let a good pound weight of bread suffice for the day' for each monk (though a superior was able to increase the allowance if it was felt that a monk's labours had been particularly onerous). In nunneries, the weekly allowance was seven pound loaves. The 'breaking of bread' was, of course, a symbolic act and in early Benedictine houses it was distributed with considerable solemnity. All the loaves from a fresh baking were suspended in a basket above the ABBOT'S TABLE in the FRATER. When the brethren were assembled, the basket 'shall descend . . . in order that the rations of God's labourers may appear to descend to them from heaven'. Once the bread had been distributed, the crumbs were collected and made into a pudding which was blessed and eaten at the end of the week. In addition to the great bakehouse, there was often provision within the church itself for the ceremonial baking of the 'single bread' – the unleavened bread used at the mass.
See also BREAD OVEN

BALDAC(C)HINO (*also* BALDACHIN, BALDAQUIN *and* UMBRACULUM) A cloth CANOPY above an altar or bishop's throne (*cathedra*). Sometimes (incorrectly) described as a *ciborium*, which is a solid canopy or *tester* of wood, stone or metal. The baldacchino, originally a medieval feature, was reintroduced into the English church by the architect Sir Ninian Comper (1864–1960). From the Italian for a richly

embroidered cloth, the word originated in *Baldacco* the Italian form of *Baghdad* where the fabric was made. There are notable examples at Liverpool Cathedral and St Paul's, London.
See also ALTARS

BALLFLOWER ORNAMENT A decorative motif (especially from the medieval Decorated period) consisting of small, widely spaced spheres in a concave moulding, each carved with a crude trefoil-like 'floret'.

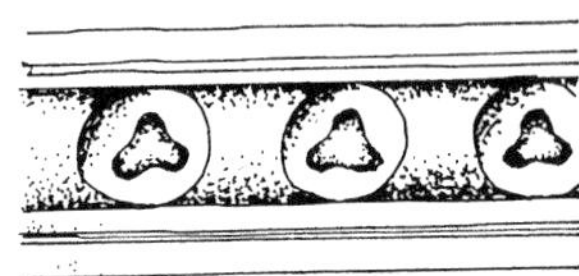

(Tom Friar)

See also MEDIEVAL ARCHITECTURE

BALNEARIUM *see* ABLUTIONS

BALUSTER A short pillar with a curving, convex outline. Used to describe the shape of vessels, the stems of candlesticks, incense boats, finials, etc. and the balustrades of altar and communion rails, staircases, copings, etc.

BANNER-STAVE LOCKERS The long staves of gonfannons and crucifixes that were such a feature of medieval PROCESSIONS were often stored in a tall, narrow recess formed for that purpose in a church wall.

BAPTISTERY That part of a church in which baptism is administered. From the third century the baptistery was often a separate, polygonal building west of the church, containing a large basin below ground level in which the candidate was submerged. An increase in infant baptism from the end of the fourth century led to the widespread practice of affusion and the use of FONTS, which were placed within the church, usually (though not invariably) near the south door, although many were later removed to the space beneath a (west) tower.

BARNS (GRANARIUM) Most of the magnificent buildings which we now describe as tithe barns were constructed by monastic communities to store the produce of their estates and granges and the tithes of their appropriated parishes (*see* GRANGE *and* TITHES).

The word barn is derived from the Old English *bereærn* meaning 'barley house', for barley was the chief crop of the Anglo-Saxon farmer. Though intended primarily to store produce, barns were used for a multiplicity of purposes and enabled farmhands to carry out many essential tasks under cover in inclement weather. They were used as shippens (for milking), for sheltering calves and for protecting ewes at lambing time. Others were provided with first-floor hay lofts and pigeon lofts, constructed within the roof gable, and some incorporated separate domestic quarters, complete with a hearth and chimney.

In the south and east of England medieval barns were usually of timber construction but elsewhere they were generally built of stone beneath a timber-framed roof with thatch or stone tiling and with narrow vertical openings in the walls for ventilation. Both in plan and elevation, these massive barns are similar in size and appearance to churches with their lofty 'naves', heavily buttressed walls, aisles and 'transepts' (*midstrays*) with tall double doors providing vehicular access to the threshing floor. This was usually constructed of closely fitted planks of oak or elm and the draught between the pairs of doors served to reduce the dust during threshing and to separate the heavier grain from the chaff. Shaftesbury Abbey's great fourteenth-century barn at Bradford-on-Avon in Wiltshire has two pairs of double doors, while the abbey barn at Glastonbury in Somerset is of cruck-frame construction and measures 26m (85ft) by 7.6m (25ft), with midstays projecting a further 6m (20ft). There are two notable fourteenth-century tithe barns in Oxfordshire at Church Enstone and Swalcliffe, and splendid examples from the fifteenth century at Abbotsbury in Dorset, originally 82m (270ft) in length, Tisbury in

Shaftesbury Abbey's fourteenth-century tithe barn at Bradford-on-Avon, Wiltshire. (Courtesy of John Mennell)

Wiltshire and Ashleworth, Gloucestershire.

Following the DISSOLUTION OF THE MONASTERIES, many monastic buildings were converted to agrarian use, such as the 'priory barn' at Latton, Essex, which was created out of the ruins of the early fourteenth-century crossing of the priory church, abandoned in 1534.

BARREL VAULT *see* VAULTING

BARTON A place-name element from the Old English *bere* or *bær-*, meaning 'barley', to *beretun* or *bærtun*, meaning 'granary farm'. The term was widely applied to a demesne farm and in particular to a monastic GRANGE which may have supported a chapelry. The proximity of a 'barton' place-name to a parish church may, therefore, suggest that the latter originated in a dependent chapelry of a monastic foundation.

BAS-RELIEF Sculpture or carving in low-relief.

BASE An architectural term used to describe the

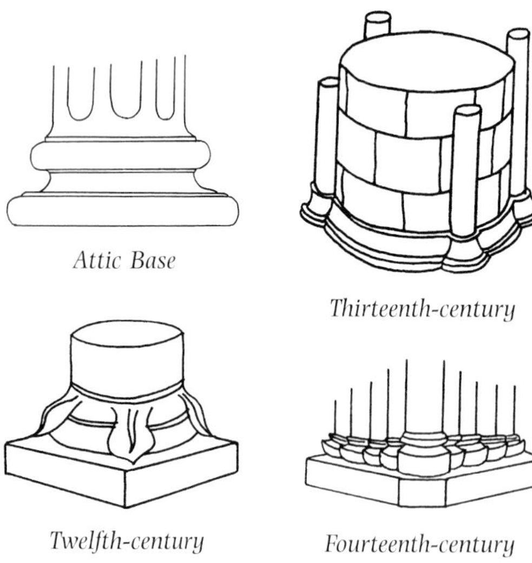

(Tom Friar)

base of a COLUMN or PIER between the shaft and the pedestal or pavement. Eleventh-century Romanesque bases usually consisted of a quarter-round moulding on a square plinth. In later work, the angles between the square and rounded sections were sometimes filled by carved decorative foliage or even animals. Some resemble the classical attic base (a concave moulding between two convex mouldings), a style which was commonly used in the Early English period of Gothic architecture (*see* MEDIEVAL ARCHITECTURE). From this developed a variety of elaborately moulded bases set on deep pedestals which were often octagonal. In the early fourteenth century bases were composed of triple rolls, which were later replaced by OGEE mouldings. In the Perpendicular period, bases were tall and slender and finely proportioned, usually with roll mouldings at the top and a double ogee and further rolls beneath. Bell-shaped bases on octagonal plinths are a feature of this later period.
See also CAPITAL

BASILICAN In the present context, the term implies a simple rectangular plan with a nave that is both higher and wider than the aisles, from which it is usually divided by colonnades (*see* COLONNADE), and with an APSE at the eastern end.

BATEMENT A vertical light in the head of a window.

BATH STONE Oolitic limestone quarried in northern Wiltshire, where it occurs in beds of up to 10m (33ft). When quarried it is damp (with 'quarry sap') and is easily cut and carved before being seasoned. This pale, golden stone was widely used for church building throughout the Middle Ages and the sixteenth century.

BATHING *see* ABLUTIONS

BATTLEMENT A crenellated parapet at the top of a wall, the indentations being *embrasures* and the raised section *merlons*. Both were originally finished with a coping, although this is sometimes missing.

BAY (i) A vertical section of wall between columns, piers or buttresses or a division of a vaulted or timber roof (*see* ARCADE, BUTTRESS, CLERESTORY, COLUMN, PIER *and* TRIFORIUM). The Normans introduced the concept into their larger churches where nave walls were articulated into bays, each separated by a tall vertical shaft which extended from floor to ceiling. With the introduction of stone vaults, this shaft (or group of shafts) terminated in a CAPITAL which supported the vault. The vault was also divided into bays by ribs which splayed upwards from the capital (*springing*) in a variety of forms (*see* VAULTING).
(ii) A recess in a room, especially one formed by a projecting window.

BEAD Originally a prayer (also *bede*) but later applied to the component parts of a necklace which were used to assist the memory when reciting the rosary, hence 'telling beads' (*see*

BEDESMAN). The famous 'Syon Beads', for example, were rosaries of either five or sixty-three beads which could be obtained from the Brigittine double house of Syon (Twickenham, Greater London) in the fifteenth century (*see* INDULGENCE). Special prayers were prescribed for their use and various symbolic meanings ascribed to the number of beads and even to the number of words in the text of the devotions. In a manuscript, now in the British Library (Harley 494), five short prayers are given, each to be followed by a 'refrain' which was to be 'sayde on every bede':

> O swete blessyd Jheus for thi holy name and thy bytter passion, save us from synne and shame and endless damnacion and bryng us to thi blysse. Amen.

In a further manuscript (Harley 541) there is also a list of indulgences which accompanied the saying of additional prayers:

> The pardon of Syon Bedez. For every paternoster CCCC dayez
> For every Ave Maria CCCC dayez
> For every credo CCCC dayez
> The summe of the pardon to the hole Sawter is 1 x Mi vij et ijC dayez

BEADSMAN *see* BEDESMAN

BEAKHEAD ORNAMENT Romanesque ornamentation consisting of mythical birds' and beasts' heads with pointed beaks or tongues (*see* MEDIEVAL ARCHITECTURE).

BEARDS *see* RASURA

BECKET A carved boss at the end of a DRIPSTONE.

BEDE-HOUSE A form of ALMONRY attached to some secular colleges in the late Middle Ages.
See also ALMSHOUSES, CHANTRY COLLEGE, HOSPICE *and* HOSPITALS

A Nave vault; B Clerestory; C Tribune or triforium; D Nave arcade. (Tom Friar)

(Tom Friar)

The north nave arcade at Durham Cathedral. (Courtesy of Derry Brabbs/www.derrybrabbs.com)

BEDE ROLL A list of benefactors to a religious community for whom commemorative prayers were to be said.
See also CHANTRY CHAPELS

BEDESMAN (*also* BEADSMAN) One who is paid or endowed to pray for others. Tiny figures of bedesmen were often carved in medieval tomb chests as symbols of the perpetual prayers which were to be offered for the deceased and his family (*see* BEAD, CHANTRY *and* MONUMENTS).

BEE-KEEPING Bees were kept for their honey and for their wax from which were produced liturgical candles and writing tablets. It was the CELLARER who was ultimately responsible for maintaining the hives which were usually kept in the outer court (*curia*).

BELFRY A bell tower or that part of a tower in which bells are housed (*see* BELLS *and* TOWERS).

BELL-HATCH (*or* BELL-HOLE) An opening in a tower vault through which bells were raised and lowered.

BELL LOUVRES Window-like openings in the walls of a tower in which sets of horizontal overlapping slats provide protection from the weather while not impeding the sound of the bells.
See also BELLS *and* TOWERS

BELLS In the monasteries 'the sound of bells was rarely absent from the air, either the small bells of the DORTER, FRATER, chapter and church or the greater bells of the tower. They seem to have punctuated every occasion throughout the day and they must have given an air of animation both within and without the monastery' (Crossley, *The English Abbey*, 1935). The great bells were rung to summon a community to prayer at the appointed Day Hours (*Diurnal*) of Lauds, Prime, Sext, None, Vespers and Compline. The onerous duty of ringing the great bell fell to a 'careful brother' selected by the Abbot, although in the later Middle Ages bells were sometimes controlled by clock mechanisms which had neither hands nor face (*see* CLOCKS). Of course, there was still a need for the bells to be rung in celebration (in some abbeys as often as forty times a year) and ringers were often rewarded with special rations or were replaced by paid servants. Only at Passiontide were the bells silent, as a sign of mourning.

Before the fourteenth century, the larger bells were normally suspended on a single spindle, but from *c.* 1300 they were mounted on wooden quarter-wheels, the spindle serving as the axle and with the rope attached to the rim of the wheel. It was then found that even greater control could be achieved when the bell was mounted on a half-wheel. At the Reformation many church bells were either silenced or removed. The task of restoring them during and after the Elizabethan period often necessitated rehanging, which provided an opportunity for further experimentation. Most bells were now mounted on a complete wheel, while the introduction of a slider and stay made it possible for the bell's movement to be halted at will.

Large medieval bells were often dedicated to a saint and were inscribed with an appropriate prayer or biblical text. Initial letters, sometimes in the form of crosses, word stops, lettering and foundry marks are of great beauty and interest, although, because of their lofty location, they remain inaccessible. Inscriptions on post-Reformation bells tend to be secular in character. They are usually (though not invariably) in English and often incorporate the name of the bell-founder and of benefactors. The bells of Sherborne Abbey, Dorset (now the parish church) are believed to be the heaviest peal of eight in the world. The tenor ('Great Tom') alone weighs 2½ tons, its inscription recalling Cardinal Thomas Wolsey (*c.* 1475–1530) who gave the bell to the abbey:

By Wolsey's gift I measure time for all,
To mirth, to grief, to church, I serve to call.

Also at Sherborne is the Fire Bell that is rung for conflagrations. It too is inscribed:

Lord, quench this furious flame:
Arise, run, help put out the same.

Change-ringing
'Ringing the changes' on peals of five, six, eight, ten or twelve bells, was introduced in the mid-seventeenth century and is almost unknown outside England. The bells are rung in a series of different orders (*changes*): on eight bells, for example, 40,320 changes are possible (this is called 'accomplishing the extent') and some 1,600 changes can be rung in an hour. The earliest evidence of change-ringing (from *c.* 1618) is a carving on the tower door-post of Buxhall church in Suffolk:

1	2	3	4	5
2	1	3	4	5
2	3	1	4	5
2	3	4	1	5
2	3	4	5	1
	2	.	.	.

It was the publication of Fabian Stedman's *Tintinnalogia* in 1668 and his *Campanologia* in 1677 that formalised a system by which the bells could make 'real music'. Stedman's method (which is still the most popular) requires an even number of bells, although (paradoxically) the changes are rung on an odd number. Thus, in a 'ring of bells' of six, 'Stedman' would be rung on the 'front five' (2–1–4–3–5) with the largest bell (the tenor) coming in behind. Inevitably, numerous variations evolved from Stedman's system and the names of those who attempted to ring Grandsire Triples, Bob Major, Stedman Caters, Tittum Bob Royal and other sequences were painted on boards and proudly displayed in ringing chambers throughout England.

All bells are considered to be feminine and are 'raised' or 'turned over' to 'speak' their Pleasures, Tittums, Superlatives and Surprises. The essence of ringing in a peal is that each bell should turn through an almost complete revolution each time the bell-rope is pulled, beginning from an inverted position (a stay on the wheel prevents a bell from performing a complete revolution).

The bells are rung from a *ringing chamber* (or *hanging chamber*) within the tower which is usually reached by ladders or a turnpike stair (*vice*). At Crowland Abbey in Lincolnshire the bells are immediately above the porch so that worshippers are obliged to pass through the circle of ringers as they enter the church. Ringing chambers often contain fascinating evidence of continuous use, sometimes dating from the seventeenth and eighteenth centuries, such as ringers' rhymes (almost invariably warning of a fine for wearing spurs or a hat in the chamber), lists of tower captains (the head ringers, also known as Bell Captains) and ringing boards on which are chalked the orders for the day. Societies of ringers (known as 'The St . . . Tower' and whose members are described as 'youths') also maintain records of their achievements.

The towers themselves (which may move during the ringing of a large peal) have an effect on the sound produced by the bells that hang within them. Old bricks soak up the sound and sweeten it, and the taller the tower, the quieter the bells in its immediate vicinity. In recent centuries, bells were usually hung about 12ft (3.6m) lower than the bell louvres in the tower walls so that the sound can rise and spread outwards.

See also CLOCKS, SANCTUS BELL *and* TOWERS
For the Central Council of Church Bell Ringers *see* APPENDIX II.

BENCHES Medieval congregations were rarely

provided with seating: they simply stood or knelt – although stone benches were sometimes attached to the walls as a concession to the elderly and infirm (hence the expression 'gone to the wall'). But with the growing popularity of itinerant preachers (notably the FRIARS who arrived in England in the fourteenth century), so the need for seating increased (*see also* PULPITS). With the introduction of an English LITURGY following the Reformation, most churches acquired some form of seating, often trestles which could be removed when the nave was required for other purposes. Nevertheless, by the late sixteenth century an increasing number of churches had installed permanent long-backed benches. These have backs with open rails or panels, bench-ends, and bookrests for the benefit of those sitting on the bench behind. Rows of benches are often (and erroneously) referred to as *pews*, which are enclosed and of a much later date. In many abbey churches and cathedrals, benches have been replaced by rows of chairs, which are more comfortable and may be removed and stored when the nave is used for other purposes.

BENEDICITE The song of praise 'Bless ye [the Lord]' attributed (in Dan. 3) to Shadrach, Meshach and Abednego as they stood together in the 'fiery furnace'. The canticle has been used in the Christian liturgy since the days of the early Church.

BENEDICTINE NUNS The Benedictine abbey of Shaftesbury, Dorset, was the largest nunnery in medieval England. By 1327 it supported a community of more than 120 Benedictine nuns, although its numbers were greatly reduced as a consequence of the Black Death (*see* PLAGUE). It owned vast tracts of land throughout Dorset and Wiltshire and maintained a HOSPICE and an almshouse at Shaftesbury and a leper hospital at Blandford Forum. However, communities such as Shaftesbury and Romsey in Hampshire were exceptional: although numerous, the majority of Benedictine nunneries were small and poor. Their chaplains were usually secular priests who held prebends in the monastic estates.
See also NUNS AND NUNNERIES

BENEDICTINES (The Black Monks) The Rule of St Benedict of Nursia (*c.* 480–*c.* 550) provided a cohesive, inclusive and individual code by which monastic life, both spiritual and administrative, could be ordered (*see* RULE). It was a perfect expression of devout sobriety, neither excessive nor fanatical, and was to become the model for all subsequent forms of monasticism in western Europe. Regular observance was based on the principle of the common life: the individual was subservient to the body corporate. But there was no *order* of St Benedict: the Benedictine Rule was simply one of several from which an abbot selected the observances by which his community lived. Successive medieval popes attempted to bring the Benedictine abbeys under a centralised constitution but the Benedictines themselves preferred to exercise reform through independent local congregations.

Throughout the DARK AGES it was the Benedictines who maintained the ideals and practice of scholarship and liturgical worship. They 'provided stability in chaotic and restless times, regulation in anarchy and continuity in a time of dissolution' (Bottomley). Indeed, their influence affected profoundly the subsequent nature of medieval society.

In England, the tenth-century clerics Dunstan, Oswald and Ethelwold reintroduced large-scale monasticism after a century of decline in the ANGLO-SAXON CHURCH. With the support of the Anglo-Saxon monarchy they introduced a strict Benedictine rule and established (or refounded) a series of monasteries, 'correcting the foolish with rods' and so antagonising the 'evil-living [secular] clerics' with their 'illegal wives' and partiality for gluttony and drunkenness, that there was even an unsuccessful attempt to poison Ethelwold in his hall at Winchester.

The Benedictines were known as the *Black Monks* because they wore a black cowl over a black, white or russet cassock, trimmed with black or white fur, and a black cape and hood (they were not referred to as Benedictines until the late Middle Ages). Prior to the DISSOLUTION OF THE MONASTERIES, there were (in England and Wales) fifty abbeys of Benedictine monks, over forty conventual priories, a similar number of lesser houses and cells, and more than sixty houses of Benedictine nuns: a total of nearly two hundred communities with some three thousand brethren and sisters, together with numerous servants, employees and dependants. Several abbey and priory churches have survived as CATHEDRALS: Winchester Cathedral Priory, for example, and the 'new foundation' cathedrals of Chester, Gloucester, Peterborough and Westminster, while many others have been adopted for parochial use. Not all are as magnificent as the parish churches of Milton (where the nave was never built) and Sherborne in Dorset, Tewkesbury in Gloucestershire and Great Malvern in Worcestershire. The majority remain as simple parish churches in which at least some part of the monastic structure survives.

See also ABBEY, CISTERCIANS *and* PRIORY

BENEDICTUS The song of thanksgiving for the birth of John the Baptist (Luke 1: 68–79) sung liturgically at Lauds and incorporated into the *Book of Common Prayer* for use at Mattins.

BENEFACTORS Those who contributed to the building, restoration or extension of a monastery or church, or who granted lands to a religious community in return for the prayers of the beneficiaries (*see* CHANTRY) and recognition as a *confrater* or honorary member of the community (*see* CONFRATERNITY).

The Norman aristocracy was particularly keen to endow large tracts of land to the monasteries. To these warrior knights, monasticism was regarded as the spiritual counterpart of their own military ethic, a perception that the Benedictines actively encouraged:

> Look carefully at the things that are provided for you by trained monks living in monasteries under a Rule; strenuous is the warfare which these castle-guards of Christ wage against the Devil; innumerable are the benefits of their struggle. Who can recount the vigils, hymns, psalms, prayers, alms and daily offerings of masses which the monks perform? These followers of Christ crucify themselves that they may please God. And so, noble earl, I earnestly advise you to build such a castle in your country, manned by monks against Satan. Here the cowled champions will resist the devil in constant warfare for your soul.
>
> *Orderic Vitalis*

For these rich and powerful men a gift to a religious house was considered to be a shrewd investment. The 'soldiers for Christ' (as Bernard of Clairvaux described his fellow Cistercians) would pray regularly for the souls of their benefactors while the benefactors could anticipate salvation through the monks' intercessions. But, as in all things, fashions changed. Initially, it was the Benedictines who attracted major endowments, followed by the more ascetic orders and, in the early twelfth century, the communities of Augustinian Canons. From the 1130s the Cistercians attracted numerous patrons, while, in the thirteenth century, the new orders of FRIARS (who did not need large gifts of land) were particularly popular. In the late medieval period, when the increasingly relaxed conduct of certain orders was attracting cynicism, the austere Carthusian order received substantial patronage.

The names of benefactors were often inscribed in a book or *bede roll* so that their generosity would be commemorated in perpetuity and, if they were ARMIGEROUS, their heraldic devices might be incorporated in the fabric of the building they had helped to endow (there are 825 shields of arms of benefactors in the vault of the Canterbury cloister which was rebuilt *c.* 1400). A relatively poor man

could qualify as a benefactor but a substantial donation was required before he could be recognised as a founder. It was not unusual for founders to join the communities they had endowed. Walter Espec, for example, one of Henry I's barons, ended his days as a humble monk at Rievaulx Abbey in 1154. Espec's patronage was typical of the great benefactors of his day. In *c.* 1122 he founded the Augustinian priory of Kirkham. This was followed, in 1132, by an endowment of land near his castle at Helmsley for the founding of the Cistercian abbey of Rievaulx. And when the Rievaulx community began to expand he made a further gift of land for a DAUGHTER HOUSE at Warden in Bedfordshire.
See also FOUNDATION (MONASTIC)

BENEFIT OF CLERGY Exemption from trial by a secular court, accorded to the medieval clergy. In England this provision was extended to all whose literacy theoretically qualified them for holy orders. Prisoners were often required to read from the scriptures in order to avoid a capital sentence for a minor offence. The test was abolished in 1706; the procedure was abolished in 1827.
See also CANON LAW *and* CLARENDON, CONSTITUTIONS OF

BIER LIGHT A tall candleholder, four of which would have been placed on the floor at the corners of a coffin when kept in a church for any length of time. Medieval bier lights were lit and placed at the corners of TOMB CHESTS to commemorate the birthday or saint's day of the deceased and when masses were said for his soul (*see* CHANTRY *and* EFFIGIES). Processional torches, which were carried on either side of the cross in processions, were of similar appearance and have heavy, removable bases so that they may be stored in an upright position or used as bier lights.

BILLET Romanesque ornamentation consisting of a series of raised rectangular or cylindrical motifs alternating with spaces (*see* MEDIEVAL ARCHITECTURE).

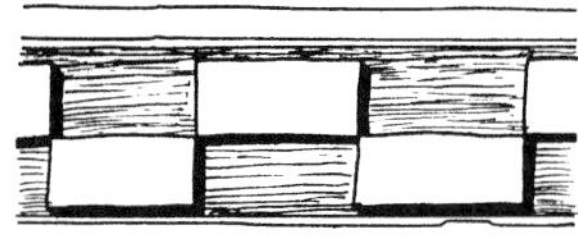

(Tom Friar)

BISHOP *see* ABBEY, CATHEDRAL PRIORY, DIOCESE *and* SIGNATURES (ARCHBISHOPS AND BISHOPS)

BISHOPS' PALACES *see* FORTIFICATION

BISHOPS' REGISTERS From the early thirteenth century, the Church began to exercise greater care in the ordering of its records. A series of papal records, which begin in 1198, are an invaluable source for English ecclesiastical history, as are royal records and bishops' registers, also dating from the thirteenth century. By the late Middle Ages diocesan administration had developed into a complex network that affected the lives of parishioners from the cradle to the grave. As a result, there are few aspects of parochial and manorial life that do not appear in the bishops' registers of the time. Entries relate to individual parishes and contain an extraordinary wealth of historical information: the identity of patrons and incumbents; priests ordained or instituted to parochial chapelries, free chapels, private oratories and chantries; licences to clergy to leave their parishes (to enter royal service or to undertake a pilgrimage, for example); entries concerning the rededication of a church or alterations in its patronal festivals; the consecration (required by Canon Law) of the extension or rebuilding of churches; details of the division or combining of parishes and the founding of chantries and oratories; records of TITHES and of disputes brought before a bishop. Such information provides invaluable evidence of demographic, political, agricultural and social change for a time when other sources are rare. There may also be incidental evidence of road and bridge building, harbour repairs, the provision of drainage and water supplies, repairs to the parish church and other communal works which were carried out, either in return for INDULGENCES (usually, of forty days) or by subscription, and recorded in the registers. Many registers have been published by local record societies and details of all the episcopal registers may be found in the *Guide to Bishops' Registers of England and Wales*. Most of the early printed registers were produced in the original Latin but later volumes are generally translated into English and include summaries and calendars.

BISHOP'S THRONE *see* CATHEDRALS

BISHOPS' TRANSCRIPTS From 1598 incumbents were required to provide their diocesan bishop with copies of entries in the parish registers. Unfortunately, in some cases the order was observed only sporadically and, in others, the returns were not scrupulously maintained. Consequently, the Bishops' Transcripts are often a poor substitute for the original registers, although they may prove invaluable where registers (or entries) are found to be missing.
See also ARCHIVES *and* BISHOPS' REGISTERS

BLACK CANONS *see* AUGUSTINIANS

BLACK DEATH *see* PLAGUE

BLACK FRIARS *see* FRIARS

BLACK MONKS *see* BENEDICTINES

BLASPHEMY Contempt of God, expressed through grossly irreverent speech, action or even thought, was once both a mortal sin and a legal offence, as was blasphemy against the Church and its saints. In Britain, it remains so only if calculated to offend believers or is likely to cause a breach of the peace.

BLAZON To describe a coat of arms or other heraldic device using the conventions and terminology of HERALDRY. Such a description is itself termed a blazon.

BLESSED SACRAMENT A term used to describe the Sacrament of the EUCHARIST, both the service and (especially) the consecrated elements of bread and wine.
See also RESERVATION

BLIND A term used to describe raised architectural features, such as arcading and vaulting ribs, between which the intervening spaces are closed.

BLIND ARCADE *see* ARCADE

BLOCK CAPITAL (*also* CUSHION CAPITAL) A Romanesque capital formed from a cube of stone the lower edges of which have been rounded off to meet the circular shaft below (*see* CAPITAL).

BLOOD-LETTING *see* PHLEBOTOMY

BONSHOMMES *see* FRIARS *and* GRANDMONTINES

BOOK OF HOURS Often the most impressive of all medieval written documents, Books of Hours were personal devotional books widely used by the devout laity from the thirteenth century. Most were embellished more or less elaborately according to the taste and pocket of the patron for whom they were prepared. Some were presented as gifts by calligraphers and illuminators in hope of patronage. Books of Hours provided a series of prayers appropriate to the eight canonical hours into which the day was divided, together with a calendar and various extracts from the divine office and psalms. They were invariably exceedingly beautiful, the illustrations providing also a wealth of information on contemporary social life.
See also MANUSCRIPT ILLUMINATION *and*

PRIMER

BOOKPLATE A sloping wooden or metal plate, with a projecting lower edge, to support an open book: as on a LECTERN, MISSAL STAND or pulpit desk (*see* DESKS).

BOOKS Books were necessary for the recitation of the offices (*see* DIVINE OFFICE), for readings in CHAPTER, the FRATER and at COLLATION and for private meditative reading which was required by the rule. Indeed, 'reading' (which included working in the SCRIPTORIUM) gradually replaced MANUAL LABOUR in the daily round (*see* HORARIUM). In 1277 the Benedictine General Chapter ordered that 'in place of manual labour the abbots shall appoint other occupations for their claustral monks according to their capacity: study, writing, correcting, illuminating and binding books.' The PRECENTOR was responsible for maintaining the service books, which were not to be removed from the church or cloister. These included the ANTIPHONARIUM, GRADUALE, MISSAL and PROCESSIONALE.
See also ARCHIVES, BOOK OF HOURS, BREVIARY, CALENDAR, CAPITULARY, CARTULARY, COLOPHON, COMMON PRAYER (BOOK OF), CUSTOMARY, ECCLESIASTICAL LIBRARIES, EVANGELIARY, FACULTY, HYMNARY, INVENTORY, LECTIONARY, LIBRARIES, LITANY, LITURGY, MANUALE, MANUAL LABOUR, MANUSCRIPT ILLUMINATION, MARGINAL INSCRIPTION, MARTYROLOGY, MONASTIC BREVIARY, MONASTICON ANGLICANUM, ORDINAL, ORDINARY (ii), PAPER, PARCHMENT, PONTIFICAL, PRIMER, PSALTER, PSALTERY, RUBRIC, SACRAMENTARY, TEMPORALE, VELLUM, VESPERALE, *and* WELSH RECORDS

BOOKS, CHAINED *see* LIBRARIES

BOROUGH, MONASTIC *see* TOWNS

BOSSES A boss is a decorative termination in wood or stone where the cross-members of a roof or ceiling intersect. In a stone vault it is a projecting KEYSTONE at the intersection of ribs and is both functional and ornamental (*see* VAULTING). In the magnificent vault of Sherborne Abbey in Dorset there are no fewer than eight hundred stone bosses and CORBELS, all elaborately carved, painted and gilded with heraldic designs, rebuses and vernacular motifs. The majority of bosses are late medieval, foliated decoration and simple QUATREFOIL and shield motifs being especially common. Unless foliated designs have acorns, haws or grapes they can be difficult to identify botanically. Popular subjects include devils and human faces; saints' emblems and symbols of the Passion; the heraldic shields, badges, rebuses and cyphers of benefactors and donors; merchants' marks; animals and symbolic beasts (such as 'Tanners' hares' which have shared ears) together with a profusion of sacred and secular legends mingled with (sometimes bawdy) everyday scenes.
See also SCAFFOLDING AND CRANES

BOY BISHOP A strange medieval custom whereby, in some monasteries, schools and rural parishes, a boy was elected to 'perform' the duties usually associated with a bishop during the three-week period from St Nicholas's Day (6 December) to Holy Innocents' Day (28 December).

BRACE Diagonal subsidiary timbers added to a structure (e.g. a door or the frame of a roof) to increase its rigidity.
See also DOORWAYS, LEDGE, MUNTIN, RAIL *and* STILE

BRACKET A flat-topped, right-angled projection of stone, wood or metal used to support a shelf, statue, candles, etc. Not to be confused with a CORBEL, an architectural feature of similar appearance which carries the distributed downward thrust of a larger structure. Both may be elaborately carved, painted and gilded. A bracket in the form of a scroll is described as a *console*.

Top left and right, and above: vault bosses from the ruined church of Hailes Abbey, Gloucestershire.

A reproduction of a boss in the choir vault at Exeter Cathedral.

BRANDAE *see* SHRINES

BRASSES (MONUMENTAL) A monumental brass is an engraved metal plate affixed as a memorial to the floor or wall of a church or to a TOMB CHEST.

There are some 8,000 brasses in England, more than in any other European country, although these represent only a small proportion of the brasses laid down between *c.* 1250 and *c.* 1650. About half of these are figure brasses (depicting a human figure) while others are engraved with heraldic devices and Christian symbols such as chalices, stylised lilies, sacred hearts and crosses and brackets. A number of later brasses are engraved with religious scenes: the Annunciation, the Nativity and the Resurrection, for example, most of which are from the early sixteenth century and fortunately escaped the attentions of the reformist iconoclasts.

Figure brasses include men, women, children, and infants in swaddling clothes as well as skeletons and shrouded figures (*see* CADAVER). Archbishops, bishops and abbots are usually depicted in their processional or mass vestments and monks and nuns in the habits of their orders (only thirty monastic brasses have survived). Judges and notaries usually have coifs (close-fitting caps), hoods, and fur-lined mantles buttoned on the right shoulder. Academics (of which there are some seventy-five examples) are usually depicted with a skull cap or raised cap, a hood (which is not always visible) and a gown, similar in appearance to a short cassock. By far the largest and most interesting category is the military brass, so called because figures are depicted in armour. Of the numerous civilian brasses, those of wool merchants often include the symbols of their trade (such as woolsacks) and merchants' marks. As a general rule, the deceased is always depicted in the attire appropriate to their status in life, although this can sometimes lead to incongruities, as in the brass to Sir Peter Legh (1527) at Winwick, Lancashire. Sir Peter was a knight but took holy orders after his wife's death and is depicted wearing a CHASUBLE over his armour!

Female figures, although not so numerous, are of equal interest and most include an element of heraldry (*see also* EFFIGIES). There are many examples of female figures in heraldic kirtles and mantles from the medieval and Tudor periods, and of women depicted in the simple white widow's veil and wimple, sideless cotehardie and kirtle of a *vowess*. A vowess (or *avowess*) was a widow who had 'avowed to live a life of chastity and obedience to God's will' but had not necessarily entered a religious community. Some of these splendid ladies were widows of the nobility and it is interesting to observe how many of them chose also to be depicted wearing the symbols of their rank – the ducal coronet of a duchess, for example.

Manufacture

Medieval brasses were, in fact, made of an alloy of copper (75–80 per cent), with 15–20 per cent zinc and small elements of lead and tin. In the Middle Ages this material was known as *latten*, and later *cuivre blanc* (white copper). Brasses originated in the Low Countries in the thirteenth century and a number were imported into England, notably from the fourteenth-century manufacturing centre of Tournai on the river Scheldt. Typical of these large, elaborate imported brasses is that of Abbot Thomas de la Mare at St Albans, Hertfordshire, which measures 2.8 x 1.5m (9ft 3in x 4ft 4in).

The majority of surviving English brasses originated from workshops established in the early fourteenth century at Norwich, York and London. The more ornate brasses were specially commissioned and engraved to a client's specification but each workshop also developed series of templates from which a cheaper 'off the peg' design could be selected and to which personal devices might be added. It may be possible to identify the different workshops from the characteristics of a particular brass but, as with effigies, early brasses portray only a stylised representation of a deceased person, not an accurate portrait.

Those who worked on monumental brasses were sometimes described as 'marblers', a possible reference to the craft of engraving INCISED SLABS from which the monumental brass developed. Indeed, it seems likely that several workshops which had traditionally produced lavishly expensive effigies turned also to the production of brasses as an alternative form of memorial which could be afforded by the average cleric, merchant or gentleman.

The first English brasses comprised a number of

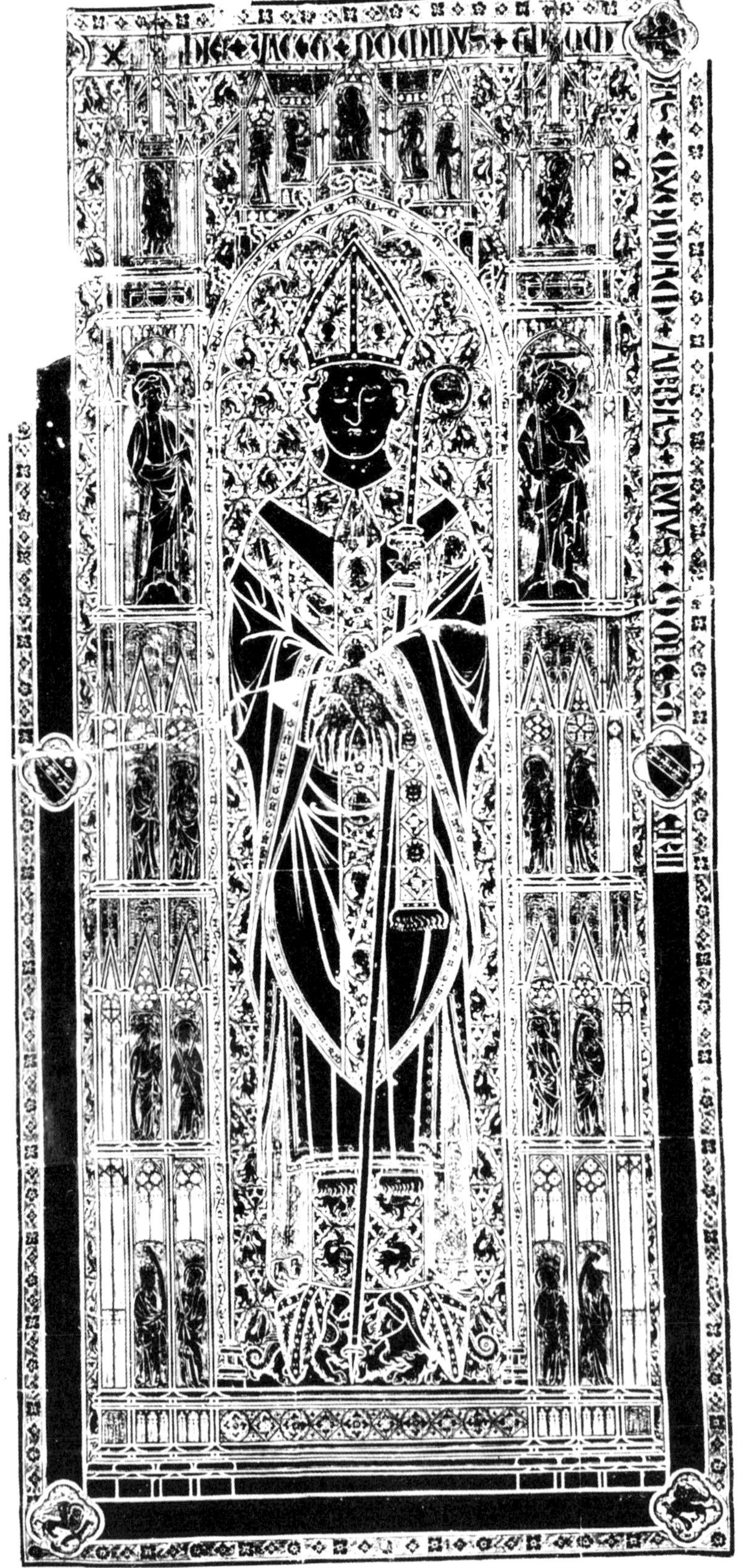

Brass to Abbot Thomas de la Mare at St Albans. (Malcolm Norris)

separate pieces, cut from a single sheet of metal, each of which was deeply engraved and set within an indentation (*matrix*) carved out of the stone slab so that the brass was flush with the surface. Each section was secured within its matrix in a bed of black pitch which also protected the metal from corrosion, although later brasses were often fixed by means of brass rivets driven into lead plugs which were compressed within holes in the slab. In many instances coloured enamels were let into the concave surfaces of the brass and this practice continued well into the sixteenth century.

Dating

Many of the earliest brasses commemorate senior clerics, who are depicted in their vestments and bearing the insignia of their office. These early figures are usually life size or slightly smaller and may be set within a decorative engraved canopy with an inscription, usually composed of separate letters, set round the edge of the brass. Decorative canopies are common to all periods and may be 'single', 'double' or 'triple', depending on the number of 'arches' depicted, and tend to reflect current architectural styles (*see* CANOPY).

Knights of this period are usually shown cross-legged with a dog or lion at their feet, long surcoat and a shield on the left arm, while their ladies may have a pet dog playing in the folds of their costumes. Invariably, military brasses contain heraldic devices which facilitate dating and identification and often provide genealogical and personal information not included in the inscription. Indeed, it was for this reason that HERALDRY was considered to be such an important component of most memorials, for it proclaimed both the authority and status of the deceased and the achievements which his descendants wished to commemorate.

From *c.* 1330 brasses were manufactured in a variety of sizes, were usually exquisitely engraved, and often included an ornate canopy. Marginal inscriptions were now incorporated within continuous strips of metal and PRECATORY SCROLLS and cross and bracket designs of great beauty were especially popular. In military brasses, the long, flowing surcoat was gradually replaced by the short, tight-fitting jupon. This was ideally suited to heraldic embellishment and yet during the period 1360–1460 only one-tenth of military brasses have figures wearing heraldic garments. Of course, it may be that it is not the jupon which is depicted in these brasses but the waisted breast-plate (*cuirass*), which was increasingly in evidence from *c.* 1350 and (in two-dimensional form) would be of similar appearance (*see also* CAMAIL PERIOD).

With the emergence of a medieval middle class there was a significant increase in the number of civilian brasses and, from *c.* 1380, male civilian figures are often depicted wearing a short sword (*anelace*) which is suspended from the belt of the tunic. Civilians usually have long hair and beards until *c.* 1410.

Fifteenth-century brasses are still well engraved but are generally smaller. Children are sometimes included, usually on separate plates below those of their parents. Some of the most magnificent brasses of the period were to be found in monastic churches although, following the Dissolution of the Monasteries, fewer than thirty remain. Of these, the finest is that of Thomas Nelond, Prior of Lewes (1433), at Cowfold in Sussex. Prior Thomas is depicted in the habit of the Benedictines, as he was head of the senior Cluniac monastery in England. There are further examples of monastic brasses at Denham in Buckinghamshire, Dorchester in Oxfordshire, Elstow in Bedfordshire, Nether Wallop in Hampshire, Norwich (St Laurence) in Norfolk and the abbey of St Alban, Hertfordshire.

Brasses from the second half of the fifteenth century (notably from the period 1470–90) show a marked deterioration in drawing and balance. The whole figure is often out of proportion and details are rendered without consideration to the constructive essentials of armour. Furthermore, brasses were a very much cheaper form of memorial than a stone or bronze effigy, so that persons thus commemorated tended to come from the lesser gentry and merchant class, who were largely unaffected by contemporary fashion. Thus we often find brasses in which figures are depicted in armour of an earlier period or in an ornate German or Italian harness which they were unlikely to have worn in real life. Nor should it be assumed that all those who are depicted in armour were of a military disposition, for it was customary for a man of note (*nobilis*) to be shown in death wearing the accoutrements of his feudal obligation of military service. Nobility and gentility were the hereditary prerogatives of the ancient warrior class: the shield was the symbol of that class and armour its uniform.

Some seventy-five brasses, mostly in the collegiate chapels of Oxford and Cambridge, are of academics. As one might expect, most were in Holy Orders and are, therefore, depicted with tonsures. Academic gowns are similar in appearance to a cassock but shorter, while Doctors of Divinity wore the *cappa clausa*, a gown divided at the front to show the hands.

During the early Tudor period (1485–1558) brasses become more numerous but, for the most part, they were poorly engraved, with excessive cross-hatching on thin metal. Mural plates (set on walls or incorporated into WALL MONUMENTS) were increasingly popular, English replaced Latin in inscriptions and there was some attempt at portraiture.

From this time, a number of brasses show figures dressed in heraldic tabards and these continued well into the sixteenth century, the complexity of heraldic quarterings increasing significantly in the Tudor period when descent from (or association with) an 'ancient' family (i.e. pre-Bosworth) was highly prized by the newly created Tudor aristocracy.

Destruction and Revival

Numerous medieval brasses (notably those which were considered to be 'popish') were torn from their matrices and discarded by the iconoclasts of the English Reformation, although many reappeared later as *palimpsests* (*see* PALIMPSEST). These were engraved on the reverse of the original (medieval) brass and the majority date from the second half of the sixteenth century, when they could be obtained more cheaply than a new plate by those seeking a brass memorial.

To her credit, Elizabeth I (1558–1603) attempted to preserve monuments by means of legislation which required that, where possible, they should be repaired and restored to the churches from which they had been removed. From about 1570 the use of figures declined in popularity and designs were generally heraldic: often a central, multi-quartered coat of arms surrounded by separate shields representing hereditary and marital connections.

Both sides in the Civil War (1642–9) destroyed thousands of brasses, often melting them down to make weapons. Those bearing religious symbols, such as the Trinity, and the beautiful cross and bracket brasses were especially vulnerable.

The monumental brass declined in popularity from the mid-seventeenth century and many brasses were damaged or destroyed as a consequence of insensitive refurbishing and rebuilding schemes in the eighteenth and nineteenth centuries. But many were also saved (and even restored) during the Gothic revival of the nineteenth century, when the brass figure set into a slab, and the brass wall monument with ornate Gothic inscriptions and the florid heraldry of the period enjoyed a revival.

For Church Monuments Society *and* Monumental Brass Society *see* APPENDIX II.

BRATTISHING Late medieval ornamental cresting consisting of carved formalised flowers or leaves

(Tom Friar)

(sometimes within a crenellated form) on (e.g.) a screen, CORNICE or PARAPET.

BRAWLING Although the word is commonly used to describe a noisy quarrel or fight, brawling was a specific offence: that of causing a disturbance in a church or churchyard.

BRAY, THE VICAR OF *see* REFORMATION, THE

BREAD In the Christian Church, bread symbolises all food and exemplifies God's providence. It was baked in huge quantities to feed monastic communities, for alms-giving and for the sustenance of guests. In BENEDICTINE houses the daily bread was distributed with extraordinary ceremony. At the commencement of a meal the loaves were placed in a basket suspended by ropes and pulleys above the abbot's table. When all were assembled the basket 'shall descend onto the abbot's table, in order that the rations of God's labourers may appear to descend to them from Heaven'. Of course, bread is associated with the Sacrament and in the western Church unleavened (unfermented) bread has always been used in the Eucharistic rite, although in the Church of England both leavened and unleavened bread are now permitted.
See also BREAD OVEN

BREAD OVEN In addition to the great monastic BAKEHOUSE, there was often provision within the abbey church itself for the baking of the 'single bread' – the unleavened bread (*obleys*) used at the mass – a task which was usually directed with great solemnity by the SACRIST. Bread ovens may occasionally be found in monastic churches: rectangular openings within the thickness of a wall, with well-constructed close-fitting stone or brick linings and an external flue. Before baking, the oven was pre-heated by a small fire of faggot-wood or furze, lit in the base of the oven. When this had died down the ashes were hastily removed and the door shut on the bread, which gently baked in the diminishing heat, supplemented by latent heat from the chimney flue.

BREAKFAST (MIXTUM) *see* FRATER

BRESSUMER (*also* BREASTSUMMER) A horizontal beam, often carved ornamentally, that carries the superstructure in timber-framed buildings and into which the first-floor joists are tenoned. The term is also used to describe a heavy beam spanning a fireplace or other opening.

BREVIARY A liturgical book containing the text (and often the music) to be used in the DIVINE OFFICE, together with certain additions such as prayers for the dead. So complex was the music that in many religious houses a number of choir books would be used during a single service: the ANTIPHONARIUM, GRADUALE, etc.
See also BOOKS, HOURS (CANONICAL) *and* PSALTER

BREVIATOR (i) The scribe responsible for drawing up a BRIEF.
(ii) A member of the almoner's staff (*see* ALMONER), usually a salaried servant, responsible for conveying a brief to other communities of an order.
See also OBIT

BREWHOUSE Beer was the staple drink of most medieval households, both secular and religious. Consequently, large quantities were required for monastic communities of both sexes: in the fifteenth century, the weekly allowance of beer to each member of certain houses of nuns was 7 gallons (32 litres)! All religious communities had a brewhouse, which was usually located in an outer court, together with a kiln for malting. The brewer was one of the sub-cellarer's assistants (*see* CELLARER) although, in the late medieval period, he was more often a paid servant. Brewhouses were often comparatively insubstantial buildings and only partial remains may have survived: at Canterbury and Fountains, for example. Beer was brewed both for the community's consumption, for hospitality and alms and (with bread) was provided as part of a servant's remuneration.

BRIEF (i) Written consent from a bishop or senior ecclesiastical official authorising collections for charitable or other worthwhile causes (*see also* BULLA).

(ii) A formal document, drawn up by the *breviator* of a religious community to record the death of a member. The brief, or mortuary roll, which requested that prayers be said for the soul of the deceased, was conveyed to the almoners of other religious houses, who sometimes endorsed the document with Latin verses praising the dead or expressing sympathy with the bereaved before returning it.

BRIGITTINES *or* BRIDGETTINES The celebrated abbey of Syon at Twickenham, Middlesex, was the only Brigittine house in England, founded and richly endowed by Henry V as a penance in 1414. The order followed a modified version of the Augustinian rule that was reformed by Saint Bridget (*c.* 1303–73), former queen of Sweden, in *c.* 1346. This permitted books to be kept as personal possessions for private study. Originally, the Brigittines closely resembled the GILBERTINE ORDER in that they were organised in double communities of canons and nuns (*see* DOUBLE MONASTERY), sharing a common church. This arrangement continued down to the sixteenth century. The order survived the Reformation and continues as an enclosed and contemplative community in Devon.

BROTHER A fellow male member of a religious order (*see* FATHER).

BUGIA (*also* PALMATORIUM *and* SCOTULA) A portable candlestick with lighted candle.

BUILDING MATERIALS *see* MASONRY

BULLA An embossed metal disc, originally lead, attached to a document as a means of authentication (*see also* SEALS). Papal edicts were sealed in this manner – hence the term *papal bull*.

BURIALS (MONASTIC) Stone coffins (or their lids) may sometimes be found at former monastic churches and these almost invariably contained the remains of distinguished members of the religious community who were granted the privilege of burial in the chapter house, east walk of the cloister or (rarely) in the church itself. Most monks were buried, without coffins, in the monastery cemetery, usually to the east of the chapter house and south of the church and approached from the cloister via a SLYPE or, in Cistercian houses, through a door in the transept. Only in Carthusian monasteries was the cloister garth used for burials (*see* CEMETERIES).

The CUSTOMARY set out in precise detail the rites that accompanied the death of a religious: Unction, Confession, Absolution and Viaticum were received while the dying man lay on a bed of sackcloth and ashes. After death, the body was washed and clothed in the habit of the order before being carried in solemn procession from the infirmary (or mortuary) to the church. There it would remain for twenty-four hours while the community kept watch and prayed. Following burial, masses were said for thirty days for the soul of the departed brother and notice of his passing was communicated by the almoner to other houses (*see* BRIEF).

The right to burial in a monastic cemetery was usually confined to brethren and confraters (*see* CONFRATERNITY), although urban monasteries sometimes provided a separate lay cemetery within its precincts. According to medieval practice, bones were exhumed after a time and conveyed to a *charnel* house near the cemetery. This was sometimes a crypt with a chapel above, as at Worcester, where a large ossuary to the north of the church was served by a college of chantry priests who were accommodated nearby. Founders (*see* BENEFACTORS) and royalty were often afforded burial in or near monastic churches: at the Cistercian abbey of Ystrad Fflur (Strata Florida)

in Ceredigion, for example, which became the burial place of the thirteenth-century princes of Deheubarth. The south porch of Beaumaris church, Anglesey, contains the splendid stone coffin of Princess Joan, illegitimate daughter of King John and consort of Llywelyn ab Iorwerth (Llywelyn Fawr, d. 1240). Joan was originally buried at nearby Llanfaes Friary (which was founded to commemorate her death) but, after various vicissitudes, her coffin finally came to rest in the parish church of Beaumaris in 1808. Her effigy is carved on the coffin lid, surrounded by Celtic-style tracery.
See also GALILEE

BURSAR Originally, the chief financial officer of a religious community, the bursar was responsible for overseeing all the revenues and expenses of the establishment. He was 'the keeper of the burse' (the purse), although, with the development of OBEDIENTIARIES, his role was increasingly restricted to those payments that were not already appropriated by other officials. Even so, he continued to scrutinise departmental accounts and was usually provided with an office for that purpose.

BUTTERY *see* LARDER

BUTTRESS A projecting support constructed against a wall to counteract the weight of roofs and TOWERS and to compensate for the structurally weakening effects of window openings. The walls of Saxon and early Romanesque stone buildings were invariably of considerable thickness, with small windows, and comparatively light timber roofs supported by tie and collar beams (*see* COLLAR BEAM). Consequently they required little reinforcement and buttresses of this period are generally wide but of low projection. The thinner walls, larger windows and heavy stone vaults of Gothic architecture required substantial buttressing with projections of greater depth at the base, reducing in upward stages to the roof level (*see*

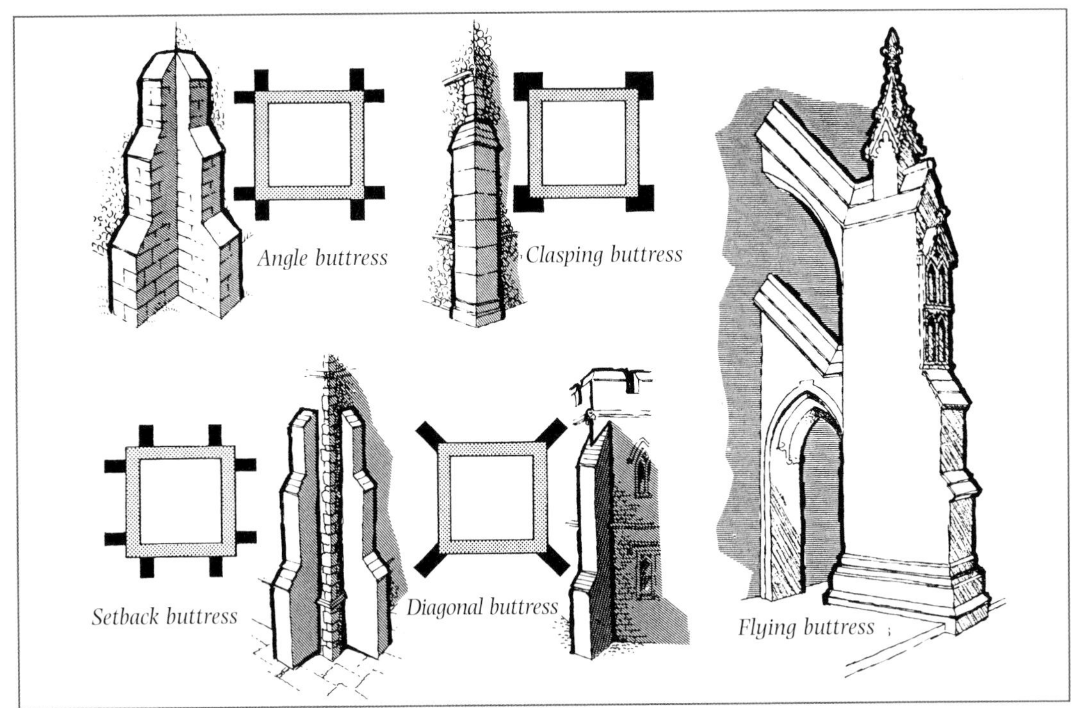

Buttresses. (Courtesy of John Ferguson)

Flying buttresses and crocketed pinnacles at Milton Abbey, Dorset. (Courtesy of Florence Morris)

BAY). During the thirteenth century *angle buttresses* were used at the corners of buildings, where they met at 90 degrees (*see* illustration). *Setback buttresses* are similar but are set back slightly to expose the corner of the building. Less common are the large, square *clasping buttresses* which enclose the corners of a tower or porch. In the fourteenth century *diagonal buttresses* were widely used. These are set diagonally, at right angles to the corners of a tower or building. The *flying buttress* (or *arch buttress*) is one by which the thrust of a vault is carried from a wall to an outer buttress by means of an arch or series of arches. The lofty stone vaults, vast windows and slender walls (often little more than cages of stone ribs) which characterise the Perpendicular style of Gothic architecture of the late fourteenth and fifteenth centuries demanded extraordinary ingenuity in order that the downward and outward thrust of roof, tower and (sometimes) spire should be evenly distributed and counteracted. Mainly through trial and error, the abutment system developed by which arches, placed at the point of greatest thrust (found to be immediately below the springing line of a vault on an internal wall) transferred the pressure through buttresses to ground level and, by means of heavy pinnacles on the buttresses themselves, successfully offset the effect of the thrust. Buttresses were sometimes incorporated into the structure of larger buildings, and may be visible from the interior, as at Gloucester Cathedral, where massive 'flying' buttresses, constructed *within* the transept walls, transfer the outward thrust of the tower to ground level. Buttresses are not confined to medieval churches: the flying buttresses of Wren's St Paul's Cathedral, London (1675–1711) are concealed behind high screen walls which themselves support the buttresses.

BYLAND CAPITAL *see* CAPITAL

C

CABLE FONT A font (usually Norman) having carved decoration in the form of a girdle of braided rope.

CABLE MOULDING (*also* ROPE MOULDING)

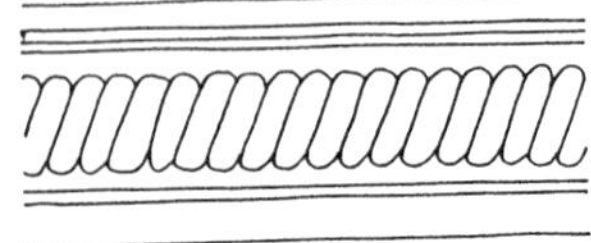

Moulding imitating a twisted rope.

CADAVER From the Latin *cadaver* meaning 'corpse', the name is applied to effigies of the dead when represented in emaciated form and on the verge of decay (*see* INTRANSI TOMB). Death, and the imagery of decay, haunted the medieval mind, especially following the plagues and pestilences of the early fifteenth century. Death was personified as a grasping skeleton, often as the 'Grim Reaper' with scythe and timeglass, and decay as worms: *humiliatus sum vermis* – 'by worms I am abused'. A startling example of a verminous cadaver may be found at Tewkesbury Abbey, Gloucestershire, where writhing worms and various snails, toads and mice feast on the corpse of a fifteenth-century abbot.

Skeleton brasses generally date from the mid-fifteenth century to the late sixteenth century and usually depict a skeleton in a knotted shroud. *Shroud brasses* are slightly different for they show a living figure wrapped in a shroud. Female shroud brasses are often strangely beautiful, for the long hair is shown flowing down the outside of the shroud.

See also BRASSES (MONUMENTAL) *and* EFFIGIES

CAEN STONE *see* MASONRY

CAPELLA ANTE PORTAS *see* PARISH CHURCH

CALDARIUM There were usually three great caldrons in a monastic kitchen: one for cooking beans, one for vegetables and a third for boiling water for washing utensils etc.

CALEFACTORIUM *or* CALEFACTORY (WARMING HOUSE) A room in the CLAUSTRAL buildings of a monastery in which a fire was maintained during the winter months (from All Saints to Good Friday) for the benefit of the monks, especially

The 'verminious cadaver' of John Wakeman, the last abbot of Tewkesbury, who surrendered the abbey to Henry VIII in 1539. (Courtesy of Geoffrey Wheeler)

those who were occupied in sedentary work in the cloister. In Benedictine houses the warming house was usually situated in the east claustral range and therefore also provided a little warmth to the dormitory above (*see* DORTER). In Cistercian abbeys it was an independent building adjoining the FRATER in the south-east corner of the cloister and conveniently close to the monks' DAY STAIR. Several warming houses had more than one fireplace: there were two at the Cistercian abbeys of Rievaulx and Roche, for example. Until the late Middle Ages the calefactorium was the only room (other than the KITCHENS and INFIRMARY) that was heated, but with the growth of private chambers (*camerae*) it became a common room for informal meetings and for restrained recreational conversation (*see* PARLOUR *and* SLYPE).

CALENDAR (i) The numerous medieval methods of calculating dates rendered calendars particularly important, and many liturgical manuscripts, private devotional works and official documents were prefixed by a calendar. Dating by reference to saints' days and religious festivals was popular in the Church and, from the thirteenth century, such dates are to be found in letters and documents. The Roman JULIAN CALENDAR, devised by Julius Caesar in 46 BC, remained in use until 1582, when it was replaced by the GREGORIAN CALENDAR, although its introduction in England was delayed until 1752.
(ii) A catalogue of documents, together with summaries of their contents.

CALLIGRAPHY *see* LETTERING

CAMAIL PERIOD A term applied to military brasses and effigies in which the figures are depicted wearing the *camail* (mail protection for the throat and neck) which was introduced into English armour during the second half of the fourteenth century.
See also BRASSES (MONUMENTAL) *and* EFFIGIES

CAMERA Private lodgings, or those of an official.

CAMERARIUS *see* CHAMBERLAIN

CANCELLI Low, latticed railings in front of, or enclosing, a communion table, usually with a broad top to facilitate the taking of communion.
See also ALTARS

CANDELABRUM A large branched candlestick or light-holder. There are various types, including the seven-branched Jerusalem candelabrum or *menorah*.
See also HEARSE

CANDLE BEAM *see* ROOD SCREEN

CANDLES It is self-evident that, in medieval churches, candles were necessary in order that the monks and canons should be able to read. But the widespread adoption of candles as ornaments, especially associated with the altar, may have developed from the early use of processional lights, which were placed beside or on the altar table (*see* PROCESSIONS). Liturgical candles were made of beeswax and were an expensive commodity, while candles used simply for illumination were of tallow. In the medieval period only one candle would be placed on the altar, others being offered as *votive lights* before images, shrines and tombs, often at enormous expense. A votive candle is one which is lit as a personal offering, usually in fulfilment of a vow or bequest.
See also ALTAR LIGHTS, LAMPS *and* TRENDAL

CANES *see* WINDOWS

CANON (i) An ecclesiastical law.
(ii) A body of writings acknowledged as genuine.
(iii) A list of canonised saints.
(iv) A member of a body of clergy serving a cathedral or COLLEGIATE CHURCH. At first the term was applied to all clergy who were members of a diocesan staff but it was later restricted to SECULAR CLERGY belonging to a cathedral or collegiate church. Residentiary canons are

permanent members of a cathedral staff who undertake administrative duties and are responsible for services. Non-residentiary canons are those who hold unsalaried posts associated with certain privileges and responsibilities.
See also CANON REGULAR *and* CLERGY (CHURCH OF ENGLAND)

CANON LAW Ecclesiastical law based on New Testament precepts. A digest of the formal decrees of various councils of the Church (*canons*) and patriarchal decisions (*decretals*) relating to doctrine and discipline. Before the Norman Conquest the courts heard all suits, both lay and ecclesiastical, with bishops and ealdormen sitting as joint judges. Such courts were disliked by the papacy and William of Normandy was able to obtain papal approval for his conquest of Britain by promising to establish separate ecclesiastical courts to consider those matters which 'belong to the government of souls'. These courts dealt not only with offences against morality and the doctrines of the Church but also with secular matters such as legitimacy and matrimonial causes (*see* COURTS (ECCLESIASTICAL)).

CANON REGULAR A member of a body of canons living under a RULE which, from the twelfth century, was usually that of St Augustine.
See also AUGUSTINIANS, CANON, CLERGY (CHURCH OF ENGLAND), GILBERTINE ORDER *and* PREMONSTRATENSIAN CANONS

CANONESS REGULAR A member of a community of women living under a RULE which, since the twelfth century, was usually that of St Augustine (*see* AUGUSTINIANS).

CANONICAL HOURS *see* HOURS (CANONICAL)

CANONICORUM Latinised place-name element indicating that a MANOR was once owned by a medieval community of canons, as at Whitchurch Canonicorum in Dorset.
See also LATIN

CANOPY (i) A roof-like projection above a statue, tomb, memorial, etc. usually of stone but also of wood or metal (*see* CANOPY (MONUMENTAL)).
(ii) A similar structure of carved wood surmounting the stalls in a medieval cathedral, collegiate chapel or former monastic church (*see* STALLS).
(iii) An ornate, tapering, tower-like structure suspended above a font (*see* FONTS *and* TABERNACLE).
(iv) An architectural or decorative motif which resembles any of the above (*see* BRASSES (MONUMENTAL)).
(v) A projecting or suspended hood (*tester*) above a pulpit or altar (*see* BALDACCHINO *and* SOUNDING BOARD).

CANOPY (MONUMENTAL) A roof-like projection above a tomb or memorial, usually of stone but occasionally of wood or metal. This type of canopy may surmount a free-standing or recessed TOMB CHEST or a hanging WALL MONUMENT, and there are examples of free-standing tomb canopies which have been adapted to form small CHANTRY CHAPELS. The undersides of these canopies were often vaulted, with floreated and heraldic painting and gilding, although much of this original work may have been lost through neglect or vandalism.

Canopies developed in the thirteenth century, principally over the tomb chests of prelates, and may have originated in the roof-like structures which were sometimes placed above shrines. The overall design of a canopy followed contemporary architectural style and decoration, indeed that above the Despenser tomb at Tewkesbury Abbey in Gloucestershire contains the earliest example of fan vaulting (1378). Heraldry was a common theme, both in the miniature bosses and spandrels of the vaulting and in the ornamentation of the moulding. The canopy of Edmund Crouchback's tomb at Westminster Abbey, for example, contains no fewer than 150 shields of arms. Canopies above recessed tombs (those which were set within a

The beautifully ornate canopied tomb of Hugh Despenser (d. 1348) at Tewkesbury Abbey, Gloucestershire. (Courtesy of Geoffrey Wheeler)

church wall) are usually less ornate, the spandrels formed on either side of the arch containing simple shields of arms, although the canopies of late Perpendicular recessed tombs often have decorative cornices with carved and gilded shields of arms and other devices such as badges, cyphers and rebuses (*see* REBUS).

With the Renaissance, Gothic pillars and arches were superseded by Roman columns, and classical pediments and entablatures which provided the 'new gentility' of the post-medieval period with an eminently suitable vehicle by which to display all, or at least the most significant, of the heraldic quarterings to which they laid claim. Every available surface was utilised for this purpose: usually a central achievement (containing all the principal quarterings) was flanked by two smaller ones above the pediment (usually of impaled arms), with the various arms acquired by marriage depicted individually in shields on the columns and pediments. Heraldic supporters were often modelled (not necessarily in stone) on either side of the central achievement or were incorporated into the overall design of the monument: flanking an obelisk, for example. Arches provided spandrels for further shields and the underside of the arch was often decorated with shields, badges and other devices. Smaller shields in a frieze along the base of the pediment, or on the back plate of a wall monument, were used to display the marriage alliances of children and ancestors and, where a monument was erected to the memory of two or more generations, the alliances of each generation would be shown. Where highly emblazoned canopies surmounted tomb chests the overall effect was even more splendid, for the chest itself would also be decorated with shields and might be surrounded by ironwork which included gilded pennants and scrollwork. A striking example is the tomb of Bishop Montague (d. 1618) at Bath Abbey.

From *c.* 1630 there was an increasing tendency towards a purer classical treatment with less decoration. Heraldry was, for the most part, confined to segmental pediments while the shield was gradually replaced by the cartouche. From the end of the seventeenth century, a single crest or heraldic cartouche might be incorporated within the canopy and, during the eighteenth century, the canopy itself became an architectural feature, eventually being replaced by the wall monument and reappearing only briefly during the Gothic revival.

See also CELURE *and* MONUMENTS

CANOPY OF HONOUR A large CANOPY (*ciborium*) above an altar (*see also* BALDACCHINO).

CANTARIST A singer in a choir and, in the Middle Ages, a member of a foundation of secular clergy (*see* COLLEGE). Adult members of cathedral choirs are known as lay clerks.

CANTICLE A prayer derived from the Bible (other than from the psalms) used in the liturgy of the Church. Most familiar are the *Magnificat*, *Nunc dimittis* and *Benedicite*.

CANTOR A member of a choir who pre-intones and leads in liturgical music. In monastic and collegiate churches the cantor stood at the great lectern on which the ANTIPHONARIUM was placed in the midst of the quire (*see* CHOIR). On major occasions there were often two or more cantors, each dressed in a surplice and cope.
See also CHURCH MUSIC

CANTORIS Literally 'of the cantor', whose cathedral or monastic stall was on the north side of the quire, the term is used to describe all those who in antiphonal singing sit on that side (*see* DECANI). It would appear that the medieval practice was for the two sides (*cantoris* and *decani*) to change places on alternate weeks. In today's cathedrals it is the side on which the precentor's stall is located (*see* PRECENTOR) and it is the trebles who sit in the cantorial stalls who usually sing the lower part in antiphonal singing.
See also ANTIPHON, CHOIR, CHURCH MUSIC, STALLS *and* VERSICLES

CAPELLA ANTE PORTAS The chapel at (or near) the outer gate of a religious house, provided for the use of visitors, servants and EMPLOYEES. Such chapels sometimes became parish churches: at Abingdon, Evesham and Westminster, for example, and at Merevale in Warwickshire, which was provided by the Cistercian community for the benefit of pilgrims.

CAPITAL A capital is the head of a COLUMN, PIER or PILASTER. Shaped like an inverted bell, most capitals comprise a flat upper stone (*abacus*) and a tapering lower section (*necking*) which is usually separated from the shaft of the pier or column by a narrow moulding. The function of a capital is to provide an area, larger than the supporting column or pier, from which an arch may spring or on which an entablature may rest.

The decoration of a capital is often a useful guide to the period or style of architecture. Romanesque piers and capitals were of massive construction: clearly, contemporary builders felt that new notions of structure were no substitute for mass. In the earliest examples both neck and ABACUS were combined in a single square or round block of stone. Early carved decoration was crude (though interesting) and included interlacing. Typical of the Norman period is the *cushion* capital, which is a cube of masonry the lower parts of which were rounded off to conform to the circular shaft of the column, leaving a flat face (*lunette*) on each of the four sides. From this evolved the *scalloped* capital, in which each of the lunettes is divided into cone shapes, beneath a square abacus. Later Romanesque capitals are deeply carved with foliated motifs, animals, birds and (more rarely in England) figures. In Gothic architecture, capitals of the Early English period were generally moulded or splendidly foliated, with a round or moulded abacus. Occasionally, human heads peer out from the foliage (*see* GREEN MEN). Specific types of foliated capital include the *crocket* capital, which has stylised leaves forming 'scrolls' (*volutes*) beneath the abacus; the *stiff-leaf* capital (with long stalks), which developed from it; and the *water-leaf* capital, which has plain, broad leaves turned over beneath the angles of the abacus (*see* STIFF LEAF ORNAMENT). Characteristic of the Decorated period is the removal of the undercut hollow beneath the abacus to form a more unified capital, usually decorated with rolls of scroll moulding or foliage. The so-called *byland capital* is a common architectural motif, consisting of broad water-leaves with banding above, and is believed to have originated at the abbey of Byland in the twelfth century. By the fourteenth century foliated capitals of oak, ivy, maple and vine leaves were carved in a more naturalistic manner and with a profusion of fruit and flowers (*see* NATURAL LEAF ORNAMENT). In the Perpendicular period of the fifteenth century octagonal capitals, often chamfered at the upper

(Tom Friar)

edge, were set on circular piers or groups of shafts and for the most part were moulded, although foliated forms may be found in some West Country churches. Carved and foliated capitals are also a feature of several larger buildings, where they are usually more stylised, of lower relief, and sometimes include figures in the form of angels. After the Reformation the Gothic style was gradually superseded by Classical forms.

CAPITULARY A compilation of legislation published by bishops for the guidance of the clergy and laity in their dioceses.

CAPITULUM A short reading (literally 'little chapter') from the rule of a religious community.

CARDINAL A member of the pope's council or Sacred College. Cardinals hold the next highest office to the pope and are nominated by him. These ecclesiastical princes comprise six cardinal bishops, fifty cardinal priests and fourteen cardinal deacons. When required, on the death of a pope, they elect a successor. Their main responsibilities are advisory and administrative and, unless expressly excused or bishops of foreign dioceses, they reside in Rome. There have been comparatively few English cardinals, the best known being Cardinals Beaufort (1377–1447), Morton (*c.* 1420–1500), Wolsey (*c.* 1475–1530) and Newman (1801–90).

CARMELITE ORDER *see* FRIARS

CARRELS *see* CLOISTER

CARTHUSIANS The Poor Brothers of God of the Charterhouse (originally the *Grande Chartreuse* in Grenoble) were a strictly contemplative order, founded by St Bruno in 1084, with a Rule dating from 1130 that required of them vows of austerity, humility and silence. Like the desert hermits of the past, each monk lived in his own cell, with its garden and patch of cultivated land, working and devoting several hours each day to prayer. His clothing was coarse and undyed and for three days a week he lived on bread and water. On other days he ate scanty rations of fish, eggs and vegetables: no meat was taken. The monks came together for the offices of Mattins, Lauds and Vespers, the other Hours being recited in their cells; and for meals only on feast-days when conversation was permitted. In order that their priories should not become too large or well endowed, numbers were restricted to a prior and twelve monks, with eighteen LAY BROTHERS, who had cells and an oratory of their own and were responsible for maintaining the meagre arable holdings, flocks and herds. The first Carthusian priory (or *Charterhouse*) in England was founded by Henry II in 1178 as part of his penance for the murder of Thomas Becket in 1170. The chosen site was then a remote and

inhospitable one at Witham in Selwood Forest on the Somerset–Wiltshire border. Two further Charterhouses were established at Hinton near Bath in 1226 and Beauvale near Nottingham in 1320. Following the onset of the Black Death in 1348–50, at a time when the endowment of monastic communities was otherwise in decline, the Carthusians enjoyed both the respect and the financial support of the nobility (*see* PLAGUE). Several priories, including the London Charterhouse in 1370, were endowed by members of the medieval court circle. The latest (and largest) Carthusian foundation in England, the House of Jesus in Bethlehem at Sheen on the Surrey bank of the Thames, was founded by Henry V (1413–22), the most puritanical of the medieval English kings. Alone among the English monastic orders, the Carthusians may be distinguished by that integrity and courage of soul which compelled them to stand against Henry VIII at the Dissolution of the Monasteries in 1536. As a consequence, nearly all were brutally executed.
See also DISSOLUTION OF THE MONASTERIES

CARTOON *see* STAINED GLASS

CARTOUCHE Scroll-like architectural decoration. Ornament in the form of a tablet or heraldic escutcheon enclosed in scrolls representing rolled-up paper.

CARTOUCHE TABLET A type of WALL MONUMENT popular in the seventeenth and eighteenth centuries. Cartouche tablets are usually made of marble and have the appearance of a sheet of paper with the sides curled up. Typically, the central section contains an inscription and, above it, a coat of arms or crest.
See also TABLET

CARTULARY A monastic or estate register-book

A Carthusian cell at Mount Grace Priory, North Yorkshire. (John Crook/info@john-crook.com)

containing details of deeds, charters, grants, property and other possessions. Also one who keeps the register and the place in which it is stored.

Monastic cartularies provide invaluable information concerning appropriated churches (*see* MEDIEVAL CHURCH) and may even contain the earliest reference to a particular parish church, including the names of incumbents, dependent chapelries and the obligations (financial and otherwise) owed by a parish to a mother church, and the rights and emoluments established for a VICAR when a religious house became the RECTOR of the parish.

CARUCATE *see* MASONRY

CASSOCK A long garment worn by the clergy and by members of a church choir. The cassock originated in the full-length robe which was retained by the clergy when, in the sixth century, shorter garments evolved for secular use. Traditionally clergy of the Church of England wear black cassocks and bishops purple. Choristers' cassocks come in a variety of colours, although only the choirs of royal foundations should wear red.
See also SURPLICE

CASTELLATED Surmounted with battlements (*see* BATTLEMENT).

CATAFALQUE A temporary tomb-like structure originally used at a Requiem Mass to represent the body in its absence. The term is now used to describe a platform on which is supported the coffin of a (usually distinguished) person during a funeral or lying-in-state.

CATERER A senior member of the cellarer's department (*see* CELLARER), the caterer supervised the kitchen staff and the serving of food at mealtimes and may also have been responsible for the bulk purchase of provisions.
See also KITCHENER *and* LARDER

CATHEDRA *see* CATHEDRALS

CATHEDRAL CHAPTER The body of canons responsible for the administration of a cathedral (*see* CANON). Chapter records include information concerning the affairs of those parishes which came within their exempt jurisdiction (*see* PECULIAR). For example, records of the visitation (*see* VISITATION (ECCLESIASTICAL)) of churches in the jurisdiction of the Dean and Chapter of York from 1362 to 1481 include details of defective church buildings, the inadequate provision of service books, and a variety of offences by clergy and laity, including non-residence, adultery, witchcraft and heresy.
See also CHAPTER

CATHEDRAL MUSIC *see* CHURCH MUSIC

CATHEDRAL PRIORY The seats (*cathedra*) of early bishoprics were established in the churches of several of the more important monasteries (*headminsters*). The monastic church thereby became a cathedral and the bishop the titular abbot of the community which, in practice, was governed by a prior (*see* PRIORY). Although accorded the style and honour of abbot, a bishop was not necessarily a member of the monastic community and exercised no authority within its CHAPTER (at Durham, in particular, the relationship was often acrimonious). It was the Benedictine archbishop Dunstan (909–88) who, with Edgar of Wessex, reformed both Church and state and established the cathedral priory as the fulcrum of regional ecclesiastical government. By the end of the medieval period, Bath, Carlisle, Canterbury, Coventry, Durham, Ely, Norwich, Rochester, Winchester and Worcester had monastic chapters: all Benedictine with the exception of Carlisle which was a house of Austin Canons. Indeed, even secular (non-monastic) cathedrals sometimes adopted a quasi-conventual plan with CLAUSTRAL buildings, chapter house, etc., as at Salisbury and Wells.
See also ANGLO-SAXON CHURCH, CATHEDRALS *and* MITRED ABBOT

CATHEDRALS A cathedral is a church that

contains the *cathedra* or throne of the diocesan bishop (*see* DIOCESE). The church of St Peter's-on-the-Wall, at Bradwell-on-Sea, Essex, is the only surviving Saxon cathedral. Constructed in 654, it sits astride the wall of the Roman fort (Othona) from which its materials were plundered. In the early church the *cathedra* was normally raised within an apse behind the High Altar, but it was removed to the PRESBYTERY in the medieval period (at Norwich it remains in its original eastward position). It is usually located on the north side of the presbytery, while a southern position signifies that a former bishop was also a monastic superior or prior. Symbols of spiritual and temporal power, bishops' thrones were immense structures: that at Exeter Cathedral is almost 18m (60ft) high, while the elevated *cathedra* above Bishop Hatfield's tomb at Durham Cathedral Priory is believed to be the loftiest of any in Christendom. Originally, a cathedral was served by a bishop and his household, but responsibility was later devolved to a separate body of clergy, an ecclesiastical corporation known as the CHAPTER.

Salisbury Cathedral.

The Middle Ages

English dioceses have always been large and cathedrals, therefore, few in number. Consequently the medieval cathedrals were able to exercise considerable regional influence and enjoyed patronage of such munificence that the scale and splendour of their architecture greatly exceeds that of most parish churches. This is particularly evident in the development of cathedrals to the east of the CROSSING, where magnificent provision was made not only for considerable numbers of clergy, but also for the SHRINES of saints, reliquaries (*see* RELICS), CHANTRY CHAPELS and royal and magnate tombs. CHAPELS were often added to the AMBULATORY for these purposes and many cathedrals built LADY CHAPELS to the east of the High Altar in response to the popularity of the cult of the Virgin during the fourteenth century. With the obvious exceptions of St Paul's in London (rebuilt by Sir Christopher Wren 1675–1710) and a number of twentieth-century cathedrals (Liverpool, Coventry, Guildford, etc.), no major English cathedral is of a single, unified architectural style. Even at Salisbury, which was constructed within a period of sixty-four years (1220–84), the tower and spire were not completed until *c.* 1380.

Of the seventeen medieval cathedrals at the DISSOLUTION OF THE MONASTERIES, seven were BENEDICTINE monastic foundations (Canterbury, Durham, Ely, Norwich, Rochester, Winchester and Worcester), as was Bath, which replaced Wells as a cathedral between 1090 and 1218 when the joint diocese was established. In these monastic cathedrals the bishop was also the titular abbot, although in practice responsibility for the monastic establishment rested with the prior, and that for the cathedral with a CHAPTER, so that they were known as CATHEDRAL PRIORIES. Of the remaining cathedrals, eight (Chichester, Exeter, Hereford, Lichfield, Lincoln, Salisbury, Wells and York) were served by *secular canons*, who followed

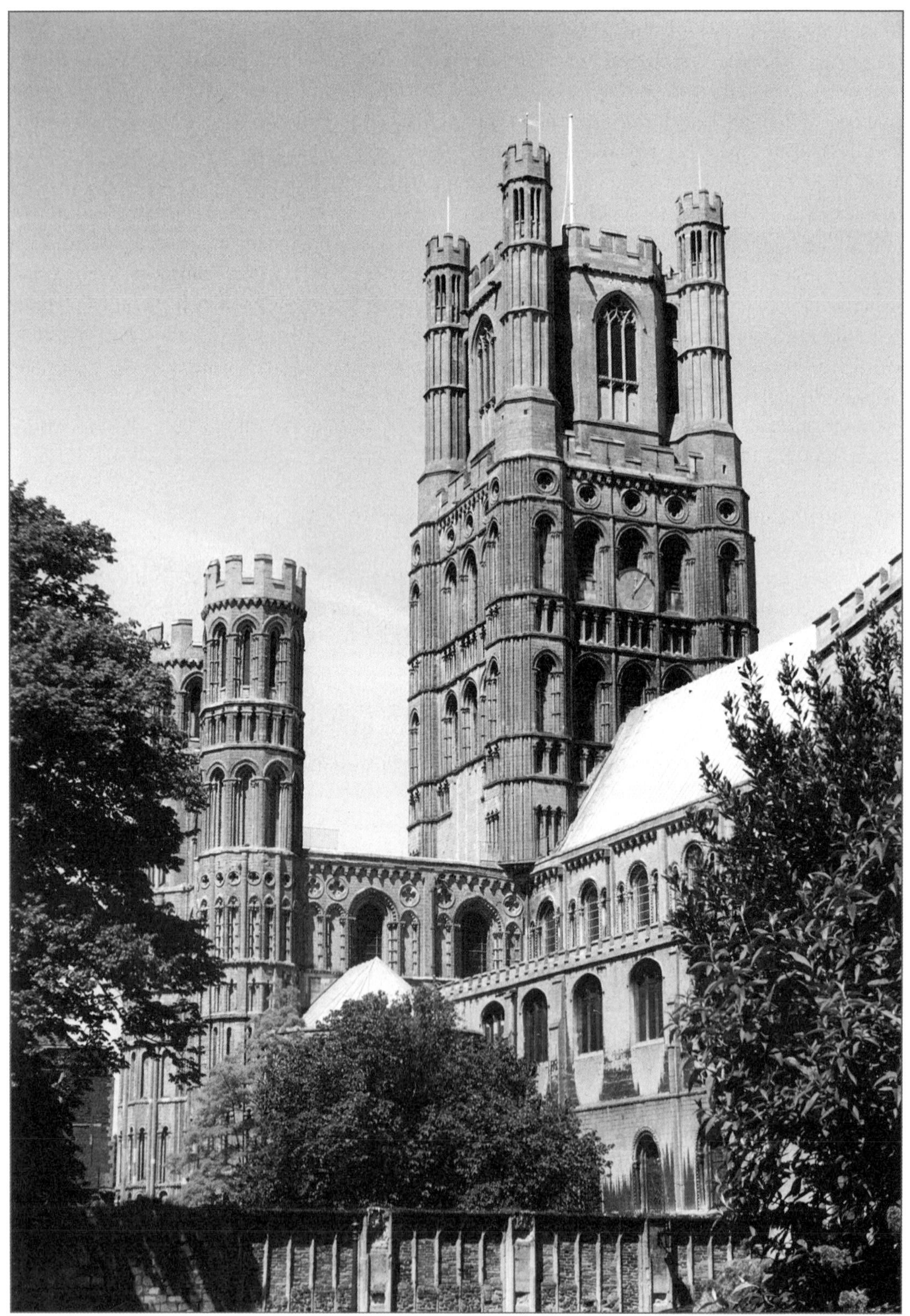

Ely Cathedral.

no rule and were free to live where they chose. They were responsible (as they are today) for the maintenance of cathedral services. The *Canons Regular* lived in accordance with a fixed code (Latin *regula* meaning 'rule') and were, in England, AUGUSTINIANS (or Austin Canons), whose rule was monastic in character, for which reason their cathedral church at Carlisle was classified as a monastic foundation at the Dissolution of the Monasteries.

Of these cathedrals of the 'Old Foundation', five are of pre-Conquest foundation (Exeter, Hereford, Lichfield, London and York) and three date from the reign of William I (1066–87) (Chichester, Sarum and Lincoln). Wells regained its former cathedral status from Bath in 1218 and in 1228 a new building at Salisbury replaced the old cathedral at Sarum – now Old Sarum – some two miles away. Secular Canons lived by means of *prebends* or benefices of income from endowed land, manors or even churches. Membership of a non-monastic cathedral chapter was restricted to prebendaries – holders of prebends – and each had his prebendal stall in the cathedral. In some cathedrals (at Wells, for example) the ancient territorial titles of prebends have been retained, although not the endowments.

The Post-Reformation Period

At the Dissolution of the Monasteries, the monastic foundations were reconstituted to become cathedrals of the 'New Foundation' and in the 1540s Henry VIII created six additional sees. The former Augustinian churches at Oxford and Bristol and the great Benedictine churches at Chester, Gloucester, Peterborough and Westminster all became cathedrals, although Westminster was 'demoted' again in 1550. No further sees were established until 1836, and of the twenty new Anglican cathedrals created since then only five are of medieval foundation: St Albans was a Benedictine abbey; Southwark an Augustinian priory; and Manchester, Ripon and Southwell were collegiate churches of secular canons (*see* POST-MEDIEVAL CATHEDRALS).

Today, Anglican cathedrals are normally administered by a chapter of residentiary canons presided over by a dean. There are also non-residentiary or honorary canons, who may have certain responsibilities and privileges, and minor canons, who are responsible for assisting at musical services but are not members of a chapter. In cathedrals of the 'Old Foundation' the *precentor* (who is responsible for the direction of the choral services) is a member of the chapter, while elsewhere he is a minor canon as is his deputy, the *succentor*.

See also CHURCH MUSIC *and* CLERGY (CHURCH OF ENGLAND)

CEILINGS *see* VAULTING

CELIBACY OF THE CLERGY In the Middle Ages celibacy was required of all those in Holy Orders. In the Church of England, the obligation of celibacy was abolished in 1549.

CELL (i) The rudimentary quarters of an individual monk in a semi-eremetical institution e.g. a charterhouse (*see* CARTHUSIANS).

(ii) A dependent house of a monastery, usually with no more than four religious. These small daughter houses were sometimes provided for convalescence, contemplation or penitentiary purposes and, as a result, were almost invariably in remote locations. The term is also applied to larger dependencies, although erroneously so.

CELLARER 'The second father of the house' was responsible for the provision of food, drink, fuel and all the day-to-day requirements of a monastic community. Through his staff he controlled the mills, malthouse, brewhouse and bakehouse, he was responsible for collecting tolls (*see* MARKETS, SHOPS AND FAIRS) and for the carriage of goods, for the staffing of granges, the production and storing of produce and the welfare of guests

and CORRODIANS. He leased and sold land and appointed overseers for the monastic estates. Most importantly, it was the cellarer who was the chief means of communication between the monastery and the outside world.
See also LARDER

CELLARIUM The great storehouse of a monastery, which often occupied the entire ground floor or UNDERCROFT of the WESTERN RANGE of claustral buildings. The entrance, which opened onto the great court, was often large enough to admit a horse and cart. The cellar at Fountains Abbey in Yorkshire was 91m (300ft) in length and vaulted in twenty-two double bays which sprang from a central arcade of columns. Originally, it was divided into storerooms, offices and FRATER for the lay brothers.
See also CRYPT

CELTIC CHURCH The term 'Celtic Church' is something of a misnomer for, while it had its own distinctive features, it was nevertheless an integral part of the universal Church – albeit a Church in which there was little uniformity of ritual or organisation. It would be more accurate to describe the 'Celtic Church' of the fifth and sixth centuries as 'the church of those who spoke the Celtic language'.

It has been argued that the Church of Dyfrig, Illtud and Dewi owed little to the Christianity of Roman Britain and that it developed from the work of peripatetic missionaries. However, it is more likely that its origins are to be found in a variety of influences and that it was in south-east Wales that these came together, notably under Dyfrig (Dubricius), a bishop who presided over a Roman form of organisation in the second half of the fifth century. Dyfrig is generally acknowledged to have been the first Celtic 'saint' and, according to legend, it was he who crowned King Arthur

The undercroft at Fountains Abbey, Yorkshire.

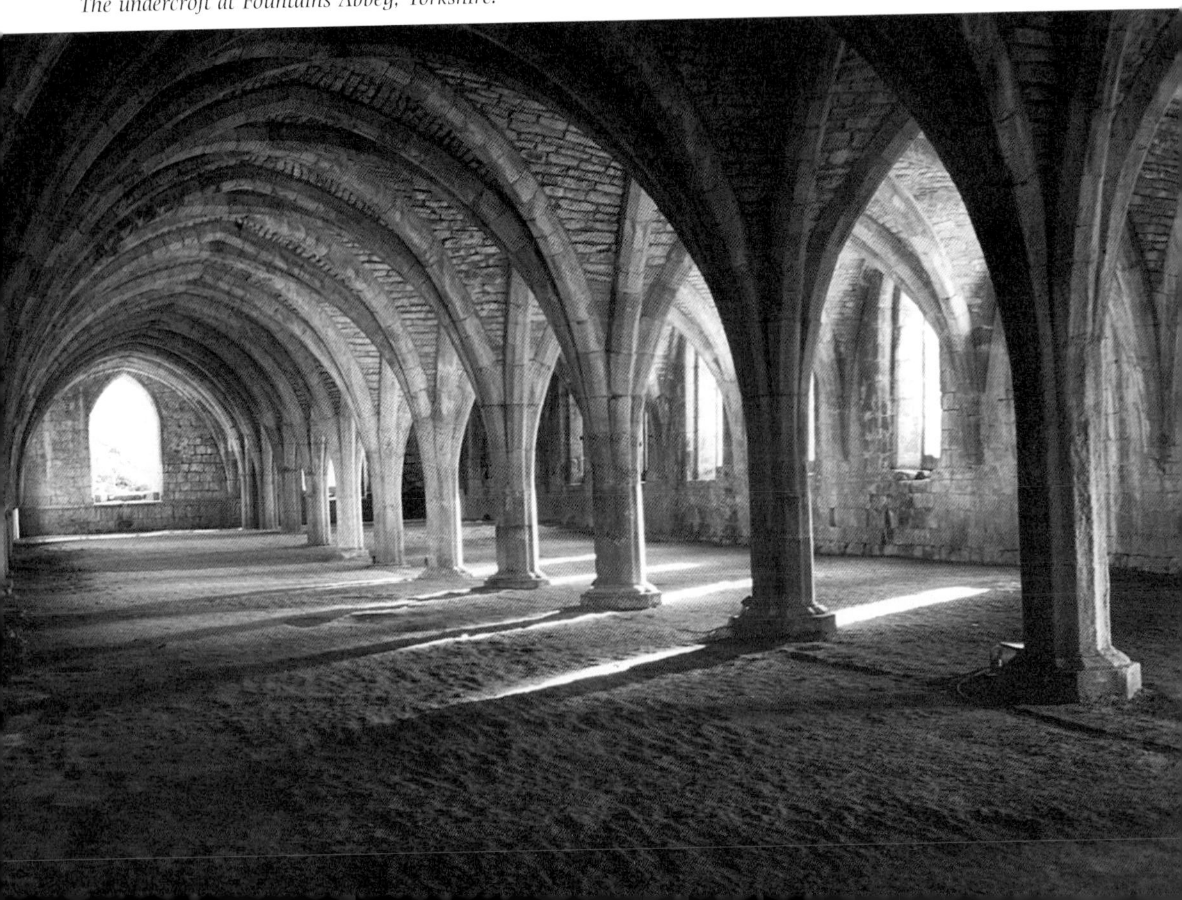

(Artorius). He was succeeded by Illtud, 'the renowned master of the Britons, learned in the teachings of the Church in the culture of the Latins and in the traditions of his own people.' Illtud was not a bishop but an abbot, which confirms that the monastic tradition had already taken root in Wales. That tradition possessed severely ascetic elements but was also characterised by scholarship and devotion. Illtud's monastery of Llanilltud Fawr (Llantwit Major, now in Vale of Glamorgan) was very different from the remote houses of his successors. It was close to the ruined villa of Llantwit (it may be that Illtud was a descendant of its former owners) and only 18km from Dynas Powys, once the seat of the kings of Glywysing. Llanilltud Fawr became the axis of the Celtic Church: Samson studied there before leaving for Dol in *c.* 520 to become the 'father of Breton monasticism'; Paul Aurelian, one of Samson's fellow students, became a leading figure in the Church in Cornwall; and Gildas, another of Samson's contemporaries, was acknowledged by the Irish to be an authority on ritual and discipline.

The Age of Saints

While Dyfrig was a bishop in an essentially post-Roman environment, the ascendancy of ASCETICISM, which was evident before his death in *c.* 612, reflected the final collapse of the economy which had sustained that environment. By the end of the sixth century, the desire of religious communities to retreat to remote and desolate places had become irresistible, no doubt encouraged by PLAGUE, which reached western Britain in 549 and is believed to have been as virulent as the notorious fourteenth-century Black Death.

This was the 'Age of Saints' when Christianity consolidated its hold on the inhabitants of Wales. In particular, it was from this time that the *llan* entered the country's toponymy. The meaning now attributed to the word is 'church' but at that time a *llan* was a consecrated enclosure in which the dead were buried and it was not until several centuries later that many *llannau* acquired churches. Associated with the ubiquitous *llan-* place-names of Wales and the Marches are the names of numerous 'saints' whose principal (and, perhaps, only) claim to fame was a gift of land on which to locate a community's burial enclosure. Such men are often described as 'founders' but, in most cases, 'benefactor' would be more precise – although inevitably, time and local pride have created legends round them. Of course, there were exceptions and there can be no denying the influence of 'saints' such as Deiniol, Padarn and Teilo (*see below*). But there is very little documentary or archaeological evidence relating to them and no way of knowing whether church dedications were contemporary or reflect a later cult.

St David of Wales

From *c.* 900 there is increasing evidence of the quite exceptional influence of David and his church, and it is not without significance that by the end of the twelfth century there were more than sixty churches dedicated to him in an area which extended from Pembroke to Hereford. *The Life of David*, written in *c.* 1090 by Rhygyfarch, the son of Julien, bishop of St David's, is the earliest of the lives of the Welsh 'saints', to which may be added material from Giraldus Cambrensis (in *c.* 1200) and the ANCHORITE of Llanddewibrefi (in *c.* 1346). From these and other sources it would appear that David (*c.* 520–89) was of the royal house of Ceredigion, the son of Sant (*Dewi Sant*), and that he belonged to a severely ascetic branch of the monastic tradition. In his day, he was the most respected leader of the Christians of Wales and is reputed to have founded twelve monasteries, including Glastonbury in Somerset and Menevia (later St David's in Pembrokeshire). The regime in all his houses was especially strict: his monks performed harsh austerities and hard manual labour, keeping no cattle to help them plough. They lived mainly in silence and on a frugal diet of vegetables, bread and water – indeed David's insistence on ABSTINENCE and his habit of immersing himself in ice-cold water as a means of subduing the flesh, earned for him the nickname *Aquaticus* – 'Waterman'. Such was his reputation that he was summoned to speak at the Synod of Brefi in *c.* 550 and (according to Rhygyfarch) he so impressed the assembly by his preaching that he was unanimously elected archbishop with authority over the whole of Wales. (This last detail is almost certainly a fabrication, intended by Rhygyfarch to invest his father's see of St David with METROPOLITAN status.) David died at his monastery of Menevia in *c.* 589. His cult received papal approval in *c.* 1120 and his relics were translated to a shrine in the cathedral of St David in 1131, and again in 1275 when the cathedral was rebuilt, financed largely from offerings at his shrine.

The Influence of Rome

Deiniol, Padarn and Teilo were contemporaries of David and were abbots, presiding over monastic communities and *clasau*, self-contained ecclesiastical communities consisting of an abbot (who might also be a bishop) and a group of hereditary canons sharing a common income but living as secular clerks (*claswyr*). The *clasau* were originally pioneering instruments of conversion, but by the twelfth century they had become well-endowed and self-indulgent communities (*see* CLAS).

When Augustine arrived in England in 597 he carried with him Pope Gregory's directive that he should exercise his authority 'over all the Christians of Britain' (*see* ANGLO-SAXON CHURCH). But when Augustine rather arrogantly sought to assert that authority in 603 he was rebuffed by the Welsh bishops, who questioned the power of the pope to impose upon them the jurisdiction of Canterbury, an archbishopric which had existed for less than a decade. Thus began the acrimonious relationship between Wales and Canterbury which was to last for more than thirteen centuries (*see* WALES, THE MEDIEVAL CHURCH IN). The most significant area of disagreement concerned the date of Easter, which in the Celtic Church was calculated by means of a system devised in 314 – unlike that of Rome which had been adopted in 457. Inevitably, the date of Easter became a symbol of freedom from the interference of Augustine and his successors. The Welsh stubbornly retained the old system until 768, but there can be little doubt that a century of isolation from the mainstream of Christendom severely weakened the influence and effectiveness of the Church in Wales.

CELURE (i) A CANOPY. (ii) The painted, panelled or vaulted section of a roof immediately above an altar or rood (*see* ROOD SCREEN).

CEMETERIES The right of burial in a monastic cemetery was usually allowed only to members of the community and confraters (*see* CONFRATERNITY). Most monastic cemeteries were located near the east end of the church, where they were approached from the cloister through a SLYPE, as at Gloucester and Worcester. However, in Cistercian houses access was more often via a door in the transept (at Byland, Rievaulx and Strata Florida, for example), an arrangement which was also found in Pre-monstratensian houses such as Easby. In Carthusian houses the cemetery was contained within the cloister garth. It was almost certainly St Dunstan who introduced the first monastic cemetery – at Glastonbury in *c.* 950 – where he enclosed it within a stone wall so that 'it seems like a charming meadow, removed from all noise of passers-by, so that it may be justly said of the holy men who lie there "Their bodies are buried in peace"'. Urban monasteries, such as Bury, sometimes provided a separate cemetery for the lay community – within the abbey precinct but with its own gate.

See also BURIALS (MONASTIC)

CENOTAPH A monument to a person or persons buried elsewhere.

CENSER *see* THURIBLE

CENSING ANGEL The figure of an angel

distributing incense.

CENTERING *or* CENTRE A temporary wooden or wicker framework used as a template in the construction of an arch or vault. Formed in the shape of the arch or vault that was being built, it was secured on scaffolding (*see* SCAFFOLDING AND CRANES) and supported the stones or bricks as they were put in place. The centering was removed once the stones were securely locked together and the mortar had set.
See also VAULTING

CERE CLOTH A cloth impregnated with wax (Latin *cera*) which is laid on the surface of an altar to prevent the linen cloths from being soiled by the oils used when consecrating the *mensa* (*see* ALTAR).

CHAINED LIBRARY *see* LIBRARIES

CHAIRS (SANCTUARY) The throne (*cathedra*) of a bishop is usually located on the north side of the sanctuary in his cathedral, while in parish churches an area is similarly designated as a place of honour for a visiting bishop. The chair which is reserved for this purpose is often of some antiquity (there are many Jacobean examples), although such valuable items of furniture are often locked away. The stone sanctuary chair at Beverley Minster in Yorkshire is of Saxon origin: the late sixteenth-century chair at Ledbury in Herefordshire is richly carved with scenes of the Journey of the Magi and the Entry into Jerusalem.

CHALICE VEIL A square of material, usually of the appropriate liturgical colour, used to cover the chalice and paten when they are not in use during the Eucharist.
See also COLOURS (LITURGICAL) *and* VEIL

CHAMBERLAIN (CAMERARIUS) A senior OBEDIENTIARY of a religious community responsible for the community's horses and wagons, including those kept at outlying granges (*see* GRANGE), and for the provision of fodder, pasturage and harness. He was also responsible for the provision, repair and laundering of CLOTHING, for the maintenance of lamps in the CLAUSTRAL and domestic buildings, for providing hot water and towels in the LAVATORIUM, for baths and for the weekly washing of feet between November and Easter, and for maintaining a fire in the warming house (*see* CALEFACTORIUM). He was also charged with engaging laundresses 'of good repute' to wash the liturgical linen and the monks' sheets, shirts, etc. Tallies were kept of all items sent for laundering, and losses were made good by deductions from the laundresses' wages.

The chamberlain had his own office (*checker*) which was usually located near the CELLARIUM or within the CURIA. In some houses the offices of Chamberlain and CELLARER were combined, in which case a *sub-camerarius* was appointed, often from the ranks of the lay brothers. The function of the chamberlain in a superior's household was similar to that of a chamberlain in any magnate establishment: he would be a member of his lord's (advisory) council and principally responsible for his financial affairs.

CHANCEL A comparatively recent term (derived from the Latin CANCELLI meaning 'lattice' or 'grating') used to describe a PRESBYTERY which is separated from the NAVE by a screen. Following the Fourth Lateran Council of 1215 (which pronounced the doctrine of transubstantiation, thereby emphasising the sacredness of the mass), it was considered necessary to enclose the presbytery by means of a screen, both to preserve the mystery of the EUCHARIST and to isolate the SANCTUARY from the secular activities of the nave. It is this enclosed space that is now described as the chancel, although in most major cathedral and monastic churches it incorporated the CHOIR and was separated from the nave by the PULPITUM.

CHANCELLOR (i) One of the four dignitaries of

CATHEDRALS of the 'Old Foundation', whose responsibilities include the cathedral library and school.

(ii) A Diocesan Chancellor is a professional lawyer who acts on behalf of the bishop in the administration of the DIOCESE. The Chancellor is usually president of the CONSISTORY COURT and is chiefly responsible for considering applications for the granting of faculties (*see* FACULTY) and for hearing complaints against clerics brought under the Ecclesiastical Jurisdiction Measure of 1963, other than those concerning doctrine or ceremonial.

CHANCERY, COURT OF The appeal court of the Province of York.

CHANT *see* PLAINSONG

CHANTRIES ACT (1547) *see* CHANTRY

CHANTRY

> Three things helpen souls most out of penance, that is devout praying, alms-giving and mass-singing . . . right as meat and drink comforteth a man when he is feeble, right so the sacrament comforteth and strengtheneth the souls that it is done for.

From the Old French *chanceries*, meaning 'to sing', a chantry was a private soul-mass, celebrated regularly for the repose of the soul of a testator and others nominated by him in his will (*see* PRIVILEGED ALTAR). It was the conviction that a regular offering of the Eucharist was the most effective means of redemption that encouraged medieval man to make financial provision in his will for a chantry – effectively a spiritual insurance policy. This was particularly so during the fourteenth and fifteenth centuries, when the LITURGY of the Catholic Church increasingly emphasised the importance of the mass. Some chantries were endowed during the lifetime of the founder, and the mass-priest would be obliged to celebrate masses for his well-being on earth and his soul after death. Chantries were also endowed by guilds and fraternities for the benefit of their members. They were, in fact, a very cheap form of endowment, for even the most humble testator could arrange for one or two masses to be said for his soul (*see* BEDE ROLL). However, it was those with the largest purses (and often the heaviest consciences) who were responsible for the erection of the magnificent late medieval CHANTRY CHAPELS and for the endowment of numerous charitable institutions such as the Hospital of All Saints (now known as Brown's Hospital) at Stamford in Lincolnshire, built in the reign of Henry VII to accommodate ten poor men, together with two poor women who were to be 'attentive and useful to the poor men in their necessities'. The residents of the Hospital of All Saints were required to recite three psalms a day for the soul of the home's founder, Thomas Brown, a prominent wool merchant, and it was a condition of admission that a candidate should not only be 'lowly, devout and poor' but also fluent in chanting 'the Lord's Prayer, the Angelic Salutation and the Apostles' Creed'. Men such as Thomas Brown were prepared to make considerable and often posthumous investments to ensure that their souls did not remain too long in the dreaded PURGATORY, a concept that was popularly established in the twelfth century and which motivated the building of numerous social institutions as well as CHANTRY CHAPELS and other memorials. In the Suffolk town of Lavenham, Thomas Spring III (known as The Great Clothier) left money to build the superb tower of Lavenham's parish church, and in many of England's great cathedrals endowments were provided to maintain choirs whose tasks included praying for the souls of the departed: at York Minster, for example, where the choristers were known as the College of the Vicars choral (*see* CHANTRY COLLEGES).

The Dissolution of the Chantries in 1547 was

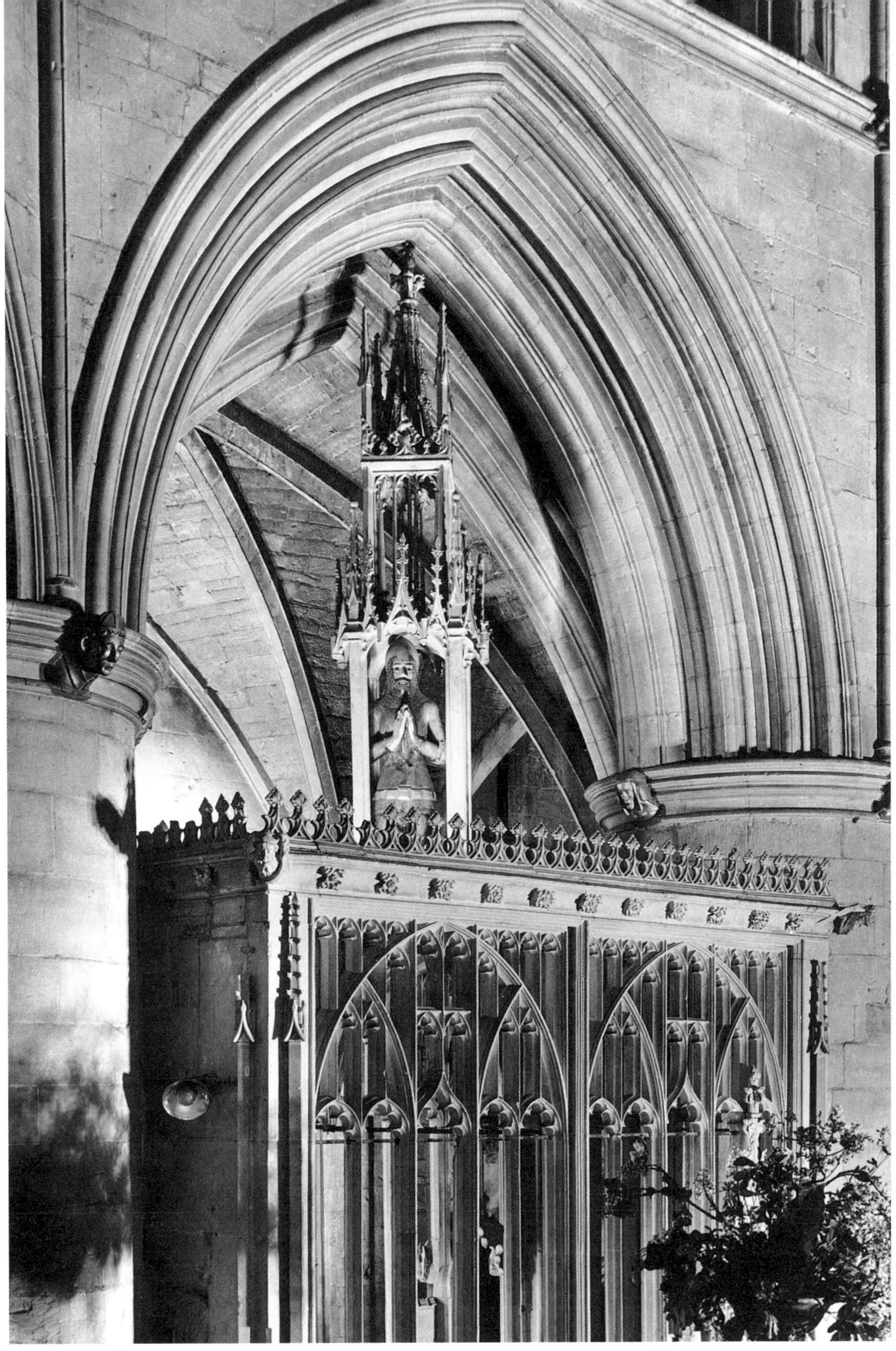

The Holy Trinity chantry chapel at Tewkesbury Abbey surmounted by the kneeling effigy of Lord Edward Despenser (d. 1375) within a tabernacle canopy. (Courtesy of Anthony Kersting)

accompanied by the confiscation of those funds of guilds and corporations which (it was claimed) had been assigned to 'superstitious objects' (*see* REFORMATION, THE). This measure had a far greater impact on community life than the more spectacular DISSOLUTION OF THE MONASTERIES, for many chantries were dependent on their investments for the maintenance of schools, almshouses, hospitals and other charitable foundations. Most significantly, the Chantries Act of 1547 confirmed official disapproval of the doctrine of purgatory and masses for 'them which be departed'. As a consequence (and because of the Crown's urgent need for resources) all chantry endowments, goods and valuables were transferred to the king. *Chantry Certificates*, which were issued in 1548, are housed at The National Archives, together with the *confiscation inventories* of 1552 (*see* APPENDIX II), and many of these have been published by local history societies. They provide an invaluable source of information concerning the nature of chantries, guilds, almshouses, schools, hospitals and other charitable foundations at the close of the Middle Ages, together with details of the plate, vestments and other valuables which parish churches had accumulated through medieval bequests and endowments.

CHANTRY CHAPELS By the fifteenth century most large churches (including monastic ones) had at least one chantry chapel in which a priest was employed to sing masses for the soul of the founder and others nominated by him in his will. Cardinal Beaufort (d. 1447) provided for three thousand masses to be said at the altar of his magnificent chapel in the RETRO-CHOIR at Winchester (*see* illustration, page 327), while successive members of the Hungerford family spent vast sums on bequests to the church so that, by the end of the fifteenth century, they had founded twelve chantries, seven anniversary masses (*obits*), a school and two almshouses. Like other forms of memorial, a chantry chapel does not necessarily mark the place of interment of the person in whose memory it was erected.

Some chantry chapels were very large: Henry VII's chapel at Westminster Abbey is a spectacular example. But the majority of chantry chapels are very much smaller and usually comprise a gilded and painted rectangular PARCLOSE of ornate stone or metal and an intricately vaulted CANOPY. (The essential difference between a canopied monument and a small chantry chapel is the presence in the latter of an altar at which masses were celebrated.) Such chapels are generally found linking the piers of the choir arcade or flanking the presbytery, and their proximity to the High Altar is usually an accurate guide to the status of those they commemorate.

It is significant that the popularity of chantry chapels in the high Middle Ages should have coincided with the flowering of the Perpendicular style of architecture, for almost without exception, the decorative detail is exquisite. At Tewkesbury Abbey in Gloucestershire, for instance, the chapel erected (*c.* 1378) for Edward Despenser (d. 1375) on the south side of the High Altar contains the earliest example of fan vaulting (*see* VAULTING) in England. From within a lofty canopy on the roof of the chapel the kneeling figure of Edward stares out at the High Altar and to the place where the sacrament house (*see* TABERNACLE) was once suspended. (There is no other known example of an effigial figure in this elevated position.) The chapel is commonly known as the Trinity Chapel, because on the east wall of the interior is a remarkable fresco representing the Holy Trinity, with portraits of Edward and his wife (Elizabeth de Burghersh) on either side of the central figures, kneeling behind angels with censers. In the corresponding north bay is a chapel within which stands the tomb of Robert Fitz Hamon, a descendant of William the Conqueror and the abbey's founder, who died in 1107. Fitz Hamon was first buried in the Chapter House of the Benedictine monastery, but his body was moved to its present position in 1241 and the chantry erected by Abbot Parker in 1397. The finest of the Tewkesbury chantry chapels is that built by Isabel

Despenser in memory of her first husband, Richard Beauchamp, Earl of Abergavenny and Worcester (d. 1421). Begun in 1422, but not completed until 1438, it has an ornate and spiky canopy and a lovely miniature fan vault within which is set the carved head of a lady – presumably that of Lady Isabella herself. There are traces of original painting in the vaulting: peacock-blue with ribs and pendants in red and gold. There are other notable examples at Boxgrove Priory in Sussex and Christchurch Priory, Dorset.

With the Dissolution of the Chantries in 1547, many chantry chapels were used for other purposes: the superb Hungerford chantry at Salisbury Cathedral, for example, was converted into an exceptionally ornate mayoral pew.

See also CHANTRY COLLEGES, PRIVILEGED ALTARS *and* SQUINT

CHANTRY COLLEGES There were two types of college of secular priests in medieval England, the earlier of which was usually created by a religious body and was based on a cathedral model with a chapter of clergy (secular canons) under a dean or provost. The collegiate chapel in the courtyard of Hastings Castle, endowed by Robert, count of Eu, in *c.* 1070, was of this type. The later, and more numerous, type was known as a chantry college because the object of their foundation was to pray for the souls of the founders and other benefactors (*see* CHANTRY). Their clergy, known as chantry priests, dwelt together in the college precincts presided over by a master, WARDEN or provost, and their constitution ensured a 'perpetual succession' of services. Although many of these colleges were small, some rivalled the cathedrals and monasteries in size and opulence, particularly in the fourteenth and fifteenth centuries, when the founding of a chantry college was often the ultimate ambition of the medieval establishment. The very rich, especially those who left no direct heir, might provide for the establishment of a college that was endowed primarily for the celebration of masses in perpetuity for the souls of the founder and his family. Many collegiate churches were also family mausoleums and there can be little doubt that they were intended to be a permanent memorial to a magnate's status and lineage. Thus, the late medieval chantry colleges were effectively CHANTRY CHAPELS on a grand scale. Several, such as St George's Chapel, Windsor and the (unfinished) collegiate church at Warkworth, were located within the walls of royal or magnate castles; while others, such as Tattershall, Staindrop, Middleham and Fotheringhay, were parish churches that were endowed as chantry colleges by noble patrons whose castles were in close proximity.

Undoubtedly one of the finest collegiate foundations, and that which inspired many others, is the Chapel of St George at Windsor Castle. The original college was endowed in 1348 by Edward III (1327–77), following the founding of the Order of the Garter in the same year. Henry III's chapel, dedicated to St Edward the Confessor, was repaired and became the collegiate chapel, rededicated to St George and the Blessed Virgin Mary. At the same time, the entire lower ward of the castle was converted to house the officials and clergy who were to serve the new college and the Order with which it was to be associated. St George's Chapel, which now dominates the lower ward of the castle, was begun by Edward IV in 1472 to celebrate his return from exile and was completed by Henry VIII in 1528. It remains the chapel of the Order of the Garter and has been accurately described as one of the greatest achievements of Perpendicular Gothic architecture.

The magnificent collegiate church at Warkworth Castle was erected in the early fifteenth century as a mausoleum for the Percy family. The church, of which only the foundations remain, was never completed but was intended to have a nave and two aisles, transepts, a tower above the crossing and a choir at the east end. The ground slopes upward from west to east, so that a pair of crypts could be accommodated beneath the chancel. The larger crypt would have contained the Percy tombs, to which the earl and his family would descend in solemn procession to celebrate the anniversaries of the deaths of their ancestors, while the smaller chamber was probably intended as a vestry. The collegiate church at Warkworth separates the inner and outer wards so that a visitor, having entered through the lofty gatehouse, would see in front of him the south façade and tower of the church and, beyond that, the spectacular mass of the keep. To heighten the dramatic effect, access to the inner ward was through a passageway constructed beneath the east end of the church.

In 1478, Richard of Gloucester (later Richard III) obtained licences to establish collegiate churches at Barnard Castle and Middleham – only three days after the execution of his brother, the Duke of Clarence. The collegiate body at Middleham consisted of a dean, six chaplains, four clerks and six choristers, and (in the words of the king's licence) was charged with the offering of perpetual masses

> for the good estate of Us, and our most dear Consort Elizabeth Queen of England, and of Our . . . brother and Anne his wife, and his heirs, while we shall live, and when we shall depart from this light, for our souls, and for the souls of the most illustrious Prince, Richard, formerly Duke of York, our father, and of our brothers and sisters, and of all the faithful departed . . .

Fotheringhay College originated in the chapel of the castle and is described in contemporary documents as 'The Collegiate church of the Annunciation and St Edward the Confessor within the castle of Fotheringhay'. Towards the end of the fourteenth century, Edmund Langley determined to refound the college on a larger scale but his plans were thwarted by his death in 1402. In 1411 Langley's son (also Edward) obtained letters patent for the transfer, and six acres of land to the south of the parish church were assigned for the collegiate buildings. However, it was not until 1415 that the parish church and college were formally united and the dean and canons replaced by a master and chantry priests. Edward was killed at Agincourt in the same year and his body is buried in the choir of the new collegiate church which was then under construction. The staff of the college consisted of a master, precentor, eleven other chaplains or fellows, eight clerks and thirteen choristers. It was established to pray for the souls of Richard II, Henry IV, Henry V, the founder and other benefactors and their families. A code of statutes was drawn up which consisted of fifty-four sections that had to be recited in the chapter house twice a year. It included legislation regarding the election of fellows, the appointment and payment of officials, the dress to be worn, the administration of corporate lands and property and the preparation of an annual balance sheet. The church building comprised two separate churches: the eastern portion, or choir, was the private collegiate church, while the western portion, or nave, was the parish church. The college was transferred into the ownership of the Duke of Northumberland following the Dissolution of the Chantry colleges in 1547. The Duke immediately removed the choir roof for the lead, and most of the collegiate buildings were demolished, although the nave, aisles and magnificent octagonal tower of the church were retained for parochial use. Intended originally as a family mausoleum, in recent years the church at Fotheringhay has become a shrine to the Yorkist dynasty, although the nearby castle is now little more than a fallen lump of masonry.

Academic Foundations

Many colleges developed as academic institutions although, in practice, there was little legal or constitutional difference between the two types of college. During the later fifteenth and early sixteenth centuries there was a significant expansion in the number of colleges at Oxford and Cambridge and many of these were endowed specifically for the better education of the clergy.

Substantial endowments made provision for increasing numbers of undergraduates and for the teaching duties of fellows, while smaller bequests provided loans for the benefit of 'poor, virtuous scholars, not vicious nor wasters nor haunters of taverns or alehouses'. Only a minority of scholars graduated as a Bachelor of Arts after four years or as a Master of Arts after a further three. Many students were the sons of nobility and gentry who were there at their own expense in order to improve their general education.

Christ Church College was founded (as Cardinal College) in 1525 by Cardinal Wolsey (*c*. 1475–1530) on the site of the Priory of St Frideswide, Oxford. Following Wolsey's fall in 1529, Henry VIII dissolved the college and, in 1532, established an ecclesiastical foundation consisting of a dean and twelve canons. This foundation survived until 1546, when the king united the recently founded see of Oxford with the College, designating what remained of the old priory church of St Frideswide as the cathedral church of the diocese. With a dean, eight canons, eight chaplains and a hundred students, it was both a cathedral and a college: one foundation with two functions. The double character of the foundation at Christchurch was once explained thus:

> There is absolutely no separation between them as if they were two distinct members in one and the same body. Neither is the Chapter an appendage to the College, nor is the College an appendage to the Chapter. They form one single foundation under one head and so intimately blended together are they in all their parts that questions involving the constitution of the one cannot be answered without including what belongs to the other.

Founded by Henry VI in 1440, the chapel of

Christ Church College, Oxford.

King's College, Cambridge is undoubtedly the finest of all collegiate chapels. The first stone was laid in 1446 but it was not until 1515 that Henry VIII completed the chapel and later exempted the foundation from dissolution in 1547. Unlike most other collegiate chapels, the original intention was that King's should be a chantry chapel, unrivalled in its scale and majesty, in which members of the college would pray for the souls of their royal patrons. Described sardonically by John Ruskin in the nineteenth century as 'a sow lying on her back with her feet in the air', the towering Perpendicular chapel was based on the royal thirteenth-century Sainte Chapelle in Paris. In many respects the audacity of its architecture and the absence of religious decoration denote the advent of the English Renaissance. Everything about it is magnificent – the intricate fan vault, for example, is the largest and most flamboyant in the world (*see* VAULTING). The superb oak organ screen was commissioned by Henry VIII and is clearly a Renaissance work – festooned with secular imagery including the cyphers of King Henry and Anne Boleyn.

Of course, there were many educational foundations outside Oxford and Cambridge. Eton College, for example, was endowed by Henry VI as a religious college with a provost, fellows, clerks and choristers to sing at divine service and a school of twenty-five 'poor scholars' under the direction of a Master. Although such places have subsequently developed as élite centres of academic excellence, in the Middle Ages their essential function remained that of commemorating patrons by prayers and intercessory masses.

Parish Church

Several parish churches have collegiate origins. The Collegiate church of St Mary, Warwick, for example, was served by a chapter composed of a dean and seven canons from 1123 to the Reformation. It was Henry, the first Earl of Warwick, who established a prebend (*see* PREBENDARY) to provide for the needs of a priest. By 1123 his son, Roger, had given sufficient property to maintain six further prebends, together with houses in Warwick to accommodate the canons, several of whom came from the chapel of All Saints in the nearby castle. The chapter met together in the church to celebrate the mass and the seven canonical offices, and in the chapter house, where their business affairs were conducted. The chancel was reserved for the College (which later came to included vicars who deputised for absent canons), together with clerics in minor orders and boy choristers. The nave was divided from the chancel by a screen and contained a parish altar and side-chapels for the townspeople. In 1544 the college surrendered to Henry VIII, who confiscated its estates, some of which were restored to the burgesses of Warwick by royal charter in 1545.

The wonderful set of twenty-eight misericords (*see* MISERICORD) in the stalls of Ludlow parish church in Shropshire suggest that this too was a collegiate foundation. But while a college-like establishment existed at Ludlow, it was not truly collegiate. Members of the influential Palmers' Guild, whose altar dedicated to St John the Evangelist was in the north-eastern chapel, endowed a number of chantries within the church. The chaplains employed to administer these chantries (ten in the late fifteenth century) were accommodated in a lodging house in College Street and shared the daily offices and duties of the church with the secular clergy while attending also to their individual responsibilities.

The Reformation

Chantry colleges were suppressed in 1547, although many were later refounded as academic institutions and some even managed to survive the Dissolution of the Monasteries in their original form. The College of St Endellion in Cornwall, for example, is first mentioned in documents dated 1260 (*Ecclesia Sancte Endeliente*) as a college of secular clergy serving the church and shrine of the sixth-century Celtic saint. In 1547 the Rector was

deprived of his living, the college members (*prebendaries*) all received their £5 pensions as dispossessed clerics and the college was presumed to be dissolved. And yet, unaccountably, there is a College of St Endellion today, its fellows claiming corporate continuity from before the Reformation. Even more remarkably, the college received a grant of armorial bearings in 1950. Grants of arms are signed and sealed by the sovereign's authority and the letters patent of 1950 would therefore appear to confirm the college's claim.
See also CHANTRY *and* CHANTRY CHAPELS

CHAPEL ROYAL Henry I (1100–35) employed a group of singers whose main duty was to provide him with music at religious services in whichever residence he was occupying at the time. In subsequent reigns, letters patent confirmed the existence of this Chapel Royal by name, although its title did not signify a particular building but a body of singers attached to the monarch rather than the church. There were several palaces in and around London where they performed, and when the court went on tour, so too did the musicians. The choir comprised boy trebles together with chaplains and singers who were dignified as 'Gentlemen of the Chapel'. At first the gentlemen took turns as accompanist, but later the post of organist brought with it considerable perquisites. Two notable holders of the post, Thomas Tallis (*c.* 1505–85) and William Byrd (*c.* 1542–1623), were granted the monopoly of music printing and publishing for twenty-one years from 1575. It was Henry VIII (1509–47) who established a

The Chapel Royal, Whitehall, London.

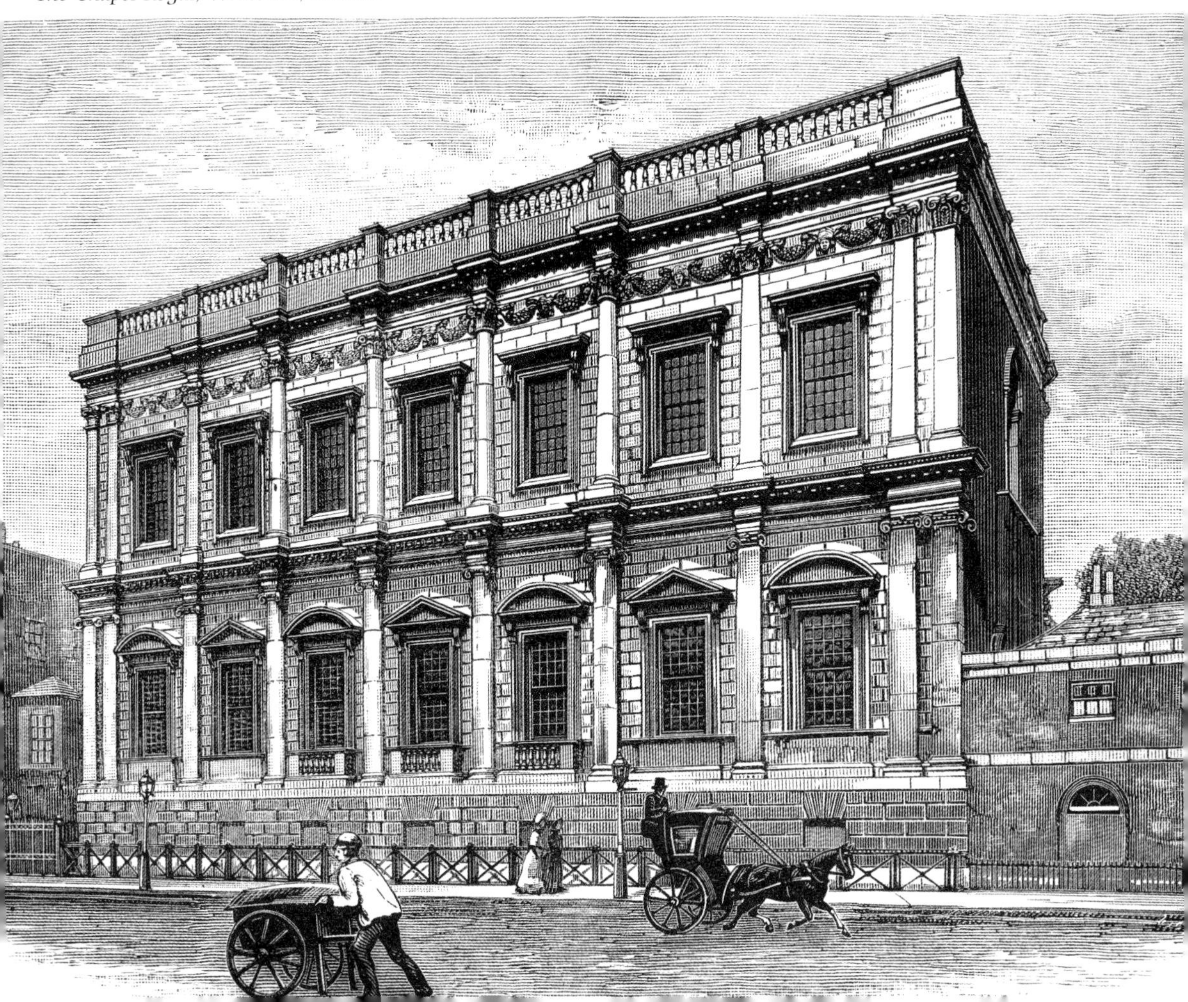

permanent home for the choir when he ordered the construction of St James's Palace.
See also CHAPELS *and* CHURCH MUSIC

CHAPELS Derived from the Latin *capella*, diminutive of *cappa* meaning 'little cape', the term refers to the cloak of St Martin of Tours, which was preserved as a sacred relic by the Frankish kings. In time, the term was applied generically to sanctuaries where holy RELICS were preserved and prayers were said and, from *c.* 800, to subsidiary churches, or subdivisions of a church, in which there was an altar.

From the eighth century, landowners began building *proprietary chapels* on their estates to augment those of the minsters (*see* ANGLO-SAXON CHURCH). Indeed, in late Anglo-Saxon England, possession of a proprietary chapel (sometimes described as a *thane's church*) was considered to be an attribute of rank. Most were served by a priest, who may also have acted as the lord's chaplain, and the estate retained the church's TITHES and other dues, while the lord exercised proprietorial rights, including the right to appoint a priest (*advowson*). Similarly, most medieval residences and castles contained private chapels (*oratories*), licensed for divine worship by a bishop, and built within the walls of a house or castle, or adjacent to it.

Most former monastic churches contain a number of minor chapels, each of which would have been used by a priest to say mass, while others were dedicated to a particular saint or provided for a specific purpose. Of these, the LADY CHAPEL, dedicated to the Blessed Virgin Mary and located at the eastern termination behind the High Altar, is usually the largest, except in Cistercian monasteries where the abbey church was itself invariably dedicated to the Virgin. Others were built into the aisles, transepts or ambulatory and may have been CHANTRY CHAPELS (*see also* PARCLOSE *and* PRIVILEGED ALTAR).

A chapel was usually provided at (or near) the gate of a religious house for the use of visitors, servants and employees (*see* CAPELLA ANTE PORTAS) and at granges (*see* GRANGE) and these sometimes became parish churches, the best-known example being the church of St Margaret at Westminster. The chapel of St Michael on the summit of Glastonbury Tor in Somerset was built by the monks of the nearby abbey for the benefit of pilgrims visiting one of the most sacred and historic sites in England. (It was on the Tor, in 1539, that the Abbot of Glastonbury was butchered for refusing to relinquish the abbey plate following the DISSOLUTION OF THE MONASTERIES.) The Glastonbury chapel may have performed a function similar to that of the fourteenth-century 'Shoe House' or Slipper Chapel at Houghton St Giles in Norfolk, which is situated about 1.6km (1 mile) from the shrine of Our Lady at Walsingham Priory. Here, the pilgrims would pause and meditate before embarking on the final stage of their journey – barefoot and penitent (*see* SHRINES).

Free chapels (*see* PECULIAR), such as the tiny thirteenth-century chapel of St Bartholomew at Corton in Dorset, were not subject to a bishop's jurisdiction, although most of the rights and privileges of these peculiars have now been revoked. Many were the chapels of former commanderies and preceptories (*see* COMMANDERY) of the military and hospitaller orders of St John of Jerusalem and the Knights Templar, usually described in documents (as recently as the nineteenth century) as *ex-parochial* and, as such, exempt from diocesan jurisdiction (*see* ST JOHN OF JERUSALEM, ORDER OF *and* TEMPLAR, KNIGHTS). Chapels Royal (*Royal Peculiars*) are private chapels attached to the royal court and are exempt from any jurisdiction save that of the sovereign, exercised through the Dean of the Chapels Royal. Other royal chapels include mausoleums, which were often constructed for that purpose during a sovereign's lifetime. The most magnificent of these is Henry VII's chapel at Westminster Abbey which is itself a royal peculiar.

Other chapels (many of them endowed by means of chantries) were built to serve HOSPITALS and at the roadside, often near bridges and fords, at

The fourteenth-century St Catherine's Chapel, built by the Benedictine monks of Abbotsbury, Dorset, on a hilltop overlooking their abbey.

SHRINES and above holy wells. At the Severn crossing near Stourport in Worcestershire, the medieval hermits (*see* HERMIT) of Redstone Rock operated a ferry on the important saltway from Droitwich; and in Devon the Starcross ferry across the Exe was maintained by monks from the Benedictine abbey of Sherborne in Dorset.

CHAPLAIN (CAPELLANUS) (i) A 'chapel priest' without a benefice who carried out the obligations of a CHANTRY.
(ii) A resident priest in a house of nuns or attached to an abbot or senior prior. A chaplain was effectively a private secretary as well as a priest, whose principal function was the administration of the Mass and Sacraments. He attended to the abbot's financial affairs, collecting his superior's allowance from the BURSAR, and supervised his household expenses and his obligation of alms-giving. In the late medieval period, the chaplain often administered the entire abbatial household and had a private chamber within the abbot's lodging. At Durham, the chaplain's office was conveniently located near that of the bursar.
(iii) The personal assistant of a bishop.

CHAPTER (i) A section (*capitulum*) of a monastic RULE (*regula*).
(ii) An assembly of the members of a religious house convened for the reading of a chapter of the rule and for the transaction of administrative and disciplinary business. In 1334 Benedict XII determined that in all houses of more than six brethren there should be a daily meeting of the community. In fact, this had been the practice in many of the larger houses since at least the eleventh century, and most communities had provided a chamber of sufficient size for the purpose (*see* CHAPTER HOUSE). The meeting usually followed the office of PRIME and began with remembrance of the martyrs celebrated on that day, prayers for the dead and, in particular, for the community's benefactors. A chapter of the rule was then read (it was from this that the meeting took its name) and this may have been accompanied by a commentary, or followed by an address, by the abbot or, in his absence, the prior (*see* PRIOR AND PRIORESS). The next part of the meeting was concerned with administrative matters: notices, correspondence, the allocation of weekly duties and reports from the community's officials regarding the management of the house and its estates (the great foundations were endowed with considerable

resources and property). Finally, the superior would announce: 'Let us now speak of our order' and guests were asked to leave. The business that followed was not divulged to anyone outside the community. This included a series of ACCUSATIONS and self-accusations concerning alleged breaches of the order's rule and the constitution of the house. These charges would be determined by the superior and punishment (often corporal) was carried out before the assembled community (*see* CUSTODIANS *and* DISCIPLINE). Discussion of chapter business outside the formal proceedings of the chapter was forbidden and there were strict rules of debate, typified by the *Constitutions* of Lanfranc (*c.* 1005–89):

> No-one shall speak privately with another or several. Whatever is said shall be audible to the superior and to the entire community. Only matters of utility and pertaining to the religious life shall be discussed. While one is speaking the rest shall keep silence. No-one shall interrupt the speaker save the president who may bid a speaker to have done if it seems to him that his words are too many or to no purpose. When the president begins to speak, even if one is already speaking, he shall cease and absolute silence shall be preserved by all present.

Meetings could be lively – and sometimes trying. Abbot Adam of Dryburgh observed that 'there is too little love and tenderness in those sitting round, no pity nor compassion whatever in the superior presiding, but there is very great discomfort and unrest in my heart as I sit there'. (*See also* GENERAL CHAPTER)

(iii) The body corporate of a religious house or other ecclesiastical institution, e.g. the canons of a cathedral (*see* CATHEDRAL CHAPTER). Like the brethren of monastic communities, the chapters of secular cathedrals met as a governing body in the CHAPTER HOUSE.

CHAPTER HOUSE Second only in importance to a community's church, the chapter house was used for meetings of the CHAPTER and, on occasions, for the Visitor's inquiry (*see* VISITATION (ECCLESIASTICAL)) and the reception of distinguished guests. It was the administrative heart of a religious community, a place where the monks or canons met every morning to hear readings from scripture and the RULE and to conduct business such as the allocation of duties and alleged breaches of discipline. The chapter houses of several of the major urban abbeys and cathedrals were also used by the secular authorities for occasional meetings, including sessions of Parliament. Henry III's magnificent octagonal chapter house at Westminster Abbey (completed *c.* 1255), described by Matthew Paris as 'beyond compare', was, from 1257, the meeting place of the king's 'Great Court', the predecessor of the English parliament, and today remains under the jurisdiction of the Crown.

In the twelfth and thirteenth centuries, abbots and (rarely) royal and noble BENEFACTORS were sometimes buried beneath the chapter house (regrettably, few tomb slabs have survived), while the bodies of deceased monks rested there before burial in the community's cemetery.

At chapter meetings, seating was allocated according to seniority: a raised seat was provided against the outer (east) wall for the community's superior, with the OBEDIENTIARIES seated on either side of him on stone benches which, in larger communities, were often arranged in two or even three tiers. A lectern (*analogium*) was provided for readings (the sockets for these have survived at several sites, including Bury St Edmunds, Byland, Cleeve and Waverley) together with book cupboards, those in Cistercian chapter houses flanking the entrance, as at Fountains and Furness, where the bays of the *armoria* are partitioned with stone. Unusually, the early twelfth-century chapter house at Worcester has a fireplace inserted in the circular wall.

Where they have survived, the chapter houses of

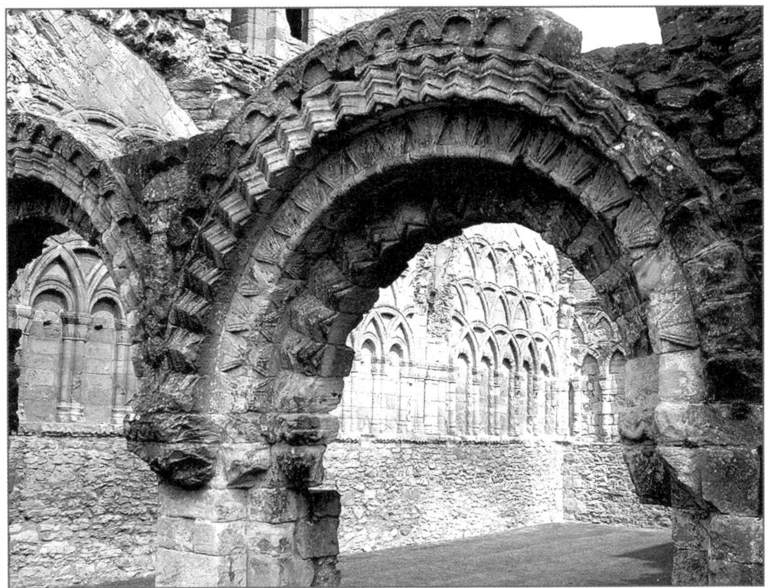

The doorway to the ruined chapter house at Wenlock Priory, Shropshire (c. 1140). The magnificent Romanesque decoration and blind arcading are typical of Cluniac buildings.

the different orders vary in size and shape and may have been extensively remodelled and enlarged to accommodate an expanding community or, as at Strata Florida, reduced in size because of contraction. Nearly all were located near the church on the ground floor of the EASTERN RANGE of claustral buildings (*see* CLOISTER), although there were exceptions, mostly at cathedrals and colleges of secular canons. At Lichfield, for example, the chapter house VESTIBULE is entered directly from the north choir aisle of the cathedral church; at Ripon the canons' chapter house is located between the choir and the south transept; and at Wells it is approached by a stair, 'unmatched in its ethereal beauty', from the north transept. The size and architectural embellishment of the doorway (often with flanking window openings) leading from the cloister to the chapter house, and of the vestibule that linked them, are indicative of the considerable importance attached to the proceedings of the chapter, indeed at Salisbury Cathedral the thirteenth-century chapter house is more sumptuous than the church which was built at the same time. The earliest chapter houses were rectangular, as at Bristol Cathedral (a richly ornamented late Norman survival), while that at Worcester (early twelfth century) was circular, and is still so within, although the strengthening of the walls in the fourteenth century resulted in the exterior becoming decagonal. It was often the case that the floor of the chapter house was excavated to a level below that of the cloister in order to allow greater height for the stone-ribbed vault. Most chapter houses were essentially aisleless halls, although the Cistercians divided their chambers with arcades of piers: of three bays at Byland, for example, and six at Fountains (one of the largest chapter houses in England). Uniquely, the magnificent APSIDAL chapter house at Cistercian Rievaulx had an AMBULATORY, possibly intended to accommodate the LAY BROTHERS during sermons. Benedictine chapter houses were usually apsidal, as at Durham, Gloucester and Shrewsbury. Many chapter houses extended beyond the eastern wall of the claustral buildings, although not invariably so. The majority were originally single-storey vaulted chambers, with the DORTER above, but in order to dignify the proceedings of the chapter many were raised to two storeys, thereby blocking access from the dorter to the NIGHT STAIR and the church. This could be overcome by vaulting the western bay of the chapter house at a lower level, thereby

The vaulting in the Chapter House at Wells, Somerset.

creating a passage above (at Bindon, Cleeve and Rochester, for example), or by building a 'detached' chapter house to the east of the claustral range (i.e. connected to it by a vestibule beneath the dorter), as at Bristol, Chester, Dore, Lanercost and Westminster.

From the early thirteenth century, most chapter houses were polygonal (probably because the acoustic was infinitely superior to that of the earlier rectangular chambers), usually with a central pier supporting the vault. However, the Cistercians continued to build in rectangular form (as at Fountains) because their rule demanded austerity. The first of the polygonal chapter houses was at Lincoln and this established an architectural fashion peculiar to England. Most were octagonal, although Lincoln's was decagonal, with a diameter of 18m (59ft). Exterior roofs were usually pointed and the walls were buttressed at each corner. As at Lincoln, most chapter houses had wooden roofs that were replaced with stone in the mid-thirteenth century. The chapter house at Wells in Somerset (*c.* 1319) is the finest in England, although by no means the largest. Beneath the windows is an arcade of fifty-one stalls with beautifully carved canopies and above, springing from a single, slender column, is a superb vault, quite unsurpassed in its architectural exuberance. The late thirteenth-century chapter house at Southwell Minster, Nottinghamshire, has the only example in England of a stone vault unsupported by a central pillar.

CHARNELS *see* BURIALS (MONASTIC) *and* OSSUARIES

CHARTER A document conferring rights on a body corporate or on an individual. A royal charter was a formal instrument by which a sovereign granted or confirmed lands, liberties, titles or immunities on his subjects in perpetuity. Charters were used particularly for grants of land and transactions of the Anglo-Saxon period, whereby land was granted to both monasteries and individuals. There are two types of *Charter Roll*, the first recording grants and the second confirmations. Both relate to the period 1199–1516, after which charters were succeeded by letters patent.

CHARTERHOUSE *see* CARTHUSIANS *and* PLAGUE

CHASUBLE An outer garment worn by priests when celebrating the EUCHARIST.

CHECKER (*also* CHEQUER) A monastic office where accounts were tallied and payments made and recorded. A cloth or board marked with

squares was used to assist calculation.
See also CELLARER *and* SACRISTY

CHEST CUPBOARD (*also* ALMERY *and* HUTCH) Chest cupboards, which were used for storing valuables and documents, were usually fitted with a heavy door or pair of doors, secured with bars and padlocks. They were usually located at the west end of a church, unlike an AUMBRY which was more likely to be in the vicinity of the PRESBYTERY.

CHEVET Meaning literally 'the head of the bed', the eastward APSIDAL termination of a church, incorporating radiating chapels – as at Cistercian Hailes Abbey, where a chevet of five chapels was constructed in 1270 as part of an imposing rebuilding scheme to accommodate a RELIQUARY for the recently acquired phial of 'holy blood'. The chevet was a noble architectural form that (regrettably) was widely abandoned in the early Gothic period to make way for a square eastern termination, presumably to provide better natural light to the High Altar. Westminster Abbey has the only Gothic chevet remaining in England and even this is not complete, the central chapel of the five having been demolished to accommodate the entrance to the chapel of Henry VII. Norman chevets at Norwich, Peterborough and Gloucester cathedrals have only partly survived.
See also SHRINES

CHEVRON MOLDING A zigzag motif characteristic of late Romanesque carving, used especially in the deeply recessed mouldings of arches.

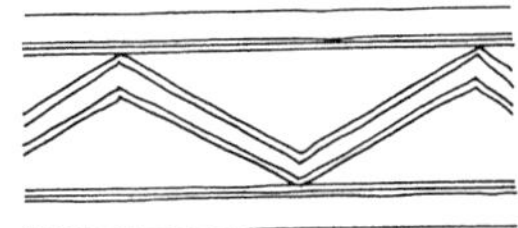

(Tom Friar)

CHILDREN The 'adoption' of orphans by religious communities, and child-oblation – the offering by parents of their children to God through the religious life – were rejected by the Cistercians, and by the twelfth century the practices had almost ceased. Initially, these children wore a version of the HABIT and served as choristers and acolytes (*see* ACOLYTE) before making their monastic PROFESSION when they 'came of age'. Later, they were brought up in separate 'schools', usually located in the conventual buildings (*see* ALMONRY) where they were maintained and educated. Should they choose not to enter the community, the monastery might pay for them to be apprenticed to a trade.
See also CHURCH MUSIC

CHILMARK STONE A Jurassic limestone quarried near Tisbury, Wiltshire. An estimated 75,000 tons of Chilmark stone was used in the construction of Salisbury Cathedral between 1200 and 1266.

CHIMERE A silk or satin gown worn by bishops and doctors of divinity.

CHOIR (*also* QUIRE) (i) A group of singers (*see* CHURCH MUSIC).
(ii) That part of a cathedral or of a monastic or collegiate church between the PRESBYTERY and the PULPITUM, a discreet and very private place enclosed on three sides, furnished with STALLS and occupied by the monks or canons when observing the *Opus Dei* (*see* DIVINE OFFICE). The onerous nature of these obligations, both physical and mental, was recognised at visitations (*see* VISITATION (ECCLESIASTICAL)), when concern was often expressed, especially regarding the ability of nuns and elderly and infirm monks to 'bear the burdens of quire with [the other duties] that pertain to religious'.

At the centre of the choir was a lectern (*see* LECTERNS), usually with four sides, on which were placed the *antiphonarium*, the *graduale* and the other great music books used by the cantors during the divine office (*see* CANTOR). Conduct in the choir was subject to strict rules (*customaries*) and was supervised by the PRECENTOR (an office

The superb late medieval canopied choir stalls and screens at the Cathedral and Collegiate Church of St Mary, Manchester. (© John Crook/info@john-crook.com)

which was retained in the post-Reformation cathedrals). Antiphonal singing alternated between the two sides (*see* DECANI *and* CANTORIS) and the rules emphasised that 'At all singing of psalms brethren ought to be careful always to make a pause in the middle, and a verse should not be begun on one side before the verse on the other is ended.' The best-known customaries, the Barnwell Observances, prohibited 'needless signs and conversation, cutting nails, writing, smiling, whittling, throwing one foot over another, stretching legs, supporting body on elbows, sitting with legs apart'. Nevertheless, the monks could obtain some relief when standing by resting their backsides on the MISERICORDS which were provided on the underside of the hinged seats. The seats themselves were inordinately heavy: 'brethren should always be careful when they get up or sit down to raise or lower the seat gently and noiselessly with the left hand' (*see* MISERICORD).

The choir was the focus of a community's daily life of prayer and was located symbolically at the centre of the church beneath (or close to) the CROSSING and with an unobstructed view of the PRESBYTERY and of the HIGH ALTAR in the SANCTUARY. It is hardly surprising, therefore, that it is almost invariably in the choirs and presbyteries of the great abbeys and cathedrals that MEDIEVAL ARCHITECTURE enjoys its most glorious manifestation: at Gloucester Cathedral, for example, which was restructured during the second quarter of the fourteenth century and marks a turning point in architectural history. Here is the first flowering of the peculiarly English Perpendicular style of Gothic architecture which lasted from the mid-fourteenth century to the early sixteenth century. At Gloucester, the eastern APSE and presbytery roof were removed and a lofty cage of delicate Perpendicular tracery erected within the great Norman arcade, with an immense window (the Crécy window) to the east of the High Altar and a delicate lierne vault above (*see* VAULTING). The result is breathtakingly beautiful. Regrettably, in many great churches the PULPITUM has been removed leaving the choir open to the nave (as at Hereford, Sherborne and Salisbury) or separated by a later CHOIR SCREEN (Ely, Winchester and Worcester).

In Cistercian houses, the LAY BROTHERS (*conversi*) had their own choir. At Rievaulx, for example, the lay brothers' choir occupied the second to seventh bays within the nave arcades and was closed to the east by a ROOD SCREEN. The monks' choir occupied the last bay of the nave and all of the crossing and was closed to the west by the pulpitum. These two areas were divided from each other by the RETRO-CHOIR, where the old and infirm monks would sit during services.

By the thirteenth century changes in practice had affected the planning of many large churches, especially of their eastern ends. There was now room to accommodate the whole of the choir within a much longer eastern arm, so that the pulpitum could be constructed to the east of the crossing leaving the transept open to the lay congregation in the nave.

See also AMBULATORY, AMPLIFIERS, MONASTIC BUILDINGS, *and* RETURNED STALLS

CHOIR MONKS *or* QUIRE MONKS Also known as *cloister monks*, those who were full members of a monastic community (i.e. not lay brethren, corrodians or employees (*see* CORRODIAN, EMPLOYEES *and* LAY BROTHERS)). The choir monks were responsible for regular observance of the DIVINE OFFICE and their lives were subject to the RULE of a particular order. In some definitions, the OBEDIENTIARIES are omitted.

CHOIR SCREEN A decorative screen that separates the CHOIR from the NAVE. In many cases a medieval PULPITUM has been replaced by a choir screen, often as a result of Georgian or Victorian restoration work. Many of these eighteenth- and nineteenth-century screens would have been better left undone: the ironwork choir screen by Sir George Gilbert Scott (1811–78) at Worcester Cathedral Priory is truly meretricious

The choir screen at Winchester Cathedral.

and should go the way of a similar choir screen at Salisbury Cathedral, which was removed in 1960. So too Scott's dreadfully dark, ponderous screen at Winchester and his grandiose marble and alabaster confection at Durham. The wooden choir screen at Beverley Minster is more successful, probably because it is functional and not merely decorative. This was also designed by Scott (1878) to carry an organ and to match the fine early sixteenth-century choir stalls. The charming Perpendicular Arundel Screen at Chichester Cathedral is hardly of sufficient substance to merit consideration as a pulpitum. Named after Bishop John Arundel (1459–78) it probably dates from the early fifteenth century. There were originally chapels in the two outer arches but these were lost when the screen was taken down in 1859. It was restored to its original location in 1961 as a memorial to Bishop George Bell (1929–58). The beautiful stone screen at Christchurch Priory was brought from elsewhere in *c.* 1320 and was installed, as a pulpitum, to separate the parishioners' nave from the canons' choir. Much restored in 1848, it once carried a rood, which would normally have been supported on a separate ROOD SCREEN to the west of the pulpitum. Undoubtedly the finest wrought-iron screen is at Derby Cathedral, a church that is full of early eighteenth-century Baroque splendours. Made in 1730 by Robert Bakewell (1682–1752), a local smith, it is a work of extraordinary elegance and delicacy.

CHOIR SISTER A nun who is required to attend choir offices in contradistinction to a lay sister who attends only certain services.

CHOIR STALLS *see* CHOIR, CHURCH MUSIC *and* STALLS

CHRISMATORY A small vessel in which holy oil (*chrism*) is kept.

CHRIST CHURCH, OXFORD (RELATIONSHIP OF COLLEGE AND CATHEDRAL) *see* CHANTRY COLLEGES

CHURCH (i) The Christian community. The New Testament teaches that the Church is not merely an association of individual disciples but an organic society established by Christ and endowed by Him with the Holy Spirit at Pentecost. It is also a tenet of the Christian faith that in addition to the Church on earth there is the invisible Church of the faithful departed. One consequence of the REFORMATION was a reformulation of the concept of the Church which no longer sought to claim its being through sacramental relationships, but through the Word of God. This is reflected in changes in the internal arrangements of the churches themselves.

(ii) A building used for Christian worship. In the Benedictine RULE, the monastic church was originally described as an *oratory* – literally, 'a place of prayer'. Consequently, unlike parish churches (the naves of which could be used for a variety of religious and secular purposes), a monastic church was designed very specifically as the focus of a community's religious observance. 'Let the oratory be what its name implies' instructed St Benedict, 'and let nothing else be done there or anything alien to this purpose be placed there.'

The church contained the PRESBYTERY, which had to be of sufficient size to accommodate the ritual associated with the SANCTUARY and the HIGH ALTAR; the CHOIR (or quire) for the observance of the canonical hours (*see* HOURS (CANONICAL)); processional spaces associated with the elaboration of the LITURGY, such as the aisles and AMBULATORY (*see* AISLE *and* PROCESSIONS) and provision for the individual ALTARS of those monks who were also priests. In Cistercian churches, the NAVE was also used by the LAY BROTHERS (the *conversi*) who had their own altar and choir to the west of the ROOD SCREEN.

In all but the smallest churches, the building was laid out in a symbolic CRUCIFORM plan, the upper (shorter) arm of the cross being the presbytery, the lower (longer) arm the nave and the transverse section usually referred to as the north and south TRANSEPT with the CROSSING between. The majority of monastic churches were entered from the CLOISTER, by doors at either end of the adjacent alley and by a NIGHT STAIR from the first-floor dormitory (the DORTER). The great western door of the nave was used only on special occasions, although in some Cistercian abbeys (*see* CISTERCIANS) (where the processional route was somewhat different to that of the BENEDICTINES) it was also used for processional purposes.

Inevitably there were variations and additions made to this basic plan: to accommodate SHRINES, for example, and the large numbers of pilgrims they attracted; and, from the twelfth century, by the addition of LADY CHAPELS, dedicated to the Blessed Virgin Mary and usually (though not invariably) located at the eastern end of the church, beyond the presbytery. All Cistercian abbeys were dedicated to the Virgin, hence the absence of Lady Chapels and the simple square eastern terminations of abbey churches such as Fountains, Rievaulx and Tintern. At Cistercian Hailes, however, the eastern termination comprised an elaborate APSIDAL cluster of five individual priests' altars, while a further six were located in the transepts and four in the RETRO-CHOIR. Such elaboration in an otherwise austere Cistercian church was almost certainly intended to dignify the shrine of the 'Holy Blood' acquired by the abbey in 1270 (see CHEVET). There are, of course, several exceptions to the cruciform plan: at Milton Abbey, for example, where the projected nave was never built, possibly as a consequence of the PLAGUE which reached Milton in 1349; and at Dore Abbey where the presbytery and transepts were restored and separated from the ruined nave when the abbey became the parish church. Unusually, the twelfth-century aisle-less nave at (Augustinian) Kirkham Priory was substantially smaller than the thirteenth-century choir, presbytery and ambulatory. The canons intended to rebuild the whole church but, everything to the east of the crossing having been completed to an impressively high standard, it seems that the money ran out! Had the work been completed, the church at Kirkham Priory would undoubtedly have been one of the finest buildings in the north of England. The (now ruined) church at Glastonbury Abbey in Somerset is believed to have been the largest enclosed space in medieval Britain. Exceeding 168m (550ft) in length, its size was commensurate with its enormous wealth and status. Glastonbury's length was equalled by that of St Albans (including the Lady Chapel) and exceeded only by Winchester Cathedral Priory (169.5m or 556ft), the longest Gothic cathedral in Europe (in fact, it once extended 13m (40ft) further to the west – as indicated by a plaque on the wall of the cathedral forecourt).

In friaries, the sermon was the principal means of mass-communication and several urban churches, with long hall-like naves, were constructed by the Dominicans to accommodate large congregations (see FRIARS).

CHURCH OF ENGLAND The English branch of the Western or Latin Church which, having rejected the pope's authority since the Reformation, has the sovereign as its titular head.

Following the Synod of Whitby in 664, unification of the Celtic and Roman traditions was finally achieved under Theodore of Tarsus (*c.* 602–90), Archbishop of Canterbury from 668, who reformed the government of the Church by dividing dioceses and extending the episcopate (*see* ANGLO-SAXON CHURCH *and* CELTIC CHURCH). The Norman Conquest of 1066, and the influence of reforming bishops and abbots from the continent of Europe, led to a restructuring of ecclesiastical administration, the introduction into England of CANON LAW and an extraordinary period of religious activity and church building. Thereafter, and despite regular disputations with the papacy, the English Church remained part of the Western Catholic Church until the sixteenth century when, against a background of religious dissatisfaction and growing national self-awareness, HENRY VIII failed to obtain a divorce from Catherine of Aragon and subsequently repudiated papal supremacy, bringing the Church under the control of the Crown (*see* DISSOLUTION OF THE MONASTERIES). Many of the king's advisers were deeply influenced by the Protestant Reformation which, in England, culminated in the Act of Supremacy of 1534 (*see* REFORMATION). This confirmed to Henry VIII and his successors the title of 'the only supreme head in earth of the Church of England'. Under Edward VI, Archbishop Thomas Cranmer (1489–1556) produced the First and Second *Book of Common Prayer* in 1549 and 1552 which (with some modifications) became the service book of the Church of England in 1559 (*see* COMMON PRAYER, BOOK OF). A further Act of Supremacy in 1559 declared Elizabeth I to be 'the only supreme governor . . . as well in all spiritual or ecclesiastical things or causes as temporal' and, in

1571, the *Thirty-Nine Articles* were adopted as the doctrinal formulary of the English Church.

Episcopacy and Anglicanism were important issues in the English Civil War of 1642–9 and led to Presbyterian reform and independency under the Commonwealth. But with the Restoration of Charles II in 1660 the Church of England was again confirmed as the established Church and repressive measures were taken against dissenters. The formal separation of the Methodist movement from the Church of England in 1791 was followed by an Anglican Evangelical revival and, in the nineteenth century, by administrative reform and the creation of new parishes and bishoprics, which reflected demographic changes brought about by the Industrial Revolution. At the same time, the Oxford Movement sought to emphasise the Catholic and apostolic character of the established church. The Enabling Act of 1919 gave to the Church Assembly authority to present legislation to parliament, and in the last century the Church of England exercised a considerable degree of control over its services through the Prayer Book (Alternative and Other Services) Measure of 1965 and the Church of England (Worship and Doctrine) Measure of 1974.

For the Church in Wales *see* WALES, THE MEDIEVAL CHURCH IN

See also CLERGY (CHURCH OF ENGLAND) *and* DEFENDER OF THE FAITH

CHURCH MUSIC In the early Church, music was used to enhance and enrich the power of worship, although it did not always meet with approval. St Augustine (354–430) confessed, 'Whenever it happens that I am more moved by the singing than by the thing that is sung, I admit that I have grievously sinned', while St John Chrysostom (*c.* 347–407) angrily observed, 'Thus does the devil stealthily set fire to the city, [using] degraded music, and songs full of all kinds of wickedness.' Originally, all music was rendered by the clergy and congregation. But from the fourth century bodies of singers comprising clerics in MINOR ORDERS and boys assisted in the music of divine services. A *schola cantorum* was established in Rome by Pope Gregory the Great (d. 604) and the custom spread through western Christendom, so that many of the medieval cathedrals and major monastic churches became centres of musical excellence and almost the only places at which a musical education could be obtained. However, in the majority of monastic churches, it was the monks alone, led by the CANTOR and sometimes supplemented by boys, who sang the eight daily offices, (*see* ANGLICAN CHANT, ANTIPHON, CHILDREN *and* PLAINSONG).

From the twelfth century, the building of Lady Chapels (*see* LADY CHAPEL) encouraged the RECRUITMENT of boy singers whose gentle, feminine voices were considered to reflect more accurately the concept of the Blessed Virgin Mary. Gradually, over the next three centuries as part-singing developed (*see* POLYPHONY), so the boys began to sing with the men and choirs were augmented with lay singers. By the sixteenth century, more than fifty English abbeys maintained choirs.

Post-Reformation

At the Reformation, the new Church of England services, although vernacular, were little different from the Roman Catholic LITURGY that preceded them (*see* COMMON PRAYER, BOOK OF). Before this time there was a clear distinction between the musical customs of the major monastic and cathedral churches, many of which had large choirs and ORGANS, and those of urban and rural parishes, which rarely had choirs but sometimes possessed a primitive organ. Following the DISSOLUTION OF THE MONASTERIES a small number of abbey or priory churches were retained as CATHEDRALS where, after making the necessary liturgical changes, the elaborate type of service was perpetuated.

This was the age of great English composers: Thomas Tallis (*c.* 1505–85), William Byrd (*c.* 1542–1623), Thomas Morley (1557– *c.* 1603), Thomas Weelkes (*c.* 1575–1623) and Orlando

Gibbons (1583–1625), all of whom learned their art as cathedral organists and (with the exception of Weelkes) were Gentlemen of the CHAPEL ROYAL. Service settings (i.e. elaborate musical settings of the Canticles (*see* CANTICLE)) continued after the Reformation but in modified form. They had now to be set in the vernacular (except in collegiate chapels where Latin remained the language of scholars), without lengthening by repetition of phrases and on the principle of one syllable to a note (though this last requirement seems to have been almost universally disregarded). The eight monastic offices were replaced by two services – Morning and EVENING PRAYER – and where the PSALTER had previously been recited once a week in monastic churches, the psalms were divided into sixty sections, one to be sung at morning and evening worship on each day of the month. Some sixteenth-century communion services survive in two forms: the Latin Mass and an adaptation that conformed with the new conditions. The new forms were sometimes described by composers as 'The Short Service' and the lengthy and complex older forms as 'The Long Service'. Antiphonal singing (by the DECANI and CANTORIS sides of the choir) is a feature of service music (*see* ANTIPHON *and* STALLS), while the traditional Anglican settings of the PRECES and VERSICLES are adaptations by John Merbecke (1510–85) of the ancient PLAINSONG. Various Elizabethan composers made 'harmonised' versions of the responses, a form now generally known as Festal Responses. From this golden age, later augmented by the prolific Henry Purcell (1659–95), flowed the magnificent body of distinctively Anglican church music which remains in the repertoire of cathedral and collegiate choirs today.

In the eighteenth century, the Church's comfortable round of services and sermons, which emphasised the importance of maintaining the established order, provided neither inspiration for the commonalty of church-goers nor a spiritual alternative to the increasingly materialistic pressures of society in general. It is little wonder, therefore, that cathedral music degenerated to a deplorable level. Despite the considerable efforts of Samuel Sebastian Wesley (1766–1837), it was the Oxford Movement (1833–45) that eventually inspired its recovery, and the Revd Walter Kerr Hamilton (1808–69) in particular. In 1841 Kerr Hamilton became PRECENTOR at Salisbury and immediately set about raising the standard of the cathedral's music. So successful was he that other cathedrals soon followed Salisbury's example. This contributed to a reawakening of the English musical tradition, inspired by the religious works of Sir Charles Parry (1848–1918), Sir Charles Villiers Stanford (1852–1924), Sir Edward Elgar (1857–1934) and Charles Wood (1866–1926), and revived by Ralph Vaughan Williams (1872–1958) and his contemporaries such as Edward Bairstow (1874–1946) and John Ireland (1879–1962), followed by Harold Darke (1888–1976), Herbert Howells (1892–1983) and Edmund Rubbra (1901–86) and, more recently, Benjamin Britten (1913–76) and Kenneth Leighton (1929–88).

Continuing in the monastic tradition, it is the precentor who has overall responsibility for a cathedral's music, assisted by the SUCCENTOR. The precentor plans the services and leads the singing by intoning the first line of each of the responses. The director of music or master of the choristers (who is usually also the principal organist) is responsible for selecting appropriate choral pieces and for the preparation and execution of the music. Today, cathedral and collegiate choirs comprise a front row of boy trebles and a back row of adult male singers (variously described as *lay clerks, lay vicars* or *vicars choral*) who sing the alto, tenor and bass lines. For antiphonal singing they are divided (as in monastic churches) between two sides: DECANI and CANTORIS. The adult male singers in several of the major collegiate choirs include both undergraduate choral scholars (*academic clerks*) and professionals (lay clerks). Most cathedrals have

Evensong at Winchester Cathedral. (© John Crook/info@john-crook.com)

associated choir schools and, increasingly, girl choristers are now recruited, usually to form separate choirs, so that the unique sound made by boy trebles is not lost.

Cathedral music both engages with the emotions and helps to convey the meaning of a text. Indeed, it is itself 'a positive act of worship, performed by an accomplished choir on behalf of the congregation' (Brett).
See also ORGANS *and* VICARS CHORAL

CIBORIUM (i) A vessel, shaped like a chalice and with a lid, used to retain the Sacramental Bread of the EUCHARIST. (ii) A large canopy or tester of wood, stone or metal above an altar or bishop's throne (*cathedra*). Originally a medieval feature, the ciborium was reintroduced into the English church by the architect Sir Ninian Comper (1864–1960).
See also ALTARS, CANOPY *and* BALDAC(C)HINO

CINQUEFOIL A figure having five radiating stylized 'petals' found both as an architectural motif and a heraldic device (*see* FOILS).

CIRCARIES The visitation districts of a medieval monastic foundation.

CIRCATOR (*also* CIRCAS) A monastic official responsible for security, particularly at night when he toured the church and CLAUSTRAL buildings (*see* CUSTODIANS, LANTERN *and* SECURITY).

CIRCULAR CHURCHES *see* MEDIEVAL ARCHITECTURE

CISTERCIANS The Cistercian Order (the White Monks) was founded in 1098 at Cîteaux (in Latin, *Cistercium*) in Burgundy by Robert of Molesme who, with others, sought to establish a strict form of Benedictinism (*see* BENEDICTINES *and* RULE). After a precarious start, the order spread rapidly during the first decades of the twelfth century, inspired by St Stephen Harding, abbot of Cîteaux (born at Sherborne, Dorset and d. 1134), and the extraordinary energy and personality of his disciple St Bernard of Clairvaux (1090–1153), so that by 1200 some five hundred houses had been established throughout Europe. The Cistercian life was one of simple communal worship, private devotion, study and meditation; and of ASCETICISM in sequestered surroundings, remote from the distractions of the outside world. Initially, there was no gradation of seniority and there were strict rules of SILENCE and diet. Worship included none of the liturgical intricacies associated with that of the CLUNIACS. The Cistercians were medieval minimalists: nothing was to distract them from their contemplative life. Their churches were to be devoid of all the opulent ornament and decoration found in contemporary cathedrals, the walls were painted white and the window glass was uncoloured. Only in the floor tiles were abstract patterns permitted. The monks themselves wore habits of undyed wool: hence they became known as the 'white monks'. The order's constitution, the *Carta Caritatis*, provided for self-regulation subject to the ordinances of the annual GENERAL CHAPTER of Cîteaux at which each community was represented. Supervision was by means of a mutual system of visitations among the 'mother' and 'daughter' houses (*see* VISITATION (ECCLESIASTICAL)). The constitution also laid down strict rules for the formation and location of new houses. They were to be founded in places 'far from the concourse of men', as colonies, or 'daughters', of existing houses, each with an abbot and at least twelve choir monks (those in full monastic orders). Unlike the Benedictine rule, that of the Cistercian's forbade receipt of the customary revenues in cash or kind (such as TITHES, rents and fees) drawn from the society they had renounced, but gifts of hitherto uncultivated 'desert' land were acceptable: indeed, an effective agriculture was an economic necessity if a community was to survive.

Although the choir monks were obliged by their rule to undertake some manual work, a substantial labour force was required to work a community's often extensive arable and grazing lands and to maintain its buildings. This work force was provided by the (often illiterate) LAY BROTHERS (*conversi*), whose religious commitment was manifested through their labours and who often outnumbered the choir monks by more than two to one. They would work either in the vicinity of the abbey or on outlying *granges* which were (in theory) located within a day's journey of the abbey, although some were more distant (*see* GRANGE). These granges were not individual cells (as in the Benedictine model) but agrarian estates, each with a farmstead and oratory, and were staffed only by lay brothers, who devoted their lives to 'turning forest, marsh and barren waste into field and pasture to the greater profit of the Lord'. The *conversi* lived as part of the full community, although their rule was less severe. The domestic arrangements provided for the two divisions of a Cistercian community are evident in the architecture of their abbeys: notably in the provision of a separate DORMITORY (*dorter*), refectory (*frater*) and choir, which was located in the nave of the abbey church to the west of the ROOD SCREEN.

The first Cistercian house in England was founded at Waverley in Surrey in 1128, but it was the foundation in 1132 of Rievaulx in the Rye Valley of Yorkshire that aroused the enthusiasm of the English for the Cistercian combination of

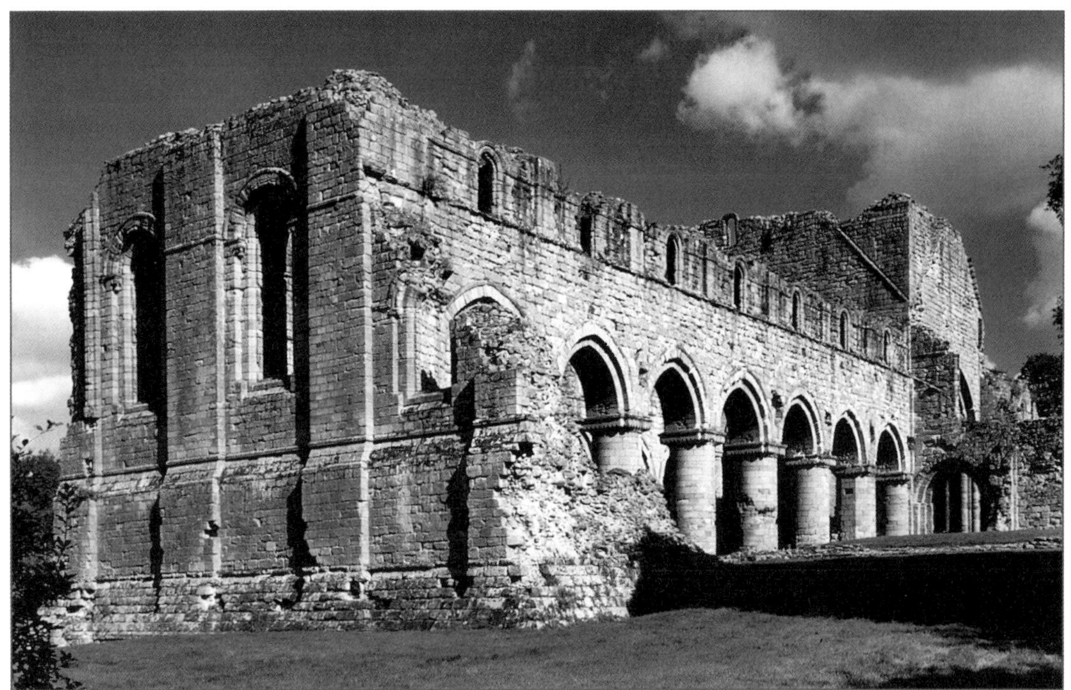

Buildwas Abbey, Shropshire. Unusually, there is no doorway in the west front of the abbey church. (Nigel Corrie/© English Heritage Photo Library)

compassion and asceticism and, by 1152, there were fifty Cistercian houses in England and Wales, some with dependent cells. When an abbey grew too large it might (with the consent of the General chapter at Cîteaux) send out twelve of its brethren to establish a new foundation under an abbot. Consequently, by the thirteenth century, the number of English and Welsh Cistercian houses had increased to seventy-five – with more than six hundred throughout Europe, including a 'family' of eleven in Scotland. In addition, there were forty English houses of Cistercian nuns, most of which were small and ranked as priories.

Cistercian abbeys, which were always dedicated to the Blessed Virgin Mary, are architecturally severe by comparison with those of other orders: presbytery, transepts, etc. are usually square-ended, chapter houses are rectangular rather than polygonal, windows contained plain glass and ornamentation of all kinds was minimal. Despite this austerity, provision was always made for a 'warming house' (*see* CALEFACTORIUM) in the vicinity of the refectory so that the brethren could dry their clothes and warm themselves.

Enthusiasm for the Cistercians caused some BENEFACTORS to endow lands that were hardly 'desert places' and the monks were often obliged to depopulate such areas, and to degrade villages into granges, by evicting tenants and demolishing their houses and even parish churches (*see* GRANGE). Even so, the Cistercians were not colonisers but entrepreneurs. They had capital and were able to purchase estates in some places from the free peasantry – and it was the peasantry who were often the driving force. In the fourteenth century the PLAGUE decimated the workforce and sheep scab ruined the wool trade. The prohibition on learning was relaxed and the architectural influences of the Gothic age become more apparent. It was also becoming difficult to recruit sufficient men who were prepared to enter into a life of such austerity as that endured by the lay

brothers. Hired labour was increasingly used and there was a move from arable farming (which was labour-intensive) to sheep breeding and the production of wool on a sometimes vast scale. Indeed, it was the enormous wealth created by the Cistercians' agrarian and industrial activities that ultimately deflected them from their high ideals and was the principal cause of their decline (*see* INDUSTRY *and* WOOL). At its peak, Fountains Abbey received a net annual income in excess of one million pounds (at today's values) and benefited from a network of fifty farms, in addition to its industrial and commercial activities. By 1500, eighty-six Cistercian abbeys together received a net income of £400,000 – ten times that of the king. Simplicity was compromised by commercial success, asceticism transmuted into complacency and minimalism reduced to ostentation and vanity – exemplified by Abbot Huby's early sixteenth-century tower at Fountains Abbey (*see* TOWERS). By the sixteenth century the Cistercian monasteries had become objects of ridicule, soft targets for the land-grabbers of the Dissolution. Today, their ruins tell the poignant story of the rise and fall of the Cistercians' utopian ideal.
See also DISSOLUTION OF THE MONASTERIES

CITATION MANDATE *see* VISITATION (ECCLESIASTICAL)

CLARENDON, CONSTITUTIONS OF (1164) A written statement compiled by Henry II at Clarendon (near Salisbury in Wiltshire) of the relationship between Church and state which had been established under his predecessors. The most controversial clause related to BENEFIT OF CLERGY and required that if a clerk in holy orders was convicted of a crime in an ecclesiastical court he should then be transferred to the secular authorities for punishment. This was vigorously opposed by Archbishop Thomas à Becket.

CLAS The *clasau* were the ancient mother churches of early medieval Wales, self-contained ecclesiastical communities consisting of an abbot (who might also be a bishop) and a group of hereditary canons, sharing a common income but living as secular clerks (*claswyr*). The *clasau* were originally pioneering instruments of conversion but, by the twelfth century, they had become well-endowed and self-indulgent communities. Nevertheless, *clasau* such as Tywyn in (modern) Gwynedd and Llandinam in Powys continued to dominate the ecclesiastical life of their respective districts well into the thirteenth century. It has been suggested that the *glas-* element in a number of Welsh place-names is indicative of a former *clas* (*glas* is normally interpreted as 'blue'): Glascwm in Powys, for example, which might have been 'The Valley of the Clas' rather than 'Blue Valley'.
see CELTIC CHURCH *and* WALES, THE MEDIEVAL CHURCH IN

CLAUSTRAL *or* CLOISTRAL Pertaining to those domestic and administrative buildings of a monastery that were arranged round the CLOISTER. The CLAUSURA was that part of the buildings from which those of the opposite sex (and sometimes lay persons) were excluded.

CLAUSTRAL PRIOR The disciplinary officer of a monastery, responsible (to the Prior) for maintaining the RULE and for correcting breaches of conduct.
See also DISCIPLINE

CLAUSURA (i) The practice of excluding members of the opposite sex from designated areas of a religious house or, in some instances, of excluding also those of the same sex who were not members of the community.
(ii) That part of a religious house from which such persons were excluded.

CLERESTORY In larger churches, the upper storey of a NAVE pierced by a series of windows (*for* illustration *see* BAY). Clerestories were

sometimes added (especially during the Perpendicular period) in order to increase the amount of light entering a building.
See MEDIEVAL ARCHITECTURE

CLERGY (CHURCH OF ENGLAND) An *archbishop* is responsible for a PROVINCE of the Church of England: either Canterbury, which covers the dioceses south of the river Trent, or York, which covers those to the north. The archbishopric of Wales was established in 1920; before that time Wales fell within the province of Canterbury (*see* WALES, THE MEDIEVAL CHURCH IN). The archbishops of Canterbury and York (Primate of All England, and Primate of England and METROPOLITAN respectively) are privy councillors and have seats in the House of Lords. Before the Reformation, archbishops of Canterbury were often appointed cardinals by the pope (*see* CARDINAL).

Bishops
Bishops, whose appointment is vested in the Crown, have jurisdiction over dioceses (*see* DIOCESE). A bishop's throne (*cathedra*) is located in the cathedral of his diocese and before the Reformation bishops were appointed by a council of canons (*see* CATHEDRALS). The bishop of London is also a privy councillor and, with the bishops of Durham and Winchester, sits in the House of Lords, with precedence over all other bishops who, until 1841, also had seats (with the exception of the bishop of Sodor and Man). Since then only twenty-one bishops sit in the Lords, any vacancy being filled by the senior diocesan bishop without a seat. In the late Middle Ages it was common practice for one or more *suffragan bishops* to be appointed (usually by the pope) to assist the diocesan bishops. An Act of 1534 made provision for the appointment of suffragan bishops by the Crown and the original list of twenty-six suffragan sees was adopted for this purpose. At that time, these suffragan sees did not relate to the dioceses, although some became diocesan sees and others were later adopted by the Roman Catholic Church. The office lapsed in 1592 and no further suffragan bishops were appointed until 1870, when the suffragan bishops of Nottingham and Dover were installed. Suffragan bishoprics are not always named after major towns in the dioceses; often the name of an ancient ecclesiastical centre has been used, such as Ramsbury in Wiltshire and Dunwich in Suffolk, or a well-known district name such as Sherwood.

A *vicar-general* is a deputy of an archbishop or bishop, an office previously held by an archdeacon. In the 1990s, a number of *Provincial Episcopal Visitors* (derogatorily known as 'Flying Bishops') were appointed to minister to those who are irreconcilably opposed to the ordination of women.

Cathedral and Collegiate Clergy
A *dean* presides over the CHAPTER of a cathedral or COLLEGIATE CHURCH – but there are exceptions. Until recently, several of the cathedrals that had been raised from parochial status (such as Birmingham) were presided over by a *provost*, while a number of collegiate churches also have a provost rather than a dean (Eton is an example). In monastic Britain, *canons* were clerks in holy orders who lived according to a rule; a monk, on the other hand, was simply someone who vowed to follow a life of austerity, meditation and prayer. Today, a canon is either residentiary, with cathedral duties, or has been appointed as a non-residentiary honorary canon in recognition of service to a diocese or as a conjunct to another diocesan appointment (such as Diocesan Director of Education). A cathedral's statutes may require that certain honorary canonries be given to the holders of specified diocesan offices: at Truro, for example, the bishop of St German's is by statute created an honorary canon. Cathedral statutes differ from one another in many details, but most allow a bishop to appoint some canons from outside the diocese. A minor canon is a clergyman attached to a cathedral or collegiate church to assist in services and is not a canon: the *precentor*, for example, who is responsible for the direction of

choral services, and his deputy the *succentor* (though, in cathedrals of the 'Old Foundation', the precentor is a member of the chapter).

In the Middle Ages the endowment of most non-monastic cathedrals was divided into *prebends*, each intended to support a single member of the chapter. Holders of prebends became known as *prebendaries* and in some English cathedrals the territorial titles have been retained, but not their incomes. In certain cathedrals (such as Wells in Somerset) prebendal stalls are reserved for honorary canons.

Diocesan Clergy

An *archdeacon* is a senior clergyman having administrative authority delegated by a bishop. He is responsible for the parishes within his archdeaconry, which may itself be subdivided into rural deaneries, each the responsibility of a *rural dean* (*see below*). In the pre-medieval Church, an archdeacon was a bishop's principal assistant ('the eye of the bishop') and the senior *deacon*. At that time deacons were accorded a rank next below that of *presbyter* (*see* PRIEST) and were chiefly responsible for collecting and distributing ALMS. During the Middle Ages the deacon was one of the three sacred ministers at the High Mass (*see* MASS *and* SUB-DEACON) but the influence of the diaconate declined and the term is now applied to those who have reached an advanced stage in preparation for the priesthood. In the early Church, a *deaconess* was responsible for caring for the poor and sick of her sex and for assisting in the baptism of women. With the increasing popularity of infant baptism in the fifth century, the office declined in importance until its revival in the nineteenth century in modified form.

The office of *rural dean* is also an ancient one but its duties were gradually subsumed by those of an archdeacon. It was revived in 1836 and the rural dean now presides over the Ruridecanal Chapter, which comprises the incumbents and clergy of a deanery, and is co-chairman of a deanery synod. An *area dean* is the urban equivalent of a rural dean.

A *rector* was originally an incumbent who received the 'Great Tithes': all the customary offerings and dues of his parish. He was responsible for the CHANCEL and the rectory and for providing service books and vestments. In many instances, benefices were annexed by corporate bodies such as monastic or collegiate foundations who then received the Great (or Rectorial) Tithes, the Lesser (or Vicarial) Tithes going to a *vicar* who was appointed by them to administer the parish. Following the Dissolution of the Monasteries, many monastic estates became the property of laymen who also acquired the right to nominate vicars (subject to a bishop's approval), together with responsibility for maintaining the chancel and vicarage. TITHES were virtually abolished in 1936 and a vicar is now appointed to all new livings, the designation rector being applicable to the incumbent of a new joint benefice or united parish or on the creation of a team ministry.

A *parson* was originally a rector, although the term is now applied also to a vicar. Before the seventeenth century a *curate* was any minister who had the CURE OF SOULS, especially a deputy who was in full charge of a parish but who could be removed by his employer. Since then the term has come to mean an assistant to the incumbent or an unbeneficed clergyman. A *perpetual curate* was the minister of a parish in which the Great Tithes had been annexed by an ecclesiastical body or lay person. More recently, concerned by the falling numbers of full-time stipendiary clergy and a decline in the number of men and women who were offering themselves for the full-time ordained ministry, the Anglican Church introduced *Local Non Stipendiary Ministers* to work as parish priests in multi-parish benefices. Now known (more appropriately) as *Ordained Local Ministers*, they are presented by their benefices as suitable candidates for the bishop to ordain, subject to satisfactory recommendation and training. Consequently, they are very much 'produced by the people for the people', working together in a collaborative ministry with the 'Priest-in-Charge' of the benefice at its head.

CHAPLAINS

Chaplains were 'chapel priests' without benefices who ministered to royal and magnate households or bodies corporate such as hospitals and nunneries. Today, they perform a similar function in relation to the armed forces and prisons or are the private secretaries of bishops.

See also MAJOR ORDERS, MINOR ORDERS *and* SIGNATURES: ARCHBISHOPS AND BISHOPS

CLERGY (PRE-REFORMATION) *see* MEDIEVAL CHURCH, MAJOR ORDERS, MINOR ORDERS, REFORMATION *and* WALES, THE MEDIEVAL CHURCH IN

CLERIC Throughout the Middle Ages, the term 'cleric' encompassed seven classes of men: four in MINOR ORDERS and three in MAJOR ORDERS. Only those in Major Orders (sub-deacons, deacons and priests) would today be recognised as 'clergy' (*see* CLERGY (CHURCH OF ENGLAND)). But in fifteenth-century England numerous conditions of men could claim to be in Minor and Major Orders. Strictly speaking, no one could claim to be in Minor Orders who had not received the 'first tonsure' at the hands of a diocesan bishop (*see* TONSURE). In practice, however, it is likely that those men who were sufficiently closely connected with the clergy often assumed the title of cleric. Doctors, lawyers, scribes, clerks of the king's household and many others were usually in Minor Orders, were thereby 'clerics' and could claim BENEFIT OF CLERGY.

Those in Major Orders were either REGULAR or SECULAR CLERGY. The regular clergy were so called because they lived according to a RULE (*regula*) and were members of a community, often segregated from the outside world. The secular clergy spent their lives in the world (*in seculo*), serving the Church as individuals. Among the secular clergy were the archbishops, bishops, archdeacons, vicars, parish priests and several other grades of ecclesiastical officer. The ranks of the regulars included communities of monks and nuns and the orders of Canons Regular who, like the secular clergy, often left their cloister and served cures. To these were added the four orders of FRIARS who, although spending some of their time in their own communities, were notably active in the wider world.

CLERK IN HOLY ORDERS The formal designation of a bishop, priest or deacon in the Church of England.

CLIPSHAM STONE A honey-coloured stone quarried in the Clipsham region of the county of Rutland.

CLOCKS In the Middle Ages, the demands of the monastic timetable (*see* HORARIUM *and* SUB-SACRIST), and its division into canonical hours (*see* HOURS (CANONICAL)), led to the development of time-keeping devices and, in particular, to mechanical clocks. These were large, weight-driven structures fitted into TOWERS (*turret clocks*) or positioned in the TRANSEPT of an abbey church near the NIGHT STAIR which led from the monks' dormitory (*see* DORTER). They had no dial or clock-hands but sounded a signal which alerted a keeper to toll a bell. In England, the first mechanical clock was installed at Canterbury in 1292; while in *c.* 1320, Richard of Wallingford, a Benedictine monk of St Albans, constructed a clock that not only indicated the time in hours and minutes but also showed the tides, the phases of the moon and the position of the sun and planets. Striking clocks were a fourteenth-century development of the turret clock and, by the end of the fifteenth century, most major monastic churches and cathedrals possessed one, as did several large town churches. Striking clocks used a weighted arm (*foliot*) as an oscillating fly-wheel controlled by a toothed wheel and an escapement mechanism. There was a clock at Exeter Cathedral as early as 1284, but this may have been a water clock. The present orrery clock on the north wall of the north tower dates originally from the late fifteenth century, although it is largely composed of replacement parts dating from the late sixteenth and seventeenth centuries. At the centre of the large dial is a globe representing the earth and around it revolves the moon, turning on its own axis to show its phases. A fleur-de-lis represents the sun which, as this is a fifteenth-century clock, revolves around the earth in twenty-four hours. It points to the hour on the outer circle of figures and to the phase of the moon on the inner circle, which is geared to revolve at a slightly slower rate. The dial at the top that records the minutes was added in 1760.

Clock mechanisms of three different periods in the north transept of Peterborough Cathedral. (© John Crook/info@john-crook.com)

A sophisticated (and charming) development of the striking clock was the clock jack (or *Jack of the Clock*) in which the bells that mark the hours and quarter hours are struck by carved and painted figures. In Britain, the earliest example is believed to be the fourteenth-century clock jack at Wells Cathedral, where two 'quarter jacks' strike the quarter hours and 'Jack Blandifer' the hours. First mentioned in 1392, its original clock mechanism is now in the Science Museum, London, having been replaced in 1880 by a 'modern' movement behind the original painted face. Wimborne Minster in Dorset has both an 'astronomical' clock and a quarter jack. The clock case is Elizabethan but the orrery face and dial are considered to be much older – there is a record of the clock being repaired in 1409. Its mechanism, which was replaced in 1695 and again in 1792, is located in the ringing chamber, where it also operates a chime. Wimborne's quarter jack, installed in 1612, was carved by a Blandford craftsman for 10*s*. The original figure was a monk, but during the Napoleonic Wars it was changed to a smart red-coated grenadier. It is apparent that most of the large clock faces that enliven our cathedrals are made up of parts from various centuries: the striking clock in the north transept of York Minster, for example, was made in 1750 by Henry Hindley using sixteenth-century figures of men-at-arms.

See also BELLS

CLOISTER From the Latin *claustrum* meaning 'an enclosed place' (hence claustrophobia), the cloister is a rectangular court surrounded by a covered and colonnaded passageway, the outer elevations of which are formed by the walls of the surrounding claustral buildings (*see* CELLARIUM, CHAPTER HOUSE, DORTER, FRATER, LAY BROTHERS, REREDORTER, SOUTH RANGE *and* WESTERN RANGE). The cloister was at the heart of a monastery: it was where the monks worked, taught, walked and meditated. The length of passageway on each side of the quadrangle is known as an *alley*, and the open area contained within is the *cloister garth* (*see* GARTH). This was often served by piped water or a well and would have been laid out with a lawn or herb garden – although the CARTHUSIANS used the cloister garth as a burial ground. The cloister was usually located on the salubrious south side of the nave of the church, although not invariably so – the suitability of a site to accommodate an efficient drainage system sometimes dictated otherwise (*see* REREDORTER). It was usually protected by a lean-to roof (*pentise*) set against the aisle of the church and the surrounding claustral buildings, although sometimes the upper storeys of these buildings projected over the cloister: at Muchelney, for example, and at Evesham where an upper floor incorporated additional carrels (*see below*) and, at St Albans, a library. In many smaller houses, and in friaries, the cloister was little more than a passage, while early Cistercian cloisters were built of wood, later to be replaced with stone.

In monastic houses, the arched openings in the cloister colonnade were usually filled with a combination of glass and wooden shutters, and the alley adjacent to the church was provided with *carrels* for individual study (except in Carthusian houses where the monks had their own cells – *see* CARTHUSIANS). Carrels were stone or timber cubicles, made draught-free by the provision of doors and canopies, each containing a desk and bench and a clear or unglazed window by which to work. At Durham, 'every one of the old monks had his carrell, severall by himselfe, that, when they had dyned, they dyd resorte to that place of Cloister and there studyed upon there books, everyone in his carrell, all the after nonne, unto evensong tyme'. On three sides of the cloister at Worcester Cathedral Priory, the window bays are separated by shallow piers, each pier pierced by a rectangular opening that enabled neighbours to see and (presumably) communicate with each other. At monasteries with strong academic traditions, additional carrels were sometimes provided in the eastern or western alleys of the cloister, together with a recessed ARMARIUM for the storage of books. Other recesses contained the community's 'duty rosters' and special notices (*see* TABULA). The western alley was sometimes used as a schoolroom where the novices were taught the principles of MONASTICISM and the complex rules of the order: there are scratched traces of children's games in the stonework of several cloisters including Canterbury, Gloucester and Norwich. *Scriptoria*, for the writing and illumination of manuscripts, were usually located in the south alley, which benefited from pure, northern light (*see* SCRIPTORIUM). Floors would be covered with rushes, straw or matting and the cloister alleys were lit by lamps at night-time and, in less austere houses, heated with braziers.

The cloister was also used for processional purposes and there is usually a processional doorway from the cloister to the church: at Lilleshall Abbey, for example, where the doorway is richly decorated with 'chevron' moulding in the

Carrels and fan vaulting in the south alley of the cloister at Gloucester Cathedral.

twelfth-century Romanesque style. The privacy of the cloister was closely guarded: at Durham 'no strangers or other persons were suffered to . . . trouble the novices or monks in their carrels while they were at their books within the cloister. For this purpose there was a PORTER appointed to keep the cloister door'. The porter (*the guardian of the cloister*) was usually provided with a seat near the entrance from the outer court and was responsible for maintaining silence in the cloister, subject to the demands of the activities that were taking place there at a particular time.

One of the finest cloisters in England is that at the former Benedictine monastery of St Peter (now the Cathedral) at Gloucester. Built to the north of the abbey church in 1375–1410 (because the town cemetery lay to the south), the cloister has one of the earliest fan vaults in England (*see* MEDIEVAL ARCHITECTURE). In the south alley are twenty recessed stone carrels, each originally provided with a wooden desk for study. In the western half of the north alley is a superb LAVATORIUM, with its own miniature fan vault, a stone trough for the washing of hands before meals (taken in the adjacent FRATER) and a nearby *aumbry* (recessed cupboard) which contained a supply of dry towels. In the centre of the east walk is the entrance to the CHAPTER HOUSE, used for formal assemblies of the community and for the transaction of the daily business of the abbey.

In several of the larger monastic houses, the INFIRMARY (or *farmery*) would be provided with its own cloister and cloister garth (at Rievaulx this became the Abbot's private garden). All double houses had two cloisters (*see* DOUBLE MONASTERY) and a number of Cistercian houses had an additional cloister for the community's LAY BROTHERS (at Byland, Fountains and Tintern, for

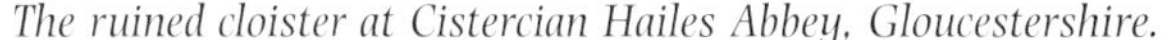

The ruined cloister at Cistercian Hailes Abbey, Gloucestershire.

example). The Augustinian Canons of Haughmond Abbey built a second cloister, separated from the main cloister by a range of refectory buildings above an UNDERCROFT. This cloister was in close proximity to the Abbot's hall and private chambers and may have been intended primarily for his use and that of his guests.

Strictly speaking, a cloister was not required in a cathedral or minster (*see* CATHEDRALS *and* MINSTERS), both of which were served by SECULAR CLERGY (*see* CANON). Unlike the monks, who were obliged by their RULE to live in a closed community, the canons of a medieval cathedral often chose not to live in the accommodation provided for them. At Lincoln, for example, the canons had lodgings in Minster Yard but they frequently appointed vicars to undertake their liturgical duties in the cathedral while they lived elsewhere. Without the imperative of a closed community, it is surprising that cloisters were built at so many non-monastic cathedrals. Indeed that at Salisbury, which was never a monastic foundation, is the largest in England. Completed in 1266, it is 58m square (190ft) with walls 5.5m wide (18ft). In such cases, it seems likely that the cloister was intended for teaching (the medieval cathedrals were centres of learning), for processional purposes and to provide the canons, chantry priests, vicars, choristers and all involved in the daily worship of the cathedral with a peaceful garden for quiet reflection and a sheltered walkway in which to exercise in inclement weather. In this regard, Salisbury is typical of non-monastic cathedrals in that it has none of the domestic claustral buildings associated with monastic cloisters, other than the cathedral's CHAPTER HOUSE, and consequently very few doors leading from it. Indeed, those cloisters that have survived intact at secular cathedrals (Lincoln and Salisbury in particular) have a more open ambience than many monastic cloisters and appear to have been designed for meditation and relaxation rather than work. At Hereford, also a non-monastic cathedral, only two sides of the original cloister remain, together with the foundations of the former decagonal chapter house, which was broken up for building stone in the eighteenth century. But, to the south-east of the chapter-house garden, and beyond the public gaze, is the cloister of the College of VICARS CHORAL, a quadrangle of fifteenth-century maisonettes that once housed the priests who sang in the cathedral choir. The Vicars Choral moved into their newly built college in 1472 for their own safety. Apparently the streets of Hereford were overrun with brigands and the journey from their quarters outside the cathedral precinct was considered to be too dangerous. The cloister is still lived in today – and, surely, there can be no more idyllic lodging in the whole of England.

However, there were also several non-monastic houses where the canons occupied claustral buildings which generally conformed more closely to the usual monastic plan. At Bolton priory, for example, an independent house of Augustinian Canons, the claustral buildings (of which only the foundations remain) included, in the EASTERN RANGE, an UNDERCROFT beneath the DORTER, a reredorter (latrines) extending to the east at the southern end, and the fourteenth-century prior's lodging which replaced the original quarters in the west range. A passage to the south of the south TRANSEPT led to the octagonal chapter house which, unusually, was not included in the eastern range but was situated to the east of it. The south claustral range contained the frater and the west range a PARLOUR to the north and cellarage to the south, with the original prior's lodging on the first floor. Most unusually, the south transept is not at right angles to the church, so that the east claustral range veers slightly to the east. Furthermore, the church (in its final form) was almost too large for the cloister: the south transept extends almost the entire length of the east claustral alley while the nave extends considerably beyond the west.

Of course, there are numerous interesting variations on the common claustral theme. At

Chichester Cathedral a large 'cloister' (the garth known as 'Paradise') is shaped like a half trapezium and abuts the church on either side of the south transept, forming a passageway from the nave to the retro-choir. It has no north alley and was substantially rebuilt in 1400, possibly to accommodate queues of pilgrims visiting the shrine of St Richard of Chichester (canonised 1262) whose relics were removed to the retro-choir in 1276. At the Premonstratensian abbey of St Agatha, North Yorkshire (now known as Easby Abbey), the thirteenth-century cloister is a singularly irregular shape: its west alley is 30m long (100ft), the north alley 29m (98ft), the south 25m (82ft) and the east 19m (63ft). A further unusual feature is the location of the dorter, which is incorporated within the west claustral range (it was usually in the east) and the guests' SOLAR and canons' reredorter, which extends in a separate building beyond the dorter in an ingenious arrangement that accommodates both the different levels on which it was built and the need for adequate drainage of the reredorter. The claustral buildings date almost exclusively from the early thirteenth century, with some late fifteenth-century additions and remodelling. At Wells, the east alley of the cloister has always been the bishop's entrance to his cathedral (from the Bishop's Palace), while the cloister garth known as the Palm Churchyard, is the burial ground for the cathedral clergy, and a long chamber above the cloister still accommodates the cathedral's library (*see* LIBRARIES). At Christ Church, Oxford, founded (as Cardinal College) in 1525 by Cardinal

The north aisle at the parish church of All Saints, Hilton, Dorset, removed from the cloister of nearby Milton Abbey in the 1530s. (Courtesy of Florence Morris)

Wolsey (*c.* 1475–1530), the late fifteenth-century cloister of the former Priory of St Frideswide was badly mutilated by Wolsey, who removed the western alley. The northern alley was restored in the late nineteenth century (*see* CHANTRY COLLEGES). Between the west range and the cloister at Cistercian Byland Abbey, North Yorkshire, a passage (or LANE) provided covered access from the foot of the DAY STAIR (leading from the southern end of the lay brothers' dormitory) to the church. The use of this passage as an assembly point for the lay brothers before they entered the nave of the church (where their services were held) is confirmed by the provision of a remarkable series of thirty-five recessed seats in the eastern wall of the passage. A similar arrangement (though without the seats) may be found at Buildwas Abbey, Shropshire (also Cistercian). A lane between the cloister and the church was a feature of several Dominican friaries and, unusually, may also be found at Salisbury Cathedral where the north wall of the cloister is separated from the south aisle of the church. The original function of the intervening space is unclear but it is now occupied by an imaginatively designed café and shop.

CLOSE *see* PRECINCT

CLOSE ROLLS These contain registered copies of private letters and documents of the royal Court of Chancery, such as conveyances, writs of summons to parliament and orders to royal officers. Letters Close were 'closed' (folded and secured with a seal), unlike Letters Patent, which were 'open' and addressed 'To all and singular . . .'. Copies of these documents were made on PARCHMENT sheets which were stitched together and stored in rolls: one or more for each regnal year. They are housed at The National Archives (*For* address *see* APPENDIX II).

CLOTHING The *habit* was the distinctive uniform worn by monks, nuns, canons and friars as members of various religious orders. The habits of the older orders consisted of a tunic and girdle, a SCAPULAR and a mantle with an attached hood or COWL (or a *wimple* for women: *see* VEIL). The habit was intended to be an outward and visible sign of commitment to a religious life. Colours and details of design varied from one order to another: for example the Benedictines and Dominicans wore black, the Cistercians white and the Franciscans grey (now brown). It was, however, the colour of the cowl from which derived the popular names for the various orders of religious: the White Monks, the Grey Friars etc. A sleeveless overall (also *scapular*) could be worn for manual work while servitors in the kitchens and frater were provided with gloves and tunics with detachable sleeves.

In a monastic community it was the CHAMBERLAIN who was responsible for the provision, repair and laundering of clothing and for preserving and replacing footwear (*see* SHOES). It was he who engaged tailors who were required to be 'trustworthy, sober, secret and not talkative . . . as they were summoned into the interior privacy of the monastery where they could hear and see the secrets of the brethren'. The chamberlain might purchase material for clothing, but more often it was produced and processed by the community – on its granges and in its MILLS and tanneries. While the Benedictine rule specified clothing that was simple and inexpensive, there were considerable differences, not only among the various orders but also among houses of the same order. Particularly variable was the degree of austerity required. While the Austin Canons of Barnwell were permitted linen, the Cistercians wore bleached and undyed wool and, because they wore no undergarments, their rough habits came into direct contact with the skin. There were differences also in the manner in which clothing was allocated. At Westminster, the brethren had their garments replaced by rotation, while their Benedictine brothers at Gloucester replaced their frocks and cowls annually, their day shoes every eighteen months, their woollen shirts every four

years and their boots every five. Undershirts, thin tunics and drawers were issued more frequently. At Barnwell Priory, the canons received their summer allowance of SURPLICE, shirt, gaiters, heavy woollen cloak and three pairs of leather shoes at Easter; while the winter issue of a lambskin CASSOCK, a pair of felt boots, a pair of woollen gaiters, two pairs of night shoes and a black lambskin with which to repair the fur hood of the cloak, was distributed on or near the feast of St Michael (29 September).
See also entries for the individual orders.

CLUNCH Chalk for building, quarried from the hard, grey-coloured beds of the Lower Chalk, sawn into blocks and dried. Often used in conjunction with brick DRESSINGS in buildings dating from the Middle Ages to the nineteenth century.

CLUNIACS Founded by William the Pious, duke of of Aquitaine, in 910, the monastery of Cluny in Burgundy was that most venerated by the Norman kings (*see* RULE). Cluniac monasticism of the late eleventh century was marked by a preoccupation with the liturgical and ceremonial: effectively to the exclusion of all intellectual, artistic or educational aspirations. The abbey was described as 'a world in itself, given wholly to the worship of God in a setting of incomparable splendour and untouched by secular intrigue'. From Cluny, the movement spread with extraordinary rapidity until some 1,500 Cluniac monasteries were established throughout Europe, each a dependent priory under the abbot of Cluny and paying an annual rent or *apport* to the mother house. The first Cluniac priory in the English province was founded in 1077 by William de Warenne at Lewes in East Sussex. Thereafter, a further thirty-two houses were founded, many as cells of Norman priories, but none, other than that at Bermondsey (founded 1087), was to rival Lewes (even so, in 1399 Bermondsey became the only Cluniac abbey in England). The best-preserved remains are at Wenlock Priory (1080) and Castle Acre Priory (1089). There were also three (or, possibly, four) Cluniac nunneries in England and Wales, notably at Fotheringhay and Northampton.

King Stephen (1097–1154) was buried in his Cluniac priory at Faversham, Kent. No doubt he had in mind the Cluniacs' reputation as 'ferrymen of departing souls': it was they who instituted All Souls' Day (2 November) as an appropriate sequel to All Saints' Day (1 November). The importance of the Cluniacs in medieval England lay not in the size or number of their houses but in the prominence and influence attained by so many of their brethren.

COAT OF ARMS *see* HERALDRY

COB Most surviving monastic ruins are, inevitably, constructed of stone. But outbuildings, and even the CLAUSTRAL buildings of poorer communities, were often built of cob, an ancient building material formed of mud, marl, chalk or gravel with dung and some form of binding material such as hair or chopped straw. Cob walls were built in 'wet' layers of about 60cm (2ft) on a foundation of MOORSTONE or boulders, each layer being allowed to set for at least seven days before the next was applied. Cob was often strengthened by the addition of horsehair or cowhair and the walls were limewashed for protection and provided with a water-repellent 'skirt' of tar at the base. A sound roof of thatch or tile is necessary to prevent a cob wall washing away into the earth from whence it came, and the eaves protrude to ensure that rainwater from the roof is projected away from the surface of the wall and does not accumulate at the base.

CODICOLOGY The study of the materials, techniques and personnel in manuscript and book production.

COENOBITE An ANCHORITE who occupies a separate dwelling, and observes a rule of SILENCE, within a monastic community.

COFFERING Decoration of a ceiling or VAULT, or the underside of an arch, with a pattern of sunken square or polygonal ornamental panels.

COFFINS (STONE) Distinguished members or confraters (*see* CONFRATERNITY) of religious communities were sometimes buried in a stone coffin which was sunk in the floor of an abbey church, chapter house or cloister so that its lid (often finely carved) was level with the floor. These may occasionally be found where they were buried, although in most monastic ruins they have been removed and the lids separated from the (now empty) stone coffins.
See also BURIALS (MONASTIC)

COLLAR BEAM A horizontal beam spanning a roof and tying the principal rafters together.

COLLAR PURLIN A timber running the length of the centre of a roof beneath the COLLAR BEAMS.

COLLATION (i) A light meal permitted on days of FASTING.
(ii) Following supper, a short reading in the chapter house or (in Cistercian houses) in the cloister. At Cleeve Abbey, Somerset, a trefoil-headed arched recess in the north alley marks the position of a seat which was occupied by the abbot during the collation.

COLLECT A short prayer, of one sentence and conveying one petition, usually read on an appointed day. In the Church of England, the collects are set out in the *Book of Common Prayer* and mostly derive from medieval sources, although some were Thomas Cranmer's original compositions.

COLLEGE A chapter of SECULAR CLERGY who held services in a cathedral (*see* CATHEDRALS) or COLLEGIATE CHURCH.
See also CANTARIST, CHANTRY COLLEGES *and* UNIVERSITIES, MEDIEVAL

COLLEGIATE CHURCH A church which is endowed for a chapter of canons and/or prebendaries but is not a cathedral.
See also CHANTRY COLLEGES

COLONNADE A row of columns supporting arches or an ENTABLATURE.

COLOPHON A brief passage at the conclusion of a handwritten document, usually giving the name of the scribe and sometimes including an expression of relief and thanks that the task has been concluded.

COLOURS (HERALDIC) The metals, colours and furs used in HERALDRY are known as *tinctures*. The metals are *Or* (gold, often depicted as yellow) and *Argent* (silver, usually depicted as white). The most commonly used colours are *Gules* (red), *Azure* (blue), *Sable* (black), *Vert* (green) and *Purpure* (purple). The most common furs are *Ermine* (white with black 'tails') and *Vair* (white and blue 'pelts'). Where a charge is represented in its natural colours it is described as *proper*. The tinctures of uncoloured coats of arms (those engraved on monuments or silver, for example) may often be determined by reference to the system of hatching developed by Sylvester Petra Sancta, a seventeenth-century writer on heraldry (*see* illustration, page 96). In documents the tinctures may be shown by means of a 'trick' – a line drawing in which abbreviations are substituted for tinctures and numbers or letters for objects (*charges*).

COLOURS (LITURGICAL) Colours used in vestments, altar frontals, etc. to mark the liturgical seasons and festivals:

White: Signifying joy: Christmas, Easter, Corpus Christi, the Feast of St Mary, Trinity and All Saints' Day (1 November) and feasts of saints who were not martyrs.

Red: Associated with fire: Whit Sunday (Pentecost), Palm Sunday, Holy Cross Day and the feasts of saints who were martyrs.

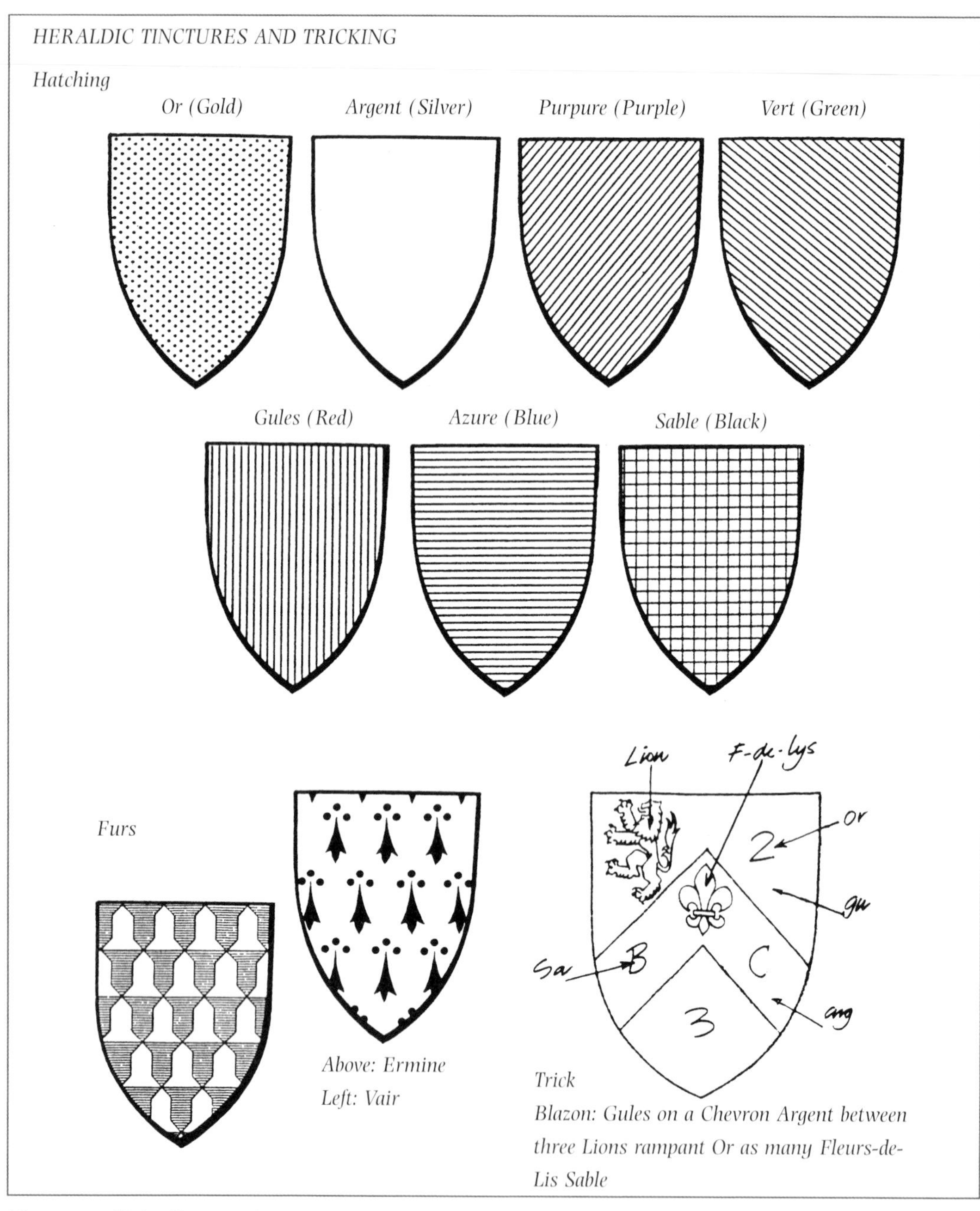

Above: Ermine
Left: Vair

Trick
Blazon: Gules on a Chevron Argent between three Lions rampant Or as many Fleurs-de-Lis Sable

(Courtesy of John Ferguson)

Green: Signifying life and hope: the periods following Trinity and Epiphany and on weekdays when no other feast or fast is kept.

Violet: Signifying penitence: Advent and Lent (in some churches unbleached linen is used during Lent to represent penitence), Rogation and Ember days.

Black: Good Friday and All Souls' Day (2 November), funerals and requiems.

COLUMBARIUM *see* DOVECOTE

COLUMN In classical architecture, an upright masonry or brick support used for structural purposes or architectural adornment. Unlike a PIER, a column invariably has both a BASE and CAPITAL. A column may be used singly, in a pair or in a group (*see* ARCADE *and* COLONNADE) or it may be wholly or partly attached to a wall or to another column. Pairs of columns are described as *coupled* and a column which has part of its surface attached to a wall is said to be *engaged*, *applied* or *attached*. A central shaft surrounded by a number of slender columns (not necessarily attached to each other) is described as *grouped*, *clustered* or *compound*. Twisted Baroque columns are sometimes described as 'barley-sugar' or *Solomonic* (after their alleged use in the Temple of Solomon), and when entwined with vine leaves they are *wreathed*. In the classical order, a column is divided into capital, shaft, base and plinth. A *fluted shaft* is one which is cut in vertical channels, and both columns and piers may be *annulated* with narrow bands encircling the shaft.
See also BAY

COMMANDERY A manorial estate and HOSPICE belonging to the military order of the Knights Hospitaller of St John of Jerusalem, usually staffed by a small complement of knights with a CHAPLAIN and servants. Such manors enjoyed certain privileges: the parish of the commandery at Dinmore in Herefordshire is entirely free of tithe, the owners of the estate benefiting from immunities granted to the Hospitallers by Pope Paschal II in 1113. Dinmore is known as an ex-parochial or *peculiar* parish for, although it possesses a parish church (one of only four dedicated to St John of Jerusalem), it forms no part of a DIOCESE, neither do the bishop nor the ecclesiastical authorities have any jurisdiction there; indeed until the mid-nineteenth century the parishioners were exempted from paying local rates. The commandery at Dinmore ranked as third or fourth in importance among the fifty or so similar Hospitaller commanderies established in England and Wales in the twelfth and thirteenth centuries. Each was in the charge of a knight of the Order, the gift of a commandery being the usual reward for outstanding service in the Crusades. In addition to providing income for the Order by the management of the estates, commanderies were regional military training centres and hospices or places of rest for those who returned injured or invalided from the Holy Land. They also afforded shelter and refreshment to travellers and sustenance to the sick and needy. Commanderies accumulated extensive tracts of land, acquired both from the Templars following their suppression in 1310 and from the endowments of *corrodians* – those who were not members of the Order but enjoyed residentiary benefits in return for their generosity (*see* CORRODY). At Dinmore, as at other commanderies, local field names evoke its past in Knights' Grove, Great St John's Meadow, etc. In the same county, at Hereford, the ruins of the fourteenth-century commandery were converted to ALMSHOUSES (the Coningsby Hospital) in 1640 by Sir Thomas Coningsby, who had acquired the nearby Dominican friary at the Dissolution of the Monasteries.

The parallel order of the Knights Templar possessed similar establishments called *preceptories* although, following the suppression of the Templars in 1312, these were transferred to the Knights Hospitaller, who also adopted the term to describe some of their later commanderies. Typically, the Hospitaller preceptory at Chibburn in Northumberland was built around a central courtyard approached through an arched gateway in a northern two-storey range of domestic buildings, and with a chapel to the south and dwelling house to the west.

Not all 'commanderies' are what they seem. The so-called commandery at Worcester, for example, was originally erected by St Wulstan in the eleventh century as an Augustinian friary for the purpose of providing hospitality for travellers who arrived at the city gate after it had been closed for the night. At the Dissolution of the Monasteries the

house gained a reprieve by subscribing to the royal supremacy, but in 1545 the hospital and its lands were transferred to the endowment of Christ Church, Oxford. The fourteenth-century great hall has survived on an impressive scale, an upper room containing a series of religious wall paintings depicting the martyrdom of St Erasmus and St Thomas Becket, the Crucifixion and the Weighing of Souls at the Last Judgement and a representation of the Trinity in the ceiling.
(*See also* ST JOHN OF JERUSALEM, ORDER OF *and* TEMPLAR, KNIGHTS)

COMMENDATOR A system, dating from the eighth century, whereby a layman was appointed to the title and income of a monastic SUPERIOR in return for military protection. Once the original purpose was lost, the system was often abused as a means of rewarding the favourites of a king or pope.

COMMISSARY COURT A diocesan court concerned with matters of probate which fell entirely within the DIOCESE.

COMMON HOUSE *see* CALEFACTORIUM

COMMON PRAYER, BOOK OF (BCP) The official service book of the Church of England and one of the finest works in the English language. The BCP contains the daily offices of Morning and Evening prayer, the forms for the administration of the sacraments (*see* SACRAMENT) and other rites, the PSALTER and (since 1552) the ORDINAL. The book was compiled in response to Thomas Cranmer (1489–1556) and others, who wished to simplify and condense the Latin service books of the medieval Church (*see* SARUM, USE OF) and to produce in English a convenient and authoritative guide for priest and people.

The first BCP (Edward VI) was authorised by the Act of Uniformity in 1549 but was revised, following Protestant criticism, and a second version was issued in 1552/3 (also Edward VI). Although, with the accession of Queen Mary (1553–8), it was never actually brought into use, the 1552 Prayer Book marks the establishment of Protestantism in the territories of the Crown of England. It abandoned the doctrine of transubstantiation, thereby confirming the distinction between the MASS and the communion service, which is the essence of the distinction between Protestantism and Roman Catholicism. The 1552 Prayer Book was reissued in 1559 (Elizabeth I) in a slightly amended form and with the Ornaments Rubric attached (a ruling that the ornaments of the Church and its ministers should be those in use 'by the authority of Parliament in the second year of the reign of King Edward VI'). During the Commonwealth the BCP was replaced by *The Directory of Public Worship*, but at the Restoration the Act of Uniformity (1662) authorised a BCP which included the 1611 (King James) Authorised Version of the Bible for the Epistles and Gospels, and this has remained in use (almost without alteration) to the present day.

A Welsh translation of the main texts of the Prayer Book (*Kynniver Llith a Ban*) was published in 1551. This was the work of William Salesbury who, in the previous year, had translated the Old Testament into Welsh.

In 1906 a Royal Commission on Ecclesiastical Discipline recommended that the Prayer Book should be revised, but the Convocations decided to retain the 1662 book and to incorporate all changes in a new book, the use of which should be entirely permissive. Although the new book was approved by the Church Assembly, it was rejected by the House of Commons in 1927 and again (following further minor revisions) in 1928. In 1955 the archbishops appointed a Liturgical Commission to prepare a revision of the BCP and, in 1965, the Prayer Book (Alternative and Other Services) Measure authorised experimentation. This was repealed by the Church of England (Worship and Doctrine) Measure of 1974, which allowed the use of alternative services on a permanent basis. These are set out in *The Alternative Service Book* (ASB) of 1980. The decision whether or not to adopt the new services is a matter for parochial church councils, subject to the advice of the incumbent. In 1994, the Synod agreed that a new 'core' Prayer Book should be published by 2000. This includes elements of both the *Book of Common Prayer* and the *Alternative Service Book*.

COMMUNION *see* EUCHARIST

COMPLINE (COMPLETORIUM) The last of the canonical hours, observed before the brethren retired for the night. Compline was established in the Benedictine Rule and included the NUNC DIMITTIS, a short lesson, psalms and a hymn, *Te lucis ante terminum*. It was preceded by CONFESSION and concluded by the singing of an ANTHEM of Our Lady and the sprinkling of HOLY WATER as the monks filed through the cloister to the dormitory (DORTER) – usually at 8.30, or an hour earlier during the winter months. The essential elements of Compline were incorporated into the service of Evensong (*see* EVENING PRAYER) in the *Book of Common Prayer*.
See also HOURS (CANONICAL), HORARIUM *and* VESPERALE

CONCORDAT An agreement between ecclesiastical and civil authorities regarding a matter of mutual concern.

CONDUCTUS A type of sacred or secular choral composition of the twelfth and thirteenth centuries, the precursor of the MOTET. At this time, the art of musical composition was that of adding voice-parts to an existing melody, the *canto fermo*. In the *conductus*, the words sung were confined to the voice singing the *canto fermo*, while other voices (usually two in number) vocalised on the principal vowel of each word.
See also PLAINSONG

CONDUIT A trough or pipe for conveying water, usually from a central conduit house where a raised tank provided water pressure. There are good examples at Durham, at Beaulieu in Hampshire and Monkton Farleigh in Wiltshire. Monastic water and drainage systems were often complex and extremely efficient. Stone-lined conduits may have been revealed by the subsequent removal of conventual buildings, as at Tintern Abbey in Monmouthshire. The well-known 'Conduit' in the marketplace at Sherborne in Dorset was constructed as a LAVATORIUM in the cloister of the nearby abbey in the early sixteenth century and moved, following the Dissolution of the Monasteries in 1539, to form a small market house and public fountain. Friaries (which were usually established in towns) were especially noted for providing public conduits of running water.
See also PLUMBING, WATER SUPPLY AND SANITATION

CONFEDERATION An obit roll of *c.* 1230, recording the death of the first prioress of Hedingham, was conveyed to 120 religious houses, all of which acknowledged its receipt with the words: 'May the soul of Lady Lucy, prioress of Hedingham and the souls of all the faithful departed, by the mercy of God, rest in peace. We concede to her the benefits of our church. We pray for you; pray for us.' Thus, confederations of abbeys formed spiritual unions, the members of which were visited annually by special messengers (*rotularius*) from each house, bearing lists of those for whom prayers were desired and exchanging expressions of greeting and mutual support.
See also CONFRATERNITY

CONFESSION (i) The tomb or shrine of a MARTYR or CONFESSOR or the church containing such a shrine.
(ii) A declaration of religious belief.
(iii) An acknowledgement of sin, either by an individual penitent in private or in the hearing of a priest (*auricular confession*), or by a congregation during an act of worship (*see* SHRIVE). The Fourth Lateran Council of 1215 made confession an

annual obligation for all Christians. In religious communities, both the mass and the offices began with a general confession and there were opportunities for confession of more particular offences (especially breaches of the RULE) before the community in CHAPTER. There were also provisions for auricular confession and spiritual council which were available to members of the community and to others. Following the REFORMATION, incumbents supervised public confessions, which were required not only by the ecclesiastical courts, but also by Quarter Sessions.

CONFESSOR (i) A priest who hears confessions.
(ii) In the early Church, one who suffered for confessing his or her faith, but excluding those who were martyred (*see* MARTYR). The term was later applied also to holy men, especially those who were pronounced as such by the pope.
See also SHRINES

CONFISCATION INVENTORIES *see* CHANTRY

CONFRATERNITY A rare honour and privilege by which a benefactor was granted honorary membership of a religious community. By becoming 'one of the family', a *confrater* could reasonably anticipate redemption through association with the piety, self-sacrifice and prayer of a religious house. He (or she) was usually allocated a place in the CHAPTER HOUSE and granted a right of burial in the monastic cemetery: King John (1199–1216), for example, who made a late entry into the confraternity of Worcester, was buried in the priory church, clothed in a Benedictine habit. Wealth was not necessarily a prerequisite: long-serving EMPLOYEES were sometimes admitted to a confraternity.
See also BENEFACTORS, COFFINS (STONE) *and* CONFEDERATION

CONGREGATION (i) A body of people who habitually attend a particular church (*see* MEDIEVAL CHURCH).
(ii) A religious society in contradistinction to a strict religious order.
(iii) A group of monastic houses, formed since the end of the medieval period.

CONSISTORY COURT A bishop's court concerned with diocesan ecclesiastical administration.

CONSOLE (i) The frame of an organ containing the keyboards, stops, pedals, etc. The GALLERY in which the console is located is known as the *organ-loft* and, in larger churches, this may be reached by a stair (*see* ORGANS).
(ii) A scroll-shaped BRACKET.

CONSTRUCTION OF MONASTIC BUILDINGS *see* ARCH, CENTERING, FOUNDATIONS (STRUCTURAL), LANTERN, MEDIEVAL ARCHITECTURE, MASONRY, MASTER MASONS AND ARCHITECTS, MASONS' MARKS, MONASTIC BUILDINGS, SCAFFOLDING AND CRANES, WINDOWS *and* VAULTING

CONTEMPLATIVE LIFE Descriptive of the austere life required of certain religious living under VOWS, which included a considerable element of contemplation and prayer.

CONVENT From the Latin *convenire* meaning 'to assemble', a convent is a religious community or the building in which it lives. Historically (and throughout this book) the term may be applied to communities of either sex, although current usage generally implies a house of nuns (*nunnery*).
See also HOUSE (RELIGIOUS)

CONVENTICLE A meeting of monks, although in the seventeenth century also a meeting (usually unlawful) of non-conformists.

CONVENTUAL A conventual is one who belongs to a religious house. A conventual mass is a public mass attended by all members of a religious community.

CONVERSI *see* LAY BROTHERS

CONVOCATION The convocations of Canterbury and York are the two ancient provincial assemblies of the English Church. Originally they consisted only of prelates, but in 1225 Archbishop Langton (d. 1228) summoned representatives (*proctors*) of the cathedral and monastic chapters. From the end of the thirteenth century, bishops, abbots (until the Reformation), deans, archdeacons and representatives of the clergy of each diocese and cathedral chapter attended, sitting together as one House. Since the fifteenth century, the bishops and lower clergy have sat as two Houses. Until 1664 ecclesiastical legislation and clerical taxation were determined by the Convocations but, with the SUBMISSION OF THE CLERGY in 1532, their powers were restricted and in 1717 they were prorogued. Thereafter, their work was entirely formal until, in 1852, the Convocation of Canterbury was reactivated, followed in 1861 by the Convocation of York. In 1969 most of the functions of the Convocations were transferred to the General Synod, although they continue to meet separately.

COPE *see* EMBROIDERY

COPE CHEST A horizontal quadrant-shaped wardrobe in which a cope is stored. Usually of sturdy timber construction with panelled sides, legs, and a lid opening in two halves decorated with foliated hinges.
See also EMBROIDERY

COPING A protective capping intended to disperse rainwater from the top of a wall.

CORBEL A projection of stone, wood or brick supporting an arch, beam, parapet or moulding.
See also BRACKET *and* DRIPSTONE

CORBEL-TABLE A series of corbels (*see above*), occurring immediately below the roof eaves, both internally and externally. The Normans were especially fond of corbel-tables, which were often elaborately carved in the forms of monsters and grotesque figures.

CORNICE (i) A moulded projection surmounting a wall, arch or building.
(ii) A plaster moulding round a ceiling.

CORONA The APSIDAL termination of a church.

CORONA CHAPEL *see* LADY CHAPEL

CORONA LUCIS A crown-shaped wrought-iron or brass chandelier. Most surviving examples are from the nineteenth-century Gothic revival. Typically, a lower (larger) circlet supports a series of drip-pans and candle-sockets on its upper rim, while the outer face may be embellished with enamelled shields and decorative pendant finials. This is suspended by chains from a smaller circlet attached to the ceiling. In monastic churches, a *corona lucis* was often the principal source of artificial light, notably in Benedictine houses such as Canterbury, where there were two huge wheel-like chandeliers, one in the nave and the other in the choir, each bearing twenty-four candles.
See also LIGHTS

CORONAL In architecture, the uppermost section of a tower.

CORRODIAN The beneficiary of a CORRODY.

CORRODY A payment by a lay person in return for accommodation in a monastery. A corrody was effectively a form of annuity that guaranteed security in old age for the corrodian and a source of capital for the monastery. Contracts varied considerably: in some cases medical care was included, as was stabling for a specified number of horses, while most set out in detail the quality of accommodation and food to be provided. Certain BENEFACTORS of religious houses or their nominees also exercised a right to board and lodging, a privilege that was often abused when abbeys were forced to accept corrodians without reimbursement. Typically, these were retired retainers and servants of royal and magnate households who were accommodated for life, often with their wives. The term was later applied to pensions and other benefits granted by a monastery. Although initially attractive as a means of raising capital, corrodies undoubtedly became a financial burden and a distraction from the religious life of a community. At the Dissolution of the Monasteries, Great Malvern Priory was subsidising no fewer than thirty corrodians. Occasionally, important 'guests' were lodged in a monastery for political reasons: John II, king of France (1319–64), was confined to the abbey of St Albans following his capture by the Black Prince in 1356, and Elizabeth Wydeville was detained at Bermondsey Abbey by Henry VII until her death in 1492.

The number of corrodians resident in monastic houses increased significantly from the fourteenth century and there is considerable evidence of former conventual buildings being converted to accommodate them – notably those that had previously been provided for the LAY BROTHERS, whose numbers had been severely depleted following the Black Death and subsequent recurrences of the PLAGUE. At Furness, Cumbria (as elsewhere), the western CLAUSTRAL range was subdivided into several smaller chambers, each with a fireplace for greater comfort. At Cleeve Abbey, Somerset, the south claustral range was remodelled in the fifteenth century and the ground floor divided into suites of rooms for corrodians, while at Tintern, Monmouthshire, a new infirmary kitchen was built in the early fifteenth century and enlarged soon thereafter, replacing an earlier structure. These new kitchens were almost certainly built to serve the increasing numbers of corrodians and retired senior monks who had taken up residence in the INFIRMARY and the adjacent private apartments.

See also COMMANDERY, HOSPITALITY *and* MONASTICISM

COTSWOLD STONE The band of oolite which runs south-west from the Humber to the Dorset coast is at its widest and reaches its greatest elevation in the Cotswolds, a range of limestone hills, largely in Gloucestershire but extending east into Oxfordshire and south-west into Wiltshire. Noted for sheep pastures and formerly a centre of the woollen industry, the wide Cotswold landscape is complemented by its buildings as in no other area of Britain. Manor houses, churches, farmsteads, cottages and entire villages are constructed of oolitic limestone or 'Cotswold stone', the colour of which varies from the richest orange-brown in the east to pale creamy greys in the south and west. High-quality freestone (*see* ASHLAR) is to be found in deep strata which are accessible only in the steep north-western escarpment.

COUNT PALATINATE *see* PALATINATE

COUNTERPOINT *see* POLYPHONY

COURSE A single horizontal row of MASONRY, brick or flint.

COURSED RUBBLE Walling of roughly dressed stone or flints set in courses (*see* COURSE). Uncoursed rubble consists of unhewn stones or flints not laid in regular courses.

COURT OF ARCHES *see* ARCHES, COURT OF

COURT OF AUGMENTATION *see* AUGMENTATION, COURT OF

COURT OF CHANCERY *see* CHANCERY, COURT OF

COURT OF DELEGATES *see* DELEGATES, COURT OF

COURTS (ECCLESIASTICAL) *see* ARCHES, COURT OF, ARCHIVES, AUGMENTATION, COURT OF, CANON LAW, CHANCERY, COURT OF, CHAPTER, COMMISSARY COURT, CONSISTORY COURT,

CLARENDON, CONSTITUTIONS OF (1164), DELEGATES, COURT OF *and* FACULTIES, COURT OF

COURTS (MONASTIC) Abbots were feudal lords and as such exercised their authority through their own courts. There is a court room above the abbey gate at Ely in Cambridgeshire and in a separate building (*Tribunal*) in the main street at Glastonbury. Many monastic GATEHOUSES also contained a prison: at Bury St Edmunds in Suffolk, for example.

COVE *and* COVING A concave MOULDING at the junction of a ceiling and a wall.

COWL A hooded garment worn by the male members of religious orders (*see* CLOTHING).

CREDENCE A niche or shelf, sometimes within a FENESTELLA, on which the elements of the EUCHARIST were placed before consecration.
See also CREDENCE TABLE *and* PISCINA

CREDENCE TABLE A small side table in the SANCTUARY on which the bread, wine and water were placed during the EUCHARIST, together with accessories required for the service. Before the REFORMATION a CREDENCE was used for this purpose.
See also AUMBRY *and* PISCINA

CREED *see* NICENE CREED

CRENELLATED From *crenel* meaning 'embrasure', an embattled parapet or a wall with loopholes (*see* BATTLEMENT *and* EMBRASURE).

CRESSET *see* LIGHTS

CROCKET In MEDIEVAL ARCHITECTURE, carved leaf-like decorative features projecting at regular intervals on the sloping sides of spires, gables, pinnacles, etc.
See also BALLFLOWER ORNAMENT, DIAPER, DOGTOOTH ORNAMENT *and* FOILS

CROP MARKS It was William Camden (1551–1623) who observed of Richborough, the Fort of the Saxon Shore in Kent, 'Age has erased the very tracks of it . . . it is at this day a cornfield, wherein, when the corn is grown up, one may observe the draughts of streets crossing one another (for where they have gone, the corn is thinner) . . .'. Crop marks are produced by variations in the quality of plant growth caused by differences in the soil and subsoil. The presence of buried walls and foundations just beneath the soil's surface will produce weak plants which are vulnerable to dry conditions, while deeper pits and silt-filled trenches retain moisture and allow for the development of a substantial root structure and more luxuriant growth. From the air such variations of vegetation (usually in a cereal crop) become more evident and may delineate the former walls and buildings of archaeological sites. Aerial photography of crop marks is particularly

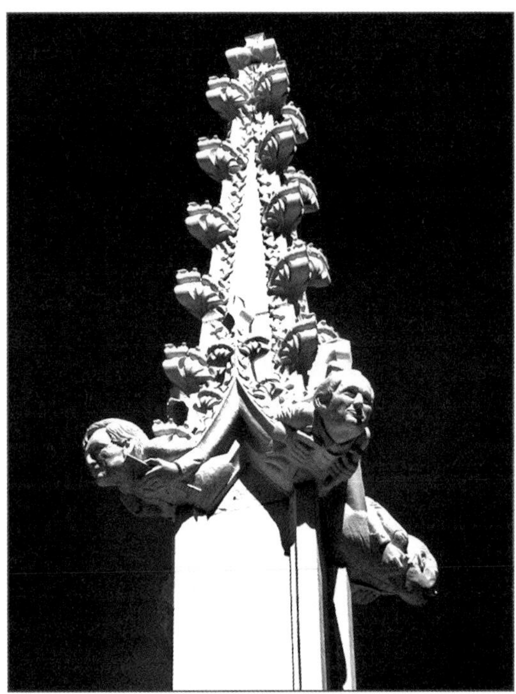

Recently carved pinnacle on the lavatorium at Gloucester Cathedral, studded with crockets and embellished with the faces of cathedral personalities.

effective when a low sun shines across a field, the different levels of vegetation casting shadows which clearly trace the structures beneath.

CROSSING The space formed at the intersection of NAVE, CHANCEL and TRANSEPT, often vaulted and with an AXIAL TOWER above.
See also MEDIEVAL ARCHITECTURE

CROWN POST A vertical post at the centre of a tie beam to support a COLLAR BEAM or COLLAR PURLIN, to which it is usually connected by means of diagonal braces.

CROZIER (*also* CROSIER) Literally 'cross-bearer', the term has come to mean the cross itself, the symbol of episcopal jurisdiction, a staff of office carried by bishops and formerly by abbots and abbesses.

CRUCIFER One who carries a cross, usually before a procession.

CRUCIFIX An image of Christ crucified, usually in the form of a three-dimensional model. Crucifixes were widely used as objects of devotion in the medieval period, as they are today in the Roman Catholic Church. Since the Reformation, they have generally been replaced by the cross in the Church of England.
See also ROOD SCREEN

CRUCIFORM In the shape of a cross.

CRUETS Vessels, usually of glass or precious metal, in which wine and water are carried to the altar for the EUCHARIST.
See also CREDENCE *and* PISCINA

CRUTCHED FRIARS *see* FRIARS

CRYPT A vaulted underground chamber, usually constructed beneath the CHANCEL of a church (and therefore in close proximity to the High Altar) to accommodate the TOMBS and RELICS of saints. As at Worcester (*see below*), there are often two flights of steps providing access and egress for the large numbers of pilgrims who visited the SHRINES. Some larger crypts (particularly those of the great abbeys and cathedrals), also contained altars which were provided for the use of individual priests or for the benefit of pilgrims who wished to pay homage at an adjacent shrine. Often, a crypt contains evidence of an earlier church: at Gloucester, for example, where the crypt extends beneath the PRESBYTERY and beyond, an APSE and AMBULATORY have survived from the original church (*c.* 1087), the VAULT springing from a series of small piers and supported by outer walls 2.5m thick (8ft). (Several of these piers were later reinforced to carry the weight of the new choir.) The crypt at York Minster was rebuilt in the late fourteenth century, the surviving remnants of beautifully incised late Romanesque piers providing a forlorn reminder of the once magnificent eastern arm of the early twelfth-century cathedral. At Ripon, the tiny crypt (reputed to be the same size and shape as the tomb from which Christ rose on Easter Day) is the only surviving remnant of the original seventh-century minster church, and is the oldest complete crypt in Britain. One of the most beautiful and atmospheric crypts, and the largest Norman example in England, is at Worcester Cathedral Priory. Begun in 1084 by Wulfstan, the only Saxon bishop who was not eventually replaced by a Norman after the Conquest, the crypt originally consisted of a central chapel, APSIDAL at its eastern end, with three arcades of eight piers separating the nave from the aisles. Pilgrims visiting St Wulfstan's shrine would descend from the church above into the south aisle of the crypt, proceed through an inner aisle to the ambulatory, where they might pause to pray at one of three polygonal chapels, and then return to the church by steps to the south TRANSEPT. The complete crypt reached to beneath the CROSSING in the west, and traces of the Norman arches may still be seen in the

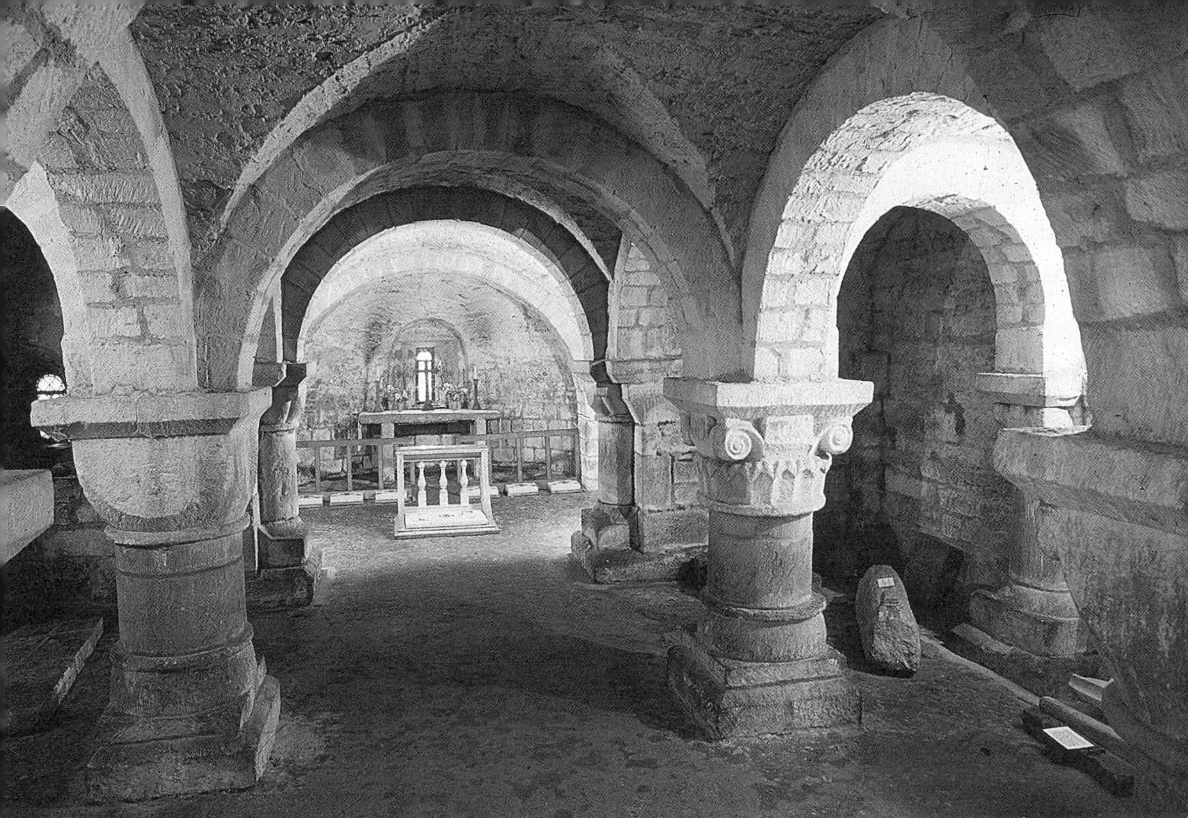

Preserved beneath the parish church of St Mary, Lastingham, North Yorkshire, is the superb Norman crypt of a Benedictine abbey, the building of which was abandoned when the community moved to York. (Courtesy of Derry Brabbs/www.derrybrabbs.com)

transepts. The crypt was completed in 1089, when a synod was held there and the monks moved into Wulfstan's new buildings. A crypt should not to be confused with a CELLARIUM or UNDERCROFT, which was of similar construction but served an entirely domestic purpose. The whole of the east end of the church at Canterbury Cathedral Priory is built over crypts. That beneath the choir was built in the late eleventh century (with fine Romanesque capitals to the piers) and extended in the early twelfth century. The other is beneath the Trinity Chapel beyond the High Altar. Both are remarkably spacious and sufficiently high above ground level to be lit by windows.

CULVERY *see* DOVECOTE

CUPBOARDS *see* AUMBRY, CHEST CUPBOARDS *and* CREDENCE

CUPOLA A small, circular or polygonal DOME crowning a roof or turret.

CURATE *see* CLERGY (CHURCH OF ENGLAND)

CURE OF SOULS Responsibility for the spiritual well-being of the common people.

CURIA (i) The papal court and its functionaries. (ii) The outer court of a religious house (*see* PRECINCT).

CURTILAGE (*also* COURTLEDGE) The monastic department responsible for the production of vegetables (*see also* LARDER).

CURVILINEAR *see* MEDIEVAL ARCHITECTURE *and* TRACERY

CUSHION CAPITAL *see* BLOCK CAPITAL

CUSP In architectural decoration the point at which two curved shapes intersect. In Gothic tracery a projecting point between two lobes of a TREFOIL, QUATREFOIL, etc. (*see* FOILS).

CUSPING A decorative feature consisting of a projection formed at the intersection of two arcs.

CUSTODIANS (CUSTODES ORDINIS) In larger houses, officials responsible for maintaining order and attending to SECURITY, including in their number (for example) the custodians of the cloister and the circators (*see* CIRCATOR). Known collectively as the *custodes ordinis*, they convened before CHAPTER in order to determine which cases of indicipline should be brought before the community.
See also DISCIPLINE

CUSTOMARY *or* CUSTUMAL (i) A customary or custumal is the book (*Liber Ordinarius*) containing the regulations and customs (the *observances*) of a particular religious community, supplementing the more general principles set out in the RULE of an order. A customary is often referred to as 'the observances' of (e.g.) Barnwell Priory.
(ii) The book containing the rites and ceremonies for services. Sometimes the two were combined in a single book.

D

DAILY ROUND, THE *see* HORARIUM

DARK AGES, THE The sixth-century British cleric Gildas described the destruction of his country by the German barbarians:

> Swords glinted all around, and the flames crackled. Foundation stones of high walls that had been torn from their lofty base, holy altars, fragments of corpses, covered as it were with a purple crust of congealed blood, looked as though they had been mixed up in some dreadful wine press.

It was inevitable that centuries of conquest and bloody resistance should acquire the epithet 'barbarous'. But this is the obverse side of the sun and, obscure though our vision of the *Dark Ages* may be, that which has been revealed to us is of a brilliant intensity.

The ancient kingdom of Northumbria was 'a land of art and culture, a haven of learning and skill' which in the seventh century became the force that first united England into a single realm. Most of this cultural creativity emanated from the Church, and from the monastic foundations in particular. The monasteries of Northumberland and Kent produced the finest illuminated manuscripts, using pigments imported from as far afield as the Himalayas. In churches, Anglo-Saxon artists established a unique and highly influential school of sculpture, while England's first poets created epic poetry that marked the beginnings of English literature. This was the age of the *Codex Amiatinus*, the world's oldest surviving Latin Bible. Weighing 75lb and requiring the skins of five hundred calves for its VELLUM pages, it was (probably) made at the monastery of Monkwearmouth (Tyne and Wear) as a gift for the pope in 716. This was the age of England's first major historian, the Venerable Bede, who produced his *History of the English Church and People* in 731; of the magnificent illuminated *Lindisfarne Gospels* and of the mystical St Cuthbert, whose beautifully carved wooden coffin may still be seen at Durham Cathedral together with an array of superb Anglo-Saxon treasures: the products, not of obscurity and barbarity, but of a highly sophisticated and cultured people.
See also ANGLO-SAXON CHURCH *and* CELTIC CHURCH

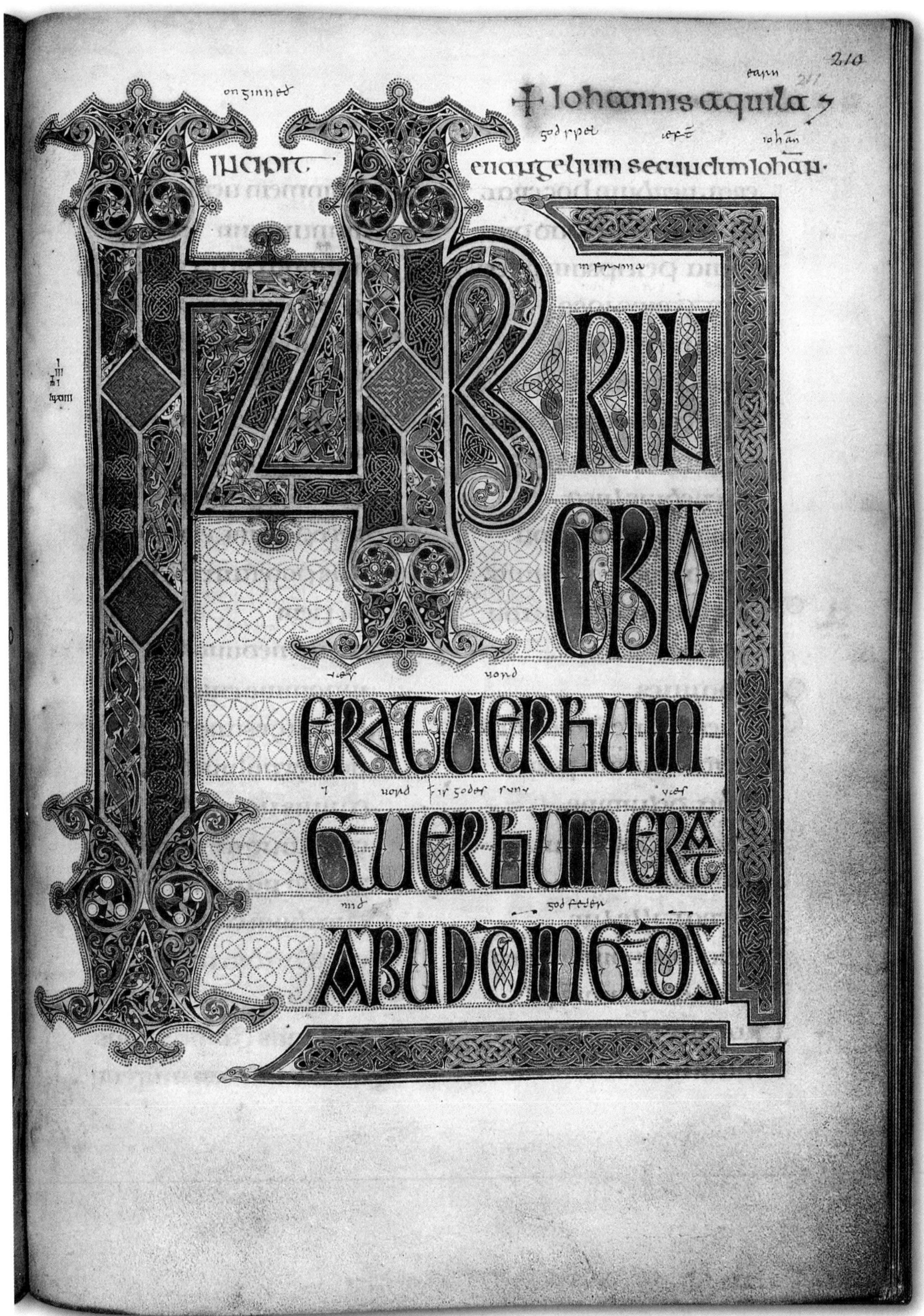

A page from the Lindisfarne Gospels: In principio erat verbum et verbum erat apud d[eu]m . . . (In the beginning was the Word. And the Word was with God . . .). (Record no: c2175–06, Cotton Nero D. IV, f.211 © British Library)

DAUGHTER HOUSE A subsidiary house of a major monastic community. Early daughter houses were established as a result of successful missions (usually consisting of twelve monks and a SUPERIOR) that achieved not only the conversion but also the active support of native ruling families, whose endowments provided for the building of a monastery and the means to maintain it. In the Middle Ages, many daughter houses were founded simply because a mother house had expanded beyond its resources, appeals to the medieval establishment almost invariably resulting in substantial benefactions and endowments. Initially, a mother house retained control over the activities of its daughter houses, which usually began as priories, although many eventually became independent and some (e.g. Cistercian Fountains) achieved even greater prestige and influence than the houses that had founded them. A number of parish churches are associated with former daughter houses: the Benedictine abbey of St Albans in Hertfordshire, for example, had eight daughter houses (and two dependent houses of nuns), of which Binham in Norfolk (the nave) and Hatfield Peverel in Essex (part of the nave) remain in use as parish churches.
See also ALIEN PRIORY *and* MONASTERY

DAY HOURS The services of LAUDS, PRIME, TERCE, SEXT, NONE, VESPERS and COMPLINE.

DAY ROOM In some houses, the equivalent of the PARLOUR and used for restrained recreational purposes; in others, a novitiates' schoolroom or a warming house (*see* CALEFACTORIUM). In Cistercian houses, the day room was reserved for those brethren who were required to carry out manual labour in the confines of the cloister. The day room at Fountains Abbey was a long chamber entered from the south-east corner of the east cloister alley. It was once vaulted in seven double bays from a central row of piers.

DAY STAIR The stair from the CLOISTER to the monks' dormitory (*see* DORTER). The day stair was

The day stair at Byland Abbey, North Yorkshire. (Jeremy Richards/© English Heritage Photo Library)

usually located near the CHAPTER HOUSE, although the position varied considerably from one monastery to another, depending on the construction of the CLAUSTRAL buildings and the custom of a particular order: the Cistercians, for example, usually located the day stair at the junction of the east and south alleys. In Cistercian houses, the lay brothers had their own dorter and stairs. It was the custom that those monks who were descending gave way to those who were ascending.

DE HAERETICO COMBURENDO A statute of 1401 by which those found guilty of HERESY in an ecclesiastical court were handed over to the secular authority to be burned at the stake.

DEACON *see* CLERGY (CHURCH OF ENGLAND) *and* SUB-DEACON

DEACONESS *see* CLERGY (CHURCH OF ENGLAND)

DEAN *see* CLERGY (CHURCH OF ENGLAND)

DEANERY The official residence or office of a DEAN.

DEATH *see* BURIALS (MONASTIC)

DEATH'S HEAD In memorials, a sculptured or engraved skull symbolising death and, by implication, both its commonality and ultimate victory through resurrection. Most death's heads date from the late fifteenth century to the eighteenth, during which period there was a preoccupation with the inevitability of death and an almost culpable desire to acknowledge, *in memoriam*, the transient nature of privilege and wealth. Many variations are to be found: some have bats' wings and others are carried by figures of children to indicate infant mortality.

DECANI Literally, the place 'of the dean', the term is used to describe those who, in antiphonal singing, occupy the stalls to the south of the choir (*see* CANTORIS *and* SUCCENTOR). It would appear that the medieval practice was for the two sides (*cantoris* and *decani*) to change places on alternate weeks. In today's cathedrals it is the trebles who sit in the decanal stalls who usually sing the higher part in antiphonal singing.
See also ANTIPHON, CHOIR, CHURCH MUSIC *and* STALLS

DECLINE OF THE MONASTERIES *see* MONASTIC DECLINE

DECORATED INITIAL In MANUSCRIPT ILLUMINATION, a VERSAL LETTER which has been embellished by the use of coloured inks and gilding.

DECORATED PERIOD *see* MEDIEVAL ARCHITECTURE

DEFENDER OF THE FAITH (FIDEI DEFENSOR) Pope Leo X conferred the title on HENRY VIII in 1521 in recognition of his treatise defending the doctrine of the Seven Sacraments. It was confirmed by parliament as an official title of the English sovereign in 1544 and has remained so to this day.

DELEGATES, COURT OF The court which considers appeals against decisions of the Prerogative Courts of Canterbury and York (*see also* ARCHES, COURT OF *and* CHANCERY, COURT OF).

DENIZATION The granting of the privileges of naturalisation to an alien, including the right to purchase and devise land (which was forbidden to aliens), but excluding the right to inherit land or to receive grants of land from the Crown. Alien priories could apply for a royal charter (in return for a substantial fee) by which they terminated all financial obligations to a foreign mother house, in return for freedom from the restrictions and penal taxation that were normally applied. It was also a requirement that a foreign SUPERIOR be replaced

by an Englishman – indeed, this was often applied to an entire community. Denization records are available for inspection at The National Archives (*see* APPENDIX II) and usually show an immigrant's place of origin.
See also ALIEN PRIORY

DESKS In churches, the term 'desk' is generally applied to a piece of furniture comprising a sloping surface on which an open Bible or other large book is supported and angled towards the reader. The most common form of lectern (*see* LECTERN) consists of an eagle carrying a desk on its outspread wings, while others may have double desks, back-to-back and with decorative gabled ends and candleholders. PULPITS also have desks, although these are usually smaller and are more correctly described as *bookplates*. They are quite often attached to an adjustable stem that is affixed to the inside of the pulpit drum. *Pulpit desks* often support a fall of the appropriate liturgical colour. A *litany desk* is intended for the recitation of the LITANY and incorporates a kneeler, as does a PRIE-DIEU which is a small prayer-desk for private devotions.
See also CREDENCE *and* MISSAL STAND

DETACHED BELFRIES *see* TOWERS

DEXTER *see* POINTS OF THE SHIELD

DIAPER In medieval architecture, a surface decoration of diamond-shaped patterns.

DIET *see* FRATER

DINNER *see* FRATER

DIOCESAN REGISTRY The official archive of a diocese, which may now be held at a county record office. Material includes details of church and cathedral administration, chapter books, BISHOPS' TRANSCRIPTS, visitation books, tithes, land holdings, probate, Compton Census returns and marriage licences.

DIOCESE A diocese is an ecclesiastical administrative territory comprising archdeaconries, rural deaneries and parishes, all subject to the jurisdiction (*bishopric*) of a bishop. In the Church of England the Crown gives a Dean and CHAPTER leave to elect a bishop, and nominates the person to be elected. A *see* is the official 'seat' of a bishop and is normally located in the cathedral (*cathedra* = 'throne') of the diocese (*see* CATHEDRALS).
See also CLERGY (CHURCH OF ENGLAND)

Medieval Dioceses
By the beginning of the ninth century episcopal sees had been established at Iona, Abercorn, Whithorn, Lindisfarne, Hexham, York, Sidnacester, Lichfield, Hereford, Leicester, Elmham, Worcester, Dorchester (Oxfordshire), Dunwich, Sherborne, Winchester, London, Rochester, Selsey and Canterbury.

Following the Norman Conquest, a conciliar decree of 1075 required that sees should be removed from rural sites to urban centres. Sherborne, for example, was transferred to Old Sarum, an ancient hilltop site to the north of present-day Salisbury, where a new cathedral and castle were built as part of a scheme which effectively remodelled an already thriving Saxon burgh to form a Norman city. Similarly, the cathedral church at remote North Elmham in Norfolk was abandoned in favour first of Thetford and then of Norwich. (Elmham's humble cathedral was converted into a moated hunting lodge, the scant remains of which were unearthed as recently as 1903.)

At the end of the thirteenth century the English dioceses comprised: Canterbury (founded in 597), London (604), Rochester (604), York (625), Winchester (662), Lichfield (669), Hereford (676), Worcester (*c.* 680), Bath and Wells (909), Durham (995), Exeter (1050), Lincoln (1072), Chichester (1075), Salisbury (1078), Sodor and Man (before 1080), Norwich (1091), Ely (1109) and Carlisle (1133); and in Wales: Bangor, St David's and Llandaff (all *c.* 550) and St Asaph (1143) (*see* MEDIEVAL CHURCH *and* WALES, THE MEDIEVAL CHURCH IN).

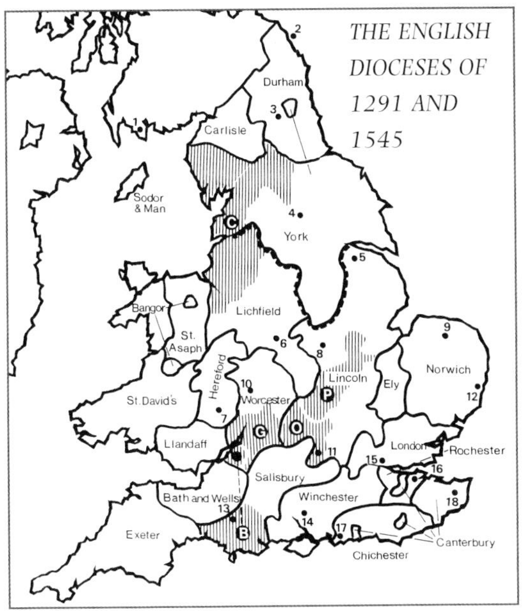

THE ENGLISH DIOCESES OF 1291 AND 1545

Anglo-Saxon Episcopal Sees

1 *Withorn*
2 *Lindisfarne*
3 *Hexham*
4 *York*
5 *Sidnacester*
6 *Lichfield*
7 *Hereford*
8 *Leicester*
9 *Elmham*
10 *Worcester*
11 *Dorchester (Oxon)*
12 *Dunwich*
13 *Sherborne*
14 *Winchester*
15 *London*
16 *Rochester*
17 *Selsey*
18 *Canterbury*

The dioceses of 1291, together with those created in 1541–5 (shaded):

C *Chester*
P *Peterborough*
G *Gloucester*
B *Bristol*
O *Oxford*

Post-Reformation Dioceses

Following the DISSOLUTION OF THE MONASTERIES a number of the English dioceses were subdivided to create a further five: Chester (1541), Peterborough (1541), Gloucester (1541), Bristol (1542) and Oxford (1545). Of these, Chester encompassed the western third of the dioceses of York and Lichfield; the creation of Peterborough and Oxford in a narrow, diagonal band across the vast diocese of Lincoln effectively divided it in two, much of the southern half being incorporated in the later diocese of St Albans (1877). Gloucester was created out of the southern half of the diocese of Worcester and the new diocese of Bristol comprised a small area north of the city, together with a large detached 'island' to the south, transferred from the diocese of Salisbury, and corresponding almost exactly to the old county of Dorset. A sixth diocese, with the Abbey of Westminster as its cathedral, lasted for only a decade, from 1540–50.

No further sees were established between 1546 and 1836, but since then twenty new dioceses have been created in response to the rapid expansion of the urban population during the Industrial Revolution and the proliferation of suburban conurbations in the present century.

Provinces

An association of dioceses is a *province* over which one of the diocesan bishops presides as archbishop. There are two English provinces: that of Canterbury, consisting of all the dioceses south of the river Trent, and that of York, which includes the remaining dioceses to the north. The Province of Wales was created out of the Province of Canterbury in 1920, and two new dioceses formed (*see* WALES, THE MEDIEVAL CHURCH IN).

Diocesan records, deposited in the ARCHIVES of diocesan registries, have mostly been transferred to county record offices.

See also CLERGY (CHURCH OF ENGLAND)

DIPTYCH (i) An altarpiece consisting of a folding pair of pictures or tablets depicting religious themes and sometimes recording genealogical and heraldic information. Many of the finest medieval diptychs originated as portable altars in royal and magnate households (*see* TRIPTYCH).
(ii) Lists of names of living and departed Christians for whom prayers are offered.

DIRGE A lament for the dead, the term originated in the Office of the Dead which included the ANTIPHON 'Dirige Domine Deus . . .' (Psalm 5: 8).

DISCALCED Bare-footed.

DISCARIUS *see* FRATER

DISCIPLINE Self-discipline was a fundamental principle of the religious life, and in meeting this obligation a monk was supported by the community in which he lived, a community that was itself bound by the 'observances' that defined the RULE of its order (*see* CUSTOMARY). Minor indiscretions were usually dealt with privately. But on those occasions when a member of the community transgressed, it was the community that was distracted from its devotions and it was therefore the community that determined the punishment (*see* ACCUSATIONS *and* CHAPTER). The internal discipline of a house was administered by the SUB-PRIOR, who, in larger houses, shared his responsibilities with the CUSTODIANS. The objective of punishment was reform (only rarely was a brother expelled) and this could vary from reducing his allowance at meal-times to solitary confinement or flagellation with a scourge tipped with lead weights. There are instances of intransigent monks being required to prostrate themselves at the church door so that the brethren had to step over them; of beatings with canes (*ferules*); of the imposition of total silence, even in choir and chapter; and (in a lighter vein) of requiring a querulous monk to wear shoes in which dried peas were placed.

DISSOLUTION OF THE CHANTRIES (1547) *see* CHANTRY

DISSOLUTION OF THE MONASTERIES (1536 and 1539) With the notable exception of the CARTHUSIANS and the Observant Franciscans (*see* FRIARS), by the fourteenth century the ascetic fervour of the religious houses had diminished significantly. There is widespread evidence of a relaxation of the observances (*see* CUSTOMARY) to accommodate the inevitable strains of life in a closed community and of a general preference for comfortable continuity rather than austerity and piety. But evidence of corpulence is not evidence of corruption and this decline in the monastic ideal was far removed from the accusations of improbity and decadence with which the monasteries were later to be charged. Indeed, there appears to have been an attempt at reform in the early sixteenth century, but by then it was already too late: the findings of Henry VIII's commissioners were predetermined. Monastic communities were by no means immune to criticism in the late Middle Ages, but it was in order to appropriate their considerable wealth and to facilitate the establishment of the royal supremacy that Henry VIII demolished the entire system (*see* AUGMENTATION, COURT OF).

The Lesser Monasteries

In 1536 the Act for the Dissolution of the Smaller Monasteries required the suppression of all religious houses with fewer than twelve monks or nuns and an annual value of less than £200 so that 'His Majesty should have and enjoy . . .' all their possessions. The annual revenues recorded in the VALOR ECCLESIASTICUS of 1535 varied considerably from one religious house to another. In Wales, for example, the abbey of Tintern was later assessed at £192, while the tiny priory of Caldey was assessed at only £5. Gilbertine Houses were specifically exempted from the 1536 Act and others (over seventy) were allowed to purchase exemptions at some considerable cost, although in all instances the reprieve was short-lived. Government policy was not necessarily one of outright confiscation; commissioners deliberately sought out vulnerability and exploited it, so that monastic communities were steadily persuaded to surrender. Confessions of sinful conduct and incompetent management were the usual instruments by which surrender was effected, and should not be taken at face value: 'forasmuch as manifest sin, vicious, carnal and abominable living is daily used and committed among the little and small abbeys, priories and other religious houses of monks, canons and nuns . . .'. The commissioners themselves were often under considerable pressure from members of the nobility and gentry who happened to covet a particular monastic estate and who were known to enjoy royal patronage. At the same time, the often rich and famous shrines were being dismantled: that of St Thomas à Becket at Canterbury was stripped of its encrusted gold, silver and jewels, which were carried away in wagonloads.

The Greater Monasteries

The Act for the Dissolution of the Greater Monasteries (of 1539) vested in the Crown all the properties so far surrendered and all remaining eligible monasteries and their vast estates. The Act did not in fact sanction dissolution per se, but, rather, safeguarded the Crown's title to the proceeds. Those who would not comply soon found themselves isolated and facing expulsion, attainder and even execution. Many were themselves tried and convicted of stealing from their own abbeys: on 15 November 1539, Richard Whyting, abbot of the most venerable monastic foundation in England, was hanged, drawn and quartered on the summit of Glastonbury Tor for refusing to release the abbey plate. Others were more acquiescent: John Blake, abbot of Cirencester Abbey (at the time the wealthiest Augustinian house in England) retired happily to Fairford with an annual pension of £200 – a substantial sum that enabled him to see out his days in comfort. After a short and often brutal finale, which included the barbarous execution of nearly all the Carthusians, the process of dispossession and dispersal was completed in 1540 and most of the religious brethren were pensioned off (though the FRIARS were not) or provided with licences to become incumbents of parish benefices.

Perhaps the most significant aspect of the Dissolution was that it was effected with so little opposition, the principal exception being the northern rebellion of 1536–7, known as the 'PILGRIMAGE OF GRACE', which was chiefly concerned with the conduct and policies of the government, of which the suppression of the lesser monasteries was but one element. No doubt the fact that the breach with Rome was essentially unopposed by the monastic orders in England facilitated the process: the dispersed brethren were not perceived as loyal adherents of the papacy and the laity readily accepted the Dissolution. The public had also been prepared for the expropriation of monastic property: preachers were commissioned to denounce the monks as 'hypocrites, sorcerers and idle drones' and to declare that 'if the abbeys went down the king would never want for any taxes again'. It is also significant that, although there was nothing to prevent the re-formation of a conventual community, no existing foundation managed to survive after 1540. Of course, the nobility and gentry who, in former times, had endowed the monasteries with gifts of land and money were now the principal beneficiaries of their suppression. But, while the rich became richer, the withdrawal of the social and welfare services provided by the monastic almonries and HOSPITALS must have had a devastating effect on many a local populace.

Destruction and Adaptation

By 1539 explicit orders had been given for the total destruction of all newly surrendered monastic buildings and for the systematic removal of all lead and other materials. Total demolition (an expensive operation) was not always achieved: comprehensive ruination invariably was. Many dilapidated buildings provided accessible supplies of ashlar and rubble for local builders, particularly in those areas (such as East Anglia) where supplies of building stone were scarce. Because of their inherent remoteness, many of the great Cistercian abbeys, such as Tintern in Monmouthshire and Fountains in North Yorkshire, were less vulnerable to plundering and remain as gaunt, skeletal

Cistercian Forde Abbey, Dorset, was dissolved in 1539. The church was destroyed but some domestic quarters survive in the seventeenth-century mansion, notably the chapter house (now a chapel), frater, dorter and kitchen. (Courtesy of Forde Abbey)

memorials to monastic exclusiveness. The twelve pre-Norman monastic cathedrals retained both their diocesan status and their lands, which were administered by a dean and chapter. Westminster Abbey became a collegiate royal PECULIAR with a dean and secular canons and, from 1540–50, was a diocesan cathedral. The new dioceses created out of the Dissolution ensured the survival as CATHEDRALS of the great medieval abbey churches of Bristol, Chester, Gloucester, Oxford and Peterborough (*see* DIOCESE). Nearly a hundred monastic churches, whose naves had long been parish churches, were retained, while others, such as Tewkesbury in Gloucestershire and Sherborne in Dorset, were purchased by local benefactors or acquired for parochial use through diocesan intervention. But such churches were invariably deprived of their claustral and domestic buildings and at some, transepts, chapels and even choirs were demolished. When monastic buildings were sold into private hands, the great church was often the first component to be destroyed. Only rarely was a church small enough to provide comfortable domestic accommodation, as at Buckland in Devon. Elsewhere, the Tudor gentry, attracted, as their monastic predecessors had been, to fertile, sheltered and beautiful locations, adapted former abbots' lodgings and gatehouses as family residences and retained the monastery kitchens, cellars, barns and outhouses, as at Beaulieu in Hampshire and Forde Abbey in Dorset. The buildings of Malmesbury Abbey in Wiltshire were acquired by a clothier and converted into a factory while the church, in part, was retained for parochial use.

Monastic Revenues

Despite the declared intention of the 1536 *Act of Suppression* that the wealth acquired by the monasteries 'for the maintenance of sin' should be 'converted to better uses', the policy of retaining monastic holdings to provide a reliable source of income for the Crown was never maintained. By 1547 the Court of augmentation (*see* AUGMENTATION, COURT OF) had received £1,338,422 from the Dissolution of the Monasteries and other suppressed institutions – a vast sum (to which should be added numerous payments for bribes, commissions and fees) and yet, by the end of his reign, Henry had squandered it all (*see* VALOR ECCLESIASTICUS). The only real beneficiaries were the 'new' Tudor gentry: the post-medieval class of ambitious and successful men who, through the acquisition of monastic estates, were able more quickly to establish their credentials. Estates were valued at twenty times the assessed value of the lands, properties and tithes to be sold, and were transferred to their new owners with comparative ease. Most were already organised in manors, administered by professional bailiffs who were unaffected by the change: few were demesne lands. When Elizabeth I ascended the throne in 1558, only a quarter of the estimated £150,000 income once available annually to the religious foundations remained in Crown hands.

See also REFORMATION, THE

DIURNAL The service book containing the DAY HOURS.

DIVINE OFFICE Described by St Benedict as the *Opus Dei* (God's work), the divine office was the duty owed to God by all members of a religious community. Inspired by Psalm 119: 164 'Seven times a day do I praise thee', it consisted of the Day Hours (services) of LAUDS (at daybreak), PRIME, TERCE, SEXT, NONE, VESPERS and COMPLINE, to which were added the long Night Hours of NOCTURN or MATTINS, all of which were sung in the CHOIR of the abbey church (*see* HOURS (CANONICAL)). This constant round of prayer was the essence of the monastic life, but in addition to the daily masses and the Hours the community also prayed for the souls of the founders and BENEFACTORS of their house and for the good estate of the living – effectively functioning as a foundation CHANTRY. A time was also reserved before each office for private prayer, while much meditative reading in the FRATER, CHAPTER, etc. was inevitably reflective.

See also BREVIARY, HORARIUM *and* LITURGY

DIVINE SERVICE A term used to describe any authorised form of Christian worship although, strictly speaking, it should be applied only to MATTINS and EVENSONG.

DOCUMENTARY SOURCES *see* ARCHIVES

DOGTOOTH ORNAMENT A form of architectural ornamentation typical of the Gothic work of the late twelfth and early thirteenth centuries. It consists of a horizontal band of raised saltires, the four limbs of which are shaped like leaves (or pointed teeth).
See also MEDIEVAL ARCHITECTURE

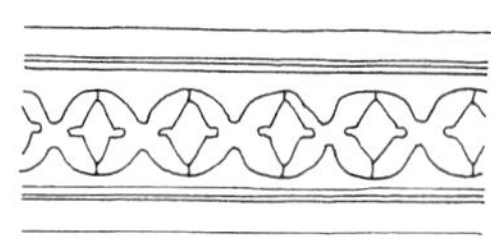

(Tom Friar)

DOLE WINDOW *see* ALMONRY

DOME A convex, rounded roof with a circular, elliptical or polygonal base. In Renaissance architecture the dome was a fundamental characteristic of design, and a variety of constructional forms was adopted. Among these was the *pendentive* which enabled a dome to be carried on free-standing piers. A pendentive is a curved triangle formed by the intersection of a dome with two adjacent arches (*see illustration*). The domical structure created thereby is known as a *sail vault* because it has the appearance of a sail when anchored at the four corners.
See also CUPOLA *and* SQUINCH

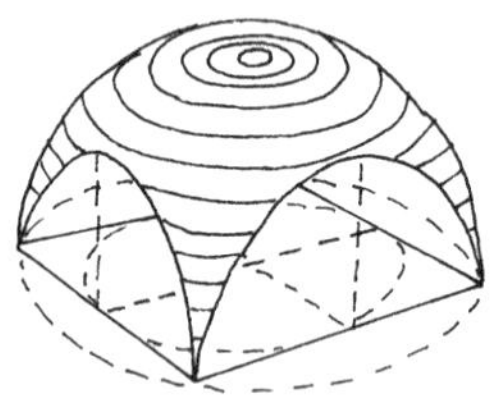

Sail vault. (Tom Friar)

DOMINICANS *see* FRIARS

DOMUS CONVERSORUM The domestic quarters of the lay brethren (*conversi*) of a Cistercian community, usually the WESTERN RANGE of conventual buildings. With the decline of the conversi in the fourteenth century, the building was often put to an alternative use: at Hailes Abbey, for example, where it became the abbot's lodging.
See also LAY BROTHERS

DONOR WINDOW A window donated to a church by a benefactor or group of BENEFACTORS (*see* WINDOWS).

DOOR-KEEPER *see* PORTER

DOORWAYS The great west doors of major monastic and collegiate churches were rarely used, indeed at several abbeys (such as Brinkburn in Northumberland, Buildwas in Shropshire, Cartmel in Lancashire and Romsey in Hampshire) there is no western doorway. They were used only on ceremonial occasions, such as the arrival of a new abbot, a visiting bishop or royalty and for Palm Sunday PROCESSIONS. Access to the nave was more usually by means of two doors from the CLOISTER which were provided for processional purposes and, in some cases, for the separate admission of the *conversi* from the LAY BROTHERS' claustral buildings to their church in the nave. There may also have been a separate entrance for the public when the church was used for parochial purposes. This is sometimes on the north side of the nave but is more usually to the west, beyond the cloister, and was often provided with a porch in which certain lay ceremonies took place (*see* PORCHES). There are examples at Malmesbury Abbey in Wiltshire and Great Malvern Priory in Worcestershire, both of which have survived as parish churches.

DORMITORY *see* DORTER

DORSAL (*or* DOSSAL) A fabric screen at the back of an altar.

DORSE The reverse side of a document.
See also ENDORSEMENT

DORTER (DORMITORIUM) In the CLAUSTRAL buildings of a monastery, the dorter was the first-floor monks' dormitory, usually (though not invariably) situated on the east side of the CLOISTER, from which it was reached by means of a DAY STAIR. Except in Cluniac houses (*see* CLUNIACS), a NIGHT STAIR led directly from the north end of the dorter to the TRANSEPT of the abbey church, and it was by this that the monks descended at midnight to attend the early offices, returning to the dorter at two or three in the morning, to sleep again until dawn. The rule of St Benedict only hints at the rigours of being awakened in the small hours: 'and when they rise for the service of God, they shall exhort each other mutually with moderation on account of the excuses that those who are sleepy are inclined to make'.

The dorter was a long, open room, illuminated throughout the night by a single light, with a series of low windows, possibly one for each of the bedsteads that were arranged along the outer walls. In a number of larger communities the dormitory range extended to the south beyond the cloister: at Benedictine Glastonbury, for example, at the Cluniac priory of Wenlock and at several Cistercian abbeys such as Furness, Neath, Tintern, Rievaulx and Fountains. Rievaulx's dorter was 75m long (245ft) and 10.3m wide (34ft), large enough to accommodate 140 monks in the 1160s, while that at Fountains was over 60m in length (197ft). (The shortening of the dormitory at Rievaulx by 30m (99ft) in the late fourteenth century is indicative of a reduction in the size of

Thirteenth-century dorter range at Forde Abbey, Dorset, where the monks' dormitory with its narrow lancet windows was built above a vaulted undercroft.

the community at that time.) Most unusually, at the Augustinian priory of Kirkham the canons' dorter was located not on the upper floor of the EASTERN RANGE, but on the same level as the cloister – because of the fall of the ground to the south. It, too, extended beyond the cloister, the southern half supported on a vaulted UNDERCROFT.

Privacy was considered to be an unnecessary luxury in many orders, as was any form of heating in the dorter, although several monastic houses eventually partitioned the dormitories to form cubicles, and warming houses were sometimes provided in the vicinity of the day stair so that the rising heat would give some relief from the cold and damp of the dorter above (*see* CALEFACTORIUM). Originally, the SUPERIOR slept in the dorter, but with the increasing responsibilities of his office (and a gradual relaxation of the rule) he withdrew into a separate chamber and, eventually, into his own lodgings. The SACRIST usually slept at the north end of the dorter, close to the abbey muniment room or TREASURY, for which he was responsible, and so that he could attend to the clock in the south transept by which he regulated the times of the offices in the church. Monks slept in their habits, except for the outer garment, on pallets: 'for bedding, let this suffice: a mattress, a blanket, a coverlet and a pillow' (Rule of St Benedict). Summoned by a bell before midnight, they rose, tidied their beds and dressed by the light of cressets (*see* LIGHTS) before entering the church by the night stair.

While the location of the dorter in the eastern range of the claustral buildings was the norm, there were exceptions. At Benedictine Durham it was in the WESTERN RANGE, as was the case at Worcester (also Benedictine), where there was a problem with supplying water to the REREDORTER (latrine) which adjoined the dorter (*see below*). At the Premonstratensian abbey of Easby the original canons' dorter was abandoned when a new western range was built in the thirteenth century. This was a three-storey building constructed against the rising slope of the river valley, so that its middle floor opened on to the cloister at ground level. The new dorter was on the upper floor, together with the prior's SOLAR, which extended south beyond the line of the refectory.

Adjacent to the dorter, and usually at right angles to it, was the reredorter or 'house of easement' (otherwise known as the *necessarium* or 'necessary house'). This was the monks' latrine, usually a long, narrow room furnished with divisions and wooden seats, venting into a channel beneath which was cleansed by flowing water (*see also* PLUMBING, WATER SUPPLY AND SANITATION).

In Cistercian houses, the larger lay brothers' dormitory was located at the opposite (western) side of the cloister, or in an entirely separate building. The west range at Fountains Abbey, the largest and best preserved twelfth-century lay brothers' quarters in Europe, was 91.5m (300ft) long. With half its length extending to the south of the cloister, it was open from end to end and provided accommodation for as many as four hundred lay brethren.

Regrettably, the upper storeys of most claustral buildings were demolished following the Dissolution and few dorters or reredorters have survived. The dorter at the Cistercian abbey of Cleeve in Somerset is a notable exception, although the roof is not original and dates to the seventeenth or eighteenth century. Today, as in the thirteenth century, the dormitory is a single open room, built to house about thirty-six monks, with ranges of lancet windows which were closed by wooden shutters. Traces of original limewash, painted with a red masonry pattern, suggest that the whole room must once have been similarly decorated and would, therefore, have been much lighter than it is today. Two later fireplaces have been inserted in the east wall and the window sills have been provided with seats. At the south end of the east wall is the doorway to the latrine, rebates in the arch head suggesting that the double doors were so arranged that there was a 'one-way' system that required the monks to enter on one side and leave by the other (there was a similar arrangement at Kirkham Priory and separate 'In' and 'Out' doors at Rievaulx). At the Dissolution, the magnificent Cistercian abbey of Forde in Dorset was abandoned, and remained a romantic ruin until 1649, when it was bought by Edmund Prideaux, Attorney-General to Oliver Cromwell, who set about transforming it into a 'palazzo' in the Italian style. Of the conventual buildings, the splendid thirteenth-century dorter range remains, its undercroft converted to a tea room for visitors to Prideaux's elegant mansion (*see* DISSOLUTION OF THE MONASTERIES).

See also EASTERN RANGE, LAVATORIUM, MONASTERY *and* UNDERCROFT

DOUBLE MONASTERY A common feature of early monasticism, a double order was a religious foundation of both men and women. Some were nunneries served by resident chaplains while others, such as those of the early twelfth-century order of *Fontrevault*, comprised distinct communities of men and women living in a double monastery under a common SUPERIOR. The two sexes occupied separate but contiguous establishments and worshipped in distinct parts of a common church, often on either side of a central dividing wall. There were five houses of the Fontrevault order in England, all of which were alien priories (*see* ALIEN PRIORY). Of these, one failed within a few years of its foundation while the others became Benedictine nunneries at the end of the fourteenth century.

The scholarship and piety of the English double monasteries, exemplified by St Hilda's foundation at Whitby, came to be widely regarded throughout Europe. Whitby's community was destroyed by the Danes in 867, while other double orders were

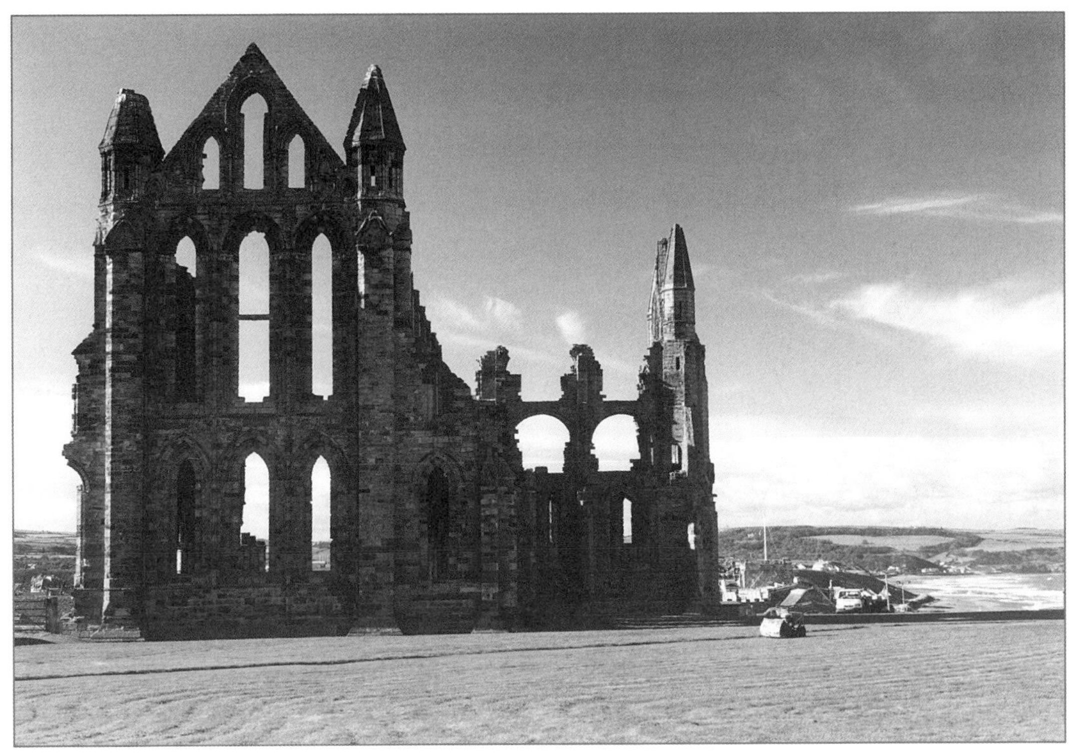

Whitby Abbey, North Yorkshire: originally a double monastery of monks and nuns founded by St Hilda in 657.

abandoned under the Benedictine Rule. However, some were later revived, notably by the GILBERTINE ORDER and the BRIGITTINES.

DOVECOTE (COLUMBARIUM) (*also* CULVERY *and* DOVECOT) South of St Michael's church at Garway in Herefordshire is a fine early fourteenth-century circular dovecot built by the Knights Templar with nesting spaces for 666 birds. Very few monastic dovecotes have survived; even that at Penmon on Anglesey (where the former priory church is now the parish church) may have been built in the sixteenth century after the priory had been dissolved. Even so, there can be no doubt that every monastic community once possessed at least one dovecote.

The Romans obtained fresh protein from birds that nested in tower-like dovecotes similar to those that were introduced into England from Normandy in the eleventh century. Medieval dovecotes are usually square or rectangular free-standing buildings of stone or brick or, from the thirteenth century, cylindrical with a conical roof and 'lantern' through which the pigeons (domesticated rock-doves with an instinct for nesting on cliff faces) could come and go as they pleased. The cylindrical shape accommodated a ladder (or pair of ladders) which revolved on central pivots to provide access to the rows of nesting holes that lined the walls. This mechanism, or *potence* (from OE *potent* meaning 'crutch'), was often so well balanced that it could be turned at the touch of a finger, enabling the culverer to remove the *squabs* (young birds not fully fledged) with a minimum of fuss. The general impression inside a dovecote was of a circular brick wall, with alternate bricks removed from floor to roof level. In fact, each hole was larger than two bricks and was several feet deep, to provide ample space for roosting and nesting accommodation for the succession of two-egg clutches produced through most of the year. Many culveries contained more than one thousand nesting holes, and with two pigeons and two young to each there could be up to four thousand birds feeding freely on the tenants' crops! This no doubt accounts for the fact that dovecotes in the medieval period were restricted to demesne and monastic lands, where they represented a significant element in the domestic economy by providing fresh meat and eggs during the winter and a constant supply of droppings (*guano*) which was used as fertiliser.

DRAINS *see* PLUMBING, WATER SUPPLY AND SANITATION

Dovecote on the manor of the almoner of Glastonbury Abbey at Shapwick, Somerset. (By kind permission of James Bond)

DRAWING FLOOR *see* MASTER MASONS AND ARCHITECTS

DRESSED STONE Worked and smoothly finished stone used in architectural features such as doorways and window openings.
See also MASONRY

DRESSER WINDOW In monastic buildings, the serving hatch, sometimes with a ROTA, between kitchen and FRATER, on either side of which was a serving table (*dresser*). There are good examples at Mattersey Priory in Nottinghamshire, where fragments of masonry from the former priory have been incorporated into the parish church, and at Muchelney in Somerset where the parish church forms part of a group with the ruins of the adjoining Benedictine abbey.

DRESSINGS Stones worked to a smooth or moulded edge and set round an architectural feature such as a doorway or window opening.

DRINK *see* FRATER

DRIP COURSE A projecting course of stonework to catch and throw off rainwater.

DRIPSTONE (*also* DRIP-MOULDING, HOOD-MOULDING *and* LABEL) A projecting moulding above an arch, doorway or window to throw off rain. The dripstone corbels (*label-stops*) of exterior windows are often carved as human heads and may assist in dating that part of the building. At Beaumaris, Anglesey, for example, a charming label-stop depicts a woman's head with a wimple, hood and veil, and hair bunched at the temple – all in the style fashionable in the reigns of the Edwardian period (1270–1330) when the church nave was built. At several cathedrals (e.g. Hereford and Gloucester) the heads of well-known members of the diocesan community have been carved into replacement label-stops and corbels (*see* CORBEL).

DRYING ROOM In Cistercian houses, a drying room was sometimes provided for the *conversi* when they returned from their labours in the fields (*see* LAY BROTHERS). Not to be confused with the monks' warming house (*see* CALEFACTORIUM), the drying room was usually located in the south-west corner of the CLOISTER, near the lay brothers' lodgings.

DURHAM, PRINCE BISHOPS OF *see* PALATINATE

EARLY ENGLISH *see* MEDIEVAL ARCHITECTURE

EARLY MASS *or* MORROW MASS *see* MASS

EASTERN RANGE In a monastery, the eastern range of CLAUSTRAL buildings which extends beyond the south (or, occasionally, the north) TRANSEPT of the church. This usually includes the SLYPE (or library in Cistercian houses), CHAPTER HOUSE and warming house (*see* CALEFACTORIUM) on the ground floor with the DAY STAIR (from the cloister) and the NIGHT STAIR (from the transept) leading to the DORTER, REREDORTER and, sometimes, a MUNIMENT ROOM on the floor above.
See also CLOISTER, SOUTH RANGE *and* WESTERN RANGE

ECCLESIASTICAL COURTS *see* COURTS (ECCLESIASTICAL)

ECCLESIASTICAL HAT *see* HERALDRY (ECCLESIASTICAL)

ECCLESIASTICAL HERALDRY *see* HERALDRY (ECCLESIASTICAL)

ECCLESIASTICAL LIBRARIES *see* LIBRARIES
For the addresses of the following ecclesiastical libraries *see* APPENDIX II: Canterbury Cathedral, Carlisle Cathedral, Church Commissioners, Exeter Cathedral, Gloucester Cathedral, Hereford Cathedral, Lambeth Palace, Norwich Cathedral, Peterborough Cathedral, St George's Chapel (Windsor Castle), St Paul's Cathedral (London), Salisbury Cathedral, Winchester Cathedral, Worcester Cathedral *and* York Minster.

ECCLESIASTICAL STRONGHOLDS *see* FORTIFICATION

ECCLESIASTICAL VISITATIONS *see* VISITATION (ECCLESIASTICAL)

ECCLESIOLOGY The study of church buildings, furnishings and decoration.

ECONOMY *see* FINANCE

EFFIGIES Figures representing a deceased person have been incorporated in church MONUMENTS since the twelfth century. The earliest effigies were of eminent ecclesiastics, carved in low relief and depicted in a standing position. In the thirteenth century, LAY figures were also represented, usually recumbent and three-dimensional, while two-dimensional figures continued in the form of INCISED SLABS and monumental brasses (*see* BRASSES (MONUMENTAL)). The earliest known military effigy is that of an unidentified knight at the Temple Church in London. Other early examples include those of King John (d. 1216, monument dated 1230) at Worcester Cathedral and William Longespee, Earl of Salisbury (d. 1226) at Salisbury Cathedral. It is generally (though not invariably) true of medieval effigies that they faced the altar: those that no longer do so may have been moved subsequent to their installation.

Through the thirteenth to the fifteenth century most monuments were carved in stone (usually Caen stone or ALABASTER), although there were some notable exceptions, including the late twelfth-century oak effigy of Robert, Duke of Normandy (d. 1134) at Gloucester cathedral.

Early effigies (other than those in magnesium limestone) were usually coated with *gesso* (a mixture of size and whiting) and painted. At Combe Florey in Somerset three cockleshells containing paint were discovered behind an effigy some five centuries after the craftsmen had departed. The effigy of Henry III (d. 1272) at Westminster Abbey was the first of a series of gilt bronze effigies created for members of the English

Effigy of William Longespee, earl of Salisbury (d. 1226), at Salisbury Cathedral.

royal family, a fashion later emulated by Richard Beauchamp, Earl of Warwick (1382–1439) in his effigy at the collegiate church of St Mary, Warwick. This magnificent tomb still retains its gilded *hearse* – a barrel-shaped metal cage originally intended to support candles – and a pall, which was removed only on special occasions. There is evidence to suggest that, while most effigies and brasses were simply stylised representations of a deceased person, splendidly lavish examples such as these were 'based on a likeness'. Indeed, when the fifteenth-century tomb of Sir Richard Croft at Croft Castle in Herefordshire was recently restored, the skulls of Sir Richard and Lady Eleanor were discovered and it was found that their bone structure corresponded precisely to the stone faces of their effigies.

Victorian antiquaries attributed all manner of explanation to the detail of effigial figures: cross-legged knights, for example, were said to indicate castration by the Saracens, while those who were depicted drawing their swords must surely have died in battle. Many effigies include the insignia of chivalric orders, of which the most common is the Order of the Garter. During the first half of the fifteenth century the 'SS' collar of the House of Lancaster appears on many figures, and again during the early Tudor period, often with a pendant of the Portcullis badge. The collar of suns and roses of the House of York is found on effigies dating from the latter half of the fifteenth century, although many were defaced after Henry Tudor's victory at Bosworth in 1485.

Heraldry

Heraldic display was particularly important because it proclaimed identity, lineage and status (*see* HERALDRY) and, with the loss of so many INSCRIPTIONS, a carved crest or shield of arms is often the only surviving clue to the identity of an effigial figure.

Until the middle of the fourteenth century a knight's effigy usually bore a shield and was clothed in an embroidered surcoat on which the arms were carved and painted. The detail of arms carved on shield and tunic may still be visible, depending on the depth of the original carving and the degree of defacement and erosion. Effigies were often richly painted, but surviving contemporary medieval paintwork and gilding is rare, and many figures were refurbished (sometimes inaccurately) at a later date. The early wooden effigy of Robert of Normandy (*see above*) is coloured, but examination of the shields on the sides of the TOMB CHEST reveals that the heraldry is not contemporaneous and it is known that the chest was replaced and

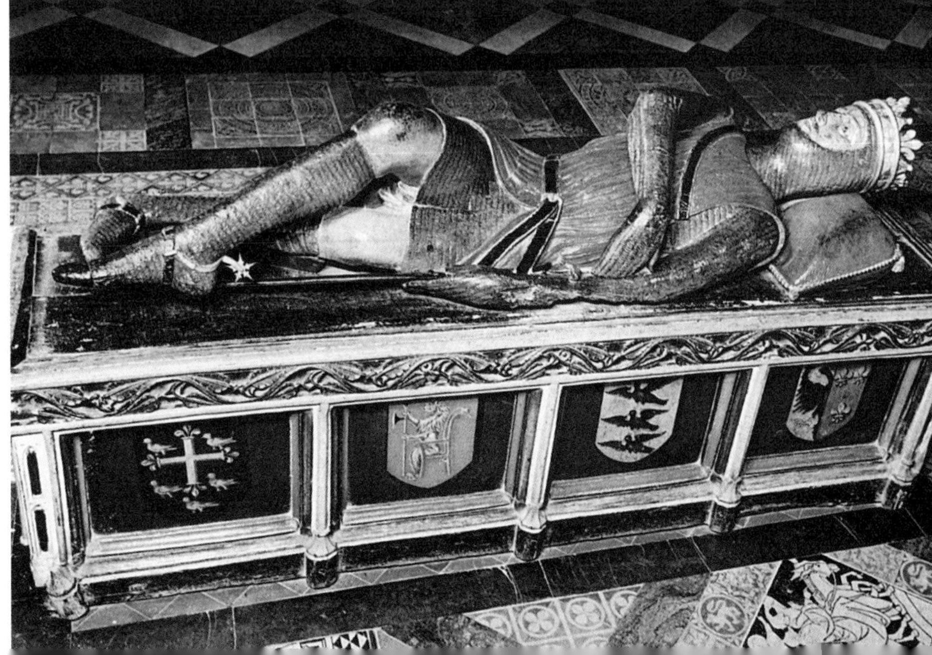

Effigy of Robert Curthose, duke of Normandy (d. 1134), at Gloucester Cathedral (the tomb chest is early thirteenth century). (Courtesy of Geoffrey Wheeler)

the effigy refurbished in the fifteenth century, and again following the Civil War.

From the mid-fourteenth century, shields of arms are more often incorporated into the fabric of the tomb chest or CANOPY and often display multiple quarterings. The importation into Britain of magnificent German and Italian armour during the fifteenth century encouraged a fashion among the nobility for discarding any form of heraldic overmantle, and effigies of the period often reflect this. There was a brief period during the late fifteenth and early sixteenth centuries when the tabard became popular. This garment was emblazoned on the sleeves and body and will be found in some contemporary effigies. The use of heraldry in medieval and Tudor effigies was not merely decorative: heraldic devices were outward and visible symbols of authority and power, and accumulated quarterings and badges conveyed details of ancestry more proudly than any inscription.

Women also bore their marital arms, on a *kirtle* (gown or outer petticoat) or *mantle* (cloak), and these appear in effigies as they would have been worn in life. The earliest example is the effigy of Matilda, Countess of Salisbury (d. 1281) in Worcester Cathedral. She was daughter and heiress of Walter de Clifford and her cloak is powdered with small shields bearing her paternal arms. Between 1280 and 1330 it was usual for women to display their arms on a mantle which was worn on ceremonial occasions. In effigies (and brasses) the sides of the garment fall forward from the shoulders and the quartered or impaled arms are emblazoned with the husband's arms on the dexter (the left when viewed from the front) and the woman's paternal arms on the sinister (the right) – the reverse of when the garment was actually worn, for it was intended to be viewed from the back. Sometimes there are 'missing' quarterings and one may reasonably assume that these are simply not visible. Thereafter, for the remainder of the fourteenth century, a close-fitting kirtle was worn beneath a sleeveless *cote-hardie*, the female equivalent of the jupon, and this was often emblazoned with the impaled marital arms. There are also instances of both mantle and kirtle being used for heraldic display, and in such cases it is always the mantle which bears the husband's arms 'in dominion' over the woman's paternal arms, which were embroidered on her kirtle. In the Tudor period heraldic kirtles and overmantles continued to be depicted in monuments, although kirtles were now loose-fitting and without a waist. But it seems unlikely that such garments continued to be worn after the mid-sixteenth century, even for ceremonial purposes, and their use in effigies and brasses is seen to decline rapidly from this time. Of course, it should be remembered that heraldic costume, as depicted in effigies and brasses, was intended primarily as a vehicle for heraldic display and does not necessarily illustrate a contemporary fashion. Many female effigial figures are dressed in the simple white widow's veil and wimple, sideless cote-hardie and kirtle of a VOWESS, although it is not unusual to find that symbols of rank have been retained – the ducal coronet of a duchess, for example.

The shield and heraldic garment were not the only vehicles for heraldic display: recumbent effigies, both male and female, often have their heads resting on cushions which may incorporate heraldic devices in the embroidery. From the fourteenth century a knight's head normally rested on a helm, to which was attached his crest, with wreath and mantling. Most effigies are depicted with their feet resting on a beast: usually a lion for a man and a dog for a woman. These figures are more often symbolic than heraldic; however, the use of other animals is almost certainly of significance.

See also BRASSES (MONUMENTAL), CAMAIL PERIOD *and* WEEPERS
For Church Monuments Society *see* APPENDIX II.

ELECTION (MONASTIC) Superiors of religious houses were elected by the members of the community, with the sovereign's permission and usually in consultation with the founder (or his successor) (*see* BENEFACTORS) or PATRON. The new

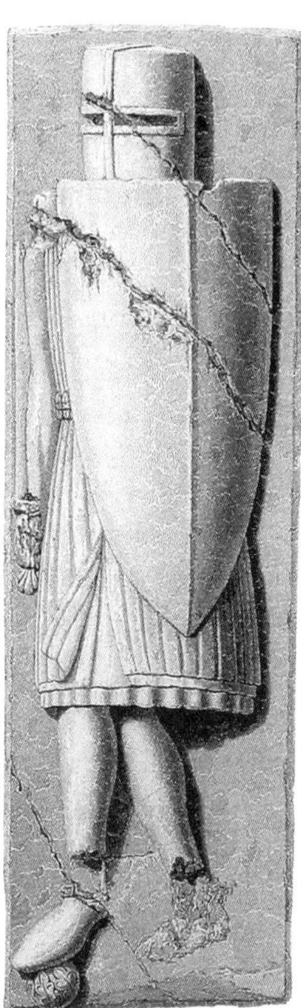

Effigies of benefactors buried in the church at Furness Abbey, Cumbria. (From *Annales Furnesienses* by T.A. Beck, 1844/Society of Antiquaries of London)

SUPERIOR was usually chosen from the more experienced and senior members of the community, although on occasions political appointments were made (usually by the Crown as patron) and members of other communities might also be appointed. Other officials were nominated by the superior.

ELEVATION, THE The raising of each of the sacred elements (*The Host*) at the EUCHARIST immediately following their consecration, a practice which is believed to have originated in the thirteenth century.

EMBRASURE (*also* CRENEL *or* CRENELLE)
(i) An opening between the merlons of an embattled parapet (*see* BATTLEMENT).
(ii) The bevelling of a wall at the sides of a window etc. (*see* SPLAY).

EMBROIDERY In the Middle Ages ecclesiastical vestments (such as copes, chasubles and maniples) were often embroidered, bishops and abbots enjoying the right to embroider their coats of arms on the orphreys of a cope or on the back of a CHASUBLE. Of the thirteenth- and fourteenth-century *Opus Anglicanum*, once the finest body of ecclesiastical needlework in western Europe, very little remains. But that which has survived, usually as fragments made into altar frontals, provides evidence of the wonderful craftsmanship which created the vestments and hangings of the pre-Reformation Church. Such reminders of the mass were anathema in protestant England and, as such, were frequently destroyed, although a number of copes (which were not mass vestments) have survived and are now mostly in museums (*see also* COPE CHEST). The most celebrated example is the late thirteenth-century Syon cope which once belonged to the nuns of Syon Abbey at Isleworth, formerly in Middlesex, and is now at the Victoria and Albert Museum (*see* APPENDIX II).

From the earliest times embroidery was regarded as an occupation suitable for the women of noble families and for nuns, but by the mid-thirteenth century other women also worked as lay professionals. Perhaps the best known of these was one Mabel of Bury St Edmunds, whose skill was highly regarded by Henry III (there are at least two dozen references to her during Henry's reign). By the end of the thirteenth century there were at least six large professional workshops in London employing some sixty or seventy embroiderers and producing both ecclesiastical and secular work. Only the finest materials were used, especially cloth of gold and velvet, with great quantities of gold and silver thread. Christian symbols were popular subjects for embroidery, as were scenes from the life of Christ and the saints, and HERALDRY, which was ideally suited to this medium. It was Henry VII who bequeathed to the Abbot, Prior and Convent of Westminster

> the hoole sute of vestiments and Coopies [copes] of clothe of gold tissue, wrought with our badges of rede Roses and Poortcoleys [portcullises], the which we of late at our propre costs and charges caused to be made, bought and provided at Florence in Italie: that is to say, the hoole Vestements for the Preist, the Deacon and Sub-deacon, and xxix Coopes of the same clothe and worke.

Such vestments and copes were extraordinarily expensive. In this instance the cloth of gold was woven to shape in Florence and made up and embroidered in England by embroiderers (mostly women, who were paid significantly less than men) under the direction of senior craftsmen in the royal workshops. But the importation of richly woven cloths, especially those from Italy, and the haste with which royal commissions had to be completed, served to undermine the embroiderer's craft in the late Middle Ages, so that embroidery was increasingly concentrated on particular areas, such as the orphreys, instead of being applied to the entire outer surface of the garment, as in the thirteenth century.

EMPTOR An agent employed by the KITCHENER to purchase provisions for the kitchen stores.

EMPLOYEES Originally, the Benedictine RULE did not envisage religious houses engaging employees from outside their communities. Each house was 'to live of its own' and this implied providing its own labour, as well as for its spiritual and material needs. Nevertheless, throughout the Middle Ages the number of employees increased steadily in response to changing economic conditions, as income through direct exploitation of resources was replaced by a rent economy (*see* FINANCE) and, particularly in the fourteenth century, as the numbers of LAY BROTHERS declined.

In the greater Benedictine houses, employees (often described as 'servants') sometimes exceeded eighty in number, and their functions, remuneration and status varied considerably. Many were menials, sometimes fugitive serfs protected by sanctuary (*see* SANCTUARY, RIGHT OF); some were freemen, salaried officials, or professionals retained for specific duties; others assisted the OBEDIENTIARIES and some were engaged as stewards, emissaries and legal representatives. Unlike the lay brothers, very few employees lived on the premises, although there is evidence that lodgings were sometimes provided beyond the CURIA for itinerant craftsmen such as bell-makers, plumbers and stone masons. In the later medieval period, other monastic employees might include altar boys, choristers and organists; servants in the FRATER, KITCHENS, ALMONRY, FARMERY, laundry and cellarer's department (*see* CELLARER); porters, millers, warreners, culverers (responsible for the DOVECOTE), gardeners, pig-keepers, shepherds and field-workers; smiths, carpenters, 'soil removers' (those who cleansed the middens), tailors and shoemakers. Nunneries usually engaged larger numbers of servants than male houses, to undertake heavy manual work and to provide protection. Surprisingly, in male houses, some employees were women, although the ordinances insisted that they should be '. . . married, sober, of good repute and honest, that all danger of detraction from evil tongues be avoided'.

In addition, the households of many monastic superiors reflected their status as feudal lords. Each would have his own CHAMBERLAIN and STEWARD, with a staff of liveried attendants, butler, secretaries (usually clerics), cooks, ostlers and servants, and a retinue of armed guards to accompany him on his travels.

ENCAUSTIC TILES The floors of most medieval churches were of compacted earth, clay or chalk and were covered with rushes for warmth and to facilitate cleaning. However, major monastic and collegiate churches were often tiled throughout.

MANUFACTURE

During the thirteenth century several methods were developed for the decoration of plain clay tiles, which were normally fired with a transparent lead glaze to produce a dark red or brown colour, although green glazes were also used. A pattern could be engraved in outline on the surface of the tile, or a design carved in relief or counter-relief on a wood-block which was then pressed into the tile. In both instances the tile was then glazed and fired to produce a patterned tile of one colour. A third method was to fill the matrix of a stamped tile with white pipeclay before it was glazed and fired. This produced the familiar brown and yellow *encaustic tile*. Occasionally the design was reversed, with a dark pattern set into a light coloured tile. Early encaustic tiles are usually 12.5–15cm square (5–6in) and as much as 2.5cm (1in) thick with a 2mm (1/10in) inlay.

By the mid-fourteenth century a flourishing English tile manufacturing industry had been established in the Chilterns, with its centre at Penn

Heraldic floor tiles at Tewkesbury Abbey, Gloucestershire. Top: Despenser, Berkeley, Beauchamp. Centre: Fitzhamon. Bottom: the bear and ragged staff device of the Beauchamps and their successors the earls of Warwick.

in Buckinghamshire. 'Penn' tiles were smaller, only 11.5cm square (4½in) and 2cm thick (¾in). It seems likely that by this time the various stages of manufacture were combined in a single process, the stamp being dipped into *slip* (a fine liquid clay which could be handled like paint) before it was pushed into the malleable tile so that the slip remained in the impression when the stamp was removed. This would explain why the slip is often very thin and some edges of the inlay may be smudged or missing. The inlay was usually flush with the surface of the tile, but a later development in technique resulted in the pattern being slightly concave.

Designs

At first tiles were produced to decorate royal and magnate palaces and important religious houses. During the fourteenth century their use spread to smaller churches and domestic buildings, although in many instances a commonality of design suggests that batches of tiles were leftovers from large monastic commissions and had been donated by a religious house to one or more of its subsidiary churches. Most designs required four tiles to complete a pattern (some required as many as sixteen) and it is often possible to identify individual tiles from a major monastery or cathedral that have been laid down inaccurately in a parish church – possibly because insufficient tiles of each type were provided to complete a pattern, or the workmen were not familiar with it.

Many designs were used in encaustic, relief and counter-relief tiles including geometrical motifs, human and grotesque heads, Christian symbols, rebuses (*see* REBUS) and heraldic devices associated with royal or monastic foundations or with the benefactors of a particular church or chantry chapel. The tiles at Neath Abbey, for example, record graphically the dependence of the house on its Anglo-Norman patrons: the Clare earls and local settler families such as the Turbervilles and the Norreys. Heraldic tiles are a considerable aid to research (*see below*), but not all lions and fleurs-de-lis are of heraldic significance. Confusingly, it is not unusual to find that a heraldic design has been carved correctly on the wood block, but the resultant impression is back to front. Tiled floors in Cistercian houses were generally composed of simple geometrical patterns, in keeping with the austerity of the order.

Medieval Tiles

Examples of medieval tiles remain throughout the country, most notably in the counties of Worcestershire and Devon, although the largest surviving thirteenth-century tiled floor in England is at Winchester Cathedral. Often tiles are not in their original position but have been rescued by nineteenth-century restorers and reset somewhere else in the church. The collection of 1,300 tiles in Great Malvern Priory comprises one of the largest collections in any parish church. Dating (mostly) from 1450–1500, and including one hundred different designs, they adorn both sides of the AMBULATORY screen and are remarkably well preserved. Although some authorities suggest that the tiles were originally made for the walls, the square tiles were placed there during Sir Gilbert Scott's restoration of the church in the 1860s. However, the larger, rectangular, tiles were indeed manufactured as wall tiles, in the kilns that were discovered close to the priory in 1833 and 1902. There was a substantial pottery and tile industry in the Malvern area from at least 500 BC down to the seventeenth century.

For the Tiles and Architectural Ceramics Society *see* APPENDIX II.

ENCLOSURE (MONASTIC) *see* PRECINCT

ENDORSEMENT That which is written on the back (*dorse*) of a document.

ENGAGED Descriptive of columns or piers which are attached to, or partly sunk into, a wall (*see* COLUMN *and* PIER).

ENGLISH ROMANESQUE *see* MEDIEVAL ARCHITECTURE

Above and right: The ambulatory screen at Great Malvern Priory, Worcestershire.

ENGROSSMENT The combining of two or more property holdings.

ENTABLATURE In Classical architecture the horizontal members above a column i.e. the ARCHITRAVE, frieze and CORNICE.

ENTAIL To bequeath an estate inalienably to a specified succession of beneficiaries.

EPISCOPACY (i) A system of Church government by bishops.
(ii) The office of bishop and the period during which such an office is held.
(iii) The bishops collectively.

EPISCOPATE The office of bishop.

EPISCOPI Latinised place-name element applied to a MANOR which was once held by a bishop.

Bishops Caundle in Dorset (until recently Caundle Bishop – the last road sign was removed in 1989) and before that Caundle Episcopi, was once held by the bishop of Sarum. (*See* LATIN)

EPITAPHS From the Greek *epitaphion* (*epi* 'upon' and *taphos* 'a tomb'), epitaphs are commemorative INSCRIPTIONS on gravestones and MONUMENTS and are of interest not only for the genealogical information they contain, but also because they epitomise contemporary social and religious attitudes.

Medieval TOMBS were themselves indicative of a man's status and dignity: the HERALDRY on EFFIGIES and BRASSES declaring his identity, lineage and authority more effectively than any epitaph. Inscriptions were usually in Latin (though some early brasses are inscribed in Norman French) and contained the briefest of details – name, dates and a religious aphorism – all modestly contained within the overall design of the monument. The tomb decorations of those who were not ARMIGEROUS sometimes included personal devices such as merchants' marks or the symbols of favourite saints. Medieval man acknowledged the commonality of death and was preoccupied with salvation. This is reflected in the monuments of the period, which are often rich but rarely ostentatious, and in simple expressions of piety and humility.

The materialism of late Tudor society is evident in many sixteenth-century monuments, which became increasingly elaborate, with exaggerated heraldic display and lengthy florid epitaphs, often written in verse. Implicit in many of these memorials is an assumption that earthly gentility would find its reward in heaven. Some of the verse was of the highest quality (Shakespeare himself is said to have composed the epitaph on the tomb of Sir Thomas Stanley (d. 1576) in Tong church, Shropshire) and many early seventeenth-century monuments, although architecturally insensitive, contain epitaphs which accurately reflect the lyricism of contemporary poetry.

While many eighteenth-century monuments are singularly ostentatious, some are also exceedingly graceful, although all too often out of keeping with their medieval surroundings. But the epitaphs inscribed thereon frequently make the most preposterous claims for the self-righteous dead in doggerel which was unlikely to enhance a poet's reputation. Biographical detail was sometimes of a singularly intimate nature, as in Bridget Applewhaite's lengthy epitaph at Bramfield in Suffolk which recalls the 'Fatigues' of her first marriage ('Born by her with incredible Patience / For Four Years and three Quarters, barring three weeks'), the 'glorious Freedom' of her widowhood and her decision to 'run the Risk of a Second Marriage-Bed' as well as the full medical details of the 'Apoplectick Dart' which after 'Terrible Convulsions, Plaintive Groans or Stupefying Sleep' eventually dispatched her, at the age of 43, on 12 September, 1773. Not all epitaphs would have been welcomed by the churchwardens: at Burford in Oxfordshire, a monument to Lord Chief Justice Tanfield, erected by his widow, complains bitterly of the inconvenience caused by having to bury him in such a backwater.

The religious upheaval of the late eighteenth and early nineteenth centuries resulted in a reaction against such commemorative excesses. Memorials, and the inscriptions they bore, became stylised and bland, just as religious observance declined into social convention. In 1843, the Revd F.E. Paget, Rector of Elfield in Staffordshire, published his *Tract Upon Tombstones* in which he stated that the erection of a tombstone should be 'a Christian act and one that shall benefit the living. The tombstones in the churchyard are, as it were, a book, from whence [visitors] draw their reflections on man's mortality and in which every new inscription is a fresh page.' A proper epitaph, he continued, 'should be characterised by Christian humility, kindness, and by a disposition to say too little rather than too much'.

In the present century there is evidence of increasing conflict between those who oppose the

cliché and the banal, and others who consider epitaphs to be a reflection of personal taste and, therefore, of contemporary society. In 1994, a CONSISTORY COURT ruled that colloquial references to 'dad', 'nanna' and 'grandad' were undignified and inappropriate, a judgement supported by the *Churchyards Handbook*, which suggests that gravestones should be raised for the benefit of posterity rather than the transient gratification of a bereaved family. Censorship of inscriptions is nothing new. In 1797 at the church of St Anthony-in-Meneage, Cornwall, the widow of Richard Roskruge suggested an epitaph for her murdered husband: 'Doomed by a cruel ruffian's hand to die!' The vicar was not impressed and substituted 'a neighbour's erring hand' as 'breathing more of Christian charity'.
See also MEMORIAL *and* WALL MONUMENTS

EQUILATERAL ARCH *see* ARCH

EREMITICAL Reclusive, as an ANCHORITE or COENOBITE.
See also HERMIT

ESTATES (MONASTIC) *see* FINANCE, GRANGE, TIMBER, VINEYARDS *and* WOOL

EUCHARIST (*also* COMMUNION, HOLY COMMUNION *and* MASS) The Eucharist (meaning 'thanksgiving') is the central act of Christian worship. The institution of the Eucharist was recorded by St Paul (1 Cor 11: 23–5) and references in the Acts of the Apostles confirm that it was a regular part of Christian worship from a very early date. The term is applied to both the sacrament in which bread and wine are consecrated and consumed and to the consecrated elements themselves, which are referred to doctrinally as the Body and Blood of Christ. Inevitably there was debate within the Church as to the sacrificial nature of the Eucharist and concerning the presence or otherwise of Christ at Communion. Belief in the doctrine of *transubstantiation* (by which the whole substance of the consecrated elements of the Eucharist are converted into Christ's body and blood, only the appearances (*accidents*) of the blood and wine remaining) was defined and confirmed at the Fourth Lateran Council in 1215. At this time, the celebrant received *Communion in Both Kinds* (or *Communion in Both Species*), other communicants receiving the bread only.

The nature of the Eucharist caused considerable controversy at the REFORMATION. Martin Luther (1483–1546) defended a doctrine of *Consubstantiation*, according to which both the bread and wine and the body and blood of Christ coexisted, each within the other, at the Eucharist. Others, notably Ulrich Zwingli (1484–1531), maintained that the Eucharist was a purely commemorative act, while John Calvin (1509–64) advocated the doctrine of *Virtualism*, according to which the faithful received the power of the body and blood of Christ through the bread and wine, denying that any change in the elements took place. The sixteenth-century reformers insisted that there was no scriptural justification for denying communicants *Communion in Both Kinds*, and the practice was restored in Protestant churches at the Reformation.

In 1548, the *Order of the Communion*, a form of words (in English) for the administration of Communion, was inserted into the Latin MASS between the Communion of the priest and that of the people. It included the *General Confession and Absolution*, the *Comfortable Words* and the *Prayer of Humble Access*, and was incorporated into the *Book of Common Prayer* in 1549 (*see* COMMON PRAYER, BOOK OF). References to the nature of the Eucharist in the *Book of Common Prayer* are ambiguous and have allowed the coexistence of a number of doctrines within the Church of England. In the Roman Catholic Church, the final session of the Council of Trent (at Trento in northern Italy, 1562–3) reaffirmed the doctrine of transubstantiation and confirmed that the Sacrifice of the Mass was expiatory.

Although in the Middle Ages church attendance at the LITURGY was general, Communion was infrequent (the Fourth Lateran Council ordered Communion at least once a year). Most post-medieval revivals have sought to increase the frequency of Communion, and weekly Communion is now common in both the Roman Catholic Church and the Church of England.

The word 'Mass' is derived from the Latin *mittere* meaning 'send forth', a reference to the dismissal of the congregation following the Eucharist. Until recently, the Low Mass (a simplified form without music) was that which was most commonly celebrated.

See also ABLUTIONS, AUMBRY, CREDENCE, EVENING PRAYER, FENESTELLA, LAMPS, LAVABO, MASS, MATTINS, PISCINA, PRESBYTERY, PYX, RESERVATION, SEDILIA, SQUINT *and* TABERNACLE

EVANGELIARY A book containing the four Gospels or those portions of the Gospels which are read at the EUCHARIST in accordance with the ecclesiastical CALENDAR.

EVENING PRAYER (EVENSONG) The service of Evening prayer as set out in the *Book of Common Prayer* combines elements of the evening offices of VESPERS and COMPLINE: the appointed psalms and lesson from the *Old Testament*, the *Magnificat*, a lesson from the *New Testament*, the *Nunc dimittis*, the Apostles' Creed and prayers. There may also be hymns and a sermon. At one time Evening prayer was said daily in most churches, even in the absence of a congregation, but is now usually observed only on Sundays, except at cathedrals and some collegiate chapels, where Choral Evensong is held also on weekdays. For many, Evensong remains the quintessence of all things English. To sit in the candlelit stalls of Gloucester Cathedral or Magdalen College, Oxford on a grey February afternoon, and to absorb the soaring splendour of Gibbons, Tallis and Byrd is to experience a sense of elation and spiritual renewal quite without equal.

See also EUCHARIST

EVENSONG *see* EVENING PRAYER

EXCOMMUNICATION The act of expelling from the communion of the Church and of imposing other deprivations on those whose actions have attracted ecclesiastical censure. In the Roman Catholic Church those who have been excommunicated (*excommunicatus toleratus*) may neither receive nor administer the Sacraments and, if pronounced *excommunicatus vitandus* by the pope, may not hold any office or dignity within the Church. Social intercourse is also discouraged. As recently as 1969 the Church of England confirmed that excommunication remains a valid form of censure.

See also ANATHEMA *and* HERESY

EXENNIA Small tokens of remembrance sent by monks to their relatives and friends. Such gifts could be obtained from the CELLARER four times a year.

EXPOSITION GALLERY A raised GALLERY in which a relic or sacred item could be observed by those beneath (*see* SHRINES).

EXTRA-CLAUSTRAL Literally 'beyond the cloister'. The term refers to activities and buildings that were usually located within the CURIA rather than in the immediate vicinity of the CLOISTER. These may have included the INFIRMARY (*farmery*), the GUEST HOUSE, the SUPERIOR'S LODGINGS, the BREWHOUSE, BAKEHOUSE, MILLS, etc.

FACULTIES, COURT OF A court established in 1534 when the granting of licences, dispensations and faculties in the provinces of York and

Canterbury passed from papal jurisdiction to that of the archbishop of Canterbury.
See also FACULTY

FACULTY (i) Authorisation by an ecclesiastical SUPERIOR for the granting of a dispensation permitting someone to hold an office or to perform a function which would otherwise be forbidden by law (*see also* FACULTIES, COURT OF).
(ii) A licence, issued on behalf of a bishop, permitting alterations or additions to be made to church buildings or churchyard for which the diocesan bishop is ultimately responsible.
See also ARCHIVES

FAIRS *see* MARKETS, SHOPS AND FAIRS

FALDSTOOL An occasional stool with folding legs. The term is also used (erroneously) to describe a litany desk (*see* DESKS) or PRIE-DIEU.
See also CHAIRS (SANCTUARY)

FAN VAULT *see* MEDIEVAL ARCHITECTURE *and* VAULTING

FARMERY A monastic INFIRMARY.

FARMING *see* BARNS, GRANGE, TIMBER, VINEYARDS *and* WOOL

FASTING A penitential discipline intended to strengthen the spiritual life through self-denial. In particular, to abstain from taking food (or specified foods) for a given period. The first full meal taken thereafter was the break-fast. In the early Church, fasting was observed on Fridays and sometimes on Wednesdays or Saturdays. Initially, fasting implied complete ABSTINENCE from food throughout the fast day, although, in the medieval period, a light meal (*collation*) was sometimes taken in the morning and evening. The eating of flesh meat was prohibited and fish was usually substituted. The medieval church imposed fasting on all, except the very young and the elderly and infirm, usually at times which alternated with the great feasts of the liturgical year such as Advent and Easter. The fast of LENT, for example, is still observed for a period of forty days before Easter and (even for many non-Christians) it remains an occasion for abstaining from some small personal pleasure.

FATHER (i) An ordained member of a religious order, with the exception of the Society of St Francis, in which all members are brothers (*see* BROTHER).
(ii) The title of a Roman Catholic priest (the term is also used by Anglo-Catholic members of the Church of England).

FATHER-GENERAL The senior monk of an order that has many houses.

FENESTELLA A canopied niche in the south wall of a PRESBYTERY containing a PISCINA and often an AUMBRY or CREDENCE and SEDILIA. The decorative moulding of a fenestella is usually compatible with the architectural style of contemporary window arches and doorways.

FENESTRAL Stones composing a traceried window.

FERETORY A shrine, above ground level, in which the RELICS of a saint were deposited and at which they were venerated (*see* SHRINES), or a chapel containing such a shrine. A feretory was usually located in a bay behind the HIGH ALTAR, separated from the PRESBYTERY by an elaborate screen. The custodian of a feretory, and of its treasures, was called a *feretrar* or *tumbarius*.

FERIAL From the medieval Latin *ferialis* meaning 'festival', the term was used to name the days of the octave of Easter: *feria prima*, *feria secunda*, etc. (first festival day, second festival day, etc.). From this the designation was transferred to the days of ordinary weeks and, in ecclesiastical usage, to any day, other than a Sunday, on which no feast was celebrated. It is sometimes used erroneously to describe an 'ordinary' Sunday on which no other feast is celebrated.

FESTIVALS Monastic life was not entirely one of abstinence and tedium. The great festivals of Christmas, Easter, Pentecost (Whit Sunday), and the Assumption of the Blessed Virgin Mary (15 August), together with that of the abbey's patron saint, were observed with considerable ceremony. The entire church would be decorated (*garnished*), the finest plate carried from the treasury to adorn the altars, the richest vestments worn by the celebrants and the whole house cleaned before the VIGIL. There would be a proliferation of bells, lights and incense, services would be longer, with more elaborate music and PROCESSIONS, and CHAPTER would be shorter. In the refectory (*see* FRATER), a greater variety of food would be served on tables decorated with festal tablecloths, while soft towels would be provided in the LAVATORIUM. In Cistercian houses, all of which were dedicated to the Blessed Virgin Mary, the feast of the Assumption was kept as the patronal festival and the feast of St Peter and St Paul (29 June) was added to the CALENDAR of major festivals. There was also a number of solemn festivals which, although not ranking among the great five, were of particular significance in certain houses. These included Epiphany (6 January), the Purification of the Blessed Virgin Mary and the Presentation of Christ in the Temple (Candlemas) (2 February), St Gregory (12 March), the Annunciation of the Virgin (Ladymas) (25 March), the Ascension (the sixth Thursday after Easter), St Augustine (26 May), St John the Baptist (24 June), the Translation of St Benedict (11 July), the Nativity of the Blessed Virgin Mary (8 September), St Michael and All Angels (Michaelmas) (29 September) and All Saints (Hallowmas) (1 November). In addition, a variety of minor and local festivals were celebrated, by modifying the rites and ceremonies associated with the DAILY ROUND of offices, while there were also occasional major celebrations such as the INSTALLATION of a superior and the reception of a visitor (*see* VISITATION (ECCLESIASTICAL)).

FEUDAL SYSTEM A medieval European politico-economic system based on the relationship of vassal and superior: the former holding land of the latter on condition of homage and military service or labour. Medieval society was divided into three estates: the clergy, the nobility and the (predominantly agricultural) workers. Each estate was dependent on the others: theoretically the Church, under the pope, was charged by God to attend to mankind's spiritual needs, while the nobility received their lands from the king on condition that they fulfilled certain obligations to those above and below them. When a noble received land (a *fief*) he became the vassal of the lord who bestowed it, and owed him military service and attendance. In return the lord offered his vassals justice and protection. Large fiefs were usually subdivided and the clergy often administered church lands held in fief from nobles. The villeins or serfs rendered service by working the land or by pursuing a craft for the benefit of the MANOR in return for security, justice and protection. Villeins were given a share in the common lands and pasture, sufficient for their own needs.

Like other great landlords, the medieval Church owed feudal obligations to the Crown, although the Cistercians attempted to avoid this obligation by accepting land where there was no indigent population (*waste land*), and developing it through a system of granges (*see* GRANGE). For three centuries after the Norman Conquest, many abbeys (as feudal tenants) were obliged to provide knight service to the king, by whom all land was held. In the eleventh century, for example, the Benedictine priory of Ely provided forty armed men while, in the twelfth century, the abbot of Peterborough had to equip sixty knights and the abbot of Bury, forty. But the obligation was at variance with the nature of a religious house and was eventually commuted to a cash payment (*scutage*). Archbishops, bishops and

royal abbots were tenants-in-chief and held baronies. They owed knight service and were required to attend parliament and to provide hospitality for others of equal rank. For this reason, the accommodation provided for religious superiors was often sumptuous and far removed from that of the humble monk.
See also HERALDRY (ECCLESIASTICAL) *and* PALATINATE

FILIATION The creation of subsidiary 'cells' or 'hives' of a (usually Cistercian) monastery, each consisting of twelve monks and a SUPERIOR. The daughter (*filia*) was an independent community but was visited by the superior of the mother house.

FILLET A narrow band between mouldings or running down the shaft of a column or pier.

FINANCE One of the principles of the Benedictine RULE was that a religious community should 'live of its own'. Initially, many of the smaller, more austere monasteries may almost have succeeded in achieving this, although even they were often obliged to purchase essential commodities, such as salt (for preserving meat). Despite endowments of land and the expansion of granges (*see* GRANGE), self-sufficiency was an ideal that was rarely realised. For the most part, communities 'lived of their own' as far as they were able: the outer courts (*see* CURIA) of many monasteries contained productive malthouses, brewhouses, granaries, dairies and bakeries, all providing for the needs of the community. Even so, increasingly, the monasteries came to depend on the world beyond their gates, not only for goods and services but also for labour – especially with the decline in the number of LAY BROTHERS that occurred following the Black Death (1348–49) (*see* PLAGUE). Very often, beyond the curia were the workshops (*see* PRECINCT) (and sometimes accommodation) for plumbers, carpenters, smiths, stone-masons and other lay-craftsmen on whose skills the abbey depended (*see* EMPLOYEES *and* INDUSTRY). Increasingly, income through direct exploitation of resources was replaced by a rent economy, the revenues of which paid for the services and goods that the monasteries were unable to provide for themselves.

Income

When a religious house was founded, except those of the MENDICANT orders, it was endowed with sufficient income to support its community of monks – usually thirteen in number. Initially, this endowment was derived from various sources, notably as gifts of money or (more often) grants of land from royal or magnate patrons (*see* benefactors) and income from manors and impropriated churches (*see* IMPROPRIATION). Income from an endowment of land depended on its successful exploitation, usually by employing direct labour, and several houses were obliged to relocate when the land was found to be unproductive. In 1154–5, for example, the Augustinian Canons of Bolton Priory moved from Embsay, four miles west of Bolton, to the present site near Skipton, having first obtained the consent of their new patroness, Alice de Rumilly.

As the monastic portfolio increased, so additional sources of income became available: rents and TITHES from property; profits from MARKETS, SHOPS AND FAIRS; fees from the extraction of minerals and the felling of timber; tolls from harbours, ferries, bridges and causeways; 'gifts in kind' such as fuel and building materials; the APPROPRIATION of rectories; the ALMS of pilgrims, donations and loans from corrodians (*see* CORRODIAN) and the thank-offerings of beneficiaries. Many monasteries also succeeded in obtaining exemptions from certain feudal obligations (*see* FEUDAL SYSTEM). Individually, the monks were not permitted to receive or retain money or private possessions. But, as bodies corporate, the greater monasteries acquired vast land holdings and were endowed with MANORS and benefices (*see* TITHES) in return for regular remembrance of the donors (*see* CHANTRY). Indeed, such was the extent of these alienations that they were limited by the STATUTE OF

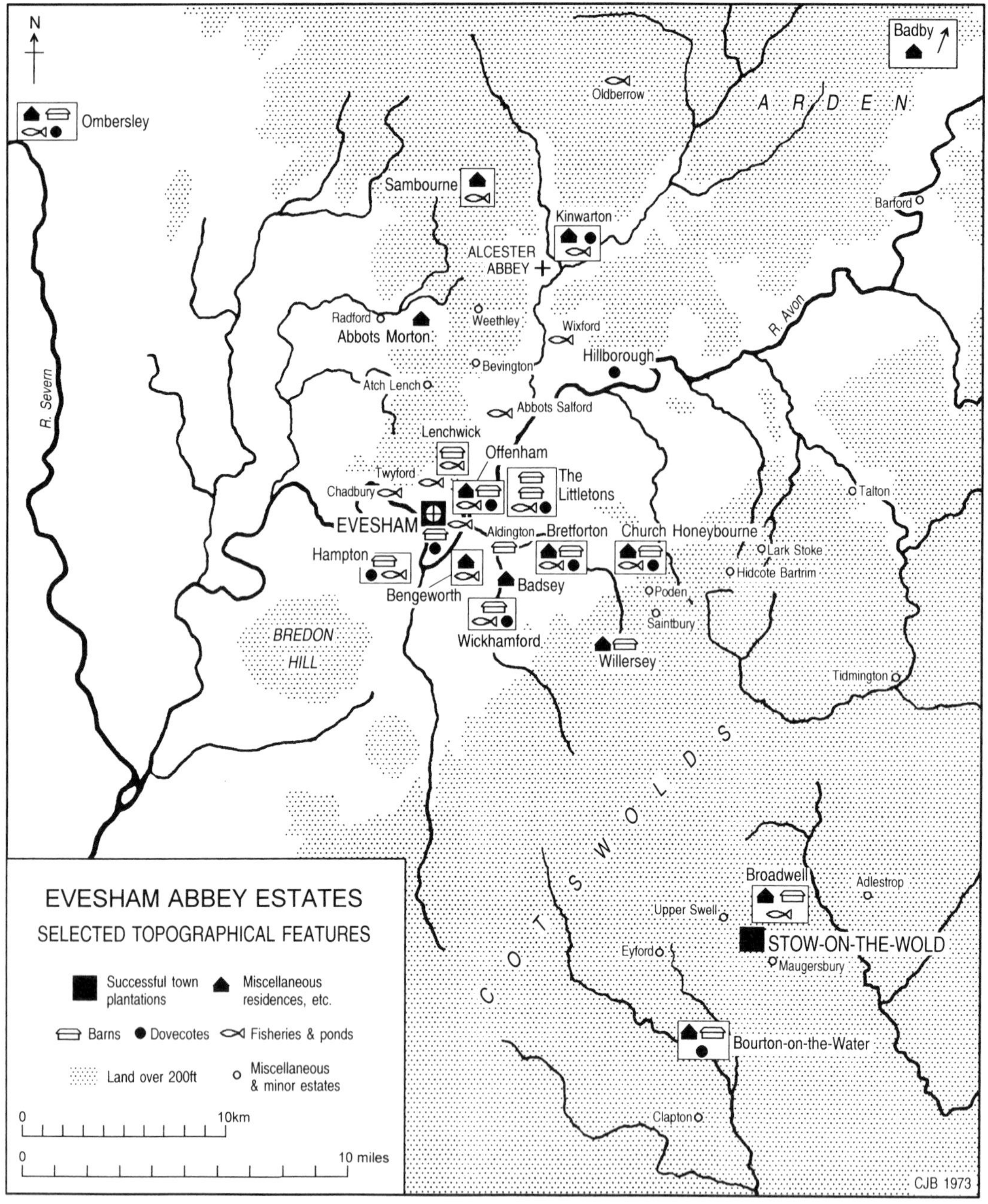

Evesham Abbey estates were distributed across complementary farming regions of the upland Cotswolds and the fertile Vale of Evesham. (By kind permission of James Bond)

MORTMAIN in 1279. For many religious communities (not only the Cistercians), it was the sale of WOOL from their numerous flocks of sheep that provided their principal source of income.

Expenditure

Despite the apparent prosperity of abbeys such as Fountains, Tintern and Glastonbury, the majority of medieval monasteries had difficulty in making ends meet. Many, notably the nunneries, barely subsisted and most, at one time or another, experienced a financial crisis. It has been calculated that while the average annual income of a major abbey such as Fountains might well have exceeded £1,000 prior to the Dissolution of the Monasteries, that of a minor house rarely reached £20.

Inevitably, much of an abbey's expenditure was devoted to providing board and lodging for its resident community which, in Cistercian houses, included the conversi who usually outnumbered the choir monks (*see* LAY BROTHERS). Expenditure also included numerous legal charges, feudal obligations and corrodians' pensions, the disbursement of ALMS, the payment of employees' wages and the provision of accommodation for corrodians and guests who, in major houses, would expect to receive a standard of HOSPITALITY appropriate to their rank. The abbey church, claustral and other buildings would have been in constant need of modification, repair and refurbishment, as would outlying granges, mills, fishponds, dovecotes and agricultural buildings. The churches and vicarages of appropriated benefices required regular maintenance and the incumbents' salaries had to be paid. Visitations (*see* VISITATION (ECCLESIASTICAL), attendance at provincial chapters and the GENERAL CHAPTER could incur considerable expenditure, as could the wider duties and responsibilities of a SUPERIOR beyond his abbey's gates. And there were natural disasters: disease (of men and beasts), the PLAGUE, fire, flood and earthquake (in 1185 Lincoln Cathedral was damaged by an earth tremor and in 1248 part of the vault was brought down at Wells Cathedral). Many houses allowed themselves to be beguiled by overambitious building projects and ran out of funds or were overtaken by events: at Milton Abbey, the construction of the nave was abandoned, almost certainly as a consequence of the Black Death, which reached Milton in 1349. There were losses due to civil unrest (*see* FORTIFICATION) and to war, especially in the marches of Scotland and Wales and during the Viking incursions of the eighth and ninth centuries. By the end of the fourteenth century, even the greatest abbeys were often facing financial crises as a result of 'compulsory ceaseless hospitality, costly lawsuits, barren lands, services and rents reduced to almost half by deaths of tenants and servants in the pestilence [the Black Death], the ruin that had befallen the monastery and its manors in frightful gales and by dilapidations and the various corrodaries and debts'. (G. Haigh)

Financial Administration

The majority of religious houses rarely succeeded in managing their finances efficiently. This was chiefly because revenues were traditionally channelled through individual offices, the OBEDIENTIARIES guarding them jealously, independent of the general fund. This was recognised by the Visitors (*see* VISITATION (ECCLESASTICAL)), who attempted to make the system more accountable, often through the appointment of a BURSAR. Clearly, the intention was that all the revenues should pass through his office, but tradition usually prevailed: the obedientiaries retained their own accounts while the bursar controlled those revenues that were not already allocated. In many cases, initial endowments were found to be inadequate and the demands of hospitality excessive. In practice, of course, it was the superior who ultimately controlled his abbey's finances, sometimes with debilitating consequences. Although he was provided with his own account, it was not unknown for an autocratic abbot to appropriate his abbey's revenues for imprudent or even dishonest purposes or to commit his house to overambitious building projects. Many houses incurred considerable debts, which had to be met by borrowing or by the granting of corrodories and the forward selling of produce. Sometimes an independent ADMINISTRATOR had to be appointed to correct the business affairs of houses whose finances had become unmanageable.

FINIAL A carved ornament on top of a PINNACLE, gable or spire: for example a sphere (*ball finial*) or a foliated fleur-de-lis.

FIRES *see* HEATING

FIRST POINTED *see* MEDIEVAL ARCHITECTURE

FISHPONDS The medieval method of preserving meat in brine was so unreliable (and the results so unpalatable) that most religious houses possessed their own dovecotes (*see* DOVECOTE), warrens and fishponds from which they obtained a regular supply of fresh protein. Of these the fishpond was of particular importance because it provided a reliable source of food for the numerous 'fish days' when no 'flesh' (i.e. red-blooded meat) could be eaten. Abstinence was especially important in religious communities whose rules determined that the forgiveness of sins and the attainment of everlasting life were contingent on austerity and self-denial. Consequently even the most insignificant of religious houses possessed its own fishpond, and many were retained when monastic buildings were converted to private homes or adopted for parochial purposes following the DISSOLUTION OF THE MONASTERIES. Carp were the most popular fish, although pike, perch, bream, roach, tench, trout and elvers were also farmed. Today, most medieval fishponds are dry, their leats silted and their sluices long abandoned. Typically, they are rectangular and flat-bottomed, with retaining embankments raised 1m (3.3ft) above ground level and with two or three adjacent *stew ponds* where young fish were raised. The grid-like outlines of ancient fishponds are sometimes evident as CROP MARKS or as linear undulations in the vicinity of former abbey churches. At Bury St Edmunds abbey the remains are known as 'The Crankles' because of their zigzag shape. They may also be marked on Ordnance Survey 'Explorer' maps.

FLAMBOYANT The final phase of French Gothic architecture in which window TRACERY is composed of wavy undulating lines. To be found in English buildings of the Perpendicular period where the resulting motif resembles interwoven curves ('flames').
See also MEDIEVAL ARCHITECTURE

FLASHING A strip of lead or other material used to protect joints against damp.

FLÈCHE (*also* SPIRELET) A slender wooden spire at the centre of a roof.

FLINT Flint is variety of quartz, consisting of irregular nodules of nearly pure silica, dark grey or black in colour, occurring in association with chalk, which provides it with its white coating. Despite its apparent ordinariness, this extremely hard and fissile mineral was of singular importance in the development of civilisation: it provided Neolithic man with implements and, when struck, it would produce fire. The Anglo-Saxons knew it as *firestone*.

In the absence of other suitable materials, and because of its strength and durability, flint is frequently found as a building material in chalk districts of south and east England and has continued in use for this purpose from the Iron Age to the present day. Before the fourteenth century, whole flints were embedded in the mortar of walls, which were further strengthened with stone and flint rubble and lacing courses of stone or brick. But from the late thirteenth century split and shaped (*knapped*) flints, with their dark facets outwards, were often used in conjunction with brick or stone to form chequer-work and other geometrically patterned surfaces (*knapping*).

A special decorative technique called *flushwork* also developed at this time. Knapped flint, set in mortar within the matrices of intricately carved FREESTONE facings, is a feature of many East Anglian churches and continued, there and elsewhere, into the sixteenth century, by which time a high standard of craftsmanship had evolved.

In Dorset, flushwork is usually set in broad horizontal strips, whereas in East Anglia it consists of thin vertical strips or squares.

FLOOR TILES *see* ENCAUSTIC TILES

FLUSHWORK *see* FLINT

FLUTING Vertical channelling in the shaft of a COLUMN or PIER.

FLYING BUTTRESS *see* BUTTRESS *and* MEDIEVAL ARCHITECTURE

FOILS Decorative figures in Gothic tracery consisting of a number of leaf-shaped curves (*lobes*) formed by small arcs separated by cusps (*see* CUSP). Most commonly used are the *trefoil* (3 lobes), *quatrefoil* (4) and *cinquefoil* (5).

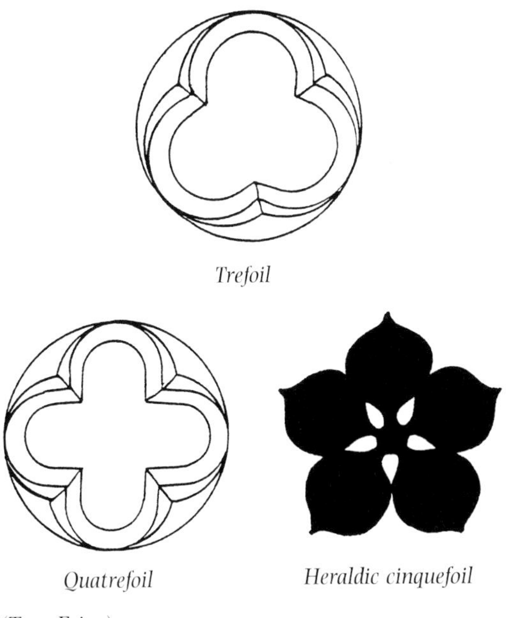

Trefoil

Quatrefoil *Heraldic cinquefoil*

(Tom Friar)

FOLIATION A decorative motif consisting of carved leaves or leaf-like shapes.

FONTREVAULT, ORDER OF *see* DOUBLE MONASTERY

FONTS A font is a receptacle for baptismal water, normally (though not invariably) made of stone. In the early Church these were large basins, set below ground level, in which the candidate was submerged in baptismal water (*submersion*). It was not until the early Middle Ages, when infant baptism, *immersion* (partial submersion) and *affusion* (the pouring of HOLY WATER over the head) became the general practice, that fonts were raised above floor level. In the Christian Church the MASS and Baptism are considered to be pre-eminent among the Seven Sacraments, baptism emphasising entry into the Christian life and the purging of sin. Consequently, every medieval church possessed its font, which was symbolically located near the entrance, at the western end of the nave (*see* BAPTISTERY). It is likely that the early CATHEDRALS possessed fonts from the outset, but those that were created following the DISSOLUTION OF THE MONASTERIES often acquired a font as the gift of a benefactor, as did former monastic churches that were adopted for parochial use.

The massive square fonts at Winchester Cathedral Priory and Lincoln Cathedral are of black polished marble imported from Tournai (now in Belgium) in the mid-twelfth century. Both fonts are supported on substantial circular 'drum' plinths and four short piers, one at each corner. The Winchester font is carved on each of its four sides with the miracles of St Nicholas (Santa Claus), the patron saint of children. Carvings on the Lincoln font depict winged lions, griffins and other beasts, fighting each other in a symbolic battle between good and evil, while, on the north side, two winged creatures resting their front legs on books may represent the ox of St Luke and the lion of St Mark, two of the four Gospel writers. There are other interesting fonts at Brecon Cathedral (Romanesque, carved with grotesque masks and fantastic beasts and birds intertwined), Chichester Cathedral (a huge, smoothly tactile font, designed by John Skelton in 1983), Coventry Cathedral (a rough three-ton boulder from

Bethlehem with a scallop-shaped bowl hollowed out by Ralph Beyer), at Ely Cathedral Priory (of Sicilian marble with an oak cover, a gift of Dean Annesley in 1687), Hereford Cathedral (a fine circular font dating from the first Norman cathedral, carved with figures of the Apostles), Liverpool Cathedral (a twelve-sided font carved from a block of French 'lunel rubane' marble, with figures of the Apostles engraved on each face), at Ripon Cathedral (an unusual font, dating from the Tudor rebuilding) and at Peterborough Cathedral (of Alwalton marble on a Victorian Purbeck base).

A number of fonts have intricately carved tabernacle-like canopies (*see* TABERNACLE): notably at Durham Cathedral Priory (a gift of Bishop John Cosin in the seventeenth century), and an extraordinarily ornate eighteenth-century canopy above a Romanesque font (of Frosterley marble) at Beverley Minster. The elaborate gilded font cover at Worcester Cathedral is a Victorian copy (1889) of a magnificent 5.5m (18ft) high Perpendicular canopy at St Mary's Church, Ufford in Suffolk.

The Lancaut font (*c.* 1140) in the Lady Chapel of Gloucester Cathedral is of particular interest. This was removed from the small church of St James at Lancaut in the Wye Valley in 1890 and donated to the cathedral in 1940. It was one of a number of lead fonts made by a highly skilled craftsman, probably working in the Bristol area in the twelfth century, of which only six have survived. The lead was cast in flat strips and then welded together to form a cylinder, the base of the font being cast last. The mould from which the fonts were made consisted of four arcades, two enclosing seated figures (probably representing the Apostles) and two with foliage. Of those that survive, four have twelve arcades, one has eleven and the Lancaut font at Gloucester has ten.

FOOD *see* FRATER

FOREST MARBLE The northern equivalent of PURBECK MARBLE, a black or dark grey limestone extracted from quarries at Frosterley in County Durham.

FORME A complete set of window TRACERY. A *forme-piece* is a section of a traceried window.

FORTIFICATION Religious houses relied heavily for protection on their status and on the principle by which 'The precincts of monks' houses and

The twelfth-century black Tournai marble font at Winchester Cathedral Priory.

granges . . . like cemeteries and churches are all by apostolic authority to be free and undisturbed by any invasion, terror or violence.' But principle was a poor defence against the unprincipled, and in 1235 the Cistercian house of Holmcultrum, near the Scottish border, was permitted to arm its servants and later to erect a small castle to protect its GRANGE at Raby, County Durham. Most monastic sites were enclosed within a hedge or low wall and ditch, and provided with a *gatehouse* at which visitors could be interrogated by a gate-keeper or PORTER (*portarius*) before entering or leaving the PRECINCT. The larger gatehouses were invariably of two storeys and often contained chambers that were used for other purposes: as offices, almonries (*see* ALMONRY) and PRISONS, for example. Gatehouses at York and Ely contained courthouses, while that at Durham provided accommodation for the prior. The passage through the gatehouse (*gate passage*) would have contained at least one gate which might be located in the centre of the passage or at one or both ends. Where there was a single gate passage (as at Kirkham and Peterborough), it would be of sufficient width and height to allow a loaded cart to enter. Alternatively, there might be two gates: one for wheeled traffic and a smaller one for pedestrians. The gates were usually closed at COMPLINE but could be opened by the porter for travellers and late arrivals. A chapel, either within the gatehouse or immediately outside its gates (*capella ante portas, see* PARISH CHURCH), is often indicative of a community that did not admit the laity to its precinct. Several abbeys had such extensive precincts that a single gatehouse was impractical: Bury St Edmunds had four, two of which are the best preserved of all the abbey buildings. The Norman Tower or Tower of St James (1120–48) was designed to be both a gateway to the abbey church and a belfry for the neighbouring church of St James, while the Great Gate (*c.* 1330s – upper storey after 1353) gave access to the Great Court and the abbot's palace. Its defences included arrow loops, a guardroom and portcullis (*see below*).

At the Cistercian abbey of Cleeve in Somerset, the gatehouse wall is inscribed with the words (in Latin): 'Stay open gate and close to no honest person.' But in the more volatile regions of the Borders, gatehouses were heavily fortified (as at Alnwick) and many outlying monastic estates were provided with pele towers for their defence (as at Nunnikirk, West Ritton and Greenleighton in Northumberland) and even castles (Carrycoats, Filton and Rytton). The monastery of Tynemouth was the largest to be located within the walls of a castle. In 1296 the monks obtained a licence to enclose and crenellate their precinct, which occupied a naturally defended promontory, washed on three sides by the sea. With a garrison to maintain, they were brought to the brink of bankruptcy many times, although (with a keep-gatehouse added in the 1390s) the castle was considered to be one of the strongest in the north. Monastic sites at Hulne and Lanercost were also heavily defended, as was the priory of Ewenny in the southern March of Wales, a dependency of the Benedictine Abbey of Gloucester. The nave of the priory church remains in parochial use, while its great defensive walls, with gates and towers, have also survived.

Bishops' Palaces

Bishops and mitred abbots (*see* MITRED ABBOT) were, of course, senior members of the medieval aristocracy with their own retinues and many episcopal castles, such as Llandaff and Llawhaden in Wales, are indistinguishable from those of secular lords. Roger de Caen, bishop of Salisbury (*c.* 1065/70–1139), was Henry I's chancellor and the greatest prelate of his day. He accumulated a huge personal fortune and built prodigiously, rebuilding his cathedral at Old Sarum (near Salisbury), founding Kidwelly Castle in Wales, rebuilding Sarum and Malmesbury castles in England and creating a fortified palace at Sherborne that was later the model for the 'sumptuous palaces' of Henry of Blois, bishop of Winchester (*c.* 1100–71). When Sherborne Castle was built between 1122 and 1137 it was almost

The south-west gateway to Sherborne Castle: a statement of Bishop Roger's power and status and a formidable defence against attack.

completely surrounded by a marshy lake. Accessible only by causeways and bridges, it was easily defendable. Typical of several Norman palace-fortresses, it consisted of a residential quadrangle surrounded by a defensive outer bailey. The inner quadrangle comprised a square keep with four ranges of buildings around a small courtyard. The outer bailey was protected by a deep ditch and a curtain wall with square flanking towers and a long, narrow barbican and water gate by which the fortress was supplied by boat. A magnificent gate house in the south-west corner of the bailey was clearly intended to be a statement of Bishop Roger's power and status. It was provided with a stone bridge (unusual for a castle at that time), the centre timber section of which could be withdrawn for defensive purposes. (The rectangular windows are sixteenth-century insertions and an earthwork to the west of the castle was probably a Civil War siege platform.) Another major project was Roger's castle at Devizes, described by Henry of Huntingdon as 'the most splendid in Europe', which included a church for the garrison. Despite his calling, bishop Roger built castles more readily than churches.

A century later, Robert Burnell, bishop of Bath and Wells from 1275 to 1292, was denied the archbishopric of Canterbury due to his fathering of numerous illegitimate offspring and the acerbic comment that his proclivity attracted. Nevertheless, he was an extraordinarily wealthy man: he controlled eighty-two manors, either in his own right or through his episcopal see, and he built a splendid residence for himself at Acton Burnell in Shropshire – in addition to his bishop's palace at Wells. Acton Burnell, with its corner towers and crenellated walls, has the appearance of a castle, but it is unlikely that defence was ever a serious consideration, despite its proximity to the Welsh border. It was essentially a defensible manor house, a residence built for comfort and as an ostentatious manifestation of the bishop's status and influence. In addition to his own lavish quarters, provision was made for a constable and other senior officials, with smaller attic rooms for clerks and secretaries.

Gaol delivery records clearly illustrate a significant increase in criminal activity during the first decades of the fourteenth century. One cause was undoubtedly a devastating rise in the price of wheat and the Great Famine of 1315–17. But, although destitution and violence were clearly linked, it was certain of the gentry (and even the parish clergy) who were chiefly responsible for organised crime, in some cases aided and abetted by patrons and maintainers among the aristocracy. It was these well-born bandits who recruited outlaws and vagabonds to their service and accelerated the breakdown of law and order that was already evident in the late thirteenth century. Furthermore, from 1294, pardons had been granted for service in the royal armies, emptying the king's gaols with violent and predictable effect. Discontent was further inflamed by a widespread failure of manorial discipline, exacerbated by the unrealised aspirations of the peasantry and the determination of manorial lords to frustrate them. And it was the Church and its senior prelates who were most often accused of avarice and sharp practice.

It was against this background of lawlessness that many abbots and bishops were obliged to defend their precincts and palaces. Henry Gower, bishop of St Davids (1328–47) fortified his country residence at Lamphey and extensively refurbished his magnificent palace next to the cathedral at St Davids. At the same time, a wall was constructed to enclose both the cathedral and the houses of the canons in the close, thereby separating the city from the secular world outside. The wall was pierced by four gates: Porth Padrig (Patrick's Gate), Porth Gwyn (the White Gate), Porth Bonying (Bonyng's Gate) and Porth y Tŵr (the Gate of the Tower), which was constructed against an octagonal thirteenth-century tower in which the cathedral bells are hung. The purpose of this enclosing wall was clearly defensive (sections of crenellations have survived), and yet there is no evidence in the palace gatehouse of a portcullis, suggesting that defence was not a major consideration. Bishop Henry's ambitious programme of works included a double set of spacious apartments on two sides of a courtyard. The eastern range appears to have been planned as private accommodation while the south wing comprised an even grander suite of apartments focussed on a great hall. (This double arrangement is evident at several other episcopal palaces such as Lincoln, Wells and Wolvesey.) Whereas one range would have been occupied by the bishops as their lodgings, the other would have been used to accommodate and entertain distinguished guests.

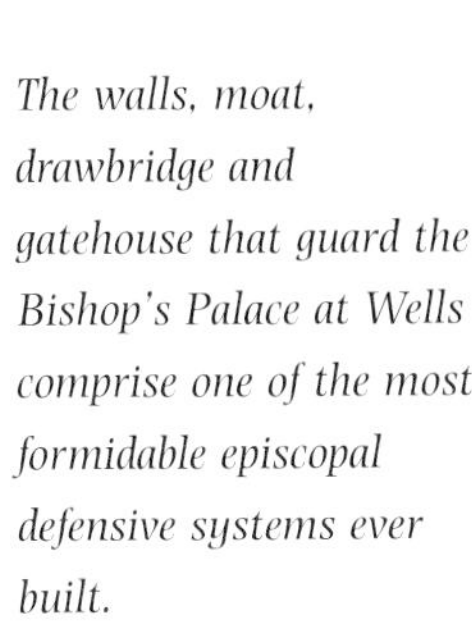

The walls, moat, drawbridge and gatehouse that guard the Bishop's Palace at Wells comprise one of the most formidable episcopal defensive systems ever built.

The great hall may also have been used for judicial and administrative purposes: the bishop of St Davids was a Marcher Lord whose tenants were obliged to appear in the episcopal courts.

Disputes between ecclesiastical corporations and their burgesses were commonplace. In 1326–7 the townspeople of two of the richest monastic boroughs, St Albans and Bury St Edmunds, had risen violently against their lords, besieging and plundering both abbeys. Consequently, monastic communities became ever more reliant on their precinct walls and gatehouses. At St Albans, abbot Thomas de la Mare rebuilt the huge fortress-like gatehouse in the mid-fourteenth century, while the (second) gatehouse at Bury St Edmunds (*see above*) at first appears to possess few military pretensions but was provided with a portcullis and arrow loops concealed by the statuary on the outer façade. A monastic precinct would have been impossibly large to defend, and these buildings should, perhaps, be considered as a type of keep-gatehouse, often serving as an almonry and exchequer, but capable of independent defence in an emergency.

In 1340, for 'the security and quiet of the canons and ministers resident there', bishop Ralph of Bath and Wells (1329–63) secured a royal licence 'to build a wall round the precinct of the houses of him and the canons and to crenellate and make towers in such a wall.' The walls, moat, drawbridge and gatehouse that guard the Bishop's Palace at Wells comprise one of the most formidable episcopal defensive systems ever built.

Lordship and Patronage

The abbots and priors of many religious houses grasped the opportunity both to enhance their status through architectural display and to dominate and overawe those over whom they exercised lordship. The massive Great Gate at St Augustine's, Canterbury, rebuilt by Abbot Thomas Fyndon between 1300 and 1309, is a wonderful confection of turrets and crenellations. Only eight years after its completion, six hundred men of the nearby manor of Minster,

> having gathered to themselves a still greater number of malefactors, approaching the manors of the abbot at Minster and Salmstone in hostile fashion with bows, arrows, swords and sticks, several times besieged them and made sundry attacks thereon, and placed fire, which they had brought with them, against the doors to burn down those manors.

Throughout the thirteenth century Battle Abbey had acquired numerous holdings of lesser landowners and had tightened its grip on the activities of its increasingly resentful burgesses. The abbey's huge, crenellated and turreted gatehouse, erected in 1338 ostensibly as a defence against French pirates, was in fact an unequivocal statement of lordship that dominated the town's marketplace and overawed its populace. Arrays of heraldic ornament on the façades of many contemporary monastic gatehouses were clearly intended to invoke the protection of the great and good. At Butley Priory, Suffolk, no fewer than five tiers of shields above the entrance include the arms of the Holy Roman Emperor, French and English kings and many of the most illustrious baronial families of East Anglia. At Kirkham Priory, North Yorkshire, the wide carriage arch of the great late thirteenth or early fourteenth-century gatehouse is surmounted by a decorative pointed gable on which is carved a series of magnate arms – all implying royal and noble patronage. Of course, this was not always the case. Worksop Priory's fourteenth-century gatehouse, although imposing, was essentially domestic in character, while the gatehouse at Tor Abbey on the south Devon coast is unambiguously defensive, intended to protect its community against piratical incursions.

By the end of the fourteenth century every major monastery was furnished with a precinct wall and gatehouse. But decades of pestilence (*see* PLAGUE) and the Peasants' Revolt of 1381 fomented discontent that proved to be even more violent than that which had preceded it. The criminal elements in the post-plague years were not the poor and desperate but people of substance: the yeomen, craftsmen and manorial officials who had led the Great Revolt and were markedly more dangerous than any previous rebel leadership. Immediately after the rebellion, the abbot of Thornton, Lincolnshire, obtained a licence to crenellate 'the new house over and about the gate' of his abbey. Although Thornton's 'new house' was primarily residential, it bristled with loopholes at several levels, each served by a purpose-built gallery. The portcullis was so large that the mechanism had to be located on the second floor, while the precinct was enclosed within a substantial wall and, in front of the gate, a moat. However, what makes Thornton unique among monastic sites is a long barbican that was added in 1389. Built entirely in brick, it comprises parallel walls, each pierced by thirteen arrow-slit embrasures and terminating in a round turret.

As at Battle and Tor abbeys, and at Michelham Priory, Sussex, proximity to the coast was undoubtedly a factor. Like his neighbour Abbot Hamo of Battle, Prior Leem of Michelham was a commissioner for coastal defence and was able to combine this responsibility with the need to secure his priory against civil unrest, for he was also a receiver of rents for the singularly unpopular John of Gaunt. Other late medieval defended monastic sites include Brecon, Powys; Hulne and Lindisfarne, Northumberland; Lanercost, Cumberland; Tavistock, Devon and Ulverscroft, Leicestershire.

FOUNDATION (MONASTIC) The minimum requirement for an independent monastic foundation was usually a community of twelve brethren and a SUPERIOR, together with an endowment to provide for their needs and a site on which to establish a religious house. It was the size of the endowment that often determined the nature and vigour of a community: the Benedictine foundation of Peterborough, for example, had an establishment of 110 in 1240, while that of Muchelney Abbey, founded in the mid-tenth century, never exceeded twenty – and was half that number when it was surrendered to

The residential gatehouse of the Augustinian canons of Thornton Abbey, Lincolnshire, rebuilt in the 1380s as a defensive work following the Great Revolt of 1381. (Courtesy of Anthony Kersting)

Henry VIII's commissioners in 1539.
See also BENEFACTORS *and* FINANCE

FOUNDATIONS (STRUCTURAL) Once the master mason had staked out the lines of a wall or building his next task was to oversee the construction of the foundations (*see* MASTER MASONS AND ARCHITECTS). We are told that, after the tower at Ely fell in 1321, Alan de Walsingham (the master mason)

> measured out in eight divisions the place where he thought to build the new tower; and he set workmen to dig and search for the foundations of the eight stone columns whereupon the whole building should be supported . . . until at last he found solid and secure ground. Then, when these eight places had been carefully dug out and firmly founded with stones and sand, at last he began . . .

It would appear from this that it was normal practice for boreholes to be dug in order to locate a solid stratum on which to build, and this would dictate the depth of the foundations. Trenches would be excavated, and filled to a variable depth with rough stone and other material to form a footing that would be of somewhat greater width than the wall to be raised on it. Foundations could be of considerable depth: writing in *c.* 1480, William Botoner of Worcester describes the foundations of the tower of St Stephen's, Bristol as being 9.5m (31ft) below ground level.

Where there was neither rock nor reasonably firm ground to build on, other measures were employed. When the tenth-century builders of Romsey Abbey first attempted to build a tower, they beat the ground 'with frequent blows of rams' in order to provide a firm foundation. But, inevitably, this proved insufficient and they were obliged to excavate a deep hole into which they rammed a mixture of stones and mortar. A more usual method was to drive in piles: at Winchester, for example, where in 1239 the Franciscans received a gift of beech trees to make piles for the foundations of their friary buildings. There is a reference, in the Calais accounts for 1468, to an engine or 'gynne called Ram, used for fixing piles'. The *ram*, or pile-driver, consisted of a hoisting apparatus of two or more poles which carried a pulley by means of which a heavy block of wood or iron (the 'ram') could be raised and let fall on the head of the pile.

In 1905, it was reported that the south and east walls of Winchester Cathedral Priory were cracking and beginning to lean outwards. Investigation revealed that the eleventh-century timber raft on which the church was constructed had begun to shrink and move as a result of changes in the water table. The unstable foundations had to be underpinned on a firm gravel stratum 7.5m (25ft) below ground level and for six years a team of 150 men worked to save the cathedral. The problem of the high water table was resolved when Francis Fox, the consultant engineer, decided to engage a deep-sea diver, William Walker. For over five years Walker worked under water and in complete darkness, progressively clearing the timber, peat and marl from beneath the walls and sealing the inflow by laying a bed of cement-filled sacks on the gravel below. The water was then pumped out and masons continued the underpinning, laying nine courses of bricks and 1.8m (6ft) of cement between the sacks and the base of the wall. To prevent further movement, ten flying buttresses (*see* BUTTRESS) were constructed against the south wall of the nave. A bronze statuette of William Walker, who 'saved this cathedral with his two hands', now stands in the RETRO-CHOIR.

An estimated 75,000 tons of stone were used in the construction of Salisbury Cathedral (1220–66) – in addition to that which was required for the (later) tower and spire which rose to the height of 123m. (404ft). That the whole edifice has not collapsed is little short of a miracle, bearing in mind that it is built on a marsh and its foundations are only 1.2m (4ft) deep. Elias of Dereham, the canon who supervised the construction for twenty-five years, knew that had his men dug deeper they would have struck the water table, and yet the only readily visible signs of this deficiency are the *sleeper walls* that spread the load of the ARCADE columns and strengthening arches at the CROSSING.

FOUNDER *see* BENEFACTORS *and* BURIALS (MONASTIC)

FOUR-CENTRE ARCH *see* ARCH

FOUR-LEAF ORNAMENT Medieval architectural ornament consisting of petals radiating symmetrically from a raised or depressed centre (*see* MEDIEVAL ARCHITECTURE).

FRANCHISE A liberty, privilege or exemption by grant or prescription.

(Tom Friar)

FRANCISCANS *see* FRIARS

FRANKALMOIGN Land granted by a lay person for the benefit of an ecclesiastical body, usually conditional upon the provision of a CHANTRY.

FRATER *or* REFECTORIUM The frater was the common dining room of a religious house. Correctly, the term should be applied to a monastic 'common room', the hall in which meals were taken being the *refectorium*. But, to the medieval monk, the fraternal breaking of bread was of the utmost significance and it is hardly surprising that the two terms have subsequently been perceived as complementary.

Mealtimes

The timing of meals varied from one order to another and, indeed, from one house to another, for much depended on the superior's interpretation of the RULE and the time of year (*see* HORARIUM). Monks broke their fast (hence 'break-fast') after the first mass of the day which followed PRIME, usually between 7 and 8 a.m. Signalled by three chimes of the bell, the meagre meal was eaten standing and in silence, while the reader invited a blessing. At its conclusion, each monk said a silent prayer for the repose of the community's benefactors. A further morning meal (*mixtum*) might be allowed for the old and infirm and for young novices who had difficulty in enduring the long period of fasting which lasted until after noon. The mixtum was taken in the frater and usually consisted of a small portion of bread soaked in beer. Dinner (*Prandium*) was the principal meal of the day – and, in some of the more austere houses, the *only* meal. It was taken shortly after noon, when it followed High Mass and the office of SEXT, or at 3 p.m. from 13 September (the eve of the Exaltation of the Cross) until the beginning of LENT. (From Whitsun to 13 September it was taken at 3 p.m. on Wednesdays and Fridays and at noon on other days.) During Lent, dinner was taken at dusk. Except at times of FASTING, there were usually two courses with bread and beer, and a choice of food was sometimes available (*see below*). When dinner was taken at noon, there might also be a light supper (*cena*) just before sunset.

Behaviour in the frater was strictly controlled, as was the food that was eaten there. The monks arrived in procession and washed at the nearby laver before taking their places (*see* lavatorium). Once grace had been sung, the meal was eaten in silence while a reader read aloud from the FRATER PULPIT. Inevitably, a sign language developed. At Syon Abbey, for example, the nuns had over a hundred signs for various types of food: fish was requested by moving the hand sideways 'in the manere of a fissh tail'; for mustard, a sister rubbed her nose with her right hand. The end of the meal was marked by a bell, and by the singing of grace, before the monks departed in an ordered procession.

The official responsible for ensuring order and cleanliness was the *Refectorian* (or *Fraterer*). Among his several duties, he had to arrange for the provision of fresh rushes for the floor, sweet-smelling flowers and herbs for the table and, in summer, fans or 'fly-traps' (*muscatorias*) for the brethren and guests. There was usually a high table (*mensa major*) at which sat the abbot, prior or sub-prior and invited guests who, in the interests of courtesy and hospitality, were permitted to converse with their hosts, but 'sparingly . . . and in a low tone'. The other tables were arranged down the sides of the hall with benches set behind them, against wall. This allowed the servers to move around easily in the centre of the room and to serve the meals over the tables. Seating was strictly hierarchical, with the junior members of the community seated nearest to the door. Novices sat at their own table, where they were supervised by the novice-master, or in a separate room. Dishes were received at the DRESSER WINDOW by the *discarius*, who placed them on the tables, beginning with the high table. In larger communities he would be assisted by *servitors*, who were appointed in rotation and took their meals with the reader and kitchen staff. The discarius was also responsible for overseeing the washing and storage of dishes and utensils, for the provision of fuel to the kitchens and the disposal of waste. The CELLARER was a senior official, 'the second father of the house', who, through his department, was responsible for the provision of food, drink and all the day-to-day requirements of a monastic community. The CATERER was a senior member of the cellarer's department who supervised the kitchen staff and the serving of food at mealtimes and may also have been responsible for the bulk purchase of provisions (*see* LARDER).

Even in the most austere of monasteries, guests were treated with generosity: the quality, quantity and choice of food were in all ways superior those enjoyed by the choir monks, lay brethren and servants, and meals were often prepared in a separate kitchen and served in the comparative comfort of a monastic GUEST HOUSE.

Diet

The quality and quantity of food served in the frater varied according to the austerity of the particular order and the time of year. The Benedictine RULE forbade the eating of meat or game (except for the sick and infirm), although this prohibition was relaxed following the GENERAL CHAPTER of 1300 and, by the late fourteenth century, meat was permitted in most religious houses because 'doctors and experience both teach that a total abstinence from meat is . . . hurtful to the system'. But even then 'flesh meat' (which included fish and poultry) was forbidden on specified days of fasting, such as Advent, Lent and Rogationtide, while the Carthusians refused to admit the relaxation and the Cistercians permitted meat to be eaten only in the INFIRMARY, MISERICORD and guest house (it also had to be cooked in a separate kitchen). The main meal of the day therefore consisted of two courses of vegetables, fish, eggs, potage (a thick soup), bread and possibly fruit and cheese – and meat, where this was allowed, usually beef or pork. Eggs were considered to be a substitute for meat: in 1333 the Durham cellarer purchased 44,140 eggs, an average of one a day for each member of the community. The restricted diet available during 'Lenten days' (the days of fasting) was sometimes made more palatable by the use of herbs and spices, while an occasional PITTANCE was allowed in celebration of a liturgical feast or some other event in the community's life.

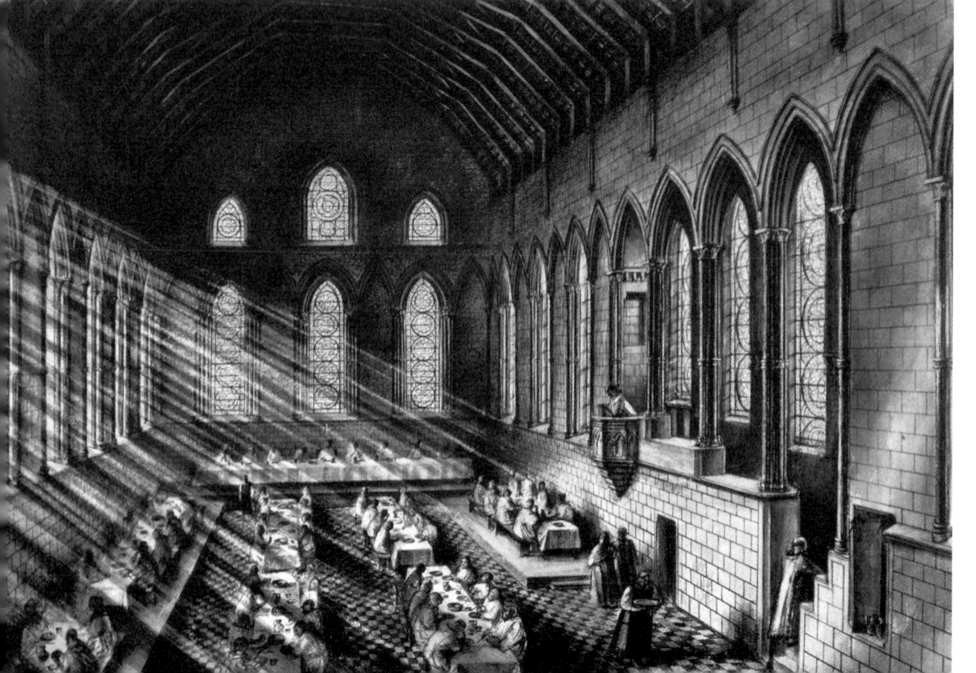

The refectory (frater) at Rievaulx Abbey, Yorkshire. (Alan Sorrell/ © English Heritage Photo Library)

In the late medieval period, feast-days were often marked with meals that were no less sumptuous than those of a magnate household. Indeed, a recent analysis of skeletons in three monastic burial sites suggests that many fifteenth-century monks were eating huge quantities of saturated fats and taking in about 6,000 calories a day. Evidence of arthritis in knees, hips and fingertips shows that the often underemployed monks were sometimes seriously obese – despite St Benedict's warning: 'There must be no danger of over-eating, so that no monk is overtaken by indigestion, for there is nothing so opposed to Christian life as over-eating.' The problem was not confined to the English monasteries: in Portugal those monks at the Cistercian monastery of Alcobaca who were unable to squeeze through a designated doorway from the frater were obliged to fast, while slimmer colleagues tucked in to 'pastry in vast abundance'. Even so, such cases may be exceptional, for there is also evidence that a relaxation of the rule in the late Middle Ages resulted in corpulence rather than obesity.

While the Benedictine rule reminded the brethren that 'wine maketh even the wise to fall away', there seem to have been no hard and fast rules concerning drink. Beer was the normal beverage (*see* BREWHOUSE), with milk offered (probably for medicinal or recuperative purposes), and wine on festive occasions – 'keeping in mind the weakness of the less robust, we think that half a pint of wine a day is sufficient for each'. Not surprisingly, water (the purity of which was extremely questionable) was rarely drunk – and then only with wine or for penitential purposes.

The Frater Building

The frater was usually parallel to the CLOISTER on the side opposite the church, either on the ground floor or raised above an UNDERCROFT. However, from the late twelfth century, refectories in the larger Cistercian houses often projected from the cloister on a north–south axis in order to accommodate a kitchen which was positioned so that meals might be served directly to the refectories of both the CHOIR MONKS and the LAY BROTHERS (*see* FRATER, KITCHENS *and* ROTA). The monks' fraters at Bylands, Buildwas, Fountains, Furness, Hayles, Roche, Tintern and Valle Crucis were all built or extended in this way, while at (smaller) Cleeve Abbey the brothers reverted to the earlier east–west orientation when the abbey was remodelled in the fifteenth century (*see below*). Of course, there were exceptions: in common with several of the smaller foundations, the monks of Cymer Abbey were so financially insecure that they never attempted to adopt the Cistercian model and the frater occupied the more conventional position – with an east–west axis, forming the southern range of the cloister.

In importance, the frater was second only to the church, for meals were perceived to be sacramental in character and symbolised the fraternal nature of the community. Consequently, they were usually imposing buildings, without aisles but with lofty timber roofs, and with devotional paintings on the east wall. The frater at Furness Abbey was one of the largest ever built by the Cistercians. Measuring 46m (150ft) in length and 12m (40ft) in width it was even larger than the refectory at Fountains Abbey, which was 33m (110ft) long and 14m (46ft) wide, while the frater at Rievaulx rose to a height of 15.2m (50ft). The undercroft of the frater often contained the great cellar in which provisions were stored, and this was sometimes provided with a fireplace, the heat keeping the provisions dry and warming the refectory above. There may also have been a BUTTERY, with a stair up to the SCREENS PASSAGE, which separated the body of the hall from the KITCHENS and pantry *see* LARDER.

Of the few refectories that have survived, that at the Cistercian abbey of Beaulieu in Hampshire now serves as a parish church, complete with FRATER PULPIT, while the most intact example, at Cleeve Abbey in Somerset (also Cistercian), has a splendid timber roof of ten bays, each of its principal trusses supported by a corbel decorated with an angel

holding a shield. Typically, the frater at Cleeve has four deep window embrasures in the south wall, together with a doorway which once gave access to the frater pulpit. The five windows in the north wall are shorter, to accommodate the cloister alley roof. Traces of a large painting of the Crucifixion, flanked by the figures of St Mary and St John, were once visible on the wall behind the dais, but these have now decayed almost beyond recognition. To the south of the refectory range, the tiled floor of an earlier thirteenth-century frater has survived almost intact. The frater at Worcester Cathedral Priory has survived as 'The College Hall', now part of the King's School and, according to Sir Edward Elgar, 'a wonderful setting for classical music . . . the acoustics were perfect'. The Worcester frater was rebuilt in the mid-fourteenth century over a Norman undercroft. It has large windows with reticulated TRACERY and on the east wall there is a sadly mutilated thirteenth-century Christ in Majesty, which was incorporated into the fourteenth-century rebuilding.
See also ABSTINENCE

FRATER PULPIT A raised lectern or balcony set in the wall near the high table of the FRATER, from which passages of scripture were read during meals (*see* READER IN FRATER). Frater pulpits were usually constructed within a window bay and often projected into the hall on corbels, the stairs concealed within the thickness of the wall or (as at Beaulieu) behind an open arcade. There was often a recessed book locker (*see* ARMARIUM) in the vicinity of the frater pulpit: at Fountains Abbey it is near the pulpit stairs. A frater pulpit is all that remains of the conventual buildings at Shrewsbury Abbey in Shropshire (now incongruously located in a car-park); while at Beaulieu Abbey, Hampshire, the frater has survived intact and is now the parish church. Its frater pulpit, which is approached by a narrow, vaulted stairway, is still used during services. While in most fraters the pulpit was located in the wall opposite the cloister, in Cistercian houses it was in the western wall.

FRATER RANGE *see* SOUTH RANGE

FRATERER *see* FRATER

FRATERNITY A religious brotherhood, a guild or group of people sharing a common interest or belief. The fraternities often attracted men of wealth and status: Richard of Gloucester (later Richard III) was a member of the fraternity of the cathedral priory of St Cuthbert at Durham.
See also CHANTRY COLLEGES

FREESTONE Easily sawn stone, usually oolitic limestone such as PORTLAND STONE or particular types of sandstone. Freestone has a fine grain, does not possess strongly marked laminations and may, therefore, be 'freely worked' with a saw and chisel.
See also MASONRY

FRIARS Greyfriars, Whitefriars and Blackfriars are common place-names in towns and cities where medieval friaries once stood. In the thirteenth century religious vocation passed to the mendicants. Theirs was an evangelising mission, particularly to the urban laity. But their churches were non-parochial and very few survived the dissolution of the friaries in 1538 (*see* FRIARY).

The two great orders of friars, the *Franciscans* (the Grey Friars or Friars Minor) and the *Dominicans* (the Black Friars or Friars Preacher) originated in the thirteenth century as adherents to the precepts of St Francis of Assisi (1181/2–1226) and St Dominic (1170–1221) respectively. Dominic was a Spaniard by birth; his objective was to prepare a team of preachers capable of counteracting the spread of heresy in southern France and he took the institutions of the Augustinian Canons as his model (*see* AUGUSTINIANS). In 1220 he is said to have met with Francis, whose influence persuaded him to adopt the Franciscan ideal of absolute POVERTY, both several and corporate, which had been adopted by the early Franciscans as the *Regula*

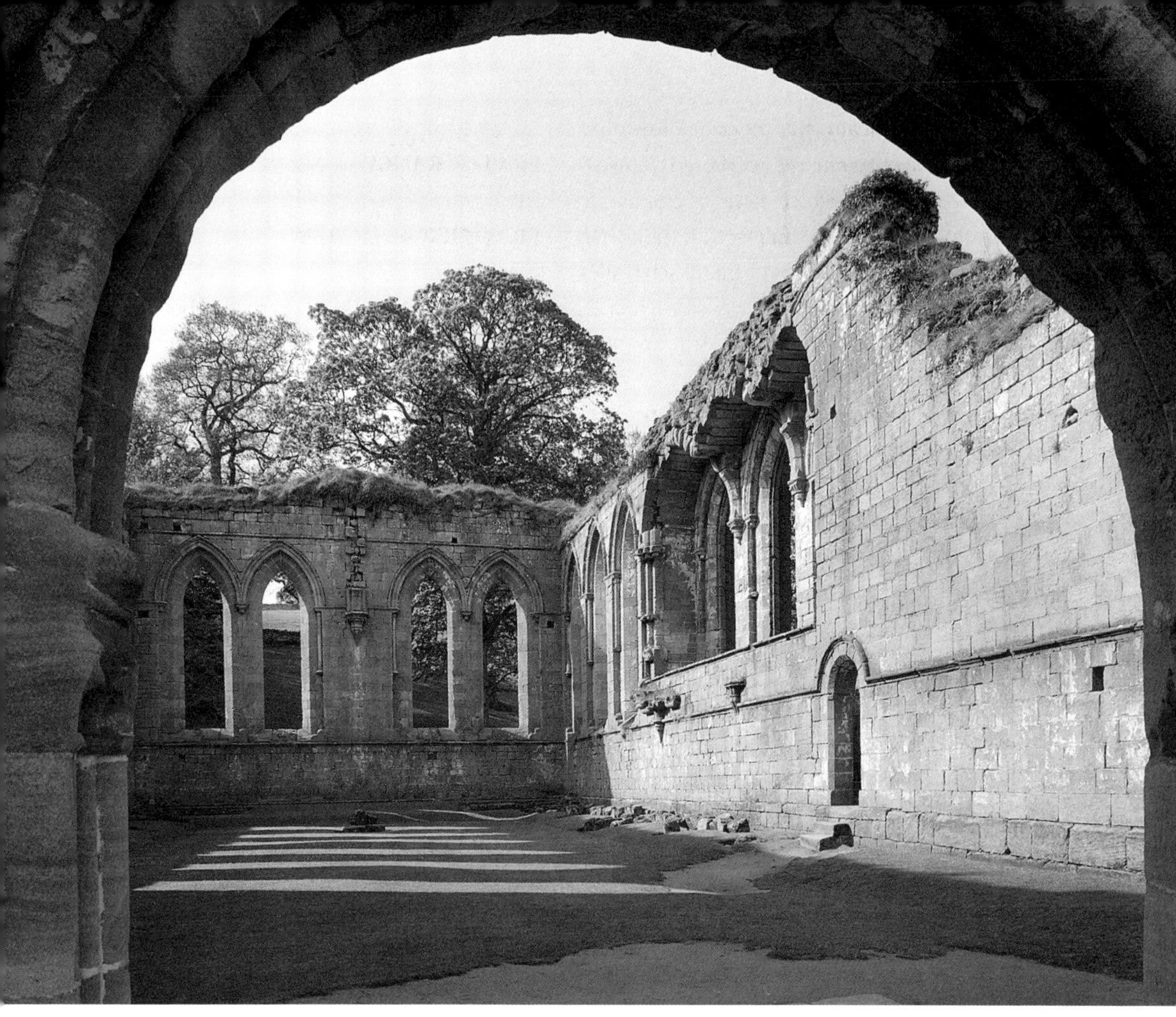

The pulpit in the west wall of the monks' refectory at Fountains Abbey, Yorkshire. To the right is the doorway to the pulpit stair. The present parapet was built in the nineteenth century and, at its southern end, covers the great corbel that once carried the reader's pulpit. (National Monuments Record/English Heritage)

Bullata (The First Rule) in 1209. The Dominican Order was established at two general chapters at Bologna in 1220 and 1221, while the Franciscans recast their First Rule in 1221 and brought it into its final form in 1223.

The Franciscans and Dominicans, unlike the monastic orders, were international brotherhoods of individuals whose members were itinerant preachers, ministering to the needs, and dependent on the charity, of those who employed them or from whom they begged. Both were MENDICANT orders (Latin *mendicare* = 'to beg') whose members did not belong to a particular religious house or community, as did the monks, and the properties needed for the administration of the orders were held on their behalf by the pope or some other PATRON. The Dominicans divided Europe into a number of provinces, each under the jurisdiction of a prior. A provincial CHAPTER, comprising representatives of the constituent houses, met annually to elect a *diffinitor*, by whom they would be represented at a GENERAL CHAPTER (which also met annually), and four *diffinitores* responsible for the administration of the chapter. For two years of a three-year cycle the general chapter was attended by the *diffinitores* and for the third by the provincial priors. A master-general of the Order was elected (for life) by an *ad hoc* general chapter.

By the 1240s the Franciscans had adopted a constitutional organisation very similar to that of the Dominicans.

The Dominicans arrived in England in 1221 and within fifty years had established some forty-six houses. The Franciscans followed in 1224, and by 1255 had forty-nine houses, more widely dispersed than those of the Dominicans, who preferred to concentrate their activities around the universities. Ironically, the Franciscans attracted to their number many of the most brilliant men of the age, and this resulted in the effective usurpation of the Dominicans' role as intellectuals and scholars and the diminution of Franciscan principles.

Other orders included the Order of the Hermits of St Augustine – the *Austin Friars* – (an order distinct from the Austin Canons) who, as their name suggests, began as communities of hermits (in the mountains of Italy) dedicated to the Augustinian rule. Like the Dominicans, they became scholars and preachers, but the order grew slowly in England, starting in small country towns and eventually moving into the larger urban centres, with some thrity-four houses. The *Carmelites* (or White Friars) also originated as a HERMIT community, located on Mount Carmel in Palestine. They were the most contemplative of all the friars, with thirty-seven English houses, some of which were remote from towns. Like the Carmelites, the smaller orders of Friars of the Holy Cross (the *Crutched Friars*), the Friars of the Penitential Sack and the Pied Friars were all under Dominican influence and their function was to teach and preach as priests and instructors among the urban laity. In 1274, the General Council of Lyon forbade these and other lesser orders to admit new members, so that those who remained were obliged to join one of the four major orders and their buildings were adapted for other 'suitable' purposes.

The *Trinitarians* (also known as the Maturins or *Red Friars*), founded in 1198, were not mendicants but an austere order of Augustinian priests. Their houses, of which there were about twelve in England and eight in Scotland, usually consisted of a prior, three priests and three LAY BROTHERS. Of these houses only traces remain at Ingham and Knaresborough, Dunbar and Peebles. The *Bonshommes* was an obscure order, possibly derived from the Friars of the Sack, introduced into England by Henry III. They wore a blue habit and followed the Augustinian rule.

The popularity of the mendicant friars in thirteenth-century England was in part attributable to their preference for going into the world instead of withdrawing from it, and partly because their poverty contrasted with the rapidly increasing wealth of the monastic foundations. But of even greater significance was the concentration of pastoral work in the towns, where the friars must have been a familiar and reassuring sight and where enormous crowds were attracted to their preaching. (The sermon was the principal medieval means of mass-communication and several urban churches, with long hall-like naves, were constructed by the Dominicans to accommodate congregations.) It was this popularity which bred increasing resentment and hostility among the lay clergy and the monasteries. Parish priests, for the most part poorly trained and held in low regard by their parishioners, were unable to compete with the sermons of the mendicants or with their competence in hearing confessions. They were also losing valuable revenues from burial fees, as people opted in increasing numbers for burial in the friars' churchyards rather than those of their parishes. The poverty and humility of the friars were characteristics with which the populace readily identified, while the unremitting acquisition of wealth which typified many of the monastic foundations was thrown into sharp relief by the comparison. The response of the late medieval 'establishment' was predictable. Misinformation found its way into the works of Chaucer and Langland and even influenced the redoubtable Wycliffe. There can be little doubt that there was some justification for criticism of the friars during the fourteenth and fifteenth centuries: observation of the First Rule had become lax and many friars employed decidedly dubious devices to extract money from patrons or to persuade young people to join their orders. Nevertheless, such criticism was by no means universal, indeed there is considerable evidence to suggest that there was no significant decline in the number or quality of bequests and benefactions to the mendicant orders until the Reformation.

FRIARY The religious house of one of the orders of FRIARS together with its church, which, unlike monastic churches, was designed to accommodate large numbers of people attracted by the friars' preaching. Most friary churches were effectively open halls, without screens or divisions, allowing uninterrupted views of the altar and preacher. A subsidiary church, reserved for the friars' private offices, was usually separated from the main church by a passage above which was a tower. Friary churches were not parochial, however, and few survived the dissolution of the friaries in 1538. Of those that did, the church of the Black Friars at Norwich is perhaps one of the most impressive (Norwich had convents of all four principal orders). Its nave, over 61m (200ft) in length, is indicative of the size of congregations attracted by the more popular preachers. The grounds of a friary were considered by many to be especially holy and were, therefore, popular places of burial.

FROSTERLEY MARBLE *see* PURBECK MARBLE

FUNERAL HATCHMENTS *see* HATCHMENTS

FUNERAL HERALDRY Funerals of the late medieval and Tudor nobility were often magnificent spectacles, not least the processions which preceded the committal in which the deceased's heraldic accoutrements were solemnly paraded in the cortège. These included his spurs, gauntlets, crested helm, shield (known in this context as a *targe*), sword, tabard, pennons and banner. After the service these symbols of chivalry would be laid up in the church, but regrettably very few early examples remain, the best known being the helm, scabbard, gauntlets, shield and embroidered surcoat of Edward the Black Prince (d. 1376) at Canterbury Cathedral (these are kept

Gateway leading to the Grey Friars, Gloucester.

near his tomb, those which hang above it being replicas).

In the sixteenth and seventeenth centuries, the Kings of Arms organised the heraldic funerals of the nobility and gentry, and the records of these magnificent occasions are contained in eighteen volumes in the archives of the College of Arms in London (*see* APPENDIX II for address). These *funeral certificates* contain much useful information, including the date and place of death and details of the deceased's descendants and of his family's heraldry. A list of fees payable to the College for the entering of certificates was issued by the earl Marshal in 1618. A fee of £45 was charged 'for a duke, duchess or archbishop' and this was reduced incrementally according to rank, a 'gentleman' paying only £2. The herald-painters also charged for executing the various escutcheons, standards, bannerols, pennons and other items that were required by the heralds for a particular funeral. Again, these 'achievements' were strictly regulated according to the rank of the deceased. For example, banners and bannerols were confined to peers and their ladies, standards (but not banners) to knights, and pennons (but not standards) to esquires. Mere gentlemen had no pennons, only 'scocheons [escutcheons] of arms', small panels on which the arms were painted (the prototypes of later HATCHMENTS).

Not only was every detail of the heraldic funeral controlled by the heralds, but also the formalities of mourning and the precedence accorded to those who participated in the ceremonial. Of Thomas Howard, the 2nd Duke of Norfolk, it was stated that 'no nobleman was ever to be buried in such style again'. Following his death in May 1524, the Duke's body lay in state for a month in the chapel of Framlingham Castle, Suffolk, in which were hung funereal drapes and numerous shields of arms. The Duke's coffin, drawn on a chariot and embellished with gold shields, was accompanied on its 24-mile progress to Thetford Priory in Norfolk by nine hundred mourners, including heralds, gentlemen of his household and numerous black-robed torch-bearers. At Thetford the coffin was placed on an enormous black and gold catafalque, adorned with seven hundred lights, black-robed wax effigies holding eight bannerols, and one hundred richly emblazoned shields of arms. The service included a procession of heralds carrying achievements of the Duke's arms and the dramatic entry of a mounted knight, wearing the dead Duke's armour and carrying his inverted battleaxe.

Several less grandiose examples of funeral accoutrements have survived, and from these may be traced the gradual evolution of the heraldic funeral from the practical equipment of medieval warfare and tournament, through the stylised, artificial helms, crests, tabards and flags of the sixteenth and seventeenth centuries to the heraldic substitute, the funeral hatchment of the seventeenth, eighteenth and nineteenth centuries (*see* HATCHMENTS).
See also HERALDRY

FUNERALS *see* BURIALS (MONASTIC), FUNERAL HERALDRY, HATCHMENTS *and* OSSUARIES

FURS *see* COLOURS (HERALDIC)

G

GABLE The triangular upper part of a wall supporting the end of a ridged roof.

GALILEE A somewhat controversial term variously used to describe a vestibule reserved as a chapel for penitents at the western end of a nave (*see* NARTHEX) or a porch enclosing the great west door. The former definition, which applies more accurately to examples in several French churches, may have originated in the 'Galilee of the Gentiles' of Matt 4:15. In England, however, a Galilee is a porch incorporated into the west end of the church for processional purposes (*see* PROCESSIONS), the name symbolising Jesus leading his disciples into Galilee following the Resurrection (Matt 28: 10). In many cases the Galilee was as wide as the church itself, and it was a characteristic feature of Cistercian churches, where it was usually constructed across the exterior of the western façade (*see* WEST FRONT). At Rievaulx, for example, the Galilee was built in the 1150s and was remodelled on at least two occasions, with solid walls replacing the original open ARCADE. At Fountains there were originally two doorways from the Galilee to the church: an elaborately moulded central doorway through which the procession would enter the nave and a plain doorway (later blocked) by which the monks entered the Galilee from the cloister and the north aisle. Corbels in the west wall of the church at Byland suggest that this type of Galilee was constructed with a sloping roof (*pentise*). In Cistercian churches, until the late thirteenth century, the Galilee was a popular location for the burial of lay patrons (at Rievaulx traces remain of eight graves).

Elsewhere, the Galilee was usually a large projecting porch. At Ely Cathedral Priory, for example, it was superimposed on the Norman west front in *c*. 1215 and is a graceful example of Early English architecture, although its original appearance has been lost following successive restorations. The Galilee at Durham Cathedral Priory (1170) is exceptional in that it is a LADY CHAPEL, its unusual position traditionally attributed to St Cuthbert's abhorrence of women. According to legend, whenever an attempt was made to construct a Lady Chapel in the usual position at the east end of the church, the Durham saint miraculously intervened, causing the foundations to collapse. It may also have been reserved specifically as an area, outside the confines of the church, in which women were permitted to worship: there is a line across the floor that marks the limit beyond which they could not pass. The Galilee at Durham has five aisles of equal height, is similar in appearance to an Islamic prayer hall and (it has been suggested) may have been influenced by Muslim craftsmen. At Glastonbury, an elongated western projection of the abbey church incorporated both a Galilee and a Lady Chapel. This was the first building to be completed following a fire in 1184 that destroyed the abbey buildings and the treasures contained therein. As at Durham, the position of the Lady Chapel is most unusual and was the result of a desire to replace on its original site the chapel of St Mary, which contained the most venerated of the lost shrines.

See also NARTHEX *and* PORCHES

GALLERY (i) In major medieval churches there is often a broad passageway constructed within the space above an aisle. This gallery, which usually opened on to the nave through an ARCADE, is known as the *tribune*. It should not be confused with the TRIFORIUM, which is a narrow wall passage or area of blind arcading immediately below the CLERESTORY. When, at the end of the fifteenth century, the monks of Gloucester replaced their thirteenth-century LADY CHAPEL with a magnificent Perpendicular structure, they incorporated an enclosed passage that connected the choir tribune on the north with its counterpart on the south. This was achieved by constructing an elaborate bridge at the west end of the Lady Chapel. This carries, beside the passage, a small chapel with an altar which was probably part of the earlier, thirteenth-century structure. For acoustic reasons the passage is known as *'The Whispering Gallery'* and is set back from the great east window of the choir (the Crécy window) so that the vast expanse of coloured glass is uninterrupted.

(ii) A tiered upper storey constructed to provide additional seating, as in the splendid baroque church of St Philip, Birmingham (1719), which became the city's Anglican cathedral in 1905.

(iii) An elevated loft from which a shrine could be observed for reasons of security (*see* SHRINES *and*

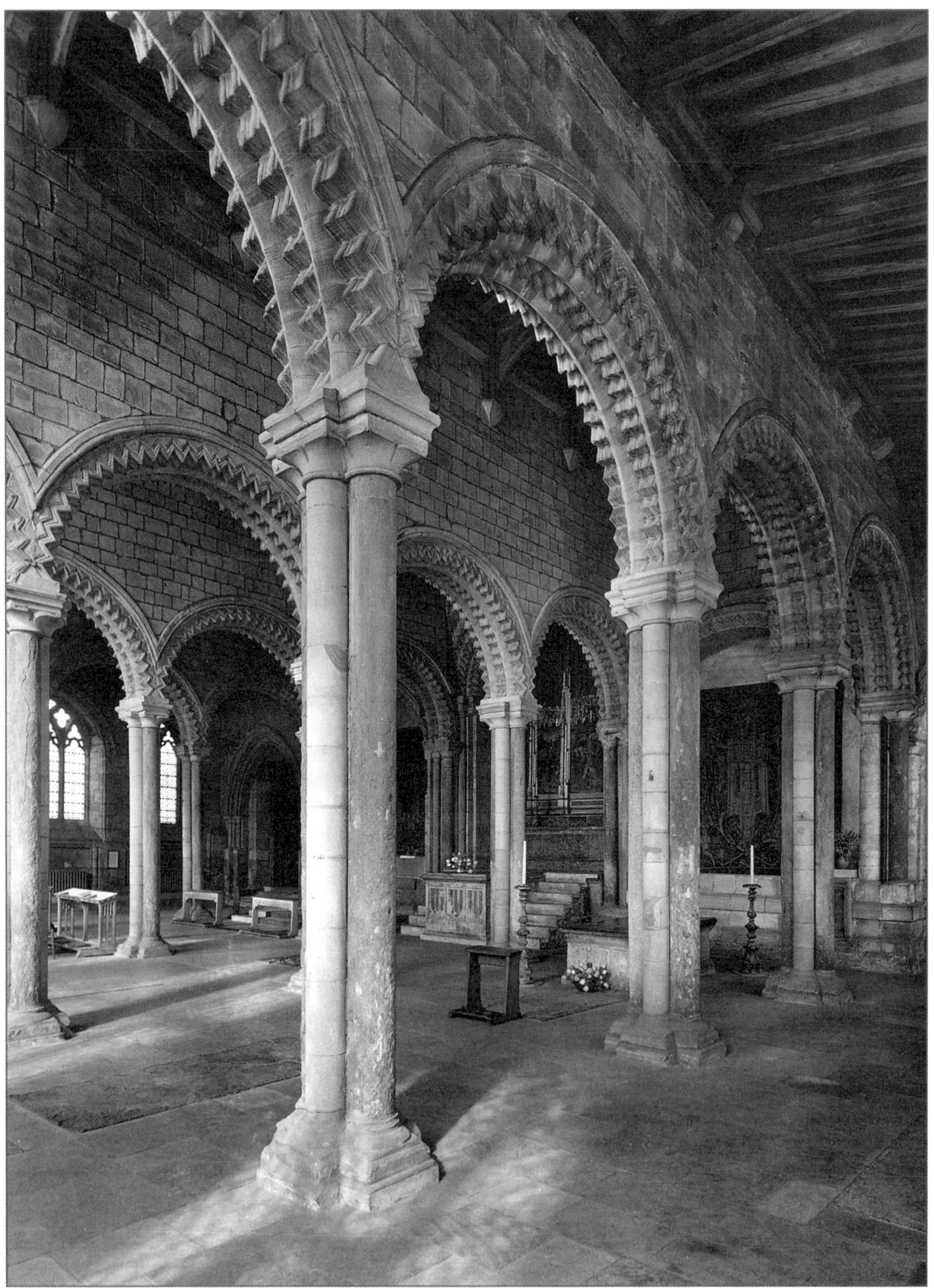

The Galilee Chapel, added to the west façade of Durham Cathedral by Bishop Hugh de Puiset in the 1170s. (Courtesy of Anthony Kersting)

WATCHING LOFT).
(iv) A raised landing or passageway, as at Fountains Abbey, where, in the fourteenth century, a gallery was constructed as an upper storey to the infirmary passage (*see* SLYPE). To the west, this led from the Abbot's Hall to a private chapel above the chapter house and, to the north, to a window opening in the south gable of the Chapel of the Nine Altars. The function of this strange gallery remains unclear, although it may be that the abbot occupied a private pew at the end of the north gallery in order to hear services conducted in the adjacent chapel (*see* SUPERIOR'S LODGINGS).
See also EXPOSITION GALLERY *and* MINSTRELS' GALLERY

GARDENER The gardener was responsible to the CELLARER and his duties included the daily supply and preparation of fruit and vegetables for the kitchens and of herbs when required by the kitchens and PHARMACY.

GARDEROBE A medieval latrine or privy, usually a single cell at the end of a short, crooked passage, within the thickness of a wall from which a shaft vented to a cesspool beneath. Others consisted of stone benches in cubicles (*gonges*) which projected on corbels high above a culvert or stream. Most latrines must have been exceedingly draughty, although those in private chambers were sometimes provided with braziers to heat water for washing. Garderobes were sometimes provided in monastic guest houses and abbots' lodgings, but choir monks and lay brethren were obliged to use the rather less congenial *domus necessaria* ('necessary house') or REREDORTER, which was usually located in the vicinity of the dormitory (*see* DORTER).

GARGOYLE The legendary *Gargouille* was a seventh-century river dragon who supposedly ravaged the city of Rouen. From the Old French *gargouille* meaning 'throat', a gargoyle is a projecting gutterstone, incorporating a lead water-spout and often carved to depict a grotesque visage, beast or figure. The function of a gargoyle was to discharge rainwater away from the walls and footings of a building. This was particularly necessary when, in the fourteenth century, ornamental traceried parapets were developed as a means of finishing off a wall. With no eaves to carry rainwater away from the building, it was necessary to provide lead bow-gutters behind the parapets and gargoyles to discharge the rainwater at regular intervals.

GARTH Derived from the Old Norse *garsr* meaning 'an enclosure', the term was originally applied to any small enclosed space, as in churchyard/churchgarth. A *cloister garth* was the area enclosed within the CLOISTER of a monastery. This was often served by piped water or a well and would be laid out with a lawn or as a vegetable or herb garden (*herbarium*) – although the CARTHUSIANS used the cloister garth as a burial ground.
See also LAVATORIUM

GATEHOUSES *see* FORTIFICATION, MONASTIC BUILDINGS *and* PRECINCT

GENERAL The title usually given to the head of a religious order or CONGREGATION, hence the Master General was head of the Dominican Order and the Minister General was the head of the Franciscans.

GENERAL CHAPTER Introduced by the Cistercians in 1119 and made compulsory by the fourth Lateran Council of 1215, General chapters of the integrated monastic orders were convened at four-yearly intervals so that order and uniformity might be maintained. General chapters were convened by a mother house and attended by the SUPERIORS (or their representatives) of the daughter houses. The decisions taken by a General Council were binding on all members of the order. Some orders, notably the Benedictines, also held triennial provincial chapters.

GESSO SOTTILE *see* MANUSCRIPT ILLUMINATION

GILBERTINE ORDER Founded by Gilbert of Sempringham (*c.* 1089–1189) in 1131, the religious communities of nuns of the Gilbertine Order (the only truly English monastic order) initially followed a simplified version of the Benedictine RULE, but as their numbers grew and LAY BROTHERS and sisters joined them, their direction was entrusted to Canons Regular following the Augustinian Rule under the control of the Master of Sempringham. The communities then took the form of 'double houses' in which there were usually twice as many nuns as canons. These double monasteries were arranged to ensure strict segregation under a single SUPERIOR. At the Dissolution of the Monasteries, there were twenty-five Gilbertine houses concentrated in Yorkshire, Lincolnshire and East Anglia, the largest of which, Watton Priory (fl. 1150), could accommodate 140 nuns and 70 canons.
See also DOUBLE MONASTERY

GLASS *see* GLAZIERS' MARKS, STAINED GLASS *and* WINDOWS

GLAZIERS' MARKS With the exception of a very small number of medieval examples, the marks and signatures found in STAINED GLASS windows are mostly from the nineteenth and twentieth centuries. Marks may identify a glazier, designer or both: the figure of a hooded friar is combined with a designer's initials in windows by the Whitefriars Glass company, for example. Monograms and signatures are widely used, as are heraldic devices and rebuses: Geoffrey Webb (1879–1954) used a spider's web, Joseph Nuttgens (1892–1982) a hazelnut, Alfred Bell (1832–95) a bell and Barbara Batt (1909–present) a bat, for example. Some are more complex: a stylised flower may be a woodruff and therefore the mark of Paul Woodroffe (1875–1954), while a wheel, half cartwheel and half ship's wheel, was used by Harry Stammers (1902–69) whose father and father-in-law were respectively a wheelwright and a mariner. One of the best known glaziers' marks is that of Sir William Comper (1864–1960), who 'signed' his work with a strawberry-leaf mark, apparently in memory of his father, who was sharing strawberries with a group of children when he died. These, and many more delightful glaziers' marks, are to be found in a splendid catalogue of *Stained Glass Makers' Marks*, edited by Joyce Little and published in 1993 by the Church Recorders section of NADFAS (*For* address *see* APPENDIX II).

GLAZING BARS The vertical and horizontal bars that secure pieces of glass within a window frame. Not to be confused with mullions and transoms, which separate the lights within a window opening.
See also MULLIONS, TRANSOMS *and* WINDOWS

GLORIA PATRI The familiar ascription of praise to the Trinity beginning with the words 'Glory be to the Father . . .' recited (or sung) at the conclusion of the psalms. Its use dates from the fourth century, and thereafter it is found in metrical form at the end of hymns in the Offices.

GODBOTE A fine imposed by the Church in respect of an offence against God.

GOSPEL (i) The teaching of Christ.
(ii) A narrative of the life of Christ, notably the New Testament Gospels of Matthew, Mark, Luke and John the authority of which was established by the mid-second century.
(iii) The stated portion of these to be read (or sung) at the EUCHARIST by the *gospeller*.

GOTHIC The style of architecture prevalent throughout western Europe from the twelfth century to the sixteenth century, characterised by the pointed ARCH (*see* MEDIEVAL ARCHITECTURE).
GOTHIC LETTERING *see* LETTERING

GOTHIC TRACERY *see* MEDIEVAL ARCHITECTURE

GRADINE A raised ledge behind an altar on which the cross is sometimes placed.
See also TABERNACLE

GRADUALE In the EUCHARIST, the antiphons sung immediately following the first Scriptural lesson. Since 1969, a psalm may be sung instead.
See also ANTIPHON

GRANARY *see* BARNS (GRANARIUM)

GRANATORIUS The 'keeper of the granary' had his own office and store, through which passed all wheat and malt corn from the granaries, both those located within the CURIA and others at outlying granges (*see* BARNS (GRANARIUM) *and* GRANGE). He was required to maintain detailed records of distribution, income and expenditure. At Durham he was described as the 'Master of the Garners'.

GRANDMONTINES An austere order, founded at the reformed monastery of Grandmont (Limoge) in 1046. Sometimes known as the 'Bons Hommes', members of the order wore a black habit and were dedicated to an observant, hermetical life. They lived in plain, simple buildings and occupied individual cells. The Grandmontine houses of Alberbury and Craswall were dissolved as alien priories (*see* ALIEN PRIORY), while a small denizen priory at Grosmont survived.

GRANGE The Cistercian monasteries of the twelfth and early thirteenth centuries accumulated vast endowments of land from Norman magnates whose admiration of Cistercian piety conveniently matched their own preoccupation with salvation. Many of these lands were so remote and fragmented that it was impossible for them to be worked directly from the abbey itself and a system of outlying farms (*grangia*) and subordinate lodges developed, staffed by lay brethren (*conversi*) and administered centrally by the abbey CELLARER. Furness Abbey in Cumbria, for example, had eighteen granges located at strategic sites throughout its estates, and at Kilnsey in Wharfedale (one of the granges of Fountains Abbey in Yorkshire) there were seven subordinate lodges, each manned by one or two LAY BROTHERS together with a cowman or shepherd. Wherever possible, granges were located within 40km (25 miles) of each other and each served both as an administrative centre and as a storehouse for produce.

So successful was the system in its early days that other monastic orders adopted it for their own estates. But during the thirteenth century endowments of land to monastic foundations declined. There was also a significant reduction in the recruitment of lay brothers, aggravated in the fourteenth century by the Black Death (*see* PLAGUE) and a more competitive labour market. Furthermore, the monastic foundations were increasingly perceived as being avaricious and corrupt and, although the Cistercian RULE required that monasteries should be detached from the evils of everyday life, the occupants of the granges inevitably experienced daily contact with local communities and were ill-equipped to cope with the numerous conflicts of interest that ensued. Difficulties in recruiting sufficient lay brothers led to the employment of local peasant labour and granges were increasingly leased to laymen, with a consequential weakening of the monastic system. The abandonment of direct management was determined by the individual needs of a particular house and of the regional economy. The changes were generally initiated at the furthest, cash-producing manors, with the home farms (which provided directly for the needs of the community) being retained well into the fifteenth century. Many of the lessees were experienced local farmers and the monasteries employed lay stewards to oversee the estates and to be accountable directly to the SUPERIOR or BURSAR.

In the late medieval period monastic granges were used also as refuges from infectious epidemics

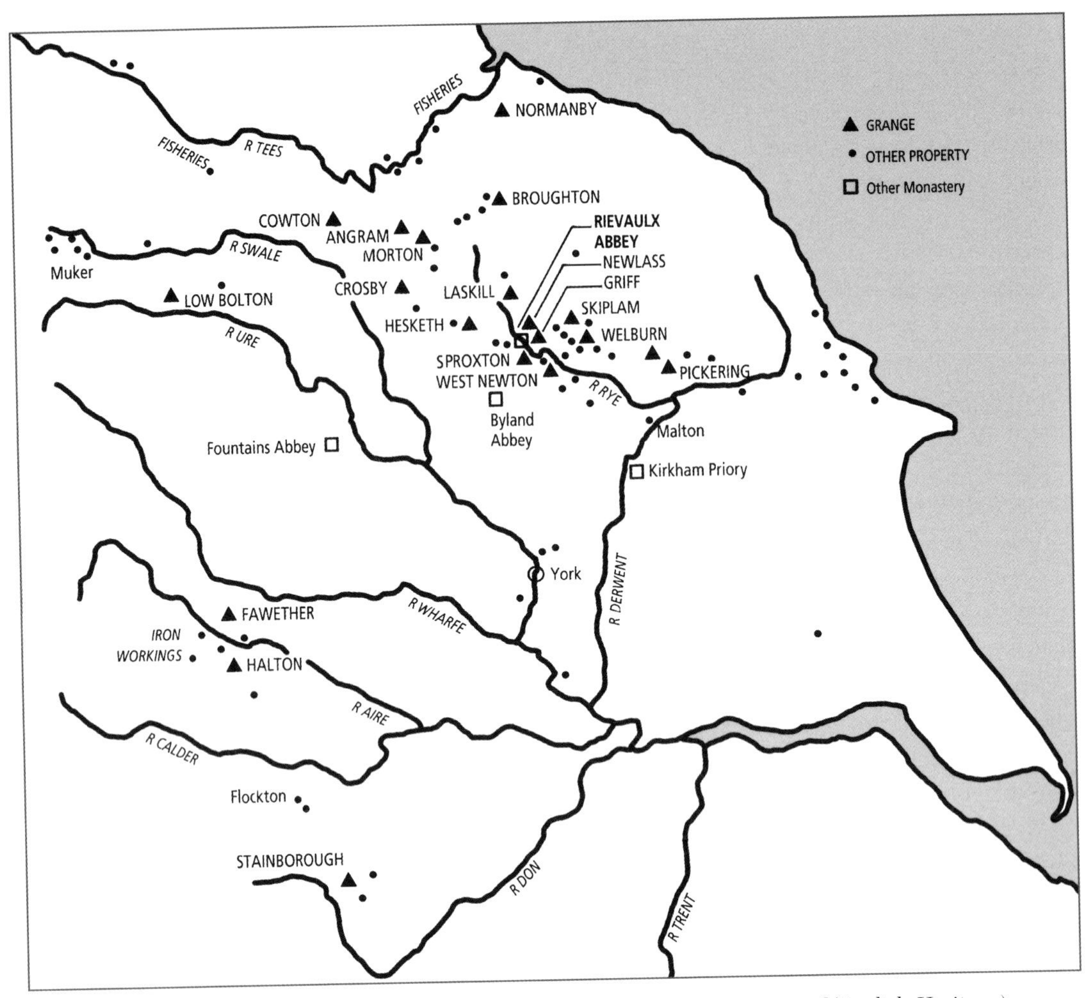

Rievaulx Abbey estates in the early thirteenth century. (National Monuments Record/English Heritage)

and as convalescent homes for sick or infirm brethren. Some became the favoured retreats of superiors anxious to escape from the demands of office. Indeed, so popular was the notion of *vacation* that fifteenth-century legislation required that an abbot should spend no more than three months annually away from his abbey.

Granges varied considerably: some were substantial complexes of purpose-built agricultural and domestic buildings, with a large barn and chapel and a substantial community of lay brothers and agricultural labourers, sometimes exceeding twenty in number and supervised by a grange master or *granger*. Others were subsidiary lodges – small farmsteads adapted to accommodate a single lay brother and one or two paid staff, augmented when necessary by local labourers. In all cases, the services of specialist staff would be required from time to time and these would be provided by the mother house.

Similarly, monastic estates varied in extent, depending on location and topography. The granges of the Cistercian abbey of Meaux, for example, varied from 85 acres at Sutton to nearly 1,500 acres at Skerne, while an average lowland grange in Yorkshire extended to some 400 acres.

By the early thirteenth century, some monastic estates were organised according to traditional manorial practice, the arable land held jointly by a religious house and its tenants, who either paid a money rent or provided labour. Both groups (the *censarii* and the *villeins*) were required to undertake customary service and were supervised by a steward or bailiff appointed by the abbey. Largely as a result of the Black Death, and the decline of the *conversi*, by 1400 this system of leasing had been adopted on the majority of monastic estates, although religious houses maintained direct control of sufficient lands to ensure adequate rents and produce to meet their needs, including those of the almonries (*see* ALMONRY). Several granges developed as settlements or were converted to domestic use following the Dissolution of the Monasteries, although not all 'Grange' place-names are genuine.
See also BARTON, FINANCE, TIMBER, VINEYARDS *and* WOOL

GRAVEYARDS *see* BURIALS (MONASTIC)

GREAT HOURS *see* HOURS (CANONICAL)

GREAT ROOD *see* ROOD SCREEN

GREAT SCHISM The period 1378–1417, during which the western Church was divided by the election of antipopes. The schism also caused bitter political dissent: the Avignon papacy was supported by France, Scotland, Castile, Aragon and some German princes; while the pope in Rome was supported by the Holy Roman Emperor, England, Scandinavia and most Italian states.

GREEN MEN One of the most powerful and enduring symbols of pagan mythology, Green men are to be found in a variety of forms in the foliated stonework and ornamental woodcarving of medieval churches throughout Europe. These male heads wreathed in foliage, which is often depicted growing from their mouths, eyes, ears and nostrils, are ideally suited to the ornamentation of capitals, corbels, bosses, misericords, candle sconces, etc. Originally a Celtic symbol of creative fertility in nature, the Green Man is closely associated with Cerunnos, the stag-horned deity who lived deep in the greenwood and who controlled all living things. The Green Man is the May King (Man-in-the-Oak or Jack-in-the-Green) of May Day ceremonies who, wreathed in garlands of oak and hawthorn (may tree), feigned death and then came to life to comfort and dance with his disconsolate May Queen. In Christian imagery, the Green Man became a symbol of Easter and Resurrection. With only a few exceptions, the medieval masons depicted the Green Man as a gentle and benevolent deity.

GREENSAND A cretacious sandstone carrying the green iron-bearing mineral glaucomite.

GREGORIAN CALENDAR The 'New Style' calendar was introduced by Pope Gregory XIII, who, in 1582, declared that 5 October should be 15 October. This was generally adopted in Catholic countries, but in England the calendar was not changed until 1752, when 3 September became 14 September. Eleven days were thereby lost from the fiscal year, the beginning of which was moved from 25 March to 6 April to compensate, and New Year's Day was changed from 25 March to 1 January. Correctly, reference to dates falling between 1 January and 25 March prior to 1753 should be referred to as, e.g. 28 January 1748/9. Pope Gregory also decreed that, of the centesimal years, only those exactly divisible by 400 should be counted as leap years.
See also JULIAN CALENDAR

GREGORIAN CHANT *see* PLAINSONG

GREYFRIARS *see* FRIARS

GRISAILLE Thirteenth- and fourteenth-century window glass to which a delicate silvery-grey coating of paint was applied, often with lightly painted leaf and stem patterns on a background of

cross-hatching and interlaced STRAPWORK. Such glass remains translucent and enhances the coolness and tranquillity of an interior. In the fourteenth century colourful painted and STAINED GLASS motifs, including human figures and armorial devices, were often inserted in the grisaille.
See also WINDOWS

GROIN VAULT *see* VAULTING

GROTESQUE (i) A decorative motif in the form of a comically distorted visage.
(ii) Decorative interweaving of foliage with human and animal forms.

GROZING IRON *see* STAINED GLASS

GUARDIAN OF THE CLOISTER *see* CLOISTER

GUEST HOUSE (HOSPITIUM) The Benedictine rule declared that 'All guests who come shall be received as though they were Christ, for He himself said "I was a stranger and ye took me in."' HOSPITALITY was therefore an essential element of monastic life and accommodation was provided for guests at even the smallest of religious houses. The usual stay was for two days and two nights, although guests who were ill were usually granted an extension in order to recuperate. In the late medieval period, there were three classes of guest: magnates, both noble and ecclesiastical, were the personal guests of the superior and shared his lodgings (*see* SUPERIOR'S LODGINGS); those of lesser rank stayed in the cellarer's *hospitium* or guest house; and the poor, pilgrims and passing wayfarers were accepted into the HOSPICE or ALMONRY, sometimes located outside the abbey PRECINCT. There were several notable exceptions: at Durham, for example, all guests were treated with equal liberality, while the term 'ever open door' apparently derives from Bardney Abbey's reputation for universal hospitality. In large communities, the guest house was often a building of considerable size, administered by the *guest-master*, who was responsible for the welfare of guests, although subordinate to the CELLARER. Most guest houses were located within the precinct but at some remove from the cloister so that 'guests should not disquiet the brethren by their untimely arrivals'. Even the remote Cistercian houses made provision for guests: Fountains Abbey had two guest houses (with fireplaces and latrines) and a guests' hall, while the guest house at Kirkstall Abbey comprised an aisled hall with transepts containing individual chambers, to which was added a courtyard complex of kitchen, service quarters and stables. Of the few monastic guest houses that have survived, the Guesten Hall of Sherborne Abbey in Dorset is one of the most impressive, although it has been modified for use by Sherborne School.

It was the *guest-master* who was responsible for the welfare of guests and for ensuring that quarters were kept in a state of readiness – clean and well provided with linen and other necessities. He was obliged to keep two hogsheads of wine 'against the coming of strangers' and to provide fodder for guests' horses. The guest-master was sometimes assisted by a *hosteller* and a staff of 'yeomen' who waited on the guests. He was subordinate to the CELLARER, from whom he received food, drink and other provisions, and he would work closely with the KITCHENER to ensure that guests were provided with refreshment, no matter how late their arrival. His office exemplified Christ's care for the homeless and destitute and was therefore filled by a brother of outstanding integrity – especially important in one who would frequently come into contact with the outside world. The rule of silence was relaxed so that he could communicate with guests, and consequently it was the guest-master who usually acted as intermediary whenever a visitor wished to speak with the SUPERIOR or any member of the community, and it was he who instructed postulants (*see* POSTULANT) and introduced to CHAPTER those who sought CONFRATERNITY.

See also ALMONRY, BEDE-HOUSE, CORRODIAN, HOSPICE, HOSPITALS *and* SHRINES

GUEST-MASTER *see* GUEST HOUSE

GULES *see* COLOURS (HERALDIC)

H

HABIT *see* CLOTHING

HAGIOSCOPE *see* SQUINT

HAGODAY *see* SANCTUARY

HALF SHAFT (*also* ENGAGED SHAFT) A pier or column partially attached to, or let into, a wall.

HALL A large communal chamber, most often found in the GUEST HOUSE or SUPERIOR'S LODGINGS of a monastery, or in place of the monastic FRATER and PARLOUR in a secular house.

HALL-CHURCH Unique among British medieval cathedrals, Bristol has side aisles rising to the same height as the nave, an arrangement similar to that of a German *hallenkirche* or hall-church. Inevitably, the absence of a CLERESTORY renders the nave vault rather dark, although the aisles are well lit by lofty windows. The Augustinians, who built the original nave (destroyed by fire in the sixteenth century), were so impoverished that they were obliged to beg food from the citizens of Bristol. The present nave and west front were designed by G.E. Street (1824–81) and completed in 1888. Coventry Cathedral, designed by Sir Basil Spence (1907–76) is, in many respects, a twentieth-century interpretation of a traditional hall-church (*see* POST-MEDIEVAL CATHEDRALS).

HATCHING *see* COLOURS (HERALDIC)

HATCHMENTS A hatchment comprises a coat of arms painted on a diamond-shaped wooden panel or on canvas within a wooden frame. Occasionally a frame will carry a brief inscription, and some hatchments include initials and a date. The word itself is a corruption of 'achievement', suggesting that it originated in the elaborate funeral heraldry of the medieval nobility. Like the earlier 'scocheon of arms' (*see* FUNERAL HERALDRY), a hatchment was carried in procession to the church, where it remained following interment. Alternatively, it may have been returned to the deceased's house following the service and hung above the door during a period of mourning, before being returned once again to the church. It is the treatment of the background which makes the hatchment unique: essentially, this is coloured black beneath those parts of a coat of arms which relate to the deceased. The system was well established by 1700, and eighteenth- and nineteenth-century illustrations and engravings and the records of antiquarian county histories indicate that there were once many more hatchments in our cathedral churches than there are today.

HEADMINSTER *see* ANGLO-SAXON CHURCH.

HEARSE (*also* HERSE) (i) A triangular stand holding fifteen candles. A hearse was used at a special form of Mattins and Lauds known as *Tenebrae*, celebrated on the last three days of Holy Week, during which the church candles were extinguished one by one (Latin *tenebrae* = 'darkness').
(ii) A barrel-shaped metal cage erected above an effigy and intended to support candles and a pall which was removed only on special occasions (*see* EFFIGIES). One of the most magnificent examples is that above the gilded bronze effigy of Richard

Beauchamp, fifth earl of Warwick (d. 1439) at St Mary's, Warwick.
(iii) A cage-like structure over a bier, although in modern usage the term has come to mean a vehicle in which a coffin is conveyed to a funeral.

HEART BURIAL The medieval practice of interring a man's heart, the seat of love and piety, in a place other than that in which his body was buried was particularly common during the thirteenth and fourteenth centuries. The separate burial of the heart and body is sometimes described in documents as 'partly buried'. Frequently, such heart burials took place in monastic churches, notably the sequestered abbeys of the Cistercian order such as Sweetheart Abbey (*Dulce Cor*) in the county of Dumfries and Galloway, where the heart of its founder, John Balliol, was buried. Similarly, the heart of a thirteenth-century bishop of Hereford was interred at Cistercian Abbey Dore in Herefordshire, the spot being marked with a miniature effigy of the bishop.

HEATING Originally, the only heated rooms in a monastery were the warming house (*see* CALEFACTORIUM), the hospitium (*see* GUEST HOUSE) and the farmery (*see* INFIRMARY) although, of necessity, there would also be fires in the KITCHENS and the workshops in the outer precinct. Later, a general relaxation of the rule was accompanied by a proliferation of smaller chambers with fireplaces, notably in the SUPERIOR'S LODGINGS and in suites of rooms for corrodians (*see* CORRODIAN). The abbey church would be unheated, and among the sacrist's many duties was the provision of a dish of warm coals at which the celebrant warmed his hands in winter (*see* SACRIST).

HEBDOMARIAN The priest responsible for celebrating all choir offices, including the daily High Mass, for saying grace in the FRATER, and for reading the lessons at Mattins and Evensong. With the exception of the SUPERIOR, all members of a religious house who were also priests were obliged to take their turn. They served for one week – from Evensong on Saturday to High Mass and None on the following Saturday – their names being posted on the TABULA and announced in CHAPTER.

HENRY VIII (1491–1547) King of England 1509–47, whose attempts to dissolve his marriage with Catherine of Aragon led to England's break with the Church of Rome and, ultimately, to the establishment of the CHURCH OF ENGLAND. The *Act of Supremacy* of 1534 did not create the sovereign's title 'supreme head on earth of the Church of England'. It merely acknowledged his right to it and defined and sanctioned the legal powers which it entailed. The Act was repealed by Mary I in 1554, but the royal supremacy was revived by Elizabeth I (under the title 'Supreme Governor') in 1559. Although Henry repudiated papal authority, his religious views remained orthodox and it was not until after his death that doctrinal Protestantism became official policy in England.

The popular image of 'bluff King Hal' is far removed from the historians' verdict. R.W. Chambers, for example, said of him 'Henry VIII destroyed more things of beauty, and more things of promise, than any other man in European history'.
See also DEFENDER OF THE FAITH, DISSOLUTION OF THE MONASTERIES, REFORMATION and SIX ARTICLES, THE

HERALDIC COLOURS *see* COLOURS (HERALDIC)

HERALDRY Heraldry (or, more correctly, ARMORY) has rightly been described as 'the shorthand of history' because it relates in symbolic form the hopes and aspirations, the achievements and failures of our ancestors. Coats of arms and heraldic badges are ubiquitous in the architecture and decoration of domestic and ecclesiastical buildings, in illuminated manuscripts and official documents, and on seals, monuments and memorials. Heraldic devices were a means of declaiming feudal authority and knightly pre-eminence. They were outward and visible signs of a man's position and influence, and of his household's status in society. The accumulated quarterings of richly emblazoned memorials and stained glass proclaimed his ancestry more proudly than any inscription. Not only is heraldry a source of aesthetic pleasure, it provides invaluable information for the historian and genealogist.

See also ARMS OF OFFICE, BRASSES (MONUMENTAL), COLOURS (HERALDIC), EFFIGIES, ENCAUSTIC TILES, FUNERAL HERALDRY, HATCHMENTS, HERALDRY (ECCLESIASTICAL), POINTS OF THE SHIELD, REBUS, ROYAL ARMS, SEALS, STAINED GLASS *and* WINDOWS.

HERALDRY (ECCLESIASTICAL) The Lords Spiritual are ARMIGEROUS, as are their sees and the chapters and bodies corporate of cathedrals and major abbeys. Sherborne Abbey in Dorset, now a parish church, continues to use the arms of its medieval foundation (a silver cross and golden crozier on a red field), for example.

In the Middle Ages, archbishops, bishops and royal abbots were tenants-in-chief and held baronies. They were ecclesiastical magnates responsible for the administration of vast estates, and held office as privy advisers in the King's Council (*Curia Regis*). Many accomplished clerics were elevated to the great offices of state and their services rewarded with the emoluments of a bishopric – a device by which the Crown was spared having to pay a substantial pension. Bishops were addressed as 'My Lord', as they are today, and many of them were also warriors, wielding not the sword (which drew blood), but the mace (which, apparently, did not). Their offices, and those of the senior pre-Reformation abbots, generated huge numbers of documents, all of which required SEALS by which they were authenticated. Ecclesiastical seals are generally oval in shape and, by the thirteenth century, were predominantly heraldic. Religious motifs from early seals were often incorporated into coats of arms: the elaborate, enthroned figure of Christ in the arms of the see of Chester, for example, first appeared in a seal of Bishop Sigefrid (1180–1204).

Bishops and Archbishops

All Anglican bishops use a MITRE instead of a crest in their coats of arms, and sometimes crossed croziers are depicted behind the shield. During their terms of office diocesan bishops impale their personal arms (on the sinister side) with those of their see but on TRANSLATION to another bishopric they change the impaled arms of office accordingly. The arms of the archbishopric of Canterbury, which date from *c.* 1350, are charged with a white *pallium* on which four crosses *fitchy* [pointed at the foot] represent the pins by which it was attached to the vestment. Behind the pallium is a gold archiepiscopal staff and the background of the shield is blue. The earliest arms of the archbishopric of York are of a similar design but with a red field, and these may occasionally be found on monuments. The present arms, which date from *c.* 1398, are red with silver cross keys (York Minster is dedicated to St Peter) and a gold imperial crown, which probably evolved from the papal tiara.

Impaled personal and diocesan arms are invaluable when attempting to establish how long a particular incumbent held office, especially when they appear on seals, the use of which can provide precise dating. They will also be found on the tombs of bishops and abbots, most of whom were buried in their cathedrals and abbey churches. Although, before the Reformation, most bishops were elected by chapter, it was usual for the pope to confirm the appointment of a king's nominee. One effect of this system was that prominent members of the royal household were frequently appointed as bishops and members of the *curia regis*. The extraordinary influence of these few families in matters ecclesiastical and secular is evident in the

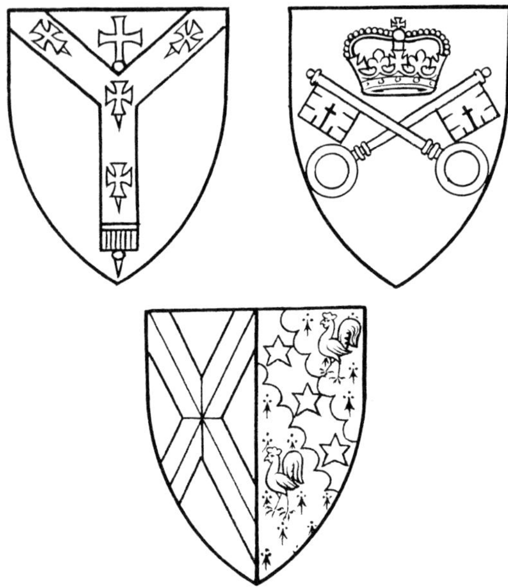

Above: Archbishopric of Canterbury. Archbishopric of York. Below: arms of office of George Law, Bishop of Bath and Wells.

ubiquity of their personal arms alongside those of the offices that they held.

Unique among the Lords Spiritual were the prince bishops of Durham, who were appointed by the king as counts palatine, head of Church and state in a vast territory which included St Cuthbert's seventh century bishopric of Lindisfarne. The PALATINATE of Durham was effectively a kingdom within a kingdom and, as defenders of the realm in the north, the prince bishops were charged with the defence of the Scottish border and maintained a standing army. The (circular) Great Seal of the prince bishops had, on the obverse, an enthroned figure of a bishop and on the reverse the bishop as an equestrian figure in full armour. By the fourteenth century the Palatinate was at the height of its military power and its warrior-bishops are uniquely commemorated in the ducally-gorged mitre and crossed sword and crozier in the arms of all subsequent bishops of Durham.

Ecclesiastical hats

Cardinals, who belonged to the highest ecclesiastical rank (and were sometimes referred to

Above: arms of the Prince Bishops of Durham. Below: arms and ecclesiastical hat of Cardinal Newman. (Both courtesy of Andrew Jamieson)

as 'old red hat'), displayed above their arms a scarlet *ecclesiastical hat*, a domed hat (*galero*) of felt with a wide brim from which depend cords, interlaced with gold thread, and tassels. These hats, which were worn by cardinals for official engagements, were instituted by Pope Innocent IV in the thirteenth century.

Interpretation

Ecclesiastical heraldry is distinctive for the manner in which colours and devices are frequently used to reflect religious concepts. As one might expect, the symbol of the cross is commonly found in ecclesiastical heraldry, although by no means exclusively so. References to saints are common: the escallop shell in the arms of Rochester, for example, was the device of St Augustine, who founded the cathedral in 604, while the *saltire* on which it is placed is the familiar 'cross of St Andrew', to whom the church is dedicated.

Many diocesan arms contain local allusions: those of Birmingham (granted in 1906), for instance, are divided *per pale indented* (vertically by an indented line) and refer to the nineteenth-century arms of the City of Birmingham which, in turn, were based on the arms of the medieval De

Bermingham family. Similarly, the arms of the diocese of Truro include, on a black border, the fifteen *bezants* (gold roundels) of the Duchy of Cornwall. Several diocesan arms contain references to the personal devices of former abbots or bishops. Those of the See of Hereford, for instance, are derived from the arms of Thomas de Cantelope, who was bishop from 1275 to 1282. The bishop's personal arms were *Azure* (blue) *three Leopard's Faces inverted jessant-de-lis Gold* (upside down and with fleurs-de-lis projecting from their mouths) but, in the diocesan arms, the field was changed to *Gules* (red).
See also REBUS

HERBARIUM The monastic herb garden, which provided raw materials for the KITCHENS and PHARMACY and sweet-scented herbs to freshen the air in the FRATER, GUEST HOUSE and INFIRMARY.

HERESY The formal denial of the authorised teaching of the Church. The Roman Catholic Church distinguished between 'formal heresy' (the wilful denial of doctrine by a baptised person) and 'material heresy' (adherence to heretical beliefs 'in good faith'), the former being a sin and subject to possible EXCOMMUNICATION.

HERMIT From the Old French *ermite*. The popular perception of the medieval hermit is of a solitary (*eremitical*), religious RECLUSE. But unlike an ANCHORITE or COENOBITE, a hermit was committed to public service as a guide, ferryman or river pilot, providing frugal hospitality and shelter to travellers (*see* CHAPELS *and* HERMITAGE).

Hermits, anchorites and ceonobites were a characteristic feature of the Celtic Church and were invariably referred to as saints. The Cornish saints Nectan and Endellion, for example, were but two of a remarkable brood of twenty-four children fathered by a sixth-century Welsh chieftain. All became hermits or anchorites and all died as martyrs or confessors for the faith, while their father, Brychan, was also celebrated as a saint in the Celtic traditions of Cornwall and Devon (the ancient kingdom of Dumnonia).

Welsh hermits lived either individually, as did Wechelen, the hermit of Llowes in Elfael, or in communities, such as the culdees of Beddgelert (Gwynedd), Ynys Lannog (Priestholm in Anglesey) and Enlli (Bardsey Island). Welsh law accorded special status to such men (*diofrydogion*), not dissimilar to that of holy men and anchorites in other societies. Even Gerald of Wales conceded that 'nowhere will you find hermits and anchorites of greater spirituality than in Wales'. At Partrishow in Powys a grille in the west wall of the church of Merthyr Issui at Patricio overlooks an ancient, narrow chapel – the site of a cell built by the Celtic St Issui, a hermit who was murdered by one of his guests and who worked various healing miracles after his death.

Several of these early hermits established hospices and other charitable foundations which later became abbeys: at Premonstratensian Cockersand, for example. The Benedictine RULE allowed a monk to choose an eremitic life, contingent upon a lengthy probation in a religious community.

HERMITAGE Many of the sites to which the term 'hermitage' is traditionally ascribed were in fact anchorages (*see* ANCHORITE) or the cells of solitary coenobites (*see* COENOBITE) and religious mystics. Because of the nature of the hermit's calling, most hermitages were located in the vicinity of routeways: at bridges, fords, ferries and causeways, and where tracks entered inhospitable country. The buildings themselves were not necessarily insubstantial, indeed some were subsidiary houses of monastic foundations. Many hermitages were created within rock piles or out of natural caves, such as the twelfth-century chambers of Blackstone Rock above the River Severn at Bewdley in Worcestershire. Some hermitages incorporated a small chapel (*see*

CHAPELS) and accommodation for travellers.

Perhaps the best example is the fourteenth-century two-storey hermitage of the Holy Trinity cut into a sandstone cliff above the river Coquet at Warkworth in Northumberland. This comprises a SACRISTY and small chapel within the rock, to which a hall, kitchen and SOLAR were added in masonry. There is evidence that the hermit kept a small farm and orchard above the cliff. Finchale Priory, County Durham, originated as the hermitage of St Godric, a colourful and heroic figure born in *c.* 1065 who, after years of travel as a sailor, merchant and pilgrim, chose the solitary life and eventually settled at Finchale, where he lived to the remarkable age of 105. In 1196 Godric's hermitage became a priory and, in the fourteenth century, a 'holiday place' for monks from the parent house at Durham. Within the ruins of the thirteenth-century priory church may be found the even earlier footings of Godric's church of St John the Baptist.

Place-names, such as Armitage in Staffordshire, may be indicative of former hermitages. But place-names can be misleading: in the twelfth century, the hamlet of Hermitage in Dorset was known as Rocombe and the 'hermitage' was a minor Augustinian priory.

HERRINGBONE A decorative zigzag pattern in a wall or floor, similar in appearance to the bones of a herring, formed by alternate rows of diagonally laid stones, bricks or tiles.

HERSE *see* HEARSE

HIGH ALTAR The principal altar of a church, usually located at the east end.
See also ALTARS

HIGH MASS *see* MASS

HISTORIATED INITIAL In documents, a VERSAL letter within which is an illustration, usually associated with the text.

HISTORICAL DEVELOPMENT OF THE CHURCH *see* ANGLO-SAXON CHURCH, CATHEDRALS, CELTIC CHURCH, CHURCH OF ENGLAND, DIOCESE, DISSOLUTION OF THE MONASTERIES, HENRY VIII, MONASTICISM, MEDIEVAL CHURCH, REFORMATION *and* WALES, THE MEDIEVAL CHURCH IN

HOLIDAYS The word holiday is, of course, derived from 'Holy Day', a major religious festival on which everyone was, as far as was practicable, required to attend MASS and to abstain from 'servile work'. The number of Holy Days steadily increased throughout the medieval period; however, there were other opportunities for monks to benefit from spiritual, mental or physical recuperation. When recovering from an illness, or when suffering from the pressures of the closed communal life, a monk could be sent to a GRANGE or retreat that was maintained by the mother house for that purpose. Here he would enjoy increased privacy and seclusion and the pleasures of a relaxed rule, although he would still be required to fulfil his religious obligations. In 1196 the former HERMITAGE of St Godric at Finchale became a dependency of Durham and, some time in the fourteenth century, it was decided to convert the priory into a 'rest home' for the Durham monks. A prior and four brethren were in permanent residence, while further groups of four monks took it in turns to spend three weeks there each year. This unusual arrangement continued until the priory was dissolved in 1538. The conventual buildings at Finchale were extensive – appropriate to a house of at least twenty brethren – while most of the time they would have been occupied by fewer than half that number. To what use the redundant buildings were put remains a mystery.

HOLY COMMUNION *see* EUCHARIST *and* MASS

HOLY ORDERS A 'clerk in holy orders' is one who belongs to the higher grades (*major orders*) of the Christian ministry: a bishop, priest or deacon.
See also MAJOR ORDERS, MINOR ORDERS *and*

PRIEST

HOLY SEE The papal bishopric of Rome.

HOLY WATER Water which has been blessed for religious purposes, and to which small quantities of salt may have been added. In the Church, water represented life and purity. Holy water was a 'sacramental': matter which could effect the assimilation of religious truths.
See also ASPERGES *and* HOLY WATER STOUP

HOLY WATER SPRINKLER *see* ASPERGES

HOLY WATER STOUP A receptacle for holding HOLY WATER, usually a stone basin set into a niche or stocle (plinth) near the church door (*see* PORCHES). Those entering the church would sign their bodies with holy water from the stoup as an act of self-consecration and spiritual cleansing. Stoups, which have no drain, were replenished regularly with holy water, which was mixed with salt, exorcised and blessed. The word is correctly *stop*, meaning a pail or basin. The practice was suppressed following the Reformation.

HONOUR POINT *see* POINTS OF THE SHIELD

HOOD-MOULD *see* DRIPSTONE

HOPTON WOOD STONE A grey, Derbyshire limestone used especially in highly polished floors.

HORARIUM The daily round of a Christian community, governed by observance of the Canonical Hours (*see* HOURS (CANONICAL)). The horarium varied according to the rules and customs of the different religious orders and was adjusted both to reflect the time of year and to accommodate major FESTIVALS, and events such as the INSTALLATION of a new abbot. The monastic day began at sunrise and ended at sunset and was divided into twelve equal 'hours', the length of which varied according to the season. In the monastic CALENDAR, winter lasted from Holy Cross Day (14 September) to Easter. The monks were summoned from the DORTER at day break in winter or sunrise in summer to attend PRIME, the first of the day offices, which was followed by an early mass for servants and manual workers during which the brethren washed in the LAVATORIUM. The priests then said masses at their private altars, while the other monks and novices attended to their studies in the CLOISTER. Except on feast-days, a light breakfast was taken (*see* FRATER) and this was followed by a simple mass (Lady Mass or Chapter Mass) and the daily meeting of the CHAPTER. During the day an office was held every three 'hours', beginning with Prime: TERCE (the third hour) was followed by a period of work until noon and the office of SEXT (the sixth hour), which either followed or preceded the solemn High Mass (*see* MASS) which, on Sundays and festivals, included a procession (*see* PROCESSIONS). The community then returned to the cloister, where they prepared for the main meal of the day (dinner or *prandium*) which was taken between noon and 2.00 p.m., depending on the season. After retiring briefly to the dorter (*see* SIESTA), the monks then attended the office of NONE (the ninth hour), and this was followed by work or a short period of RECREATION until VESPERS at sunset. This was the longest of the day offices and was sometimes followed by a simple meal (*cena*) accompanied by a solemn grace and prayers. Following a further period of work or private devotions the brethren would meet in the chapter house or cloister for COLLATION before attending COMPLINE. They would then process to the dormitory (*see* DORTER) for a few hours' sleep until summoned once again by the bells for the long night office of MATTINS, which began after midnight and was followed by LAUDS. They would then return to their dormitory by the NIGHT STAIR to sleep until dawn. Any spare moments during the day were occupied by the duties that were allocated to them by the chapter or by a brief visit to the PARLOUR.

Inevitably, the daily round varied considerably

among the different orders, from one house to another, and from one season to the next. A further complication, particularly evident before the introduction of CLOCKS, was the accurate keeping of time. The problem was especially acute in the early morning, when the sequence of services was so rapid that the slightest miscalculation could disrupt the horarium for the remainder of the day.

At the Benedictine monastery of Canterbury the winter horarium in the late eleventh century consisted of eight hours of services (the *Opus Dei* or *divine office*), three hours of study and contemplation and (at most) four hours of work. From this it will be seen that few of the offices fit neatly into the model horarium described above:

2.30 a.m.	Rise. Prayers with psalms. Nocturns and prayers for the royal house. Mattins and Lauds of the dead. Mattins of All Saints.
5.00–6.00	Study.
6.00–6.45	Lauds. Psalms and prayers for the royal house. Anthems.
6.45	Prime. Seven penitential psalms. Litany of the saints.
7.30–8.00	Study and wash.
8.00	Seven psalms. Terce. Psalms for the royal house. Chapter or Morrow Mass. Chapter meeting followed by psalms for the dead.
9.45–12.00	Work.
12.00	Sext. Psalms and prayers for relatives etc. High Mass.
1.30	None. Psalms and prayers for relatives etc.
2.00	Dinner with readings.
2.45–4.30	Study or work.
4.30	Vespers. Psalms and anthems. Vespers of All Saints. Vespers of the dead.
5.30	Study.
6.15	Compline. Psalms.
6.30 p.m.	Retire.

See also DIVINE OFFICE *and* MONASTICISM

HOSPICE (HOSPITIUM) A lodging for pilgrims and travellers, especially one maintained by a religious order. Hospices were sometimes located in the outer precinct of a monastery or friary (*see* FRIARS) but more often they were to be found in neighbouring towns or serving busy ports and routeways. A hospice that was under the direct control of a major religious house usually reflected the rules and customs of that house and was managed by a prior. However, many were administered independently, indeed some became priories in their own right. At St Bartholemew's, Smithfield, the priory and hospice coexisted, each with its own staff and identity. A hospice usually included a chapel, a hall (*frater*) where meals were taken, a dormitory (*dorter*), wash-place (*lavatorium*) and latrines (*reredorter*). Some university colleges originated as hospices or 'halls', supervised by a warden or master.
See also ALMSHOUSES, GUEST HOUSE, HOSPITALS, INFIRMARY *and* (*for* pilgrims) SHRINES

HOSPITALITY *see* ALMONRY, BEDE-HOUSE, CORRODIAN, GUEST HOUSE, HOSPICE, HOSPITALS, (*for* pilgrims) SHRINES *and* SUPERIOR'S LODGINGS

HOSPITALLER, KNIGHTS *see* ST JOHN OF JERUSALEM, ORDER OF *and* COMMANDERY

HOSPITALS There were more than a thousand hospitals in medieval England. Also known as *mallardies* and *masendews* (a corruption of *Maison Dieu*), medieval hospitals were charitable institutions founded by religious houses, guilds and private individuals or groups of BENEFACTORS, and were concerned as much with housing the elderly and infirm as tending the sick (*see also* ALMSHOUSES). Many hospitals were established as a form of CHANTRY, where the residents were invited to pray for the souls of those on whose charity they depended. Most served the needs of specific groups of people such as wayfarers and pilgrims (*see* HOSPICE), aged or sick priests, orphans and lepers. The inmates of leper hospitals (known as *lazar houses* after St Larazus) were required to wear a distinctive habit of a grey coat and scarlet hat. Typically, the Leper Hospital of St Margaret and St Antony at Wimborne in Dorset was founded in the thirteenth century with encouragement from the pope, who granted an INDULGENCE of a year to anyone who contributed to its building or to its maintenance. Christ's Hospital in London was founded by Edward VI (1547–53) on the site of the Grey Friars, originally as a foundling hospital (for deserted and illegitimate children) although it soon became the famous Blue Coat School. There were also monastic hospitals (*see also* INFIRMARY), but most of these were dissolved following the Dissolution of the Monasteries in 1536/9 – notable exceptions being St Bartholomew's ('Barts'), St Thomas's and the Bethlehem hospital for the mentally ill ('Bedlam'), which were refounded under lay control. In the late medieval period, when many monastic houses were attracting censure, hospitals provided a popular alternative form of endowment. Even so, they too sometimes suffered from PLURALISM and from abuses of their generosity, notably by the imposition of corrodians (*see* CORRODIAN). The withdrawal of the social and welfare services provided by the monastic almonries and hospitals must have had a devastating effect on many a local populace following the Dissolution of the Monasteries in 1536 and 1539 and the Dissolution of the Chantries in 1547.

All hospitals resembled formal religious communities and both staff and inmates wore uniforms, similar to that of the Austin Canons (*see* AUGUSTINIANS), often with a distinctive badge on the right breast. In most cases the superior (a master, prior or WARDEN) followed a religious RULE (most frequently that of St Augustine), as did his staff of brethren and sisters, who would be assisted by LAY BROTHERS, lay sisters and servants. There would also be a CHAPLAIN and a visiting staff, such as physicians and barber-surgeons. All would be expected to recite the DIVINE OFFICE in the hospital chapel which, as in all religious houses, was the centre of community life. Chapels would be dedicated to an appropriate saint: St Lazarus (for lepers), St Christopher (travellers), St Thomas of Canterbury and St Julian the Hospitaller, for example. In some cases a hospital exercised a prescriptive right to use a chapel in a nearby parish church, while others made their chapels available for parochial use. Those hospitals that were founded and maintained by monastic houses were sometimes located within, or adjacent to, the abbey precinct. They were not confined to urban centres: many were in remote locations, such as Killingwoldgraves in Yorkshire, which was founded before 1169. Several of the larger hospitals were fully conventual and assumed a status that exceeded that of many lesser priories.

In most hospitals the accommodation was similar to that in a monastic INFIRMARY: a large (usually heated) hall in which the bedheads were arranged against the outer walls as in a traditional hospital ward. The altar of an adjacent chapel might be visible at one end of the hall and there would be a kitchen and sometimes a refectory. The hospital of St Mary at Chichester provides a typical example. In some hospitals, the hall was partitioned to provide individual cubicles.

Theoretically, no one in need of care would be turned away and patients often received exemplary personal attention, with daily washing and regular changes of clothing and bed linen. The sick were provided with food, shelter and medical care until they either recovered or died. Casual visitors received a meal, hot water for washing and a bed for the night or a charitable gift (*dole*) of food, clothing or money. As in other religious houses, festivals were marked by an enhanced diet and larger portions at meal times. Should a patient die in hospital, he would receive a Christian burial and a mass would be said for the repose of his soul.

Most hospitals were suppressed, either with their parent houses at the DISSOLUTION OF THE MONASTERIES in 1536/7 or in 1547 with the Dissolution of the Chantries (*see* CHANTRIES).
See also ALMONRY, AUGUSTINIANS, BEDE-HOUSE, GUEST HOUSE *and* COMMANDERY

HOSPITIUM *see* GUEST HOUSE *and* HOSPICE

HOSTELLER In a religious house, the guest-master or his assistant, who was responsible for the administration of the HOSPICE, GUEST HOUSE or ALMONRY.

HOURS (CANONICAL) The monastic day, from sunrise to sunset, was divided into twelve equal parts called the *canonical hours*. At the heart of the daily services was the chanted recital of the Psalter: the entire Book of Psalms, which was recited during the course of each week in a round of daily prayer known as the *Opus Dei* ('the Work of God'). Services (*canonical offices*) were conducted according to the BREVIARY. The seven day hours were LAUDS (at dawn), PRIME, TERCE, SEXT, NONE, VESPERS and COMPLINE, while the night hours were NOCTURN or MATTINS. In this arrangement, Benedict was following the Book of Psalms, which states that: 'At midnight I rose to give praise to thee' and 'Seven times a day have I given praise to thee'. To the Canonical Hours, which came to be known as the *Great Hours*, were added various commemorative and festive services, prescribed private prayers and a daily service in the CHAPTER HOUSE, following Prime, called *Pretiosa* at which prayers were said for 'departed brethren' and BENEFACTORS.

Benedict stated that the first psalm at the first service of the day should be chanted slowly, 'in order that all may assemble in time', and that the monks should sleep dressed and ready for prayer: 'Being clothed they will thus always be ready, and rising at the signal without any delay may hasten to forestall one another to the Work of God, let them gently encourage one another, on account of the excuses to which the sleepy are addicted.' He recommended that the timetable should not be too onerous and that the eight offices should be sufficiently short to allow time for private STUDY and MANUAL LABOUR. However, as time passed the services became more elaborate and time-consuming. The MASS, which was originally celebrated only on Sundays and on the feast of St Benedict, became a daily celebration – to which a second was added. This ritual elaboration was particularly intensive in Cluniac monasteries (*see* CLUNIACS) where, on numerous feast-days, most of the working day was spent in church. Indeed, the founding of the Cistercian and Carthusian orders was based, in part, on a belief that excessive amounts of time spent in church and a preoccupation with ritual could arrest spiritual development: 'Candlesticks as tall as trees, great masses of bronze of exquisite workmanship, dazzling with precious stones, what is the point of all this? Will it melt a sinner's heart? O vanity of vanities – no, insanity rather than vanity' (St Bernard of Clairvaux). The CISTERCIANS changed the timetable, allowing more time for work, study and private contemplation. They insisted on simplicity in the decoration of their churches, on austerity and a reduction in the elaboration of their services. The CARTHUSIANS required their monks to undertake most of the day offices through solitary prayer in their cells, and consequently the majority of Carthusian churches are small by comparison with those in the great Benedictine monasteries.
See also CLOCKS, DIVINE OFFICE, HORARIUM *and* MONASTICISM

HOUSE (RELIGIOUS) From the Latin *convenire* meaning 'to assemble', a convent is a religious community or the building in which it lives. Historically (and throughout this book) the term may be applied to communities of either sex, although current usage generally implies a house of nuns. A monastery was a religious community of men, a nunnery a community of nuns and a friary a community of friars. The houses of the Knights Templar were commanderies and those of the Knights Hospitaller preceptories (though following the persecution and papal suppression of the Templars in 1312, their commanderies were transferred to the Hospitallers) (*see* TEMPLAR, KNIGHTS *and* ST JOHN OF JERUSALEM, ORDER OF). The terms abbey and priory denote rank: an abbey was generally of superior status to a priory, although there were exceptions. All Cluniac houses were dependencies of Cluny and, therefore, priories. Carthusian houses and those of regular canons were usually priories, while large Benedictine abbeys to which cathedrals were attached are usually called cathedral priories because they were administered by a prior, a bishop being the titular abbot.

In almost every religious house, the choir monks or nuns would be outnumbered by the other members of the community: the oblates, novices, conversi, confraters, corrodians, guests, chaplains, stewards and various employees sometimes outnumbered the religious by more than four to one (*see* CHAPLAIN, CORRODIAN, EMPLOYEES, LAY BROTHERS, NOVICE, OBLATE *and* STEWARD).

HYMNARY A medieval book containing the metrical hymns of the DIVINE OFFICE arranged according to the liturgical year.

HYMNS From the Greek *hymnos* meaning 'song of praise', a hymn is a song used in Christian worship. St Augustine defined a hymn as 'the praise of God by singing', to which might be added 'by a congregation'. Hymns are characterised by non-biblical texts in metrical and stanzaic form. Hymnody in the Church derives from the singing of psalms in the Hebrew Temple. It developed systematically following the legalisation of Christianity by the Emperor Constantine in 313, notably in the Byzantine Church. In the West, during the second half of the fourth century, St Hilary of Poitiers composed a book of hymn texts (*c.* 360) and St Ambrose of Milan instituted the congregational singing of psalms and hymns. These early hymns, which were sung to simple 'folk' melodies, derived from contemporary Christian Latin poetry. Hymns were a fixed part of the Benedictine monastic office, although they were not generally used in the Roman LITURGY until the thirteenth century. By the late fifteenth century, liturgical music was sung by trained choirs (*see also* CHURCH MUSIC) although congregational singing was re-established by the Lutheran Church in Germany at the REFORMATION. The early German hymn melody (*chorale*) was unharmonised and unaccompanied, although harmonised versions, used by combinations of congregation, choir and organ, appeared later. While some were new compositions, others drew on a variety of PLAINSONG, vernacular and secular sources. Important early collections of hymn texts include those of Martin Luther (1524), Johann Gottfried Walther (1524) and George Rhau (1544). French, Scottish and English Calvinism later promoted the singing of metrical translations of the PSALMS, unaccompanied and in unison. The English Psalter used only a few metres, while the common metre 8–6–8–6 (representing the number of syllables in each line) remains the archetypal English hymn metre.

The Congregationalist hymn writer Isaac Watts (1674–1748) provided the impetus for the development of English hymnody in the late seventeenth century. His *Horae Lyricae* (1706), *Hymns and Spiritual Songs* (1709) and *Psalms of David Imitated* (1719) included such well-known hymns as 'Jesus shall reign where'er the sun', 'When I survey the wondrous cross' and 'O God, our help in ages past'. The evangelical revival of the mid-eighteenth century under John Wesley (1703–91) and Charles Wesley (1707–88), the founders of Methodism, finally established hymnody in England, Charles Wesley's poems employing a variety of experimental metres and John Wesley's translations introducing a number of fine German hymns.

The Church of England officially recognised

hymn singing in 1820 following a controversy concerning the singing of hymns at a Sheffield church. The Oxford Movement stimulated new compositions, the use of plainsong melodies and translations of medieval hymns. *Hymns Ancient and Modern*, edited by H.W. Baker (1821–77) in 1861 (and subsequently revised on many occasions) incorporated many of the traditional office hymns and was characterised by austerity of style and conformity to the *Book of Common Prayer* (*see* COMMON PRAYER, BOOK OF). Two influential collections which were published at the turn of the century were the *Yattendon Hymnal* (1899), compiled by the poet Robert Bridges (1844–1930) and *The English Hymnal* (1906), edited by Percy Dearmer and the composer Ralph Vaughan Williams (1872–1958), which contains many plainsong and traditional folk melodies. *Songs of Praise* (Vaughan Williams and Martin Shaw), first published in 1925, was a 'national' hymnal intended for use by Christians of all denominations. Theologically, it was markedly liberal, even more so in the second edition published in 1931.

I

ICONOCLASM The antithesis of the veneration of images. An *iconoclast* is one who destroys or defaces religious images.

ILLNESS *see* INFIRMARY

ILLUMINATION, MANUSCRIPT *see* MANUSCRIPT ILLUMINATION

IMAGE SCREEN A stone screen comprising tiers of niches, each of which contains a carved image: the WEST FRONT of Exeter Cathedral, for example.

IMPOST A wall bracket on which rests the end of an arch.

IMPROPRIATION The annexation or assignment of an ecclesiastical benefice to a lay proprietor or body corporate. When, as a consequence of the DISSOLUTION OF THE MONASTERIES, many benefices which had formerly been appropriated to monastic houses passed to lay rectors (*see* LAY RECTOR), it became necessary for 'perpetual curates' to be appointed in order to undertake the duties of impropriated benefices.
See also APPROPRIATION

INCENSE A spice or gum which gives off a sweet smell when burning. The smoke of incense symbolises prayer. In the western Church, incense has been used since the sixth century for ceremonial purposes, although the legality of its use in the Church of England has long been a matter of dispute.

INCISED SLABS Among the earliest examples in Britain of these engraved stone memorials (*see* MEMORIAL) is a collection of over two hundred, dating from the eighth to the tenth centuries, at Clonmacnois in Ireland. But it was during the period from the eleventh century to the mid-fourteenth century that coffin-shaped slabs, usually incised with a simple cross (*cross-slabs*), became numerous. These were usually of hard sandstone, although there were regional variations: Purbeck and other marbles in the south of England, gritstone in Derbyshire and Northumberland, and Bath and Ham stone in the south-west, for example. In the western Highlands of Scotland a vigorous Celtic school developed using mica-schist, and by the Reformation alabaster was widely used in the English Midlands. Human figures first appeared in the twelfth century. These were often of priests, although there were also early military figures, such as that of a knight at Sollers Hope in Herefordshire. Unlike brasses (*see* BRASSES (MONUMENTAL)) and

EFFIGIES. British incised slabs rarely depict heraldic figures, most armorial display being confined to coats of arms or small shields. Such slabs, which were almost invariably laid in the church floor, were clearly liable to wear, and many were eventually lifted and set upright against a wall or raised on to a plinth. An even greater number have been lost or their detail has been defaced. Some incised slabs may have been embellished with inlaid materials, especially those imported from the Low Countries. Regrettably, little remains of the pitch and painted lead (and occasionally copper or enamel) with which the figures were coloured.

Ledger Stones

During the seventeenth century incised slabs, depicting full-length figures, were replaced by *ledger stones*. These were usually of black marble (*see* TOUCH) or local stone such as slate, and bore a simple but finely carved inscription and a deeply incised roundel containing a coat of arms or other device. Ledger stones, which remained popular to the mid-nineteenth century, are indicative of intramural burials. They are the capping stones of brick-lined burial shafts which could accommodate up to six coffins stacked one above the other and separated by horizontal iron bars. Consequently, a ledger stone may have been chipped at the edges when raised with crowbars for the interment of further deposits. A number of ledger stones may also be found on tomb chests and table tombs (*see* TOMB CHEST).

INCOME *see* FINANCE

INCUBATION Of pagan origin, the practice of sleeping in a church, or within the precinct of a church, in anticipation of experiencing a divine revelation or of being cured of disease. Inevitably, certain churches acquired reputations for efficacious incubation.

INDENT A matrix in a slab from which a monumental brass (or a section thereof) is missing (*see* BRASSES (MONUMENTAL)).

INDULGENCE (i) Exemption of an individual from ecclesiastical law.

(ii) Remission by the Church of temporal penalties still due after penance and ABSOLUTION. The practice of granting indulgences presupposes that sin is punishable either on earth or in PURGATORY, even when a sinner has been reconciled to God. There are several degrees of remission: plenary indulgences remit all temporal punishment (*see* PRIVILEGED ALTAR), partial indulgences remit a portion, temporal indulgences last only for a given time, indefinite or perpetual indulgences last until revoked, personal indulgences apply only to a specified person or confraternity, and local indulgences are obtainable only at a particular place. From the twelfth century, the granting of indulgences became commonplace, plenary indulgences being especially susceptible to abuse.

A number of religious houses acquired reputations for the granting of indulgences: the Brigittine double house of Syon (Twickenham, Greater London) for example, was popular for the many indulgences it could offer to pilgrims. In 1425, at the request of Henry V, the pope granted the house the so-called Vincula indulgence, remission of punishment for sins equivalent to those available at Rome on the feast-day of St Peter ad Vincula (1 August). Visitors could obtain indulgences of five hundred days on the fourth Sunday in Lent and at Lammastide (1 August) and the brethren also blessed special rosaries (known as 'Syon Beads'), a practice which existed in the mid-fifteenth century but was not confirmed by the pope until 1500 (*see* BEAD). Indulgences could be obtained through acts of charity. In the mid-fifteenth century, for example, the archbishop of York granted an indulgence of forty days to all who assisted in the rebuilding of a flood-damaged bridge on the river Trent at Kelham in Nottinghamshire, while in 1488 a similar indulgence was granted to

those who contributed to the refurbishing of the church of St Mary-le-Strand in London, which had been desecrated by thieves.
See also SHRINES

INDUSTRY Most religious communities were obliged to undertake some form of industrial activity in order to survive (*see* FINANCE). From the twelfth century, wool, metals, agricultural surpluses and a variety of manufactured goods were offered for sale at MARKETS, SHOPS AND FAIRS. Coal was mined at Monk Seaton (a cell of the Benedictine priory of Tynemouth, Northumberland), the mighty cathedral priory of Durham had mines at Ferryhill and Gateshead, while a mine at Finchale (a dependency of Durham) had its own horse-powered pumping station in 1486. There were iron-workings at Jarrow Priory in County Durham and Kirkstall Abbey in Yorkshire and iron was mined at St Bees Priory in Cumberland (now a parish church) and Byland Abbey in Yorkshire. Kirkstead Abbey in Lincolnshire had four forges for smelting and working iron, while Bolton Priory (also in Yorkshire and, in part, a parish church) owned several lead mines. At Cistercian Rievaulx, the river was diverted to provide a reliable water supply to the domestic buildings (*see* PLUMBING, WATER SUPPLY AND SANITATION), a series of FISHPONDS, water meadows and millponds for the tanning and other MILLS along its course. The Yorkshire moors were rich in mineral deposits, and throughout their tenure the monks of Rievaulx excavated the valley floor on an industrial scale, controlling the entire iron-making process from mining, through smelting, to the production of artefacts. By the fifteenth century the Cistercians had made ground-breaking advances in technology, radically increasing the amounts of iron produced, by developing huge furnaces (often measuring 5m square) and water-powered bellows. At its peak, Fountains Abbey had a net annual income in excess of £1 million (at today's values) and benefited from a network of fifty farms in addition to its industrial and commercial undertakings.

Tiles were manufactured commercially at Repton Priory in Derbyshire and at Great Malvern Priory in Worcestershire. Medieval floor tiles (*see* ENCAUSTIC TILES) from Malvern are still to be found in cathedrals and parish churches throughout southern England and beyond. By the fifteenth century, the wealth created through the responsible management of these and numerous other industrial enterprises contributed significantly to the resources of the Church which, at that time, possessed nearly one third of the total wealth of England.
See also TIMBER, VINEYARDS *and* WOOL

INFIRMARIAN, INFIRMARER *or* MASTER OF THE FARMERY The monastic official responsible for the administration of the INFIRMARY (*farmery*) and the PHARMACY – and for the feeding of any monastic prisoners (*see* PRISONS). He was expected to be 'gentle, good-humoured, kind, compassionate to the sick and willing to gratify their needs with affectionate sympathy'. Most religious houses were served by a PHYSICIAN, who was sometimes a member of the community, but infrequntly so. The barber-surgeon responsible for blood-letting was, at that time, considered to be an inferior physician (*see* PHLEBOTOMY)

INFIRMARY (FARMERY) When, through sickness or infirmity, a monk could no longer carry out his duties he would confess his incapacity in CHAPTER. The SUPERIOR would then grant the monk discretion concerning which conventual duties he should undertake. However, if his symptoms were serious, or should his health deteriorate further, the monk would be admitted to the infirmary (*farmery*).

A monastic infirmary was a religious house in miniature, with its own chapel, DORTER and FRATER, and its own kitchen where 'more subtle and delicate meats' could be prepared for the aged, sick and convalescent monks. It was to the infirmary that elderly monks retired (*see* STATIONARIES), there to be treated with special consideration. These were the *sempectae* or *stationarii* – monks who had been

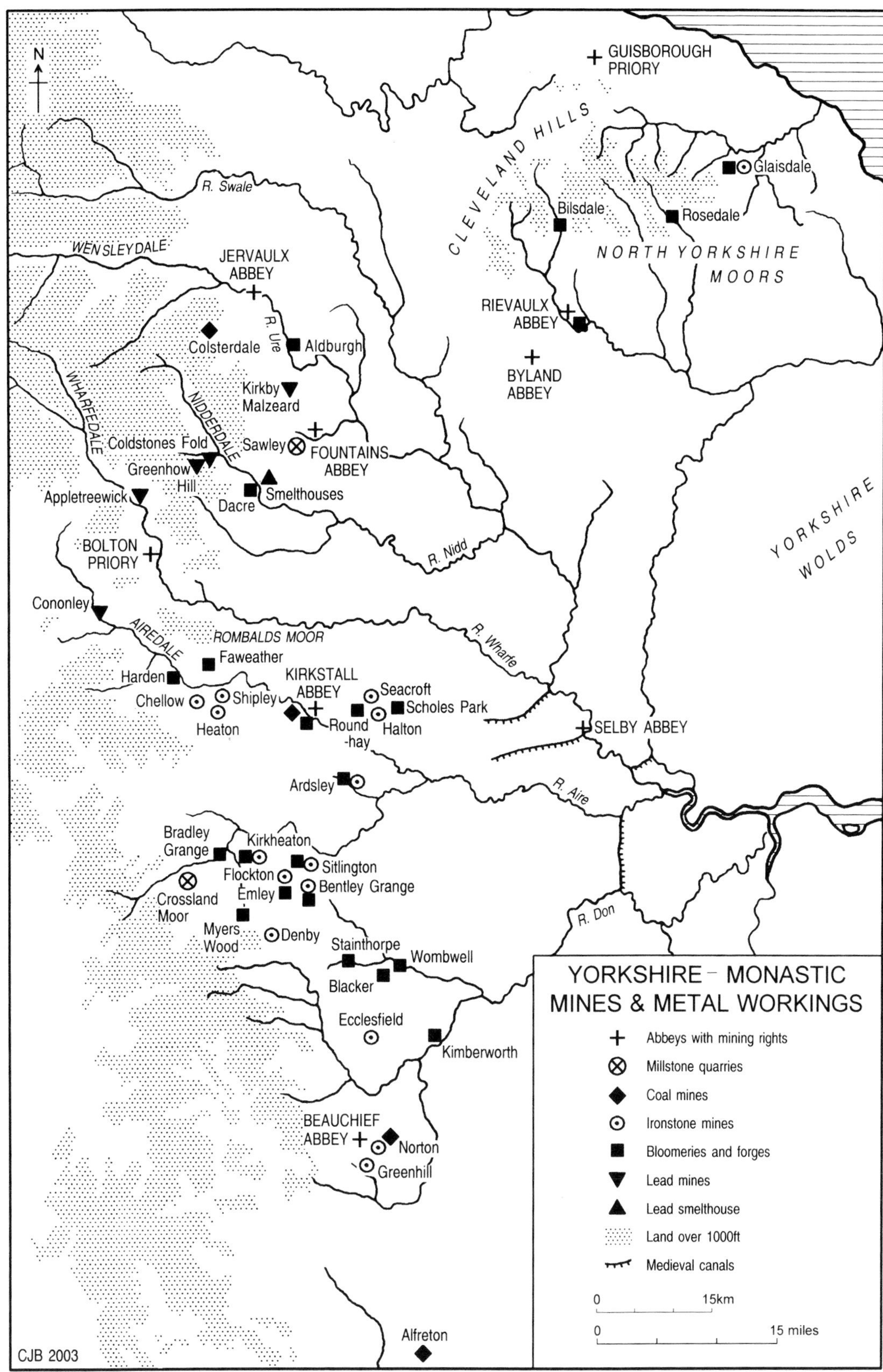

(By kind permission of James Bond)

professed for fifty years and whose age demanded some relaxation of the monastic RULE. They, and the other inmates of the infirmary, were allowed a fire, provided with special diets (including meat) and permitted to observe a less onerous office. All monks visited the infirmary at regular intervals for blood-letting which was considered to be a medical necessity, after which they spent three days convalescing (*see* PHLEBOTOMY). This was seen by many as a welcome break from the austere routine of community life.

A major house would almost certainly have had its own trained PHYSICIAN, who might also be its INFIRMARIAN. Its library would have included works on medicine and it would probably have had a PHARMACY, which was heavily dependent on the efficacy of herbal remedies. The physician might be a monk, although in the later medieval period he was more likely to have been a layman from outside the community. The *barber-surgeon*, who was responsible for blood-letting was, in effect, a junior physician.

The infirmary was usually located to the east of the CLOISTER, away from the noise of the CURIA. Most infirmaries had the same simple church plan as medieval HOSPITALS, the 'nave' being the hall and the 'chancel' containing the chapel (as at Canterbury and Peterborough), although several later farmeries had separate chapels and were sometimes grouped round a cloister (as at Thetford, Waverley and Winchester). In a Charterhouse (*see* CARTHUSIANS) the sick brethren were attended in their individual cells and, when they died, were buried in the cloister garth.

The monks' infirmary at Cistercian Fountains Abbey comprised a vast group of buildings that included an infirmary hall, a two-storey range of chambers, a chapel, kitchen, scullery, frater (dining hall), latrines and cloister, all served by a CONDUIT house and a complex plumbing system (*see* PLUMBING, WATER SUPPLY AND SANITATION). In order to accommodate the buildings within the confines of the narrow valley, Abbot John of Kent (from 1220 to 1247) was obliged to build over the river. He did so by constructing an 82.3m (270ft) long platform on four parallel stone-vaulted tunnels. The infirmary hall, now ruined, was one of the most impressive aisled halls in medieval England. Measuring 55m (180ft) by 23.7m (78ft), it had a central nave of eight bays, two bays wide and with aisles on all four sides. There were fireplaces in the north and south aisles and there may also have been a central fireplace. When the hall was first built in the early thirteenth century the beds would have been ranged along the aisles, the central space being kept free. However, the beds were later screened with curtains to provide privacy and reduce drafts, and from the fourteenth century these were replaced with stone or timber partitions. As was often the case, the infirmary buildings at Fountains were extended, modified and adapted many times. The late thirteenth-century infirmary complex at Furness Abbey contained another splendid Cistercian hall. Measuring 38m (125ft) in length and 15m (50ft) in width, it appears to have been roofed with a single span, possibly a surprisingly early example of a hammer-beam roof. The Furness infirmary was provided with a chapel, latrines, and a detached octagonal kitchen linked to a servery at the eastern end of the hall by a covered passage. In common with most Cistercian infirmaries, that at Tintern Abbey was rebuilt in stone in the thirteenth century. Measuring 33m (107ft) by 16m (33ft), it may have had a chapel at its eastern end. Brethren who wished to leave the infirmary in order to visit the abbey church or the conventual buildings were usually protected from the elements by a covered passage (SLYPE), that at Tintern being a particularly fine example, linking the south alley of the infirmary cloister with the north transept of the abbey church.

Care of the sick was considered to be the principal objective of the Benedictine rule: 'so that in every deed [the sick] may be served as Christ for He himself said "I was sick and ye visited me" and "What you have done to one of these little ones, ye have done unto me"'. No one was turned away, and

Firmary Lane, Ely.

many religious houses maintained separate infirmaries for the benefit of the sick and infirm from beyond their walls. There was a second infirmary 'without the south gate' at Durham, while the parish church of St Thomas at Ramsey in Cambridgeshire may once have been the hall of an infirmary or HOSPICE located outside the gatehouse of the Benedictine abbey (*see also* HOSPITALS). A number of Cistercian abbeys maintained a second infirmary for the *conversi* (*see* LAY BROTHERS). At Fountains, for example, the lay brothers' infirmary was (like the monks' infirmary) built on tunnels over the River Skell and against the west wall of the reredorter. It comprised a large aisled hall of six bays with tall octagonal piers, each bay being illuminated by a two-light window. A door in the east wall led to the ground-floor latrines while a second door in the southern bay of the west wall led to a kitchen. With the demise of the lay brothers in the fourteenth century, the infirmaries at Fountains, Roche and several other Cistercian abbeys were converted to use as guests' halls.

With a decline in the size of monastic communities in the later Middle Ages, many buildings that were originally provided for large numbers of choir monks and lay brethren became redundant and were either converted to other uses or, as in the case of the infirmaries at Byland and Cleeve, demolished, and the stone reused in later buildings. At Rievaulx the twelfth-century infirmary was remodelled in the fifteenth century to provide a grand residence for the superior, and its cloister became the abbot's garden. Similarly, at (Premonstratensian) Easby Abbey the canons' infirmary was remodelled, possibly in the fifteenth century, to form the abbot's lodging. Elsewhere, former infirmary buildings have been subsumed by later development. At Ely, for example, the twelfth-century aisled hall has lost its roof and the blocked arches of its arcades now form the sides of a street called Firmary Lane, at the eastern end of which is a stone wall with a twelfth-century doorway that separated the hall from the infirmary chapel (which has also lost its roof). At the end of the lane the sanctuary of the chapel stands within the nineteenth-century brick building that now forms part of the Chapter Offices. The twelfth-century infirmary at the Cluniac priory of Wenlock formed part of a quadrangle of conventual buildings on the south side of the church. The infirmary and prior's lodgings which were part of this quadrangle were converted into a private residence after the priory was dissolved in 1540, and remain so today.

INK Most medieval and early modern texts were written in inks made from a mixture of oak-galls, iron sulphate and gum arabic, although natural dyes and walnut juice were also used and a darker but less stable ink was produced from carbon, gum and water.

See also PAPER, PARCHMENT, PENS, SCRIPTORIUM *and* VELLUM

INNS *see* SHRINES

INQUISITION, THE An ecclesiastical court established for the detection and punishment of heretics in *c.* 1232. The officials of the Inquisition were chiefly Dominicans and Franciscans, whose methods of interrogation rarely included torture (although this was accepted practice in judicial procedures of the time). Those accused of HERESY were tried before an inquisitor assisted by a jury of clerics and laymen. Penalties for heresy included confiscation of goods, imprisonment and (in capital cases) surrender to the secular authorities for execution by burning. In 1542 the Inquisition was assigned by Pope Paul III to a church department, known as the *Holy Office* or *Congregation of the Inquisition*. This became the final court of appeal in trials for heresy and, ultimately, an organ of papal government.

INSCRIPTIONS The reading of inscriptions is often a difficult task that requires not only a knowledge of LATIN and French but also an ability to decipher the lettering itself. On monumental BRASSES, for example, Norman French in Lombardic script was generally used during the period 1250–1350, Latin inscriptions in black letter usually date from the period 1350–1500, while English, in Tudor black letter or capitals, was used from 1500–1650 *see* LETTERING). But, of course, there are many exceptions. At Brightwell Baldwin in Oxfordshire an inscription in English commemorates one 'John ye Smith' who died in 1370; while many of the clergy continued to commission MONUMENTS with Latin inscriptions long after the Reformation.

Norman French inscriptions are usually short, with a name and a brief prayer: *Sire: John: Daubernoun: Chivalier: Gist: Ici: Deau: Sa: Alme: Eyt: Mercy*, for example, on a brass at Stoke d'Abernon in Surrey. Such an inscription requires only a rudimentary understanding of modern French and a little guesswork ('gist' would now be 'gît'). But Latin inscriptions in black letter are often very difficult to decipher. Vowels are usually omitted, and a bar is placed above a preceding letter (or elsewhere) to indicate the omission. Dates are almost invariably inscribed in Roman numerals and most Latin inscriptions of the period begin with the words 'here lies' and end with an abbreviated prayer, 'on whose soul may God have mercy'. Where an inscription is set in a continuous metal strip or inscribed round the edge of a monument, the first word is usually in the top left corner and may be marked with a cross. Common phrases include: *hic jacet* ('here lies'), *orate pro anima* ('pray for the soul of'), *cui' aie ppiciet de' ame* (an abbreviation for 'on whose soul may God have mercy').

English inscriptions are, of course, easier to read, although spelling can be erratic. Common abbreviations are:

AMDG *ad majorem Dei Gloriam*: To the greater Glory of God
HIS *hic iacet sepultus*: Here lies buried
HMP *hoc monumentum posuit*: He erected this monument
INST *in nomine Sanctae Trinitatis*: In the Name of the Holy Trinity
MS *memoriae sacrum*: Sacred to the memory
RIP *requiescat in pace*: May he rest in peace

The most common archaic words to be found in commemorative inscriptions are:

almys: alms
armiger: one entitled to bear arms
auncynt: ancient
aungeles: angels
awtere: altar

bles: bliss
capellanus: chaplain
certes: certainly
cheyffe: chief
comes: earl
consul: councillor
crysten: christian
decanus: dean
deptyd: departed
dominus: master
eccles: church
eke: also
elemosinarius: almoner
erchdiakn: archdeacon
eyre: heir
fadyr: father
ffro: from
generosus: gentleman
gent: gentleman or gentlewoman
halud: hallowed
hem: them
maden: made
mci: mercy
mede: merit
miles: knight
moder: mother
or: our
p: per, pro or prae
pannarius: draper
pelliparius: tanner
pish: parish
prepositus: provost
pson: parson
quere: choir (chancel)
redecion: redemption
relict: widow
sowlys: souls
steven: staves of music
s'teyne: certain
thred: third
twey: two
wen: think
whylom: once
wot: know
XPS: Christus
yat: that
yistis: gifts
ys: this

See also EPITAPHS, LAPIDARY, PRECATORY SCROLL *and* WALL MONUMENTS

INSTALLATION The induction of a CANON or PREBENDARY to a stall in a CATHEDRAL or COLLEGIATE CHURCH.

See also CLERGY (CHURCH OF ENGLAND)

INSTITUTION The admission by a bishop of a new incumbent to the spiritual responsibilities of a parish. Institution is usually followed by induction.

INTERDICT An ecclesiastical punishment whereby the faithful are excluded from all matters spiritual, other than the Communion of the Church (*see also* EXCOMMUNICATION). A general interdict applied to an entire population or that of a defined district, a local interdict was confined to a particular place and a personal interdict was directed only at a specified person or persons. In 1207 Pope Innocent III consecrated Stephen Langton, an English cardinal, as archbishop of Canterbury, but King John declined to receive him and vented his anger on the monks of Canterbury, at least sixty of whom were sent into exile. The following year the pope issued an interdict against the realm of England under which all church sacraments (*see* SACRAMENT) were withheld except baptism and extreme unction. The king retaliated by ordering the confiscation of church property and other measures, including a requirement that the parish clergy should ransom their mistresses (described in one document as *sacerdotissis*: literally 'women priests': clearly, the scribe possessed a sense of humour). The interdict was not lifted until 2 July 1214.

INTRANSI (*or* TRANSI) TOMB Medieval double-decker tombs with two EFFIGIES of the same person: splendour and piety above and pathetic and cadaverous mortality beneath. From the Latin *transeo* meaning 'to cross over', an intransi tomb is remarkable in that it has two effigies of the deceased: one in which he is depicted in his former earthly glory and, beneath, one in which he is revealed in the emaciated, worm-eaten form to which he has gone. Bishops and abbots are often commemorated in this way, thereby declaring that they acknowledged the transitory nature of their earthly lives and the ultimate irrelevance of their accumulated power and wealth.
See also CADAVER, MONUMENTS *and* TOMBS

INTRINSECA *see* PLACE-NAMES (MONASTIC AND ECCLESIASTICAL)

INTROIT The opening act of worship in the mass, usually the singing of a psalm or a part thereof.

INVENTORY A list of possessions, goods and chattels, often with a valuation.

J

JACKS OF THE CLOCK Carved and painted human figures which strike the bell of a clock. In Britain, the earliest example is believed to be the late fourteenth-century jack-clock at Wells Cathedral, where two 'quarter jacks' strike the quarter hours and 'Jack Blandifer' strikes the hours.
See also CLOCKS

JESSE TREE Christ's descent from Jesse, the father of King David, depicted in a church window, wall painting, etc. in the form of a *Tree of Jesse*, which springs from the recumbent body of Jesse and terminates in the Virgin and Holy Child, with the intermediate descendants represented on foliage scrolls branching out from each other. Of several fine examples, that in the church of St Mary the Virgin at Shrewsbury is one of the best, and was probably transferred there from a friary church in the town.

JESSE WINDOW *see* JESSE TREE

JESUS ALTAR The votive mass (the *Jesus Mass*) was celebrated at the Jesus altar every Friday. This stood in front of the ROOD SCREEN in the

NAVE.
See also NAVE ALTAR

JOINERY *see* WOODWORK

JUBE *see* ROOD SCREEN

JUBILATE Psalm 100, the first words of which are 'Make a joyful noise unto the Lord'. According to the *Book of Common Prayer*, the Jubilate may be sung or said as an alternative to the BENEDICTUS at Morning Prayer. In the *Alternative Service Book* it is offered as an alternative to the VENITE.

JULIAN CALENDAR The calendar introduced by Julius Ceasar in 46 BC, in which the standard year has 365 days and every fourth year is a leap year of 366 days. The GREGORIAN CALENDAR was introduced in 1582 to compensate for the ten days that had accumulated as a result of the Julian calendar being 11 minutes and 10 seconds too long, although the change was not effected in England until 1752.

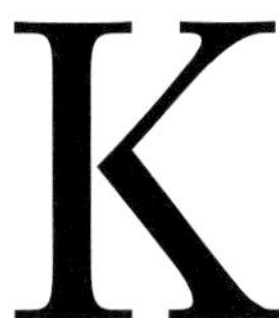

KENTISH RAG A grey-green sandy limestone quarried in Kent. Used extensively for architectural dressings and as facing stone because of its hard, impervious characteristics.

KETTON STONE A cream-coloured limestone quarried in Rutland.

KEY A boss (*see* VAULTING).
KEYSTONE *see* ARCH *and* BOSSES

KINGS AND QUEENS *see* RULERS OF ENGLAND AND OF THE UNITED KINGDOM

KING'S BOOKS, THE *see* VALOR ECCLESIASTICUS

KIRTLE *see* EFFIGIES

KITCHENER (COQUINARIUS) In a religious house, the official responsible for supervising the KITCHENS, for the work of the cooks and their (often numerous) assistants and for planning meals 'according to traditional allowances and observances', particularly with regard to FASTING, ABSTINENCE and religious festivals.
See also CATERER *and* EMPTOR

KITCHENS Of all the surviving monastic buildings in England, none is more redolent of the power and status of a religious superior than the abbot's kitchen at Glastonbury Abbey. As head of the second richest monastic foundation in Britain, the Abbot of Glastonbury enjoyed many of the perquisites of a medieval magnate and was expected to provide appropriately lavish HOSPITALITY for his eminent guests (*see* FEUDAL SYSTEM *and* SUPERIOR'S LODGINGS). Of the magnificent abbot's quarters at Glastonbury, begun by John de Breynton (1334–42), only the south-west angle of the great hall and the splendid kitchen remain. The kitchen is a detached, square building with heavily buttressed walls, on top of which an octagonal sloping roof reaches up to a central octagon, with two trefoil-headed windows on each face, and above this a second, smaller octagon with a pointed roof. These octagons form the louvred chimney through which smoke escaped via a system of flues from fireplaces in each of the four corners of the kitchen. At Glastonbury there were also kitchens serving the monks' refectory (*see* FRATER), INFIRMARY and GUEST HOUSE, although of these only the footings of the frater kitchen have survived. This was also a substantial square building, detached from the other conventual buildings in case of fire and

The late fourteenth-century Abbot's kitchen at Glastonbury Abbey, Somerset. (Courtesy of John Mennell)

linked to the frater by a covered passageway. The Glastonbury kitchen was one of a comparatively small number of high-status examples that included Battle Abbey, Canterbury and Durham.

Although the larger monasteries often added separate kitchens to serve the frater, infirmary, guest house and abbot's lodging, initially the majority of religious houses had only one kitchen providing for the needs of the whole community. In smaller houses this was often a simple rectangular chamber incorporated within the western range of the claustral buildings, adjacent to the monks' frater in the south range – or attached to it, as at Easby Abbey.

Only vegetables and legumes were cooked in the frater kitchen: the Benedictine RULE forbade meat except to the weak and sick, although superiors were permitted to modify the rule on certain festive occasions. Consequently, several monasteries built special kitchens for that purpose and to provide meat dishes for corrodians and guests (*see* CORRODIAN *and* MISERICORD). By the late fourteenth century it was generally acknowledged that 'a total abstinence from meat is contrary to nature and hurtful to the system', and there was a general relaxation of the rule, except during periods of fasting. At Fountains Abbey, the infirmary kitchen was rebuilt in the fourteenth century to provide a meat diet that gradually replaced the strict vegetarian diet of the early Cistercians. The kitchen was separated from the infirmary hall by service yards (to protect against fire) and was linked with both the hall and the infirmary chambers by passages. It was a rectangular building, with a stone vault (again, to protect against fire) and divided by a cross-wall into a wide northern and narrow southern room. The northern room was the main kitchen, with two great fireplaces in the dividing wall. In the north-east angle of the room a stone grid in the floor was fitted with wooden trap-doors through which waste was discharged into the river beneath. Further ovens were added in the late fifteenth century, including a bread oven in an annex built against the west wall. The southern room was a scullery, of which the stone floor and gutters have survived together with a fifteenth-century fireplace.

Originally, cooking and the preparation of food was undertaken by all the brethren in turn. But while this practice continued in Cluniac and Cistercian houses, elsewhere there was a tendency towards engaging paid servants under the direction of a KITCHENER. The OBSERVANCES of the various orders set out in considerable detail the furniture and utensils that were to be provided for the efficient ordering of a monastic kitchen. Water was to be heated in three cauldrons (*caldaria*): one for cooking legumes, one for vegetables and another for washing dishes, cloths and utensils. Four large water cisterns were to be provided for conserving beans, for washing vegetables (this

Plate 1: Salisbury Cathedral, described by Thomas Hardy as 'the most graceful architectural pile in England'.
(© John Crook/info@john-crook.com)

Plate 2: Above: *Fountains Abbey, Yorkshire: Abbot Huby's Tower, the west front of the church and the lay brothers' range – the largest and best preserved in Europe.* (© English Heritage Photo Library)

Plate 3: Below: *The Pilrow Cut near Mark, Somerset: a canal cut by Glastonbury Abbey as part of its thirteenth-century programme of water management in the Somerset levels. A small port was established at Rooks Bridge and carriage along the canal to Glastonbury continued until at least 1500. Schemes such as this were huge undertakings requiring considerable resources, both human and financial.* (By kind permission of James Bond)

Plate 4: Above: *The Cistercian abbey of Rievaulx, North Yorkshire, became one of the most celebrated monasteries in England. Within a few years of its foundation in 1132, its community had grown to 140 monks and 500 conversi (lay brethren).* (Courtesy of Derry Brabbs/www.derry brabbs.com)

Plate 5: Below: *The magnificent Norman west front of Castle Acre Priory, Norfolk.* (Courtesy of Derry Brabbs/www.derrybrabbs.com)

Plate 6: The enormous mid-fourteenth-century east window at Gloucester Cathedral. As large as a tennis court, it forms a giant triptych filled with tiers of canopied figures. The heraldry in its lower lights is said to commemorate the knights who fought with Edward III at the battle of Crécy in 1346. (© John Crook/info@john-crook.com)

Plate 7: Fan vaulting in the chapel of King Henry VII, Westminster Abbey. (© John Crook/info@john-crook.com)

Plate 8: The late thirteenth-century chapter house steps at Wells Cathedral. In 1459 an upper doorway was made, connecting the steps to the Chain Gate and the Vicars' Close. (© John Crook/info@john-crook.com)

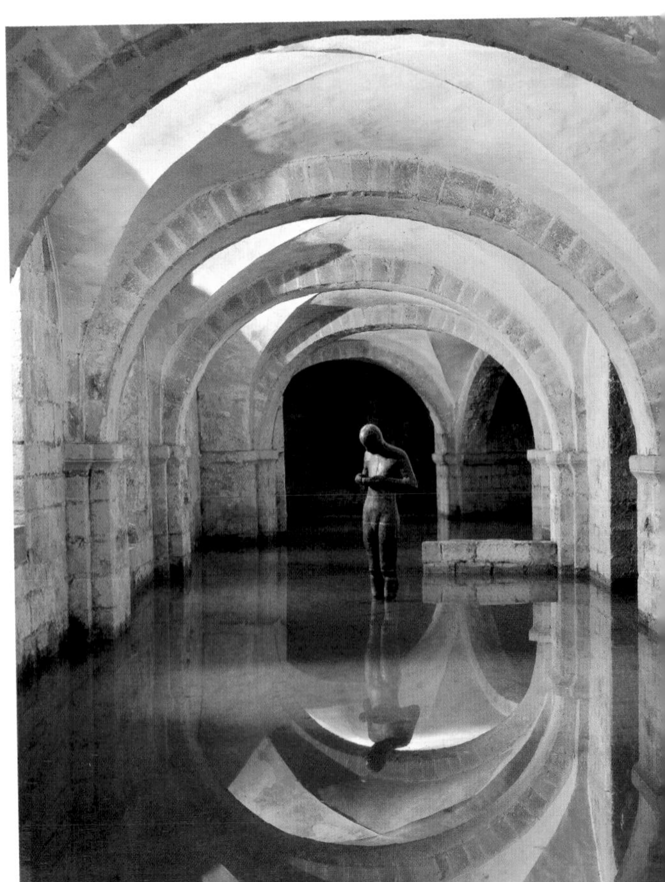

Plate 9: Antony Gormley's sculpture Sound II in the flooded north aisle of the crypt at Winchester Cathedral. (© John Crook/info@john-crook.com)

Plate 10: The spectacular timber vaults and lantern above the octagon at Ely Cathedral. (© John Crook/ info@john-crook.com)

Plate 11: Versal letters from the Winchester Bible, the finest of the great twelfth-century illuminated Bibles. Distinguished by its extraordinary size and the sumptuousness of its decoration, the skins of more than 250 calves were used to produce its vellum pages. The decorated initial letters were designed and painted by a team of six artists, employing gold leaf and (even more expensive) lapis lazuli from Afghanistan. (© John Crook/info@john-crook.com)

The great kitchen of the Bishop's palace at Lincoln. (Jeremy Richards/© English Heritage Photo Library)

required a constant supply of running water), for washing up and for storing hot water for shaving, tonsuring and the weekly MAUNDY (*see* LAVATORIUM).

In Cistercian houses the principal kitchen was almost invariably located so that it could serve both the monks' frater in the SOUTH RANGE of the claustral buildings and that of the LAY BROTHERS in the west. In order to accommodate the kitchen in this position, the monks' frater in Cistercian houses was usually constructed on a north-south axis, extending at right angles beyond the cloister (there are exceptions: at Cymer Abbey, for example, where financial insecurity prevented the monks from adopting the usual Cistercian arrangement). Typically, at Fountains Abbey the kitchen occupied the western part of the south claustral range, where it serviced both fraters (evidence of the revolving 'dumb waiters' by which food was passed to the servers in the frater has survived both here and at Rievaulx Abbey – *see* ROTA). To the south of the kitchen was a service yard, where fuel and other non-perishable commodities were stored, a covered passage (*pentice*) running along the frater wall to a latrine, and a bridge across the river by which the kitchen was supplied. At the centre of the kitchen was a great double fireplace, the hearths built back-to-back beneath a chimney that rose through the centre of the building. To reduce the risk of fire, the roof was vaulted in stone on either side of the chimney.

Many monastic kitchens had service yards similar to that at Fountains and the various offices (pantry, buttery, scullery, etc.) were usually located in close proximity (*see* LARDER *and* SCREENS PASSAGE). There are, of course, monasteries where the claustral buildings are located to the north of the church (at Cistercian Dore, Buildwas and Tintern, for example.) In such cases, the frater kitchens are to be found in the north-east corner of the cloister, again serving both the monks' frater and that of the lay brothers.

At Cistercian Rievaulx, as elsewhere, there is evidence of various stages of construction and modification, the surviving form dating from the fourteenth century when (like the chapter house and dormitory) the frater kitchen was reduced in size to serve a smaller community. At the Cluniac priory of Thetford, a wine store (*buttery*) was located at the west end of the frater, with the kitchen to the south and a well between them. In the fourteenth century the original kitchen was demolished and the buttery converted to the monastic kitchen. Fourteenth-century modifications such as these reflect a decline in the numbers of choir monks and (particularly) lay brothers in many communities. Even so, several houses also experienced a corresponding increase in the number of corrodians seeking accommodation. At Tintern, for example, a new infirmary kitchen was built in the early fifteenth century and enlarged soon thereafter, replacing an earlier structure. These new kitchens were almost certainly built to serve the increasing numbers of corrodians and retired senior monks who had taken up residence in the infirmary and the adjacent private apartments.

KNAPPING *see* FLINT

KNIGHTS HOSPITALLER *see* ST JOHN OF JERUSALEM, ORDER OF

KNIGHTS TEMPLAR *see* TEMPLAR, KNIGHTS

KNOP A carved motif: an ornamental knob or the stylised bud of a flower.

L

LABEL (i) A small, stylised 'scroll' inscribed with a religious aphorism or prayer and located, for example, near the head of a figure in a monumental brass (*see* PRECATORY SCROLL).
(ii) *For* architectural label *see* DRIPSTONE.

LABEL STOP Carved architectural decoration at the termination of a label (*see* DRIPSTONE).

LABOUR *see* MANUAL LABOUR

LADY CHAPEL A subsidiary chapel dedicated to the Blessed Virgin Mary, usually (though not invariably) located at the eastern termination of a major church beyond the HIGH ALTAR. From the eleventh century onwards many larger churches were constructed or remodelled to a cruciform plan with the lower, elongated limb of a LATIN CROSS forming the NAVE, the upper limb the CHOIR and PRESBYTERY and the lateral limbs the north and south TRANSEPT. The presbytery around the altar was usually APSIDAL, but many were rebuilt after *c.* 1150 to provide a square termination, and in larger churches a RETRO-CHOIR or AMBULATORY was added with radiating CHAPELS. Of these, the most important is often a Lady Chapel, usually of late medieval date, its size and architectural splendour reflecting a contemporary cult-like veneration of the Blessed Virgin Mary (*see* MARY, THE BLESSED VIRGIN). Regrettably, few Lady Chapels escaped the attentions of the iconoclasts at the Reformation, and consequently much of their elaborate and often exquisitely executed detail has been lost.

St Bernard promoted veneration of the Virgin Mary, and consequently all Cistercian abbeys were dedicated to Our Lady, making a separate chapel superfluous. Even so, the elaboration of the east

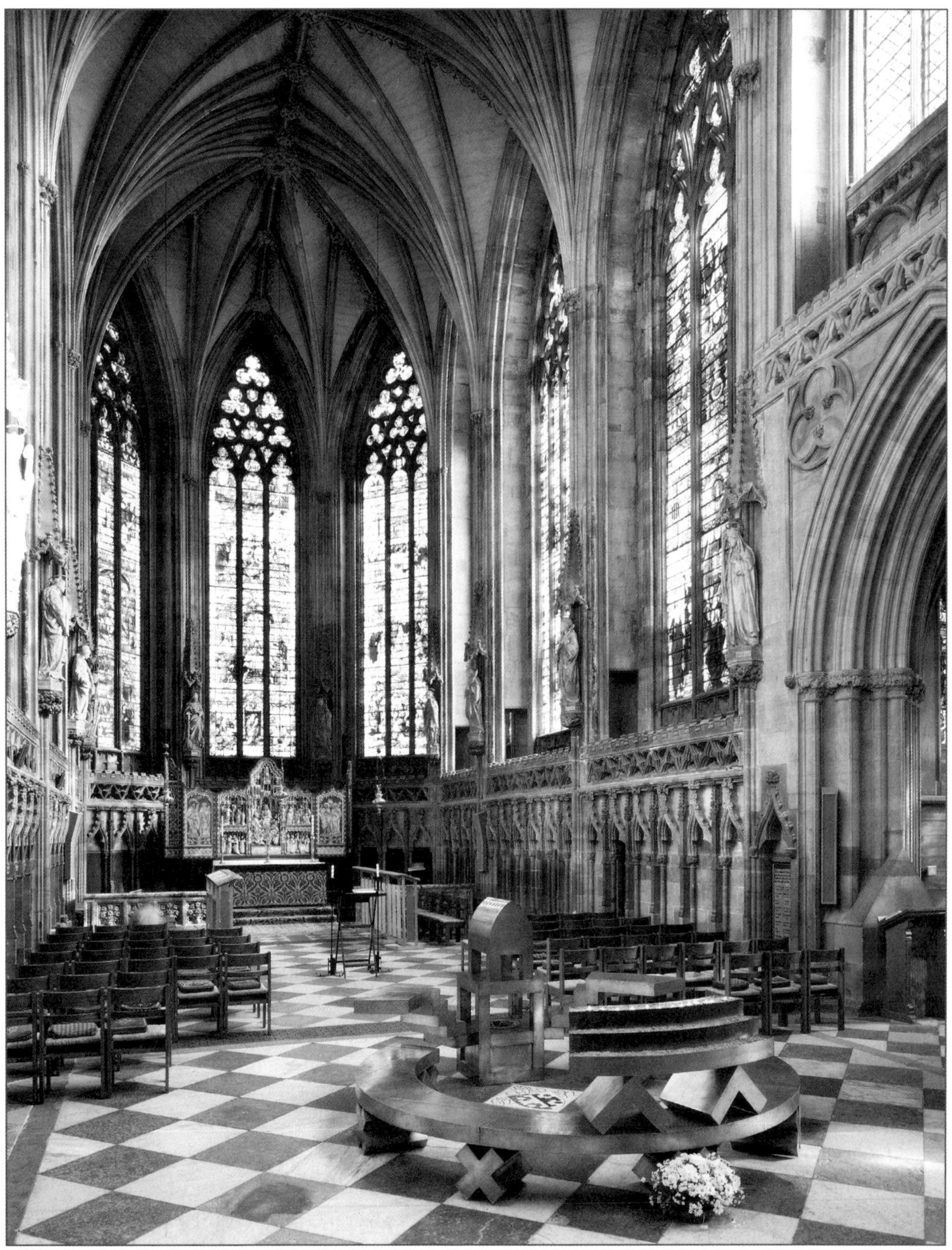

The Lady Chapel at Lichfield Cathedral, renowned for its Herckenrode glass, installed in 1803. (© John Crook/ info@john-crook.com)

end, which distinguishes a major church from a minor one, may be found in a number of Cistercian churches: the remarkable thirteenth-century Chapel of the Nine Altars at Fountains, for example, or at Hailes Abbey, where a ring of subsidiary chapels was constructed in the late thirteenth century to provide a dignified setting for the shrine of the Holy Blood (*see* CHEVET).

The majority of Lady Chapels are to be found in the great cathedrals and, for the most part, these date from the late thirteenth and fourteenth centuries, when the cult of the Virgin Mary was at its height. Those at Chichester, Exeter, Gloucester, Hereford, Lichfield, Llandaff, St Albans, Wells, Winchester and Worcester are among the best. The eastern bay of the Winchester Lady Chapel was rebuilt in *c.* 1500, possibly as a thank-offering by Elizabeth of York, whose son, Arthur, was baptised there in 1486. A series of contemporary mural paintings on the south wall depict legendary miracles of Our Lady, although the work is so fragile that they are covered by panels on to which the original paintings have been copied. Gloucester's Lady Chapel, completed in *c.* 1482, is one of the finest and represents the final flowering of the Perpendicular style of MEDIEVAL ARCHITECTURE, that had its birthplace here. A lofty vault is supported on a series of arches that are now almost entirely filled with tall, painted glass windows. It is the third chapel to stand on the site, replacing earlier Romanesque and thirteenth-century buildings. At its western end the new construction was made to carry a passageway connecting the choir tribune on the north with its counterpart on the south. This was achieved by constructing an elaborate bridge at the west end of the Lady Chapel which carries, beside the passage, a small chapel with an altar. For acoustic reasons the passage is known as 'The Whispering Gallery', and is set back from the great east window of the choir (the Crécy window) so that the vast expanse of coloured glass is uninterrupted.

Several of the larger parish churches have Lady Chapels: Christchurch Priory and Sherborne Abbey in Dorset, for example, while the chapel at Romsey was demolished in 1544 when the townspeople bought the abbey for £100. Only when, as at Southwell Minster, the church itself was dedicated to the Virgin was a Lady Chapel considered unnecessary (Southwell became a cathedral in 1884). Salisbury Cathedral, which is also dedicated to the Virgin, had no need of a Lady Chapel; nevertheless a fine eastern chapel was built, but was dedicated to the Trinity. Unusually, Sherborne Abbey has a Lady Chapel despite its dedication to St Mary the Virgin. The two eastern bays of the thirteenth-century chapel were demolished by the Governors of Sherborne School at the Reformation and the western bay was converted into a house for the headmaster. The Tudor east window which once illuminated the upper floor of these apartments is still in evidence, as are the royal arms (used by the School) on the external south wall. The chapel was restored to the abbey and reconsecrated in 1934 and it may be that, with such a complex history, the dedication is not the original.

The Lady Chapel at Tewkesbury Abbey was demolished in 1541: the stonework of the former arch is visible in the exterior eastern wall of the AMBULATORY, while the upper of the two windows was originally also the west window to the Lady Chapel. On each side of the ambulatory is a group of chapels, seven in number (including the destroyed Lady Chapel), a similar arrangement to that at Westminster Abbey, where the chevet forms the eastern termination of the Chapel of Henry VII, also known as the Lady Chapel. This magnificent chapel, considered at the time to be 'a wonder of the world', was commissioned in 1503 by Henry VII (1485–1509). He intended it to be a burial place for Henry VI (1422–61) but it was Henry VII himself who was finally buried there in an elaborate tomb. As such, its designation as a Lady Chapel is of doubtful validity. The fine Lady Chapel at York Minster is flanked by the chapels of St Stephen and All Saints. It is the same height as the choir and in plan has the appearance of a retro-

The magnificent Chapel of Henry VII at Westminster Abbey. Sometimes described as the Lady Chapel, it also serves as the chapel of the Most Honourable Order of the Bath. (Mansell/Time & Life Pictures/Getty Images)

choir. At Canterbury, the original apse surrounding the (present) presbytery was lost in the fire of 1174. However, two of the chapels that projected from this apse were saved and incorporated in the rebuilding which included the Trinity Chapel (also known as St Thomas's Chapel), in which stood the shrine of the murdered archbishop Thomas à Becket. Canterbury's Trinity

Chapel occupies the eastern location where one would expect to find a Lady Chapel, although it is closer in function to a retro-choir. To the east, it extends into a small apsidal *Corona chapel*, just 8m (27ft) in diameter, said once to have been the site of a RELIQUARY containing Becket's TONSURE. It now houses St Augustine's chair, constructed from Petworth marble in 1205, on which archbishops of Canterbury are enthroned.

There are, of course, exceptions to the general rule: not all Lady Chapels were built at the eastern end of the church. At Glastonbury Abbey the first building to be erected following a devastating fire of 1184 was a Lady Chapel which replaced the old church of St Mary, the most venerable of the destroyed shrines. This magnificent Romanesque building has survived, its proportions marred only by the insertion of a crypt by Abbot Beere in *c.* 1500. Unusually, it is located at the western end of the church, separated from the nave by a GALILEE. It was the same Abbot Beere who, in the late fifteenth century, added the Edgar Chapel at the eastern end of the church. This had the appearance of a Lady Chapel but was intended to contain monuments to Edgar and other Saxon kings whom the abbey claimed as it founders. At the Cluniac priory of Thetford, the east end of the church was rebuilt in the thirteenth century and, although there was clearly an opportunity to provide a Lady Chapel at the east end, it was built to the north of the High Altar. There is a spiral staircase at the west end of the chapel which led to a gallery in which a monk would be on duty during pilgrims' visiting hours (*see* WATCHING LOFT).

Most Lady Chapels were square-ended, although a few had polygonal apses (as at Lichfield and Wells), and only a small number rose to the full height of the adjacent choir (as at Bristol and, again, Lichfield). The integration of the Lady Chapel with the main building is especially sophisticated at Wells, where it forms part of an octagonal composition extending into the retro-choir, which is a lower structure. One of the most spectacular Lady Chapels, at Ely Cathedral, has the widest Gothic vault in England, spanning 12m (40ft), and is ornamented throughout with elaborate fourteenth-century carving. 'When one imagines the sculpture which has been lost from its niches, the bright paint once on its stonework and the brilliant colours of its vanished stained glass, one gets some impression of the overwhelming richness of its original impact and the deep reverence felt by the medieval congregation for the mother of Christ' (Lucy Archer). Had the Lady Chapel at Ely been built in the usual eastern position it would have trespassed on the abbey's cemetery. It was therefore constructed as a detached building on the north side of the church between the presbytery and the transept from which it is entered. Following the Reformation, the Lady Chapel became one of Ely's parish churches, and was known as Holy Trinity Church until 1938.

A number of twentieth-century cathedrals have Lady Chapels: at Liverpool it was the first part of the cathedral to be completed (in 1910) following the laying of the foundation stone in 1904. Designed by Sir Giles Gilbert Scott and his mentor G.F. Bodley, it is located to the south east of the SANCTUARY and is reached by a staircase from a gallery opening out of the south choir aisle. But, unlike the original Lady Chapels, in which the daily LADY MASS was celebrated, the Liverpool chapel has its own organ and entrance and is used regularly for a variety of services, especially for baptisms, weddings and funerals. Nevertheless, the window glass celebrates the lives of women, both from the Bible and from the history of the church, and there is a statue of the Virgin Mary by Giovanni della Robbia, a fifteenth-century Italian sculptor.

LADY MASS Also known as the *Morrow Mass*, the Lady Mass was a votive MASS to the Blessed Virgin Mary which was usually celebrated in the LADY CHAPEL (except in Cistercian abbeys, where it was celebrated in the choir). The Mass of the Blessed

Virgin Mary was sung in the morning throughout the year, except on Good Friday and Easter Eve, and such was its importance that it was usually attended by the entire community.

LAIRSTAL A grave located within a church. The stone covering of such a grave may be described as a *lairstone*.

LAMPS The practice of burning a *sanctuary lamp* (with a red light) before the altar, and to indicate the presence of the reserved SACRAMENT (a white light), dates from the thirteenth century. A further lamp (with a blue light) was also burned before images of the Mother and Child. Lamps of this type (sometimes described as *aumbry lamps*) are usually suspended from the ceiling by means of a chain and ring from which three shorter chains support an ornamental drip-pan with pendant finial. Sanctuary lamps are generally of highly polished brass, the red, white or blue light emanating from a slow-burning candle or oil lamp within a cylindrical funnel of coloured glass.
See also ALTAR LIGHTS, BIER LIGHT, CANDELABRUM, CANDLES, CORONA LUCIS, HEARSE, LANTERN, LIGHTS, PRICKET, STRAP SCONCE *and* TRENDAL

LANATUS Buried in wool.

LANCET *see* ARCH, MEDIEVAL ARCHITECTURE *and* WINDOWS

LANE An unusual feature found in some Cistercian monasteries: a covered passageway between the west alley of the CLOISTER and the LAY BROTHERS' range of claustral buildings. Lanes, which varied considerably in width, ran the entire length of the cloister, passing through the frater range to the south and with a door to the church in the north. They were separated from the cloister by a wall and were almost certainly provided to allow the lay brethren to move about without disturbing the monks' activities in the cloister. At Byland Abbey, for example, the lane provides segregated access to all the lay brothers' buildings and facilities, to their (separate) cloister in the south and to the church in the north. A series of thirty-five niches, used as seats, suggests that it was here that they assembled before entering the nave of the church for services. A similar space separated the cloister from the church in some friaries.

LANTERN (i) A circular or polygonal turret-like structure, often surmounting a dome, for the purpose of admitting light and air. In churches, a lantern will usually be found above the CROSSING, where the vault is omitted, and there may be a series of windows in the upper story of a central tower.
For the Lantern at Ely Cathedral Priory *see* TOWERS.
(ii) A portable lamp, the windows of which were originally made of sliced animal horn (hence 'lanthorn'). In religious houses, night-time processions were led by a junior monk carrying a lantern. The CIRCATOR also carried a lantern when patrolling the conventual buildings in search of monks who were not at VIGIL. If he discovered a sleeping brother he would wake him by placing the lantern before his eyes. The errant monk was then obliged to take the lantern, find another brother in a similar condition, and repeat the process.
See also LIGHTS

LANTERN TOWER A tower in which there is no vault immediately above the crossing, the space extending upwards and lit by upper windows (*see* LANTERN *and* TOWERS).

LAPIDARY That which is engraved on stone.

LAPS AND ROLLS The usual method of constructing a lead roof is for lengths of lead to be laid with their edges overlapping. The 'laps' are then 'rolled' to make them waterproof.

LARDER The *Larderer* was the monastic official responsible for the acquisition, storage and preparation of provisions. Bread was the province of the *pantry*, utensils and equipment were maintained by the *scullery* and table linen by the *napery*. Wine was the concern of the *buttery* and vegetables were provided by the *curtilage*. In the monastic hierarchy, the CELLARER was charged with overall responsibility for all these departments, together with the produce of the dairy, mill and BREWHOUSE. Beneath him was the *Caterer*, who was accountable for the work of the KITCHENS and the refectories (*see* FRATER). The *Kitchener* managed the preparation of meals, while administration of the refectories was the responsibility of the *Refectorian* or *Fraterer*.

LATH AND PLASTER Material used for ceilings, and for the internal walls of timber-framed buildings, consisting of a framework of interlaced or parallel laths (usually split hazel or willow) covered with layers of plaster which often contained a bonding agent such as horsehair.

LATIN An Indo-European language of the Italic group, and the ancestor of all Romance languages. Latin was originally the dialect of small communities living along the lower Tiber, a district of Italy known as Latium. With the increase of Roman political control, the language spread throughout Italy and into western and southern Europe and the western Mediterranean coastal regions of Africa. It became the official language of the Roman Empire and remained the international medium of communication in western Europe throughout the Middle Ages, notably in matters of law, scholarship and the LITURGY. It remained the official language of the Roman Catholic Church until the mid-twentieth century.

LATIN CROSS A plain cross with an extended lower limb.

LATRINES *see* REREDORTER

LATTEN *see* BRASSES (MONUMENTAL)

LAUDS A short office, observed at dawn, which (until 1911) included five groups of psalms sung antiphonally (*see* ANTIPHON). The fifth of these comprised Psalms 148–150, known as the *Laudes*, in which the word *laudate* ('praise ye') recurs. In the *Book of Common Prayer*, elements of Lauds and MATTINS were combined to form the service of Morning Prayer.
See also DIVINE OFFICE, HORARIUM *and* HOURS (CANONICAL)

LAVABO The washing of a priest's fingers following the offering of the OBLATIONS at the EUCHARIST. The lavabo was usually carried out at a PISCINA in the PRESBYTERY or in an ancillary chapel, indeed a second piscina was sometimes provided for this purpose, and the term is often applied to this.
See also ABLUTIONS, CREDENCE *and* FENESTELLA

LAVATORIUM *or* LAVER The monastic washing place (*lavatorium*) was usually located in (or adjacent to) the CLOISTER and near the entrance to the refectory (*see* FRATER). It was here that the monks performed their morning ABLUTIONS (following PRIME), washed their hands before meals and celebrated the weekly MAUNDY. Shaving, which for the tonsured monk (*see* TONSURE) meant the head as well as the face, was performed every third week when the community gathered in the cloister and shaved one another. The senior monks shaved first and benefited from a sharp razor, warm water and dry towels – luxuries denied the novices, who came last in the queue.

There were two types of lavatorium. The first consisted of a long trough, usually recessed within an alcove, lined with lead or pewter and fed by brass piping: as at the Augustinian houses of Kirkham in Yorkshire and Hexham in Northumberland (where the lavatorium is now in the police station!). Kirkham's thirteenth-century lavatorium was in the west cloister, where two

The lavatorium in the cloister of Gloucester Cathedral.

arched recesses with fine tracery panelling have survived, as have the chases for the piped water supply. The beautiful lavatorium at the Benedictine abbey of Gloucester (now the cathedral) occupies four bays at the west end of the north alley, where it projects 2.4m (8ft) into the cloister GARTH. Internally it is 14.3m (47ft) long and two metres (6ft 6in) wide, with a superb fan vault, eight windows towards the garth and eight tall arches by which it is entered from the cloister, each with a glazed traceried opening above. The Gloucester laver was vividly described by the Very Revd Seiriol Evans in 1974:

> There was a good deal of hand-washing decreed in the routine of the cloistered monk, and he approached the lead-lined water trough through the arches of the cloister walk; here, under the diminutive fan vault, he found a broad ledge, with leaden tanks full of water upon it, so arranged so as to discharge into the trough. Drain holes led the dirty water away and carried it by means of a gully into a tank sunk in the cloister garth. The tank was sluiced by a stream called the Fulbrook which ran through it. Opposite the lavatorium a recess [*aumbry*] accommodated the towel cupboard. After drying their hands, the monks would form up in a double row at the refectory door to await the senior monk who would preside at dinner.

Inevitably, those houses with the largest communities required the most extensive facilities. At Cistercian Fountains, for example, the lavatorium occupied the entire length of the south alley, set deep in a wall arcade on either side of the refectory doorway. The stone bench that once supported the semicircular troughs has survived, as has the inner side of the troughs, which were once lined with pewter and supplied with running water from lead pipes. Not all Cistercian lavers were as impressive: at Cleeve Abbey the lavatorium occupied a single arched recess in the south alley.

The second type of lavatorium was a detached circular or polygonal structure, projecting into the cloister GARTH and built round a large, central basin. One of the finest examples is the 'Conduit' at Sherborne in Dorset, a sixteenth-century hexagonal lavatorium which was removed from the Abbey at the Dissolution of the Monasteries and set up as a public fountain in the nearby marketplace. At Wenlock Priory, the base of a lavatorium (here erroneously described as the lavabo) has survived in the cloister garth, together with the lower section of the extraordinary free-standing water vessel it contained. Built in *c.* 1220, the lavatorium was an octagonal building with open arcades supporting a roof. Within this, water was fed into a circular cistern, from which it flowed through the mouths of sixteen carved heads into a shallow circular trough where sixteen monks could wash simultaneously. The trough had plugholes for drainage and was supported on an elaborately carved, circular base.

Both types of lavatorium were often embellished with ornate architectural decoration: the wonderful fan vaulting at Gloucester, for example. The lavatorum at Durham was described in contemporary documents:

> Within the Cloyster garth, over against the Frater House dour, was a fair Laver or Counditt [conduit] for the Monncks to washe ther hands and faces at, being maid in forme round, covered with lead, and all of marble, saving the verie utter-most walls; within the which walls you may walke round about the Laver of marble, having many little cunditts or spouts of brasse, with cockes of brass, rownd about yt.

Larger houses were often provided with several lavers (there were four at Canterbury) and some were reserved for specific purposes. Towels were

The remains of the lavatorium at Wenlock Priory, Shropshire.

kept in a nearby cupboard (*see* AUMBRY), sometimes a recess in an adjacent wall, and were changed on Sundays and Thursdays. The lavatorium was the responsibility of the CHAMBERLAIN, whose many and diverse duties included the provision of hot water and soap when required, together with a whetstone and a supply of sand so that the brethren could clean and sharpen their knives.
See also CONDUIT, PLUMBING, WATER SUPPLY AND SANITATION *and* REREDORTER

LAVER *see* LAVATORIUM

LAY A member of the laity: one who is not ordained into the clergy.
See also LAY BROTHERS *and* LAY CLERK

LAY ABBOT A layman who was appointed to the title, revenues and privileges of an abbacy. An abuse of royal or papal authority which almost invariably resulted in economic and spiritual dissipation.
See also COMMENDATOR

LAY BROTHERS Lay brothers were accepted as members of religious orders from the eleventh century, a time when an increasing number of monks were ordained as priests and, therefore, excused MANUAL LABOUR. Lay brothers were not bound to the recitation of the DIVINE OFFICE and were generally occupied in manual work, although they were usually required to attend a daily mass and to recite a short office.

In Cistercian houses (*see* CISTERCIANS), there were often twice as many *conversi* (laymen who had 'turned' to the service of God) as there were CHOIR MONKS. The conversi, who included skilled craftsmen such as masons, dedicated themselves to a simple life of work and prayer. They lived according to their own version of the Cistercian rule (the *Carta Caritatis*) and took vows of poverty, chastity and strict obedience. Like the choir monks, the conversi were also bound by vows of ABSTINENCE and SILENCE but they were allowed a more nourishing diet – because of the nature of their work. For the same reason they rose an hour later than the monks and observed a simplified office and modified HORARIUM. They worshiped in the nave of the abbey church and were provided with their own segregated lodgings, which included a refectory (*see* FRATER), dormitory (*see* DORTER) and DAY ROOM or PARLOUR in the WESTERN RANGE of the claustral buildings, together with a separate latrine block (*see* REREDORTER) and, in larger houses, an INFIRMARY. In some monasteries, the lay brothers had their own CLOISTER: at Fountains and Tintern, for example (*see also* LANE).

In the late twelfth century there were 70 monks and 120 conversi at Waverley Abbey in Surrey, while at mighty Rievaulx in Yorkshire there were 140 monks, 240 conversi and 260 lay servants. Consequently, the accommodation provided for the lay brethren was often extensive. At Fountains the surviving twelfth-century west range of claustral buildings is 91.5m (300ft) long and vaulted in twenty-two double bays, twelve of which comprised the lay brothers' frater, while the dormitory above ran from one end of the building to the other and was capable of accommodating as many as four hundred conversi. This dorter was the largest of its kind and hardly typical: its size suggests that the numbers of monks and lay brethren at Fountains exceeded even those at nearby Rievaulx. The lay brothers' refectory at Hailes was more representative: occupying just five bays, it has a raised floor level at the southern end, suggesting that there was a high table and, therefore, a hierarchy among the conversi similar to that in the monks' refectory. Small communities of conversi managed outlying granges (*see* GRANGE) and were attached to houses of Cistercian nuns where the sisters were unable to undertake heavy manual work. Although they took the monastic vows of poverty, chastity and obedience, the conversi were not permitted to become choir monks and consequently were denied a literary education.

The twelfth-century lay brothers' range at Fountains Abbey, Yorkshire, is the largest and best-preserved example of its kind in Europe. (National Monuments Record/English Heritage)

Conversi wore a modified form of the Cistercian habit: a white cloak and tunic with a cowl which was shorter than that of a monk and which covered only the shoulders and chest.

Occasionally, the lay brothers rebelled. In 1206, the abbot of Margam was attacked by his conversi, who claimed that they had been badly treated. They pulled the CELLARER from his horse, barricaded themselves in their dormitory and refused to provide food in the monks' refectory. When the rebellion was finally subdued, the errant lay brothers were ordered to walk from Margam to Clairvaux in France (the mother house of the Order), and were then dispersed to different Cistercian monasteries.

From the mid-fourteenth century, lay brethren began deserting the monasteries in large numbers, attracted by improved wages and working conditions as a result of a labour shortage following the Black Death (*see* PLAGUE). Consequently, the dormitories, reredorters, infirmaries and refectories that had been provided for the lay brethren were often reduced in size or converted to other uses. At Rievaulx, for example, the twelfth-century infirmary was remodelled in the fifteenth century to provide a grand residence for the SUPERIOR, and its cloister became the abbot's garden. At Roche, the splendid lay brothers' infirmary was adapted to serve as a GUEST HOUSE, while at Furness (as elsewhere) the western claustral range was subdivided into several smaller chambers, each with a fireplace for greater comfort. These may have been intended to accommodate increasing numbers of corrodians (*see* CORRODY) or guests. It is ironic that shortly after its construction the great fourteenth-century nave of Tintern Abbey was effectively abandoned by the lay brethren for whom it was built. In common with other monasteries, the depleted Tintern community was obliged to use its nave for processions and little else, although some of the bays in the north and south aisles may have been converted to chapels, either as chantries (*see* CHANTRY) or as individual altars at which those monks who were also priests could celebrate a daily mass.

LAY CLERK An adult male member of certain cathedral or collegiate choirs.
See also CHURCH MUSIC *and* VICARS CHORAL

LAY INVESTITURE *see* NORMANS, THE

LAY OFFICIALS In the late medieval period many religious houses employed laymen to administer their estates. Chief among these were the offices of STEWARD, bailiff and receiver. It was the steward who exercised the authority of a community's superior in matters which were brought before non-ecclesiastical courts.
See also ADMINISTRATOR

LAY RECTOR A layman or institution (such as a monastic house) who is in receipt of the rectorial TITHES of a benefice (*see* MEDIEVAL CHURCH, THE).

LAY VICAR *see* CHURCH MUSIC

LAZAR HOUSE A hospital for lepers (*see* HOSPITALS). The term is derived from St Lazarus, the patron saint of lepers, and from the nursing order of that name. The first leper hospital in England was founded at Harbledown, Kent in *c.* 1100.

LEAD A heavy, soft, grey-coloured metal widely used in the glazing of churches, as a roof covering or sealant, as piping, and as a lining in fonts. In Britain, lead was first used by the Romans for water pipes because of its durability and resistance to corrosion. In the medieval period it was used in the complex plumbing systems of religious houses (the Franciscans were acknowledged to be expert in the use of lead piping – *see* PLUMBING, WATER SUPPLY AND SANITATION) and to cover the vast timber roofs of abbey churches where, if correctly laid, it would form a single impervious sheet and could therefore be set on a low-pitched or flat roof. Unlike SLATES AND ROOFING TILES it did not require constant repair and, unlike thatch, it was not flammable.

Lead was a particularly expensive commodity. In 1310, three *fothers* of lead (sufficient to cover about 150sq ft) were purchased at Boston fair for £9 12*s* and transported to Exeter for the rebuilding of the cathedral. The accounts show that 'weighing, marking, customs and carriage to the water cost 5*s* 9*d*; carriage to Topsham by sea 18*s*; discharging it there 17*d* and carriage to Exeter 3*s* 5*d*'. One wonders why the canons of Exeter did not obtain their lead from the much closer Mendip mines in Somerset.

At the Dissolution of the Monasteries lead was an obvious target for Henry's commissioners (together with brass and bell-metal). A lead roof was stripped and rolled in sections and melted into ingots, using wooden furnishings from the church as fuel. The ingots were then stamped with the king's crowned Tudor rose device and stacked in the roofless nave to await collection. At Rievaulx Abbey in Yorkshire, the overzealous commissioners failed to secure the nave walls, the upper sections of which collapsed, burying the lead ingots beneath tons of rubble. They were discovered during excavations in 1920 and used for the reglazing of the Five Sisters window at York Minster in 1923.

LEADED LIGHTS *see* WINDOWS

LECTERNS A lectern is a bookstand to hold liturgical books. Medieval lecterns were usually (though not invariably) located on the north side of the HIGH ALTAR, where they supported the *Gospels* during the mass. In monastic and collegiate churches, several lecterns were provided for different purposes (*see* FRATER PULPIT, for example). The CANTOR stood at the 'Great Lectern' on which the ANTIPHONARIUM was placed in the midst of the choir and from which the liturgical readings (*lessons*) that were an essential element of the offices were declaimed. Quite often a second, often double-sided, lectern was used when there was more than one cantor. Following the REFORMATION most lecterns were replaced in parish churches by reading DESKS in the nave, from which the scriptures were read at Mattins and Evensong. In cathedrals there are often several lecterns: one in the nave, a second in the choir and another in the Lady Chapel, for example.

There are three types of lectern: (i) a revolving two- or four-sided reading desk supported on a pillar, (ii) a similar one-sided desk, usually of nineteenth- or twentieth-century origin and (iii) an eagle (or, rarely, a pelican – the mystical emblem of Christ) with outstretched wings, usually standing on a sphere supported by a baluster stem and circular moulded base. The eagle was the symbol of St John the Evangelist, whose words 'soared up into the presence of Christ', just as the eagle of the medieval bestiaries renewed itself by flying into the sun. Most lecterns used today reflect the neo-Gothic style of the Victorian period, are of nineteenth- or twentieth-century origin and are generally made of wood, latten (*see* BRASSES (MONUMENTAL)) or brass.
See also MISSAL STAND

LECTIO DIVINA *see* ARMARIUM

LECTIONARY A book containing extracts from the scriptures which are to be read at services on specific days. Originally, such passages were marked in the margins of Bibles but were later collected in separate books, each relating to a particular service: the MISSAL for the mass, for example.

LECTOR A reader and, as such, a member of one of the MINOR ORDERS.

LEDGE A horizontal timber to provide rigidity to a door.

LEDGER STONES *see* INCISED SLABS

LENT The period of forty days before Easter, a period of penitence, ABSTINENCE and FASTING during which Christians recall Christ's suffering in the wilderness. The name is derived from the Anglo-Saxon word *lenct*, meaning 'spring', a period of enforced frugality in agricultural communities when the winter stores of food were running low. In the early Church, the period of abstinence did not usually exceed three or four days but, from the fourth century, it appears gradually to have been extended to forty days. At first, abstinence was rigorous: only one meal a day was permitted and the eating of flesh (including fish) was forbidden. In monastic communities a strict fast was prescribed (though in the later Middle Ages this was sometimes supplemented by raisins and figs) and this could not be broken before VESPERS. Eventually, the penitential character of Lent came to be expressed through abstinence from pleasurable activities, alms-giving, and increased religious devotion, rather than strict observance of a lengthy and rigorous fast.

LEPER HOSPITALS *see* HOSPITALS *and* LAZAR HOUSE

LETTERING The word calligraphy is derived from the Greek *kalos* and *graphos* meaning 'beautiful writing'. The writing found in medieval manuscripts and elaborately decorated books of hours varies from the formal 'book hands' of professional and monastic scribes to informal or cursive handwriting used for personal business purposes. (*Cursive*, from the Latin *curro* meaning 'to hasten', is the running characteristic of writing done at speed, often with a slope to the right.)

Uncial is a form of writing in large, rounded characters commonly found in manuscripts from the fourth to the eighth century, such as the magnificent seventh-century Lindisfarne Gospels in which both uncials (capital letters) and half-uncials (lower case letters) are used. Medieval book hands were mostly varieties of 'Textur' (known as *black letter* from *c.* 1600), a narrow, angular hand which forms a rich pattern on the page. With the exception of Italy, black letter was the staple book hand of medieval Europe and Scandinavia, although it is often described as Old English or Gothic. In manuscripts, uppercase letters are referred to as *majuscules* and lowercase letters are *minuscules*, although for most other purposes the terms capital letters and lowercase letters will suffice. A *serif* is a short cross line at the end of a stroke in a letter: hence the term *sanserif*, a style of lettering in which serifs are omitted. A *versal letter* is an ornamental capital letter at the beginning of a verse or paragraph in an illuminated manuscript. Significantly larger than the letters of the accompanying text, a versal is often colourfully embellished and gilded with floriated or decorative motifs and may include scenes and figures from contemporary life (*see also* MANUSCRIPT ILLUMINATION).

With the spread of literacy in the fourteenth century, the cursive element in writing became more common. Documents of the period continued to be written in varieties of black letter, including a less formal version known as *Gothic Cursive* or *Bastard Hand*. The introduction of printing and, in England, the demise of the monastic *scriptoria* following the DISSOLUTION OF THE MONASTERIES, resulted in a rapid decline in the writing and decoration of manuscripts. But legal, ecclesiastical and state documents continued to be handwritten, either in a new humanist hand from Italy (*Renaissance Italic*) or in modified versions of earlier hands such as *Tudor black letter*.

Blackletter

Gothic Cursive

Renaissance Italic

(Courtesy of Anthony Wood)

LIBRARIES All religious houses possessed a library, the size of which reflected the status of the monastery, although not necessarily its size. Initially, collections were small and were usually housed in a cupboard (*armarium*) in the north-east corner of the CLOISTER or in the VESTIBULE of the CHAPTER HOUSE. In several Cistercian houses, a narrow chamber was sometimes utilised for this purpose, usually between the north transept and the chapter house, as at Rievaulx and Tintern. Later monastic libraries occupied whole rooms, together with ancillary book cupboards strategically placed in the church and conventual buildings. At Worcester Cathedral Priory a library chamber was provided above the south aisle of the church, while at Bury, Norwich and St Albans an upper storey was added to the claustral buildings. BOOKS, which were the common property of the house, were usually borrowed and copied in the SCRIPTORIUM or donated by BENEFACTORS. The library was administered by the ARMARIUS, who was also responsible for the scriptorium. Individual members of the community could borrow books '*ad usum*' for a fixed period but they had to be returned, checked and reissued on the first Monday of LENT.

Medieval books were, of course, extremely rare and usually written on continuous rolls of

The chained library at Hereford Cathedral.

PARCHMENT or VELLUM, which only later may have been cut and arranged into folio form (*see* MANUSCRIPT ILLUMINATION). Even during the century after Mainz-born Johannes Gutenberg (1400–68) produced the first printed Bible and Psalter in 1456, significant collections of books were to be found only in the libraries of major religious and academic houses and those of the most eminent magnates.

One of the many consequences of the DISSOLUTION OF THE MONASTERIES (1536–9) was the dispersal of the monastic libraries and the destruction of many irreplaceable manuscripts: the sheets of parchment and vellum serving as tinder to light the fires of the supression. In part, this was the result of contemporary attitudes to the old libraries, most beneficiaries of the Dissolution of the Monasteries preferring the *de rigueur* printed folios of William Caxton (*c.* 1422 to *c.* 1491) and his successors to the inconvenient and archaic manuscripts of the early Church. Consequently, those libraries that are found in many of our medieval cathedrals today date from the sixteenth century or later, although many contain earlier manuscripts that survived the iconoclasts' flames. Even so, we know that, at the Dissolution, the library at Bury St Edmunds contained over two thousand books and Canterbury four thousand. Even the modest Premonstratensian abbey of Titchfield had, by 1400, acquired a fine library of more than a thousand books.

Just as today collections of rare books are protected from theft by sophisticated electronic devices, so the librarians of the post-medieval period looked to the security of their extremely valuable collections. The famous chained library at Hereford Cathedral is the largest of its kind to have survived. Each of its 1,500 handwritten and printed books has a chain attached to the front edge of one cover and to a rod on the bookcase. Only by turning a key to release the rod may a book be removed or added. Wooden desks and benches, placed conveniently between the oak bookcases (installed in 1611), facilitate study without the necessity of releasing the books from their fetters. The library, which was housed in the Lady Chapel, was removed to a fine new building to the west of the cloister in 1996. This also contains the extraordinary *Mappa Mundi* ('Map of the World'), one of the most elaborate medieval maps in Europe. It was painted by Richard of Haldingham, (d. *c.* 1313) who was Treasurer of

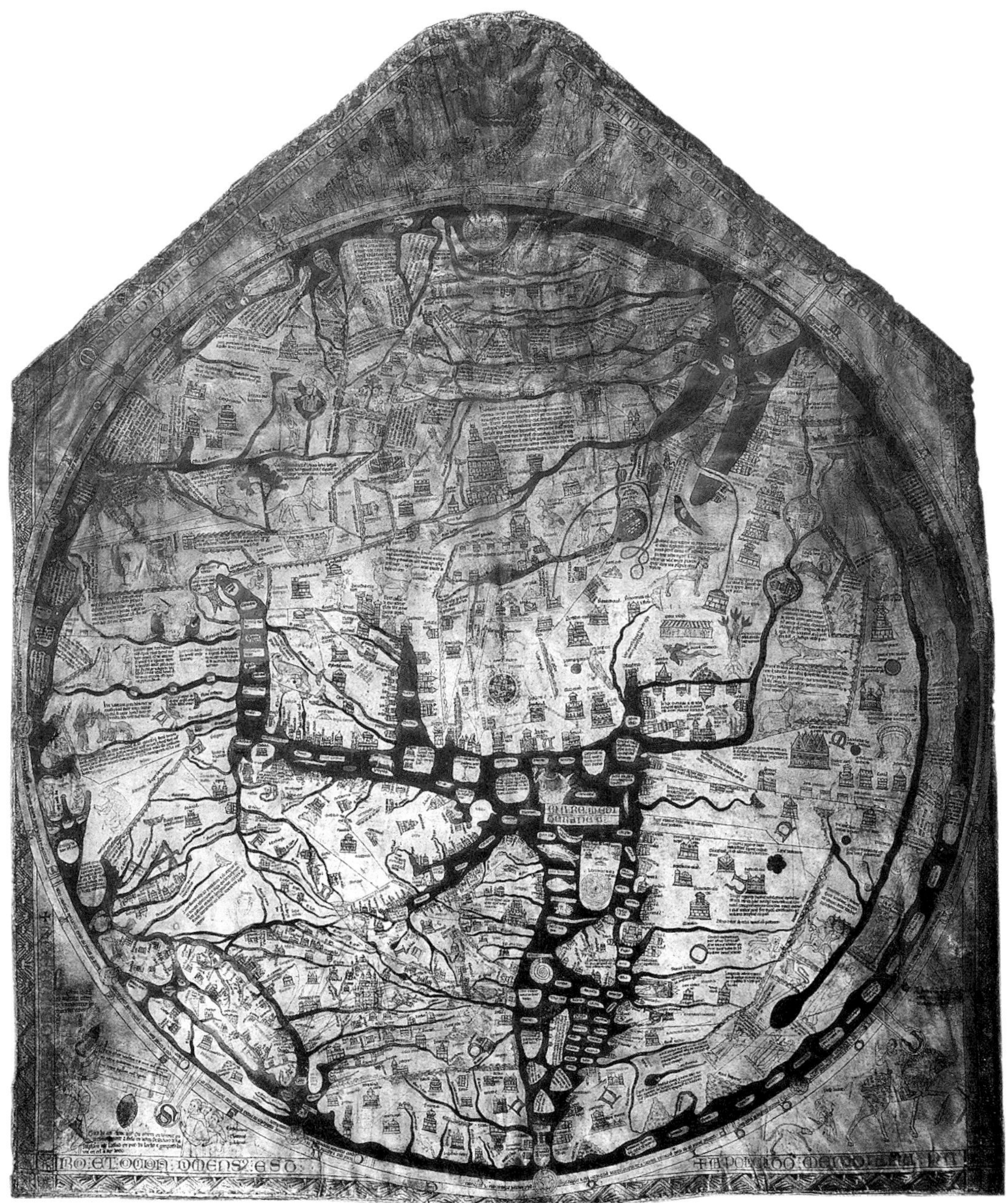

The Mappa Mundi. (Courtesy of Dean & Chapter of Hereford Cathedral and the Hereford Mappa Mundi Trust)

Lincoln Cathedral and a prependary of Hereford. The prominence given to Lincoln on the map suggests that he painted it there in *c.* 1275. The map, worked on vellum, embodies all the fundamental medieval beliefs concerning the shape and nature of the world, which is drawn with Jerusalem at the centre and with east at the top. All Saints' Church, also in Hereford, has a notable library of over three hundred books and there are other 'chained libraries' at Cartmel Priory in

Lancashire and Wimborne Minster in Dorset (both now splendid parish churches). Most medieval missals, psalters, gospels and other liturgical books are now in museums, although individual chained books may still be found in parish churches: at Cumnor (Berkshire), Kingsthorpe (Northamptonshire) and Sherborne St John (Hampshire), for example.

The medieval cathedrals were centres of learning, and consequently acquired large numbers of books. The library at Wells was built over the east cloister range in the fifteenth century – a bequest of Bishop Bubwith (d. 1424) who left 1,000 marks for the purpose. It is one of the longest medieval reading rooms in England, illuminated by numerous small windows that are a characteristic of medieval schools and libraries. It suffered greatly during the Commonwealth but at the Restoration Dean Creyghton began its refurbishment and in 1685 its present bookcases and panelling were installed. It now contains about six thousand books, covering such diverse subjects as theology, law, medicine, travel, languages, botany and mathematics, and includes important collections from the sixteenth to the eighteenth centuries, the archives of the Chapter from the tenth century to the present day, and the beautiful *Hayles Psalter*, an illuminated medieval manuscript written by a famous one-eyed Brabantin scribe for the abbey of Hailes in Gloucestershire.

The fabric of England's great cathedrals suffered considerably from neglect following the abolition of cathedral chapters in 1643. The medieval library at Lincoln (*c.* 1422) was no exception, indeed it had already been damaged by fire at an earlier (unrecorded) date. In 1674 the cathedral's dean, Michael Honywood, commissioned Sir Christopher Wren (1632–1723) to design a new library to house both the one hundred medieval manuscripts that had survived the fire and his own collection of over five thousand books. The elegant Wren Library was built over an open loggia or walkway on the site of the then ruinous north claustral range. The truncated exterior of the original library was faced in ASHLAR in 1789, in order that it should blend with the Wren building, while its roof retains mostly original timbers, bosses and carved angels.

See also ARCHIVES, ECCLESIASTICAL LIBRARIES *and* PORCHES.

LIERNE *and* LIERNE VAULT *see* VAULTING

LIGHTHOUSES Medieval chantries were often established for the benefit of seafarers, notably a number of beacons or lighthouses which were erected above chantry chapels and maintained by chantry priests (*see* CHANTRY). The best-known examples are the rocket-shaped fourteenth-century lighthouse and chapel on St Catherine's Down on the Isle of Wight and the lonely Norman chapel on St Aldhelm's Head in Dorset, which once supported a fire basket on its roof (*see* CHAPELS).

LIGHTS Monastic buildings must have been very dark places at night and somewhat depressing on overcast days. *Cressets* were the most common form of lighting. These were either stone bowls or stones in which holes were carved and into which cooking fat or grease and floating wicks were placed to provide multiple lamps. Some cresset stones were portable and contained three or four such holes; larger ones were too heavy to be moved and held perhaps twenty or more cressets (a cresset stone with thirty holes may be seen at Brecon Cathedral). They were positioned to provide light at hazardous corners, in the DORTER and REREDORTER, at the foot of the NIGHT STAIR and in the church. After sunset, lamps were placed in the CLOISTER and tallow candles were used to illuminate tables in the FRATER. Children and novices were provided with a LANTERN when moving around the precincts after dark while the CLAUSTRAL PRIOR and the CIRCATOR carried 'dark lanterns' so that they might not disturb the sleeping brethren when carrying out their night-time duties. Liturgical candles were made of beeswax and were an expensive commodity, while

candles used simply for illumination were of tallow. In the medieval period only one candle would be placed on the altar, others being offered as *votive lights* before images, shrines and tombs, often at enormous expense. Wax tapers provided light at the altars and LECTERNS and accompanied PROCESSIONS. In Benedictine churches, a CORONA LUCIS was often the principal source of artificial light, notably at Canterbury, where there were two huge, wheel-like chandeliers, one in the nave and the other in the choir, each bearing twenty-four candles.
See also ALTAR LIGHTS, AUMBRY LAMP, BIER LIGHT, CANDELABRUM, CANDLES, HEARSE, LAMPS, LANTERN, LIGHTHOUSES, PRICKET, ROOD SCREEN, STRAP SCONCE *and* TRENDAL

LIGHTS (WINDOW) The openings between the MULLIONS and TRANSOMS (*see* WINDOWS).

LIMEWASH Quicklime (unslaked lime) boils with intense heat when water is added. For centuries limewash was made by packing coarse waste fat in a tub of quicklime and adding water, the effect of which was to heat and distribute the fat. When it was used as an external wall covering on a building, the fat content of limewash did not dissolve in the wet, thereby making the coating waterproof.

LINENFOLD Sixteenth-century wooden panelling carved with stylised fabric in vertical folds, one piece of 'linen' filling each panel.

LINTEL A horizontal stone or beam spanning an opening and supporting the wall above (*see also* ARCH *and* PIER).

LITANY A form of prayer comprising a series of supplications said or sung by a priest, deacon or CANTOR, to which the congregation responds. The Anglican Litany is a free translation and adaptation of the chief Roman Litany. It first appeared in English as a separate book in 1544 and in Henry VIII's *Primer* of 1545, in which it was described as the 'Common Prayer of Procession', the rhythmical alternation of prayer and refrain being especially appropriate for processional use. In the *Book of Common Prayer*, the Litany is a 'general supplication' to be said or sung after Morning Prayer on Sundays, Wednesdays and Fridays.
See also MATTINS *and* VERSICLES

LITANY DESK *see* DESKS

LITERATE One who has been admitted to HOLY ORDERS without a university degree.

LITTEN A burial ground.

LITTLE OFFICE OF OUR LADY, THE The Office of Our Lady, the Blessed Virgin Mary, was introduced in the late eighth century by the Benedictine reformer, Benedict of Aniane. Originally it was a short service, a supplement to the Great Hours in honour of the Blessed Virgin Mary (*see* HOURS (CANONICAL)). But such was its popularity that in the thirteenth century it became a separate office and inspired the Marian cult of the late Middle Ages (*see* LADY CHAPEL *and* MARY, THE BLESSED VIRGIN).

LITURGICAL COLOURS *see* COLOURS (LITURGICAL)

LITURGY Derived from the Greek for 'a public work', the liturgy is the form of service used in the celebration of the EUCHARIST (*see also* MASS). But in ordinary English usage the term has come to imply all forms of service authorised by the Church, in contradistinction to private devotional worship. It is also used to describe the texts by which services are ordered and the study of such texts. In England, the evolution of the liturgy has affected significantly the development of the church, its architecture, art, music and ritual.

Before the Reformation all the countries of western Europe shared a common (Roman) liturgy, although there were numerous local modifications. In England, for example, the rites (*uses*) practised at Salisbury differed from those of York and Hereford, although by the late Middle Ages it was the Salisbury rite (the *Use of Sarum*) that had been adopted for use in most English cathedrals and parish churches and this was to provide much of the material for the first *Book of Common Prayer* (1549) (*see* COMMON PRAYER, BOOK OF *and* SARUM, USE OF).

The liturgy followed that of the BENEDICTINES: a daily celebration of High Mass and the seven canonical offices (*see* DIVINE OFFICE *and* HOURS (CANONICAL)) which were observed throughout the Middle Ages by a rapidly increasing number of clergy, chaplains and chantry priests (*see* CHANTRY). But for the laity, there were usually three services, on Sundays and Holy Days: MATTINS followed by mass, in the morning, and EVENSONG in the afternoon. The mass was of special significance, increasingly so following the Fourth Lateran Council of 1215, which pronounced the doctrine of transubstantiation, thereby emphasising the sacredness and mystery of the mass. In parish churches this resulted in a weakening of the intimate relationship between priest and people, so evident in Anglo-Saxon and Norman churches, where there was no physical separation of the SANCTUARY from the nave (*see* CHANCEL); and as belief in the potency of the mass increased, so the sacrament was received less often. Communion was administered only after CONFESSION, which was then so thorough that it was normally made only once a year, before Easter. Nevertheless, a regular reaffirmation of faith was required and this was achieved by witnessing the ELEVATION of the Host. Consequently, in cathedrals and parish churches High Mass on Sunday was the best-attended service of the week, the other offices attracting modest congregations and, in many instances, none at all. Of course, in the Middle Ages, the laity was denied the Precious Blood of Christ (the wine) and received only the Host (the consecrated wafer of the Eucharist).

Neither was there a *Book of Common Prayer* to conveniently set out the liturgy in a single volume. In the Middle Ages, there were so many services, and so many variations and accretions, that several books were provided, one for each service or part thereof (*see* BOOKS). These included the MISSAL, or mass book, which set out all the variations of the service required for Sundays, saints' days and festivals and, in the great abbey churches and cathedrals, this would be supplemented by other books containing specialised elements of the rite: the Epistle Book, the Gospel Book and the GRADUALE (or *Grail*) which contained the music. The MANUALE (or *Ritual*) set out the offices of baptism, marriage, visitation of the sick and the burial of the dead, while the BREVIARY attempted to provide an abbreviated edition of the daily offices and the main prayers and collects, although even this ran to four volumes, one for each season of the year, and contained 'optional extras' such as the *Placebo* and the *Dirige*, the evening and morning offices for the dead. Two of the more convenient service books which were used by both the clergy and the congregation were the PSALTER, which brought together the Old Testament psalms, and the BOOK OF HOURS, which was a compendium of the most frequently used liturgical material. There was also the PONTIFICAL, which set out the services and prayers to be used only by bishops, at confirmation and ordination, for example.

It should be remembered that, for the laity in the cathedral nave, the ritual of the liturgy would be hardly visible or audible. The PRESBYTERY was separated from the nave by a ROOD SCREEN and PULPITUM, while much of the service was spoken *sotto voce* by the celebrant – and in Latin. It was the Elevation of the Host which was the culmination of the mass, for it signified that transubstantiation had taken place (*see also* SQUINT). There were no hymns and only occasional sermons and, before the fifteenth century, no seating other than a stone bench at the foot of the nave wall for those who were too

weak to stand (hence the saying 'gone to the wall'). Only during liturgical PROCESSIONS, was the congregation able to witness the proceedings at close quarters. The effect was to create a sense of mystery and symbolism, reinforced by an occasional glimpse of the ritualistic movements of the celebrant beyond the screens, by the brilliance of the plate and vestments, and by the messages conveyed in sculpture, paint and stained glass. There can be no doubt that, while the doctrines of the Church were, for the most part, beyond the understanding of the commonalty, the regular performance of ritual, augmented by the special ceremonies associated with the various feast-days, provided medieval communities with a sense of stability and security and created an intense attachment to the mother church.
See also ANGLO-SAXON CHURCH, MONASTICISM, MEDIEVAL CHURCH *and* WALES, THE MEDIEVAL CHURCH IN

LOCULUS (i) A recess in an altar in which relics were kept.
(ii) A recess in a vault for holding a coffin or urn.

LOCUTORIUM *see* PARLOUR *and* SLYPE

LOGGIA A covered veranda, open on at least one side.

LOLLARD A term of contempt, of Dutch origin, meaning 'mutterer' or 'mumbler', conferred on those who professed to follow John Wycliffe (*c.* 1330–84) in his opposition to the established order within the English Church. They rejected priestly authority and advocated evangelical poverty in imitation of Christ, and the studying of the scriptures in the vernacular. Official attitudes to the Lollards varied considerably, but they were generally considered to be heretics and were often violently suppressed.

LONG AND SHORT WORK Typical of Anglo-Saxon structures, alternate long vertical and short horizontal stones set in the termination of a wall to provide additional strength, for example, to the corners of a tower or a doorway jamb.
See also QUOIN

LOW MASS *see* MASS

LUCARNE A dormer window in a church spire.

MADONNA (Italian = 'My Lady') The Blessed Virgin Mary when represented in statues and paintings.

MAGDALENES From St Mary Magdalene, the term was often adopted as a title by medieval religious communities of penitent women.

MAGNIFICAT From St Luke's Gospel (1: 39–55), the hymn sung by the Blessed Virgin Mary when her cousin Elizabeth greeted her as the mother of Christ ('My soul doth magnify the Lord . . .'). The Magnificat is a CANTICLE in the office of VESPERS and was incorporated into the Anglican Evening Service in the *Book of Common Prayer*. Together with the NUNC DIMITTIS, the Magnificat has been set to music by numerous composers and is regularly sung in cathedral and collegiate chapels at choral evensong (*see* EVENING PRAYER).

MAJESTAS A representation of Christ in Majesty. The majestas was one of the few images allowed by the Cistercian RULE and was usually placed in a prominent position as a reminder of the Last Judgement and, therefore, of the purpose of the religious life.

MAJOR ORDERS The senior grades of the Christian ministry: bishops, priests and deacons (*see* CLERGY (CHURCH OF ENGLAND)). From the thirteenth century, the office of SUB-DEACON was considered to be the lowest of the major orders in the Roman Catholic Church until it was suppressed in 1972.
See also MINOR ORDERS

MAJUSCULE *see* LETTERING

MALLARDY (*also* NURCERY) A medieval hospice, specifically for the sick.

MANDATUM *see* MAUNDY

MANOR *see* FEUDAL SYSTEM

MANUAL LABOUR Manual work, and the spiritual values of 'honest toil', were emphasised by St Benedict in his RULE: 'At fixed times, the brothers ought to be occupied in manual labour; and again, at fixed times, in reading.' The BENEDICTINES were expected to work in the monastic gardens, in the workshops of the CURIA and on the monastic estates, those with special skills to 'work at their crafts in all humility'. Each choir monk was responsible for some aspect of the community's administration, either as a senior member of the CHAPTER (*see* OBEDIENTIARIES) or as a junior official in a domestic department, and many developed a particular skill: in the SCRIPTORIUM, for example.

However, a greater emphasis on STUDY, especially in Cistercian houses (*see* CISTERCIANS), and the CLUNIACS' preoccupation with matters spiritual meant that lay brethren were recruited in increasing numbers to carry out many of the routine tasks that had previously been undertaken by the monks (*see* LAY BROTHERS). Belatedly, the Benedictine GENERAL CHAPTER held at Canterbury in 1277 ordered that 'in place of manual labour the abbots shall appoint other occupations for their claustral monks according to their capacity: study, writing, correcting, illuminating and binding books'. The contribution of the lay brethren should not be underestimated: by their labours they converted waste land to pasture, the abbeys became the engine rooms of agricultural innovation, and they laid the foundations of the country's economic prosperity.

During the first decades of the fourteenth century climatic changes resulted in a series of poor harvests, causing starvation and malnutrition which, by the 1330s, had debilitated the peasant population of Europe. Recent evidence has shown that by 1341, eight years before the arrival of the *Black Death* in England (*see* PLAGUE), many villages were already depopulated and their lands left uncultivated. It is now clear, therefore, that climatic change, urban overpopulation, frequent livestock murrains and famine preceded the plague and, by reducing immunity to disease, contributed to its virulence. Inevitably, this led to a dramatic decline in the number of lay brethren in the monasteries and secular EMPLOYEES (usually described as 'servants') were increasingly engaged to do much of the work, including tasks that required a particular expertise. Within the inner precinct, the monks continued to work in the SCRIPTORIUM, the SACRISTY and the other purely monastic departments. But by the late medieval period their time was devoted more to reading and study than to manual labour – and they worked in silence 'unless the need of the work constrain someone to speak'. Even before the arrival of the plague in 1349, most monastic houses had at least as many servants as choir monks. At Canterbury, in 1322, for example, the CELLARER alone had the following staff:

steward of the gatehouse and two porters
keeper of the pantry and his boy
keeper of the cloister gate and his boy
keeper of the guest house pantry
watchman
scullion and his boy
soup maker

scullion of the refectory and his boy
first and second cooks and their boys
salter and his boy
kitchen stoker
potter
kitchen waiter
drawer of wine and beer and his boy
cellarer's esquire
cellarer's groom
cellarer's carter
two purveyors
hunter and his boy
porter of the guest house and his boy
general servant
gaoler

In the nunneries, the sisters specialised in spinning and needlework, the richly embroidered liturgical vestments fashioned by English nuns earning a reputation across Europe as the 'opus anglicanum'. Throughout the Middle Ages, large numbers of male servants were engaged by the nunneries to carry out those tasks that the nuns were physically incapable of undertaking and to administer their estates (*see* NUNS AND NUNNERIES).
See also INDUSTRY

MANUALE (Latin = 'a book of convenient size') A medieval book containing the forms prescribed for the administration of the Sacraments.

MANUSCRIPT ILLUMINATION A manuscript is a book or document written by hand. Although paper making was known in Spain and Italy by the twelfth century, PARCHMENT and VELLUM were the chief materials used for writing throughout medieval Europe until the development of printing in the late fifteenth century. Parchment was ideally suited to ornamentation as well as writing, and some of the finest artistic works of the Middle Ages are the illuminated manuscripts produced in the *scriptoria* of monastic houses (*see* SCRIPTORIUM).

A manuscript that is described as illuminated is one that is decorated in colours and gold. When the page is held at an angle and the gold is caught by the light, it appears to possess a lustrous quality unequalled by other forms of decoration. The gold, either in the form of a powder mixed with a suitable water-based medium and used as a pigment, or in the form of gold leaf, was applied either directly to the working surface or on a plaster ground of *Gesso sottile* (deactivated calcium sulphate, lead carbonate, an animal glue and sugar). This plaster ground was applied either with a quill pen or painted on and dried hard, flexible and raised. The leaf was then applied, and was polished with an agate burnisher.

In Britain the early medieval schools of Ireland and Northumbria produced manuscripts of extraordinary skill and originality in the interlacing and counterpointing of geometrical and animal patterns and subtle variations of colour. The best known of these Celtic manuscripts are the *Lindisfarne Gospels* and the *Book of Kells*. In Europe, the Byzantine tradition, with its florid use of gold and vermilion, continued into the Carolingian period to produce works in which the emphasis was on illuminated ornamental motifs. In England the (incomplete) twelfth-century *Winchester Bible* contains the work of five different artists and, in its obvious Byzantine influences and its emphasis on naturalistic elements, is one of the finest and most innovative products of the illuminator's art. The *Winchester Bible* is a quite remarkable work – 'a quarry from which all the liturgy and other readings and lections in the church's year are taken' (Paul Binski).

From the end of the twelfth century the art of the miniaturist flourished, notably in the production of the great Bibles. (The work of the miniaturist is not concerned with that which is small but with the use of red lead for colouring, the Latin verb *minire* meaning 'to colour with red lead'.) In the later Middle Ages increasing use was made of enlarged and ornamented versal letters in which illustrations of biblical and naturalistic scenes were inserted. Beautifully

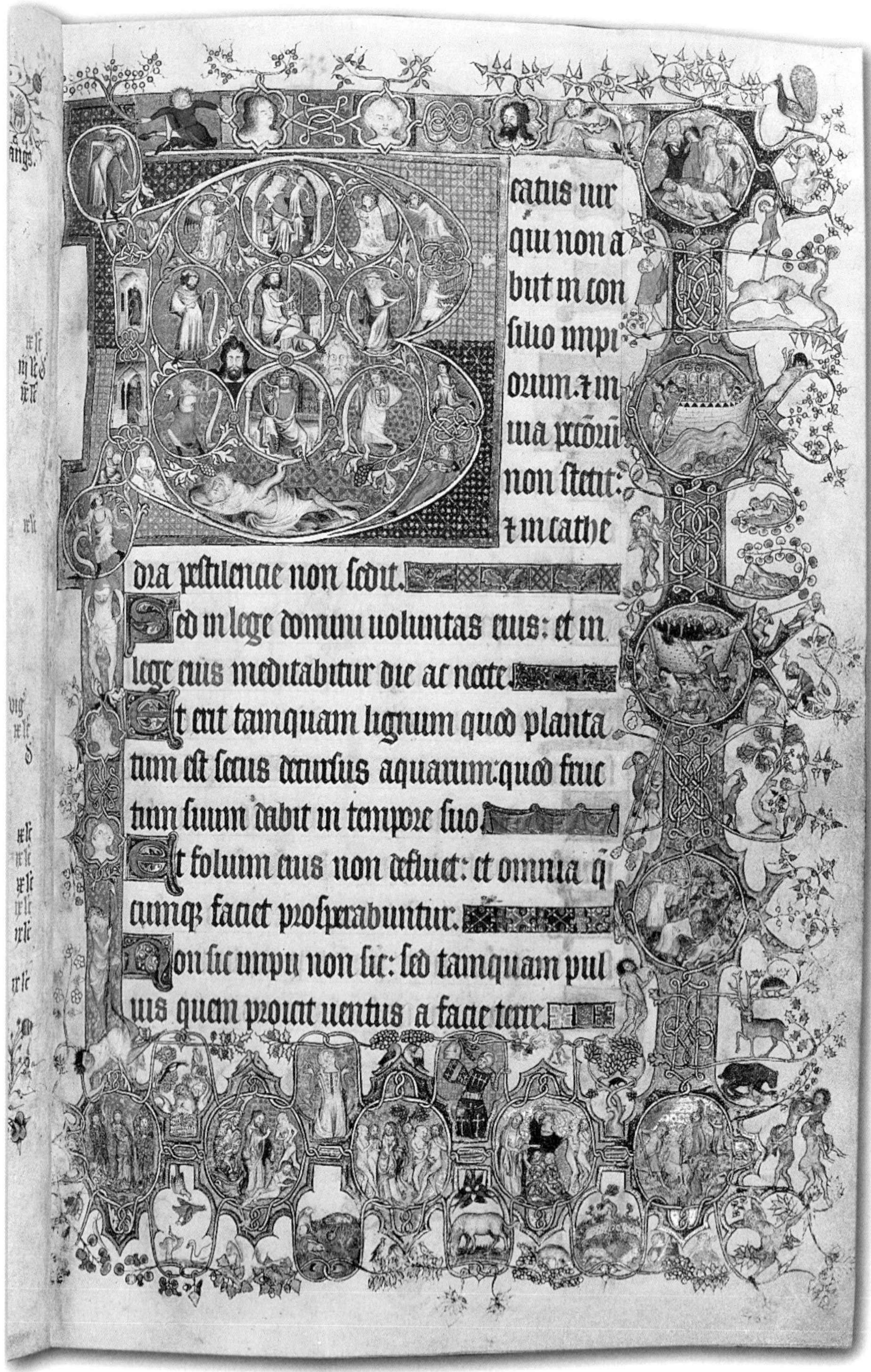

The Beatus page from the St Omer Psalter, executed c. 1325 for members of the St Omer family of Mulbarton, Norfolk, whose portraits appear in medallions beneath the text. (Record no: c3099–03 Yates Thompson 14, f.7 St Omer Psalter CC272. © The British Library)

illuminated breviaries, psalters, missals and books of hours were commissioned by medieval magnate families as gifts to superiors and as benefactions to religious houses. These contained exquisitely executed illustrations of the agrarian year, biblical scenes, devotional texts and the lives of saints and martyrs, often identified as the patron saints of the recipients. Quite often we are given an insight into the character of the artist, many of whom were blessed with a sense of humour. The pages of the wonderful fourteenth-century *Macclesfield Psalter* teem with bestial curiosities, puns and bawdy jokes. The margins include numerous rabbits – allusions to the earl of Warenne who commissioned the work (before being excommunicated for multiple adultery!) – and jokes, including a bare-bottomed man pulling a dragon's tail, a dog dressed as a bishop and a man reeling in shock from a giant skate that swims towards him across the page. The book was made in East Anglia, probably at Gorleston, which at the time was pre-eminent in Europe for manuscript illumination.
See also LETTERING

MAPPA MUNDI *see* LIBRARIES

MARBLE A granular crystalline limestone, although the term is loosely applied to any stone of a similar appearance which takes a high polish. A rich and costly material, marble was frequently used for embellishing major medieval churches, notably in altars, colonnettes, flooring and SCREENS. Both imported and local English marbles were used, the best known being the almost black marble obtained from quarries on the Isle of Purbeck in Dorset (*see also* PURBECK MARBLE *and* TOUCH).

MARGINAL INSCRIPTION An inscription contained within the margin of (e.g.) a monumental brass. The opening word of such an inscription is usually preceded by a cross.
See also INSCRIPTIONS

MARKETS, SHOPS AND FAIRS In the early medieval period the English monasteries were developing trading links internationally, importing luxury items such as gold, spices and wine, and exporting wool. They were to become the engines of economic power. Localised commodities such as salt and lead were traded nationally; corn, cattle and fish regionally; and perishable produce, such as vegetables, fruit and eggs, were sold in local markets. Tenth-century commerce was generally unregulated until Edward the Elder (900–25) decreed that all buying and selling should take place openly in a marketplace and within the jurisdiction of a reeve. As permanent communities developed in the vicinity of abbeys and castles, so markets and fairs flourished, and by the late tenth century tolls were exacted by the magnates and monastic superiors who organised and controlled the movement of goods between their estates.

During the Middle Ages fairs emerged as seasonal gatherings, sometimes on the periphery of towns or at prominent sites in the surrounding countryside, whereas markets were held weekly and always in towns or larger villages, where there was a focus of community activity. After the Norman Conquest many of these customary markets and fairs were recorded in Domesday Book and eventually they were regularised under the Norman kings by the granting of charters that permitted the receipt of revenues. The acquisition of a market charter was obviously of great financial advantage to a manorial lord or monastic superior, who would receive the tolls and taxes and the fines exacted for breaches of trading regulations, and to the Crown, from whom the privilege was almost invariably purchased.

By the end of the medieval period there were approximately 2,170 markets operating throughout England and Wales, of which some 333 had been initiated or acquired by monastic houses. Occasionally a grant of a market was only partial: in 1283, for example, John de Vescy gave the Cistercians of Rufford half the profits from his market at Rotherham, a full grant being confirmed

A fifteenth-century shop row on the edge of the abbey precinct at Tewkesbury, Gloucestershire. (By kind permission of James Bond)

ten years later. The Benedictines of Canterbury Cathedral Priory held eleven markets – in addition to those held by the archbishop – while Westminster Abbey had five markets in the Home Counties and three more in the south Midlands. But these were exceptional: while the Benedictine abbeys of Bury St Edmunds, Glastonbury, St Albans, Peterborough and Ramsey each had markets in half a dozen different places, the great houses of the other orders rarely held more than two.

Triangular or wedge-shaped marketplaces immediately outside the abbey gates are characteristic of towns promoted by monasteries before the Norman Conquest (at Abingdon and Peterborough, for example), while broad main streets or rectangular marketplaces are indicative of new towns planned after the Conquest. In some cases a new marketplace was superimposed on an older settlement. When Bishop Losinga of Thetford relocated his see in 1095 he founded a new Benedictine cathedral priory at Norwich and laid out a large, rectangular marketplace (Tombland) outside its west gate, demolishing a number of dwellings and the church of St Michael in the process. Several towns (including Norwich) had more than one market, reflecting different proprietorships, or provision for the sale of different commodities.

Many monastic houses had market stalls, often temporary structures which eventually became established as permanent shops with dwellings above. Indeed, shops were a lucrative source of rental income: Vale Royal owned at least thirteen shops at Chester in 1299 (mostly occupied by cobblers); a bequest to Evesham Abbey in 1366 included thirty-six shops off Leadenhall Street in London; while in 1376 Rewley Abbey owned twenty-three shops in Coventry. Rows of shops were particularly favoured by monastic houses: the fine terrace of twenty-three half-timbered dwellings with ground floor shops built by Tewkesbury Abbey in the mid-fifteenth century may still be seen today.

Medieval fairs were generally annual occasions and of greater significance to a local populace than markets. They usually took place (or commenced) on the *feriae*, the feast or holy days of the local church to whose patronal saint the fair was often dedicated. On such days men were freed from labour ('holy day' became 'holiday') to engage in both the business and sociability of the fair. Most fairs originated in the thirteenth and fourteenth centuries in the new towns and seigniorial boroughs, and were concerned not only with trade and commerce but also with entertainment and the propagation of news and ideas. Many fairs grew to national (even international) importance, and lasted for several days. And because they were held regularly at a fixed time and fixed place, they became centres of banking and commerce and contributed to the intellectual and cultural development of medieval Europe.

The exclusive right to hold a fair was established through a royal or magnate charter, which specified the day or days on which it was to be held. Enterprising manorial lords, monastic houses and burgesses who obtained charters profited from the revenues that could be raised through farming out stalls or 'pitches' to lessees. Several of England's major international fairs belonged to Benedictine abbeys, including Bury St Edmunds, St Ives and Westminster, while some four hundred of the lesser fairs were held by monastic houses. Fairs inevitably attracted merchants who were able to offer exotic and high-quality goods not normally available at markets, and for this reason many continued to be held until the distribution of merchandise was transformed in the nineteenth century by the advent of the railway age and an efficient postal service. But the anticipated profits which encouraged many medieval magnates to apply for charters did not always materialise: establishing a fair was a speculative business, and while many fairs flourished or specialised, others became moribund.

See also FINANCE

MARKS, MASONS' *see* MASONS' MARKS

MARKS, WINDOW *see* GLAZIERS' MARKS

MARTYR From the Greek word meaning 'witness', the term was originally applied to the Apostles, who were witnesses of Christ's life and resurrection. Later, it came to mean those who were persecuted for their faith and, ultimately, those who suffered death in His name. In the Middle Ages, martyrs were venerated as potent intercessors, as were their RELICS (*see also* SHRINES).

MARTYRIUM (*also* MARTYRION) A building or memorial constructed above the tomb (or relics) of a MARTYR, or (rarely) a church erected to the memory of a martyr.

MARTYROLOGY An official register of Christian martyrs (*see* MARTYR). The earliest examples are calendars containing details of the martyr's name and place of death, and the date on which he/she was commemorated. From the ninth century it was the practice in most religious houses for the day's entry in the martyrology to be read during the office of PRIME.

See also NECROLOGY

MARY, THE BLESSED VIRGIN (BVM) In the Greek, *Theotokos*, 'the God-bearer', Mary, mother of Christ, daughter of Joachim and Anne, and betrothed to Joseph at the time of the Annunciation. The doctrine of the Assumption of the Blessed Virgin Mary was formulated in the sixth century and the feast-day (15 August) was widely observed in the Middle Ages, although omitted from the *Book of Common Prayer* in 1549. But while belief in the Assumption roused little opposition in the pre-Reformation period, the doctrine of the Immaculate Conception was the subject of vigorous disputation. Reformers, while acknowledging Mary's humility, also reacted strongly against what they perceived to be the excessive devotion of the Roman Catholic Church.

Belief in the humanity and the intercessory powers of Christ's mother was apparent even in the early fourth century, while in the medieval period it reached almost cult-like proportions, promoted by her special devotees the Cistercians and the Franciscans (all Cistercian abbeys were dedicated to the Blessed Virgin Mary). The cult found popular expression in the Hail Mary, Rosary and Angelus, in the rededication of churches and the building of LADY CHAPELS, and in pilgrimages to SHRINES such as Walsingham. Other feast-days are the Nativity of the Blessed Virgin Mary (8 September), the Annunciation of the Blessed Virgin Mary (25 March), the Purification of the Blessed Virgin Mary (Candlemas, 2 February) and the Visitation of Our Lady (2 July).

See also LITTLE OFFICE OF OUR LADY, THE

MASONIC LODGE *see* MASTER MASONS AND ARCHITECTS

MASONRY Medieval monastic buildings were usually constructed of local materials, which is why they sit so comfortably in the landscape: Peterborough was built of local stone hewn from its own Barnack quarries; Durham was constructed of carboniferous limestone; Chester of red sandstone; Gloucester of oolitic limestone from the Cotswolds. Even so, most of the great abbey churches incorporate materials that could only have been obtained at considerable expense: dark, fossiliferous limestone from the Isle of Purbeck and black marble from Tournai in Belgium, most commonly found in the shafts of clustered piers; the fine white stone of Caen in France which, from the Norman Conquest, was more widely used than any English stone. Others 'quarried' earlier buildings for materials: St Albans utilised FLINT and Roman brick while Winchester's limestone was transported across the Solent from the Isle of Wight. It has been estimated that 75,000 tons of Chilmark stone were used in the construction of Salisbury Cathedral between 1220 and 1266 (the upper sections of the tower and the spire were added half a century later).

In Britain, most of the stone structures that have survived from before the sixteenth century are of rubble construction. *Rubble* is not a derogatory term but describes stones of different sizes, laid in a variety of ways and bound with lime mortar. *Squared coursed rubble*, for example, is walling of roughly square stone laid in horizontal courses (also described as *regular coursed rubble*), while *square-necked rubble* is walling in which small stone blocks (*snecks*) are inserted to prevent a wall being weakened by long, vertical joints. The term *random rubble*, on the other hand, describes stones of different shapes and sizes laid without any discernible pattern, while *coursed random rubble* consists of similar unshaped stones laid in horizontal courses. Cut and squared (*dressed*) stone was exceedingly expensive and was generally used only for facings and dressings such as mouldings, quoins, sills, merlons, window tracery, lintels and arches (*see* ARCH). *Ashlar* is masonry made from smooth, finely cut blocks of stone that are tooled on the external face. Thin walls, such as those of parapets or screens, might be constructed of ashlar blocks dressed on both faces which were known as *through stones* or, more commonly, *parpains*. While the walls of many abbey churches were often faced with dressed stone, in practice it was the thickness of the random rubble and the quality of the mortar which provided strength and stability. Walls were generally constructed with a soft core of rubble and quicklime between outer skins of masonry, the lime remaining flexible and enabling the wall better to respond to the downward and outward thrust of the building.

It has been estimated that, in the Middle Ages, the cost of transporting stone for a distance of 19km (12 miles) was equal to the cost of the stone itself, although clearly this depended on the terrain and on whether movement by water was an option. Stone for the Cathedral Priory at Norwich was purchased at Caen (*see below*) in 1287 for £1 6*s* 8*d*; its carriage by ship to Yarmouth was £2 10*s* 8*d*; transferring it to barges cost 2*s* 2*d*; carriage in six barges to Norwich cost 7*s* 2*d* and from the wharf to the cathedral a further 2*s*. The Abbey of Bury St Edmunds enjoyed the right of quarrying at Barnack, near Peterborough, but required confirmation from the Abbot of Peterborough of its right to carry the stone by water to the River Nene. Similarly, in 1176, the pope was obliged to confirm Sawtry Abbey's right to use 'the ditch which they had made at their own cost to carry stone for the building of their church' to conclude a long and often acrimonious dispute with Ramsey Abbey.

Wherever possible local stone was used, and many monasteries were built of stone from quarries opened in the vicinity of the site. Limestone for the construction of Fountains Abbey was quarried from the walls of the valley in which it stands, while local 'marble' was used for architectural details. Where stone was not immediately available, or where there were insufficient quantities, a patron might donate a quarry on his land and make the necessary arrangements for transporting the stone. Towards the end of the twelfth century Osmund de Kent granted the Cistercian community at Meaux, in the East Riding of Yorkshire, a quarry on his estates at Brantingham '120ft [36.6m] long and 8 perches [5m] broad together with all the quarrying rights in a carucate of land, less 24 perches, with storage for the stone and free access to the Humber by which it could be conveyed to the abbey'. (A *carucate* was as much land as a team of oxen could plough in a season.) The Abbey of Meaux was fortunate: communities that were less well endowed were often obliged to buy or hire a quarry for their operations, or buy the stone from privately owned commercial quarries. When the quarry was in the neighbourhood of the site, the same men would be employed first as quarrymen and then as masons. But if the stone had to be brought to the site from a distance, it was usually purchased ready cut. Most stone was supplied in blocks, rough-hewn (*scappled*) to convenient sizes. Normally stones were sold by the hundred, although sometimes sizes were specified. Another measure was the *ton* or *tonne-tite* which was based on the weight of a tun of wine (2,000lb or 90kg).

Stones in standard shapes and sizes and DRESSED STONE for ornamental work were usually supplied from quarries ready worked and cut to measure according to a master mason's detailed specifications. Indeed it is likely that from early in the fifteenth century mouldings were increasingly purchased 'off the shelf', even for the finest applications. Consequently, much late medieval moulding of the Perpendicular period is of uniform craftsmanship and lacks individuality (*see* MEDIEVAL ARCHITECTURE).

When a quarry was opened the soil strata would be removed, together with the top layer of inferior stone (*rag*), which might be used for filling walls. In 1371, the clerk of the works at York Minster, the master mason and others spent a day selecting a quarry, after which 46*s* 8*d* was spent on removing the top soil and inferior strata before the *freestone* was reached. Freestone (usually oolitic limestone or particular types of sandstone) has a fine grain, does not possess strongly marked laminations and may, therefore, be 'freely worked' with a saw and chisel. (Medieval builders were expected to lay stone in a wall in the same position as it lay in the quarry, although there is ample evidence that they did not always bed their stone correctly.) Heavy steel-tipped iron wedges and *malls* were used to extract blocks of stone, which were then reduced in size by further splitting (*plugging and feathering*) and sawing to the required dimensions. The final tooling was performed either at the quarry or on site in the masons' lodge. In 1278 a group of masons was paid 100*s* 'for ten hundreds of stones which they dug from the quarry and cut, prepared and worked in full at their own costs' during the construction of Vale Royal Abbey.

As one would expect, certain sources of stone were more highly prized than others. London drew largely on quarries in Kent and Surrey, the Maidstone district in particular supplying large quantities of hard KENTISH RAG which had been used for the walls of Roman Londinium. For finer work, freestone was extracted from quarries in the neighbourhood of Reigate and Mersham in Surrey. In 1252, no fewer than 23,000 freestones were purchased at a cost of £72 from the Reigate quarries for the rebuilding of Westminster Abbey and thereafter, throughout the fifteenth century, 'there flowed every year a stream of stone, of varying volume, from the Reigate hills down to Westminster'. In 1477, '9755ft [2,973.3m] of Teynton [Oxfordshire] stone, measured by Henry Jenyns, chief mason' were bought at 2*s* a foot for St George's Chapel at Windsor, while in 1360 over 1,000ft of 'crestes' and 'tables' were brought down by water from quarries near Stamford to Surfleet and Lynn and shipped from there to Windsor. Barnack stone was considered to be the best in East Anglia, while stone from northern quarries was widely used from at least the middle of the fourteenth century. In 1395 the walls of Westminster Hall were raised with stone from the Yorkshire quarry of Marr, while in *c.* 1417 ships were sailing south carrying stone from Cawood, Doncaster and Stepleton in Yorkshire for the building of Sion Abbey near London. In 1347 William Hamele of Weymouth supplied sixty-eight 'great stones of Bere' for the king's chapel at Westminster for £11, while two years later the accounts show a payment of £4 6*s* 8*d* for '100 great stones of Bere, whereof fifty were worked as voussoirs for the heads of doors and windows . . . and 50 were in the rough'. Stone from Portland in Dorset (according to local tradition 'the best building stone in the world') was also widely used: at Exeter Cathedral in 1303, at Westminster in 1347 and, in the seventeenth century, for Christopher Wren's mighty St Paul's Cathedral in London (completed in 1711). A major characteristic of the medieval period was the use of PURBECK MARBLE. This is not a true marble but an almost black, fossiliferous limestone that occurs in two narrow strata in quarries on the Isle of Purbeck, Dorset. Purbeck marble, which came into fashion at the end of the twelfth century, is capable of taking a very high polish and was used for high-status decorative work, notably in monumental effigies and the shafts of clustered piers (*see* MONUMENTS *and* PIER). The northern equivalent of Purbeck marble is *Frosterley marble*, a black or dark-grey limestone extracted from quarries in County Durham.

Undoubtedly the finest building stone in Europe was the pure white stone from the quarries at Caen in Normandy, which was in constant demand throughout the medieval period, especially from the mid-thirteenth century. *Caen stone* was used in the rebuilding of Canterbury Cathedral Priory in 1175; two shiploads of 'freestone from Caen' were purchased for Westminster Abbey in 1252 at a cost of £24 18*s*, while no fewer than seventy-five shiploads of Caen stone, comprising 89,200 'parpayns' (stones dressed on two parallel faces) were delivered to the Tower of London in 1278 at a cost of £332 2*s*. The quality of Caen stone made it particularly suitable for detailed carving (*moulding*): in June 1494, the Prior and Convent of Canterbury ordered considerable quantities of Caen stone for the completion of the tower know as 'Bell Harry' and other buildings 'affecting the honour of God and the use and beauty of our church'. One William Feraunte was appointed as the Prior's agent to procure stone 'of sufficient quality, from which quarries it is well known that our whole church was built of old'. During the next three years over £1,035 was spent on building and refurbishment, of which two fifths was for 'canestone, with carriage, cranage and customs, 1132 tons at various prices'.

A characteristic of eighteenth- and nineteenth-century classical architecture was *rustication*. Introduced by Inigo Jones (1573–1652) from Renaissance Italy, rustication was a method of providing contrasting textures in stonework by projecting square ashlar or decorative blocks of stone forward from the recessed mortar courses, usually at basement level or in the lower storeys of buildings and on columns. These projecting blocks were usually ornamented: banded, chamfered, diamond-pointed, frosted and rock-faced (all of which may be easily identified) and vermiculated – carved to represent the random path of worms.

Mortar and Cement

Mortar, composed of lime and sand, was used to bind together the stones or bricks of a wall. The usual proportions were one part of lime to three parts of sand. Lime, which is produced by burning limestone or chalk, was either obtained from kilns constructed near the building site or purchased ready-burned. For major building works, kilns could be of considerable size: a kiln built at York in 1400 required 3,300 bricks and 33 loads of clay for its construction. Huge amounts of timber were needed to feed the kilns: at Windsor, in 1275, the Hundred Rolls complain that five hundred oaks in the forest of Wellington had been used to fire the king's two lime kilns, while in 1229 the abbot of Abingdon permitted the king to clear the timber from 26 acres of woodland for three kilns producing lime for work on Oxford Castle and the town walls. Coal was also used, where it was available – either from pits or from the sea. In 1278 huge amounts of 'sea-coal' were used to make lime for work on the Tower of London, leading to complaints from the citizenry, while in 1291 coal from Newcastle upon Tyne was used to fire the kilns at Corfe in Dorset. Old mortar was often reused, either by reburning or by pounding it together with new. At Pevensey in 1288 we find men 'digging stones and old mortar where the wall had been thrown down . . . making old mortar and new'.

Whereas the preparation of lime was a comparatively skilled task, sand could be dug, sieved and carried by unskilled labourers. It is self-evident that even larger quantities of sand were required than of lime: the Dover accounts for 1226 record payments of over £20 for 11,160 seams of sand and 11,000 'loads' (a *seam* was a unit of measurement equal to one packhorse load). The mixing of mortar by 'mortermen' was also unskilled work, and was sometimes carried out by women. There is a reference in the Westminster accounts for 1399 to 'a sieve in which to sift burned lime for the making of free mortar', which was probably a type of mortar that was used for plastering the exposed surfaces of walls. But where a wall was particularly exposed to the elements, a cement composed of wax and pitch or resin was applied in a molten condition. The medieval mortermen were not averse to experimenting with a variety of supplements – including, at Silverston in 1279, sulphur and 'a pennyworth of eggs'. In 1349, at the Tower of London, the foundations of 'the turret beside the Thames opposite the King's Exchange' were in urgent need of repair. The accounts for the works include references to 'an iron pan in which to heat cement', 'a caldron bound with iron in which to make cement', 'and iron ladel and an iron slice, with a tripod, to serve the masons for making cement'. There is also a reference to 'tylpuodre for making cement fore the foundations of the turret', which confirms that the Roman practice of pounding crushed tiles in with the mortar continued into the medieval period. When used on the outer face of a wall, this type of mortar was believed to be less pervious to rain.

See also ALABASTER, ANCASTER STONE, ASHLAR, BATEMENT, BATH STONE, BECKET, BRACKET, CAEN STONE, CLUNCH, COB, CORBEL, COTSWOLD STONE, DRESSED STONE, DRIPSTONE, ENCAUSTIC TILES, FENESTRAL, FILLET, FLINT, FLUSHWORK (*see* FLINT), FOREST MARBLE, FORME, FOUNDATIONS (STRUCTURAL), FREESTONE, FROSTERLEY MARBLE (*see* PURBECK MARBLE), GARGOYLE, GREENSAND, KENTISH RAG, KETTON STONE, KEY, KNAPPING (*see* FLINT), LAPS AND ROLLS, LEAD, LATH AND PLASTER, LINTEL, MARBLE, MASTER MASONS AND ARCHITECTS, MOORSTONE, MULLIONS, OGIVE, PENDANTS, PORTLAND STONE, PURBECK MARBLE, QUARREL, QUARRY, RAG *and* RAGSTONE, RAGWORK,

RESPOND, SCAFFOLDING AND CRANES, SCONCHON, SEVERY, SLATES AND ROOFING TILES, TOUCH, TRANSOMS, VAULT, VAULTING, VICE *and* WELDON STONE

MASONS' MARKS Devices used by stonemasons to mark their work. Each mason had his distinctive mark, which could be passed from father to son. They were usually hastily and shallowly incised and measure about 5cm (2in) in height. The marks were numerous and varied and include simple cyphers, geometrical patterns, and rune-like symbols. Registers of marks were maintained by the medieval masons' guilds, both to avoid duplication and to ensure that bad workmanship could be traced. Most medieval masons were peripatetic craftsmen who often worked in teams. It is therefore possible to trace the movements of a particular mason or group of masons from one commission to the next through identification of their marks. Masons' marks may also assist in the dating of buildings and in studying the various phases of construction.
See also GLAZIERS' MARKS

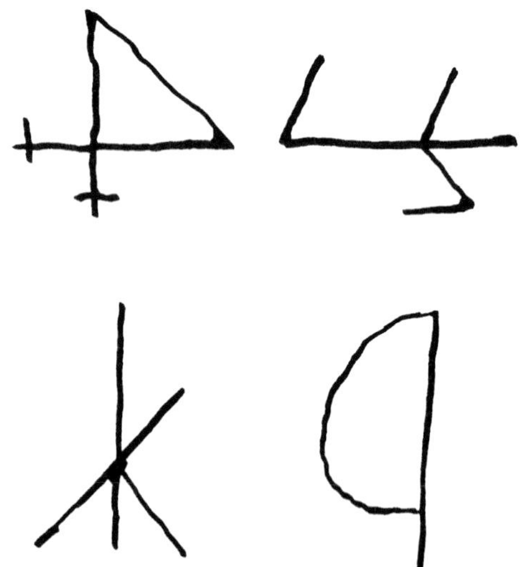

(Courtesy of Andrew Jamieson)

MASS A title for the EUCHARIST or Holy Communion, dating from at least the fourth century, and most widely used during the Middle Ages. The word mass is derived from the ecclesiastical Latin *missa* (from *mittere* meaning 'to send forth'), a reference to the dismissal of the congregation following the Eucharist. Medieval theology emphasised the propitiatory and sacrificial nature of the mass, and priests were expected to say the mass each day. One consequence of this was a significant increase in the numbers of monks entering the priesthood and a corresponding increase in the celebration of masses. This in turn affected the development of ecclesiastical architecture, notably in the provision of numerous side ALTARS, and the institution of chantries (*see* CHANTRY, CHEVET *and* PRIVILEGED ALTAR).

The mass, so men believed, was a re-enactment of Christ's supreme sacrifice and, as such, was an effective means of attracting God's mercy. Every testator in the fourteenth and fifteenth centuries therefore endeavoured to provide in his will for the celebration of soul-masses on the anniversary of his death, 'for the well-being of the living and for the repose of the dead', and in order to curtail the trials of PURGATORY. These private masses were celebrated by chantry priests at side altars and in the CHANTRY CHAPELS and CHANTRY COLLEGES of the magnate classes.

The High Mass (*Missa Solemnis*) was the normal form of the mass at which the celebrant was always assisted by a deacon and SUB-DEACON. But it was the Low Mass, without music and incense and with the assistance only of a single SERVER, that was most commonly observed in the churches and chapels of medieval England (*see* LITURGY *and* MEDIEVAL CHURCH). At that time, of course, the laity was denied the precious Blood of Christ (the wine) and received only the consecrated wafer of the Eucharist (the Host).

In religious houses, the Morrow Mass (*Missa Matutinalis*) at 8.00 or 8.30 a.m. (mass was not permitted before dawn) was followed by High Mass (*Missa Major*) at noon. In some communities, the Morrow Mass was known as the Lady Mass because it was celebrated in honour of the Blessed

Virgin Mary in the LADY CHAPEL. In houses other than those of the Benedictine and Cistercian orders, it was known as the Chapter Mass (*Missa Capitularis*), because it preceded the daily meeting of the CHAPTER. In the later Middle Ages, the Morrow Mass was attended by half the community's priests, the other half saying private masses (*missa familiaris*) at side altars located throughout the church. There were also occasional masses for the dead (*Requiem*), and to mark special occasions such as visitations, while daily masses were celebrated in the INFIRMARY and for the lay brethren (*see* LAY BROTHERS).

See also ABLUTIONS, ALTARS, AUMBRY, CREDENCE, FENESTELLA, LAVABO, PISCINA, PRESBYTERY, RESERVATION, SANCTUARY, SEDILIA *and* SQUINT

MASTER MASONS AND ARCHITECTS Initially, it would have been the missionary monks themselves who constructed the wattle and daub walls and thatched roofs of their churches and monasteries. However, in *c.* 670, Benedict Biscop (*c.* 628–89) built monasteries at Monkwearmouth and Jarrow, 'being the first person who introduced into England builders of stone edifices and makers of glass windows', while it was Wilfrid (634–709) who, as bishop of York, 'made many buildings by his own judgement but also by the advice of the masons whom the hope of liberal reward had drawn hither from Rome' (William of Malmesbury). From this, it would appear that Wilfrid was not lacking in ideas – neither, indeed, was King Alfred who, in fulfilling a vow to build a monastery at Athelney, 'made a church . . . contrived in a new manner of building' and allocated a portion of his income 'to craftsmen whom he constantly employed in the erection of new buildings in the manner surprising and hitherto unknown to the English' (ibid.).

While the chapter of a medieval abbey or cathedral exercised a general oversight of building operations, it was very often an eminent abbot or bishop who dictated the specification and design. Senior churchmen were widely travelled and were heavily influenced by the buildings and architectural styles they saw in continental Europe. But while the great medieval cathedrals and abbey churches were the products of genuine religious fervour, there was nothing amateur about their design or construction. It was the professional lay architects who translated a patron's architectural aspirations into practice – men who were usually masons by training and who were engaged on long, lucrative contracts. Inevitably, there was a large measure of experimentation in both the design and the construction of medieval churches, and sometimes the master masons made costly (and occasionally fatal) mistakes. Inadequate FOUNDATIONS and structural miscalculations caused towers to collapse at Winchester in 1107, Gloucester in 1170 and Worcester in 1175, for example. In some cases structural weaknesses had a less immediate effect. In 1322 the Norman tower of Ely Cathedral Priory collapsed, destroying the three bays that remained from the Norman choir, together with parts of the nave and transept (*see* LANTERN). During the eighteenth century the efforts of the Hereford chapter to prop up the west tower of their cathedral proved to be too little too late and the tower collapsed in 1786, taking the west end of the nave with it (*see* WEST FRONT).

Some medieval architects seem to have been singularly unpleasant characters whose advice was not always welcomed. When John, Abbot of St Albans (1195–1214), rebuilt the west front of his church 'very many picked masons were summoned together over whom was Master Hugh de Goldclif, a deceitful and unreliable man but a craftsman of great reputation, by whose advice an elaborate design with carving, unnecessary, trifling, and beyond measure costly', was adopted (*Gesta Abbatum*).

There can be little doubt that a medieval master mason performed a dual role. In consultation with his patron he was responsible for the overall design of a building and thereafter for preparing working drawings (*plattes*) that could be interpreted by those working under him. In the majority of cases he superintended the execution of his own designs, but if his employer was a major ecclesiastical magnate, then he could usually rely on a surveyor and clerk of the works to attend to day-to-day supervision. As a senior freemason, he was also responsible for much of the detail, supervising the preparation of the sectional drawings (*moulds*) for architectural features such as the mouldings of arches and window tracery.

Beneath the master mason was a large and varied team of specialists that included masons, carpenters, glaziers (*see* WINDOWS), tilers (*see* SLATES AND ROOFING TILES), plasterers, painters, plumbers (*see* PLUMBING, WATER SUPPLY AND SANITATION), metal workers, roofers (working with LEAD) and scaffolders (*see* SCAFFOLDING AND CRANES). Unlike the other artisans, skilled masons and glaziers were in great demand and would often travel long distances to work on a new building. There would also be a force of general labourers, recruited from the local community and sometimes augmented by the monks themselves. Indeed, we read that at Gloucester Abbey in 1242 'the new vaulting in the nave was finished, not with the help of wrights as formerly, but by the spirited courage of the monks there'. And it was not unknown for a religious superior to join the artisans: in 1100 Abbot Hugh of Selby 'every day, putting on a workman's smock, he used with the other workmen to carry on his shoulders to the wall stones, lime, and anything else required for the work; and every Saturday he received his wages as one of the workmen and bestowed them upon the poor'. Not all craftsmen worked on site: some masons would prepare stone in the quarries (the reduced weight of the dressed stone saving transport costs), while joiners could prepare almost everything in their workshops and transport the finished work to the building site. However, the majority of stonemasons lived on site in temporary lodges, hence their strong sense of brotherhood and the development of craft guilds (*masonic lodges*) to protect their interests. Work (which continued from sunrise to sunset) lasted from March to October, when any unfinished masonry was covered with straw to prevent frost damage. In the winter only a small number of highly skilled masons would be retained, to work on detailed pieces of tracery and statuary in the masons' lodge.

The rules of the Strassburg masons are likely to be an accurate indication of practice throughout Europe at the end of the fifteenth century: 'If anyone contracts for a work and gives a plan for it . . . the work shall not be cut short of anything in the design, but he shall execute it according to the plan which he has shown to the lords . . . so that nothing be altered in the building.' Furthermore, 'No one who has not served his time as a craftsman or been employed in a lodge, and does not know how to execute carved or designed stonework from the ground plan shall undertake such work.' The authority of the masonic lodge is clearly in evidence: 'No craftsman . . . shall teach anyone that is not of our craft to make extracts from the ground plan, or other usages of masonry.' From this, it is evident that a qualified mason was expected to be able to draw and interpret a plan and to carve mouldings from a sectional drawing (*see* MOULDING). In addition to a practical knowledge of stonecraft, master masons would also have worked on the production of plans, elevations, sections and detailed drawings. These were made in the *trasour* or 'tracyng house', the drawing office of the master mason, and were then converted by carpenters into wooden templets for use by the masons working on the carved mouldings of a building ('template' is a nineteenth-century term).

Very few architectural drawings have survived from the medieval period. Many were, by their nature and use, impermanent and it is hardly surprising that most were disposed of once a particular piece of work was finished. Nevertheless, there is abundant evidence that the master masons of the period did, indeed, make such drawings: 'tracing floors' have survived in the chapter house vestibule at York Minster and above the north porch at Wells Cathedral, for example. It was on these vast 'drawing boards' that were traced the designs for critical pieces of a building's construction – a thin wash of lime plaster or gesso providing a background which could easily be re-applied when a new tracing was required. The masons' loft at York still contains a remarkable collection of (mostly) early nineteenth-century templets, shapes of wood and blackened zinc from which the sections of stone tracery were sculpted.

MASTER OF NOVICES *see* NOVICE

MATERIALS *see* MASONRY

MATRICULARIUS *see* SUB-SACRIST

MATRIX A cavity within which a thing is embedded e.g. the hollow in a slab to receive a monumental brass (*see* BRASSES (MONUMENTAL)).

MATTINS (*or* MATINS) From the Latin *matutinus*, meaning 'of morning', the Breviary office for the night which, until the eleventh century, was known as *vigilae* from the vigils (*see* VIGIL) of the early Church. Originally it was observed at midnight, but the Benedictine rule prescribed it for the 'eighth hour of the night' (2.00 a.m.). In importance Mattins was equal to all the day offices together and, for many centuries, was known as *Nocturns*, being composed of several divisions each defined as a *nocturn*. The number of nocturns varied according to the ecclesiastical calendar: three on Sundays and major feast-days, for example, and a single nocturn on weekdays (*feria*). Each nocturn consisted of three psalms with their antiphons, versicle, paternoster and a short prayer (*Absolutio*) together with three lessons, each preceded by a benediction. The term Mattins is now more commonly used to describe the service of Morning Prayer in the Church of England which, as set out in the *Book of Common Prayer* (BCP), is essentially an abbreviated form of the medieval office, with supplements from *Prime*. The BCP service includes the *Venite*, *Te Deum* (or *Benedicite*) and *Benedictus* (or *Jubilate*) together with prayers and the psalms and lessons appointed for the day.

See also EUCHARIST, EVENING PRAYER, HOURS (CANONICAL) *and* HORARIUM

MAUNDY The maundy ritual of washing the feet of the poor is an act of love and humility which commemorates Christ's washing of the Apostles' feet at the Last Supper (John 13). In most religious houses a daily maundy (*Mandatum* or *Pedilavium*) was observed, during which a monk (selected by rotation from the brethren and supervised by the ALMONER) washed the hands and feet of a specified number of the poor. At a weekly maundy, the brethren who were on duty in the kitchen and FRATER washed the feet of the superior and brethren, usually in the CLOISTER and in the vicinity of the LAVATORIUM. (At the Cistercian abbey of Strata Florida in Powys a stone-lined basin, with steps at either end and located at the centre of the crossing, may have been used for this purpose.) The annual ceremony of the Great Maundy was held in Benedictine houses on the Thursday of Easter week, when the poor, equal in number to the brethren, were admitted to the abbey church. After the singing of the psalms and collects for the day, they were taken to the lavatorium, cloister or chapter house, where each monk would wash a pauper's feet, kiss his mouth and eyes and then serve him with a meal.

In the Middle Ages, the annual Maundy Thursday ceremony (which originated in the sixth century or even earlier) was also performed by royal or other eminent persons and was commonly followed by the distribution of clothing, food or money. Except in the Roman Catholic Church, all that remains in Britain of this ritual is the distribution by the sovereign of specially minted silver (*Maundy money*) at a Maundy service which is usually held at a cathedral. From the time of Henry IV (r 1399–1413), the number of recipients has corresponded to the number of years of the sovereign's age.

MEALS *see* FRATER *and* KITCHENS

MEAT *see* FRATER, KITCHENS *and* MISERICORD

MEDALLION (i) A bas-relief of circular, oval or rectangular form.
(ii) A circular tablet, ornament or panel.
(iii) A small decorative panel of stained glass in a traceried window.

MEDICINE *see* INFIRMARY

MEDIEVAL ARCHITECTURAL ORNAMENT *see* BALLFLOWER ORNAMENT, BEAKHEAD ORNAMENT, blind arcade (*see* ARCADE), BRATTISHING, CAPITAL, CORBEL-TABLE, CROCKET, DIAPER, DOGTOOTH ORNAMENT, FOILS, FOUR-LEAF ORNAMENT, MEDIEVAL ARCHITECTURE, TREE OF LIFE *and* TUDOR ROSE

MEDIEVAL ARCHITECTURE

Components of a Medieval Church

Early Norman churches were constructed on a simple BASILICAN two-cell plan with a short, dark NAVE and apsidal SANCTUARY (*see* APSE). From this basic, two-cell church there developed the three-cell church (consisting of a nave, PRESBYTERY and sanctuary), the cruciform church (nave, presbytery with PORTICUS and sanctuary) and the larger aisled church (with nave, AISLES and sanctuary). Three-cell and cruciform churches often had a central tower above the presbytery.

From the twelfth century, many cathedrals and large monastic churches were constructed or remodelled on a *cruciform* plan with the lower, elongated limb of a *Latin cross* forming the nave, the upper limb the CHOIR and presbytery, and the lateral limbs the north and south TRANSEPT (*see* MONASTIC BUILDINGS). The architecture of a monastic church was both functional and symbolic, the desire for spirituality being expressed through light, harmony and proportion. Indeed, it is now generally acknowledged that the dimensions of a monastic church, and of its various elements, were determined by reference to numbers and ratios that were themselves possessed of mystical or biblical significance. But form also followed liturgical function – 'a spatial expression of spiritual necessity' combined with 'a fiscal expression of the church's ritualistic needs' (J. Meades).

The presbytery in the vicinity of the sanctuary and HIGH ALTAR was usually apsidal, but many were rebuilt after *c.* 1130 to provide a square termination (*see* CHEVET) to which a RETRO-CHOIR or AMBULATORY were added (*see* ALTARS, CHANTRY CHAPELS, CHAPELS, LADY CHAPEL *and* SHRINES). To the west of the presbytery, the STALLS of the body corporate lined the walls of the choir, separated from the nave by a massive PULPITUM (*see also* RETURNED STALLS). One bay to the west of the *pulpitum* was the ROOD SCREEN and in front of that, the NAVE ALTAR (the *Jesus altar*), at which the laity – or, in Cistercian houses, the lay brethren – participated in the EUCHARIST.

The naves of large medieval churches usually consist of three storeys: an ARCADE, separating the nave from the aisles, a TRIFORIUM or tribune, and a CLERESTORY forming an upper level above the aisle roofs. In most cases, TOWERS were constructed above the CROSSING, where the four limbs of the building meet, and these sometimes carry a spire. During the twelfth and thirteenth centuries many timber roofs were replaced with stone vaults (*see* VAULTING) which, together with the weight of the tower, required considerable structural support and the provision of buttresses both at ground level and within the buildings themselves (*see* BUTTRESS).

The FRIARS, whose evangelical mission and commitment to preaching distinguished them from the monks and canons, built large churches specifically for that purpose. These churches had naves with wide aisles and broad arcades, while the choirs were long and often without aisles.

A small number of churches followed the Rotunda of Constantine's Church of the Holy

Sepulchre in Jerusalem, notably those of the Knights Templar and Knights Hospitaller (*see* ST JOHN OF JERUSALEM, ORDER OF *and* TEMPLAR, KNIGHTS). Of these, only four remain: the Temple Church in London (1185), the church of the Holy Sepulchre at Cambridge (*c.* 1130, restored 1840), Northampton (*c.* 1125 and much extended) and Little Maplestead in Essex (*c.* 1340, restored 1850). Originally, these churches were circular (or, at Little Maplestead, hexagonal), with an inner ring of arcaded piers, a central conical roof and a lower roof above the circular, outer aisle. The church at Garway in Herefordshire, extraordinary for its eccentric spatial organisation, massive linked tower and remote location, was once a circular Templar church, although very little evidence remains of its former shape.

Classification of Styles

The familiar classification of medieval architecture – *Norman*, *Early English*, *Decorated* and *Perpendicular* – was devised by Thomas Rickman (1776–1841) and first published in his book *An Attempt to Discriminate the Styles of English Architecture from the Conquest to the Reformation* (1817). Other forms of classification have been advocated, but those that attempt to apply specific dates to what was essentially an evolutionary process ignore both transitional elements – which are present in the gradual movement of one architectural phase to the next – and significant regional variations. Rickman's classification is firmly established; however, the dates given below are intended only as a very approximate guide to his architectural periods. Furthermore, architectural features were frequently added to those of an earlier period: at Gloucester Cathedral, for example, where a fourteenth-century remodelling of the eleventh-century choir resulted in the construction of a spectacular Perpendicular stone-ribbed 'cage' which masked the original Norman arcade and was extended upward into a magnificent new clerestory and vault. Very few medieval churches have survived that are of a single architectural style: most have been altered, extended or rebuilt and therefore have features from a variety of periods. Salisbury, the paragon of the Early English style, is a notable exception.

English Romanesque (*c.* 1066–*c.* 1190)

Rickman's *Norman* phase is that which is now described as *English Romanesque* and is easily recognised through the builders' preoccupation with solidity, exemplified by massively thick walling, small window openings and (in larger churches such as Durham, Gloucester and Tewkesbury) arcades of immense piers (*see* PIER) supporting semicircular arches (*see* ARCH). The great churches, like Norman castles, were both centres of Norman administration and monuments to the permanence of Norman power – manifested, for example, in the overwhelming solidity of Winchester's Romanesque north transept (1079–93). Durham is the best-preserved Romanesque cathedral in England, closely followed by Peterborough and Norwich.

Romanesque was a style of art and architecture prevalent in Europe *c.* 1050–1200 that reached its fullest development in central and northern France. As the name suggests, Romanesque architecture was inspired by the classical buildings of ancient Rome and the BASILICAN plan, with its nave, aisles and APSIDAL termination, which was adopted in Romanesque churches. In central Europe, Romanesque masons developed variations of classical themes, using the semicircular arch, arcading and tunnel vaults, and their buildings were vigorously decorated with foliated and other motifs. In northern and western Europe a more austere Romanesque style reflected Carolingian influences rather than those of classical Rome, and from this developed a distinctive Norman style which was evident in English church building even before the invasion of 1066. The CRYPT of Worcester Cathedral is a striking example of early Norman work (1084), with plain piers on simple, square bases, cushion capitals and a groined roof with square-edged transverse arches. The finest

Norman APSE in England is at Norwich Cathedral (early twelfth century), where it is surmounted by a perfectly proportioned fourteenth-century clerestory and later vault, while the massive semicircular arches above the crossing at St Albans Cathedral are entirely in their original form. Undoubtedly the most majestic of Norman naves is that at Durham (1093–1133), where the enormous piers are incised with a variety of geometric patterns and support semicircular arches decorated with characteristic chevron moulding (*see below*).

Eleventh-century masonry was massive, with walls up to 7.3m (24ft) in thickness at the base to provide structural stability and to compensate for poor-quality mortar and wide jointing. Window openings were small, so that the walls should not be weakened, and decoration was minimal (*see* WINDOWS). But in the twelfth century there occurred an extraordinary intensification in the scale and complexity of church building. By *c.* 1130 walls were less massive, windows larger, and the masonry more finely jointed, naves were longer and sometimes aisled, sanctuaries had square terminations, and there was an increasing use of carved ornament.

Early *mouldings* had been cut very sparingly with shallow hollows, fillets and chamfers, but later Romanesque work was profusely carved, mostly in geometrical forms, the most common of which are the familiar zigzag (*chevron*) decoration used in the deep mouldings of round arches, cylindrical motifs (*billets*) alternating with spaces in hollow moulding and, from *c.* 1130, blind arcading (*see* ARCADE). Sculptural decoration in doorway arches, capitals and tympana included floreated and animal forms, human figures, biblical scenes and monsters. Typically English is *beak-head ornament*, in which the heads of birds and beasts were carved in hollow mouldings so that the beaks or tongues overlapped into adjacent round mouldings. Anglo-Norman sculpture was an extraordinary pot-pourri of influences: from Scandinavian to Levantine and from Celtic to Byzantine. Many of the sinuous and diabolical creatures depicted in British Romanesque carvings are of Celtic origin, while others were introduced through the importation of highly decorated eastern silks. This merging of Christian and pagan motifs, which was to continue well beyond the Romanesque period, is best observed in the ornamental carving of smaller churches such as Adel and Birkin in Yorkshire (both *c.* 1160), Elkstone in Gloucestershire (*c.* 1170) and Brinsop and Kilpeck (*c.* 1130–40) in Herefordshire. Of the carvings executed by the celebrated Herefordshire School, those at Kilpeck are by far the best preserved: a magnificent TREE OF LIFE tympanum above the south doorway, a curious doorpost with warriors, possibly Celtic, hidden among interlaced vines, and an exceptionally varied (and occasionally *risqué*) carved CORBEL-TABLE. The south porch of Malmesbury Abbey in Wiltshire contains 'the richest ensemble of Romanesque carving in England . . . a great carved Pentecost broken into two halves, each with six Apostles. Almost nowhere else in England does one find figures on such a scale or in such profusion' (Harbison). In Wales, the integration of Celtic and Romanesque motifs in the south door of Penmon Priory and the chancel arch of Aberffro (both in Anglesey) is indicative of an accelerating process of cultural assimilation.

Gothic (*c.* 1175–*c.* 1550)

Gothic was the architectural style current in medieval Europe from the late twelfth century to the mid-sixteenth century. The term was first used by the sixteenth-century painter, architect and historian Giorgio Vasari (1511–74) to imply disapprobation of all things medieval. For him,

Opposite: *The apsidal presbytery (1118–40) at Peterborough Cathedral: despite the insertion of later tracery into the windows, it is one of the purest Romanesque interiors in England.* (© John Crook/info@john-crook.com)

Gothic architecture symbolised barbarism, and that of the Renaissance intellect: the verticality of faith versus the horizontality of enlightenment.

Rickman identified three phases of the Gothic style – *Early English*, *Decorated* and *Perpendicular* – each dependent on that which preceded it and fashioning that which followed. Each phase grew further away from the solidity that characterised Romanesque architecture and closer to the 'seemingly ethereal fragility' (Yarwood) of the late fifteenth century. Above all, the medieval architect was attempting to achieve an appearance of lightness and elegance, a space enclosed by glass, in direct contrast to the heavy sturdiness of the Romanesque and, unlike Classical and Renaissance buildings, the great medieval churches were therefore conceived from within. How the medieval builders would have rejoiced in Sir Joseph Paxton's splendid Crystal Palace, constructed in Hyde Park for the Great Exhibition of 1851. Larger than Wren's St Paul's, the luminescence of its 900,000sq ft of glass and the pure functionalism of its construction were precisely the architectural objectives which motivated medieval church builders for four centuries. It was this relentless quest for unattainable perfection (equated in the medieval mind with the greater glorification of God) that inspired architecture of the most extraordinary ingenuity and audacity, and in particular the development of the stone vault and abutment (*see* VAULTING). And it was the master mason of Durham Cathedral Priory who led the way. Although essentially Romanesque, its architecture was nevertheless extraordinarily innovative and radically ahead of its time. By its completion in 1133 Durham's masons had rib-vaulted the building throughout and had introduced flying buttresses to counteract the outward thrust of the vault – nearly three decades before Gothic architecture developed in northern France.

The 'heavenward thrust' of glass and stone created that feeling of emotional ascension which is the essence of Gothic architecture. And yet these great medieval buildings are essentially functional: every piece of stone is critical to the equilibrium of the building and (as at Richard Roger's twentieth-century Lloyd's building in London) no part of the structure is deliberately concealed. As in a house of cards, weight is distributed and structural stability is maintained by translating the outward thrust of an arch into the downward thrust of a corresponding pier or buttress. Nothing is superfluous: even a PINNACLE is part of the structural equation, adding its weight to a buttress or corner tower.

As the Middle Ages progressed so too did man's understanding of structure, and his ability to apply new engineering techniques. Buildings became larger, higher, lighter and the geometry ever more complex.

The *Early English* phase (also *First pointed* or *Lancet* from the characteristic narrow, pointed *lancet window*) lasted from *c.* 1175 to *c.* 1265. It is endowed with a certain austerity of form and a beauty of proportion, best seen (in its most developed form) at Salisbury Cathedral in Wiltshire, built between 1220 and 1266. The vaulting has plain quadripartite ribbing; tiers of lancet windows pierce the walls of the aisles, clerestory and transepts in pairs and threes; and the tall piers of the nave have clustered shafts of black Purbeck marble and simple moulded capitals in a characteristic inverted bell form. Decoration is minimal and consists mostly of finely carved but formal stiff-leaf foliation, mainly in capitals and in window and doorway mouldings, together with DIAPER and DOGTOOTH ORNAMENT and crockets (*see* CROCKET). Salisbury's interior is magnificent but, because of its joyless perfection, it is also the most austere of all English cathedrals. Notable examples of the Early English style are the magnificent west front of Peterborough Cathedral (*c.* 1238), the Galilee Porch at Ely (1215) and the Lady Chapels at Hereford (*c.* 1220–30) and Llandaff (late thirteenth century).

The need for *tracery* (ornamental stone mouldings within a window, *see* WINDOWS) arose

The nave of Salisbury Cathedral – a building of singular, though somewhat severe, architectural unity, 'the paragon of the Early English style'. (© John Crook/info@john-crook.com)

from the Early English practice of grouping two or more lancet windows beneath a single arch head (DRIPSTONE or *hood-mould*) that was intended to direct rainwater away from the openings. This created an awkward space (*spandrel*) between the window openings and the arch head, which at first was carved and pierced to provide the earliest form of tracery (*plate tracery*). From this simple device developed a variety of forms by which the Gothic phases are most readily identified. From the mid-thirteenth century single windows were divided by slender stone 'bars' (*bar tracery*) to provide larger areas of glass, one of the earliest forms being *Y-tracery* in which a Y-shaped mullion divides the window into two narrow vertical lights and a smaller top light. This later developed into *intersecting tracery* in which two or more mullions intersect each other in curves at the head of the arch.

The *Decorated* phase (also *Curvilinear, Flamboyant, Geometric* or *Mid-Gothic*) refers to the middle pointed style of window tracery, which lasted from *c.* 1250 to *c.* 1370. The increased width of buildings, achieved through advances in vaulting, created a need for greater internal illumination: windows became larger and wider and clerestories higher. This in turn increased the height of the nave and resulted in the development of the *arch buttress* (or *flying buttress*), which conveys the thrust of the vault and main roof over and beyond the aisles (see BUTTRESS). The increase in window size was accommodated by an equilateral arch and several mullions giving three, five, seven and even nine lights and ever more complex tracery. At first this was essentially geometrical, with circles, quatrefoils and trefoils (*see* CUSP *and* FOILS), but in the fourteenth century flowing or curvilinear tracery evolved, based on the OGEE form of double-curving lines producing flowing flame-like shapes. Reticulated tracery was a development of this, circles forming a lattice of ogee shapes. Many scholars now divide the Decorated period into *Geometrical* (Early Decorated) and Curvilinear (Late Decorated) phases, while others prefer the term *Mid Gothic*. The east window at Ripon Cathedral (late thirteenth century with nineteenth-century glass) is one of the finest examples of geometrical tracery in England, while the west window at York Minster (1338–9) exemplifies the ornate, flowing tracery of the later curvilinear style.

Decoration also became more elaborate, in the areas of stone carving, coloured window glass (see STAINED GLASS) and painted and gilded stonework. Carved ornament became increasingly vigorous and dynamic, with intense and detailed naturalism evolving into more stylised forms, the symmetrical four-leaved flower and BALLFLOWER ORNAMENT, for example. The nave of Exeter Cathedral (1275–1369) is a superb example of this period, as is the Lady Chapel at Lichfield Cathedral (completed 1330) in which nine enormous windows fill the entire space above the arcading of the lower wall. Lincoln Cathedral has one of the most highly decorative interiors in England, celebrated for the depiction in stone of natural foliage and smiling human faces expressing an inner joy – man and nature both part of the same joyous creation.

The Decorated style is best understood as a fusion of architecture and ornament to create special effects. Illusionistic and transcendental, the style aimed to convey the mystical experience of God.

English medieval architecture reached its apogee in the *Perpendicular* or *Rectilinear* style of *c.* 1330 to *c.* 1550, a time of almost frenetic architectural activity when numerous churches were refurbished, extended and even rebuilt – despite the ravages of the PLAGUE. Although lacking the richly carved detail of the Decorated period, the Perpendicular was a truly sumptuous and audacious style, characterised by the delicate vertical tracery of windows and stone panelling (from which the term 'perpendicular' is derived) with regular horizontal divisions and slender fluted piers leading upward into an exuberance of intricate fan-shaped vaulting (*fan vaulting*), exemplified in the magnificent vaults of Sherborne

The Decorated style: the nave of Exeter Cathedral with its exquisite tierceron vaulting – probably the finest in Europe. (© John Crook/info@john-crook.com)

Gothic window tracery: 1. Y-tracery (13th century); 2. intersecting tracery (13th century); 3. geometrical tracery (early 14th century); 4. reticulated tracery (14th century); 5. panel tracery (late 14th century); 6. panel tracery (late 15th and early 16th centuries). (Doreen Yardwood)

Abbey, Dorset (1425–85) and the Chapel of King's College, Cambridge (1446–1515) (see VAULTING). Windows of the period are significantly wider and the arches flatter, those of the late Perpendicular and Tudor Gothic periods being of the four-centre type. Rectilinear or panel tracery features both in windows and in wall panels and is characteristic of British architecture of the period. This form of tracery incorporates both MULLIONS and TRANSOMS, thereby creating rows of small glass 'panels' (lights), with more complex tracery confined to the upper tiers within the arch. There are numerous wonderful examples of Perpendicular architecture in our abbey churches and cathedrals: in the presbytery (1348) and Lady Chapel (1499) at Gloucester; in Canterbury's magnificent nave, rebuilt between 1391 and 1405; and in Henry VII's Chapel at Westminster Abbey

The magnificent Perpendicular nave of Canterbury Cathedral was designed and built by Henry Yevele between 1377 and 1405. (Courtesy of Anthony Kersting)

(1509), with its quite extraordinary fan vault, justly acclaimed as the finest of Perpendicular buildings.

The late Gothic builders very nearly achieved the perfection sought by their thirteenth-century predecessors. Their buildings are lofty, spacious and brilliant, with a minimum of masonry supporting a maximum area of glass. But by the beginning of the sixteenth century, technical virtuosity and decorative richness seem almost to have become an end in themselves.

See also CONSTRUCTION OF MONASTIC BUILDINGS *and* LANTERN

MEDIEVAL CHURCH, THE The extraordinary proliferation of churches in the twelfth century was indicative of both the Norman establishment's enthusiasm for its reformed Church and the vitality of the Church itself. With the gradual demise of the old MINSTERS (*see* ANGLO-SAXON CHURCH), thousands of newly established parishes acquired their own churches, many of which occupied earlier Anglo-Saxon or Celtic sites. In the towns there was a corresponding increase in the number of churches: by the end of the twelfth century there were over a hundred in London, thirty-five in Lincoln and fourteen in York. Church building was also considered to be a sound investment, producing both financial and spiritual rewards.

Most new churches were paid for by manorial lords (or groups of landholders), who endowed land and a priest's house and thereafter claimed a major proportion of the TITHES and other revenues of the parish and exercised the right to select the priest (*see* ADVOWSON *and* PATRON). Even those churches which in *Domesday Book* are shown to be attached to specific estates may have shared their profits among a number of landholders. Similarly, in the towns an apparent multiplicity of churches may be explained by the building and endowment of churches for the benefit of groups of wealthy burghers or for the extended households of successful merchants. A church was regarded as the property of the patron, and as such it could be rebuilt or enlarged, regardless of the wishes of the parishioners, or even demolished and removed to a new site. In particular, a church and its revenues could be bequeathed to a religious house, a practice known as APPROPRIATION. It has been estimated that, by 1200, one-quarter of English parish churches had been annexed to monastic houses and that this number had more than doubled by the end of the fifteenth century (*see also* CARTULARY).

Medieval Endowments

The medieval cathedrals exercised considerable regional influence, both ceremonial and commercial, while many abbeys promoted themselves as cult centres, with saints' SHRINES and reliquaries attracting pilgrims, sometimes in great numbers, and thereby stimulating the local economy. The corporate ownership of property, and particularly the endowment of land, ensured the continuing affluence of the cathedrals and monasteries up to the end of the thirteenth century, but the fourteenth and fifteenth centuries witnessed a gradual decline in this support and a corresponding diversion of patronage into the building and remodelling of parish churches.

In part, this was attributable to the piety of individual parishioners, anxious by their good deeds to secure eternal rest (*see* CHANTRY). It was also inspired by rivalry, both individual and corporate. In the neighbouring wool- and cloth-producing communities of Cullompton and Tiverton in Devon, for example, architectural emulation reached ostentatious proportions, while at Swaffham Prior in Cambridgeshire the rival manorial churches of St Mary and SS Gyriac and Julia stand within each other's shadow, sharing a common churchyard.

Inevitably, civic pride reflected that of the individual and *vice versa*: the magnificent Perpendicular churches of East Anglia and the Cotswolds are indicative not only of the prosperity of local industry, but also of the pre-eminence of the merchants and manufacturers whose MONUMENTS and CHANTRY CHAPELS rivalled those of the nobility and whose HERALDRY eloquently advertised the pervasive authority of the late medieval establishment, even in death. In such areas there were few churches that did not benefit in the fifteenth century from an endowment for the addition of a tower, clerestory or aisle, while numerous BENEFACTORS, both individual and corporate, provided for the building of hospices, ALMSHOUSES and SCHOOLS, many of which may still be found in the vicinity of a parish church.

Of course, not all parishes prospered, and there is ample evidence of abandoned churches following depopulation or contraction in the size of the population, and of churches which were neither rebuilt nor enlarged because of the declining influence of their patrons or the reduced circumstances of their parishioners. Throughout the Middle Ages, the Welsh Marches suffered deprivation, as did parts of East Anglia and Yorkshire in the late medieval period. Demolished chancels, aisles and chapels at churches such as Ovingdean in Sussex, Merton in Oxfordshire, Chepstow in Gwent and Cley-next-the-Sea in Norfolk, and even the reduction of naves (maintenance of which was the parishioners' responsibility), are vividly indicative of the fluctuating fortunes of many medieval communities and those upon whose patronage they depended.

Organisation

From 1072 the diocesan structure was reorganised under Archbishop Lanfranc of Canterbury (*c.* 1010–89). Those Saxon bishoprics which were located in remote, rural areas were removed to major towns such as Lincoln (from Dorchester-on-Thames), Chichester (from Selsey) and Chester (from Lichfield), while Sherborne in Dorset and Ramsbury in Wiltshire were combined to create a new bishopric at Old Sarum (to the north of present-day Salisbury). The see of Elmham in Norfolk was transferred to Thetford (and later to Norwich), and in Somerset, the see of Wells was moved to Bath. At the beginning of the twelfth century the creation of two further dioceses, Carlisle and Ely, completed the pattern of diocesan administration which was to last, almost without alteration, until the REFORMATION (*see* DIOCESE).

Also during the eleventh century, CANON LAW defined more clearly the financial and other parochial obligations of the laity (*see also* TITHES), while parish boundaries were delineated more precisely so that every man knew in which church he should attend the MASS, where his children should be baptised and his daughters married, and in which churchyard he should be buried. By the twelfth century, dioceses were subdivided for administrative purposes into archdeaconries, rural deaneries and parishes, while Church discipline was organised through a series of ecclesiastical courts (*see* COURTS (ECCLESIASTICAL)).

The 'regular' clergy (in contradistinction to the 'secular' clergy) included monks and nuns (*see* MONASTICISM), canons regular (*see* CANON REGULAR), FRIARS and members of the military orders (*see* TEMPLAR, KNIGHTS *and* ST JOHN OF JERUSALEM, ORDER OF), all of whom lived according to rules (*see* RULE) imposed by the heads of their orders and were subject to the ultimate authority of the pope. Members of the regular clergy (with the obvious exception of nuns) could be ordained priests and could become bishops – but not archdeacons or parish priests. All regular clergy were celibate, as were the secular clergy above and including the office of sub-deacon, although this requirement was not strictly enforced until the end of the eleventh century. All clergy were subject to Canon Law which, on occasion, came into conflict with the civil law.

The Secular Clergy

Before the Reformation, there were over 9,000 parishes in England, each with its rector or vicar. A rector was a parish priest whose TITHES were not impropriate (*see* IMPROPRIATION), whereas a vicar had identical responsibilities but in a parish where the tithes were subject to APPROPRIATION. Most parish priests performed their religious duties reasonably assiduously, either in person or by means of a deputy, and assisted by members of the MINOR ORDERS. They were responsible for 'the cure of souls', for celebrating the MASS and observing the Canonical Hours (*see* DIVINE OFFICE) and the various feast-days and FESTIVALS, and for visiting the sick and providing instruction. While many university-trained priests found employment as chaplains (*see* CHAPLAIN) in the households of the nobility and gentry, most parish priests came from the lower classes of society and received only an elementary education, although standards improved during the fifteenth century. Each was 'presented' to his living by a PATRON, who might be an eminent layman, a bishop or abbot, or even the king. Few benefices provided an income of any substance and the majority of parish priests enjoyed a standard of living little better than that of a better-off peasant. The vicars of appropriated parishes suffered particularly badly, the rectorial tithes (those which were profitable and easily collected, such as corn and hay) being the prerogative of a religious house (*see also* LAY RECTOR), while the vicarial tithes (such as garden produce, milk and cheese) were more difficult to assess and of less value. Those priests who accepted appointments as domestic chaplains were often rewarded with a rectory and engaged a curate to perform the duties, while continuing to receive the revenues of the living – for a patron, an economical way of rewarding service. The *Paston letters* of 1479 describe the Oxnead rectory in Norfolk as having a 'little and reasonably pleasant church', a 'well repaired parsonage', two orchards, a dovecote and 22 acres of land which, together with tithes, produced about £10 a year from which the rector would be obliged to deduct alms and payments for the repair of the chancel and his curate's stipend. 'It is but an easy cure to keep for there are not 20 persons to be yearly houseled [given the sacraments]', the implication being that there would be adequate time for more lucrative activities.

By far the most useful sources of information relating to the medieval clergy are the BISHOPS' REGISTERS. These include records of ordinations, inductions, patrons, changes of benefice and an extraordinary wealth of detail concerning the day-to-day work of a diocese and its parishes. Here too are the wealthy pluralists (*see* PLURALISM) and non-residents, many of them eminent administrators or Crown servants, and the wrong-doers – who (in the nature of things) feature more prominently in the records than their more virtuous (and numerous) colleagues.

Church Interiors

One of the pleasures of entering an ancient church is to experience the delicate play of light on mellowed stone and burnished wood, the reassuring texture of flint, brick and alabaster, and the hushed calm of continuity. But it was not always so. In the late Middle Ages the interiors of churches, other than those of the more austere monastic orders, would have been very different from the quiet, sober places they are today. Then, they blazed with brilliantly painted stone and woodwork, brightly coloured glass (*see* STAINED GLASS), lurid WALL PAINTINGS, gilded SCREENS and candlelit roods (*see* ROOD SCREEN), a profusion of LIGHTS, pyxes (*see* PYX), statues and ALTARS, a flamboyant conjunction of the sensual and the spiritual, primitive faith concealing a desperate need of salvation. Indeed, the vigour and intensity of medieval vernacular decoration convey an extraordinary sense of insecurity, a pervasive preoccupation with the transitory nature of life and the inevitability of death:

> For under the sunne a man may se
> Thys world ys butte a vanyte.
> Grace passeth gollde
> And precyous stoon,
> And god schal be god
> When goolde ys goon.

Even the smallest church was liberally decorated with wall paintings in which the glory of redemption was contrasted with the horrors of hell and eternal damnation (*see* PURGATORY), while numerous late medieval chantries (*see* CHANTRY), endowments and benefactions provide ample evidence of man's attempts to secure salvation for himself and his family at a time when 'visitations of pestilence, famine and fire' were regular occurrences. For the most part, the tenets of the Christian faith (the incarnation, atonement, redemption, the sacrifice of the mass and so on) were incomprehensible, especially as the ceremonies of the Church were conducted in Latin, and the religious and allegorical themes of paintings, stained glass and even play-acting were intended to instruct and to edify. But when the theology of Rome failed to satisfy, or was beyond a plain man's understanding, then dimly perceived images of past traditions were summoned in its place. Vestiges of paganism are evident in many surviving wall paintings, and in the carved images of monsters and demons so characteristic of English Romanesque stonework. For, just as many churches occupied earlier pagan sites, so the fabric of medieval worship was composed of two, sometimes conflicting, sometimes interchangeable, strands: the theological warp of Rome and the weft of an obscure primitive past.

For medieval church buildings *see* LITURGY *and* MEDIEVAL ARCHITECTURE.

See also ANGLO-SAXON CHURCH *and* WALES, THE MEDIEVAL CHURCH IN

MEMBRANE A sheet of parchment sewn with others to form a roll.

MEMENTO MORI Literally, 'remember to die' (though, more aptly, 'remember that you must die'), a *memento mori* is a human skull or any other object serving as a reminder of the transient nature of life and of the inevitability of death. Frequently found carved in MEMORIALS, tombs and gravestones and painted on HATCHMENTS.

See also CADAVER *and* MORTHEAD

MEMORIAL An object, institution or custom established to preserve the memory of a person or event.

see BRASSES (MONUMENTAL), BURIALS (MONASTIC), CARTOUCHE TABLET, CENOTAPH, CHANTRY, CHANTRY CHAPELS, CHANTRY COLLEGES, EFFIGIES, FUNERAL HERALDRY, EPITAPHS, HATCHMENTS, INCISED SLABS, INSCRIPTIONS, LEDGER STONES (*see* INCISED SLABS), LETTERING, MASS, MEMENTO MORI, MONUMENTS, OBELISK, STAINED GLASS, TABLET, TOMB CHEST, WALL MONUMENTS *and* WEEPERS

MEMORIAL TABLETS *see* WALL MONUMENTS

MENDICANT Mendicant FRIARS were members of those unendowed orders which were forbidden to hold property. Consequently they worked or begged for a living (Latin *mendicare* = 'to beg') and were not bound to a particular religious house. In the Middle Ages they worked mainly in towns and enjoyed extensive privileges, including exemption from episcopal jurisdiction and faculties for preaching and hearing confession.

METALWORK *see* ALTAR CROSS, BELLS, BRASSES (MONUMENTAL), CANDELABRUM, CORONA LUCIS, hatching (*see* HERALDIC COLOURS), HEARSE, LAPS AND ROLLS, LEAD *and* PARCLOSE.

METROPOLITAN The title of a bishop who exercises both diocesan and regional authority.

See also PRIMATE

MEZZANINE In a building an additional storey between two others, usually entered from a half-landing.

MIDDLE POINTED *see* MEDIEVAL ARCHITECTURE

MILITARY ORDERS Founded in response to the capture of Jerusalem by the Saracens in 1076. Members of the military orders were warrior-monks whose institutions exercised considerable political influence throughout medieval Europe (*see* TEMPLAR, KNIGHTS *and* ST JOHN OF JERUSALEM, ORDER OF).

MILLS Like dovecotes (*see* DOVECOTE) and FISHPONDS, wind- or water-powered mills for grinding corn into flour were an essential part of the medieval economy and there is often evidence, documentary or archaeological, of a former mill within, or in close proximity to, the outer court (*curia*) of a monastery or in the vicinity of a GRANGE. Most religious houses were situated close to a river and the majority of monastic mills were powered by water. There are rare surviving examples at Abingdon and Fountains (*see below*) although, more often, it is traces of a mill leat or mill pond that have survived.

Milling soke was a feudal monopoly exercised by most (though not all) lords of the manor, including monastic landlords. In practice many mills were leased to tenant millers, and manorial custom required that the peasants should have their corn ground in the lord's mill on payment of a toll (*multure*), usually one-sixteenth of the grist ground, although from the thirteenth century the toll was usually commuted to a money payment. The lord, who was responsible for major repairs, had first claim on his mill for grinding corn from the demesne lands, while the peasants could be fined for grinding their corn at home or for patronising a rival mill. No fewer than eighty mill stones (*querns*), confiscated in 1274 from the recalcitrant tenants of the Abbot of Cirencester, were later used to pave the abbey floor.

Windmills were numerous by the end of the twelfth century but, for the most part, these were primitive fixed structures and they could only be operated when the wind was blowing from a particular quarter. Later *post mills* had box-like weatherboarded bodies that could be rotated on a strong central post to catch the prevailing wind. The characteristic mill mound, in which the post was embedded, may be mistaken for a tumulus.

Some six thousand watermills were recorded at the time of the Domesday survey (although there were undoubtedly many more). Medieval watermills were of four types: the *click mill* (positioned horizontally across a stream), the *undershot mill* (a vertical wheel, the lower section of which came into contact with the water), the *overshot mill* (in which water was directed to the top of the wheel) and the *breastshot mill* (in which water was directed into 'buckets' at a point level with the wheel's axle). There were also *tidemills*, dating from the late fourteenth century, a type of undershot mill driven by water impounded at high tide.

Early references to mills are not always reliable because many are contained in documents that were forged by monastic houses in order to establish claims to ancient privileges that did not exist. The earliest authentic record is that of an 'adultarine' mill (one which operated unlawfully in direct competition to manorial mills) at Bury St Edmunds, Suffolk, in 1191. There are many references to thirteenth-century mills in contemporary documents and several illustrations in manuscripts such as the *Windmill Psalter* of *c*. 1270.

The corn mill at Fountains Abbey is the best-preserved monastic watermill in Britain. It was fed by a leat, drawn from the River Skell just outside the western wall of the outer precinct, that ran parallel to the river for 244m (800ft) before entering the mill. To the west was a mill pond, the water from which drove two water wheels within the mill. Built in the 1140s, the mill continued in use until 1937. The original mill was a two-storey building with a single undershot wheel at its southern end. In the 1150s the lower storey was buried beneath a dam to create the mill pond and a new single-storey mill with two wheels was built over it. An upper storey with a large granary was added in the early thirteenth century.

MINIATURE A full-page illustration, originally in red lead (*minium*) but later coloured and often illuminated (*see* MANUSCRIPT ILLUMINATION).

The mill at Fountains Abbey, Yorkshire, remained a working mill until 1939. The lower floor is from the late 1130s while the mill was extended and an upper floor added as a grain store in the mid-thirteenth century. (By kind permission of M. Aston)

MINISTER (Latin *minister*, meaning 'servant') One who is charged with the performance of spiritual functions within the Church. The 'Sacred Ministers' were the deacon and sub-deacon who, with the celebrant, officiated at the mass and were provided with designated seats (*sedilia*) in the SANCTUARY. In the Church of England, one who administers at a service – not necessarily a priest.
See also CLERGY (CHURCH OF ENGLAND)

MINOR CANON A cleric attached to a cathedral or COLLEGIATE CHURCH. Minor canons were not members of a CHAPTER.
See also CLERGY (CHURCH OF ENGLAND)

MINOR ORDERS The ranks of the Roman Catholic ministry below the MAJOR ORDERS (*see* ACOLYTE *and* LECTOR).

MINORESS A female member of the strictly contemplative order of Friars Minor, otherwise known as the *Poor Clares* after their co-foundress St Clare of Assisi (1194–1253), who was canonised 1255. The order received its first RULE in 1219 and by the fifteenth century was considered to be the most austere of all the women's orders. The 'Minories' place-name may be indicative of the location of a former house, although archaeological remains are rare. In 1958 St Clare was designated by the pope as the patron saint of television because, at Christmas 1252, when she was in her cell at San Damiano, she 'saw and heard' a service being held in the church of St Francis in Assisi. The order was re-established in the nineteenth century.
See also NUNS AND NUNNERIES

MINORITES The Franciscan Friars Minor (*see* FRIARS).

MINSTERS (MONASTERIUM) Anglo-Saxon minsters were religious communities, usually comprising a priest and a group of secular assistants (collectively known as *familia*), that served as centres of conversion and administration from the seventh century, prior to the development of a system of ecclesiastical parishes (*see* ANGLO-SAXON CHURCH). In Wales, *clasau* performed a similar function, although these were usually staffed by an abbot and hereditary canons (*see* WALES, THE MEDIEVAL CHURCH IN). A minster settlement usually consisted of a church and thatched outbuildings surrounded by a wooden palisade or a wall of turf and stone. They were almost invariably established on Saxon royal estates and served vast territories (*parochium*), their missionaries protected by royal or thegnal patronage in recognition of the administrative and cultural services provided by the minster staff.

Gradually the peripatetic clergy of the minsters were replaced by priests attached to proprietorial *chapelries*, strategically located daughter churches ancillary to the minsters and dependent on them. Chapelries were of two types: those with a burial ground and those without, a distinction which in some cases was perpetuated even into the nineteenth century. While many chapelries were later abandoned as settlements declined, a number continued as dependent churches for several centuries. Others became parish churches or continued as subsidiary chapels within the parochial system.

Evidence of former minsters remains, surviving not only in documents such as charters, monastic and cathedral records, court proceedings, land grants and bishops' records, but also in place-name elements such as the *eccles-* of Ecclesfield in West Yorkshire and Eccleston in Cheshire, derived from the Latin *ecclesia* or 'church' (Welsh: *eglwys*). More obviously, Kidderminster in Worcestershire was 'Cydda's minster' and Sturminster in Dorset was 'the minster by the River Stour'. Many others are as yet unidentified, although remnants of Saxon stonework (which was used only in major buildings) may be indicative of a church's former minster status. Even when no Saxon work remains, the historical relationship of a group of churches may indicate that one was traditionally superior to the others and may well have been a Saxon minster.

Some historians use the term 'minster' in its vernacular sense when describing 'family monasteries': small communities established by noblemen on their estates, governed by relatives and administered by dependants.

MINSTRELS' GALLERY The precise function of the so-called 'Minstrels' Gallery' above the north nave arcade at Exeter Cathedral remains a mystery. The gallery is a carved stone balcony that projects from a large room located above the north aisle and was clearly added at some time after the construction of the triforium and clerestory in the 1330s. The gallery's musical associations may be deduced from the figures of fourteen angels, each playing a musical instrument, that have been inserted into recesses in the face of the balcony. However, during conservation it was observed that the angels' wings had been trimmed to fit the recesses and that they are therefore not in their original position. Perhaps it was an EXPOSITION GALLERY associated with a RELIQUARY. Or it may have been used, as it is sometimes used today, for antiphonal singing.

MINUSCULE *see* LETTERING

MISERICORD (i) From the Latin *misericordia*, meaning 'mercy', a monastic dining room which was set apart for the use of those whose health or age required some relaxation of the strict RULE. Various terms such as 'loft' (at Durham), 'deportum' (Canterbury), 'seyny' (Peterborough) and 'oriel' (St Albans) will also be encountered to describe dining rooms for the aged and infirm. It was in the misericord that meat was served as an exception to the rule (*see* FRATER). However, by the fourteenth century there were many religious

The minstrels' gallery above the nave of Exeter Cathedral. (© John Crook/info@john-crook.com)

houses where the numbers dining in the misericord exceeded those in the frater. Indeed, the refectories of several major Benedictine houses were severely depleted except at the major feasts, that at Westminster, for example, being divided to provide a separate room for meat-eating. The misericord at Fountains Abbey was originally the infirmary latrine (a row of seven shafts may still be seen in the southern wall). In the late fifteenth century the building was extensively remodelled to form a ground-floor hall measuring 17.6m (58ft) by 6.7m (22ft). From this, and from other late medieval remains (such as the misericord at Furness Abbey), it is evident that, even in Cistercian houses, by this date meat from the infirmary kitchen could be eaten in the misericord, not only by the sick but by the community in general.

(ii) A hinged wooden seat which, when tipped up, presents a corbel-like projection for the user to rest on when in a standing position. Usually found in the choir STALLS of cathedrals and former monastic and collegiate churches, most date from the mid-thirteenth century to the late fifteenth (*see also* RETURNED STALLS). Their function was to provide support and relief for the monks or canons who were able to rest without sitting as they stood through interminable divine offices (*misericordia* = 'mercy'). Where misericords have survived, every stall seems originally to have been provided with one, suggesting that it was not only the elderly and infirm who had need of them.

By the mid-fifteenth century, the enigmatic imagery of the carved misericord had acquired a tradition of its own. Many designs are unique but others, or variations of them, were widely used by carvers, who appear to have worked from design books. These would be submitted to the patron or chapter, who would then select those designs which were considered appropriate to a particular church, at the same time commissioning others that were entirely new. Each collection therefore has its own unique flavour and reflects the tastes of a period as well as local influences, and even contemporary political allegiances. Fifteenth-century Ludlow in Shropshire, for example, was thrust into the forefront of national politics, being one of the principal strongholds of Richard, Duke of York (1411–60). In Ludlow church Yorkist badges (such as the Falcon and Fetterlock and the white rose) are much in evidence among the thirty-two misericords and in the splendid BOSSES of the chancel roof immediately above the stalls.

Most misericords consist of a raised central motif (beneath the corbel) between two subsidiary carvings (known as *supporters*) that are generally different in design and subject matter from the centrepiece. Heraldic symbolism was ideally suited to such carvings, as were images culled from the medieval bestiaries and from folklore and legend, moral allegories and cautionary tales. Sacred subjects are comparatively rare, while sports, jesters, romances, satires (notably on monks and musicians) and domestic scenes were especially popular. Many themes are singularly abstruse. Typically, at Beverley Minster in Yorkshire, there is a misericord in which a man is depicted shoeing a goose – an illustration of the (then) popular maxim that, if you meddle in something you don't understand, you may as well try to shoe a goose. Woodcarvers used a system of identification similar to that of the masons: several of the misericords at Ludlow are distinguished by a carver's mark of an uprooted plant, for example.

There can be little doubt that, following the Reformation, many sets of monastic and collegiate stalls provided fuel to melt the roofing lead salvaged by Henry VIII's commissioners. Fortunately, many have survived in our medieval cathedrals and in abbey churches, such as Sherborne, that were retained for parochial use. Others were retrieved and transferred to parish churches: at Tansor in Northamptonshire, for example, where the mid-fifteenth-century misericords originated in the collegiate chancel at nearby Fotheringhay, and an exceptionally fine set of early fifteenth-century misericords and richly carved and canopied stalls at Whalley in Lancashire, which were rescued from the abbey church. The church of St Botolph at Boston, Lincolnshire ('the largest and most important parish church in England'), has a fine set of sixty-four late fourteenth-century misericords beneath a nineteenth-century canopy. There are also numerous instances of misericords that have been removed from their original stalls and rearranged during restoration.

MISSAL A liturgical book containing the words and ceremonial directions for the celebration of the MASS and, from the tenth century, combining in one book the devotions which had previously appeared in several. Development of the missal was encouraged by the medieval practice of saying private masses. Many were presented as gifts to benefactors and are exquisitely illuminated.

MISSAL STAND A sloping book stand used by the priest at the altar. Two types are especially common: the wooden ledger stand with scrolled and foliated end panels and a scalloped bookplate edge, and the brass pedestal stand with a revolving bookplate and trumpet-shaped base.
See also DESKS *and* LECTERNS

MITRE The liturgical headdress of an archbishop or bishop and (until the Reformation) of certain mitred abbots (*see* MITRED ABBOT), a tall cap, shaped at the front and back like an inverted shield, and deeply cleft from one side to the other. Mitres are usually covered with embroidered satin and have two fringed *infulae* or

Misericords in the church of St Laurence, Ludlow, Shropshire.

The mitre of the Prince Bishops of Durham. (Courtesy of Andrew Jamieson)

lappets (ribbons) at the back. The mitre is also a symbol of episcopal or abbatial dignity, and Anglican archbishops and bishops ensign their coats of arms with a *mitra pretiosa* of precious metal, either jewelled or chased and jewelled. This was the mitre used by pre-Reformation bishops, while the *mitra simplex*, a plain white mitre, is that depicted in the heraldry of abbots of the Roman Catholic Church. Uniquely, in the arms of the bishop of Durham the mitre is depicted within a ducal coronet as a symbol of the temporal jurisdiction exercised by the medieval prince bishops of the PALATINATE.
See also HERALDRY (ECCLESIASTICAL)

MITRE ARCH *see* ARCH

MITRED ABBOT The head of a major monastic house who was permitted (by papal authority) to wear a MITRE and other episcopal insignia and to carry a CROZIER. The privilege, which required confirmation by the metropolitan and diocesan bishops, was extended also to the priors of cathedral priories (*see* CATHEDRAL PRIORY). By the late fifteenth century there were twenty-nine mitred abbots, most of whom were BENEDICTINES.

MIXTUM *see* FRATER

MONACHISM *see* MONASTICISM

MONASTERIA *see* ANGLO-SAXON CHURCH *and* MINSTERS

MONASTERY A community devoted, both severally and corporately, to the service of God. A monastic community (*family*) could be of men or women who were bound by VOWS of poverty, chastity and obedience both to the RULE of their order and to their SUPERIOR.

MONASTIC BREVIARY The BREVIARY used in religious houses which followed the Benedictine RULE.

MONASTIC BUILDINGS Many former abbey and priory churches escaped demolition at the DISSOLUTION OF THE MONASTERIES and became cathedrals and parish churches. In a number of cases, traces of conventual buildings have also survived: at Sherborne Abbey in Dorset, for example, where the former 'guesten hall' and undercroft now serve as libraries for Sherborne School and the former Abbot's Hall is the school's chapel.

Celtic and Anglo-Saxon monasteries were austere habitations, enclosed within a protective wall or bank and consisting of little more than a church and a few ancillary buildings (*see* ANGLO-SAXON CHURCH *and* CELTIC CHURCH). The church of the missionary community founded in 786 by Offa of Mercia at Peterchurch, Herefordshire, has survived in its original form, although it was rebuilt by the Normans in 1130. It is of particular interest in that, instead of the usual chancel arch dividing the church into two sections, there are three arches dividing it into four. This was the model adopted by Rome at the time: the APSIDAL east end and altar were reserved for the clergy; the next compartments, the SOLEAS and the PRESBYTERY, were for the prior and those of the community who were ordained; and finally the NAVE was occupied by the other brethren.

In the eleventh century the CLUNIACS had established a regular plan for their monasteries which, with modifications to accommodate the characteristics of a particular site and the needs of the various orders, became the model in England. The most notable exceptions were the houses of the Carthusian order (*see* CARTHUSIANS). These consisted of one or more courts around which were arranged separate cells for each monk. The brethren met in church only for Vespers, the night office and mass, the lesser offices being said in the privacy of the monks' cells, where they slept, ate, worked and prayed.

At the beginning of the thirteenth century there were over one thousand monasteries in England. They varied considerably in both resources and size: Fountains was immense, Cymer was diminutive. Many monastic churches were less than 30m (100ft) in length, while others, such as Winchester and St Albans, were five times that size (*see* CHURCH). And therein lies the danger of attempting to describe a 'typical' monastery. As will be apparent from the pages of this book, each is fascinatingly unique.

The Site

Land was gifted to religious houses for a variety of reasons. Cistercian Flaxley Abbey in Gloucestershire was founded in the 1150s by the son of the earl of Hereford to mark the place where his father had died in a hunting accident on Christmas Eve 1143. Not all endowments were as opportune. Many were of land that was otherwise of little value or was too costly to develop. For the monastic buildings, a site had to be comparatively level, with a reliable water supply for drinking, cooking, washing, flushing and drainage, and to replenish FISHPONDS and mill leats (*see* MILLS). The nature of an order's vocation also defined the suitability or otherwise of a particular site. The CISTERCIANS and PREMONSTRATENSIAN CANONS demanded that their houses should be 'far from the concourse of men' in remote valleys, on inaccessible islands surrounded by marshes, and in forest clearings. The houses of the mendicant FRIARS, on the other hand, were almost invariably in towns. Some convents were founded to venerate the shrine of a saint or to commemorate a major historical event: Battle Abbey, for example, was traditionally said to have been founded to fulfil a vow made by Duke William of Normandy before he invaded England in 1066. (More prosaically, in 1070 the papal authorities imposed heavy penalties on the Normans for the bloodshed of the Conquest and the founding of the abbey was William's penitential response.) The richest monasteries were early English foundations that had acquired undeveloped land before the twelfth century, and those of the Cistercians that were invariably situated in remote areas where there were fewer constraints on development.

As monastic sites became permanent, complex systems of conduits (*see* CONDUIT) and stone-clad drains and sewers were constructed, many of which are still in evidence, as at the Cistercian abbey of Tintern in Monmouthshire (*see* PLUMBING, WATER SUPPLY AND SANITATION). Ideally, the site would be north of a stream flowing from west to east (as at Fountains Abbey), although often it was necessary for a natural watercourse to be diverted and the conventual buildings to be arranged accordingly (at Rievaulx, for example, where the River Rye was deflected three times in the twelfth century). Space for expansion and quietude was essential: at Thetford in Norfolk the Cluniac priory became so beleaguered by urban housing that it had to be moved to a new site outside the town. The availability of substantial quantities of minerals, BUILDING MATERIALS and firewood was also an important consideration: Byland Abbey in North Yorkshire was moved four times in fifty years before a satisfactory site was found. The church was usually constructed on the highest point of the site, with the conventual buildings to the south. Occasionally the eminence on which the church was built did not relate well to the natural drainage of the site, to other topographical features (such as rivers) or to urban encroachment (which restricted development to the south). In such cases, the CLAUSTRAL buildings were laid out to the north of the church – as at Buildwas, Forde, Tintern, Gloucester and Sherborne, for example.

The Precinct
The enclosed monastic PRECINCT was entered by means of a gatehouse at which visitors could be identified and their credentials checked before being admitted (*see* FORTIFICATION). Many gatehouses had separate side entrances for pedestrians, while a central vaulted gate passage would be of sufficient height to allow for the movement of heavily laden wagons. Chambers above the gatehouse were often used as a courtroom or schoolroom and occasionally a small prison was incorporated into the building, as at the Benedictine priory at Ely in Cambridgeshire. Some gatehouses were CRENELLATED, while others (notably those of the Cistercians) included a chapel for the use of LAY BROTHERS. At Westminster, a parish church (St Margaret's) was built outside the abbey gatehouse for the benefit of the lay community.

Having passed through the gatehouse, the visitor entered the *curia*, a busy outer court where the monastic world met the secular. Here were located all the conventual buildings of a self-sufficient and self-contained community: a great barn (often of considerable size, *see* BARNS), granary, bolting-house (where corn was sieved), bakery, malthouse, brewery, smithy and STABLES, together with a house and dining hall for monastic servants. Beyond the *curia*, and separated from it, were the abbey church and the claustral buildings to which only the brethren were permitted access.

The Claustral Buildings
As the name suggests, the claustral (or cloistral) buildings were arranged around the CLOISTER, a covered and colonnaded passageway surrounding a rectangular open space or GARTH. In most cases, this was located to the south of the abbey church, the aisle of which abutted the north side of the cloister (for what follows, this is assumed to be the case, although there were notable exceptions such as Gloucester and Tintern). On the other three sides of the cloister were the most important domestic and administrative buildings of the monastery: the chapter house, dormitory (*dorter*), refectory (*frater*), kitchens, and the great monastic storehouse (cellarium) which often occupied the entire undercroft of the WESTERN RANGE. The cloister walks (*alleys*) were used for processional purposes and for silent work and meditation.

The CHAPTER HOUSE was normally within, or connected to, the EASTERN RANGE of claustral buildings in the upper storey of which was the DORTER or monks' dormitory with the latrines (*reredorter*) on the same floor and, in most Benedictine monasteries, a CALEFACTORIUM (warming house) below. A DAY STAIR, which gave access to the dorter, was usually located in or near the south east angle of the cloister. The refectory or FRATER was on the south side of the cloister and in Cistercian houses was usually set at right angles to, and south of, the cloister alley. A LAVATORIUM, where the monks washed after rising and before meals, was usually located in the vicinity of the frater. The monastery's KITCHENS were also near the frater, either in the adjacent western range of claustral buildings or in a separate building, to reduce the risk of fire. Chimney flues and ovens were set within the thickness of walls, and around the kitchens ancillary buildings housed the pantry, buttery, bakery and other domestic offices (*see* LARDER).

The guests' chambers (*hospitium*) and abbot's (or Prior's) lodgings were often (though not invariably) in the vicinity of the claustral buildings (*see* GUEST HOUSE *and* SUPERIOR'S LODGINGS). The lodgings would normally include a parlour, dining room, bedchamber and chapel but, as many abbots rose to positions of political influence, so their responsibilities for entertaining eminent guests

A reconstruction of Byland Abbey as it might have appeared at the end of the fifteenth century. (Simon Hayfield/ © English Heritage Photo Library)

1	*Nave*
2	*Choir*
3	*Cloister*
4	*Dormitory (dorter)*
5	*Chapter house*
6	*Monks' latrine (reredorter)*
7	*Day room*
8	*Meat kitchen*
9	*Abbot's lodging*
10	*Warming house*
11	*Refectory (frater)*
12	*Kitchen*
13	*Lay brothers' latrine (reredorter)*
14	*Lay brothers' dormitory (dorter)*
15	*Barn*

(and their households) increased. Separate dining halls were provided at several monasteries, adjacent to the abbot's chambers and with suites of guests' rooms beneath. From the thirteenth century a number of abbots had three-storey houses built, with dining halls on the middle floor and a parlour and bedchamber above. Some even had their own kitchens, the most splendid of which was the Abbot's kitchen at Glastonbury Abbey in Somerset (*see* KITCHENS). Such opulence was not always of the abbot's choosing but was expected of him by his peers – the magnates and prelates who relied on the monasteries for HOSPITALITY.

In Cistercian monasteries the western range of claustral buildings was originally used to accommodate large numbers of *conversi*, who usually outnumbered the choir monks (*see* LAY BROTHERS). They were provided with a common room and refectory on the ground floor and a dorter and reredorter above. As the numbers of lay brothers declined in the fourteenth century, their quarters were often adapted for use as accommodation for guests (*see* CORRODY) and for administrative purposes.

The INFIRMARY (*farmery*) was usually built beyond the eastern claustral range and was intended both for the sick and infirm and for those who were too old or too deranged to cope with the stringent demands of monastic life. Dietary rules were relaxed for those in the infirmary and, as these often included guests, food was obtained either from the abbot's kitchen or from a separate kitchen attached to the infirmary. The great hall of an infirmary contained at least one large fireplace and had its own lavatorium and latrines. The beds were arranged between pairs of high windows in the side walls and faced a central space, as in a modern hospital ward. Many infirmaries were of considerable size, indicative of the practice of *phlebotomy* or blood-letting, which was considered to be a medical necessity. Following phlebotomy, a monk was required to rest for three days during, which time he could enjoy rich food in the MISERICORD and relaxation in the monastery gardens, could rise late, and was excused choir. Consequently the frequency of blood-letting was, in most orders, restricted: four times a year for Cistercians, five times for Carthusians and eight for the Austin Canons.

While eminent members of the monastic community might be buried beneath INCISED SLABS in the chapter house or cloister (or, from the fifteenth century, in the abbey church itself), most brethren shared a common grave in the monastery's cemetery, which was approached by means of a covered passageway from the cloister (*see* SLYPE). The slype was generally used for conversation, which was forbidden in the cloister itself, and in some monasteries it developed into a library, although books were generally stored where they were needed: in the SACRISTY, the choir, the cloister or the frater (*see* LIBRARIES).

The Church

The cruciform CHURCH usually stood on the north side of the cloister, the longer (western) arm of the nave providing shelter to the claustral buildings without cutting out the sunlight. Although the interiors of Anglo-Saxon and Romanesque churches were often dark, later Gothic buildings were constructed to admit as much natural light as possible (*see* MEDIEVAL ARCHITECTURE). The principal door was at the west end and was often set within an imposing façade and sometimes flanked by twin towers, as at Durham (*see* WEST FRONT). Eastward was the NAVE, with aisles to the north and south separated by arcades of massive piers (*see* AISLE, ARCADE, PIER *and* ARCH) above which rose the tribune or TRIFORIUM and CLERESTORY. Some naves were of extraordinary length: Norwich, for example, is 76m (250ft) long. At the eastern end of the nave, were the ROOD SCREEN, the CROSSING and PULPITUM, and above the crossing the tower (*see* TOWERS). East of the pulpitum, and at a higher level than the nave, was the CHOIR (or *quire*), with its carved wooden STALLS, each provided with a MISERICORD and a desk for service books. The stalls were raised on a stone base as protection against damp and this sometimes contained an acoustic chamber (*see* AMPLIFIERS). In the midst of the choir was the lectern (*see* LECTERNS) and, at the west end, the abbot's stall (*see* RETURNED STALLS). To the east were the PRESBYTERY and the raised SANCTUARY in which was the High Altar (*see* ALTARS). In larger churches, CHAPELS to the east of the sanctuary were linked by an apsidal aisle or AMBULATORY, as at Tewkesbury Abbey in Gloucestershire (*see* CHEVET), or RETRO-CHOIR, screened from the High Altar by a REREDOS. Of these chapels, the most important was the LADY CHAPEL, usually of late medieval date, its size and architectural splendour reflecting a contemporary cult-like veneration of the Blessed Virgin Mary (*see* MARY, THE BLESSED VIRGIN).

English monasteries were rich in RELICS, particularly of native saints, and these were often retained in ornate canopied SHRINES, few of which survived the Dissolution of the Monasteries. Kings, princes and magnates sought burial in or near the sanctuaries of the great abbeys and numerous CHANTRY CHAPELS were erected for this purpose in the fourteenth and fifteenth centuries. Many shrines and royal tombs became so popular that additional accommodation had to be provided for the thousands of pilgrims who travelled from all over Europe to offer prayers and supplications and to swell monastic coffers. In the TRANSEPT, the northern and southern arms of the cruciform building, were side-chapels and subsidiary altars for those monks who were also priests. A door in the north wall of the northern transept led to the community's burial ground, and from the southern transept a doorway opened to the NIGHT STAIR by which the monks descended from their first-floor dormitory (*dorter*) to attend the night office. Doors at each end of the south aisle gave access to the cloister: both were used for processional purposes, while that at the western end of the aisle was also used by the lay brethren, who worshipped in the nave.

MONASTIC, CANONICAL AND MENDICANT ORDERS *see* AUGUSTINIANS (*for* Austin Canons or Canons Regular), BENEDICTINES, BRIGITTINES, CANON REGULAR, CARTHUSIANS, CISTERCIANS, CLUNIACS, FRIARS (*for* Austin Friars, Bonhommes, Carmelites, Crutched Friars, Dominicans, Franciscans, Friars of the Holy Cross, Friars of the Penitential Sack, Red Friars *and* Trinitarians), GILBERTINE ORDER, GRANDMONTINES, HOLY ORDERS, MAGDALENES, MEDIEVAL CHURCH, MENDICANT, MILITARY ORDERS, MINORESS, MONASTICISM, NUNS AND NUNNERIES, PREMONSTRATENSIAN CANONS, RELIGIOUS ORDERS IN THE ANGLICAN CHURCH, RULE, SAVIGNIAC ORDER, TRAPPIST *and* VICTORINES

MONASTIC DECLINE The history of western MONASTICISM is one of alternating decline and revival, not only of individual houses but also of entire orders. In the ninth and tenth centuries many monastic communities suffered from repeated Viking incursions: their buildings were sacked and destroyed and their brethren slain or dispersed in a land where lawlessness was endemic. Furthermore, the religious communities of Britain were at that time isolated both from the mainstream of European religion and from one another. The Benedictine Rule, in particular, was susceptible to laxity because of its inherent moderation, and many abbots exploited their autonomy, not for the advancement of their houses, but in order to attract the patronage of powerful lords. That monasticism survived was due to a small number of determined and able men who set out to restore moral values by first reforming the monasteries (*see* ANGLO-SAXON CHURCH *and* BENEDICTINES).

The CISTERCIANS, whose sacrificial quality of life attracted numerous benefactions and endowments, acquired vast estates which they managed so efficiently that they became the victims of their own success. As landlords they could not avoid being part of feudal society, they became institutionalised and, as their administrative responsibilities multiplied, so they were forced to increase their establishments with *conversi* (*see* LAY BROTHERS) and paid officials. By contrast, the arrival of the FRIARS in the thirteenth century brought renewed vigour and an innovative form of religious commitment with which the monasteries could not compete. At that time, many religious houses had already begun to relax their original principles of austerity and, in the face of increasing public hostility, monasticism suffered an acute crisis of identity in a society that was abundantly endowed with religious houses.

For many houses debt was a perennial problem, caused by bad harvests, diseased stock, natural disasters, legal disputes, improvidence and even corruption. But the principal cause of debt was almost invariably the abuse of HOSPITALITY. Corrodians could be forced on a monastery by a patron or magnate as a cheap form of retirement annuity (*see* CORRODY), while self-invited guests, often accompanied by their retinues, demanded high standards of accommodation for long periods. Even deserving travellers could be a drain on a monastery's resources, especially if it was located on a pilgrimage route or near a port.

The economic and psychological repercussions of the PLAGUE were evident in the monasteries, as elsewhere: the Black Death severely reduced the number of monks, perhaps from 9,000 to 4,500, and although this number had recovered to almost 7,000 by 1377, it then remained static until the Dissolution of the Monasteries. From the mid-fourteenth century, lay brethren began deserting in large numbers, attracted by improved wages and working conditions as a consequence of a labour shortage following the Black Death. Society generally became increasingly acquisitive and materialistic. Endowments were diverted from the monasteries to parish churches, where numerous additions and improvements were effected by benefactors whose generosity reflected their status in society as much as their religious devotion. A recent account of monastic life in the fifteenth century paints an appalling picture of drunkenness, gluttony, licentiousness and racketeering at (of all places) the abbey of Westminster. Presumably, this cannot have been exceptional. And yet, while there is clear evidence of increasing laxity, occasional scandal and sporadic civil unrest (*see* FORTIFICATION), widespread decadence and corruption are more difficult to prove (the reports of Henry VIII's commissioners are hardly to be trusted!). It was at this time that the deeply devout Henry V (1413–22) founded a new Charterhouse at Sheen and a house of Brigittine nuns across the river at Syon. These were the last monasteries to be founded in medieval England and they were to be renowned for the strictness of their observance. Henry was anxious to preserve the quality of the religious life in the monasteries, and in April 1421 he summoned to Westminster a GENERAL CHAPTER of the Benedictine order at which he claimed to be the 'patron' of English monasticism. He spoke forcibly of the need for fidelity to the Benedictine rule and, in particular, attacked those abbots who had separate lodgings and lived apart from their brethren, 'which was neither a part of the Rule nor the founder's intention'.

Ironically, towards the end of the fifteenth century, there were signs of renewed vigour in the Church and of a willingness to acknowledge the need for monastic reform. What the outcome might have been had not the DISSOLUTION OF THE MONASTERIES intervened is a matter for conjecture (*see* REFORMATION).

MONASTIC PLACE-NAMES *see* PLACE-NAMES

MONASTICISM (*also* MONACHISM) Monasticism is generally believed to have originated in the Egyptian wilderness, where St Antony (251–356) lived for twenty years in the most rigorous seclusion. In 305 he was persuaded to leave his hilltop retreat by the supplications of numerous anchorites (*see* ANCHORITE) and to found a monastery, a group of separate and scattered cells, near Memphis. In 355, the venerable hermit (then over 100 years old) journeyed to Alexandria to dispute with the Arians. But, conscious that his end was approaching, he retired to his desert fastness and died.

Monasticism, then an extreme form of ASCETICISM, was introduced into the West in the fourth century. Monks followed an austere, disciplined life devoted to prayer and work, secure from worldly distraction (*see* MONK). Their objective was to achieve personal sanctification in fulfilment of the solemn threefold vow of poverty, chastity and obedience (*see* VOWS). They were not required to become priests and only the clerical order could administer the sacraments (*see* SACRAMENT). Like the ordained clerks, monks received the *tonsure*, the circular shaved patch on the crown of the head, which signified commitment to the Church (though not necessarily ordination). From the sixth century, as a result of papal influence, a distinction was made between the clerical order, which served the spiritual needs of lay people under the authority of a diocesan bishop, and the monastic order, which was devoted to a cloistered existence. In practice, however, the distinction was frequently blurred: many monks were also priests (or even bishops) and, by the beginning of the seventh century, were exercising significant influence beyond the precincts of their monasteries. Most early monastic communities comprised just twelve monks and a SUPERIOR (a *family*), in imitation of Christ and his apostles, and they were essentially democratic: superiors were elected and there was no distinction made among the brethren with regard to background or class. The only distinctions recognised by St Benedict were those of obedience and charity. In practice, of course, a monk needed to be literate, which implied membership of an educated class. A monk's day was divided between prayer and work: observance of the DIVINE OFFICE (the *Opus Dei*) and labour (*see* MANUAL LABOUR), which developed to include scholarly research, teaching, manuscript illumination and the copying of manuscripts (*see* SCRIPTORIUM). Consequently, many monasteries became the intellectual and artistic engine rooms of European civilisation.

From the eighth to the twelfth centuries, Benedictine monasticism was the only form of religious life in western Europe (*see* BENEDICTINES *and* ANGLO-SAXON CHURCH). Thereafter there was a proliferation of monastic, canonical and mendicant orders, the most significant period of monastic expansion in Britain lasting from the Norman Conquest of 1066 to *c.* 1220 (*see* MEDIEVAL CHURCH). Although from that time the religious houses remained numerous and their prosperity increased, their popular credibility declined in an age of deprivation and uncertainty, exacerbated by the Black Death of the mid-fourteenth century (*see* MONASTIC DECLINE *and* PLAGUE).

During the thirteenth century, one-third of a typical monastic community consisted of choir monks and two-thirds of lay brethren, paying guests (*corrodians*), visitors and servants. The largest community in England was that of the Benedictine abbey of St Alban in Hertfordshire, where there were

The Cistercian Melrose Abbey in the fifteenth century. (Alan Sorrell)

one hundred monks. But elsewhere, at the great Cistercian and Benedictine houses, establishments usually numbered between sixty and seventy, and in the houses of other orders perhaps no more than thirty. Of a population in thirteenth-century England of about three million, one out of every 150 persons was a monk, canon or nun. There were some 4,000 Benedictines, 3,000 Cistercians, 500 Cluniacs and 200 Carthusians – monks, who were not necessarily clerics, but men who had vowed to pursue a life of austerity, contemplation and prayer 'outside the gates of the world'. Of canons, who were clerks in holy orders and lived according to a RULE, there were some 3,000 Augustinians, 1,000 Gilbertines and 800 Premonstratensians (*see* CANON REGULAR). In addition there were about 7,000 nuns of the various orders and 500 Knights Templar or Hospitaller (*see* MILITARY ORDERS). By the fourteenth century, the half-dozen largest Benedictine houses each contained some fifty monks, and a second tier, together with those of the Cistercians, twenty or thirty. The houses of the Augustinian and Premonstratensian canons had generally fewer than twenty, while a large number of small priories and cells of all orders had fewer than a dozen (*see* MONASTIC DECLINE).

Lay Brethren

Lay Brothers (and, in Gilbertine houses, lay sisters) were an important element of the monastic population. They were not bound to the recitation of the divine office and were generally occupied in manual and domestic work, although the Cistercian *conversi* included many skilled craftsmen (*see* LAY BROTHERS). In the mid-twelfth century the converse outnumbered the monks in Cistercian houses by three to one, and the Carthusians, Austin Canons and Benedictines also recruited lay brothers in large numbers. But during the thirteenth century their numbers declined steadily, so that by 1350 few remained in the monastic communities. In part, this was the result of market forces, but in many monasteries the often tense relationship between monks and lay brethren had proved to be incompatible with the objectives of monastic life. As the numbers of lay brethren decreased, so a veritable army of wage-earning servants moved in. It is estimated that in the thirteenth century there were 40,000 servants in religious houses (twice the number of monks, canons and nuns), many of whom lived with their families in the PRECINCT. Their tasks ranged from curers of herrings to keepers of the wax and cressets (lamps) while Worcester Priory maintained a crew of five boatmen on the River Severn.

Of course, domestic help was needed not only to free the monks of routine chores but also to provide for the numerous guests who comprised about one-sixth of a monastery's population. Many temporary guests were accommodated without charge, but others generated a substantial income through *corrodies* – annuities of land or money made over to a monastic foundation in return for guaranteeing the comfort and security of the benefactor in old age (*see* CORRODY).

Superiors

Ironically, it was the possession of vast tracts of land (obtained through corrodies and endowments) and numerous manorial estates and granges (*see* GRANGE) that eventually diverted monastic energy away from quiet contemplation and prayer to the administration and commercial exploitation of property, and promoted many an abbot to the dual status of spiritual leader and magnate, responsible to the brethren by whom he was elected, to the tenants of his estates and (if he was called upon to hold office) to the Crown. His instructions came as from God, and in his monastery he was both good shepherd and autocrat, elected for life. But in practice, many abbots lived as ecclesiastical magnates with their own households and retinues, dispensing patronage and exercising political and judicial authority. In such cases, responsibility for the day-to-day life of a monastery and the welfare and conduct of the monks was delegated to an abbot's deputy-general, the PRIOR (*see also* PRIORIES).

Plate 12: Christopher Wren's magnificent choir at St Paul's Cathedral, London. (© John Crook/info@john-crook.com)

Plate 13: *Canterbury Cathedral has one of the finest collections of twelfth-century stained glass in the world.* (Courtesy of Derry Brabbs/ www.derrybrabbs.com)

Plate 14: Highly dramatic stained glass by Morris and Company in the east windows and west tower window of Birmingham Cathedral. Designed by Sir Edward Burne-Jones (1833–98) it includes a depiction of the Ascension (illustrated) of 1884–85. (Jonathan Berg/Birmingham Picture Library)

Plate 15: John Piper's (b. 1903) shimmering baptistry window at Coventry Cathedral was executed by Patrick Reyntiens in 1962. It contains 195 panels of brilliantly coloured glass, moving from darker reds, blues and greens at the periphery to a brilliant sunburst of white and gold at the centre. It is rightly considered by many to be one of the finest stained-glass windows in the country. (Courtesy of Geoffrey Wheeler)

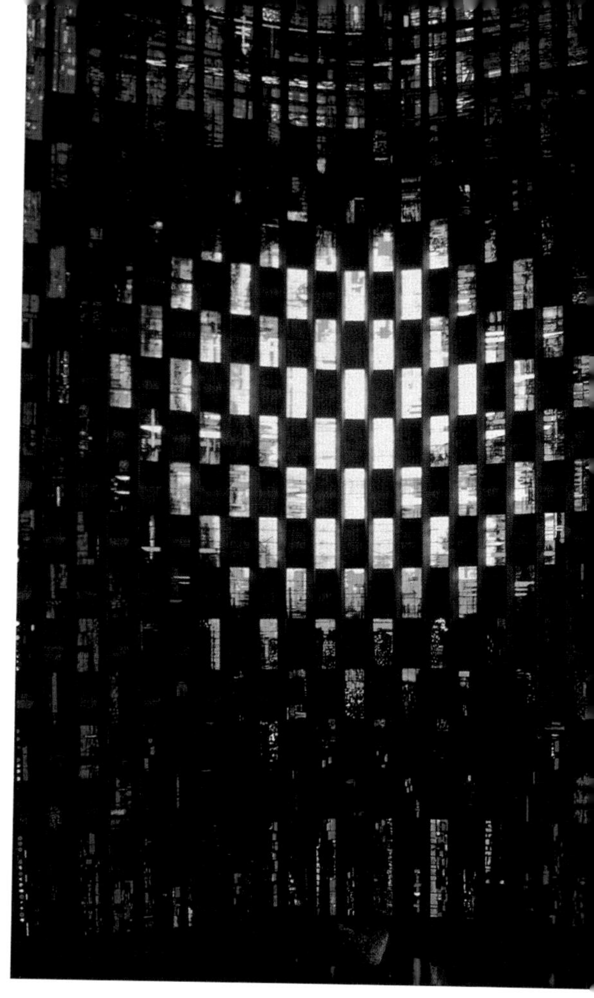

Plate 16: Window designed by Marc Chagall (1889–1985) at Chichester Cathedral. Made by Charles Marq of Reims in 1978 it depicts Psalm 150: 'Praise ye the Lord . . . Praise him with the sound of the trumpet; praise him with the psaltery and harp.' (© John Crook/info@john-crook.com)

Plate 17: The magnificent early thirteenth-century west front at Wells Cathedral – an image screen containing 297 medieval figures. (© John Crook/ info@john-crook.com)

Plate 18: The dramatic early thirteenth-century west front at Peterborough Cathedral has three gigantic, deeply recessed portals that rise 26m (85ft) to the full height of the walls.

Plate 19: Lincoln's west façade is an immense mid-twelfth-century stone screen with the original late Norman west front at its core. Three large recessed Romanesque portals correspond with the nave and aisles within. (© Judges of Hastings; (01424) 420919; www.judges.co.uk)

Plate 20: The carvings on Bishop Oliver King's elegant sixteenth-century west front at Bath Abbey form a quite extraordinary confection – including angels climbing ladders to heaven on the stair turrets. (© John Crook/info@john-crook.com)

Plate 21: Unusually, the cloister garth at Gloucester Cathedral is located to the north of the church. Gloucester's sumptuous fifteenth-century tower commands the Severn Vale like a beacon. (© John Crook/info@john-crook.com)

Plate 22: The historic core of Durham lies within an incised meander of the River Wear. At the southern end is the great Norman cathedral while its northern flank is protected by the castle – seat of the prince-bishops of Durham. The Palatinate over which they ruled was effectively a kingdom within a kingdom and, as defenders of the realm in the north, the prince-bishops were charged with the defence of the Scottish border. (© John Crook/info@john-crook.com)

Plate 23: The nave and high altar at Westminster Roman Catholic Cathedral. Constructed between 1895 and 1903, the design was modelled on Justinian's church of the Holy Wisdom in Constantinople and San Vitale at Ravenna, Italy. (© John Crook/info@john-crook.com)

Obedientiaries

The *obedientiaries*, or monastic officials, usually numbered between fifteen and twenty depending on the size of the monastery, although Cistercian houses were not organised on hierarchical principles (*see* OBEDIENTIARIES). The senior obedientiaries were the prior and *sub-prior(s)*; the SACRIST or *sacristan*, who, with the *sub-sacristan*, was responsible for the abbey church; and the CELLARER who, with the *sub-cellarer(s)*, was responsible for the properties of the monastery, including all revenues, rents and patronage. The cellarer also exercised supervision over the various domestic departments and was responsible for the maintenance of the monastery buildings; for the acquisition of food, drink, clothing, fuel and livestock, and for tenants, lay brethren and servants. Responsible to the cellarer were the *kitchener*, who ensured that meals were of a suitable quality and served on time (*see* KITCHENS); the *refectorian*, who organised the refectory (*see* FRATER); the *hosteller*, who ran the GUEST HOUSE and the *infirmarian*, who had charge of the infirmary. The *almoner* provided for the needs of the poor and infirm who could not leave their homes, and gave food, clothing and money to pilgrims, beggars and lepers who called at the monastery gate (*see* ALMONRY). The PRECENTOR maintained the monastery library and was also responsible for its music.

Admission

By 1200, the practice of offering children in infancy to be educated as *oblates* in religious communities had been abandoned, and thereafter the age at which a POSTULANT could make application for admission to a monastery or nunnery was generally between 17 and 19. Once admitted, a postulant became a NOVICE and was required to give all his possessions to the monastery or to the poor, although his clothing was kept so that he could re-enter the world if he so wished or if he was required to leave. The Novice Master instructed the novices in the RULE and prepared them for the demands of monastic life. He also gave lessons in reading, singing and comportment. The noviciate lasted for a year, at the end of which time the novice (if accepted) made his VOWS and swore obedience to the Rule.

The Daily Round

The primary responsibility of a monastic community was to recite the DIVINE OFFICE, the eight Canonical Hours or services of the *Opus Dei* (*see* HOURS (CANONICAL)), and each day's pattern was determined by the hours of daylight (*see* HORARIUM). At the March and September equinoxes, for example, when night and day each last twelve hours, the brethren rose from a seven-hour sleep at 2 a.m. to attend the 'night watch' meditation of NOCTURN and MATTINS. The Day Hours began with LAUDS ('praises'), which was recited at first light, and PRIME at sunrise. Then followed TERCE (third hour), SEXT (sixth hour), NONE (ninth hour), VESPERS (at sunset) and COMPLINE (sung to 'complete' the hours before retiring at dusk). All eight hours consisted of psalms, hymns, lessons, antiphons, versicles, responses and prayers, led by the PRECENTOR and his deputy the SUCCENTOR, and sung in PLAINSONG. The Hours did not include CONFESSION, which was made at the daily meeting of the CHAPTER, in the presence of the abbot and brethren. During services, the CHOIR MONKS occupied the STALLS and the LAY BROTHERS the nave, and each had their own entrance to the church. The intervals between the Hours were devoted to work, with a two-hour rest period following None, and the daily meal taken after Vespers (*see* HORARIUM). The rules and customaries demanded acceptance of hierarchy, obedience to superiors, and courteous deference to age and office. The brethren were required to wash their hands before and after eating and levity was not permitted, especially in the FRATER. The monks at Ely Cathedral Priory were warned that if they persisted 'in holding their parliament at the door of the frater, they would be put on bread and water until they promised better obedience'.

F.H. Crossley, in his *The English Abbey* (London, 1935), describes monastic life in terms that make its apparent popularity difficult to comprehend.

> They [the monks] spent their time in innumerable services and study, living a dull existence in silence, shut away from the world and its excitement, for they lived on a low diet and suffered much from indigestion, a prey to habits which cut across the precepts of good health, and the constant and periodical bleeding were weakening. The average life of a monk was 55 years. The picture of a monk's life during an English winter is not to be envied, with no heating in the monastery, the dorter icily cold when he rose for the long night service, going half asleep in the dark to a freezing church, perhaps filled with a clinging fog, and being expected to sing and pray with fervour for an hour and a half.

No wonder that a medieval monk wrote:

> I cannot endure the daily tasks. The sight of it revolts me. I am tormented and crushed down by the weight of the vigils and I often succumb to the manual labour. The food cleaves to my mouth, more bitter than wormwood. The rough clothing cuts through my skin and flesh down to the very bones. More than this, my will is always hankering after other things, it longs for the delights of the world and sighs unceasingly for its loves and affections and pleasures.

See also MONASTIC BUILDINGS

MONASTICON ANGLICANUM A collection of monastic charters and other sources relating to English monasticism and medieval collegiate churches compiled between 1655 and 1673 by Sir William Dugdale (1605–86).

MONK In its early form, the term was used to describe a religious who lived a solitary life (*see* COENOBITE) but it came to include all members of a closed religious community of men, living according to a RULE and subject to a tripartite vow of poverty, chastity and obedience. It should not be applied to Canons Regular (*see* CANON REGULAR) or to members of the MENDICANT or MILITARY ORDERS. There were two classes of monk: choir (or quire) monks (*see* CHOIR MONKS) and LAY BROTHERS. Of these, the choir monks were the senior brethren, whose principal function was to observe the DIVINE OFFICE. They were, of necessity, literate, and were often the younger sons of the nobility and gentry. Many monks were also ordained priests, but not necessarily so.
See also MONASTICISM *and* NUNS and NUNNERIES

MONUMENTAL BRASSES *see* BRASSES (MONUMENTAL)

MONUMENTAL INSCRIPTIONS *see* INSCRIPTIONS *and* LETTERING

MONUMENTS Monuments, erected within a church to perpetuate the memory of an individual, invariably reflect the fashions and foibles, aspirations and *folies de grandeur* of a particular class at a particular time. They can provide a wealth of information concerning the fluctuating fortunes of individuals and communities, the way people lived, their appearance and clothing, how and at what age they died, and how they (or their relatives) hoped they would be remembered. Monumental INSCRIPTIONS and HERALDRY are invaluable sources for the researcher (*see also* EPITAPHS), while changing artistic and architectural styles reflect both contemporary tastes and attitudes to religious observance. Memorials vary in size from large, elaborate, canopied monuments to modest tablets (*see* WALL MONUMENTS) affixed to a wall. Monuments do not necessarily mark the place of interment, which may be some distance away or even at another church. Many have been moved – to accommodate an organ, for example. In what follows, it should be remembered that only the 'great and good' of society enjoyed the privilege of being commemorated in their diocesan cathedrals and abbey churches.

The Medieval Period

Memorials developed from the practice of carving designs on stone coffin lids and on grave covers that were exposed in a church floor. The earliest surviving lids are from the eleventh century and are carved in shallow relief with simple decorative designs, usually foliage or Christian symbols such as the fish and key. The tapering grave cover, engraved with a cross, is typical of a style that lasted into the thirteenth century. Several have survived (though not always in their original locations) and may be even older than the buildings that house them.

It is likely that depiction of the human form was reserved, in the twelfth century, for eminent ecclesiastics, the earliest known example in England being that of Abbot Gilbert Crispin (d. 1117) at Westminster Abbey. In these early monuments the image was recessed into the slab, but from the beginning of the thirteenth century it was often placed on a TOMB CHEST and carved in a three-dimensional effigial form (*see* EFFIGIES). Throughout the medieval period, painted ALABASTER or PURBECK MARBLE effigies were widely used to commemorate members of the nobility and eminent knights and clerics, the familiar recumbent attitude signifying mortality and humility. Before the mid-fourteenth century, legs and arms were depicted in a variety of positions but thereafter legs are rigidly straight and hands closed together in veneration and prayer. One of the earliest military effigies is that of William Longespée, Earl of Salisbury (d. 1226) in Salisbury Cathedral, which provides evidence of the early systematic use of hereditary armorial devices (*see* HERALDRY). The heads of effigies may rest on pillows (sometimes held by angels) or on helmets, and their feet on beasts, usually (though by no means invariably) a lion for a man or a pet dog for his lady. Tiny bedesmen (*see* BEDESMAN) may also be found, carved in the folds of clothing or at a figure's feet.

Tomb chests were also highly decorated and usually reflect contemporary architectural styles, although many were subsequently replaced and are therefore of a later date than the effigies they bear. Tomb chests, with or without effigies (or, occasionally, with brasses) could be free-standing or recessed within a wall and were sometimes surmounted by an ornate CANOPY, as at Ewelme in Oxfordshire where the late fifteenth-century monument to the Duchess of Suffolk (complete with CADAVER) is possibly the finest of its type in England. (Free-standing canopied tomb chests were the precursors of the late medieval CHANTRY CHAPELS.) Two-dimensional figures continued to be engraved in INCISED SLABS and, from the late thirteenth century, in monumental brasses (*see* BRASSES (MONUMENTAL)). The figures in effigies and brasses are generally stylised, as it was the accompanying heraldry that announced the identity, lineage and status of the deceased – although some of the more lavish examples are idealised portraits, 'based on a likeness'. It became the practice to place man and wife (or wives) side by side (and sometimes holding hands), but their children were not usually represented, except as WEEPERS around the sides of the tomb chest or by armorial shields illustrative of marital alliances. The figures carved on a tomb chest may help in dating: weepers occur from the late thirteenth century, angels from the late fourteenth century and saints in the fifteenth century.

The development of armour and costume may be traced through effigial figures and brasses, although it should be remembered that memorials are not necessarily contemporaneous with the death of those they commemorate: many were prepared years (or even decades) beforehand, while

Tomb and effigy of Sir Christopher Matthew (d. 1526) at Llandaff Cathedral.

others were commissioned retrospectively and may be in a later style. Similarly, dating a memorial by reference to the armour or costume of a figure can be fraught with difficulties. An effigy at St David's Cathedral in Powys, alleged to be that of the Lord Rhys of Deheubarth (d. 1197), is of a knight in fourteenth-century armour, for example.

Sixteenth Century

Throughout the ages, a substantial portion of the surplus wealth of communities has been expended on the burial places of their leaders. But from the mid-fifteenth century there are signs of increasing expenditure on the commemoration of less distinguished members of society, indicative of the notion that everyone has the right to be interred beneath masonry. In the Tudor period, great families and those of the 'new gentility' and the merchant class were often commemorated in sumptuous monuments. The recumbent figure continued into the sixteenth and seventeenth centuries, but may be somewhat stiff in appearance. There was also a proliferation of undevotional postures, reflecting, no doubt, changes in religious attitudes brought about by the Reformation: reclining casually on an elbow, for example. Kneeling figures (often at a prayer desk) and demi-figures are also in evidence, and these may be included in a wall monument (*see* WALL MONUMENTS) that has no tomb chest. Two distinctive types of memorial that date from the late sixteenth and early seventeenth centuries are the triptych, a hinged set of three painted panels, and the OBELISK, a tall, four-sided tapering pillar, usually placed on a plinth. Renaissance forms and decoration superseded the Gothic, characterised by STRAPWORK, grotesques, cherub-heads and allegorical figures.

Seventeenth Century

Many Jacobean monuments are singularly impressive, lavishly coloured and adorned with heraldry, the armour and costume of kneeling or recumbent figures being particularly striking. Children are often included, usually carved in relief or painted on a frieze, with the boys in descending order on one side of their deceased parent(s) and the girls on the other. A skull held by a child is also indicative of early mortality.

During the late sixteenth and early seventeenth centuries heraldry proliferated, often ostentatiously so, reflecting the changing nature of armory from the practical to the ceremonial and symbolic. It was now necessary to provide artificial helms, gauntlets, tabards and other items of FUNERAL HERALDRY which, in the previous century, would have been readily available; and it was at this time (*c.* 1627) that funeral HATCHMENTS were introduced as inexpensive substitutes for the elaborate trappings of the heraldic funerals of the nobility and gentry. Unfortunately for the genealogist, heraldic errors abound: from elementary mistakes committed by restorers with little understanding of armorial practice, to multi-quartered shields that are either inaccurate or incomplete.

The seventeenth century witnessed the development of Classical architecture which, inevitably, influenced the design of church monuments. Tomb chests became unfashionable, columns and pediments predominated and, while kneeling effigies remained in hanging monuments, figures were carved in more natural poses. Indeed, at the church of St Michael at St Albans in Hertfordshire, Francis Bacon is depicted in a seated position and appears to be fast asleep, while, at Culford in Suffolk, Lady Bacon is also seated – surrounded by her family and with her first husband recumbent beneath her feet!

Eighteenth Century

Black and white MARBLE superseded alabaster at the end of the seventeenth century and colour was confined to an occasional (and diminutive) heraldic motif. The ostentatious sculpted memorials of the period often dominate the churches in which they were erected, standing figures (indicative of self-glorification rather than humility) reflect the spirit of the times, while contemporary epitaphs relate in the most pompous and verbose manner the innumerable merits of the deceased. There are also many memorials that reflect the flamboyant Baroque style of late seventeenth- and early eighteenth-century architecture. Imposing figures were often modelled to capture a significant moment in the deceased's life and ornate carved fruits, garlands and cherubs' heads were incorporated into designs, particularly in wall monuments.

As the eighteenth century progressed, there was an inevitable reaction against the excesses of the Baroque and a reversion to more classical styles, indeed figures were often depicted in classical costume (or armour), surrounded by images of ancient Rome. From *c.* 1750 the architectural canopy was superseded by the two-dimensional pyramid, a large slab of black or grey marble set vertically against a wall, while the earlier tomb chest was reintroduced as the SARCOPHAGUS, which often had figures of the deceased, his family or allegorical characters sitting or leaning against it. The area at the base of the monument was usually devoted to biographical or genealogical details, or incorporated a frieze depicting a scene from the deceased's life, particularly of those who had enjoyed successful military or naval careers. Busts, small portrait medallions, amorini, urns, cartouches and symbols of mortality are ubiquitous.

Many eighteenth-century monuments appear extraordinarily vulgar to our modern eye, especially when insensitively located in a Gothic building. Even so, many memorials, while no less ostentatious, are exquisitely sculpted. At Milton Abbey in Dorset, Caroline Damer (d. 1775), recumbent and cushioned in white marble, is watched over pensively by her widower, Lord Milton, who leans nonchalantly on his right elbow. The Damer monument, wonderfully sculpted by Agostino Carlini to Robert Adam's design, is pathetic rather than vulgar and is greatly enhanced by its location in the north transept of the former abbey church, where its scale is entirely in keeping with the massive fifteenth-century transept walls and memorial window.

Nineteenth Century

In the nineteenth century the classical Roman style was superseded by a restrained neo-classicism inspired by Greek designs, again in black and white marble (white was increasingly popular). The two-dimensional pyramid motif was replaced by the STELE, a rectangular slab surmounted by a low, triangular pediment, and recumbent effigies are again in evidence. The size of nineteenth-century monuments varied from small inscribed tablets to large hanging monuments with an inscription in the base and a sculpted relief figure, usually an angel or the deceased, in classical Greek dress, resting against an urn or sarcophagus.

The Greek revival continued into the second half of the century, when it was overtaken by the Gothic revival. Inevitably, there was a return to the 'medieval' tomb chest and alabaster effigy, sometimes surmounted by a canopy, and to the figured monumental brass. But most Victorian effigies combine a variety of medieval influences and rarely reproduce accurately the style of a particular period. Brass wall monuments and plaques were also popular, with their now familiar 'Gothic' lettering and decorative capital letters.

Twentieth Century

From the end of the nineteenth century, large funeral monuments became unfashionable and, in most cases, impracticable. A notable exception is the tomb chest and effigy of T.E. Lawrence (Lawrence of Arabia, d. 1935), finely sculpted in marble by Eric Kennington, in the Saxon church of St Martin at Wareham, Dorset. But, for the most part, twentieth-century memorials take the form of simple commemorative wall tablets and window glass, or the provision of church furniture and fittings as bequests 'in memoriam'.

See also BRASSES (MONUMENTAL), BURIALS (MONASTIC), CANOPY (MONUMENTAL), CEMETERIES, EFFIGIES, EPITAPHS, HEART BURIAL, INCISED SLABS, MONUMENTS, OSSUARIES, PLAGUE, SHRINES, TOMB CHEST, VAULT, WALL MONUMENTS *and* VISCERAL TOMBS

For the Church Monuments Society, the Royal Commission on Historic Monuments *and* the Monumental Brass Society *see* APPENDIX II.

MOORSTONE A granite quarried in the west of England and used for buildings, paving and monuments.

MORNING PRAYER *see* MATTINS

MORROW MASS The early morning mass celebrated between TERCE and CHAPTER (*see* HORARIUM). A chapel at Newland in the Forest of Dean, Gloucestershire, was founded in the fifteenth century for a priest who was required to say Morrow Mass twice a week for the local miners before they began their long and dangerous day underground.

MORTAR AND CEMENT *see* MASONRY

MORTHEAD A death's head, a symbol of mortality and the transient nature of life, either painted (as in HATCHMENTS) or sculpted in (e.g.) the form of a skull (*see* MEMENTO MORI).

MORTMAIN Mortmain means, literally, 'dead hand' and, in the present context, it is the hand of the Church. Land which was granted by laymen to ecclesiastical bodies such as monastic foundations became free of escheats and reliefs, thereby reducing the revenues of the manorial lord. (Escheated estates were those that reverted to a lord when a tenant died without heirs or committed a felony which incurred the forfeiture of his estate.) Various medieval Statutes of Mortmain prohibited the transfer of land without a lord's consent and restricted the ability of the Church to acquire property in this way.

MORTUARY CHESTS At Winchester Cathedral Priory, a series of Renaissance chests containing the bones of pre-Conquest monarchs and bishops, was placed on the screens between the presbytery and ambulatory by Bishop Richard Fox (1501–28), who was responsible for rebuilding the presbytery aisles in the late 1520s. The bones were originally brought into the cathedral from the Old Minster site in 1158 by Henry of Blois (*c.* 1100–71), bishop of Winchester and grandson of William the Conqueror. One of the four chests contains the remains of King Canute while two others are later replicas.

MOS TUTONICUS The separation, by dismemberment and boiling, of bodily fat and bones in order that the skeleton of a deceased person might be returned home for interment (e.g. from the Crusades) while the remainder of the corpse was buried at the place of death. At the end of the thirteenth century, Pope Boniface VIII (*c.* 1234–1303) attempted to prohibit the practice because the chapels of churches were sometimes used as 'appropriate kitchens' for this purpose. The body of Henry V (1387–1422) was dismembered, boiled and well spiced before it was returned from the castle of Bois de Vincennes (on the outskirts of Paris) for burial in Westminster Abbey. *See also* HEART BURIAL

MOTET A form of unaccompanied polyphonal chant which superseded the CONDUCTUS, although both were in use from the thirteenth century to the

One of four surviving mortuary chests at Winchester Cathedral. (© John Crook/info@john-crook.com)

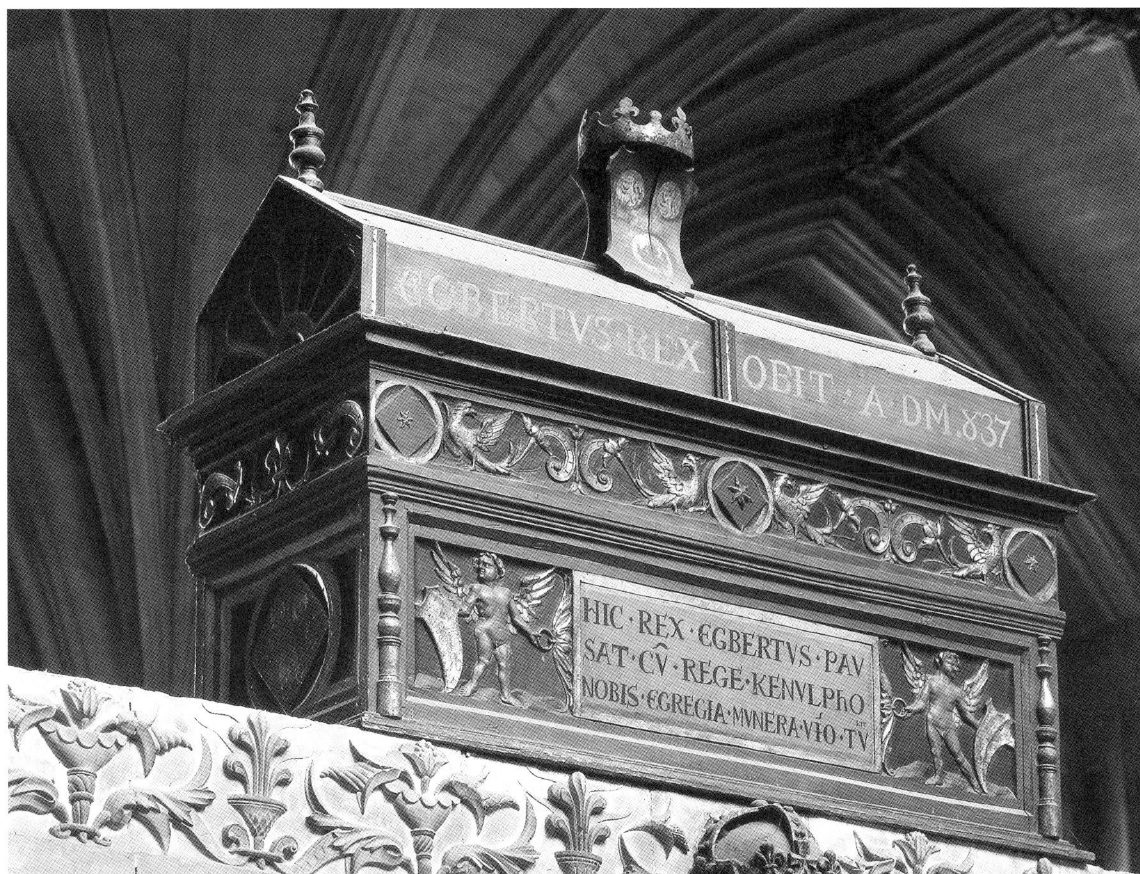

early sixteenth century. The motet was not a setting of any part of the ordinary of the MASS but was the equivalent of what (in the Protestant Church) is now called an ANTHEM. Motets (*sanctiones sacrae*) were introduced into the service at the OFFERTORY, the ELEVATION of the Host and during processions and other ceremonies for which the LITURGY did not prescribe any other text to be sung. The motet reached its apotheosis at the end of the sixteenth century in the works of Giovanni Palestrina (*c.* 1525–94), William Byrd (1542–1623) and others.
See also CHURCH MUSIC *and* PLAINSONG

MOULDING A modelled surface to (e.g.) an arch, panel, capital or entablature, which may be purely decorative, intended to define or accentuate the architectural character of a building, or designed to protect a vertical surface by projecting outwards in order to deflect rain and snow, as in (e.g.) a CORNICE or hood-mould. In some instances (notably in MEDIEVAL ARCHITECTURE) mouldings are both functional and decorative and may be carved ornamentally and/or painted. In most cases, mouldings are characteristic of certain periods of building and are useful when attempting to identify a particular architectural style.

MOVABLE FEASTS Annual ecclesiastical festivals that do not occur on a fixed day in the secular calendar.

MULLIONS Vertical bars dividing the lights of a window.
See also GLAZING BARS, TRANSOMS *and* WINDOWS

MULTIFOIL Composed of a number of FOILS e.g. the head of a traceried window light.

MUNIMENT ROOM A muniment was a title deed, documentary evidence of a right or privilege, although the term has come to include other archival material that requires safe-keeping. Religious communities accumulated numerous legal documents and these were usually stored in a muniment room. That at Fountains Abbey was vaulted, with four bays, similar to the monks' warming house (*see* CALEFACTORIUM) on the ground floor below, and was designed with security in mind. It was approached from the DAY STAIR by a short vaulted passage with two doors, its windows had iron bars, and its (third) inner door was locked with a draw-bar buried in the masonry. Because of its location above the warming house the muniment room remained at a constant temperature and its valuable contents were protected from fire by stone-vaulted ceilings above and below. Fountains Abbey had more than 3,500 title deeds relating to its extensive estates. Furthermore, the abbeys were regularly used by patrons, corrodians and local magnates as depositories for their legal documents, which would also have been kept in the muniment room. In the sixteenth century a similar room at nearby Rievaulx Abbey was described as the 'howse of euidence'.
See also SACRISTY *and* TREASURY

MUNTIN A vertical framing piece between door panels, openings (*lights*) in screens etc. Not to be confused with a window MULLION.
See also BRACE, LEDGE, RAIL *and* STILE

MURAL PAINTING *see* WALL PAINTINGS

MURAL TABLET *see* TABLET *and* WALL MONUMENTS

MUSIC, CHURCH *see* AMPLIFIERS, ANGLICAN CHANT, ANTHEM, ANTIPHON, ANTIPHONARIUM, BELLS, CANTICLE, CANTOR, CANTORIS, CHOIR, CHURCH MUSIC, CONDUCTUS, DECANI, DIVINE OFFICE, EVENING PRAYER, GALLERY, GRADUALE, GREGORIAN CHANT (*see* PLAINSONG), HYMNARY, HYMNS, INTROIT, LAY CLERK, LITURGY, MOTET, ORGANS, PLAINSONG, PRECENTOR, PRECES, PSALMS, PSALTER, REQUIEM, RESPONSES (*see* PRECES *and* VERSICLES), STALLS, SUCCENTOR *and* VERSICLES

MUSTARDIUS *see* SALTER

NAPERY *see* LARDER

NARTHEX In early churches, a vestibule that extended transversely across the western end of the building, separated from the NAVE by a screen or wall. Also known as a *galilee* or *antenave*, in the Middle Ages it was often set aside for the exclusive use of women and penitents.
See also GALILEE *and* PORCHES

NATIONAL MONUMENTS RECORD (NMR) Formerly part of the Royal Commission on the Historical Monuments of England, the National Monuments Record is now run by English Heritage. It is England's national archive of heritage information and contains over twelve million items covering architecture, archaeology, aerial photographs and maritime sites in England. The NMR collections include three million photographs of buildings; almost total coverage of the country in aerial photographs; data on most known archaeological sites; textual records for buildings, including the Listed Buildings Information service; 50,000 measured drawings; and an extensive reference library. The NMR offers a wide range of services that are freely accessible to the public. There are research rooms and other facilities at Swindon and London.
For address *see* APPENDIX II.

NATURAL LEAF ORNAMENT Architectural ornament characteristic of the late thirteenth and fourteenth centuries, particularly in the treatment of capitals (*see* CAPITAL). Unlike earlier STIFF LEAF ORNAMENT, the carved foliage of ivy, vine, oak, rose and other plants is characterised by its naturalness and rich, undulating form.
See also MEDIEVAL ARCHITECTURE

NAVE From the Latin *navis* meaning 'ship', the nave is the main body of a church which, from the late twelfth century, was usually separated from the CHANCEL by a ROOD SCREEN or, in monastic churches and cathedrals, from the CHOIR by a rood screen and PULPITUM (*see also* PRESBYTERY).

In the pre-Reformation parish church, the MASS was celebrated in the *sanctum sanctorum* to the east of these screens, while sermons were preached in the nave and parishioners gathered there for worship, assisted in their supplications by the terrifying images of the Doom and other salutary WALL PAINTINGS. Most medieval congregations stood in the body of the nave, although a stone ledge was sometimes provided so that the elderly and infirm could 'go to the wall' to rest (*see also* BENCHES). Some naves were hardly large enough to accommodate more than a few people: at St Edwold at Stockwood in Dorset, for example, where the tiny nave measures just 6m by 3.6m (20ft by 12ft). When of sufficient size, the nave of a parish church also performed a variety of other functions: it was a venue for guild plays and processions, for parochial assemblies and the church ales which the Puritans found so distasteful, and might even be used for transacting business.

Many naves were extended laterally by the addition of an AISLE or aisles, and sometimes vertically by the raising of a CLERESTORY, many of which date from the fifteenth century. Several churches (known as *hall churches*) have aisles that are as large as the nave itself: the collegiate church of St Mary at Warwick, for example, much of which was rebuilt (by William Wilson) following a fire in 1694. At Leominster Priory in Herefordshire there are three 'naves': to the north is the old monastic church with a fine Norman ARCADE, in the centre is the nave of the thirteenth-century parish church and to the south a large fourteenth-century aisle embellished with superb Decorated ornament. At Milton Abbey in Dorset, the projected nave

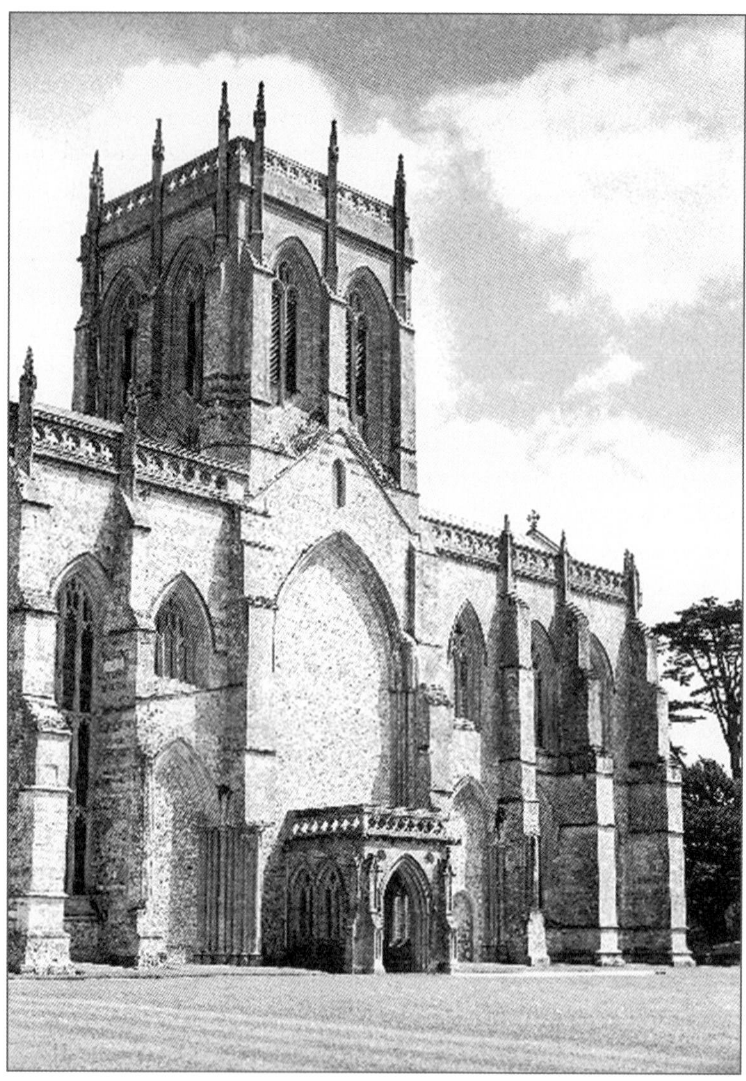

Milton Abbey, Dorset, where the building of the nave was abandoned, possibly as a consequence of the Black Death.

was never built – possibly as a consequence of the PLAGUE which reached Milton in 1349 – and the great fourteenth- and fifteenth-century church (now a daughter church of nearby Milton Abbas) consists only of choir, TRANSEPT and tower. At Sherborne, also in Dorset, a second nave was added at the west end of the abbey in the late fourteenth century to provide a large chapel-of-ease (All Hallows) for the townspeople. This was demolished at the DISSOLUTION OF THE MONASTERIES, when the abbey church was acquired for parochial use, although the springing for the arches is still visible in the masonry of the west wall of the abbey nave (*see* PARISH CHURCH). Elsewhere, several former monastic churches were found to be much too large for parochial purposes and their naves were either truncated or demolished, as at Abbey Dore in Herefordshire where nothing remains of the once magnificent early thirteenth-century nave (76m (250ft) long), which fell into disrepair following the abbey's suppression in 1536. Fortunately the choir and transept were restored in the early seventeenth century and are now a spacious, and evocative, parish church. At Upholland in Lancashire, the chancel of the former Benedictine priory now forms the nave of the parish church, while Carlisle in Cumbria must surely be one of the most extraordinary cathedral churches in England. Built by a priory of Augustinian Canons in the early twelfth century, the church had a fine Romanesque nave of seven bays, five of which formed the parish church of St Mary. By the late fourteenth century, the choir and presbytery had been extended from two bays to eight, creating a dignified and beautifully proportioned space (with one of the finest Decorated windows in England) that now accommodates both the choir and the cathedral's congregation. During the Commonwealth (*c.* 1649) the five western bays of the nave were ruthlessly demolished by the parliamentarians, who needed the stone for their fortifications, and all that can be seen today of the original church are the two eastern bays of the nave, the south transept and part of the crossing. The church today is, therefore, completely reversed: the nave having been reduced to two bays and the choir and presbytery increased to eight.

The BENEDICTINES and AUGUSTINIANS generally admitted the laity to the naves of their churches and these sometimes became parish churches, as at Brecon Priory (now the Cathedral), Binham and Wyndonham priories in Norfolk, Shrewsbury Abbey in Shropshire and Tynemouth Priory in Northumberland. In these larger churches a NAVE ALTAR (the *Jesus altar*) was located in front of the rood screen, one bay west of the pulpitum (*see also* RETRO-CHOIR). In some cases parishioners exchanged their rights in the nave for use of the chancel and transept: at Boxgrove Priory in Sussex and the Augustinian priory of St Bartholomew, Smithfield, for example. This willingness to share their churches with a wider lay community explains the survival of so many Benedictine and Augustinian churches, but parochial rights were rarely granted in the churches of Cistercian, Cluniac or Pre-monstratensian foundations, hence their almost universal destruction following the Dissolution of the Monasteries. In Cistercian churches the nave was the church of the LAY BROTHERS (*conversi*). It had its own nave altar and was separated from the rest of the building by stone screens, both at the eastern termination and between the pillars of the nave arcades. However, it should not be forgotten that where a church served a religious community the principal purpose of its nave was to provide an imposing and dignified space for the frequent PROCESSIONS that emphasised the order and discipline of the community and symbolised its corporate commitment to follow Christ. The churches of the FRIARS were entirely different: their naves were designed for preaching, and to accommodate large congregations, and were therefore provided with wide aisles and broad arcades.

The naves of many of the great medieval abbeys, priories and cathedrals are extraordinarily long: 76m (250ft) at Norwich, for example, and 87m (285ft) at St Albans. They are also very tall, with each BAY consisting of three vertical stages (ARCADE, tribune or TRIFORIUM and CLERESTORY) so that as much light as possible could be admitted to the interior, while complex VAULTING was required to support (and distribute) the weight of the roof. The nave at Westminster Abbey (begun by Henry III in the thirteenth century but not completed until after 1375) is 31.4m (103ft) high and 11.75m (39ft) wide. It is the tallest vault in Britain and its extraordinary French Gothic proportions inspire that feeling of spiritual elation which is the essence of medieval architecture. The nave of York Minster is the widest in England and, after Westminster Abbey, the tallest.

In theory, there was no structural need for the nave to be any longer than the transepts and yet, in English churches, it was almost invariably so.

The proliferation of secondary altars may be one explanation: several thirteenth- and fourteenth-century altarpieces have survived on the north side of the nave at St Albans, for example. And during the medieval period the nave was often used for secular and judicial purposes, whereas on the Continent such business appears to have been conducted in a NARTHEX or atrium. However, the long naves of English cathedrals are best accounted for by the fact that, where both monks (or canons) and laity had to be provided for, the church was effectively divided in two: the monks occupying the east end (the presbytery, choir and transept – and sometimes, as at Norwich and Westminster, the first two or three bays of the nave) and the laity the nave itself where they were provided with their own altar (the *nave altar*) in front of the rood screen. In Cistercian abbeys it was the numerous conversi who occupied the nave and it was there that they observed a modified office.
See also BAPTISTERY *and* CROSSING

NAVE ALTAR (*also* JESUS ALTAR) An altar set up at the east end of the NAVE in front of the ROOD SCREEN. Originally, this was the *Jesus altar* at which the Cistercian lay brethren worshipped or, in Benedictine and Augustinian churches, the laity. The practice of worshipping at a nave altar has come to be associated with recent liturgical changes, but there are numerous precedents, both medieval and post-Reformation (*see* ALTARS).

NECESSARIUM *see* DORTER *and* REREDORTER

NECROLOGY A list of the dead to be remembered in the prayers of a religious house. A general necrology was a similar list used in groups of houses within a particular order.
See also MARTYROLOGY

Opposite: *The nave at Ely Cathedral, looking west.*

NEW FOUNDATION *see* CATHEDRALS

NICENE CREED A creed is a statement of faith, a formal summary of Christian beliefs or principles. There are two Nicene creeds, the longer of which is found in the THIRTY-NINE ARTICLES and is used in the EUCHARIST.

NICHE A shallow recess in a wall.
see AUMBRY, BREAD OVEN, CREDENCE, FENESTELLA, HOLY WATER STOUP, PISCINA, SEDILIA *and* SQUINT

NIGHT OFFICE *see* MATTINS *and* NOCTURN

NIGHT STAIR In MONASTIC BUILDINGS, a staircase providing direct access from the DORTER to the church (usually via the south TRANSEPT) for those attending the Night Office (*see* MATTINS *and* NOCTURN). Few night stairs have survived, although there is a splendid example at Hexham Priory in Northumberland. Occasionally, where space was restricted the night stair was reduced to a spiral staircase, as at Ewenny Priory in Glamorgan, where the nave has survived as a parish church. Unusually, there was no night stair at Gloucester and the monks descended to the cloister by means of a dormitory stair in the east cloister alley.

NINE LESSONS AND CAROLS, FESTIVAL OF The annual Festival of Nine Lessons and Carols in the chapel of King's College, Cambridge, was instituted almost by chance in 1918 when Eric Milner-White, chaplain and later dean of the college, returned from the First World War and decided to mark Christmas Eve with a service modelled on one devised in 1880 by the bishop of Truro. The poignancy of his reference to 'all those who rejoice with us, but upon another shore, and in a greater light' remains a powerful evocation of

The night stair at Hexham Priory, Northumberland. (Courtesy of Derry Brabbs/www.derrybrabbs.com)

the war that had just ended. In 1928 the BBC broadcast the King's College service and it rapidly became a national institution, followed by cathedrals and college chapels throughout the land.
See also CHURCH MUSIC

NOCTURN An early name for the office of MATTINS, derived from the units (*nocturns*) of which it was composed and which varied in number according to the significance of the day in the ecclesiastical calendar.
See also HOURS (CANONICAL) *and* HORARIUM

NONE A short office, the last of the Little Hours of the BREVIARY. The ninth hour of prayer (about 3 p.m.) consisting of a hymn followed by psalmody, a short reading, response and closing prayer.
See also HOURS (CANONICAL), HORARIUM, TERCE *and* SEXT

NORMAN ARCH *see* ARCH *and* MEDIEVAL ARCHITECTURE

NORMAN ARCHITECTURE *see* MEDIEVAL ARCHITECTURE

NORMANS, THE

> You may see in every village, town and city churches and monasteries rising in a new style of architecture.
>
> *William of Malmesbury*

The Norman Conquest of 1066 had a dramatic impact on religious life in England. William of Normandy was a pious and austere man, an enthusiast for ecclesiastical reform and a patron of a growing number of intellectually brilliant Norman monasteries. The invaders were fierce warriors, able administrators and the greatest builders of their time, their immense churches and castles symbolising the authority and permanence of conquest. But under William's supervision the insular, conservative and traditionalist ANGLO-SAXON CHURCH was reformed rather than oppressed, a policy that was facilitated by the appointment of Norman churchmen to vacant abbacies (a process begun by Edward the Confessor (*c.* 1003–66) on his return from exile in 1042) and, in particular, by the installation of an eminent European Benedictine as their head. In August 1070 the Saxon Archbishop Stigand was deposed and replaced as archbishop of Canterbury by Lanfranc (*c.* 1005–89), formerly prior of Bec in Normandy and abbot of Duke William's own foundation at Caen, a man with a formidable reputation as a scholar, and the king's appointee.

Inspired by the vigorous Norman monasticism of Caen and Bec, Lanfranc had little understanding of Anglo-Saxon spirituality and even less sympathy for its saints: 'These Englishmen among whom we are living have set up for themselves certain saints whom they revere. But sometimes when I turn over in my mind their own accounts of who they were, I cannot help having doubts about the quality of their sanctity.' Under his leadership local saints were removed from the liturgical calendar, their shrines were dismantled and their mean churches were replaced by more commanding stone buildings. Until his death in 1089 he relentlessly pursued a policy of standardisation, bringing English liturgical practice and monastic customs and observances into line with those of France and Italy. 'For the Normans, every emphasis was on the virtues of the new' (Platt). Inevitably, such a policy was bitterly opposed by many English brethren: at Glastonbury, for example, the newly imposed Abbot Thurstan was faced with open rebellion when he attempted to introduce a revised liturgy, so much so that he was obliged to resort to armed force:

> There was a disgraceful contention between the abbot of Glastonbury and

> his monks; so that after altercation they came to blows. The monks being driven into church bewailed their miseries at the holy altar; but the soldiers, rushing in, slew two of them, wounded fourteen and drove away the rest.
>
> *William of Malmesbury*

Not all Norman churchmen were as brutal as Thurstan. Indeed, the century that followed the Norman Conquest was a time of considerable achievement for the Benedictine Order in England (*see* BENEDICTINES). For the most part, the churchmen who were brought over from Normandy were a distinguished and dedicated group: Abbot Serlo (1072–1104), for example, transformed the monastic community at Gloucester, increasing the number of monks from ten in 1072 to one hundred in 1104, while a series of notable abbots at St Albans established the abbey's reputation for the quality of its liturgy and its artistic and intellectual excellence. While in numerous small, enclosed communities the Anglo-Norman divide was often painfully apparent, the two nations, living together under one rule, eventually came to terms, their new abbey churches and cathedrals, built by English craftsmen in a style imported from continental Europe, providing a permanent record of that sometimes tenuous reconciliation.

In 1066 there were some forty-eight monastic houses still functioning in England, all of them south of a line from the Humber to the Severn. After the Conquest the Normans rapidly founded new monasteries (Battle, Chester, Colchester, Shrewsbury and York were all founded in the late eleventh century), created dependencies of Norman houses (*see* ALIEN PRIORY), and revived a number of moribund northern foundations such as Whitby, Jarrow and Wearmouth. But it was William's predecessor, Edward the Confessor, who introduced into England the architectural style that we now describe as Romanesque (*see* MEDIEVAL ARCHITECTURE). When Edward came to build his great abbey church at Westminster he built it in the style and on the scale of the churches that were being built in Normandy – it was said to be very similar in design to the abbey church of Jumièges, which was being constructed at the time of his return from exile in 1042. The Confessor's new church was consecrated on 28 December 1065 – just one week before his death. Soon after the Conquest, in the 1070s and 1080s, cathedrals and abbey churches of similar monumental proportions were begun at Canterbury, Ely, Lincoln, St Albans, Winchester and Worcester. These were followed, before the end of the century, by others at Durham, Gloucester, Norwich, Tewkesbury and elsewhere. Buildings on such a scale must have overwhelmed the native population, establishing once and for all the durability of Norman rule. They were, literally, awesome – confirming incontrovertibly that the Church was intended to be a powerful engine of state control.

In 1070 the abbey of Peterborough was given to Turold, a monk of Fécamp who enjoyed a redoubtable, war-like reputation. When he arrived with a hundred men-at-arms at his back, the abbey's tenants, led by Hereward 'the Wake', rebelled rather than relinquish their lands to the Normans. Abbot Turold's retinue was by no means exceptional. The bishops and major abbots of Anglo-Norman England were in every sense the equal of their lay counterparts – men of considerable wealth and status, with large households of dependants to maintain. In return for service to a spiritual lord, laymen could be given knights' fees (Abbot Turold made substantial grants of land in knight service to two of his nephews), while clerks could be appointed to archdeaconries, an office only recently introduced from Normandy and one that brought with it substantial financial benefits. Furthermore, when the Norman churchmen who were promoted to oversee the vast dioceses of Anglo-

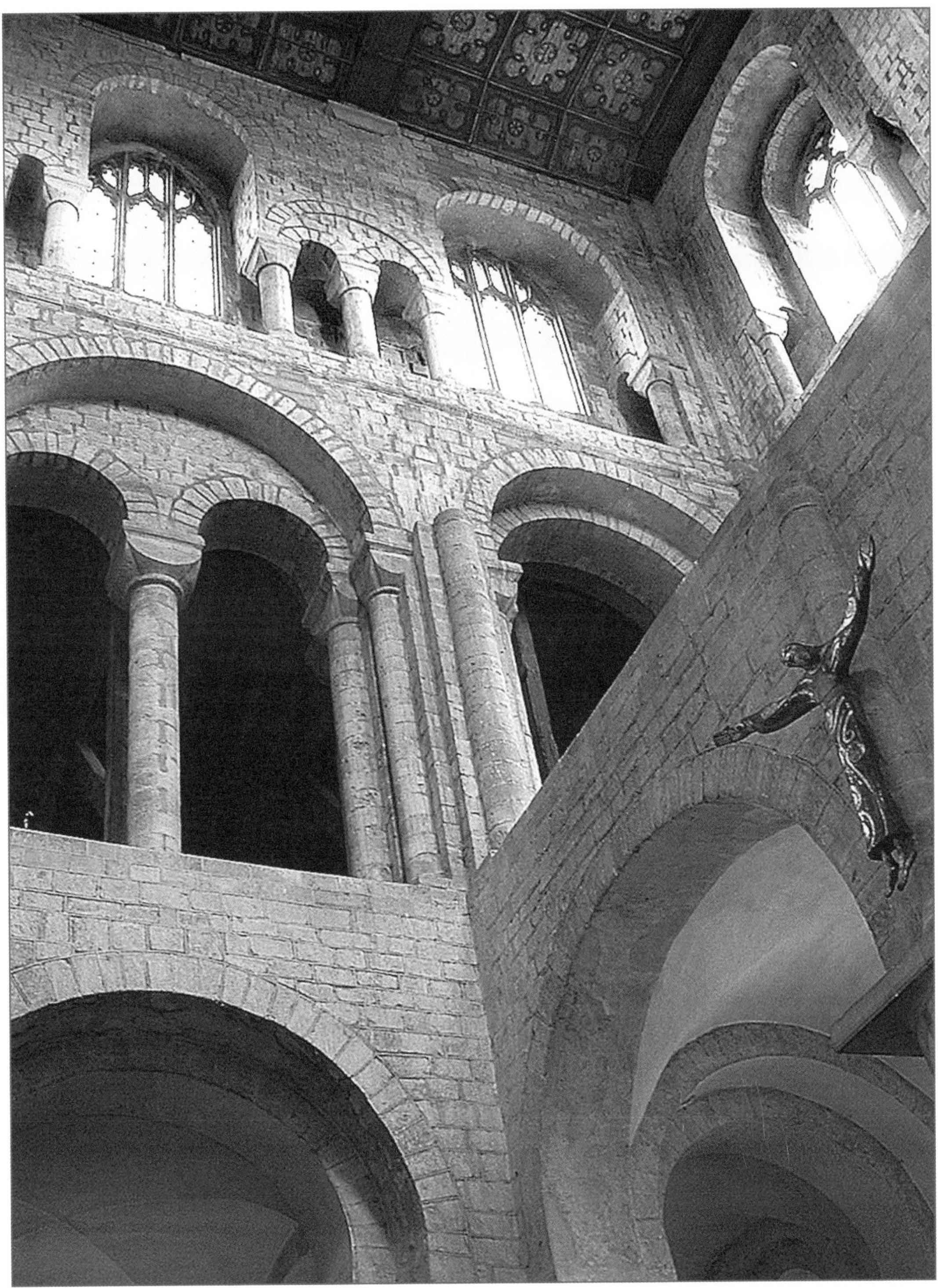

The massive Norman north transept at Winchester Cathedral.

Saxon England met in CONVOCATION in 1075, they determined to apply CANON LAW to their own advantage. This stated that episcopal sees in small townships should be discouraged, and consequently the see of Sherborne was moved to Salisbury (Old Sarum), Selsey to Chichester and Lichfield to Chester – populous locations that increased significantly the bishops' income and patronage (*see* DIOCESE). In Norman England it was the king who appointed men to ecclesiastical offices and they were expected to reciprocate: they held their lands of the king and it was to the king that they owed knight service and other feudal obligations (*see* FEUDAL SYSTEM). This principle applied to those of English descent as well as to the Normans. Wulfstan, the first bishop of Worcester (1062–95) was the head of two very different households: his biographer records that he dined sometimes with his monks and at others with his knights. However, such an arrangement did not sit comfortably with canon law. King William and his sons assumed that they should appoint the bishops who were their vassals and, in many cases, served as their officials in government. But the practice was severely condemned by many churchmen, as was *lay investiture* by which the king performed the symbolic granting of a bishop's ring and staff on his appointment. Eventually, in 1106, a compromise was reached: in England new bishops first did homage to the king for their lands and then received their ring and staff of office from their fellow bishops.

In the years that followed the Conquest it was Normandy that provided the impetus for monastic reform. But in the later eleventh and early twelfth centuries, as Anglo-Norman society became more diverse and sophisticated, new influences began to be felt. The monopoly of the Benedictine Order was broken by the arrival in England of the CLUNIACS (at Lewes in 1077), the Augustinian (or Austin) Canons Regular (at Colchester Priory in 1093) (*see* AUGUSTINIANS) and, ultimately, the CISTERCIANS (at Waverley, Surrey in 1128).

NOTARY A professional scribe. A notary authenticated each document for which he was responsible by drawing a distinctive notarial symbol at its foot.

NOVICE When a POSTULANT was admitted to a religious house he or she was required to serve a probationary period as a novice. This usually lasted six to seven years, during which time the novice learned the liturgical USES of the house, studied grammar, read the Bible and commentaries and perhaps learned illumination, but otherwise received no specific training. In some houses the novices were provided with their own communal accommodation, where they might 'meditate, eat and sleep'. In most houses there would be no more than six novices at any time. They wore the HABIT of the order and followed its RULE (with some concessions to their age) and were able to leave at any time without penalty. All members of the community were expected to advise or reprove the novices, although it was the *Novice Master* who was responsible for their material, intellectual, social and spiritual needs. Novices were required to leave CHAPTER immediately after the sermon, to make frequent CONFESSION and to spend even more time in the abbey church than the monks. They were educated in the monastic school (usually in the west alley of the cloister) until they had acquired a basic understanding of the services and scriptures and of the minutiae of monastic behaviour (including, for example, how to sit correctly in the latrine). This was followed by more advanced teaching from the Novice Master or tutor, while those who showed particular promise 'and had a pregnant wit withal' might be sent to study advanced divinity at a university. At Tewkesbury and Durham, the novices were provided with their own garden and bowling green, while graffiti evidence has survived in the cloisters of Canterbury, Gloucester, Norwich and Westminster of board games such as 'fox and geese' and 'nine holes'. Having served his period of training, 'if the brethren approve of his behaviour

and he of their way of life', the novice would appear before Chapter and, if elected, would read his formal profession 'before the High Altar in the church in the presence of all the community' (*see* VOWS). There followed a solemn blessing of the COWL and investment by the superior: 'May the lord clothe thee with the new man who is created according to God in righteousness and the sanctity of truth.'
See also OBLATE *and* RECRUITMENT

NOVICE MASTER *see* NOVICE

NOVITIATE *see* NOVICE

NUNC DIMITTIS The *Song of Simeon* (Luke 2: 29–32): 'Lord, now lettest thou thy servant depart in peace . . .'. Part of the office of COMPLINE, from which it passed into the service of Evensong in the *Book of Common Prayer*, where it follows the second (New Testament) lesson (*see* EVENING PRAYER). In Compline, the Nunc dimittis has its traditional PLAINSONG, but in the Anglican service it is usually spoken responsively or sung to an ANGLICAN CHANT. Together with the MAGNIFICAT, the Nunc dimittis has been set to music by numerous composers and is sung in this form in most cathedrals and collegiate chapels.

NUNS AND NUNNERIES A nun is a member of a religious order of women. In the medieval period, a nun could live within a community or (in exceptional cases) as an anchoress (*see* ANCHORITE). Communities of nuns which, in most respects, were similar to monasteries (*see* MONASTERY), are known as nunneries (a *convent* is a religious community of either sex). In the Middle Ages, about 20 per cent of religious were women. Nunneries increased in number from twelve in 1066 to 152 in the early fourteenth century, while at the DISSOLUTION OF THE MONASTERIES there were some 136 nunneries and two thousand nuns (also known as *monachae*, *nonnae* or *sanctimoniales*), almost half the nunneries containing fewer than ten sisters and only four having more than thirty. When compared with the monasteries there was a similar contrast: only seven nunneries had annual incomes that exceeded £450, while at least half the remainder received less than £100. This largely reflected their origins and location: of the seven wealthiest, five were BENEDICTINE houses in the former Anglo-Saxon kingdom of Wessex, while the other two were royal foundations (Dartford and Syon).

With the exception of the Gilbertines (*see* GILBERTINE ORDER) and lay sisters, nuns appear to have been recruited almost exclusively from the upper classes of medieval society. Several nunneries established 'finishing schools' for young ladies of gentle birth, while others acquired reputations as refuges for widows of noble rank and the relicts of traitors whose titles, lands and possessions had been forfeited. A nun's family was usually expected to pay a dowry of between £12 and £20 at her PROFESSION. Most nuns were, of course, *illitteratae*: having no Latin they were obliged to recite the offices by rote. Even so, the spiritual and liturgical life in nunneries was not far removed from that of men of the same order, although much time must have been passed in reading, embroidery, clothes-making and in the teaching of young children in the conventual schools. In the context of the times, the nunneries were liberating for women, for whom they provided spiritual fulfilment.

Because nuns could not provide priests from their number, chaplains had to be appointed, either from the ordained brethren of a DOUBLE MONASTERY or by means of a prebend (*see* PREBENDARY) or CHANTRY, in order to administer the sacraments and to provide religious instruction. The Church's deep unease concerning female sexuality resulted, initially, in a strict prohibition against going beyond the convent walls and of any but the most limited visits of laity from outside. A *custos* or lay steward was usually engaged to administer a convent's lands, while men were employed as servants to undertake heavy manual work.

Place-names can sometimes provide clues to the location of former nunneries: at White Ladies Aston, Worcestershire, for example (*see* PLACE-NAMES).
See also CANONESS REGULAR, BENEDICTINE NUNS, BRIGITTINES, CISTERCIANS, MAGDALENES, MINORESS *and* VOWESS.

O

OBEDIENTIARIES The officers of a religious house who exercised departmental responsibilities ('obediences'). Most obedientiaries managed their own revenues and maintained accounts which were presented at quarterly meetings of CHAPTER. Their terms of office ended with the appointment of a new SUPERIOR, to whom they surrendered their keys. Some offices were particularly demanding and in such cases the RULE was often relaxed: obedientiaries might be excused certain services and permitted to leave the monastery precinct, for example. Typically, at the Austin priory of Barnwell, Cambridgeshire, there were a prior, SUB-PRIOR, third prior, PRECENTOR, SUCCENTOR, SACRIST, SUB-SACRIST, CELLARER, SUB-CELLARER, granger, receiver, fraterer (*see* FRATER), KITCHENER, CHAMBERLAIN, HOSTELLER, INFIRMARIAN and ALMONER in addition to a number of minor or rotational offices. At Durham and Canterbury there were twenty-five major officials, some with subordinates; at Westminster 60 per cent of the monks held office of some kind. It is likely, therefore, that in smaller houses the majority of the brethren would have been allotted special responsibilities and that individual monks would have held a number of offices.

The duties of the various obedientiaries were usually very precise: in the tailor's shop, for example, the sub-almoner was responsible for providing the needles and the sub-chamberlain the thread; while the SACRIST was required to provide the dorter bell and the chamberlain the cord with which to ring it. On the other hand, other duties were allocated on a weekly or day-to-day basis (*see* TABULA)
See also FINANCE *and* MONASTICISM

OBELISK A tapering, usually four-sided .stone pillar, named *obeliskos* ('little spit') by the Greeks after the copper-capped pyramidions of Egyptian pillars. These belonged to the Sun God and were placed before Egyptian temples, where they reflected the rays of the sun. Many were carried off as trophies and inspired a variety of similar forms throughout the ancient world, eventually arriving in Britain in the Classical architecture and church MONUMENTS of the eighteenth century.

OBIT The office for a dead person (*see* CHANTRY). An anniversary or other commemoration of a death. An *obituary* was originally a monastic register of deaths, but has come to mean a biographical account of a deceased person or a published record of his death. An *obit roll*, on which were inscribed the names of deceased brethren, was conveyed to sister houses by a messenger described as a ROTULARIUS (or BREVIATOR, if a lay servant).

OBITUARY *see* OBIT

OBLATE From the mid-sixth century, the Church permitted parents to dedicate their infants to a religious life by placing them in a monastic community where they were cared for until the age of 15. These *pueri* or *infantes* were taught reading and singing, were excused the night office and had their own CHAPTER. The child was presented as an oblation (an offering) at the offertory in the mass, a petition (promising stability, conversion and obedience) being bound in its right hand by an altar cloth. Once the dedication was made, there could be no release – even when the young person reached maturity. The practice continued until the end of the twelfth century. Later, the term came to be applied to laity who lived in a monastery but who did not take full religious vows.

OBLATIONS (i) The wafers of unleavened bread offered for consecration in the EUCHARIST.
(ii) An offering presented at the mass for the benefit of the clergy, the poor, the infirm, etc.

OBSERVANCES A synonym for the regulations or customs of a religious house (*see* CUSTOMARY *and* RULE).

OBSERVANTS *or* OBSERVANTINES Those members of the Franciscan order who claimed to 'observe' the primitive rule of St Francis as confirmed in 1223 (*see* FRIARS).

OBTUSE ARCH *see* ARCH

OCCASIONAL OFFICES Those offices in the *Book of Common Prayer* which are used only as occasion requires e.g. Baptism and Visitation of the Sick.

OCTEOCHOS *see* YEAR, LITURGICAL

OCULUS (*also* OEIL-DE-BOEUF) From the Latin meaning 'an eye', a round or oval window usually with radiating glazing bars. Not to be confused with a ROSE WINDOW or wheel window.

OECUMENICAL An oecumenical council is a worldwide assembly of bishops and other ecclesiastical representatives whose decisions are binding on all Christians. According to CANON LAW, an oecumenical council of the Roman Catholic Church may be convened only by a pope and its decrees promulgated by the HOLY SEE. They are thereby infallible.

OEIL-DE-BOEUF *see* OCULUS

OFFERTORY (i) The worshippers' offering of bread and wine to be consecrated at the EUCHARIST. This was often commuted to an offering of money.
(ii) The offering of gifts (usually money) during a service.

OFFICE, DIVINE *see* DIVINE OFFICE

OFFICIALS, MONASTIC *see* OBEDIENTIARIES

OGEE A double continuous curve (like an 'S'). An *ogee arch* has two ogee curves meeting at the apex (*see* ARCH).

OGIVE (i) A diagonal ogee-shaped rib in a vault (*see* VAULTING).
(ii) An OGEE arch above a door or window opening.
(iii) An ogival compartment is a space delineated by a border consisting of two ogees.

OLD FOUNDATION *see* CATHEDRALS

'OLD-STYLE' Usually a reference to the CALENDAR prior to its reform in 1752, by which New Year was defined as 1 January and the English calendar was brought into line with those of European countries by the omission of the eleven days 2 to 14 September 1752.

OPUS DEI *see* DIVINE OFFICE

OR *see* COLOURS (HERALDIC)

ORDERS *see* MONASTIC, CANONICAL AND MENDICANT ORDERS

ORDINAL (i) A medieval manual intended to acquaint a priest with the offices to be recited in accordance with the variations of the ecclesiastical year.
(ii) In the Church of England, 'The Form and Manner of Making, Ordaining and Consecrating of Bishops, Priests and Deacons' (*see* ORDINATION).

ORDINARY (i) An ecclesiastical superior, e.g. a bishop.
(ii) Those parts of the MASS that do not vary according to the ecclesiastical calendar.
(iii) In HERALDRY, an ordinary is one of a number of bold rectilinear charges, also known as the Honourable Ordinaries.
(iv) An ordinary of arms is a reference book which lists the heraldic descriptions (*blazons*) of shields of arms alphabetically by the charges they contain. Proficiency in the use of blazon is essential if an ordinary is to be used to identify arms. The best known ordinary is J.W. Papworth's *Ordinary of British Armorials*, first published in 1874 and reprinted in 1977 (pub. Five Barrows).

ORDINATION Admission to the Christian ministry through the ceremonial laying-on of hands by a bishop. References to ordination and to prayer and the laying-on of hands occur in the New Testament (e.g. Acts 6: 1–6 and 13: 1–3). In the early Church, a distinction was made between the 'missionary' ministry of prophets and apostles and the 'settled' ministry of bishops, presbyters and deacons. By the mid-thirteenth century, the ministry was arranged in orders which, by the end of the medieval period, were generally accepted to be seven in number, a distinction being made between the three MAJOR ORDERS of bishop, priest and deacon and the four MINOR ORDERS of acolyte, exorcist, lector and doorkeeper. (Bishops and priests were sometimes considered to be a single major order to which were added deacons and sub-deacons.) Ordination has always taken place in the context of the EUCHARIST and may be performed only by a duly consecrated bishop. The medieval form of ordination (which usually took place on one of the Ember Days) was extremely elaborate, while that of the Anglican Church was first set out in 'The Form and Manner of Making, Ordaining and Consecrating of Bishops, Priests and Deacons' (the *Ordinal*) of 1550, which was based on the (medieval) rites of the *Sarum Pontifical*. This was followed by further ordinals in 1552, 1559 and 1662, none of which makes provision for the minor orders. In the consecration of bishops, the medieval practices of anointing, of the putting on of gloves and of the receiving of a ring and MITRE were omitted, while in the Ordering of Priests the Tradition of the Instruments (the solemn delivery of the paten and chalice) was replaced in 1552 by the presentation of a Bible (deacons receive a book of the Gospels). In all the ordinals, the formula which accompanies the laying-on of hands includes the words 'Receive the Holy Ghost' and 'Whose sins thou dost forgive, they are forgiven; whose sins though dost retain, they are retained.'
See also CLERGY (CHURCH OF ENGLAND)

ORGAN LOFT *see* CONSOLE

ORGAN SCREEN A stone or timber screen between the choir and the nave on which is located an organ. This could be a medieval stone PULPITUM or a later timber or stone CHOIR SCREEN specially designed and built for the purpose.

ORGANS The old Scottish name for an organ, 'kist o' whistles' (chest of whistles), describes very accurately the fundamental construction of all organs before the introduction of the pipeless electric version in the 1930s. Pipes of varying lengths are placed upon a box (*wind chest*). When in rows (*ranks*), each row of pipes possesses a special tone-character. The box is furnished with an even supply of wind from a bellows by means of *feeders* or, in modern organs, by an electrically driven rotary fan. So that all the ranks do not sound together, wooden *sliders* are made to pass beneath the mouths of the pipes, each slider controlling a single rank. Holes in the sliders correspond with the mouths of the pipes so that when the slider is pushed in, the rank is 'stopped'. Hence, the knobs which control this operation are known as *draw-stops*, or merely *stops*. (The set of pipes controlled by a draw-stop is also known as a *register*.) In modern organs the sliders are usually replaced by valves and the draw-stops by balanced slips of ivory.

In order that the pipes of a rank should not sound together, the mouth of each pipe is provided with a hinged 'lid' (*pallet*) controlled by a series of articulated rods (*trackers* and *stickers*) collectively known as the *action*. The action in a modern organ is usually controlled pneumatically (common from 1880–1930), electronically or by a combination of the two. The action is connected to a hand keyboard (*manual*) or (for certain ranks) a foot keyboard (*pedal board*). The organist therefore selects the required tone-colours by pulling out the appropriate stops, thereby placing certain ranks on 'standby'. He then depresses those keys which, either singly or in combination as chords, will open the mouths of those pipes through which he wishes the air to pass, thereby allowing them to 'speak'.

Collectively, the arrangement of keyboards and stops is known as a CONSOLE and, in larger organs, there may be several manuals, each of which controls what is effectively a separate organ. These organs are usually linked by means of *couplers*, so that two or more manuals (and the pedal organ) can be operated simultaneously from a single keyboard. The most important manual is the Great Organ, which has the solid-sounding, louder stops. The Swell Organ is enclosed in a *swell-box*, one side of which consists of movable shutters which can be opened and closed by means of a special pedal. (The swell-box principle is now applied to most manuals, usually with the exception of the Great Organ.) The Choir Manual contains a number of softer, sweet-toned stops which are ideally suited to accompaniment, while the Solo Organ contains certain stops of an orchestral quality which are most effectively used on their own, against an accompaniment on another manual. In the largest organs there may be an Echo Organ devoted to delicate stops with a 'distant' sound. The organs of most parish churches have just one or two manuals (the Great and Swell) and a pedal organ, those in cathedrals and collegiate chapels may have four or even five. While the chief stops of a manual are 2.6m (8ft) in length, the normal pitch of a pedal organ is an octave below that of the manuals and its pipes are therefore significantly longer, ranging from 4.9m (16ft) to (very rarely) 19.5m (64ft). Pipes are made of metal (usually zinc or an alloy of tin and lead), or wood, which is commonly used for the larger pipes. While most of the pipes are located within the body of the organ (*organ case*), the visible front pipes are usually arranged in groups of short pipes (*flats*) or in projecting clusters (*towers*) of longer pipes. These are often elaborately decorated with diaper patterns and arranged according to their length to form an attractive composition. Where the tin content is high, the pipes may have a mottled appearance known as *spotted metal*.

Historical Development

Of course, the instruments used in churches today are far removed from their medieval predecessors, although the fundamentals remain unchanged. An organ is recorded at Malmesbury, Wiltshire in the eighth century and, by the tenth century, 'portative organs' accompanied the singing of PLAINSONG in most monastic churches and were carried in processions. These were portable instruments consisting of a single rank of pipes and a small keyboard, and their use continued throughout the Middle Ages. *Positive organs* were those that could not be moved, the greatest of which (allowing for poetic hyperbole) being at Westminster in the tenth century. This had two manuals (played by two performers) each of twenty notes, each note having ten metal pipes, making four hundred pipes in all. It is said to have required seventy 'blowers' to operate the twenty-six bellows and the 'keys' were so heavy that they had to be depressed with the fist. A fourteenth-century document at Worcester records payments to a musician 'to thump the organs, teach the quire boys and instruct any of the monks who wishes to learn the art of organ-thumping'. Such organs merely thundered out the plainsong melodies, and so led the singing.

The organ at Chichester Cathedral was originally mounted on the choir screen but was moved to the north transept shortly before the disastrous collapse of the spire in 1861, thereby escaping serious damage. (© John Crook/info@john-crook.com)

By the end of the fifteenth century most parish churches possessed an organ and many abbey churches had several, each with a different function and, therefore, with different characteristics. At Durham, for example, there were three 'paires' of organs in the quire, one near the Great Rood (*see* ROOD SCREEN) (for the Jesus Mass) and another for public services in the GALILEE.

In the sixteenth century, the new Church of England services, although vernacular, were little different from the Roman Catholic liturgy that preceded them (*see* COMMON PRAYER, BOOK OF). Before this time there was a clear distinction between the musical customs of the major monastic and cathedral churches, which had large choirs and organs, and those of urban and rural parishes which rarely had choirs but (surprisingly) often possessed a primitive organ (*see* CHURCH MUSIC). Following the DISSOLUTION OF THE MONASTERIES several abbey or priory churches were retained as CATHEDRALS, where the elaborate type of service was perpetuated. But, even in the major churches, there was no repertory of organ music and no independent 'organ parts' in anthems or service music. The instrument simply augmented the choir voices and accompanied plainsong unisonally.

At the Reformation many organs were removed from parish churches or allowed to decay. The decline was temporarily reversed by the appointment of Archbishop William Laud (1573–1645), a high-churchman who opposed the prevailing Calvinist theology and sought to restore something of pre-Reformation liturgical practice. But his reforms were widely resented and he was impeached by the Long Parliament, imprisoned in 1644 and executed in the following year. The Puritans considered that instrumental music distracted the mind and soul from divine worship and in 1644 an Act of Parliament required the removal of organs from churches. In many areas implementation of the act was rigorous: organs were smashed and the pipes were carried off to be used for more mundane purposes. According to John Evelyn (1620–1706), London innkeepers 'translated the organs out of the churches and set them up in taverns, chanting . . . bestial bacchanalias to the tune of those instruments which were wont to assist them in the celebration of God's praises'.

The restoration of Charles II in 1660 resulted in a revival of the craft of organ-building and the arrival in England of several eminent organ-builders from the continent, notably Bernhard Schmidt ('Father Smith', 1630–1707) together with his two nephews from Germany, and Renatus Harris (of English parentage, 1652–1724) from France. This revival was stimulated by the rebuilding (by Christopher Wren and others) of London's churches following the Great Fire of 1666. At that time, the churches of the City of London competed with each other in the excellence of their organs, both in the tone of the instruments and in the beauty of their cases. Despite the bombing of the Second World War, many of these have survived, notably at St Clement's, Eastcheap and St Magnus, London Bridge, St Stephen's, Walbrook and St Sepulchre's, Holborn. The most important nineteenth-century organ-builders were Hill, Willis, Gray & Davison, and Walker (there is usually a name-plate on the console) and there are several examples of organ cases which were designed by eminent Victorian architects such as Bodley, Pearson, Pugin and Scott. With the exception of the organs in some London churches and a number of cathedrals and collegiate chapels, very few early organs have survived, although many rebuilt organs incorporate parts from earlier instruments.

ORIEL A curved or polysided window projecting from an upper floor. Unlike a bay window, an oriel window does not reach the ground but is either cantilevered or supported by means of a CORBEL or BRACKET.

ORIENTATION Tradition has it that medieval churches were invariably constructed with the

CHANCEL to the east for symbolic reasons: that Jerusalem is in the east, that the rising sun represents Christ, the Sun of Righteousness, and that the Second Coming would be from that quarter. Inevitably, this tradition was compounded by Victorian ecclesiologists, many of whom were obsessed with symbolism. It was they who devised the notion of the 'weeping chancel': one that inclines slightly to the north of the east-west axis (as at Bridlington Priory) and supposedly represents the head of Christ on the Cross. But such deviations are entirely due to medieval masons not caring too much about geometrical niceties when altering or extending earlier buildings.

Although the reason for the eastern orientation of churches remains a mystery, the practice was consistent and is likely to have been symbolic. But it was also practical: in these northern climes, natural early morning light was needed for the mass which was celebrated at dawn in the SANCTUARY or adjacent chapels (*see* MEDIEVAL ARCHITECTURE). In some cases, the exigencies of a site made an eastern orientation impossible: at Rievaulx, for example, where the abbey church in its narrow valley is aligned more nearly north and south than east and west.

OSSUARIES Charnel houses, where the bodies or bones of the dead were kept. Ossuaries are most often associated with churches where overcrowded graveyards could no longer provide for the needs of a (usually urban) community. In some instances endowed charnel chapels were provided in which prayers were offered for the souls of the dismembered dead. The medieval ossuary and chapel in the churchyard of Old St Pauls, London were revered by the populace as exemplifications of immortality. Crypts were often used as ossuaries. The antiquary John Aubrey, writing in the seventeenth century, described the ossuary beneath the cathedral at Hereford: 'the largest Charnel-house for bones that I ever saw in England. In 1650 there lived amongst these bones a poor woman that, to help out her fire, did use to mix deadmen's bones: this was thrift and poverty: but cunning alewives putt the ashes of these bones in their Ale to make it intoxicating.' At Worcester Cathedral Priory, the construction of the LADY CHAPEL in *c.* 1224 encroached on the monks' cemetery and the remains of the dead were removed to a charnel chapel erected for the purpose near the north porch. The chapel was dedicated to Thomas the Martyr and daily masses were said there for the repose of the souls whose dismembered remains lay in the CRYPT beneath.

OSTENSORY A receptacle in which an object of religious devotion was displayed.

OVENS *see* BREAD OVENS

OUTBUILDINGS, MONASTIC *see* PRECINCT

OUTER COURT *see* PRECINCT

OUTER PARLOUR *see* PARLOUR

OVENS *see* BREAD OVEN

OYLMENT A small opening in window TRACERY.

P

PAINTINGS *see* WALL PAINTINGS

PALATINATE The word *palatine* means 'pertaining to a palace' and the palatine counties were those over which Norman magnates and their successors exercised royal jurisdiction. The original counties were those of the Welsh March (ruled by the earls of Chester, Shrewsbury and Hereford) and the Scottish borders (ruled by the prince bishop of Durham). The palatinates were necessary for the defence of William the Conqueror's new realm, but elsewhere the holdings of the nobility were dispersed to prevent the concentration of magnate power.

The *prince bishops* of Durham are unique in the history of England. They were appointed by the king as *counts palatine*, head of church and state in a vast territory that included all the lands between the Rivers Tyne and Tees, land around Crayke and Northallerton in Yorkshire, and an area along the River Tweed in Northumberland known as 'North Durham': Norhamshire, Islandshire, including Holy Island, and Bedlingtonshire. This was St Cuthbert's diocese: the seventh-century bishopric of Lindisfarne which, from 995, was administered from Durham, the customary dues of its vast estates recorded in 1183 in what is now called the *Boldon Book*. The Palatinate was effectively a kingdom within a kingdom and, as defenders of the realm in the north, the prince bishops were charged with the defence of the Scottish border. By the fourteenth century the Palatinate was at the height of its military power, its warrior-bishops uniquely commemorated by the ducally crowned mitre and sword in the coats of arms of all subsequent bishops of Durham. They had their own chancellor, exchequer and mint; they administered the civil and criminal law; granted charters for markets and fairs; and exercised rights of forfeiture. Inevitably, the bishops' authority was reduced under the Tudor kings, nevertheless in 1585 the bishop of Durham was the largest landholder in the country, with eighty manors worth £2,500 annually. The failure of the Northern Rising in 1569 succeeded in suppressing local opposition to the bishop's traditional domination of local affairs, and single-faction politics continued in County Durham until the mid-nineteenth century. The bishop's powers were finally vested in the Crown in 1836 and the palatinate courts were abolished by the Courts Act of 1971.
See also HERALDRY (ECCLESIASTICAL)

PALIMPSEST A manuscript on which the original writing has been effaced to make room for new material. Also a monumental brass which has been turned and re-engraved on the reverse (*see* BRASSES (MONUMENTAL)).

PANTRY *see* LARDER

PAPAL BULL *see* BULLA

PAPER Paper was first used in England as a writing surface from the fourteenth century, but was not manufactured here until the late fifteenth century, and even then only in small quantities.
See also INK *and* PARCHMENT

PARAPET A low wall erected along the outer edge of a structure for reasons of safety or to conceal guttering etc. A parapet may be plain, battlemented, pierced or carved ornamentally, and was a characteristic of the Perpendicular period of MEDIEVAL ARCHITECTURE. Battlemented parapets were sometimes added to churches in the nineteenth century as 'Gothic' features, despite the fact that contemporary architects disliked such elaboration and preferred the simplicity of the Early English style.
See also PINNACLE

PARCHMENT A writing surface made from the treated skins of sheep or goats. The lighter 'flesh' side was preferred for formal documents, but both sides were used in the writing of rolls and books.
See also MANUSCRIPT ILLUMINATION, SCRIPTORIUM *and* VELLUM

PARCLOSE A stone, timber or metalwork screen separating a chapel or subsidiary altar from the body of a church. More specifically, a screen or a set of railings enclosing a chantry chapel (*see* CHANTRY CHAPELS).

PARDONER A 'pardon' was an alternative name for an INDULGENCE. In the Middle Ages, shares in

Half of the twelfth-century church of Malmesbury Abbey, Wiltshire, is preserved in Anglican use. (Courtesy of Derry Brabbs/www.derrybrabbs.com)

indulgences were hawked by pardoners, a practice that was denounced by Geoffrey Chaucer, John Wycliffe and others.
See also SHRINES

PARISH CHURCH A number of monastic communities made provision for public worship, either within or adjacent to their abbey churches. The BENEDICTINES generally permitted public access to their naves or provided separate chapels (a *capella ante portas* – literally 'chapel by the gate'), as at Abingdon, Bury St Edmunds and York. At Crowland and Leominster an AISLE was set aside for the purpose; or a TRANSEPT, as at Chester. But parochial use invariably intruded on the monastic offices and a number of houses built separate parish churches, as at Coventry Abbey and Rochester Cathedral Priory, where the parish church was located in the outer court, and at Evesham where two churches were built within the abbey precincts. Several Benedictine churches later became parish churches (at Brecon, Bridlington and Tynemouth, for example), while at Binham Priory, Norfolk, seven of the original nine bays of the Norman nave were retained for parochial use. Binham's nave has lost its aisles, but its cool interior, with Norman arcading incorporating huge gallery openings, is unlike that of any other parish church in the county. Simon Jenkins described Binham as 'a ghost, fragment of a priory in a field surrounded by ruins'.

At Sherborne, Dorset, the nave of the Benedictine abbey was used for public worship until the end of the fourteenth century, when the abbot, who was RECTOR of the parish and appointed SECULAR priests as his vicars, had a new church, dedicated to All Hallows, built against the west end of the abbey church as a chapel of ease for the townspeople. Early in the fifteenth century the work of rebuilding the abbey church was begun by Abbot Brunyng (1415–36) and continued by Abbot Bradford (1436–59). The new choir seems almost to have been completed when a quarrel flared up between the abbey and the town concerning the rights of the parishioners to have their own font in All Hallows. The dispute was exacerbated when the monks moved the abbey font and narrowed the doorway leading from the south aisle into the AMBULATORY of All Hallows. Despite the intervention of Bishop Neville of Salisbury, the quarrel led to the burning of the abbey church, recorded a century later by John Leland:

> after the variance growing to a plain sedition, by the men of an Earl of Huntingdon, lying in those quarters and taking the townsmen's part, and the bishop of Salisbury the monks part, a priest of All Hallows shot a shaft with fire into the top of that part of St Mary's Church that divided the east part that the monks used from that which the townsmen used; and the partition, chancing at that time to be thatched in the roof [a temporary cover for the building works], was set on afire, and consequently the whole church, the lead and bells melted, was defaced. Then Bradford, Abbot of Sherborne, persecuted the injury, and the townsmen were forced to contribute to the re-edifying of this church.

Reminders of the conflict remain in the scorched limestone walls of the choir, a roof boss in the choir vault depicting the flaming arrow, and the narrow, pointed doorway inserted into the wider Norman one at the west end of the south aisle. After the fire, All Hallows became an independent parish church and when the abbey was finally surrendered in 1539 at the Dissolution of the Monasteries its church was acquired by Sir John Horsey, a privy councillor and chief steward of the

Cistercian Abbey Dore, Herefordshire, restored as a parish church by Lord Scudamore in 1634. (Courtesy of John Mennell)

monastery, who then sold it to the 'Vicar and parish of Sherbourn for 100 marks to them and their successors forever'. During the 1540s All Hallows was demolished, and the abbey has served as the parish church of Sherborne since the Reformation.

Some of England's greatest parish churches were similarly acquired by purchase from their new owners following the DISSOLUTION OF THE MONASTERIES: Great Malvern Priory and the abbeys of Romsey and Tewkesbury, for example. Unlike the BENEDICTINES and AUGUSTINIANS the CISTERCIANS, CLUNIACS and PREMONSTRATENSIAN CANONS rarely granted parochial rights, and consequently few of their churches have survived, (Cistercian) Abbey Dore, Herefordshire, being a notable exception.

PARLOUR (*also* AUDITORIUM, LOCUTORIUM *or* SPEKE HOUSE) A room in a religious house where the rule of SILENCE was relaxed to allow necessary conversation (*parler*), including the preparation of CHAPTER business. There were often two parlours: one (the inner parlour), either adjacent to or replacing the SLYPE, was reserved for the use of the community, while the other (the *outer parlour*), sometimes located in the west claustral range, was where meetings took place with merchants, artificers, etc. from the outside world. Typically, at Cistercian Fountains, the inner parlour was a dark and cheerless passage, between the CHAPTER HOUSE and the slype in the east claustral range, the outer parlour originally occupying the two northern bays of the lay brothers' range, with a wide door to the inner court and a smaller door opening onto the cloister alley. Stone benches along the side walls of the inner parlour have survived at Rievaulx. The term *auditorium* was also used to describe a monastic schoolroom.
See also CALEFACTORIUM

PAROCHIUM *see* ANGLO-SAXON CHURCH *and* MINSTERS

PARVIS (*also* PARVISE) Literally, 'Paradise', the term was originally applied to the atrium in front of St Peter's in Rome. Thereafter it was used to describe the court between the west end of a monastic church or cathedral and the outer wall of its PRECINCT. The word is also used to describe the western portico of a church and a porch with a room above, although such use is possibly erroneous (*see* PORCHES).

PASTORAL LETTERS Official letters addressed by a bishop to all members of his diocese. Encyclical letters are those that are addressed only to the clergy.

PASTORAL STAFF A stave, surmounted by either a cross or a shepherd's crook, carried for ceremonial purposes by a bishop and (in the medieval period) by a senior abbot or abbess (*see* CROZIER).

PATRON The right to nominate a clergyman to a living (*see* ADVOWSON) is exercised by a diocesan bishop or by some other person or body corporate, either lay or clerical, known as the patron. In the Middle Ages, monastic and collegiate foundations were often patrons of benefices. As such they nominated priests to livings and received the rectorial TITHES (*see* APPROPRIATION *and* MEDIEVAL CHURCH, THE).

PATRONAGE *see* BENEFACTORS

PECTORAL CROSS A cross, often of precious metal, worn on the breast and suspended by means of a chain around the neck. In the Church of England, use of the pectoral cross is now generally confined to bishops.

PECULIAR A church or parish (or group of parishes) that is exempt from the jurisdiction of the bishop in whose diocese it is situated. Peculiars usually derived from the possession of land in one diocese by a senior church dignitary who held office in another, or from privileges granted to special groups of religious such as the Knights Templar (*see* COMMANDERY). The *Royal Peculiars* are churches connected with royal palaces or castles: St George's Chapel at Windsor Castle and Westminster Abbey, for example, which are exempt from any jurisdiction other than that of the sovereign. In 1318 Wimborne Minster, Dorset, was declared a royal peculiar by Edward II, although the benefits and exemptions granted thereby hardly survived the king's death in 1327. Even so, the choir continued to wear scarlet cassocks, indicative of royal preferment, until the last century. Most of the privileges associated with monastic and cathedral peculiars have been abolished.

PECULIUM A monk's personal allowance, intended originally for distribution to the poor. From the fourteenth century it came to be used for the purchase of medicines, spices and other small 'items of comfort' and was supplemented by a clothing allowance. By the sixteenth century these two allowances produced an annual income of about one pound – known as *wages*. The practice was contrary to the notion of property held in common, but persisted until the suppression despite various attempts at reform.

PEDILAVIUM *see* MAUNDY

PEDIMENT In classical architecture, the triangular gable above the ENTABLATURE of a portico or a decorative feature over a door, window or niche. The horizontal base moulding may be incomplete (*broken pediment*), the apex of the triangle may be omitted (*open*), or the top members may be curved and scrolled (*segmental*).
See also TYMPANUM

PENAL CODE Religious communities lived by the RULE of their orders and by the regulations and conventions of a particular house (*see* CUSTOMARY). DISCIPLINE was, of necessity, strictly observed for the benefit of the body corporate and required sincere CONFESSION and repentance, manifested in the imposition of additional duties, the performance of an unpleasant task (*penance*) or, in extreme cases, corporal punishment (in CHAPTER) or even imprisonment and solitary confinement (*see* PRISONS). Those who held office could be demoted, thereby relinquishing their status in the community's strictly observed hierarchy. It was a principle of monastic life that sanctions for transgressions should be welcomed without demur as just and positive. Following a monk's public confession in chapter, the superior would determine the punishment and this would be carried out either privately or in public. Penance could also be performed voluntarily and secretly in reparation for an individual's faults or those of another. In the hour following the office of PRIME there would always be a confessor in the chapter house ready to hear private (*auricular*) confessions.

PENANCE *see* ABSOLUTION, PENAL CODE, SHRINES *and* VISITATION (ECCLESIASTICAL)

PENDANTS Stone infill in VAULTING.

PENDENTIVE *see* DOME

PENDLE *see* SLATES AND ROOFING TILES

PENS Before the eleventh century pens were made from dried reeds. Thereafter, until the nineteenth century, the quill pen was used. This was formed from a goose feather (though feathers of swans, ravens, crows and even turkeys were also used), the hollow quill of which retained a small quantity of INK which was released by gentle downward pressure on the nib while writing. When used as pens, feathers were always stripped down to the quill, the larger end being carefully shaped and split with a penknife to form the nib. Metal nibs date from the mid-nineteenth century, and fountain pens from the end of that century.

The pens and animal-hair brushes used for producing the magnificent illuminated manuscripts of the medieval period were themselves kept in superb pen-cases: one mid-eleventh-century example at the British Museum is made from walrus ivory, obtained from Lapland through Viking traders and carved with mounted warriors in combat with a dragon, two lions, and a pair of archers in the act of shooting birds from a tree. It is likely that mouse whiskers were used for the most delicate details.
See also INK, PARCHMENT, SCRIPTORIUM *and* VELLUM

PENSIONS At the DISSOLUTION OF THE MONASTERIES superiors of religious houses who cooperated with the king's commissioners were usually awarded pensions of between £60 and £100. These were met from the resources of the dissolved house until such time as they could be replaced by stipends from benefices created in the newly constituted church. Other brethren received a pension of no more than £5 as a reward for their cooperation, the alternative, for resistance, being imprisonment or even death.
See also CORRODY

PENTISE *or* PENTICE A covered walkway, porch or gallery, with a sloping roof attached to the wall of an adjacent building (*see* CLOISTER *and* GALILEE).

PERPENDICULAR PERIOD *see* MEDIEVAL ARCHITECTURE

PETRA SANCTA, SYLVESTER (SYSTEM) *see* COLOURS (HERALDIC)

PEWS *see* BENCHES

PHARMACY The INFIRMARIAN of a religious house was expected to be skilled in the use of herbs, obtained either from the community's *herbarium* or purchased elsewhere (where there was an infirmary cloister, the cloister GARTH was often cultivated as a herb garden). His pharmacy was usually located within the infirmarer's chambers, and most monastic LIBRARIES included reference books (*herbals*) to assist him. Sage was provided for those who had been bled (*see* PHLEBOTOMY) and monastic observances required the infirmarer always to have 'ginger, cinnamon, peony and the like', ready in his cupboard.
See also INFIRMARY

PHLEBOTOMY Many monastic infirmaries (*farmeries*) were of considerable size, indicative of the practice of *phlebotomy* or therapeutic blood-letting, which was considered to be a medical necessity (*see* INFIRMARY). Those being treated were described as 'minuti' (from the Latin *minutio* meaning 'diminishment'), while the period of treatment and recuperation was then known as *seynies*. Following phlebotomy, a monk was required to convalesce for three days in the infirmary, during which time he could enjoy rich food and relaxation in the monastery gardens, could rise late, and was excused attendance at choir. Not surprisingly, seynies came to be viewed as holidays by the brethren, and consequently the frequency of blood-letting was, in most orders, restricted: four times a year for Cistercians, five times for Carthusians and eight for the Austin Canons. The barber-surgeon responsible for blood-letting was, at that time, considered to be an inferior physician. He would be engaged to attend larger communities once a week and special facilities were provided for the purpose. In the late medieval period the Benedictines often sent their minuti away from the abbey infirmary to outlying granges (*see* GRANGE) that effectively became convalescent homes.
See also RASURA

PHYSICIAN A physician was often engaged to attend the sick of a religious community and was one of the very few secular who were permitted unrestricted access to the INFIRMARY (*farmery*).

He worked closely with the INFIRMARIAN, who was responsible for dispensing drugs and 'cordials' and for the administration of the infirmary and the PHARMACY.

PIER A support of brick or masonry carrying a LINTEL or the downward thrust of an ARCH. Romanesque piers were not solid: they were effectively tubes filled with rubble. Structurally stronger than solid piers, they were also cheaper and quicker to construct. Ideally, the circumference of these early piers was equal to their height – the circle of the pier symbolising spirituality and the square formed by 'unrolling' the outer casing of the tube representing the material world. A pier is composed of four parts: the ABACUS (from which the arch springs), the CAPITAL (immediately below the abacus), the SHAFT (which may be oval, rectangular or multiform), and the BASE. In MEDIEVAL ARCHITECTURE the term is synonymous with *pillar*, but it is not the same as COLUMN or PILASTER, both of which have a capital and base of a classical order. An arch which springs from a pier is called a *pier arch*, while a *half-pier*, which is set within a wall and carries one end of an arch, is known as a *respond*. *Fluting* is vertical channelling in the shaft and a pier that is surrounded by clusters of attached or detached shafts is a *compound* or *clustered pier*. An ENGAGED PIER (also *applied* or *attached*) is one where part of its surface is in contact with a wall. A slender pier dividing a large doorway is known as a *trumeau*. Except in churches of the more austere orders, it was not uncommon for piers to be decorated with geometrical patterns – usually these were painted, although at Durham the nave piers were deeply sculpted with geometrical patterns.
See also ARCADE *and* BAY

PILASTER A rectangular classical column partly built into, partly projecting from, a wall.

PILASTER STRIP Correctly, the term PILASTER should be applied only to classical architecture. Nevertheless, the term 'pilaster strip' is often used to describe a *lesene*: a shallow pier, without capital or base, attached to a wall. Pilaster strips are a characteristic feature of Anglo-Saxon architecture.

PILGRIMAGE OF GRACE, THE (1536–7) A multiple insurrection in the northern counties of England, motivated by widespread resentment of Thomas Cromwell's ecclesiastical, administrative and fiscal reforms. The Pilgrimage of Grace was, in essence, a huge and popular demonstration of disgust. It encompassed the northern lords, whose traditional independence was threatened by Cromwell's new, centralised (southern) administration, and many who were oppressed by Cromwell's novel taxes and consequently distrusted the king's new, 'low-born' counsellors. Above all, there were those who deeply resented the religious changes, again imposed centrally, and wished to return to the customs of former times. Yet even within these forces of religious conservatism there were disparate elements: some wishing to return to Rome and others accepting the royal supremacy but seeking the restoration of their ancient practices and privileges. In particular the DISSOLUTION OF THE MONASTERIES, a highly visible operation that affected the structure of society, provided a focus for discontent. King Henry VIII responded at first with incredulity and then with ferocity – tempered by the practicalities of the situation (there was no standing army, and loyal forces were difficult to muster) and the advice of the Duke of Norfolk, who had been entrusted with pacifying the North. A general pardon for all offences committed before 7 December 1536 was granted to those north of Doncaster. Even so, over two hundred rebels were eventually executed, including Robert Aske, the leader of the Yorkshire rebels.
See also REFORMATION, THE

PILGRIMAGES *see* SHRINES

PILGRIMS *and* PILGRIMS' WAY *see* SHRINES

PILLAR *see* PIER

PILLAR PISCINA A free-standing PISCINA.

PINNACLE A miniature spire constructed as a decorative termination to a BUTTRESS or PARAPET, but more particularly to provide additional weight in order to counteract the outward thrust of a vault or spire (*see* VAULTING).

PISCINA A stone basin in which a priest rinsed the chalice and paten after MASS (*see* ABLUTIONS). A piscina is usually set within a FENESTELLA (a canopied niche) in the south wall of the PRESBYTERY, and this may also contain SEDILIA (seats), a CREDENCE (shelf) and AUMBRY (cupboard). Evidence of piscinas elsewhere in a church is indicative of former side-chapels and altars (*see also* SQUINT). A small number of piscinas have survived in PORCHES, although they are similar in appearance to a HOLY WATER STOUP. His fingers having been in contact with the Elements (the Host and the Wine, which were believed to have been transubstantiated into the body and blood of Christ), and with the sacred vessels in which they were contained, the priest would wash them over the piscina (*see* LAVABO). From the piscina a drain conveyed the water (itself sanctified through contact with the Elements) to the consecrated ground outside. Some late thirteenth- and early fourteenth-century piscinas have two basins: one for the vessels and the other for the hands.

PISTRINUM The monastic BAKEHOUSE.

PITTANCE A modest addition to a normally frugal monastic meal, usually in celebration of a liturgical feast or some other event in the community's life.

PLACE-NAMES (MONASTIC AND ECCLESIASTICAL) The extraordinary number and diversity of monastic place-names bears witness to the prosperity of the medieval Church. Most names originated in endowments of lands, for the benefit of both a religious order and the soul of the benefactor, or were granted in return for corrodies (*see* CORRODY). Some recall the sites of minor religious houses, usually dependencies or granges (*see* GRANGE); and a small number commemorate former abbeys, as at Cerne Abbas in Dorset (*abbas*, from the Latin for 'abbot'). Typical are names such as Abbotsbury ('the manor of the abbot'), Friar Waddon ('the hill of the friars where woad grew'), Whitchurch Canonicorum ('the stone church of the canons'), Toller Fratrum ('land by the Toller stream belonging to the brethren' of Forde Abbey') and Maiden Newton ('the new homestead of the sisters'), all in Dorset; White Ladies Aston ('the eastern homestead of the [Premonstratensian] Canonesses') in Worcestershire; Newton Abbot ('the new homestead of the Abbot') and Monkton ('the homestead of the monks') in Devon; the two villages of Stoke Prior, one in Herefordshire and the other in Worcestershire ('the prior's place' or possibly 'the prior's cell') and Fryerning ('the place of the brothers') in Essex. Place-name elements such as the Latin *monachorum* ('of the monks') and *sororum* ('of the sisters') are self-evident, but not all are strictly monastic: the 'brothers' who dwelt at Fryerning were Knights Hospitaller, and canons could be either priests in canonical orders or the secular canons of a cathedral who held prebends (*see* PREBENDARY). At Canons Ashby in Northamptonshire a fragment of the former priory remains in Anglican use, Nunthorpe in Yorkshire was 'the [dependent] community of the nuns', while Nunney in Somerset was 'the island of the nuns' (though an alternative interpretation is 'the island of *Nunna*'). Place-name elements such as the Welsh *llan* and the Cornish *lan* (both meaning 'church') and *clas* (the Welsh for a monastic community or college) are indicative of ancient Celtic religious sites, while *kirk* ('church'), *minster* (*see* MINSTERS), and (in some instances) *stoc* ('monastery' or 'cell') and *stow(e)* ('holy place', 'hermitage' or 'monastery') have similar Anglo-Saxon connotations. *Stow(e)* in particular is often joined with a saint's name as a first element (as in Bridestowe, Edwinstowe, Felixstowe, etc.) meaning 'a place dedicated to Saint Bride, Saint Edwin, Saint Felix, etc.'. Minster place-names are ubiquitous: Yetminster, Wimborne Minster, Minster Lovell, Minsterworth, and so on.

It should be noted, however, that many monastic and ecclesiastical place-names indicate the possession of an estate rather than the existence of a religious community, as Tooting Bec reminds us that it once formed part of the considerable possessions of the great Norman house at Bec and had a Benedictine cell, while, in Dorset, the manor of Stour Provost was held by the Provost and Scholars of King's College, Cambridge who, in 1830, still maintained small lifehold tenements and pastures open to common grazing. Similarly, many feudal affixes have ecclesiastical origins: in Somerset, for example, the manor of Templecombe was held by the Knights Templar and the present parish incorporates the former manor of Abbas Combe, which was held by the Abbess of Shaftesbury. (*For* 'Temple' place-names *see* TEMPLAR, KNIGHTS.) In Dorset, the medieval Caundle Episcopi, once held by the bishops of Sarum, became Caundle Bishop and remained so until recently, when it was translated to Bishops Caundle (Latin *episcopus* = 'bishop'). But place-names can be deceptive. In the same group of villages Purse Caundle is believed to have derived from the Old English *preost*, meaning 'priest', as it was a manor of Athelney Abbey. But there is also evidence of a thirteenth-century armigerous Purse family whose Dorset ancestors are said to have held a manor of that name from 1055. Place-names can originate in local traditions which are not always accurate: in the twelfth century, the hamlet of Hermitage in Dorset was known as Rocombe and the 'hermitage' was, in fact, a minor Augustinian priory.

Street names may also afford clues to the location of a former religious house. At Bicknacre in Essex, for example, where Augustine's Way and Priory Lane refer to the former priory of Austin Canons, although Monks' Mead in the same town is clearly a later (and erroneous) designation. London has many ecclesiastical street names, notably Canongate, Minories and St Sepulchregate, while Blackfriars, Whitefriars and Greyfriars are common in many towns (*see* FRIARS). Names of individual buildings may be indicative of former ecclesiastical use: Abbey, Chantry, Grange, Hermitage, Priory are obvious examples, but they should always be approached with caution.

See also SECUNDA

PLAGUE During the first decades of the fourteenth century climatic changes resulted in a series of poor harvests, causing starvation and malnutrition which, by the 1330s, had debilitated the peasant population of Europe. Recent evidence has shown that, by 1341, eight years before the arrival of the *Black Death* in England, many villages were already depopulated and their lands left uncultivated. It is now clear, therefore, that climatic change, urban overpopulation, frequent livestock murrains, and famine preceded the plague and, by reducing immunity to disease, contributed to its virulence.

The Black Death of 1349–50 first arrived in Britain through ports in the West Country (traditionally Melcombe Regis in Dorset) and, until recently, was generally believed to have been a form of bubonic plague, although it is now suggested by some experts that it was caused by a highly infectious virus (*haemorrhagic plague*) that was spread by humans – possibly itinerants seeking work.

The fourteenth-century pandemic probably originated in Mongolia in the 1320s and reached Europe by *c.* 1347. Amazingly, there was no attempt to prevent its spreading across the English Channel or even to discourage contact with the stricken Continent. Indeed, two weeks before the plague's arrival the Archbishop of York was warning of its inevitability, and of 'the sins of men, whose prosperity has made them complacent and who have forgotten the generosity of God'. Presumably, he was not referring to the emaciated peasantry. When it finally struck, the only provision made by the establishment was the excavation of mass grave-pits. At Clerkenwell, outside the walls of London, 50,000 corpses were buried in a 13-acre cemetery established by Walter de Manny, who later founded a Carthusian monastery on the site as a memorial to the dead. This later became the *Charterhouse*, the cloister, chapel and gatehouse of which have survived, as have the foundations of the original cemetery chapel in which penitential services were held during the Black Death. At Clerkenwell a small leaden cross was placed on the chest of each victim before burial.

Estimates of the numbers who died during the Black Death vary enormously, but at least 20 per cent of the population must have perished, and some historians have proposed figures of 40 or even 50 per cent. 'To our great grief the plague carried off so vast a multitude of people that it was not possible to find anybody to carry the corpses to the cemetery,' wrote a fourteenth-century monk of Rochester in Kent, 'mothers and fathers carried their own children on their shoulders to the church and dropped them in the common pit . . . such a terrible stench came from these pits that hardly anyone dared to walk near the cemeteries.' The nobility and gentry, with a more reliable diet and a marginally greater perception of hygiene, fared somewhat better, although neither rank nor privilege brought immunity: at Crich in Derbyshire a local knight, William de Wakebridge, erected a tiny CHANTRY chapel to the memory of his wife, father, two sisters and three brothers, all of whom had been cut down by the plague in the summer of 1349. At Gloucester the terrified inhabitants barred the city gates to refugees fleeing from plague-stricken Bristol, while at Winchester the populace was urged to parade barefoot round the marketplace and to recite the seven penitential psalms three times a week – but to no avail, for well over half the population perished.

As a result of depopulation many settlements became moribund, although (contrary to popular belief) only a small number of villages were abandoned as a direct result of the plague. Monastic communities were not immune: the Black Death severely reduced the number of monks, perhaps from 9,000 to 4,500, and although this number had recovered to almost 7,000 by 1377, it then remained static until the Dissolution of the Monasteries. In the spring and summer of 1349, when the pestilence was at its height, at least half the community of Westminster Abbey was carried off, as were the abbot and most of his monks at the great abbey of St Albans. Even so, few religious houses were utterly extinguished at that time, although many small communities were reduced to near ruin: Wothorpe in Northamptonshire being but one (particularly well documented) example. For many houses, religious life was brought to a temporary halt, while for the majority recovery in the form of RECRUITMENT became impossible.

So too on the manors: on the Titchfield estates in 1348–9 the tenants of the Premonstratensian abbey lost almost 60 per cent of their number, and when the plague returned in 1361–2 a further 92 of the original 515 tenants died. On the Cambridgeshire manors of Crowland Abbey some 57 per cent of the tenants at Cottenham died, as many as 70 per cent at Oakington and 48 per cent at Dry Drayton during the period October 1348 to January 1350. For a century and more, plague was endemic in England. After the Black Death itself, the pestilence returned in 1361 and 1368–9 and thereafter, until the end of the medieval period, there was scarcely a decade when the greater part of the country was free of it. Christ Church, Canterbury, was one of the few houses that escaped comparatively lightly from the first outbreak in 1348–9; thereafter it was the victim of repeated epidemics in every decade of the fifteenth century except for the last. The Christ Church obituary lists show that at least 16 per cent of the monks died of plague, while others of their community were carried off by diseases of comparable virulence. The effect on recruitment was dramatic, not least on the monastic estates. Consequently, we find that Battle Abbey suffered a drop in income of nearly one-third by the 1380s, a deficit from which it never fully recovered. Durham Priory similarly suffered a reduction in receipts, especially in SPIRITUALITIES such as TITHES. Significantly, at Battle and Durham, and at Selby Abbey in Yorkshire, little of architectural substance was added to their churches after the 1340s (Selby had spent lavishly on a splendid new choir only a few years before the arrival of the plague). At Milton Abbey in Dorset, the construction of the new church stopped abruptly some time after 1348, leaving only the choir, and a green space where the nave should have been (the transept was added during the abbacy of William Milton (1481–1521)). The reconstruction of the nave at Worcester Cathedral Priory was halted for several decades, with the result that a new master mason introduced a new style of building when work eventually recommenced.

Lay brethren began deserting the monasteries in large numbers, attracted by the improved wages and working conditions that resulted from the labour shortage following the Black Death. Consequently, conventual accommodation was often converted to other uses, or even demolished (*see* LAY BROTHERS). Particularly exposed were the poorly endowed communities of nuns: at the small Cistercian house of Legbourne, Lincolnshire, the abbess complained that she was unable to maintain the lands in good order 'on account of the dearth of cultivators and rarity of men, arising out of unwonted pestilences and epidemics', while at Easebourne, Sussex, a community of Augustinian canonesses was obliged to appeal for help as a result of 'epidemics, death of men and of servants'. Their complaint must have been familiar at that time: 'few tenants can be found willing to occupy the lands in these days, and the said lands, falling into a worse state, are so poor that they cannot supply the religious women with sufficient support for themselves or for the repair of their ruinous buildings'.

The anxious search for recruits and new manorial tenants inevitably resulted in a lowering of standards, a weakening of morale and a corresponding decline in support for the monastic ideal. Patronage of the POSSESSIONER houses declined significantly, and it was to reclusive orders such as the Carthusians, to the mendicants (*see* FRIARS) and to chantry priests that benefactors of the period now turned most readily. But, as the Benedictine John of Reading observed after the second onset of the plague in 1361, the mendicant orders were often unable to reconcile this newly diverted patronage with the principles of their rule:

> This Mammon of iniquity is thought to have hurt the religious houses most of all; but it dealt the mendicant orders a mortal wound. For these latter found so much superfluous wealth flowing to them from their confessions and the legacies of their penitents, that they would scarcely deign to receive the offerings of the faithful. Without more ado, little heeding their profession and their rule, which consist in mendicant poverty, they gathered from all sides superfluous equipment for their rooms, their tables and their horses, being tempted thereto by the devil.

Furthermore, many priests had given their lives in the service of their plague-stricken communities and had to be replaced: in the diocese of Worcester alone, there were 217 new institutions to benefices in 1349, compared with only 14 in the previous year. Inevitably, it was to the monasteries that hard-pressed diocesan bishops looked for recruits. When, in 1351, Abbot William of Bury obtained papal permission to have ten of his monks ordained as priests – even though they had not attained the statutory age for ordination – he acknowledged that: 'because of the lack of monks who were also priests, at the time of the plague, which in time past was raging in these parts, because of those who are missing, this monastery is known to be in need of monks who are also priests, who can celebrate mass and other divine services'. Abbot William's monks were ordained prematurely and served as priests in the community – but their loss gravely affected the religious life of the abbey at Bury, as elsewhere. Similarly on the estates: while it was not difficult to find tenants for the better lands, they did not share the commitment of their predecessors. They were more captious than previously, and less disciplined: former relationships, established as the result of centuries of continuity, were lost.

PLAINSONG (*also* PLAINCHANT) The term is applied to the large body of traditional ritual melody of the Latin rite and is inextricably associated with monastic worship, especially that of the BENEDICTINES. Before there was any central authority to call upon, each monastery had its own musical tradition, derived entirely from the skill and experience of its singers. Consequently every 'performance' was unique. The term 'plainsong' emphasises the unadorned nature of the music, its free rhythm depending on accentuation of the words of the LITURGY, sung in unison and with a single line of melody. Plainsong is unaccompanied and its scales (*modes*) run from D, E, F and G, the only accidental being a flattened B. It was introduced into England by Augustine in 597 but was largely lost at the REFORMATION, although it continued in the VERSICLES and Responses and influenced the development of ANGLICAN CHANT. Promoted by the Oxford Movement, plainsong enjoyed a revival in the nineteenth century and has subsequently been used (in modified form) for the PSALMS and in the liturgy generally.

Plainsong is synonymous with *Gregorian chant*, named after Pope Gregory the Great (d. 604) during whose papacy services were reorganised, choral scholars and choirs were established in the Roman churches, and the plainsong repertory was reviewed and expanded.

See also ANTIPHON, CHURCH MUSIC *and* POLYPHONY

PLATE TRACERY *see* MEDIEVAL ARCHITECTURE

PLUMBING, WATER SUPPLY AND SANITATION Monastic communities required substantial volumes of water and produced vast quantities of liquid waste, especially from the KITCHENS, INFIRMARY (*farmery*), LAVATORIUM (wash-house) and REREDORTER (latrines) (*see* ABLUTIONS). This was collected in a main drain that usually traversed the site, its route dictated by the gradient. Those buildings that produced the most waste were carefully sited along its course so that when water was reused, that which was most heavily polluted entered the drain at its lowest level. Rainwater from roofs was collected, and fed into the system following use. Collection and drainage systems were often extraordinarily sophisticated and were provided with conduits (*see* CONDUIT), sluices and subsidiary drains, syphons and balancing tanks or *spurgels* for clearing the water and correcting its pressure within the distribution system. LEAD was used for gutters, spouts and pipes (although these may have been of wood lined with lead), while the main drain was often constructed of fine masonry: at Monk Bretton and Fountains in Yorkshire and at Tintern in Monmouthshire, for example.

While medieval houses depended for their water on natural sources such as wells, the monasteries frequently had elaborate systems of water supply connected with various parts of the conventual buildings and often brought water from a considerable distance. In *c.* 960 the Abbot of Abingdon was recorded as having made 'the water course that runs under the dormitory to the stream that is called Hoke', although this was probably little more than a stream for flushing the abbey's drains. In the late twelfth century the Benedictine abbey at Canterbury (later the Cathedral Priory) obtained a grant of land containing springs, and installed a complex water supply system, the plan of which has survived. This shows that a circular conduit house was built close to the source, and from this water was carried through an

At Fountains Abbey, Yorkshire, it was the River Skell that provided the main drain and consequently the conventual buildings were positioned so that the river passed beneath, or in close proximity to, those that produced the most waste.

underground pipe that passed through five oblong settling tanks. It then passed directly to the lavatorium in the infirmary cloister – a raised cistern that fed a washing basin below. From there another pipe led to a second lavatorium in front of the refectory, similar to that at Durham (*see* LAVATORIUM). Within the lavatorium, a central pillar supported a cistern from which two pipes ran north and east, the former beneath the refectory, scullery and kitchen, supplying each by means of a standpipe and cock, and across the court to the bakehouse, brewhouse and guest hall, with a branch to the bath-house. The eastern pipe supplied a third lavatorium in front of the infirmary hall and a tank in the town cemetery. The waste from both these branches ran into a stone pond east of the church, and from there a pipe ran to a tank beside the Prior's chamber and on to 'the Prior's water tub', where it was joined by the waste from the bath-house and flowed into the main drain beneath the reredorter. All the rainwater from the roofs of the church and claustral buildings was fed into this drain, which finally ran beneath the court and into the city ditch. The system was designed so that a hollow pillar above the main pipe in the infirmary court could be used in emergencies: 'should the aqueduct fail, water can be drawn from the [adjacent] well and being poured into this column will be supplied to all the offices'. At the angle of every pipe, where it was turned into a vertical position to feed a tank, a short horizontal branch terminated in a stopcock. These were marked on the plan as '*purgatorium*' and were used to flush ('purge') sediment from the pipes. So efficient was the system that only minor modifications for the removal of rainwater were required before the monastery was dissolved in 1540.

Water was often conveyed considerable distances: when Walter de Banham became sacrist at Bury St Edmunds in *c.* 1200 he 'enclosed in lead the aqueduct from its head and spring for a distance of two miles [3.2km], and brought it to the cloister through ways hidden in the ground'. In 1215 the water supply to the Cistercian abbey of Waverley suddenly gave out, so that a monk, Simon, was required to find another spring and, 'after great difficulty, inquiry and invention, and not without much labour and sweating', brought the water to the monastery by underground pipes – a distance of 521m (570yd).

Quite often, the position of conventual buildings was dictated by the proximity of the water supply and the need for regular and reliable flushing. At Worcester, for example, there was a problem with providing water to the reredorter, which was moved, together with the adjacent dorter, from its customary position in the east claustral range to the west, incidentally creating additional space to accommodate the sumptuous chapter house. At Kirkham Priory the fall of the land required the reredorter, kitchens, infirmary and prior's lodgings to be accommodated in an arc of buildings that followed the course of the stone-lined drain for 91m (100yd) to the east of the church and cloister. At Fountains Abbey it was the River Skell that provided the main drain, and consequently the conventual buildings were positioned so that the river passed beneath, or in close proximity to, those that produced the most waste: the monks' and lay brothers' infirmaries, their latrines and the refectory and infirmary kitchens and sculleries. The regular flushing of drains was essential to the well-being of a community and, occasionally, claustral buildings were located to the north of an abbey church because of the more favourable topography (*see* REREDORTER).

The buildings of Cistercian abbeys rarely survived the Dissolution of the Monasteries, and consequently watercourses and drains have often been exposed within the ruined foundations: at Byland, Furness, Hailes and Tintern, for example. From these, and from surviving documentary evidence, it is clear that many monastic systems of water supply and sanitation were unequalled in their engineering and hydraulic sophistication, even by those of ancient Rome.
See also FISHPONDS *and* MILLS

PLURALISM The holding simultaneously of two or more benefices, offices or sinecures (*pluralities*).

POINTED ARCH *see* ARCH

POINTS OF THE SHIELD The heraldic term *dexter* is derived from the Latin meaning both 'right' and 'favourable' and is used to describe the right-hand side of a shield of arms (the left when viewed from the front). Those who were right-handed were considered to be dexterous and to exercise dexterity. *Sinister* is similarly derived from the Latin, meaning both 'left' and 'perverse' and in heraldry is used to describe the left-hand side of a shield of arms (the right side when viewed from the front). In the Middle Ages, to be left-handed was considered to be unnatural and, therefore, 'sinister'. Charges placed in the top portion of the shield are said to be *in chief* and those in the lower portion *in base*. There are three reference points in a shield: *fess point* at the centre (A) with *honour point* above (B) and *nobril point* below (C) (*see* illustration).

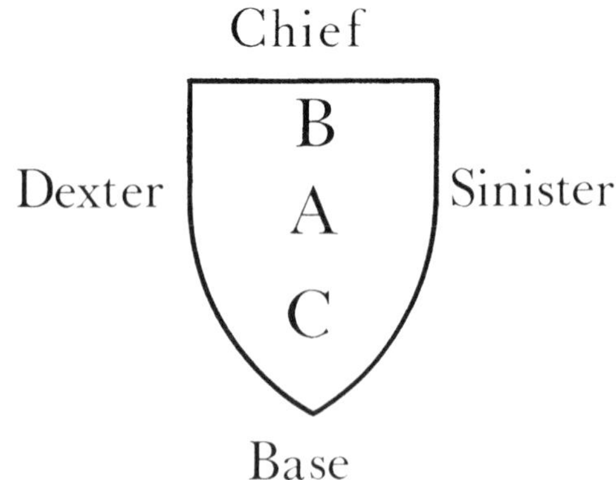

(Courtesy of John Ferguson)

POLYPHONY Music 'of many voices' in which any number of parts move in apparent independence, although fitting together harmonically. The term is frequently applied to the great age of unaccompanied choral music exemplified by the works of Thomas Tallis (*c.* 1505–85), Giovanni Palestrina (1525–94), William Byrd (1543–1623) and their contemporaries. Tallis, known as 'the father of English cathedral music', was organist at Waltham Abbey at the Dissolution of the Monasteries, when it is conjectured that he became 'a gentleman of the Chapel royal'. His MOTET '*Spem in alium*', written in forty parts, overshadows any other English piece of the period. *Counterpoint* has the same meaning, such music being *contrapuntal*.
See also CHURCH MUSIC

PONTIFICAL The liturgical book containing the services to be performed only by bishops at confirmation, ordination, etc. (*see* LITURGY).

POOR CLARES, THE *see* MINORESS

PORCHES From the late thirteenth century there would normally be a porch on the south side of the nave of a parish church. This would usually be furnished with stone or wooden benches and a HOLY WATER STOUP. The porch not only sheltered the entrance from the weather but also served a number of liturgical and legal purposes: marriage contracts were made there and ceremonies such as the churching of women after childbirth and the ABSOLUTION of penitents began at the church door. Those monastic, secular

The south porch at Gloucester Cathedral.

The elaborate, three-storied south porch at the church of St John the Baptist, Cirencester, Gloucestershire. (Courtesy of John Mennell)

and mendicant houses that admitted the public to their churches (*see* NAVE) sometimes provided a porch, the great west door being reserved for processional purposes. These porches were usually (although not invariably) located on the north side of the nave, the CLOISTER (to which the public were not admitted) occupying the south side. The porch was often a major architectural element: there are fine examples at Worcester, Salisbury and Gloucester cathedrals and Sherborne and Tewkesbury abbeys. Late medieval monastic porches sometimes developed into TOWERS to emphasise the importance of the entrance and to provide additional space for the conducting of secular business outside the monks' precinct. Parochial rights were rarely granted in the churches of Cistercian, Cluniac or Premonstratensian foundations, and consequently porches are rarely found attached to their churches, a GALILEE at the west end of the nave being a more common feature of Cistercian churches, as at Fountains and Rievaulx. Some porches were of two or more storeys and the upper rooms might be used as schoolrooms, courtrooms or as a MUNIMENT ROOM. The elaborate, three-storied south porch at the church of St John the Baptist, Cirencester was built in *c.* 1490 by the canons of the Augustinian abbey for the transaction of secular business. It was adopted for use as a town hall in the seventeenth century and returned to the parish church a century later.

PORTER Responsible for security of the CURIA or outer court, the porter was often a lay employee who had lodgings in the gatehouse (*see* FORTIFICATION). He checked the credentials of visitors before directing them to an appropriate obedientary, and supervised the admission of wayfarers after nightfall. Within the precinct, monastic porters were responsible for the security of the church and CLOISTER (*see* CUSTODIANS) and for overseeing contacts between the kitchens and infirmary and the outside world.

PORTICUS A side-chapel or porch-like chamber entered from the main body of a church. Porticus formed the 'arms' of Saxon and Norman cruciform churches.

See also MEDIEVAL ARCHITECTURE, TOWERS *and* TRANSEPT

PORTLAND STONE The Isle of Portland, the 'Gibraltar of Wessex', was described by Hardy as a 'huge lump of freestone' jutting into the Channel from the Dorset coast: strange, bleak, almost treeless and with cliffs on every side. Its fine, hard, oolitic limestone was first introduced to London by Inigo Jones in 1619 in the King's Banqueting House in Whitehall, and Christopher Wren chose Portland stone for the rebuilding of London after the Great Fire of 1666, notably in the new St Paul's Cathedral and fifty-one City churches. The stone was quarried in immense blocks, trolleyed down short slipways, and winched by 'slingers' onto barges to be transported along the south coast and up the River Thames. Wren's wineglass device may still be discovered on huge, discarded blocks of stone in the quarries of east Portland, a few of which are worked today. Portland stone is not confined to Portland, however. Further east, the Tilly Whim Caves near Durlston were once quarried (a *whim* is a stone-miner's windlass), and the stone extracted from quarries at Chilmark in Wiltshire for the construction of Salisbury Cathedral in the thirteenth century also belongs to the Portland series.

POSSESSIONER An endowed religious community, the term is usually applied to the older orders such as the BENEDICTINES, AUGUSTINIANS and CISTERCIANS, in contradistinction to the 'advocates of evangelical poverty' such as the MENDICANT orders.

POST-MEDIEVAL CATHEDRALS The iconoclasm that followed the REFORMATION in England manifested itself under Thomas Cromwell (*c.* 1485–1540), when the monasteries were the principal target; under Elizabeth I (r. 1558–1603), in an attempt to purge the country of her sister's 'popery'; and under Oliver Cromwell (1599–1658) during the Commonwealth of 1649–60. All three onslaughts were directed primarily against images and RELICS, but the first included also the destruction of numerous monastic houses, notably those in remote locations that could not be adapted for parochial use (*see* DISSOLUTION OF THE MONASTERIES). The cathedrals suffered less from iconoclasm than from neglect, aggravated by their widespread use as barracks and prisons during the Civil War. Canterbury, Chichester, Durham, Winchester, Exeter, Hereford, Worcester, Chester, Oxford, Norwich, Peterborough, Lincoln, Old St Paul's in London and (above all) Lichfield and Carlisle all suffered substantial damage at that time.

But, in many respects, the indifference of the Georgian period was even worse. Stained glass that had escaped the iconoclasts was either removed wholesale (as at Salisbury in 1788) or allowed to disintegrate through neglect. Screens, pulpits and reredoses were casually removed, while, in the 1790s, the interior of Canterbury was covered with whitewash. In 1834, Augustus Pugin remarked of Ely Cathedral:

> Here is a church, magnificent in every respect, falling into decay through gross neglect. There is no person appointed to attend to the repair of the building, and the only person who has been employed during the past sixty years is a bricklayer. Not even common precautions are taken to keep the building dry . . .

Ely was hardly exceptional. It is little wonder, therefore, that much of what is seen today is Victorian restoration – much of it oppressive and insensitive but, nevertheless, laudable in that it saved many of our great cathedrals from further deterioration, if not ruination. Only one new cathedral was built during the post-Reformation period: St Paul's, London.

St Paul's Cathedral

By the mid-seventeenth century the old cathedral was in a state of decay and the central tower was in imminent danger of collapse. Before its spire was destroyed by lightning in 1561, St Paul's had been the longest and tallest cathedral in Europe: measuring over 178m (585ft), its total length was greater even than Winchester's, while its tower and lead-covered timber spire rose to 149m (489ft), 26m (85ft) taller than Salisbury's tower and stone-clad spire (*see* TOWERS). An alarming report, prepared by Christopher Wren (1632–1723), concluded that 'the Tower from Top to Bottom and the adjacent parts are such a heap of deformities that no Judicious Architect will think it corrigible by any Expense that can be laid out upon new dressing it'. He therefore proposed replacing the tower with a dome (which, he suggested, should be built before demolishing the tower), recasing the Norman piers of the nave with new stone and generally providing the church with a classical 'make-over' following Inigo Jones's earlier remodelling of the west front in 1633–40. Wren's plans were accepted by the authorities, but before he could begin work the cathedral was engulfed by the Great Fire of 1666.

Although not entirely destroyed, it was decided that the medieval building was in a dangerous condition and should be demolished. During the following decade Wren proposed several designs for the cathedral's replacement including a centrally planned church with a large dome 36m (120ft) in diameter. This was rejected by the commissioners, who considered it to be too far removed from the English tradition. (Interestingly, Wren's early plans for St Paul's included a long building with galleries on either side, the galleries supported by rows of shops beneath.) Eventually he produced a more conventional scheme with a long nave, choir and transepts – and a dome. It is clear that Wren disliked this scheme, and the royal warrant of 1675 included a clause that enabled him 'to make some variations, rather ornamental, than essential, as from time to time he should see proper'. Consequently, Wren was able to redesign his new cathedral as it was constructed – an early 'design and build' project that took thirty years to complete and which cost £738,845 5*s* 2*d*.

Despite its appearance (and Wren's protestations), beneath its magnificent dome and Classical PORTLAND STONE shell the new St Paul's is a conventional cruciform church with nave, choir and transepts and a number of architectural characteristics inherited from its medieval predecessor – including flying buttresses, which were concealed behind a curtain wall. Even the vast space beneath the dome is a variation of the crossing at Ely, where, after the collapse of the tower in 1322, the crossing piers were dispensed with and the tower replaced by a spectacular octagon and lantern (*see* TOWERS). Nevertheless, St Paul's is essentially Roman: a ceremonial space, stately and dignified, and yet detached and aloof. Its most impressive features are the central space beneath the dome, the sumptuous decoration and fittings, and the dome itself – a dome within a dome, an octagonal central space 31m (102ft) in diameter roofed by an inner dome of plaster-faced brick, above which a tall brick cone supports an upper dome, lightly constructed of timber sheathed with lead, and a delicate Baroque lantern. The whole rises 111m (214ft) – just 12m (40ft) shorter than Salisbury's spire (*see* colour plate 1).

The New Anglican Cathedrals

In 1836, for the first time in three centuries, a new Anglican diocese was created and the ancient church of Ripon Minster, North Yorkshire, was designated as its cathedral. Thereafter, a number of new dioceses were established (*see* DIOCESE) to serve rapidly expanding industrial conurbations, few of which possessed a church of sufficient size or grandeur to compare with the ancient cathedrals. Consequently, a number of 'parish church cathedrals' were designated to serve the new dioceses: Manchester (diocese created in 1847), Newcastle upon Tyne (1882), Wakefield (1888), Birmingham (1905), Southwark (1905), Chelmsford (1913), Bury St Edmunds (1914), Sheffield (1914), Coventry (1918), Bradford (1919), Blackburn (1926), Derby (1927), Leicester (1927) and Portsmouth (1927). Although not in the same league as the major medieval cathedrals, they all have some outstanding features: Newcastle's great crown steeple (*c.* 1448), Southwark's sixteenth-century reredos (restored in 1833), the fifteenth-century south porch at Chelmsford and Derby's splendid choir screen by Robert Bakewell (1730), for example. More recently, the western extension and flanking towers at Portsmouth Cathedral, begun in 1935 by Sir Charles Nicholson and completed in 1990 by Michael Drury, are a great success; whereas the truly dreadful portico at Sheffield Cathedral is a sad memorial to the brutality of 1960s architecture. At Manchester, the first of the 'parish church cathedrals', a range of collegiate buildings dating from 1421 now houses the famous Chetham's School of Music and, despite bomb damage in 1940, the church's magnificent late medieval choir stalls, screens and roof survive. Although of modest proportions, the cathedral church of St Philip, Birmingham, is a Baroque gem. Designed by Thomas Archer (1668–1743) in 1725, it acquired a fine presbytery in 1883 with superb windows by Burne-Jones (*see* STAINED GLASS) and became the city's cathedral in 1905.

St Albans Abbey became a cathedral in 1877 – exactly eight centuries after work began on the present building. Unlike many of the other new cathedrals its considerable size and distinguished history recommended it for the purpose. Its nave is second only in length to that at Winchester, while its early Norman tower was largely built of bricks salvaged from the nearby Roman town of Verulamium. Regrettably, the building was heavily restored in the twenty years after it became a cathedral and before a dean and chapter were appointed. Much of the restoration work was undertaken by Sir Edmund Beckett (later Lord Grimthorpe 1816–1905), an exceedingly wealthy lawyer and an amateur architect. Because he was paying for the scheme Beckett was able to proceed without constraint, with the result that much of the exterior bears little resemblance to the earlier building. However, the interior is still imposing, as is the recently rebuilt and restored shrine of St Alban (1308).

Had Henry VIII determined, in 1539, that the great Benedictine abbey of Bury St Edmunds should become a cathedral, then in 1914 the new diocese would have acquired a building worthy of the name. Bury was once the greatest and wealthiest of the English religious houses and, after Old St Paul's and Winchester, its church was the largest in England. But few have vanished so completely as Bury, following its systematic demolition. In 1914 the sixteenth-century church of St James became the cathedral, located next to the Norman St James Gate in the wall of the monastic precinct and close to the west end of the former abbey church.

The splendid collegiate church of Southwell Minster in Nottinghamshire became a cathedral in 1888. Before this time it shared with Ripon and Beverley minsters the status of pro-cathedral, its prebendaries assisting in the administration of the very large diocese of York. With the exception of the Perpendicular west window and early fourteenth-century pulpitum, the nave and transepts are pure Romanesque, the huge semicircular arches of the triforium nearly matching in size those of the arcade beneath. From the north choir a passage leads to the beautiful, late thirteenth-century, octagonal chapter house, built in the Decorated style and renowned for its leaf carvings. Southwell's is the only chapter house in England with a stone vault unsupported by a central pillar.

The diocese of Liverpool was created in 1880, but it was not until 1904 that the foundation stone was laid for the immense Cathedral Church of Christ, a project that was not completed until 1978. The architect, Sir Giles Gilbert Scott (1880–1960), was only 22 when his scheme was selected out of more than a hundred submitted in competition, although his designs were modified several times as building continued. The cathedral occupies a site high on a ridge overlooking the River Mersey and is built of a pink and somewhat sombre sandstone. Despite its Gothic appearance, in conception the building most resembles St Paul's: it is symmetrical (with the exception of the projecting Lady Chapel and chapter house at the east end), it has a vast central space at the crossing beneath the Vestey Tower (named after the family who paid for the tower as a family memorial) and the nave and choir are of equal length. Unlike St Paul's, the central space is flanked by pairs of transepts, with large porches occupying the space between each pair. Everything about the building is huge: it is one of the largest churches in the world, its magnificent tower rises to over 100m (331ft), it has one of the world's biggest organs and the heaviest of its thirteen bells

The Anglican Cathedral, Liverpool. (Paul Ellis/AFP/Getty Images)

('Great George') weighs 16.5 tons. The central space is 64m (210ft) long and 26.5m (87ft) wide, and the vaults are over 35m (116ft) high – that beneath the central tower rising to 53m (175ft).

Not all newly created cathedrals serve industrial conurbations. The ancient diocese of Cornwall (931–1043) was reconstituted in 1876 and a new cathedral built at Truro to replace the dilapidated parish church of St Mary. The driving force behind the scheme was the newly appointed bishop Edward White Benson (1829–96), who became Archbishop of Canterbury in 1882. The architect was J.L. Pearson (1817–97), and his cathedral, built in grey granite, represents 'the swansong of the late but impressive Gothic Revival in the thirteenth-century French medieval style' (Yarwood). It comprises a traditional cruciform plan with three tall towers and spires, and is much admired – although Alec Clifton-Taylor describes it as 'a scholarly building' but 'alien to Cornwall'.

The diocese of Guildford was created out of the diocese of Winchester in 1927 and its new cathedral, built on a magnificent site to the north-west of the town, was begun in 1936. The architect was Sir Edward Maufe (1883–1974) and his building, in a simplified, almost emasculated, Gothic style, is characteristic of the time. Built almost entirely of red brick, it has an austere but distinguished exterior that respects its location – indeed, its bricks are of the same type of clay as that on which it stands (750 piles were sunk deep into the clay in order to carry the weight of the structure). Its strong central tower is crowned with a golden angel that faces into the prevailing wind. The interior brickwork is hidden beneath plaster rendering with limestone dressings, and has a cool spaciousness, with open vistas to the great golden dorsal curtain at the east end. Ferro-concrete was used for the construction of the nave vault, which has a wider span than that of any other English cathedral. Building was halted by the outbreak of the Second World War and was not resumed until 1952. The cathedral was finally consecrated in 1961.

In 1095, the great Benedictine abbey of Coventry was designated a cathedral priory. At that time it was one of the richest and most influential houses in the Midlands and it was the only English cathedral to be destroyed at the Dissolution of the Monasteries. The foundations of the east end of this once immense church were discovered in 1955 just beyond the west wall of the new cathedral. It was found to have been 122m (400ft) long, with a large, semicircular ambulatory around the High Altar. When the new diocese of Coventry was created in 1918 the fourteenth-century parish church of St Michael became its cathedral. With the exception of its magnificent tower and spire – at 91m (300ft) the third highest in England – and the now consolidated outer wall, the building was destroyed in an air raid in 1940. It was replaced by

Truro Cathedral.

Coventry Cathedral. (© John Crook/info@john-crook.com)

the present building, which was consecrated in 1962. The architect, Sir Basil Spence (1907–76), was selected by competition in 1951 and work began three years later. Spence's design was criticised by some for being too modern and by others for being too traditional. It is certainly true that, unlike Liverpool and Guildford, it does not follow the Gothic tradition in plan, and its axis is almost at right angles to that of the earlier cathedral. But, as Spence admitted, his sandstone, green slate, concrete and copper-covered cathedral is, in many respects, a traditional HALL-CHURCH in design: it has a wide nave with aisles, and arcades of piers, a stellar vault, canopied choir stalls, presbytery, High Altar and reredos. But its proportions are entirely modern – made possibly by the strength of reinforced concrete – and the great south door is entered from a glass atrium that incorporates the walls and traceried windows of the earlier building. Spence created a church of considerable dignity and elegance, ideally suited to decoration by some of the most eminent artists of his day: Graham Sutherland's 22m (72ft) high tapestry *Christ in Glory*, the glowing baptistery window by John Piper and Patrick Reyntiens, John Hutton's lofty engraved glass entrance screen, the cleverly angled nave windows by Lawrence Lee, Keith New and Geoffrey Clarke, Sir Jacob Epstein's striking sculpture of *St Michael and the Devil* and Elizabeth Frink's bronze eagle lectern are works of far greater creative quality than those that furnish any other contemporary cathedral.

New Roman Catholic Cathedrals

While the Church of England was facing up to its urban responsibilities by adapting parish churches as cathedrals, the Roman Catholic Church, 'emancipated' by the Roman Catholic Relief Act of 1829, began creating new dioceses and building cathedral churches in the industrial conurbations. Several of these nineteenth-century cathedrals were designed by A.W.N. Pugin (1815–52), who had converted to Roman Catholicism in 1834. He embraced his new faith with passionate fervour, expressing his emotions through architecture – and the 'Second Pointed Style' of medieval architecture (*c.* 1280–1340) in particular. Birmingham (begun in 1839), Newcastle upon Tyne (1844), Nottingham (1841) and Shrewsbury (constructed to Pugin's designs by his son, E.W. Pugin, in 1853) are characterised by austere exteriors and rich, darkly Byzantine interiors. Southwark Cathedral, begun in 1840 but much reduced from his original design, was Pugin's greatest London church. But it was much criticised by John Ruskin, was destroyed by bombing in 1948, and was rebuilt by Romilly Craze in 1953–8.

Of all the new Roman Catholic cathedrals four are pre-eminent: Norwich, Westminster, Liverpool and Clifton (Bristol). The Cathedral Church of St John the Baptist at Norwich was built between 1884 and 1910 for the 15th Duke of Norfolk who also commissioned the remarkable French Gothic church at Arundel which became the cathedral of the new diocese of Arundel and Brighton in 1965. With the creation of the diocese of East Anglia in 1976, the church of St John at Norwich was designated as its cathedral. It is England's finest Victorian Roman Catholic cathedral: 84m (275ft) long, with a long aisled nave, transepts, stone vaulting, flying buttresses and an imposing central tower – all in the Early English style (*see* MEDIEVAL ARCHITECTURE). It was designed by Sir George Gilbert Scott (1811–78), who was also responsible for the restoration of the Anglican cathedrals at Hereford, Winchester, Ely, Salisbury, Lichfield and Peterborough and Westminster Abbey (much of this work was excessive, but without his timely intervention much more of the structure of these great buildings would have been lost).

The Metropolitan Cathedral of the Most Precious Blood, St Mary, St Joseph and St Peter at Westminster is both the most important Roman Catholic cathedral in England and the finest. Built between 1895 and 1903 to designs by J.F. Bentley (1839–1902), the banded pattern of the exterior originated in the Italian cathedrals of Siena and Orvieto – although there the banding is of black and white marble, whereas at Westminster it is in red brick and white stone. Similarly, the magnificent 87m (285ft) high campanile is reminiscent of the bell tower at Siena. Westminster is an immense neo-Byzantine building – 12.5 million bricks were used in its construction. It was intended to accommodate great ceremonial occasions and consequently it is exceptionally wide: 47.5m (156ft), compared with a total length of 110m (360ft) (*see* colour plate 23).

The contrast with the new steel and concrete Metropolitan Cathedral of Christ the King at Liverpool could not be greater. Built in 1962–7, it was an exception: a building of stark beauty in an age of architectural brutality. Designed by Sir Frederick Gibberd (1908–84), it sits on the crypt of Sir Edward Lutyens's (1869–1944) abandoned cathedral, an immense building that, had it been built, would have been the largest cathedral in the world – 207m (680ft) long with a dome 51m (168ft) in diameter and 155m (510ft) high. Work began in 1930 but the project was abandoned nine years later. Gibberd's building is wonderfully innovative and could not be further removed from a conventional cruciform church. Constructed on a circular ground plan, it resembles a huge marquee, with a glass lantern and stainless-steel corona above. The spatial handling of the interior and the use of both natural and artificial light create something of the spiritual quality of its great medieval predecessors. Chapels are inserted in the outer walls, squeezed between the great, sloping

The Roman Catholic Metropolitan Cathedral of Christ the King, Liverpool. (Scott Barbour/Getty Images)

buttresses that offset the thrust of the 2,000-ton lantern. A 190-ton white marble altar is located at the centre of the vast circular interior space, 61m (200ft) in diameter, beneath a delicate metal BALDACCHINO and illuminated by the huge lantern, filled with coloured glass. There is seating for more than 3,000 people. The external concrete surfaces have been faced – the chapels and porches with Portland stone and the ribs with pale-grey mosaic. The roof is of grey aluminium.

The Cathedral Church of St Peter and St Paul was built in 1970–3 on a new site at Clifton, Bristol. Designed in 1965 by F.S. Jennett, R. Weeks and A. Poremba of the Percy Thomas Partnership, it replaced the inadequate pro-cathedral of the Apostles in Bristol which had been begun in 1834 but never completed. The new cathedral is built entirely of concrete, on a hexagonal plan, all its proportions derived from an equilateral triangle – symbolising the Holy Trinity. The High Altar stands at the focus of a quadrant, ensuring uninterrupted sight-lines for congregations at the mass (how different from the medieval notion of the *sanctum sanctorum*). The Portland stone altar is located beneath a pyramidal lantern surmounted by a concrete flèche that contains a cross and two bells. There is seating for nearly 1,000 people, and large doorways, called St Peter's and St Paul's, lead to bridges over car parks beneath. The overall effect, especially of the interior, is one of composed simplicity.

POST-MEDIEVAL MONASTERIES A number of religious houses have been established since the Middle Ages, several of them as Anglican communities (*see* RELIGIOUS ORDERS IN THE ANGLICAN CHURCH). Of the 'second spring' of Roman Catholic abbeys, most (such as the Benedictine abbey of Buckfast in Devon) are built in the early Gothic style favoured by the traditional school of Victorian and Edwardian architects. (The rebuilding of Buckfast's ruined tenth-century abbey began in 1907 and was completed in 1938.) However, the new Benedictine abbey of Prinknash, (pronounced 'Prinage') was architecturally innovative and even (for its time) controversial. The Prinknash community was established soon after 1928, when Benedictines from Caldey Island, Pembrokeshire (the 'Island of Saints'), were given an ancient manor house that sheltered beneath the Cotswold scarp near Painswick in Gloucestershire. Built as a GRANGE (St Peter's) by the abbots of Gloucester, it later belonged to the lords Chandos of Sudeley and was occupied by Prince Rupert in

1643. When the monks arrived, plans were made for a neo-Gothic abbey church and cloister, but the Second World War intervened and a new building, modern both in design and construction, with a temporary church in the crypt, was finally opened in 1972 with a temporary church in the crypt. Built of 2,500 tons of yellow Guiting limestone, the building projects audaciously from the scarp 'on a glorious but impractical hill, in the midst of a little forest of beech, and commanding Elysium' (Horace Walpole, who visited Prinknash Park in 1774). The design is by F.G. Broadbent and the wonderful glass in the crypt, as well as most of the fittings, was made by the monks, who supported themselves by the produce of their estate and a highly successful pottery. Most regrettably, it is understood that the community has been obliged to close both the pottery and the monastic buildings and to return to St Peter's Grange. At the time of writing, the future of the splendid building has yet to be determined.

POSTERN A small private entrance in the wall of a monastic PRECINCT.

POSTULANT One seeking admission to a religious order. Initially, a postulant would be accommodated near the monastery gate where he would undergo testing before presenting himself on three consecutive days before the CHAPTER, humbly petitioning to be accepted as a NOVICE.
See also RECRUITMENT

POT METALS *see* STAINED GLASS

POULTRY, THE *see* LARDER

POVERTY One of the three monastic vows: 'They venerate poverty, not the penury of the idle and the negligent, but a poverty directed by a necessity of the will, sustained by the thoroughness of faith, and approved by divine love.' Private possessions were not permitted, although, as bodies corporate, many monasteries accumulated considerable wealth and, in the later medieval period, even individual monks were allowed a small personal allowance.

PRAEMUNIENTES A clause contained in a parliamentary summons requiring bishops to

The Benedictine abbey of Prinknash, Gloucestershire. (By kind permission of Richard Sale)

arrange for a specified number of other clergy (notably abbots) to attend at a particular session of parliament. In 1295, for example, thirty-seven Benedictine and sixty-two Cistercian abbots were summoned, although this number was exceptional and in the parliament of 1302 the numbers were reduced to twenty-three and twenty-one respectively.

PRANDIUM The main meal of the monastic day (*see* FRATER *and* HORARIUM).

PRAYER *see* DIVINE OFFICE

PRAYER BOOK, THE *see* COMMON PRAYER, BOOK OF

PREACHERS, ORDER OF (THE DOMINICAN ORDER OF FRIARS PREACHER) *see* FRIARS

PREBEND *see* CLERGY (CHURCH OF ENGLAND) *and* PREBENDARY

PREBENDARY The title-holder of a cathedral benefice. The endowments of most medieval non-monastic cathedrals were divided into prebends, each of which was intended to support a single member of the chapter. In some cathedrals (such at Wells in Somerset) the territorial titles remain, although not the income.
See also CATHEDRALS *and* CLERGY (CHURCH OF ENGLAND)

PRECATORY SCROLL A stylised scroll containing a supplicatory prayer. Precatory scrolls are a common feature of monumental brasses where they are usually engraved near the hands or mouths of figures, like the 'speech bubbles' of a modern strip cartoon (*see* BRASSES (MONUMENTAL) *and* LABEL).

PRECENTOR The director of music and principal cantor in a religious house, a senior obedientiary and one of the three custodians of the community's seal (*see* OBEDIENTIARIES). The precentor's duties included organising the music for the services (all of which were sung), conducting choir practices, rehearsing readers and ordering PROCESSIONS. He was also responsible for ensuring that the service BOOKS were properly notated and in good repair and often doubled as a community's librarian (*see* ARMARIUS), annalist, archivist and chronicler. He was in absolute control of the choir: 'what he arranged to be sung had to be sung and what he decided to be read had to be read'. His position was to the north of the choir (hence, CANTORIS) and his deputy, the SUCCENTOR, occupied that to the south (*see* DECANI).

The ancient monastic office was retained in the post-Reformation cathedrals, where the precentor is responsible for the direction of choral services. The office is that of a minor canon or chaplain, except in cathedrals of the 'Old Foundation', where the precentor is a member of the cathedral chapter.
See also CHURCH MUSIC *and* CLERGY (CHURCH OF ENGLAND)

PRECEPTORY *see* COMMANDERY

PRECES The plural of *prex* meaning 'prayer', preces are short petitions uttered by the priest and responded to by the choir or congregation. In the Church of England, those prayers that precede the Creed are called preces and those that follow it are VERSICLES.
See also CHURCH MUSIC

PRECINCT The symbolic withdrawal from the world of a religious community was marked by physical boundaries defining the precinct within which the brethren lived. The precincts of medieval monasteries were often extensive: that at Jervaulx Abbey extended to 100 acres and at Glastonbury Abbey to 60 acres, containing not only the abbey church and claustral buildings, but also numerous stores, barns, workshops, cattle-sheds, mill, smithy, stables, cemetery and charnel house. Sometimes even a monastery's orchards, vegetable gardens and vineyards were enclosed within a wall or embankment and ditch. The inner precinct, in the immediate vicinity of the abbey church and claustral buildings (the *close*), was itself surrounded by the *curia* or outer court, which contained the guest-house, dairy, scullery, bakehouse, brewhouse, granary and other buildings necessary to the efficient running of the community. It was in the curia that contact was made with the outside world, although monks were not permitted to leave the claustral enclosure without permission (which was assumed, in the case of certain monastic officials). The Cistercians often had a further court, beyond the main gatehouse of the curia, in which they located noisy or offensive activities such as the smithy and tannery. Today, former precincts may be identified by reference to the delineation of later streets and house plots, to fragments of walls (notably at St Mary's, York) and to the location of gatehouses, several of which continue to provide access to the close of a cathedral or major church (*see* FORTIFICATION).

A number of cathedrals have retained their medieval closes: that at Norwich Cathedral Priory is the largest, delineated by the original precinct and entered by three gates – one a water gate from the River Wensum. The precinct at the cathedral priory at Durham (Palace Green) was constrained by the narrowness of its site and the present open space between the cathedral and the castle (Palace Green) was covered with houses until the twelfth century, when they were considered to be a health hazard and were demolished. As the name suggests, Palace Green is surrounded by buildings that were once closely associated with the cathedral and the prince bishops of Durham but are now largely used by the university (*see* PALATINATE). Sadly, at Gloucester Cathedral the close (College Green) is covered by a car park, just one example of the vandalism that has been inflicted on that once noble city since the 1960s.

The closes of non-monastic cathedrals would originally have served a different purpose: that at Hereford, for example, was open land in the Middle Ages, when it was the site of St Ethelbert's fair, and was later the city's only graveyard until 1791. (There was a time when any Welshman discovered in Hereford's precinct could be shot on sight!) The close at Wells is especially attractive, and allows the splendid west front to be viewed to advantage, while Exeter's close was opened up when the church of St Mary Major was demolished in 1971. The finest close in England is at Salisbury, where a wide area of grass allows uninterrupted views of the magnificent cathedral. It was effectively a gated suburb of the medieval town, enclosing the bishop's palace and canons' lodgings within a high wall of stone plundered from the earlier cathedral at Old Sarum and entered by four gates which were locked at night. Lichfield's close, with its ditch

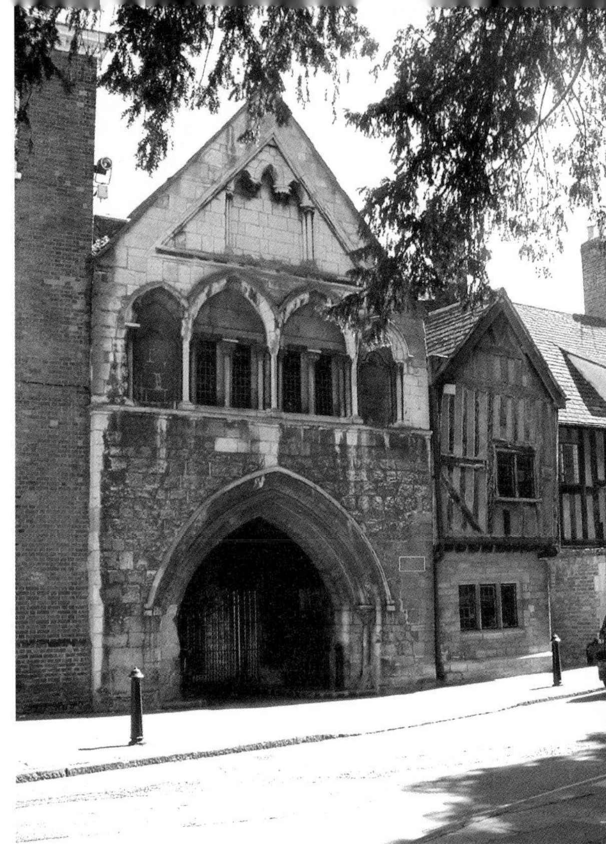

St Mary's Gate was the main entrance to the monastic outer court of what is now Gloucester Cathedral. It was from the room above that the dean and chapter witnessed the burning of Bishop John Hooper in 1555 (see illustration, page 318).

and stone walls, became a fortress during the Civil War when it was subjected to three sieges: as a result many of the medieval buildings were destroyed and the wall dismantled.
See also FORTIFICATION *and* MONASTIC BUILDINGS

PREDELLA (i) A platform, formed by the uppermost of the SANCTUARY steps, on which the priest stood when celebrating the mass.
(ii) A shelf behind an altar or communion table on which a REREDOS is supported or a is TRIPTYCH placed.

PRELATE A high-ranking cleric in the medieval Church, usually a bishop or the superior of a religious house.

PREMONSTRATENSIAN CANONS The 'White Canons' belonged to an order of canons regular founded in 1120 by the saintly Norbert of Prémontré near Laon. Norbert was a friend of Bernard of Clairvaux, the charismatic leader of the early CISTERCIANS. The Premonstratensian rule was that of St Augustine, with additional austerities and an emphasis on manual work (*see* AUGUSTINIANS). Their habit comprised a white cassock, a long white cloak and hood and a white cap. As with the Cistercians, their churches were dedicated to Our Lady and they were governed from a mother house at which annual chapters were held. Despite their preference for remote sites, the Premonstratensians often worked in the community as parish priests (some became bishops) and in hospitals. They arrived in England in 1143 and eventually had thirty-one abbeys, each consisting of an abbot and twelve canons, together with conversi (*see* LAY BROTHERS), servants and dependents.

PRESBYTERY The eastern area of a major church, surrounding the SANCTUARY. In the Middle Ages the presbytery was reserved for the clergy: literally, 'the place of the presbyters', the 'elders' of the early Church. In a cathedral, the bishop's throne (*cathedra*) was originally located in an apse behind the High Altar, but was removed to the PRESBYTERY in the medieval period.

Eleventh-century Benedictine presbyteries were apsidal and surrounded by an AMBULATORY and subsidiary chapels, as at Canterbury (St Augustine) and Bury St Edmunds. Of the two Norman apses to have survived in major English churches, that at Norwich Cathedral Priory is surmounted by a later clerestory and vault, while the apse at Peterborough is one of the purest Romanesque interiors in England (*see* APSE). From the twelfth century these apsidal presbyteries were generally superseded by presbyteries with square terminations, although there are examples where presbyteries were later extended and apsidal ambulatories added to provide for additional chapels: as at Battle, Hailes and Tewkesbury abbeys, all in the thirteenth century (*see* CHEVET).

At the eastern end of the presbytery was the sanctuary, a slightly raised area immediately surrounding the High Altar (*see* ALTARS *and* REREDOS) and separated from the presbytery by a single Sanctuary Step (the *gradus presbyterii*). In the churches of major abbeys, priories and cathedrals there were also flights of steps separating both the presbytery and the sanctuary from the CHOIR, so that the ceremonial could more easily be seen. In parish churches, and in those of the more austere monastic orders, such as the Cistercians and Carthusians, there was usually no architectural division between the presbytery and the NAVE. But following the Fourth Lateran Council of 1215 (which pronounced the doctrine of transubstantiation, thereby emphasising the sacredness of the MASS), it was considered necessary to enclose the presbytery of a parish church by means of a screen (*see* ROOD SCREEN), both to preserve the mystery of the EUCHARIST and to isolate the sanctuary from the secular activities of the nave. It is this enclosed space that is now described as the CHANCEL (from the Latin *cancelli* meaning 'lattice' or 'grating'), the term 'presbytery' being used (erroneously) as a synonym for 'sanctuary'. In the

Among the most beautiful in England, the presbytery at Norwich Cathedral is an extraordinary blend of Romanesque and Perpendicular architecture. (© John Crook/info@john-crook.com)

medieval cathedrals and major monastic churches, this separation of choir from nave was marked by a PULPITUM, together with a rood screen. There are several instances in English cathedrals of the pulpitum and rood screen having been removed or replaced by a (usually Victorian) screen, leaving the choir and presbytery visible from the west end of the nave – at Hereford, Peterborough, Salisbury and Worcester, for example.

The majority of English cathedrals have square eastern terminations, the apsidal presbyteries and ambulatories at Canterbury, Gloucester and Norwich being notable exceptions. Despite Victorian restorations, many medieval presbyteries have retained one or more of the architectural features that were provided for the celebration of the mass. These may include an AUMBRY, CREDENCE, FENESTELLA, PISCINA, SEDILIA and SQUINT.

The presbytery and choir were, of course, the focus of worship, and consequently considerable sums of money were often expended in order that the architecture and decoration should reflect the solemnity of their function. At Gloucester Cathedral a fourteenth-century remodelling of the eleventh-century choir and presbytery resulted in the construction of a spectacular Perpendicular stone-ribbed 'cage' that masked the original Norman arcade and was extended upward into a magnificent new clerestory and vault – an achievement that 'leaves one gasping with admiration at its brilliant audacity' (Alec Clifton-Taylor). In 1252 the presbytery at Ely Cathedral Priory was rebuilt and extended in order to accommodate increasing numbers of pilgrims to St Etheldreda's shrine, which was located between the choir and the sanctuary. *See also* MEDIEVAL ARCHITECTURE *and* MONASTIC BUILDINGS

PRETIOSA *see* HOURS (CANONICAL)

PRICKET A stand with one or more upright spikes on which votive candles are fixed.
See also LIGHTS

PRICKING The practice of making a pattern of small holes in a sheet of parchment in order to guide the ruling of lines.
See also RULING

PRIE-DIEU From the French 'pray God', a small prayer-desk for private devotions (*see* DESKS).

PRIEST Early English versions of the New Testament distinguished between *presbyter* ('elder') and *sacerdos* ('sacrificing minister'), but by the eleventh century the word 'priest', which is an etymological contraction of *presbyter*, was ambiguously used for both. With the spread of Christianity, the presbyters adopted more fully the functions of priests and as the parish priest became the normal celebrant of the EUCHARIST, and customarily exercised the power of ABSOLUTION, his supernatural functions and powers were emphasised and he acquired a position outside the feudal hierarchy while remaining subordinate to his bishop, the validity of his position being dependent on ORDINATION. The medieval perception of the priesthood was therefore almost exclusively concerned with the mass. This was later rejected by the Reformers, although the term 'priest' was retained in the *Book of Common Prayer*, apparently to ensure that deacons would not celebrate the Holy communion.

Members of monastic communities were not necessarily priests, although many monks were ordained clerks and were permitted to administer the sacraments: baptism, absolution, confirmation (the prerogative of a bishop), ordination of clerks, matrimony, communion, unction for the sick and dying, and the casting out of evil spirits.
See also CLERGY (CHURCH OF ENGLAND) *and* HOLY ORDERS

PRIEST'S DOOR A small door, usually in the south wall of the PRESBYTERY or CHANCEL, by which the priest entered the church.

PRIMATE The title of the bishop of 'the first see': the Archbishop of Canterbury is 'Primate of All England' and the Archbishop of York is 'Primate of

England'.

PRIME Dating from *c.* 395, the first of the canonical hours observed at daybreak and sometimes followed by Prime of the Blessed Virgin Mary. Similar in structure to COMPLINE.
See also HOURS (CANONICAL) *and* HORARIUM

PRIMER (*also* PRYMER) A devotional book containing the Little Office of the Blessed Virgin Mary, the Seven Penitential Psalms, the fifteen Gradual Psalms, the Litany of the Saints and the Office for the Dead.

PRINCE BISHOP *see* PALATINATE

PRIOR *and* PRIORESS *see* PRIORY, HOSPICE *and* SUPERIOR

PRIORY A religious house presided over by a prior or prioress. The head (superior) of a monastic house was either an ABBOT (abbess) or prior (prioress) and it is not always possible to draw a clear distinction between the two titles (*see* SUPERIOR). Under the Benedictine influence the term came to denote a monk who ranked next to the abbot and acted as his deputy. It was later applied also to the heads of small houses that were dependencies of abbeys (*see* CLUNIACS) and to the heads of mendicant houses (*see* FRIARS), although in practice several priories attained religious eminence and economic prosperity which greatly exceeded that of many abbeys. All Cistercian, Premonstratensian and Victorine houses were abbeys and all Carthusian and Cluniac houses were priories, being daughter houses of the Grand Chartreuse and Cluny (although, anomalously, the Cluniac house of Bermondsey was an abbey). The great Benedictine foundations were abbeys, as were some Augustinian houses, but the majority of smaller houses of both these orders, and those of the Gilbertines, were priories. Furthermore, the Benedictines distinguished between *conventual priories*, which were self-governing houses, and *obedientiary priories*, which were dependencies of abbeys. Where a bishop was also titular abbot, the community would be administered by a prior and its church was designated as a CATHEDRAL

Leominster Priory, Herefordshire. (Courtesy of Roy Morgan)

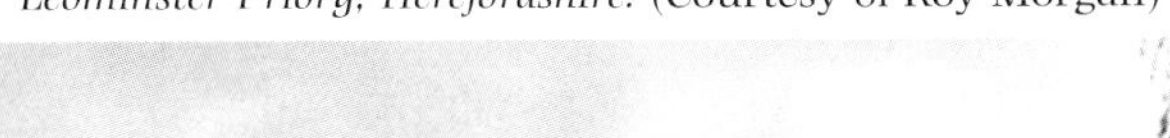

PRIORY: at Durham and Ely, for example. A prior's deputy was a *sub-prior*. At the DISSOLUTION OF THE MONASTERIES a number of priory churches were acquired for parochial use: Bolton in Yorkshire, Great Malvern in Worcestershire and Leominster in Herefordshire, for example.
See also ALIEN PRIORY, CATHEDRALS, MONASTERY *and* MONASTIC BUILDINGS

PRIORY CELL A religious community of no more than three members.

PRISONS Recalcitrant and unruly monks were dealt with in chapter (*see* PENAL CODE). Sanctions for serious offences included imprisonment and even solitary confinement, and cells were provided for the purpose. Furthermore, as feudal lords, the superiors of major monastic houses exercised temporal jurisdiction in their own courts, and convicted felons could be held in a monastic prison. These were often located in an abbey gatehouse, as at Ely and St Albans. At Fountains there was a range of cells on the ground floor beneath the abbot's lodging, each with its own latrine (*garderobe*), and a staple in the floor to which a prisoner's shackles were attached. These cells were accessible from the courtroom to the west and from the abbot's hall by a newel stair added to the north wall of the house. When the southernmost cell was excavated in the nineteenth century the words *vale libertas* ('farewell freedom') were found inscribed into the wall, the use of Latin suggesting that the occupant had been a monk rather than a common felon. A particularly secure prison at Durham was known as the 'lying house'. This was located beneath the infirmarian's chamber and was 'ordained for . . . great offenders'. A second cell, adjacent to the chapter house, was used for monks who had committed minor offences.

PRIVATE MASS A MASS celebrated individually by a single priest, assisted by a SERVER or ACOLYTE. An increasing emphasis on the propitiatory element of the eucharistic sacrifice encouraged priests in the belief that they had a duty to say a daily mass. In the monasteries this resulted in an increase in the number of monks who were also ordained priests and a proliferation of subsidiary altars. Private masses were said either at the priest's discretion and for his own purposes, or in fulfilment of obligations such as chantries (*see* CHANTRY).

PRIVATE PROPERTY A monk's vow of poverty required him to renounce all private property: 'he had absolutely not anything; neither a book, nor tablets nor a pen – nothing at all'. He was provided with the essentials – a bed, food and medical care – and items such as clothing and bedding were lent to him 'according to need'. Even so, by the twelfth century there was evidence of laxity, although this was strongly resisted by reforming superiors. By the fourteenth century a monk received a small personal allowance (*peculium*). This was intended originally for distribution to the poor, but it came to be used for the purchase of medicines, spices and other small 'items of comfort' and was supplemented by a clothing allowance. By the sixteenth century these two allowances produced an annual income of about one pound – known as *wages*. The practice was contrary to the notion of property held in common, but persisted until the suppression of the monasteries, despite various attempts at reform.
See also PITTANCE

PRIVILEGED ALTAR An altar at which a plenary INDULGENCE could be obtained for a soul in PURGATORY through a celebration of the MASS.
See also ALTARS, CHANTRY

PROBATION *see* NOVICE *and* POSTULANT

PROBATIONER A young chorister in training. In some choirs, probationers wear cassocks but not surplices.

PRO-CATHEDRAL A church in which is located a

bishop's throne (*cathedra*) pending the erection of a permanent building.

PROCESSIONAL CROSS A cross carried on a staff before a liturgical procession.

PROCESSIONAL TORCHES *see* BIER LIGHT

PROCESSIONALE The book containing the litanies, hymns and prayers prescribed for use in PROCESSIONS.
See also BOOKS

PROCESSIONS Liturgical processions, which were either festal or penitential, usually took place before the principal celebration of the EUCHARIST on feast-days and were of such importance that they influenced the architecture of churches, both large and small. In monastic communities, there was a procession of the entire convent every Sunday before High Mass. Led by the PROCESSIONAL CROSS, torches, THURIFER, priests and novices it visited each of the subsidiary altars in turn (including those in the claustral buildings) before returning to the choir for the singing of the High Mass. Provision had to be made for the processional route (*see* AISLE, AMBULATORY *and* DOORWAYS), and the stations occupied by certain participants in the procession were often marked in the church floor: at Easby Abbey in Yorkshire, for example, where traces of incised circles remain. The NAVE provided a separate and self-contained place of worship which sometimes served as a parish church or, in Cistercian houses, was used by the *conversi* for worship (*see* LAY BROTHERS). But its main purpose was to provide an imposing and dignified space for the frequent processions which served to emphasise the order and discipline of a religious community and symbolised its corporate commitment to follow Christ. The BENEDICTINES had both east and west doorways between the church and the CLOISTER so they could include three sides of it in their processional circuit. The CISTERCIANS followed a slightly different route and sometimes preferred to re-enter the church through a special porch covering the west door of the nave. These porches came to be known as Galilees because the abbot who led the procession was seen as Christ leading his disciples into Galilee (*see* GALILEE).

Processions occasionally left the precincts, especially where religious houses were located in towns. At Durham the community of the cathedral priory processed through the city on St Mark's Day to the church of St Mary le Bow, where a High Mass was celebrated. There were similar celebrations on Palm Sunday, Holy Thursday, Whit Sunday and Trinity Sunday, but the greatest processions were those in honour of Corpus Christi, when the members of town guilds and parishes thronged the streets with their crosses, banners and relics, led by a crystal monstrance containing the Body of Christ. Rogation days were universally marked by processions, accompanied by the singing of litanies and the 'beating of the bounds'. At York, the Rogation procession included a dragon (representing the devil), which was stored in the tower of St Olave's, next to the gate where the procession emerged from the minster precinct.
See also BANNER-STAVE LOCKERS

PROCTORS FOR THE CLERGY Elected representatives of the Anglican clergy who, with the members *ex officio*, constitute the Lower Houses of the Convocations of Canterbury and York (*see* CONVOCATION).

PROFESSION A solemn oath, including the VOWS of poverty, chastity and obedience, required of those wishing to enter a religious order. In the Middle Ages the minimum age at which profession could be made was 18 for monks and 25 for lay brothers.

PRONE A medieval vernacular office which followed the sermon in the High Mass. It included such matters as the announcement of banns of marriage and notices concerning fasts and feast-days.

PROVINCE A major ecclesiastical unit of administration comprising a number of contiguous dioceses. The term originated in the provinces of the Roman Empire, which provided an organisational framework for the early Church. In England, the archbishops of Canterbury and York exercise jurisdiction over their respective provinces.
See also CLERGY (CHURCH OF ENGLAND) *and* DIOCESE

PROVINCIAL EPISCOPAL VISITOR *see* CLERGY (CHURCH OF ENGLAND)

PROVOST *see* CLERGY (CHURCH OF ENGLAND)

PSALMODY *see* PSALTER

PSALMS Psalms are sacred songs accompanied by stringed instruments. The (Old Testament) Book of Psalms, which is used in both Jewish and Christian worship, is the oldest book of songs still in use. Some of the psalms are accredited to particular authors (seventy-three to David, twelve to Asaph and so on) but the accreditations are more recent than the psalms themselves and some are demonstrably incorrect. The popular belief that the entire PSALTER was written by David is no longer tenable, although many of the psalms date from the early period of the monarchy in Israel and the book is most probably a collection of anthologies. They include a number of imprecatory psalms which, in whole or in part, invoke divine vengeance (e.g. Psalms 58, 69, 109 and 137). The psalms comprise the essential element of the offices of the Roman BREVIARY and, to some extent, of the Anglican services of Morning and Evening prayer (*see* MATTINS *and* EVENING PRAYER). They are sung antiphonally (*see* ANTIPHON), either by priest (*cantor*) and choir or by the two sides of the choir (*decani* and *cantoris*), or recited responsively by the minister and congregation. The English version of the psalms sung in churches (the 'Prayer Book Version') dates from the sixteenth century and the translations of Tyndale and Coverdale. These were revised by Cranmer for the 'Great Bible' of 1539 and were retained in the prayer book when the Authorised Version of the Bible was issued in 1611.
See also ANGLICAN CHANT, CHURCH MUSIC *and* PLAINSONG

PSALTER A collection of PSALMS. The psalter (or *psaltery*) so dominated the life of religious houses that the monastic hours were called *psalmodia principalis* and the lesser hours (the Hours of the Blessed Virgin Mary) the *psalmodia secundria*. The core of worship consisted of the daily recitation of the psalter during the seven divine offices (even this division was derived from the psalmist's 'Seven times a day will I worship thee') (*see* DIVINE OFFICE) and the psalter would undoubtedly have been known by heart by many of the brethren. Psalters were superseded by *breviaries*, liturgical books containing not only the psalms but also the hymns, lessons, responsories, Canticles, etc. used in the divine office. As with breviaries, medieval psalters are often beautifully illuminated and are not always as sober as one might expect: the pages of the wonderful fourteenth-century *Macclesfield Psalter* teem with bestial curiosities, puns and bawdy jokes (*see* MANUSCRIPT ILLUMINATION).

Metrical psalters, which contain metrical versions of the psalms, were first introduced into England under Edward VI (1547–53). The *New Version of the Psalms*, a metrical psalter compiled in 1696 by Nahum Tate (1652–1715) and Nicholas Brady (1659–1726), was widely used in parish churches until the early nineteenth century. *Psalmody* is the study of the music for metrical versions of the psalms and for HYMNS.
See also SERVICE BOOKS

PSALTERY (i) An ancient and medieval stringed instrument.
(ii) A book containing the PSALMS and other

matter for recitation at the divine office (*see* PSALTER).

PULPIT DESK *see* DESKS

PULPITS A pulpit is an elevated platform (Latin: *pulpitum*) for a preacher or reader. In monastic houses, a sermon would be delivered to the brethren by the superior or his deputy, either from the lectern (which was located in the midst of the choir) or while seated on a raised chair in CHAPTER. There was always a pulpit or reading desk in the FRATER, from which passages of scripture were read by the READER IN FRATER during meals: the frater at Beaulieu Abbey has survived as the parish church and its FRATER PULPIT is still used during services.

In medieval cathedrals and abbey churches that were used for parochial purposes, there was usually a pulpit attached to a pillar on the north side of the NAVE and to the west of the ROOD SCREEN. The earliest pulpits are from *c.* 1340, although most surviving pre-Reformation examples are from the fifteenth and early sixteenth centuries. Medieval pulpits were constructed of stone or oak and are similar in shape to a wineglass, with a slender, splayed stem and tall, narrow 'drum' with traceried panels which sometimes contain carved or painted motifs depicting the likenesses of the Four Evangelists or familiar preceptors such as the Four Doctors of the Latin Church. One of the few medieval choir pulpits to have survived is the beautiful Prior Silkstede's pulpit at Winchester Cathedral Priory. Delicately carved in oak, with a winding stair and an ornate canopy, it was constructed during a fifteenth-century refurbishment of the cathedral's presbytery.

Liturgical changes effected by the REFORMATION resulted in a greater emphasis on direct communication between the priest and his congregation, and the pulpit acquired a more central role in worship, as did the reading desk (or *reading pew*) from which the priest conducted the services. In 1547 Edward VI ordered that each parish should provide 'a comely and honest pulpit', and this was repeated in the Elizabethan Injunctions of 1559. In the seventeenth and eighteenth centuries canopied pulpit and reading desk were often combined to form 'double-decker' pulpits, with the pulpit above the desk and each having its own means of access. These pulpits were often provided with a *tester* or overhead SOUNDING BOARD, which amplified and directed the voice of the preacher, together with an iron stand for an hourglass. Sounding boards have survived in a number of cathedrals, including Lincoln, Peterborough and Salisbury. In the eighteenth century there was, for a time, an enthusiasm for moving the pulpit halfway down one side of the nave and for rearranging the seating to face the preacher. In the nineteenth century there was, again, a change of emphasis and a return from preaching to the administration of the sacraments. As a consequence, many reading pews and tiered pulpits were removed, encouraged by Victorian ecclesiologists in their enthusiasm for all things medieval. Most cathedrals now have two pulpits: one in the nave and a second between the presbytery and the choir. These are, for the most part, Victorian 'Gothic' in style and of variable quality. However, the intricately carved Victorian nave pulpit at Worcester Cathedral Priory, although anachronistic, is finely executed in a variety of marbles, and the bronze and marble art nouveau pulpit at Ripon Cathedral (1913) is exceptionally beautiful. There are several instances of pulpits being moved from other churches: at Carlisle Cathedral Priory, for example, where a finely carved sixteenth-century pulpit, originally from the church of St Andrew, Antwerp, was installed as a memorial to a former dean. In recent times a distinction has been made between the 'traditional' sung services in the choir and 'congregational' services (with greater participation) in the nave. This practice (which has sound medieval precedents) has required the provision of a NAVE ALTAR and, in some cases, a

One of the few medieval choir pulpits to have survived is the beautiful Prior Silkstede's pulpit at Winchester Cathedral Priory. (© John Crook/info@john-crook.com)

new lectern and pulpit, several of which are of outstanding design and craftsmanship.
See also LECTERNS

PULPITUM From the Latin *pulpitum* meaning 'platform', a pulpitum is a massive transverse stone screen that separates the NAVE from the CHOIR. The majority of the great abbey churches and all the medieval English cathedrals once had both a ROOD SCREEN and a pulpitum. Each was possessed of an entirely different function, and whereas nearly all the medieval rood screens have been dismantled, several pulpita have survived. (Among the cathedrals, St Albans is a notable exception: there, the stone rood screen remains but the pulpitum has gone.) A pulpitum usually extended between the piers of the CROSSING, although there are several 'double' structures that occupy the depth of an entire bay: at Kirkstall Abbey in Yorkshire, for example, at Gloucester (but not the present screen – *see below*) and at Norwich Cathedral Priory, where the choir occupies the first two bays of the nave (in order to shut off public access to the cloister) and the pulpitum the third. Thus, the position of the pulpitum varied according to the needs of the resident community and the physical relationship of the choir to the nave – although it was always to the east of the rood screen. The original arrangement is not always immediately apparent: at Malmesbury in Wiltshire, for example, where the pulpitum enclosed the first bay west of the crossing and its western wall now forms a REREDOS for the altar of the parish church. By the thirteenth century changes in practice had affected the planning of many large churches, especially of their eastern ends. There was now room to accommodate the whole of the choir within a much longer eastern arm, so that the pulpitum could be constructed to the east of the crossing, leaving the TRANSEPT open to the lay congregation in the nave.

The pulpitum was usually pierced by a central doorway, flanked by altars in the western elevation, and with an internal stair to the platform (*loft*) above. On occasions the loft was used as a gallery for singers, and it often housed a portable organ (*see* ORGANS). It was also adorned with paintings or statues of historical and religious figures, set in tabernacles, whose achievements were intended to inspire the beholder. The Latin *pulpitum* is a 'platform' or 'stage', suggesting that it was from here that public sermons were preached before the development of PULPITS. But, in monastic houses, sermons were usually given from the president's chair in CHAPTER or from the choir lectern, and the main function of the pulpitum was to provide a solid screen for the RETURNED STALLS in the choir, thereby securing for the monks or canons both privacy and protection from draughts during the long hours of

The early fourteenth-century Great Screen at Exeter Cathedral. (© John Crook/info@john-crook.com)

the DIVINE OFFICE. Today, a surviving pulpitum is often surmounted by an organ, an arrangement that is not without its critics. Indeed, opinions are divided on the architectural merit, or otherwise, of the structure itself – imagine Peterborough with a pulpitum!

There are several fine examples, notably at Canterbury, Exeter, Lincoln, Rochester, St Davids, Southwell and York, all of which carry organ cases. Exeter's Great Screen of 1317–25 still retains its subsidiary altars on either side of the central passageway, although in both the rear wall was pierced in the 1870s to create openings to the choir beyond. In the earlier Norman church the screen chapels were dedicated to St Mary and St John Baptist. Thirteen panels, painted in *c.* 1590 directly on to the stone surface of the screen, replaced earlier carved figures. The west side of Lincoln's magnificent early fourteenth-century pulpitum is renowned for its Decorated Gothic stone carving. Characterised by the use of ogee arches (*see* ARCH) and elaborate surface decoration (once gilded and painted), Alec Clifton-Taylor rightly observed that 'It would not be possible to find a better illustration of the magnificence of Decorated art at its best. One other English cathedral, Southwell, has a smaller screen of comparable splendour and of much the same date.' At St Davids Cathedral, the splendid fourteenth-century pulpitum incorporates a compartment containing the tomb of Bishop Henry de Gower (1328–47), who undertook a major remodelling of the cathedral and built the remarkable bishop's palace (*see* FORTIFICATION). Unusually, Gower's pulpitum was surmounted by a rood loft that was removed in 1571. The charming Perpendicular Arundel Screen at Chichester Cathedral is hardly of sufficient substance to merit consideration as a pulpitum. Named after Bishop John Arundel (1459–78), it probably dates from the early fifteenth century. There were originally chapels in the two outer arches, but these were lost when the screen was taken down in 1859. It was restored to its original location in 1961, as a memorial to Bishop George Bell (1929–58).

Not all pulpita are what they seem. The splendid fourteenth-century pulpitum at Gloucester was described by St John Hope in 1897 as comprising 'two stone walls – the one to the west end of the quire, against which the stalls were returned, and the other west of it between the first pair of pillars. The western wall was broader than the other, and had in the thickness of its southern half an ascending stair to a loft or gallery above, which extended over the whole area between the two walls'. This magnificent pulpitum survived *in situ* until 1741 when Bishop Benson (1734–52) replaced it with a screen designed by William Kent (1685–1748). In turn, this screen was replaced by the present pulpitum in 1819. Designed by Sir Robert Smirke (1780–1867), it makes no pretensions to being a pulpitum in the medieval sense. However, with its great, crowned organ case, it does serve to conceal the abrupt change of architectural style between the nave and choir.

The pulpitum should not to be confused with the *chancel screen*, which replaced the rood screen in numerous parish churches, or with the choir or organ screen which, in several cathedrals, replaced the medieval pulpitum. Typically, the wooden organ screen at Beverley Minster was designed by Sir George Gilbert Scott to match the fine, early sixteenth-century choir stalls, and was expertly made by James Elwell of Beverley in 1878–80. Not all choir screens are successful: that at Worcester Cathedral Priory (also by Scott, 1877) is truly awful in its pretentiousness. It should go the way of a similar ironwork choir screen at Salisbury Cathedral, which was removed in 1960.
See also MEDIEVAL ARCHITECTURE, MONASTIC BUILDINGS *and* SCREENS

PURBECK MARBLE Used by the Romans in Britain and much favoured by the church builders and monumental masons of thirteenth- and fourteenth-century England and Normandy, Purbeck marble is a not marble at all but a dark, shell conglomerate which is capable of taking a very high polish and occurs in two narrow strata in the Isle of Purbeck in Dorset. Its use became fashionable towards the end of the thirteenth century when, stone from a quarry near Worth Maltravers was used in work at Lincoln Cathedral. Thereafter, there was hardly a great church in the land into which slender Purbeck marble shafts were not introduced in the thirteenth and fourteenth centuries (*see also* EFFIGIES). Its northern equivalent is *Frosterley marble*, a black or dark-grey limestone extracted from quarries at Frosterley in County Durham.
See also MASONRY *and* TOUCH

PURGATORY Purgatory and Hell are not synonymous. Described by Eamon Duffy as 'the out-patient department of Hell', Purgatory is 'the third place', a transient state occupied by repentant sinners who have died in grace. Hell is for the unrepentant and is a place of eternal torment (*poena sensus*) and exclusion from God's presence (*poena damni*). The concept is believed to date from the twelfth century and was intimately associated with profound social and intellectual changes, particularly attempts to introduce THIRD ORDERS between the powerful and the poor, the clergy and the laity. Medieval man did not believe that Purgatory held out hope of remission from Hell. Rather, Purgatory was a state of temporal punishment beyond the grave, a long and painful process of probation and expiation, preparing not-

yet-worthy Christians for Heaven. Without the concept of Purgatory, the medieval practice of offering prayers and masses for the dead would have been untenable. The Reformers argued that this doctrine was unnecessary: when a sinner repented and put his faith in Jesus, he or she was immediately justified by God, adopted as a child into the heavenly Father's family and made God's friend. In the words of Paul: 'Those whom he justified he also glorified' (Rom. 8: 30). God's grace short-circuited Purgatory.
See also CHANTRY, INDULGENCE, MEDIEVAL CHURCH, PRIVILEGED ALTAR *and* WALL PAINTINGS

PURPURE *see* COLOURS (HERALDIC)

PYX (i) A receptacle in which the reserved host is retained. Specifically, a small silver or silver-gilt box in which the BLESSED SACRAMENT is conveyed to the sick, wrapped in a *corporal* and carried in a pyx-bag slung about the priest's neck.
(ii) A box in which samples of new coinage were stored prior to their being tested for purity (*assayed*). A crypt beneath the magnificent CHAPTER HOUSE at Westminster Abbey contained a royal treasury which extended into an adjacent room known as the Pyx Chamber or the Chapel of the Pyx. The chamber was created out of the northern part of the UNDERCROFT to the monks' DORTER and is a low, square room with a massive central pillar supporting four bays of vaulting. It was here that the Trial of the Pyx was held, a procedure dating from 1281 at which new coins were compared with standard specimens (known as trial plates) in the presence of independent witnesses. At the dissolution of the abbey in 1540 the CHAPTER HOUSE and Pyx Chamber were used as a repository for government records, a function that continued until 1863, when it was transferred to Goldsmith's Hall. The chamber was also a chapel and an altar and PILLAR PISCINA have survived against the east wall.
See also RESERVATION *and* TABERNACLE

PYX-SHRINE *see* TABERNACLE

QUARREL An opening in TRACERY for a QUARRY.

QUARRY (i) One of a series of small diamond-shaped glass panels within a window (*see* STAINED GLASS). Stamped quarries, mass-produced and decorated with monochrome motifs, are characteristic of the nineteenth century.
(ii) An unglazed floor tile.

QUARTERING In HERALDRY, the method (known as *marshalling*) whereby a shield of arms is divided to display both the paternal arms and those acquired through marriage to heraldic heiresses.

QUATREFOIL A figure with four radiating stylised 'petals' found both as an architectural motif and an heraldic device (*see* FOILS). Quatrefoils in Gothic tracery often contain heraldic shields, especially those found in the side panelling of a TOMB CHEST.

QUIRE *see* CHOIR

QUOIN From the French *coin* meaning 'corner' or 'angle' a quoin is the external angle of a building and *quoins* or *quoin stones* are the dressed stones (*see* DRESSED STONE) forming the angle. In Anglo-Saxon buildings, *long and short work* comprises quoins laid so that long vertical slabs alternate with short horizontal ones.

R

RAG *and* RAGSTONE A hard, coarse stone that is not FREESTONE.

RAGGLE The remains of a roof line preserved in the stonework of an adjacent building.

RAGWORK Rubble walling, usually a weathering face, composed of polygonal stones.
See also MASONRY

RAIL (i) A horizontal member in the framework of a panelled door.
See also BRACE, LEDGE, MUNTIN *and* STILE
(ii) *For* other types of rail *see* BENCHES, PARCLOSE *and* STAIRCASES.

RAINWATER HEAD A box-shaped metal structure (usually of lead or cast-iron) in which water from a gutter is collected and discharged into a down-pipe.

RASURA Except for mendicants and (in some houses) the lay brethren, the growing of a beard was not permitted as it was considered to be indicative of pride. The monthly shaving of the monks (the *rasura*) was a solemn occasion regulated by the customaries of a particular house and normally conducted in the cloister, near the LAVATORIUM. Shaving included tonsuring (*see* TONSURE), and each monk was responsible for washing his own head in preparation. Hot water, towels and soap were provided by the CHAMBERLAIN, and the senior brethren were shaved first: 'because in the beginning the razors are sharp and the towels dry'. They were required to attend the office when summoned, unless their shaving had already begun. Professional barber-surgeons were often engaged in the larger houses and they may also have carried out the regular blood-letting (*see* PHLEBOTOMY). From the thirteenth century the frequency of shaving increased to fortnightly in winter and twice in three weeks during the summer.

READER IN FRATER The office of Reader in Frater, although not one of the OBEDIENTIARIES, was of considerable importance. Silence was observed during mealtimes in the FRATER so that his words could be heard: the Barnwell Observances enjoined the assembled brethren, 'nor let your mouths only take in food but yet your ears also hunger after the word of God'. The Reader was selected by the PRECENTOR and was blessed in choir on Sunday, the day before he began his week's responsibilities. Dinner was preceded by a second blessing before the reader entered the FRATER PULPIT and the meal did not begin until he had read the opening sentence of the passage that had been selected by the precentor. Readings were taken from the scriptures and from commentaries, the entire Bible being read during the course of a year.

READING *see* BOOKS

REBUS A rebus is a pictorial pun on a name (*non verbis sed rebus*). Many early seals include simple rebuses, and the concept almost certainly predates

Rebus of Abbot William of Milton Abbey, Dorset. (Courtesy of Florence Morris)

HERALDRY. Rebuses were especially popular in medieval ecclesiastical circles and were widely used as personal devices and to decorate the fabric of buildings, chapels and tombs. At Milton Abbey in Dorset, for example, a stone CORBEL is carved and painted in the form of a windmill on top of a wine barrel (*tun*), the rebus of a former abbot of Milton; while at Canterbury, one Thomas Goldstone, Prior of Christchurch, used a gold flint stone ensigned with a mitre.
See also GLAZIERS' MARKS *and* MASONS' MARKS

RECESS *see* AUMBRY, BREAD OVEN, CHEST CUPBOARD, CREDENCE, NICHE, PISCINA, SEDILIA *and* SQUINT

RECLUSE A religious who lives apart from the world (*see* ANCHORITE *and* COENOBITE). Not all recluses were genuinely EREMITICAL: in the medieval period, many occupied guests' rooms in religious houses and even engaged servants and private chaplains.

RECORDS *see* ARCHIVES

RECREATION In some houses of the less austere orders simple recreation was sometimes permitted during the hours between None and Vespers (mid- to late afternoon). For children, especially, and for novices and the sick and infirm, small indulgences were allowed – in addition to occasional pittances and relaxation of the rule of SILENCE. In the later medieval period some religious communities maintained country houses as retreats and convalescent homes for those brethren seeking spiritual or mental recuperation (*see* GRANGE). Practical hobbies, including weaving and the making of clocks and musical instruments, were sometimes encouraged, as was music-making, which was acknowledged as spiritually uplifting. Board games and (restrained) ball games were sometimes permitted, indeed late medieval Durham had a 'bowlinge allie' for the novices and even employed travelling players as part of their festal celebrations. Sometimes recreational activities went too far: in the fourteenth century the monks of Canterbury St Augustine were prohibited from playing games of chess and dice, from attending duels, cock-fighting and dog-baiting, and from hunting with hounds in the woods. On the other hand, the Cistercians of Jervaulx were permitted to keep a pack of mastiffs to protect their flocks from wolves.

RECRUITMENT Until the twelfth century there were two sources of recruitment: young adults who chose to enter a community and children (*oblates*) who were pledged to the monastic life by their parents. In the early twelfth century the historian Orderic Vitalis described how he was sent from his home in Shrewsbury to the monastery of St Evroul in Normandy:

> My father, Odeler, wept as he gave me, a weeping child to Rainald the monk, and sent me into exile for your [Christ's] love – nor ever after saw me. A small boy did not presume to contradict his father, but I obeyed him in all things, since he promised that I should possess paradise with the innocent. And so I left my country, my parents, all my kindred and my friends. At ten years old I crossed the Channel, and came, an exile, to Normandy, knowing no one, known to none. Like Joseph in Egypt, I heard a tongue I knew not. Yet by your grace I found among the strangers every kindness and friendship.

The CISTERCIANS rejected the practice, insisting that no one who had not reached the age of 16 should be admitted to their houses, while in Benedictine communities by the early twelfth century the OBLATE system was already in decline.

By the late medieval period, the larger houses were regulating their size to correspond with their incomes. Novices usually entered between the ages of 18 and 21 and were mostly drawn from an abbey's estates. The majority were the sons of freemen and therefore came from the middle ranks of rural and urban society, while very few came from the knightly or magnate classes where there was a dearth of male heirs. The most significant constraint on membership was an expectation that novices would bring with them endowments of money or land. It was therefore virtually impossible for a woman from an impoverished background to become a nun, while impecunious men could at least become LAY BROTHERS, if not full members of a community.

Inevitably, the motives for wishing to join a monastic community varied considerably. Some were attracted to the ascetic life and the Cistercians, in particular, exerted a powerful sense of vocation. For some, family expectations were important, while many nuns regarded the religious life as an acceptable alternative to marriage and motherhood. Indeed, for women from the aristocratic or gentle families, it was the only 'career' available to them. Naturally, there were times when a particular religious order or house was more 'fashionable' than others and therefore attracted more recruits. In the thirteenth century, recruitment by the FRIARS reduced significantly the number of men entering the established monastic orders and, from the mid-fourteenth century, those who might previously have considered work as lay brethren (*conversi*) turned instead to the buoyant labour market created by the Black Death (*see* PLAGUE). While all the monastic orders had suffered a general decline in membership by the fifteenth century (*see* MONASTIC DECLINE), there was a late revival – notably among the austere orders such as the CARTHUSIANS and Observant Franciscans (*see* OBSERVANTS).

Once monks and nuns had taken their final VOWS they were obliged to remain members of their orders for life, although under certain circumstances they were permitted to move from one house to another. Inevitably, there were those who came to regret their decision, and there are numerous records of *apostates* – those who ran away. A monk who deserted his community thereby committed a crime, and a warrant for his arrest could be issued by a secular authority. When apprehended, he would be returned to his house 'to be chastened according to the rule of his order'.

> One brother John Bengeworthe, a monk, who had been imprisoned for his ill desert, brake prison and went into apostasy, taking with him a nun of Godstow, but he has now been brought back to the monastery and is still doing penance.
>
> (Records of Eynsham Abbey, 1445)

RECTILINEAR TRACERY *see* MEDIEVAL ARCHITECTURE

RECTOR (i) A *clerical rector* was originally an incumbent who received the 'Great Tithes': all the customary offerings and dues of his parish. He was responsible for the CHANCEL and the rectory and for providing service books and vestments. In many instances, benefices were annexed by corporate bodies such as monastic or collegiate foundations who then received the Great (or Rectorial) Tithes, the Lesser (or Vicarial) Tithes going to a *vicar* who was appointed by them to administer the parish.

Following the Dissolution of the Monasteries, many monastic estates became the property of laymen (*lay rectors*) who also acquired the right to nominate vicars (subject to a bishop's approval), together with responsibility for maintaining the chancel and vicarage.
See also APPROPRIATION, CLERGY (CHURCH OF ENGLAND) *and* LAY RECTOR
(ii) The head of a college that may enjoy rectorial rights: as at Exeter and Lincoln colleges, Oxford.

RED FRIARS *see* FRIARS

RED LETTER DAYS Specific days, sometimes printed in red in the *Book of Common Prayer*, for which a proper Collect, Epistle and Gospel are provided. Important feast and saints' days were

similarly inscribed in red in ecclesiastical and monastic calendars and came to be known as 'red letter days', for which adequate warning and preparation was required.
See also RUBRIC *and* RUBRICATOR

REFECTORIAN *see* FRATER *and* LARDER

REFECTORY *see* FRATER

REFORMATION, THE This somewhat imprecise term covers a complex series of changes that took place in the western Church between the fourteenth and seventeenth centuries. Reformers of Catholicism such as John Wycliffe (*c.* 1330–84), Martin Luther (1483–1546) and John Calvin (1509–64) rejected the authority of the papacy, both religious and political, and sought authority in the original text of the scriptures through vernacular translations (*see* ROMAN CATHOLIC CHURCH). They claimed justification (salvation) by faith, rejecting the Catholic doctrine of transubstantiation (the conversion at the EUCHARIST of the bread and wine into the body and blood of Christ) and the adoration of the Virgin and the saints, and denounced malpractices and abuses within the Church such as the sale of indulgences (*see* INDULGENCE).

The Reformation in England

The Reformation was not a natural fulfilment of what had gone before but a violent disruption. In England, medieval Catholicism was neither exhausted nor decayed. Its vigour, richness and creativity were undiminished and it retained a strong hold on the loyalty and imagination of the English people right up to the 1530s, when the break with Rome occurred.

The English Reformation was a violent act of state rather than a popular movement, an insular process responsive to particular social and political forces which themselves arose from a long-standing monarchical policy of extending the sovereignty of central government. Reform was occasioned by papal procrastination concerning the 'King's Great Matter' – the dissolution of HENRY VIII's marriage with Catherine of Aragon – which led to Henry's repudiation of papal authority in England and a series of Acts of Parliament in 1534 which severed financial, judicial and administrative links with Rome, and to the SIX ARTICLES of 1539, the first authoritative statement of the doctrines of the English Church. In particular, the Act of Supremacy of 1534 confirmed to Henry and his successors the title of 'the only supreme head in earth of the Church of England' (*see* CHURCH OF ENGLAND). It was followed by legislation intended (in Thomas Cromwell's words) to make Henry 'the richest Prince in Christendom'. By the Annates Acts of 1534 the Crown, as successor to the pope, claimed the first year's revenues of each benefice, together with one tenth of the income from all succeeding years (the *annates*); acts of 1536 and 1539 authorised the DISSOLUTION OF THE MONASTERIES, in 1538 the religious SHRINES were dismantled, the relics destroyed and their treasures confiscated, and in 1547 the chantries were suppressed (*see* CHANTRY). Also in 1547, the year of the king's death, several of the traditional ceremonies of the medieval Church were abolished and an order made for the removal of all images 'from wall and window'. This resulted in the lime washing of WALL PAINTINGS (which, ironically, served to preserve them), the destruction (or defacement) of religious statues and the smashing of windows, although many escaped destruction – probably because of the cost of replacing them with clear glass.

Despite his break with Rome, Henry VIII consistently opposed the Reforming Movement and remained a convinced traditionalist in matters of doctrine and Church government, and it was not until after his death in 1547 that doctrinal Protestantism became official policy. The Act of Uniformity of 1549 required that the (first) *Book of Common Prayer* should be used in Anglican worship (*see* COMMON PRAYER, BOOK OF). This was followed by a second act in 1552, which authorised use of the (second) *Book of Common Prayer* and prescribed severe penalties for non-compliance and fines for non-attendance at Anglican services. The 1552 Prayer Book marks the establishment of Protestantism in the territories of the Crown of England. It abandoned transubstantiation, thereby confirming the distinction between the MASS and the communion service that is the essence of the distinction between Roman Catholicism and Protestantism.

With the accession of Queen Mary in 1553, Roman Catholic forms of worship were restored, and in 1555 there began a series of religious persecutions which acquired for the queen the epithet 'Bloody Mary'. The fanaticism of the Queen's supporters and advisers, and the unpopularity of her marriage with the king of Spain, undoubtedly increased popular support for the objectives of the Reformers. Mary died in 1558

In 1553, Bishop John Hooper (b. 1495) was burned for heresy outside the gate to his cathedral close, a victim of Mary Tudor's purge of Protestant clergy. A Victorian memorial now marks the place of execution.

and a further Act of Supremacy in 1559 declared her successor, Elizabeth I (1558–1603), to be 'the only supreme governor . . . as well in all spiritual or ecclesiastical things or causes as temporal'. In the same year, the third Act of Uniformity required that a revised version of the Prayer Book should be used in all churches and weekly fines imposed for non-attendance at services. In 1563 the THIRTY-NINE ARTICLES were published and in 1593 the Conventicle Act reinforced the penalties for non-attendance at services and for holding secret assemblies (*see* CONVENTICLE).

Thus, the sixteenth century was a period of unprecedented religious upheaval, one which witnessed the dismantling of many long-established rituals of community life and presented both parishioners and clergy with acute and perplexing problems of belief and conduct. In most places, there is little evidence of hostility to the Roman Catholic Church which, in the 1530s, was still held in high regard. In early sixteenth-century wills, for example, the most common bequest was to the parish church and to the chapels of chantries and guilds that were accommodated therein. For an essentially conservative people, whose religious beliefs were focused on the mystery of the Latin Mass, the introduction of a vernacular Bible and liturgy (*see below*), the destruction of familiar and comforting religious images and the prohibition of popular festivals and observances must have had a profound effect. And yet, with some notable exceptions (*see* PILGRIMAGE OF GRACE), most parishioners appear to have conformed to the doctrinal and liturgical changes that were imposed upon them by the combined authority of Church and State. Inevitably, a common reaction to such fundamental (and often contradictory) changes was one of helpless resignation. Documentary sources (including the lists of incumbents which are to be found in most churches) show that a remarkable number of the clergy simply shifted their position to accommodate each new change and, while a few were no doubt openly or privately cynical, most succeeded in avoiding trouble. One such was Simon Aleyn, the celebrated Vicar of Bray, who succeeded in retaining his Berkshire benefice through all the changes: 'being taxed by one for being a turncoat and an unconstant changeling, Not so, said he, for I always kept my principle, which is this, to live and die the vicar of Bray'.

Cohabiting clerics were a phenomenon throughout medieval Europe, but in 1549 the clergy of the new English Church were permitted to marry. There can be little doubt that, to the ordinary priest, respectability for his 'wife' and legitimacy for his children were above all the factors that made Protestantism acceptable to him. While in 1530 Henry VIII ruled over an essentially medieval society, by 1570 England was (outwardly, at least) whole-heartedly Protestant.

The redistribution of lands and property that followed the DISSOLUTION OF THE MONASTERIES had a considerable impact on many parishes. In some, the churches of former abbeys or priories were acquired for parochial use and were often reduced in size in order to accommodate a community's needs and financial resources. Others received the fittings from demolished monastic churches or even parts of their fabric: the tiny church of Hilton in Dorset, for example, has a striking series of traceried windows in the north wall, which were removed from the cloister of nearby Milton Abbey in the 1530s. Impropriated parish churches (those which, in the Middle Ages, were annexed to a religious house) acquired lay patrons, members of the Tudor establishment who had received (or purchased) monastic buildings, estates and privileges at the Dissolution. Medieval abbots were often rectors (*see* RECTOR), and as such received the major revenues and tithes of impropriated parishes. These rights were also transferred to the new lay rectors (*impropriators*), who thereby assumed responsibility for maintaining the chancels of their impropriated churches and for appointing perpetual curates to the benefices.

It was the suppression of the chantries in 1545 that resulted in the greatest impoverishment of community and civil life. Official disapproval of the doctrine of PURGATORY ('vain opinions of purgatory and masses satisfactory to be done for them which be departed') led inevitably to the Chantry Act of 1547 and the confiscation of those chantry funds which had been assigned to so-called 'superstitious objects'. As a consequence, innumerable endowments, ranging from schools and hospices to the provision of wax for candles, were terminated simply because they were designed to provide perpetual masses for the souls of their founders. The Chantry Act was followed by a further confiscation of church possessions in 1552 (because, as the official records readily admit, 'the King's majesty had need presently of a mass of money'), leaving only the bare essentials for worship. CHANTRY CHAPELS, with their altars removed, remained in the ownership of the families that endowed them and several continued in use as burial places or were adapted to serve as family pews.

The New Liturgy and Church Furnishings

With the religious pendulum swinging first one way and then the other, there was an understandable reluctance to perpetuate the expansion of church building and refurbishment which had characterised the fifteenth and early sixteenth centuries (*see* MEDIEVAL ARCHI-TECTURE). Resources that had previously been used to endow chantries and to beautify churches were now diverted to more secular purposes. Even before the Reformation, the classical influences of the Renaissance were increasingly apparent in architectural decoration, window glass and MONUMENTS; and HERALDRY, which emphasised the authority of the Tudor dynasty and the credentials of the post-medieval establishment, was ubiquitous – often ostentatiously so.

In 1549, the second year of Edward VI's reign (1547–53), the first English Prayer Book was issued and the revised LITURGY contained therein resulted in changes in the internal arrangement of churches. The aim of the reformers, led by

Archbishop Cranmer (1489–1556), was to increase public participation in the services of the new English Church. In the 1549 Communion service, for example, the congregation was instructed to remain in the nave until the Offertory. This part of the service (the Ante-Communion) was conducted by the priest from a reading pew in the nave, not from his old stall in the chancel. At the Offertory, priest and people moved into the CHANCEL for the Communion, depositing their offerings of money in an oak chest provided for the purpose. Thus the chancel was no longer the *sanctum sanctorum* of the priests, and communion was now received by the congregation in both kinds (i.e. both bread and wine). The parson was also required to use the reading desk for the revised offices of Mattins and Evensong so that the congregation could see and hear him clearly. In 1550 an order was made for the removal of the old stone ALTARS and these were replaced by wooden communion tables that were erected in the centre of the chancel so that the people could approach them from all sides. With the publication of the second Prayer Book in 1552, many of the remaining ceremonies were abolished, as were the traditional vestments, and orders were given for the removal of those 'superstitious images' which had not been taken down in accordance with earlier legislation.

Following the fanaticism and persecution of Mary's reign (*see above*), Queen Elizabeth attempted to reconcile the divisions within the English Church. A series of injunctions was issued which were intended to prevent extremists from taking the law into their own hands. Chancel screens were to be retained (or rebuilt), although the figures of the rood were to be taken down, together with the rood lofts which, in the late medieval Church, had often accommodated a choir (*see* ROOD SCREEN). These choirs, which had 'performed' the elaborate music of the period, were frowned upon by the reformers. Congregational singing was to be encouraged, although an ANTHEM was permitted following the third collect at Mattins and Evensong. From this time until the nineteenth century, the parish clerk led the singing of the congregation from a desk in the nave, while choirs (of singers and instrumentalists) were usually located at the west end of the church, either on a raised platform or in a gallery which, in a number of cases, was constructed from the materials of the former rood loft. Communion tables were to be kept against the east wall of the SANCTUARY except during the communion service, when they were moved into the centre of the chancel and turned so that the narrow ends faced east and west, thereby enabling the communicants to kneel at all four sides. Seats were sometimes provided along the chancel walls for the communicants, an arrangement which is still evident at several churches. At this time celebrations of the communion took place only once or twice a quarter, on '*Sacrament Sundays*'. On other Sundays the morning service consisted of Mattins, the Litany and Ante-Communion, the sermon being of particular importance (*see* PULPITS). Churches were, of course, unheated and in many parishes high-sided box pews were erected in order to keep out draughts. With increasing literacy, texts replaced medieval wall paintings, which the reformers regarded as primitive and 'superstitious'. The Creed, the Lord's Prayer, the Ten Commandments and other biblical texts (*sentences*), sometimes painted within a (modestly) decorative border, now adorned the walls of post-Reformation churches for the instruction of congregations, where once pitchfork-wielding demons and gaping hell-mouths had terrified their medieval predecessors.

See also VALOR ECCLESIASTICUS

REGISTRAR A functionary responsible for maintaining the monastic register and all the legal documents of a particular house – deeds of gift, endowments, conveyances, charters, etc.

REGNAL YEARS In the Middle Ages documents were dated by reference to the year of the

sovereign's reign: thus, a document of the third year of the reign of Henry VI (1422–61) would be shown as such (and in modern calendars as 3 Henry VI). In later records the *Anno domini* year either replaced the regnal year or was given in addition to it. Regnal years began on the first day of a reign and continued until the same day twelve calendar months later. One exception is King John (1199–1216), whose rule began on Ascension Day (a movable feast): therefore each of his regnal years commences on Ascension Day and not on the calendar anniversary of his succession.
See also RULERS OF ENGLAND AND OF THE UNITED KINGDOM

REGULAR One who lives in a religious community and is bound by its RULE – in contradistinction to a secular, who lives in the world. As the name suggests, the life of a regular (also known as a *religious*) was strictly regulated so that 'Personal standing is merged in the equality of each and all, there is no inequitable mark of exemption, except the greater sanctity which is able to put one man above others.' This 'equality of each and all' applied to all members of an order who were required to do nothing of their own will: 'Everything they do is at the motion of the prelate's nod . . .'.
See also AUGUSTINIANS

RELICS Relics are the material remains of a saint after his death and sacred objects with which he had been in contact. The bodies of martyrs were venerated from the mid-second century, and in Rome attracted cults whose members worshipped at the martyrs' tombs. Indeed, the Second Council of Nicaea in 787 ordered that no church should be consecrated without relics. The veneration of relics was approved for the English Church by the Council of Constantinople in 1084, but the cult was never as popular in Britain as it was in continental Europe where its influence increased significantly during the Crusades. Nevertheless, quantities of relics, mostly spurious, were brought back from the Holy Land to be displayed in richly decorated *reliquaries* and carried before processions at religious festivals. Many gave rise to superstitious practices, vestiges of which are discernible today.

In the Middle Ages, the cult acquired a theological foundation. The unique dignity of the bodies of the saints as receptacles of the Holy Spirit was emphasised, together with the sanction given by God in making them the occasion of miracles. Consequently, several great churches became the repositories of saints: notably Canterbury (St Thomas of Canterbury), Durham (St Cuthbert), St Albans (St Alban), Westminster (St Edward the Confessor) and Winchester (St Swithun). Such relics attracted innumerable pilgrims to the more famous SHRINES at which prayers of supplication were offered in the hope of salvation and cures for a multiplicity of ailments. So lucrative were these activities that it has been suggested that the acquisition of relics and the building of shrines came to be an obsession with many Benedictine abbots. The Carthusians and Cistercians, on the other hand, eschewed the practice lest pilgrims should invade their precincts – of the Cistercian houses only Hailes (the Holy Blood) and Rievaulx (St William of Rievaulx) possessed significant relics. The doctrine was later confirmed by the Council of Trent, convened at Trento in northern Italy from 1545 to 1563, which defined the doctrines of the church in opposition to those of the REFORMATION. In England, shrines and relics were suppressed at the Reformation, although many churches have dedications that allude to their former possession.

In practice, of course, the medieval church benefited significantly from its monopoly of relics and the sale to pilgrims of officially sanctioned tat. However, it has recently been argued that the financial benefits to the religious houses may have been exaggerated.

RELICT A widow.

RELIGIOUS ORDERS IN THE ANGLICAN CHURCH The nineteenth-century revival of religious orders in the Anglican Communion was inspired by the Oxford Movement, and by Edward Pusey (1800–82) in particular. It was Pusey who, in 1841, received the vows of Marian Hughes, the first superior of the Convent of the Holy and Undivided Trinity at Oxford (1849), and it was he who established the community at Park Village, Regent's Park in London, which later merged with Priscilla Sellon's Society of the Holy Trinity at Davenport (1848) (now at Ascot Priory in Berkshire). Other communities include those of St Mary the Virgin at Wantage in Oxfordshire (1848), St John the Baptist at Clewer in Somerset (1852) and St Margaret at East Grinstead in Sussex (1855). These were 'active' communities which combined a religious life with public service, notably in the slums of the great cities. The first 'closed' (contemplative) community, the Sisters of the Love of God, was founded at Fairacres, Oxford in 1907. The first religious order for men was the Society of St John the Evangelist (the 'Cowley Fathers'), a society of mission priests and laymen founded by Richard Benson near Cowley, Oxfordshire in 1865. This was followed by the Society of the Sacred Mission at Kelham, Nottinghamshire (1891) and the Community of the Resurrection founded by Charles Gore (at Oxford, 1892) at Mirfield, Yorkshire. The English Order of St Benedict moved from Caldey Island, Dyfed to Nashdom Abbey in Buckinghamshire (via Pershore in Worcestershire) when the majority of the Caldey Island community submitted to Rome in 1913 (*see* POST-MEDIEVAL MONASTERIES). An English Franciscan order was established after the First World War at Hilfield in Dorset (1921) and was constituted as a religious community in 1931. There are now nine orders of men in the Church of England, one mixed community (the Community of the Glorious Assumption at Burton upon Trent) and thirty-six orders of women. Most are members of the Advisory Council for Religious Communities.

RELIQUARY A receptacle for RELICS, often made of precious metals and richly decorated (*see* SHRINES).

REQUIEM A form of MASS offered for the repose of the souls of the dead. The name is derived from the opening words of the introit which (until recently) was used at all such masses. The Requiem Mass was popularly known as the *Black Mass*, from the medieval custom of using black vestments.

RERE-ARCH An internal arch to a gothic window, supporting the inner part of a wall's thickness and characteristic of thirteenth-century lancet windows.

REREDORTER Known as the *domus necessaria* (the 'necessary house'), the reredorter was the latrine block in the conventual buildings of a religious house. It was usually located at the end of the upper-floor dormitory (*see* DORTER), either as a continuation of the eastern claustral range or at right angles to it, depending on the disposition of the water supply that ran beneath or alongside it. Indeed, the reliable provision of water for flushing the reredorter drain was of such importance that it often determined the position of the other monastic buildings (*see* PLUMBING, WATER SUPPLY AND SANITATION), and in some cases the conventual buildings were located to the north of an abbey church rather than to the (more usual) south because of the fall of the land: at Tintern, Forde and Buildwas Abbeys, for example, where allowance was made for the sloping topography and natural drainage towards a river.

The reredorter usually comprised a row of cubicles set against an outer wall and separated by stone or timber partitions, each cubicle provided with a wooden seat and a window. The partitions were usually carried on transverse arches above a stream or drain that carried the waste away and the drain would be screened within the basement by stone side walls. This was not always the case, however. At Durham Priory, for instance, it would appear that there were rows of cubicles on both sides of the reredorter and that the partitions were carried on two substantial pillars:

> Also there was a faire large house and a most decent place adjoyninge to the west syde of the said Dortre [dormitory], towards ye water, for ye moncks and novices to resort unto called the previes, which was made with two great pillars of stone that did beare up the whole floore thereof, and every seate and particion was of wainscott close of either syde verie decent so that one of them could not see another, when they weare in that place. There was as many seates or previes on either side as there is little windowes in ye walles which wyndowes was to gyve lighte to every one of the saide seates.
>
> *The Rites of Durham*

At both Neath and Furness Abbeys the reredorter was contained within a separate building parallel to the dorter and linked to it by a bridge, while at Worcester Cathedral Priory the dorter and reredorter were moved to the west range of the claustral buildings because of a problem with the water supply. At Byland Abbey, an earlier reredorter was replaced in the thirteenth century, again because of drainage problems, and this was built at a right angle to the east end of the old reredorter and with a more efficient drainage system.

As at most Cistercian monasteries, Byland also had a LAY BROTHERS' reredorter. This was a large building that projected from the south end of the lay brothers' dorter in the west claustral range. The remains of its stone channel may still be seen running down the centre and screened from the ground floor by walls that supported a row of latrine seats at first-floor level. At the Premonstratensian abbey of St Agatha, North Yorkshire (now known as Easby Abbey), the early thirteenth-century dorter was incorporated within the west claustral range from the outset (*see* CLOISTER). Beyond this, a building containing both the guests' SOLAR and the canons' reredorter extends towards the River Swale, an unconventional but ingenious arrangement that accommodates the different levels on which it was built and the need for adequate drainage. At Fountains Abbey, as originally planned the drain was to have run down the centre of the monks' reredorter, with a narrow room to each side. However, in the course of building the plan was changed and the drain was moved to the south side of the building where it could be directly flushed by the river. Reredorters were often substantial buildings, depending on the size of the community: that at Canterbury contained fifty-five seats and was 46m (150ft) long, while at Lewes it was 48m (158ft) long and had sixty-six seats. Both were large houses, but it is hard to imagine that such a significant proportion of the community would wish to avail themselves of the facilities simultaneously.

Additional reredorters were often provided for the infirmary and to serve the lay brothers' quarters – notably for the numerous *conversi* of Cistercian houses. Individual latrines or garderobes (*see* GARDEROBE) were more often found in the guesthouse and superior's lodgings. It was not uncommon for brethren to fall asleep in one of the reredorter cubicles and the CIRCATOR was charged with waking them 'with consideration and solicitude'. He was not to touch them but 'modestly he should make the slightest noise which is sufficient to waken them'.

REREDOS An ornamental stone or timber screen, often supported on a shelf (*predella*), and covering the wall behind an altar or filling the space between two piers to the east of a SANCTUARY. A screen that separates the High Altar from a shrine (or shrines) to the east is sometimes described as a SHRINE SCREEN. Many late medieval wooden reredoses were richly decorated with painted panels set together in a wooden frame

The magnificent late fifteenth-century reredos behind the high altar at St Albans Cathedral is similar in style to that at Winchester Cathedral. (© John Crook/info@john-crook.com)

(*retable*), but of these none has survived *in situ* in England. Stone reredoses are composed of tiers of ornate canopied niches, each containing a stone or ALABASTER figure sculpted in high relief and originally brightly coloured and gilded. Regrettably, few of these figures escaped the attentions of Cromwell's iconoclasts, and most surviving reredoses contain little more than empty niches – like rows of broken teeth – or are Victorian replacements. A notable (and dramatic) exception is the magnificent stone reredos at Christchurch Priory in Dorset (*c.* 1360). Known locally as the Jesse Screen, it has retained much of its original detail. The lower figures illustrate the Old Testament ancestry of Jesus, with Jesse flanked by David and Solomon, while the 'Epiphany' panel above depicts the Christmas story. Fortunately, the Victorians resisted the temptation to replace the figures that are missing from nine of the niches. Winchester Cathedral Priory's late fifteenth-century 'Great Screen' is a wonderful confection of delicate canopied niches and figure carving. Again, the original figures were pulled down at the Reformation but, in this case, the Victorian replacements are reasonably sympathetic (they include a small effigy of Queen Victoria). The remains of some of the original statues may be seen in the Triforium Museum. Almost identical in scale, style and date is the splendid reredos at St Albans Cathedral. It too has a large Crucifixion as the focal point, it is pierced by doors on either side of the High Altar, and the figures that occupy its niches are Victorian replacements. There is a rare Tudor reredos at Southwark Cathedral. Donated by Bishop Ford of Winchester to the Augustinian Priory in *c.* 1520, it was heavily restored, and its figures replaced, in 1833. The fourteenth-century half-height reredos at Beverley Minster has beautifully patterned carving and figure sculpture, although the western elevation was largely renewed in 1826 and covered with statues and mosaics in 1897. The reredos at Milton Abbey, Dorset, must once have been one of the finest in England. It was badly damaged at the DISSOLUTION OF THE MONASTERIES and the twenty-six ornately carved figures destroyed. It was restored (in plaster) by James Wyatt in 1789 but, devoid of its figures, it serves only to remind us of the iconoclasts' idiocy. Undoubtedly one of the finest features of Durham Cathedral Priory (or, indeed, of any church in England) is the Neville Screen, a singularly beautiful, late fourteenth-century, pierced shrine screen of Caen stone, perfect in its proportions and once containing 107 statues, all richly gilded and painted, the centre one representing the Virgin Mary with Saint Cuthbert and St Oswald on either side. A gift of Lord John Neville in *c.* 1380, the screen was wrought in London and brought by sea to Newcastle.

There are several post-medieval reredoses, most of them Victorian and some of them of notable execution: W.D. Caroe's reredos at Brecon cathedral, for example, with its rows of apostles and saints set in niches and panels. It is said to be based on the intricately decorated style of the early sixteenth century. A magnificent painted reredos by A.W.N. Pugin (1815–52) at Leeds Roman Catholic Cathedral was made in 1842 for an earlier church that was demolished in 1902 and the reredos transferred to the new cathedral on its completion in 1904. The immense tapestry of Christ in Majesty at Coventry Cathedral is a late twentieth-century equivalent of the medieval reredos. Designed by Graham Sutherland (1903–80) it is 22m (72ft) high and fills the entire north wall of the presbytery.

See also RETABLE, SCREENS *and* TRIPTYCH

RESERVATION The practice of reserving the Host (the consecrated bread of the EUCHARIST) for the purpose of Communion. In the early Church, the faithful kept the sacrament in their homes, but from the fourth century it was reserved in churches, either in the SACRISTY or in a special receptacle provided for that purpose: a wall-cupboard in the sanctuary (*see* AUMBRY), a TABERNACLE suspended above the altar, or a PYX on the altar. The presence of the reserved Host was signified by the burning of a lamp with a white flame (*see* LAMPS).

RESONATORS *see* AMPLIFIERS

RESPOND A half-pier, bonded into a wall or PIER and carrying one end of an ARCH.

RESPONSES *see* PRECES *and* VERSICLES

RETABLE A ledge behind an altar or a decorative altarpiece. Very few medieval examples have survived, the Westminster Retable being a notable exception – despite its use as a cupboard lid in the seventeenth century and as part of a display case in the eighteenth. At that time it was given a coat of green and white paint – 'a victim less of Reformation iconoclasts than of Georgian tourism'. It was almost certainly commissioned for Westminster Abbey by Henry III (1207–72), who had just remodelled the entire building in the fashionable Gothic style. Originally it would appear to have been made of solid gold studded with jewels. The oak for the panels came from an English tree felled in *c.* 1235, the lead white paint from the Mendips, the glass from France and the intense blue lapis lazuli from Afghanistan.
See also ALTARS, DIPTYCH, REREDOS *and* TRIPTYCH

RETICULATED TRACERY *see* MEDIEVAL ARCHITECTURE

RETREAT A period spent in meditation and contemplation (and often in silence), removed from the distractions of the outside world. Some religious communities maintained country houses as retreats and convalescent homes for those brethren seeking spiritual or mental recuperation (*see* GRANGE *and* RECREATION).

RETRO-CHOIR Opinion is divided concerning the correct definition of this term. Logically, one meaning of the Latin *retro* is 'behind' and consequently the term retro-choir is sometimes used to describe the area immediately to the east of the CHOIR and PRESBYTERY, a space that was often constructed on a grand scale when the eastern wing of a church was extended to accommodate a notable shrine and the multitude of worshippers attracted to it. At Winchester Cathedral Priory, for example, a magnificent vaulted hall to the east of the High Altar, built in the thirteenth century to house the relics of St Swithun, and now described as the retro-choir, contains the towering Perpendicular CHANTRY CHAPELS of Cardinal Henry Beaufort (episcopate 1405–47), William Waynflete (1447–86), Bishop Richard Fox (1501–28) and Bishop Stephen Gardiner (1531–55). It seems almost that each successive bishop was intent on outdoing his predecessor in the grandeur of his monument, although the cadaver in Richard Fox's INTRANSI TOMB is a salutary reminder of the transient nature of life. The late thirteenth-century Angel Choir at Lincoln Cathedral is sometimes described as a retro-choir because it is immediately to the east of the presbytery. Built to accommodate the translated remains of St Hugh (canonised 1220), it too contains a number of tombs and chantry chapels, deliberately erected in close proximity to the saint's shrine (which was destroyed at the Reformation), and was provided with entrances to the north and south for the benefit of pilgrims. Its splendid great east window (*c.* 1275) is 18m (60ft) high and is the first Gothic eight-light window. There being no Lady Chapel or REREDOS, the window provides a wonderful backdrop to the High Altar. A similar space between the presbytery and Lady Chapel at Chichester Cathedral is described in the guidebook as a retro-choir, although here, as elsewhere, the space is more correctly an AMBULATORY.

The alternative definition of retro-choir is applied, in medieval monastic and secular churches, to the space to the west of the choir between the PULPITUM and ROOD SCREEN. When

The chantry chapels of Cardinal Beaufort (d. 1447) and (left) Bishop Fox (d. 1528) in the south aisle of the ambulatory at Winchester Cathedral Priory. This vaulted hall to the east of the high altar is frequently described as the Retro Choir – but erroneously so? (© John Crook/info@john-crook.com)

viewed from the High Altar (the focal point of any church) this area would, indeed, be 'behind the choir'. It was here that PROCESSIONS came together, having divided when entering from the nave via two doorways in the rood screen, before proceeding into the choir through the central passageway of the pulpitum. The retro-choir was a characteristic of Cistercian churches (although not exclusively so) and usually contained two subsidiary altars, one on either side of the pulpitum doorway. It also provided accommodation during the choir offices for elderly or infirm monks and those who arrived too late to enter the choir. There is some structural evidence of former retro-choirs at a number of Cistercian abbeys, including Buildwas and Byland (although at both the rood screen appears to have had a single doorway). At Neath Abbey the foundations of the side walls of an enclosed retro-choir have survived. The retro-choirs in English medieval cathedrals were lost when rood screens were demolished following the Reformation.
See also MEDIEVAL ARCHITECTURE

RETURN The point at which a length of wall, moulding or pipe changes direction, e.g. in the DRIPSTONE of a doorway or window opening.

RETURNED STALLS Those sections of the STALLS in the CHOIR of a monastic or collegiate church or cathedral which have their backs to a PULPITUM and therefore face east and are at right angles to the other stalls. The returned stalls were usually occupied by senior priests and visiting dignitaries.

REVESTIARIUS A sacrist's assistant, responsible for the maintenance of vestments and church fabrics and for ensuring that these were changed according to the liturgical seasons and festivals (*see* COLOURS (LITURGICAL)).
See also SACRIST *and* SACRISTY

RIB *and* RIBBED VAULT *see* VAULTING

RIDDEL CURTAINS *and* RIDDEL POSTS From the French *rideau* ('curtain'), riddel curtains screened an altar on three sides or at each end. They were supported by riddel posts at the corners of an altar, each of which was often surmounted by a carved and gilded angel or ornate candle-holder. Riddel curtains were a medieval feature that was reintroduced by the ecclesiastical architect Sir Ninian Comper (1864–1960) in the early twentieth century.

RINGERS' FLOOR The storey of a church tower in which the BELLS are rung.

RITUAL *see* LITURGY, PROCESSIONS *and* REFORMATION, THE

ROMAN CATHOLIC CHURCH That part of the Christian Church which is in communion with the pope, whose office is acknowledged to be in succession to St Peter and the Apostles in whom Christ invested the power of the Holy Spirit. Its doctrine is characterised by a strict adherence to tradition, together with a belief in the infallibility of the living voice of the Church. It has a complex hierarchical organisation of bishops and priests with the pope at its head. Supernatural life is mediated to individual Christians by members of the hierarchy in the seven sacraments, and the MASS is at the centre of liturgical life.

Catholicism was the religion of England and Wales prior to the REFORMATION (*see* MEDIEVAL CHURCH), but following the Acts of Uniformity of 1552 and 1559 the political climate deteriorated and strict anti-Catholic legislation was introduced. Catholics were tolerated during the Protectorate (1653–9) but persecuted following the Restoration (1660). They were prevented from holding civil or military office by the Test Act of 1673 and from membership of parliament by the Test Act of 1678. In 1778 the Catholic Relief Act enabled Catholics to own land, but it was received with hostility, culminating in the Gordon Riots of 1780. The Catholic Emancipation Act of 1829 removed many constraints, such as discrimination against Catholic teachers and schools, but it was not until 1871 that Catholics were readmitted to the universities.

ROMANESQUE *see* MEDIEVAL ARCHITECTURE

ROOD *see* ROOD SCREEN

ROOD BEAM (*also* CANDLE BEAM) *see* ROOD SCREEN

ROOD LOFT *see* ROOD SCREEN

ROOD SCREEN From the Old English *rōd* meaning 'cross', a rood is a carved image of Christ crucified (a crucifix). A notable feature of Saxon religious art, roods were commonly placed above the doorways of churches, although few have survived the attentions of the iconoclasts and the depredations of the weather. The medieval *Great Rood* was a carved and painted crucifix, erected on a pedestal above a wooden or stone rood screen which, in major monastic and secular churches, extended between the nave piers (usually one bay west of the PULPITUM) and separated the RETRO-CHOIR from the NAVE. The rood was flanked by the figures of the Blessed Virgin Mary and St John the Evangelist and was usually supported by a *rood beam* which, with the rood screen, sometimes carried a raised platform or *rood loft*. The loft was entered by means of a *rood stair*, a flight of steps that provided access to the Great Rood, which was covered with a veil during Lent, and to the rood beam on which candles were lit on festive occasions (hence the alternative name '*candle beam*'). The upper part of a rood screen was usually open, the apertures filled with unglazed traceried lights, while doorways on either side of the NAVE ALTAR afforded access to the retro-choir. Both loft and screen were usually richly decorated with coloured and gilded carving, the panels below the tracery of the screen sometimes containing painted figures of the saints.

Just as the death and resurrection of Christ dominates Christian theology, so the Great Rood, the symbol of Redemption, dominated the naves of medieval churches. The Great Roods were dismantled by order of the Privy Council in 1548 and consequently most of the roods that are now found in churches date from the Gothic revival of the nineteenth century and from the work of ecclesiastical architects such as Sir Ninian Comper (1864–1960). A Comper rood screen was installed at Wakefield Cathedral in 1950, while an imposing modern rood and rood beam dominate the nave and chancel at Norwich's early twentieth-century Roman Catholic Cathedral. At medieval Peterborough a striking rood figure (1975) by Francis Roper is suspended high above the nave. The rood figures on the early fourteenth-century strainer arch at Wells Cathedral are less successful. They were made in 1920 by G. Tovi to Sir Charles Nicholson's design and are (in Alec Clifton-Taylor's opinion) 'unfortunately of no artistic merit'. Most cathedral rood screens were of wood and, deprived of their function, did not survive the Reformation. Exceptionally, at St Albans Cathedral it is the pulpitum that has been demolished and the stone rood screen that has survived. The rood itself has gone and the screen now supports an organ for which it was never intended. The foundations of former rood screens, and sometimes the sockets that once supported the rood beam, may still be seen in the ruins of several monastic churches, notably at Lilleshall Abbey in Shropshire and Roche Abbey, Yorkshire, where the bases of both the pulpitum and rood screen have survived (see illustration, page 330).

ROOD STAIR *see* ROOD SCREEN

ROOF BOSSES *see* BOSSES

ROOFING TILES *see* SLATES AND ROOFING TILES

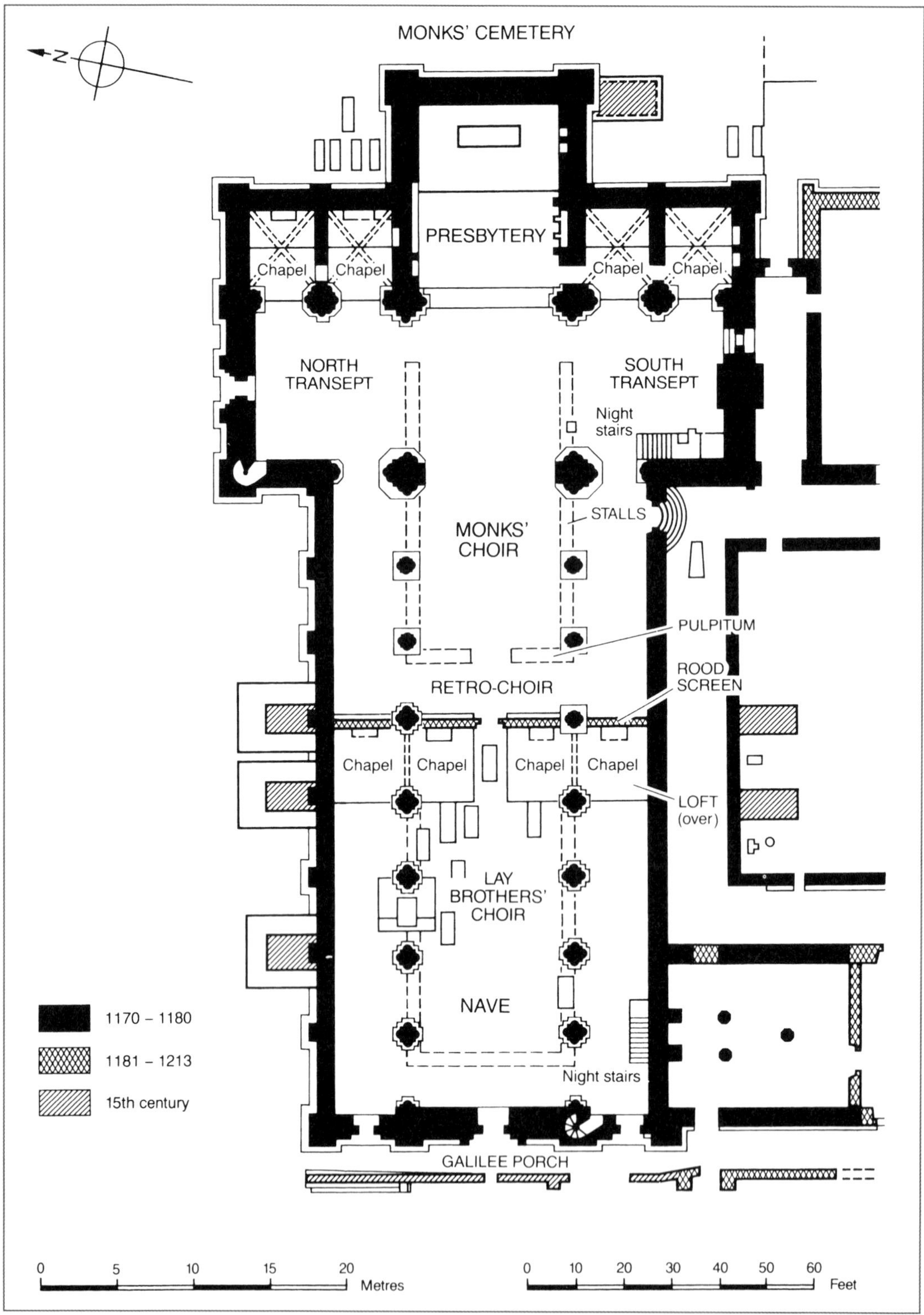

Plan of the church at Roche Abbey, South Yorkshire, showing the position of the rood screen, retro-choir and pulpitum that separated the lay brothers' church from the monks' choir. (© English Heritage Photo Library)

ROOFS The roofs of early timber-framed conventual buildings, and those of workshops and outbuildings in the curia, were usually thatched or covered with tiles or shingles (oak tiles). As resources became available, the claustral ranges, the infirmary, guests house and superior's lodgings were roofed with slates (*see* SLATES AND ROOFING TILES) and the church with LEAD.
See also VAULTING

ROSE WINDOW A circular window with a complex traceried design similar in arrangement to the petals of a rose. This type of window is often confused with the *wheel window*, which is also circular but has tracery that radiates from a central hub like the spokes of a wheel. Consequently, the term is often used generically to mean any large circular window. In order to accommodate their shape and size, these circular windows are usually found in the gable-ends of transepts (*see* TRANSEPT). But, for some reason, they were never as popular in Britain as they were in continental Europe, and rose or wheel windows are rarely found in the west gables of English naves as they are in France. More often, a circular motif is incorporated in the upper lights of a traceried west window: as at Exeter and Worcester cathedrals. This may have the appearance of a rose or wheel window, but is simply one element of a larger design.

The wonderful 'Bishop's Eye' window in the southern gable of the Great Transept of Lincoln Cathedral is often described as a rose window, but the intricate bar tracery recalls two immense veined leaves and it is, therefore, neither a rose window nor a wheel window. It is filled with fragments of glass of various ages and origins reassembled from other parts of the cathedral – with dazzling effect. Its partner, the 'Dean's Eye' in the north transept, is a unique survival in England: a thirteenth-century rose window (*c.* 1210) with its original glass intact. Measuring 7m in (23ft) diameter, it depicts scenes and symbols representing the Passion, the Last Judgement and the Kingdom of Heaven – little of which detail would have been discernible to those standing below. Unfortunately, the most magnificent of England's rose windows has not survived. In *c.* 1300 a new east end was added to the medieval St Paul's Cathedral in London and this incorporated seven tall lancet windows surmounted by a rose window measuring over 12m (40ft) in diameter. Similarly, there were two fine rose windows in the transepts at Westminster Abbey, although not those that are seen today. That in the north transept has glass designed by Sir James Thornhill (1675–1743) showing eleven of the apostles (Judas Iscariot was not included), while the glass in the south transept window was replaced in 1902. A large rose window in the east wall of the Chapel of the Nine Altars at Durham Cathedral was inserted by James Wyatt (1746–1813) in *c.* 1795. It replaced a medieval window and is of poor design and execution – even so, the early morning light that floods the chapel and presbytery can be wonderful. There are examples of modest wheel windows at Oxford Cathedral (at the east end) and at Beverley Minster (the transept). The wheel window in the south transept of York Minster is similar to those that were once a feature of a number of Cistercian churches, where they were found in the west gable of the nave: at Byland Abbey, for example, which may have been the model for the York window, and at Fountains Abbey where a twelfth-century wheel window at the west end was later replaced by a large traceried window.
See also MEDIEVAL ARCHITECTURE, STAINED GLASS *and* WINDOWS

ROTA A mechanism for dispensing food without the need to communicate: typically a turntable device within the DRESSER WINDOW.

ROTULARIUS The messenger who conveyed the obit roll from one religious house to another (*see* OBIT).

ROTUNDA A circular room or building, usually with a domed roof (*see* MEDIEVAL ARCHITECTURE).

ROUND CHURCHES *see* MEDIEVAL ARCHITECTURE

ROYAL ARMS The royal arms will often be found painted, and sometimes gilded, on boards affixed to the interior walls of churches. They were erected as tokens of loyalty to the Crown and obedience to the sovereign as head of the Church, and consequently all but a very small number date from after 1534 when Henry VIII assumed the title of 'Supreme Head on Earth of the Church of England' (*see* HENRY VIII *and* REFORMATION). Royal devices from earlier periods will also be found in glass, furnishings, memorials, etc., but their function is mainly commemorative.

Following the succession of the Catholic Mary I, most royal arms were removed from churches, but the practice was again reversed by her successor, Elizabeth I, for whom several examples are to be found. The practice continued through the early Stuart period and in 1614 the Archbishop of Canterbury instructed a painter-stainer to 'survey and paynte in all the churches and chappells within the Realme of England, the Kinges Majesties Armes in due form, with helmet, crest, mantell, and supporters as they ought to be, together with the nobel young princes'. In 1631, the Archbishop again issued instructions that the royal arms should be painted or repaired, together with the ten Commandments and 'other Holy sentences'.

During the Commonwealth (1649–60) many examples of the royal arms were destroyed or defaced, while others were taken down and hidden or turned round and the Commonwealth arms painted on the reverse. Following the restoration of Charles II in 1660, a statute requiring that the royal arms should be displayed in all churches resulted in many old boards being brought out of hiding and repainted, or new ones being made. Wherever the Commonwealth arms were displayed they were to 'be forthwith taken down; and that the King's Majesty's Arms be set up instead thereof'.

ROYAL PECULIAR *see* PECULIAR

R.R. Abbreviation for *regni Regis*, meaning 'in the –th year of King –'.

RUBBLE The term does not necessarily imply inferior construction: walls built of roughly cut stones of differing shapes and sizes, bound with lime mortar and sometimes laid in courses, are singularly durable.
See also MASONRY

RUBRIC A textual heading, usually in red ink. In the present context, ritual or ceremonial directions in a service book which were often picked out in red ink. The celebrated 'Black Rubric' was the 'Declaration on Kneeling' which was added at the last moment, and without parliamentary authority, at the end of the Holy communion service in the 1552 *Book of Common Prayer*. When the rubrics were later printed in red, the fact that the 'Declaration' was not authorised was indicated by printing it in black.
See also RED LETTER DAYS

RUBRICATOR A scribe who specialised in painting and illuminating uncial letters and, in particular, highlighting the RED LETTER DAYS for which adequate preparation was required.
See also LETTERING

RUFF Dating from the sixteenth century, a projecting starched frill worn as a collar by choristers, usually of cathedral or collegiate choirs.

RULE (REGULA) The constitution which set out the principles and practices of the monastic or regular life. The fundamental rule was that of St Benedict (*see* BENEDICTINES), which was

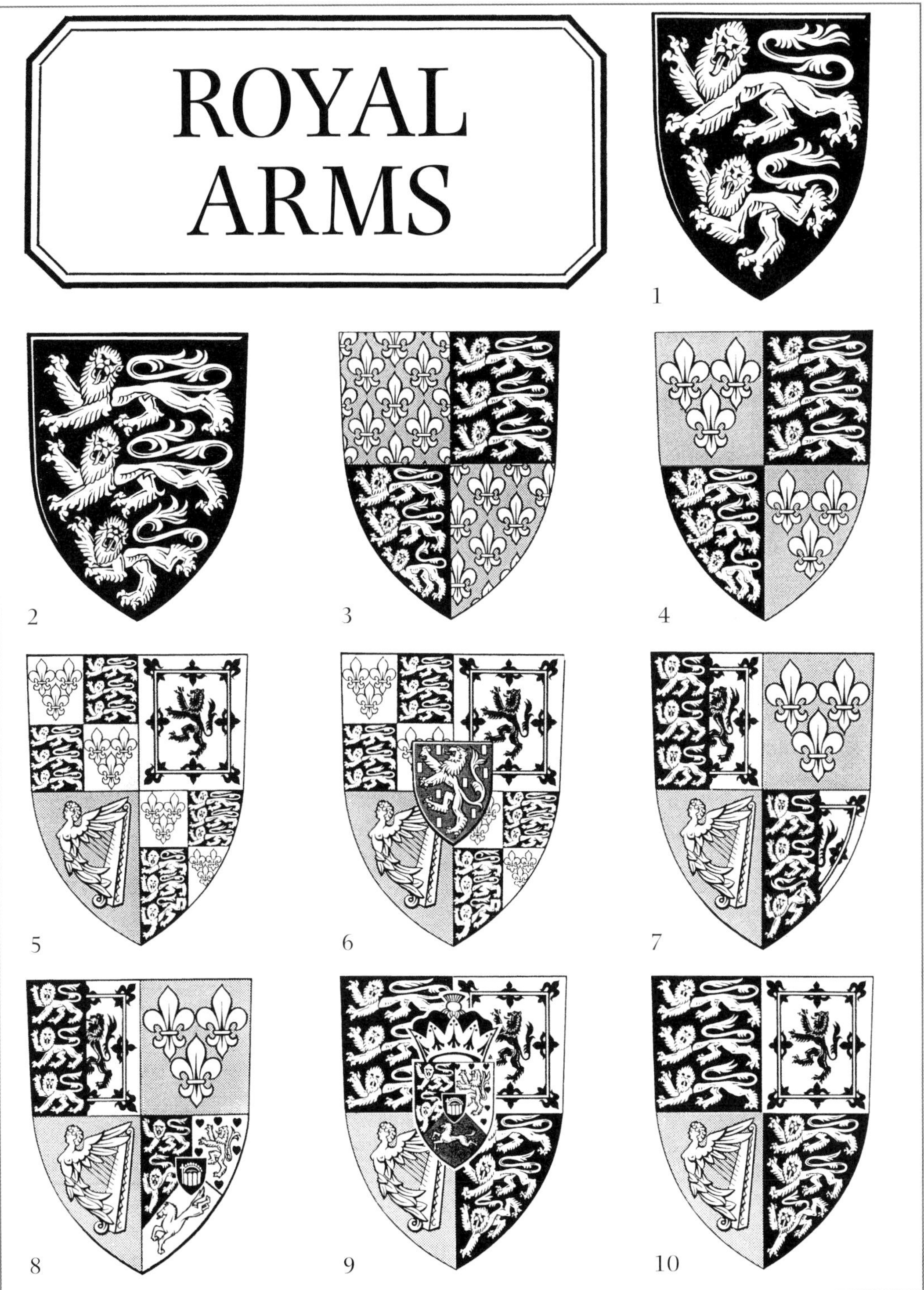

Royal Arms: 1. The Norman kings (attributed); 2. 1195–1337; 3. 1337–1405; 4. 1405–1603; 5. 1603–88 and 1702–7; 6. 1688–1702; 7. 1707–14; 8. 1714–1801; 9. 1801–37; 10. 1837–present. (Courtesy of John Ferguson)

modified and developed by later orders such as the CISTERCIANS and CLUNIACS. the Benedictine rule has been described as

> wholly lacking in eccentricity. It does not expect heroic virtue. It is full of provisions for exceptions, changes and relaxations in its rules; yet at the same time it insists that rules must be kept, once made. The monk must live to a timetable, and he must be doing something all the time, even if this only takes the form of eating and sleeping in order to enable him to labour afresh. The rule is classless and timeless: it is not grounded in any particular culture or geographical region, and it will fit into any society which will allow it to operate (P. Johnson).

The other determining rule was that of St Augustine (*see* AUGUSTINIANS), which provided a structure for the canons regular and within which the Christian life might be lived to the full (*see* CANON REGULAR). The rule was supplemented by regulations (*observances*), contained in a CUSTOMARY, that were intended to accommodate the customs and idiosyncrasies of a particular house.
See also MONASTICISM *and* OBSERVANCES

RULERS OF ENGLAND AND OF THE UNITED KINGDOM

Saxon	
Edwy	955–959
Edgar	959–975
Edward the Martyr	975–978
Ethelred the Unready	978–1016
Edmund Ironside	1016
Danish	
Cnut	1017–1035
Harold I	1035–1040
Harthacnut	1040–1042
Saxon	
Edward the Confessor	1042–1066
Harold II (Godwinson)	1066
Norman	
William I	1066–1087
William II	1087–1100
Henry I	1100–1135
Stephen	1135–1154
Plantagenet	
Henry II	1154–1189
Richard I	1189–1199
John	1199–1216
Henry III	1216–1272
Edward I	1272–1307
Edward II	1307–1327
Edward III	1327–1377
Richard II	1377–1399
Lancaster	
Henry IV	1399–1413
Henry V	1413–1422
Henry VI	1422–1461
York	
Edward IV	1461–1483
Edward V	1483
Richard III	1483–1485
Tudor	
Henry VII	1485–1509
Henry VIII	1509–1547
Edward VI	1547–1553
Mary I	1553–1558
Elizabeth I	1558–1603
Stuart	
James I of England and VI of Scotland	1603–1625
Charles I	1625–1649
Commonwealth (declared in 1649)	
Oliver Cromwell (Lord Protector)	1653–1658
Richard Cromwell	1658–1659
Stuart	
Charles II	1660–1685

James II	1685–1688
William III and Mary II	1689–1702
Anne	1702–1714
Hanover	
George I	1714–1727
George II	1727–1760
George III	1760–1820
George IV	1820–1830
William IV	1830–1837
Victoria	1837–1901
Saxe-Coburg-Gotha	
Edward VII	1901–1910
Windsor	
George V	1910–1936
Edward VIII	1936
George VI	1936–1952
Elizabeth II	1952–

See also REGNAL YEARS

RULING The lines, delineated by PRICKING, which were incised or drawn on a writing surface both to guide the writing and to contain it within margins. Before the mid-twelfth century, ruling was done with the dry point of a sharp implement. Thereafter, lead was used until the beginning of the fifteenth century, from which time lines were usually drawn in INK.
See also MANUSCRIPT ILLUMINATION

RURAL DEAN *see* CLERGY (CHURCH OF ENGLAND)

RUSTICATION *see* MASONRY

S

SABLE *see* COLOURS (HERALDIC)

SACCARIUM The monastic exchequer.

SACRAMENT 'An outward and visible sign of an inward and spiritual grace given unto us, ordained by Christ himself, as a means whereby we receive the same, and a pledge to assure us thereof' (*The Book of Common Prayer*). As many as thirty Sacraments have been listed at various times but the seven Sacraments of Peter Lombard's *Sentences* (compiled 1155–8) are those that were defined by the Council of Trent in 1545–7: Baptism, Confirmation, EUCHARIST, Penance, Extreme Unction, Orders and Matrimony. In the Church of England, Article 25 of the THIRTY-NINE ARTICLES differentiates between Baptism and Eucharist ('two Sacraments ordained of Christ our Lord in the Gospel') and the other five ('commonly called Sacraments'). Traditional Catholic theology differentiates between the 'matter' (the material element: the bread and wine of the Eucharist and the water in Baptism) and the 'form' (the consecratory words, e.g. 'This is My Body' and 'This is My Blood' in the Eucharist).

SACRAMENT HOUSE *see* TABERNACLE

SACRAMENTARY A liturgical book used for the celebration of the MASS until the thirteenth century. The Sacramentary contained the Canon of the Mass together with the Collects, Prefaces and other prayers, but not the Epistles or Gospels. From the tenth century sacramentaries were gradually superseded by Missals (*see* MISSAL).

SACRILEGE Violation or profanation of anything holy, whether it be a person, object or place publicly dedicated to the worship of God.

SACRING BELL *see* SANCTUS BELL

SACRIST *or* SACRISTAN In religious houses, the sacrist was a major obedientiary (*see* OBEDIENTARIES) responsible for the fabric of the church, its furniture, fittings and supplies. His responsibilities included the cleanliness of the church and its repair and security, together with the design and construction of fittings, altars and windows, decoration, inscriptions and wall paintings. He was charged with the care of all clocks, bells, ornaments and lights, for vestments, church plate, shrines, reliquaries and other treasures for which he kept inventories. Indeed, in the later Middle Ages, the duties of the sacrist became so wide-ranging that he was provided with an office (*see* SACRISTY) and a number of assistants including the SUB-SACRIST, TREASURER, REVESTIARIUS and *master of works*. The responsibilities of the various obedientiaries were extraordinarily precise: for example, the sacrist was responsible for providing a bell in the dorter, but it was the CHAMBERLAIN who supplied the cord by which it was rung! The sacrist usually had his own revenues, derived from offerings and dues and from monastic estates, and could engage a clerk of works (*custos*) to oversee major building and reconstruction projects. The sacrist usually slept at the north end of the dorter, close to the abbey MUNIMENT ROOM or TREASURY, for which he was responsible, and so that he could attend to the clock in the south transept by which he regulated the times of the offices in the church.

SACRISTY The sacrist's office (*see* SACRIST). The sacristy could be a room or suite of rooms annexed to a church or contained within it. Originally it was a single, secure chamber where the vestments, altar cloths and liturgical vessels were kept and maintained (for this reason it is sometimes described as a VESTRY, although the two were often combined). As the sacrist's responsibilities increased, so too did the space his department occupied, and towards the end of the medieval period the sacristy might comprise a number of chambers including workshop, storeroom and administrative office (*see* SACRISTY). It was in the CHECKER that the sacrist and his assistants transacted estate business, maintained the abbey records and kept the community's accounts. Ease of access from the PRESBYTERY and from the NIGHT STAIR (which descended from the DORTER where the sacrist slept) was clearly an imperative. In a number of Cistercian houses the sacristy was entered from the south transept, as at Cleeve, Kirkstall, Neath, Roche and Vale Crucis, while at Tintern and Buildwas it occupied a narrow chamber in the east claustral range and could only be entered from the north transept of the abbey church. At Fountains and Rievaulx abbeys (both Cistercian) the sacristy was located to the south of the presbytery aisle, while at (Benedictine) Durham and (secular) York Minster it was to the north. Quite often the community's valuable library was contained within an adjacent chamber – also a characteristic of Cistercian houses. The foundations of an unusual fifteenth-century octagonal sacristy, entered from the south presbytery aisle, have survived at the Cluniac priory of Much Wenlock, while at Ingham Priory the checker was accommodated above the church porch. Some houses had two sacristies (at Thetford and Castle Acre, for example) while in others the sacristy and vestry were combined in a single chamber. At Easby Abbey there is evidence of a clear distinction between the functions of the sacristy, a large chamber entered from the south transept, and the vestry, which was entered directly from the presbytery. It is said that, following the battle of Tewkesbury in 1471, the monks from the nearby abbey collected pieces of armour from the battlefield, cut them into strips and used them to reinforce the inner side of the sacristy door.

See also MUNIMENT ROOM *and* TREASURY

SADDLE BARS *see* WINDOWS

SAIL VAULT *see* DOME

ST JOHN OF JERUSALEM, ORDER OF Among the many new religious orders that came into being in the eleventh and twelfth centuries were the military-religious orders of the Knights Templar and Knights Hospitaller. Both originated in the decades following the capture of Jerusalem by the crusaders in 1099 and the establishing of the Christian Kingdom of Jerusalem which stretched from northern Syria to the Sinai desert. Knights of the Hospital of St John of Jerusalem provided shelter and care for the sick, poor and weary pilgrims who visited the holy places, while the Templars guarded the holy places of Jerusalem, protected travellers and lived according to the RULE of Bernard of Clairvaux. Both orders were endowed with substantial revenues, property and lands in the new kingdom and throughout Catholic Europe. Within a few years of their foundation most of their brethren, while living under VOWS of religion, were conventual knights (their priests were known as *chaplains*) and the two orders played an increasingly significant role in the defence of the Christian settlements in Palestine and Syria and in the administration of the Kingdom of Jerusalem. They constructed and garrisoned castles and fought alongside crusading forces in the perennial wars against the Egyptians and Turks. The convent of each order was situated in the Holy Land, with dependent priories and estates throughout Europe. Each order had about fifty preceptories or commanderies (*see* COMMANDERY *and* PRECEPTORY) in the British Isles, many commemorated by place-names such as St John's Jerusalem in Kent, St John's Wood in London, Templecombe in Somerset, Temple Guiting in the Gloucestershire Cotswolds and Fryerning in Essex – 'the place of the brothers'. Driven from Palestine with the rest of the Catholics in 1291, the Hospitallers took over the island of Rhodes, off the coast of Asia Minor, which became their base for naval operations against Muslim shipping. The island was ruled as a semi-independent state until 1522, when it was seized by the Ottoman Turks and the knights removed to the island of Malta, which they held as a sovereign power from 1530 until 1798. Following the persecution and papal suppression of the Templars in 1312 (*see* TEMPLAR, KNIGHTS), most of their properties were transferred to the Hospitallers. From 1312 to their dissolution by Henry VIII in 1540, the English Knights Hospitaller comprised a minor, though well-endowed, branch of an international order, drawn (as required by its statutes) from the ARMIGEROUS families of the nobility. Discipline was firm and a knight's vow of obedience to the rule was strictly observed. Chastity and poverty were also required, although in practice a successful knight could enjoy his possessions until they were claimed by the order at his death. The Hospitallers' English headquarters were at St John's Priory, Clerkenwell in London and it was there that an aspiring knight would undertake his novitiate before travelling to Rhodes, where several years of military service against the Muhammadans would normally lead to promotion to the rank of Commander. As a senior member of the order he would be responsible for the administration of its estates and finances, serve as a diplomat, or be seconded into royal or magnate service. The arms of the order were a plain white cross on red and its HABIT was black with the badge of a white 'Maltese' cross on the shoulder.
For the Order of St John Library and Museum *see* APPENDIX II.

SAINTS The practice of invoking and venerating the saints and martyrs has long been an element in Catholic devotion. They are perceived as being accessible as a medium of intercessionary prayer: because of their holiness they are close to God and yet they also remain close to man, whose nature they share. From the eighth century, the lives of the saints were read at MATTINS, but various councils found it necessary to curb the excesses and superstition of popular devotion. In the early Church, bishops controlled the cult of the saints in their dioceses, but the veneration of some saints spread beyond regional limits and the resulting problems sometimes required papal intervention. The first historically attested canonisation is that of Ulrich of Augsburg in 993. In *c.* 1170 it was asserted that no one should be venerated as a saint without the authority of the Roman Church and this became part of CANON LAW. In the Roman Catholic Church, *canonisation* is the definitive sentence by which the pope declares a dead person to have entered into heavenly glory and ordains that a new saint should be recognised throughout the Church. (*Beatification* is slightly different in that it permits the public veneration of a faithful Catholic in a particular church, diocese, religious order or country.) The cult of the saints was repudiated by the reformers, notably the Calvinists, who objected that it was not specifically recommended in the scriptures.

SAINTS, AGE OF *see* CELTIC CHURCH

SALTER In the medieval period there was usually insufficient fodder to maintain livestock throughout the winter, and meat and fish could be preserved only by dry salting or by curing in brine. Religious communities therefore consumed inordinate quantities of salt. On the monastic estates, animals other than breeding stock were killed in the autumn, the 'season' beginning on St Martin's Day (11 November). The salter was an assistant to the KITCHENER and was responsible for purchasing the huge quantities of salt required at that time. It was often considered necessary to take mustard and other spices with food in order to disguise the taste (or the ineffectiveness) of the salt. Consequently, the salterer was sometimes descibed as a *mustardius* because it was he who was responsible to the kitchener for preparing seasonings and sauces. Salt was also one of the ingredients used in the production of HOLY WATER and was blessed for this purpose before the High Mass. Because of its preservative quality, it was considered to be a symbol of incorruptibility, and a small quantity was retained from the blessing so that a pinch could be added to the saltcellars in the FRATER.

SALVE REGINA Recited at the end of the COMPLINE, the *Salve Regina* was one of the oldest Marion antiphons (*see* ANTIPHON). As devotion to the Blessed Virgin Mary increased, so too did the complexity of the musical setting.

SANCTORALE That section of a MISSAL or BREVIARY in which are set out the offices peculiar to particular saints' days.
See also TEMPORALE

SANCTUARY That part of a church containing the altar or, if there are several ALTARS, the High Altar. The terms sanctuary and PRESBYTERY are considered by some to be synonymous but, correctly, the former is contained within the latter and is often raised above it at the east end (*see* PREDELLA).
See also LITURGY and MEDIEVAL ARCHITECTURE

SANCTUARY CROSSES Medieval roadside crosses erected to delineate the boundaries of an ecclesiastical liberty within which certain privileges were enjoyed (*see* FRANCHISE *and* SANCTUARY, RIGHT OF). There were eight such crosses around Ripon, of which only one, the Sharrow Cross, survives.

SANCTUARY LAMP *see* LAMPS

SANCTUARY, RIGHT OF From the Latin *sanctus*, meaning 'inviolable', is derived the Right of Sanctuary which, in medieval England, was of two kinds: ecclesiastical and secular.

Ecclesiastical sanctuary developed through usage from the Saxon period and originally applied only to that area in the immediate vicinity of a bishop's throne (*cathedra*) and to the precincts of certain religious houses. In 431 this was extended to include the CURTILAGE of a church, or an area defined as such. Having claimed the right of sanctuary, a fugitive could not be forcibly removed, contravention of the laws of sanctuary being a form of SACRILEGE punishable by excommunication. Within forty days the fugitive was permitted to take an oath before a coroner, by which he confessed his crime, swore to abjure the realm (leave the country) and submit to banishment. Thereafter, dressed in a white robe or sackcloth and carrying a wooden cross, he would travel to an agreed port and board the first available ship. Such journeys had to be completed within an allotted time and by a prescribed route. This was by no means an easy task: in the fourteenth century the walk from Yorkshire to Dover had to be accomplished in nine days. The right of sanctuary could also be exercised by those who were the victims of brigandage or raids from rapacious neighbours. Indeed, entire communities were sometimes accommodated within a church tower and storage would be provided for their goods and cattle. Many churches possessed sanctuary knockers (*hagodays*): brass rings, often with escutcheons in the form of some monstrous beast. By grasping the ring of the hagoday, a fugitive could claim sanctuary from his pursuers. The most celebrated sanctuary knocker is at Durham cathedral priory where 'serten men that dyd lie alwaies in two chambers over the church dore . . . that when any such offenders dyd come and knocke, straight waie they were letten in at any our of the nyght'. Giraldus Cambrensis, writing at the end of the twelfth century, described 'the churches in Wales [which] are more quiet and tranquil than those elsewhere. Around them the cattle graze peacefully not only in the churchyards but outside too with the fences and ditches marked out and set by bishops to fix the sanctuary limits' (*see* SENTRY FIELD). In some cases, the right of sanctuary (Welsh *braint*) extended as far as 'the cattle go to feed in the morning and return in the evening', a privilege which was sometimes grossly abused.

Another type of ecclesiastical sanctuary, confirmed by William I in 1070, applied to twenty-two abbeys and cathedrals where sanctuary could

The sanctuary knocker on the north door of Durham Cathedral.

be claimed for life. This resulted in numerous complaints of abuse, indeed the abbey of Westminster acquired an unenviable reputation as a 'base for systematic robbery'. In 1529, coroners were instructed to ensure that those who abjured the realm should be branded with the letter 'A' on the back of the thumb. In 1540 the right of sanctuary was abolished for those believed to be guilty of murder, rape, burglary, highway robbery or arson. James I effectively abolished the right altogether in 1623, although in some places sanctuary for debt was recognised well into the nineteenth century.

Secular sanctuary relied upon a royal grant and in theory might be applied to any FRANCHISE where a lord exercised *jura regalia*. For this reason, secular sanctuary is often confused with ecclesiastical sanctuary, for fugitives frequently sought refuge in a church in franchise, especially in ecclesiastical liberties such as Beverley and Durham. The privileges of secular sanctuary were

restricted to seven cities in 1540 and were abolished in 1773.
See also SANCTUARY CROSSES

SANCTUS BELL (*also* SACRING BELL) A bell rung at the saying of the *Sanctus* ('Holy, holy, holy . . .') at the beginning of the MASS and to focus attention at the consecration and ELEVATION of the Host.

SANITATION *see* PLUMBING, WATER SUPPLY AND SANITATION

SARCOPHAGUS A stone coffin, the lid of which may be decorated with a simple Christian motif. The term is also used to describe a structure on which a coffin is rested, or a monument (*see* MONUMENTS) depicting the same. The original sarcophagus was a limestone used by the Greeks to make coffins and believed to consume the flesh of corpses.

SARUM, USE OF (SARUM RITE) The medieval modification of the Roman rite used in the cathedral of Salisbury in Wiltshire. Traditionally ascribed to St Osmund, it was compiled by Bishop Richard le Poore (d. 1237) and was revised (as the *New Use of Sarum*) in the fourteenth century. Adopted by several other dioceses in the later Middle Ages, it formed the basis for the first *Book of Common Prayer* of 1549 (*see* USES).

SAVIGNIAC ORDER The abbey of Savigny, the mother house of the Savigniac congregation, owed its origins to St Vitalis of Mortain (d. 1120). Originally a secular clerk, Vitalis chose to join a disparate group of religious individuals in the wild Craon Forest, pursuing the life of a HERMIT and itinerant preacher. In *c.* 1105 he discovered a secluded valley near the village of Savigny on the borders of Normandy, Brittany and Maine, where he was joined by a group of like-minded disciples. Together they established a religious community that soon attracted the patronage of the rich and powerful. In *c.* 1112 the community was recognised as an abbey which, under the leadership of Abbot Geoffrey (1122–39), expanded into a flourishing monastic order with more than thirty houses throughout Europe.

The Savigniacs were introduced into Britain by the Anglo-Norman Count Stephen of Mortain (later King Stephen). A colony was established at Tulketh, Lancashire, in 1124, although three years later it moved to the beautiful Vale of Nightshade at Furness, Cumbria. The order's rapid expansion resulted in a structure that lacked both accountability and control. This was recognised by Abbot Serlo (1140–53), who, impressed by St Bernard of Clairvaux, petitioned for his entire order to be absorbed into the Cistercian community (*see* CISTERCIANS). The merger was ratified at the GENERAL CHAPTER of 1147. Notable Savigniac communities that became Cistercian houses included Buildwas, Byland, Furness and Neath – and Jervaulx, which (apparently) was established without the consent of the Abbot of Savigny.

SAXON CHRISTIANITY *see* ANGLO-SAXON CHURCH

SCAFFOLDING AND CRANES Scaffolding used in the construction of medieval stone or brick buildings usually consisted of a platform supported on trestles for low-level work, and more elaborate structures – not dissimilar to those used today – for working above head-height. The uprights (*spars*) were most often of alder, although other types of timber were used. These and the horizontal ledgers (sometimes described as *putlogs*) were lashed together with ropes of bast (or some other fibrous material) or withies, and the lashings were tightened by driving in wedges (*warrokes*). Shorter lengths of timber inserted into *putlog holes* in the wall supported the ends of the ledgers. Hurdles formed both the platform 'for the masons to stand upon' and 'the way onto the scaffold'. Employers often undertook to provide the necessary scaffolding and the temporary timber or wicker structures (*centering*) required to keep an arch or vault in place during construction (*see* ARCH, CENTERING *and* VAULTING). In 1324, when particularly long standards were required for the construction of the LANTERN at Ely, the large sum of £2 8*s* was paid 'for 24 fir trees for stagyngg [staging]'. Scaffolding represented a major item in the cost of rebuilding the nave at Westminster Abbey, with its vault more than 30m (100ft) above the ground. In 1472–3, when preparations were being made for the roofing, there were three scaffolds: the *inferior* (lower), *superior* (intermediate) and *supremus* (highest). From 1482 to 1490, 'the carpenters had been occupied chiefly in moving the scaffolding from severy to severy [compartments of vaulting] as the work advanced. The scaffolding was elaborate. Each portion of the great scaffold, upon which the centres stood and where the masons worked, was floored and shut off by partitions from wind and weather' (Rackham). To avoid the expense of erecting a scaffold when undertaking repairs, a platform was often bracketed out from a wall or a cradle lowered from above. At Hadleigh Castle in 1365 a 'cradel' was hired 'for taking down the scaffolding round two towers and blocking up the holes' – presumably the putlog holes in which the ledgers of the scaffolding had rested.

A variety of baskets, barrels and other receptacles for carrying materials are to be found in medieval illustrations, while large blocks of stone were lifted separately using rope 'slings' or pincer-like iron 'grips' which were attached to hemp lifting ropes. While the hodmen were capable of carrying small quantities of material on to the scaffolding, it was necessary to have some sort of machine for hoisting heavier loads. In 1222 we find tallow bought 'for greasing the machines for lifting timber and water', while at Westminster in 1333 tallow was used 'for greasing the pulleys and beams for lifting up great blocks of marble'. This type of mechanism, known as a 'gin' or *verne*, consisted of a rope running over a wheel fixed above the position to which the stone was to be delivered, one end of the rope ending with a hook and the other passing round an axle rotated by a wheel. Again during the construction of the lantern at Ely, iron bands, a hoop, brass hinges and great iron nails for the brass wheels were provided for the verne and 6*s* 8*d* was paid to Master Thomas the carpenter for 'setting up le ferne'. A common form of crane incorporated a *falcon* or *hawk*, a horizontal spindle that passed through the upper end of a vertical post and carried a pair of brass pulley wheels on iron axles. The records of Vale Royal Abbey, Cheshire refer to the men who operated these cranes as *falconarii*. A particular form of grip, the reversed grip, was used to swing large pieces of stone (such as BOSSES) over the space between the vaulting ribs and lower them accurately into position. This type of grip consisted of two crescent-shaped irons suspended from a ring, with their convexities facing outwards. The lower ends of the irons were inserted into holes drilled obliquely into the stone so that the strain on the ring would hold them in position. Among the stores at Westminster in 1399 were 'a machine called wynde, a machine called brokke, and 4 vernes'. The 'brokke' or *brake* was a type of capstan, while 'wynde' probably refers to a *windas* or windlass mechanism, both of which were turned by hand. Medieval hoists of this type have survived above the north-west gable at Peterborough Cathedral and in the tower at Salisbury Cathedral, where most of the original fourteenth-century scaffolding also remains – just as it was erected within the spire. The Salisbury hoist measures several metres in diameter, was operated by four men, and is still functional. That at Peterborough measured 3m (10ft) in diameter and had a power to weight ratio of ten to one. This could be doubled by the use of block and tackle, and it has been calculated that a man of average weight could have raised a block of stone weighing 1.5 tons to a height of 30m (100ft) in about a quarter of an hour. Furthermore, the machine

The reconstruction of an abbey church. (CADW (Crown Copyright). Drawing by Chris Jones-Jenkins)

could have been dismantled by three men in fifteen minutes when required in another position. Other lifting machines were powered by treadmills: in 1488 the sum of 6*s* 8*d* was paid at Clarendon 'to four workmen running in the great wheel for 4 days'. This type of wheel features in several medieval illustrations of cranes and in numerous documents: a 'great wheel' is mentioned in the Westminster Abbey accounts in *c*. 1482–90, for example. It was located above the nave vault and was moved, with the scaffolding, from one bay to the next. An example of a treadmill has survived in the early sixteenth-century Bell Harry Tower at Canterbury Cathedral Priory.
See also FOUNDATIONS (STRUCTURAL), MASONRY *and* MASTER MASONS AND ARCHITECTS

SCAPULAR Part of the regular monastic HABIT, a sleeveless garment worn over the shoulders at the front and back and reaching almost to the feet.
See also CLOTHING

SCHISM Formal separation from the unity of the Church (*see* GREAT SCHISM). Schism was not considered to be heretical because it did not result from doctrinal differences. Priests in schism did not relinquish their authority to celebrate the Eucharist and bishops could continue to ordain priests.

SCHOLA CANTORUM *see* CHURCH MUSIC

SCHOOLS Although the early monasteries were perceived as centres of learning, they were intended to be 'schools of Christ' where the spiritual growth of the brethren was sacrosanct. A classical education was therefore considered to be both an irrelevance and a diversion. Nevertheless, a monk required a certain degree of education and religious, literary and musical instruction was given during the novitiate, together with training in the minutiae of the HORARIUM and monastic behaviour (*see* NOVICE *and* OBLATE). In the late medieval period, some monasteries maintained houses of instruction at the universities where opportunities were available for academic study.

Providing educational opportunities for the wider community was, initially, the responsibility of a bishop and his clergy but, by the twelfth century, it seems to have passed to the superiors of the monasteries and (despite concern that ALMS might be diverted from the indigent poor) a number of monastic schools were established at this time – notably at the Benedictine abbeys of Gloucester and Reading. Many urban houses provided education for poor children through their almonries (*see* ALMONRY), while nunneries often supplemented their meagre incomes by accepting young girls as boarders, despite frequent prohibitions of the practice which was seen as a distraction from their principal function. Several abbeys built schoolrooms near their gates: at Bury St Edmunds, for example, where in 1180 Abbot Samson engaged a school master and provided him with a building in School House Street. Other almonry schools included those at Canterbury, Durham, St Albans and Westminster. Some of these were 'grammar schools' while others, known as *song schools*, provided a choir for the daily LADY MASS and for services to which the public were admitted in the abbey or cathedral church. In *c.* 1318 a large school house was attached to the almonry at York Minster for that purpose while, at Durham, the song school occupied part of the dorter UNDERCROFT. Song schools offered a broad curriculum that included mathematics, reading, writing and Latin as well as a variety of musical skills. Pupils, who received free tuition and sometimes board, were usually few in number (there were only six at Durham) but the education they received significantly enhanced their career prospects. Tuition was usually the responsibility of a secular clerk, who would receive a stipend from the monastery or cathedral and was provided with board and lodgings. The medieval song school tradition has survived in today's cathedral choir schools (*see* CHURCH MUSIC).

Following the DISSOLUTION OF THE MONASTERIES in 1536–39, monastic song schools were displaced, together with the small schools that were sometimes attached to medieval chantries (*see* CHANTRY). Their purpose had been the training of priests, and rote learning, particularly of Latin, grammar and music, predominated. The grammar schools by which they were replaced continued to teach in Latin, but there was a greater emphasis on analysis and on an understanding of classical literature, science and theology, which were at that time considered to be the fount of learning. The contemporary development of printing meant that books were more readily available, although usually only for the preceptor's use, and paper also, so that the boys were able to keep journals or 'common place books' in which extracts from the texts were carefully copied and indexed.

The purpose of the 'new' secular grammar schools was to provide the sons of the emerging middle class with a suitable career. With the decline of the Church, the governance of late Tudor and Stuart England was increasingly the concern of secular administrators, drawn from the swelling ranks of well-educated young men. Latin not only continued as a necessary adjunct to the study of mathematics, medicine and the law, but was also the European language of diplomacy and trade, and classical literature provided many of the precepts for political life. Nevertheless, stimulated by the introduction of an English Bible and prayer book, the use of the English language, both in administration and in business, was increasing rapidly. Many of these sixteenth-century educational foundations remain today and are often known as the King's School, Henry VIII's School, King Edward's School and so on. Such titles do not necessarily imply that they were founded by the sovereign whose name they bear or, indeed, during that sovereign's reign. Many, including the majority of cathedral schools, were refoundations of earlier monastic or chantry schools: King's School at Sherborne in Dorset, for example, was reputedly founded by St Aldhelm, the first bishop of Sherborne (d. 709), and reconstituted in 1550 during the reign of Edward VI.

'SCISSOR ARCHES' *see* TOWERS

SCONCE A wall-bracket holding a candlestick.

SCONCHON Splayed stone (*see* SPLAY).

SCREENS Monastic churches and those of secular canons were divided by screens in order to separate the various functions. The NAVE, to which the public was admitted (or, in Cistercian monasteries, the LAY BROTHERS) was separated from the RETRO-CHOIR by a ROOD SCREEN in front of which was a nave altar. The retro-choir was separated from the CHOIR by a stone PULPITUM and the choir itself was enclosed within its STALLS (*see also* RETURNED STALLS). In Cistercian churches, where the lay brothers attended their own offices in the nave, the aisles were often separated from the nave by screens within the nave arcade. The PRESBYTERY was usually separated from the AMBULATORY by a REREDOS or SHRINE SCREEN while subsidiary chapels and CHANTRY CHAPELS had their own screens (*see* PARCLOSE). All these screens would have been richly painted and gilded, their niches filled with the sculpted figures of saints, apostles and luminaries. In the majority of cathedrals, the medieval pulpitum has been demolished or replaced by CHOIR SCREENS (*see also* ORGAN SCREEN). There were also numerous screens in the conventual buildings: the CARRELS in the cloister, the cubicles in the DORTER, REREDORTER and INFIRMARY and the SCREENS PASSAGE in the FRATER and abbot's hall, for example.

SCREENS PASSAGE A passageway separated from a medieval hall by a decorative timber or stone screen (*see* SCREENS). The abbot's hall and guests' hall of a monastery were very similar in both function and design to the great halls of magnate castles and palaces. At one end of the hall was a passage from which three doorways led to the pantry, the buttery (*see* LARDER) and (in the centre, via a corridor) the KITCHENS. On the other side, and running across the width of the hall, was a screen pierced by a single doorway or pair of doorways and often with a gallery above. This was the standard arrangement, although it would often be modified in order to accommodate the confines of the site and the arrangement of the buildings. The screen was intended to reduce draughts from these doorways, and enabled the domestic staff to carry out their duties unobserved by guests in the hall. A similar passage was sometimes incorporated in the monks' refectory in order that they should not be distracted from the reading (*see* FRATER).

SCRIBE *see* SCRIPTORIUM

SCRIPT *see* LETTERING

SCRIPTORIUM

> Every word you write is a blow that strikes the devil.
>
> St Bernard of Clairvaux (1090–1153)

Calligraphy and illumination were ideally suited to the monastic vocation because they could be undertaken in SILENCE. The work of a monastic *scribe* – the transmission of God's word in a form so skilled and beautiful that it brought credit to his house, to his order and to his God – was an entirely appropriate occupation for a MONK. Book production included also the supply and preparation of materials (*see* INK, PARCHMENT, PENS *and* VELLUM) and the binding of manuscripts. The scriptorium was the writing-room of a monastery, where documents were written, illuminated and painted (*see* MANUSCRIPT ILLUMINATION). In Benedictine houses, the scriptorium was usually located in the south alley of the CLOISTER, where the scribes benefited from the pure, northern light. They were often provided with individual compartments (*see* CARRELS) to reduce drafts and encourage privacy and silence. At Chester, the cloister alley next to the church was wider than the others in order to accommodate a large number of scribes – indeed, it was nonetheless inadequate, and the scriptorium was continued into the west alley. In some monasteries the scriptorium was housed in a separate building: at Wenlock Priory it was in a room above the south aisle of the church, at Selby it was above the SACRISTY and at both Norwich and Evesham it was extended into a chamber above the north alley. In theory it was the duty of the scriptorium to provide the service books for use in choir, and therefore it came within the jurisdiction of the PRECENTOR (*see* ARMARIUS). In practice, however, many other magnificent works were produced, including numerous chronicles (histories) and transcriptions of manuscripts, both religious and pagan.

SCULLERY *see* LARDER

SEALS A seal (*sigil*) is a piece of wax, lead or paper, impressed with an individual design and attached to a document as a guarantee of authenticity. The piece of stone or metal upon which the design is engraved, and from which the impression is taken, is called a *matrix*.

Important documents carried seals which often bore distinctive devices which alluded to the names of their owners even before the inception of HERALDRY in the mid-twelfth century. Ecclesiastical bodies generally used religious symbols on their seals and these were often translated into later coats of arms. The dual authority of the lords spiritual is exemplified by the seal of Bishop Odo of Bayeux (d. 1097): on one side is the image of a powerful magnate, an equestrian figure bearing the sword of secular power, while on the other is the tonsured clerk with the ring and the staff – the symbols of a bishop's office.

Medieval seals were usually circular in shape, pointed ovals being used by ecclesiastics, cathedrals and religious communities, although not exclusively so. By the thirteenth century, the administrative offices of abbots, priors, bishops and cathedral chapters were producing numerous legal documents, all of which required authentication by means of seals. These seals were often so large, and

Second seal of Richard of Bury, bishop of Durham 1334–45. (Courtesy of Geoffrey Wheeler)

the documents so numerous, that *privy seals* were used for purely administrative purposes. These were smaller and, therefore, less ornate than great seals and usually bore a simple shield within a decorative interstice and legend. A *secretum*, perhaps a signet ring, was generally used for private matters and, because of their small size, these often bore devices other than coats of arms.

Seals are most often found singly, but may also represent the different parties to a contract. The normal practice in such cases was to prepare a number of copies of a document, each copy (*chirograph*) being sealed by all the parties to the agreement. The *Constitutions of Clarendon* (1164) were prepared in this way, but the three identical documents were never sealed. *Magna Carta* (1215) was sealed by King John's 'five-and-twenty over-kings', while one of the most remarkable surviving medieval documents, a letter to the pope, was sealed (but not delivered) by the ninety-six barons summoned to the Lincoln Parliament of Edward I in 1300.

In England, the Great Seal of the realm has always been two-sided, like the coinage, with a different device on each side. The first 'great' seal of England was probably that of Edward the Confessor (1003–66), but that which provided a model for later English monarchs was the seal of William I (1066–87), which was engraved on the reverse with the *majesty* (a depiction of the king seated in state) and on the obverse an equestrian figure, also of the king. Subsequently, the faces were reversed: the majesty becoming the obverse and the equestrian figure the reverse.

Inevitably, from the early thirteenth century it became fashionable for the magnates also to engrave their seals with equestrian figures of themselves in armour, complete with heraldic shields, horsecloths and banners. The lords spiritual were no exception and (like Bishop Odo before them) they would depict themselves in both the trappings of secular authority and the vestments of their office. Unique among the prelates were the prince bishops of Durham who, as lords palatine, bore an equestrian figure on one side of their (circular) seals and a majesty on the other (*see* PALATINATE).

A seal was required in order to enter into a contract and to conduct business. Officially, possession of a seal was therefore restricted to 'kings and great men only', but by the end of the twelfth century it was common practice for the major OBEDIENTIARIES of religious communities to use departmental seals, and these had to be handed in, together with the keys to their offices, on the death of the SUPERIOR. The great seal of an abbey was the joint responsibility of the three senior obedientiaries, each of whom held a different key to the case in which it was kept, thereby ensuring that it could not be used for official purposes without the consent of all three. As lords spiritual, superiors were permitted to use personal seals, but other members of the community were not. Abbot Samson of Bury St Edmunds (1135–1211) was obliged to enquire which of his monks held personal seals – 'and thirty three seals were found'. It would appear, therefore, that most of the Bury monks had seals and several of them were trading to their own benefit. One Geoffrey Russ, a monk-warden responsible for four of the abbey's manors, was found to have gold and silver to the value of two hundred marks in his chests, most of which must have represented the profits of land.

For the papal bull *see* BULLA.

SECULAR (i) One who is not bound by a monastic RULE (*see* REGULAR). *Secular canons* were clergy serving a CATHEDRAL or COLLEGIATE CHURCH. Although they were not members of a monastic order, and were not obliged to observe a monastic rule, they were nevertheless required to live a quasi-monastic life of celibacy and discipline. Initially, they lived as a community, often in accommodation that resembled the claustral buildings of a monastery (see CLOISTER), and were subject to the authority of a CHAPTER to which

they all belonged. But, by the fourteenth century, there was a tendency towards laxity: lodgings were often at some remove from the cathedral and some secular canons even enjoyed the appurtenances of a benefice while appointing a deputy to undertake their cathedral duties. Chichester, Exeter, Hereford, Lichfield, Lincoln, London, Salisbury, Wells and York were all medieval secular cathedrals.
(ii) Pertaining to matters civil in contradistinction to matters ecclesiastical.
(iii) Concerned with that which is not spiritual.

SECULAR ARM In CANON LAW, the term is used to describe the state or any lay authority concerned in ecclesiastical cases. Following trials for HERESY, for example, condemned prisoners were usually handed over to the secular arm for punishment.

SECULAR CANONS *see* SECULAR

SECULAR CLERGY Priests who live in the general community as distinct from the 'REGULAR' clergy who are members of religious orders.

SECUNDA Latin element of a monastic place-name, signifying a second foundation. The Augustinian house of Llantony in Monmoutshire grew so large that most of the canons moved to a new site near Gloucester in 1136. A nucleus remained at Llantony which became a PRIORY CELL of the new house which was known as Llantony Secunda.
See also PLACE-NAMES (MONASTIC AND ECCLESIASTICAL)

SECURITY Responsibility for the keys to a community's church and its claustral buildings rested with the second-in-command – the prior or sub-prior. Once the buildings had been secured at night by the CIRCATOR the keys were kept in his possession until the following morning, when they were returned to the CUSTODIANS and porters (*see* PORTER) The principal OBEDIENTIARIES held the keys to their respective departments, but these had to be handed in on the death of the SUPERIOR so that they could be redistributed (together with their departmental SEALS) by his successor.

SEDILIA Stone seats built within the south wall of a PRESBYTERY, often with an adjacent PISCINA. Sedilia were provided for the priest who celebrated the mass and for the deacon and sub-deacon who assisted him. The seats were sometimes stepped and would be occupied according to rank, the highest (and that nearest the altar) being for the celebrant. In some churches, nineteenth-century remodelling has raised the CHANCEL floor so that the seats of the sedilia appear to be uncomfortably low (*see* FENESTELLA).
See also ABLUTIONS, AUMBRY, CREDENCE, LAVABO, LITURGY *and* MASS

Fenestella with piscina and sedilia. Here, the sanctuary floor has been raised during a nineteenth-century restoration, making the seats of the sedilia appear uncomfortably low.

SEE The *cathedra* (throne) of a bishop (*see* CATHEDRALS) and the jurisdiction which this represents (*see* DIOCESE).

SEGMENTAL ARCH *see* ARCH

SEMPECTAE *see* STATIONARIES

SENTENCES (i) From the Latin *sententia* meaning an exposition of thought, medieval sentences were compilations of opinions which, by the thirteenth century, had evolved into accepted theological propositions.
(ii) Mural texts, maxims of Christian doctrine, which often replaced earlier WALL PAINTINGS following the Reformation.

SENTRY FIELD A West Country term for a field in the vicinity of a church where at one time there was a right of sanctuary (*see* SANCTUARY, RIGHT OF).

SEQUESTRATION A legal procedure by which sequestrators are appointed to administer the emoluments of a vacant benefice for the benefit of the next incumbent.

SERMON A discourse on a religious or moral subject, delivered during a religious service (*see* PULPITS).

SERVANTS *see* EMPLOYEES

SERVER One who assists in the SANCTUARY, especially at the EUCHARIST. A server's duties include the conveying of the bread and wine to the communion table and washing the celebrant's hands. He or she may also be the CRUCIFER.

SERVICE BOOKS *see* BOOKS (for a list of individual entries), LIBRARIES, MANUSCRIPT ILLUMINATION, PRECENTOR *and* SCRIPTORIUM

SERVICES *For* conventual services *see* DIVINE OFFICE, HORARIUM, HOURS (CANONICAL), LITURGY, MEDIEVAL CHURCH, MASS *and* PROCESSIONS.

The Laity
For the laity in the Middle Ages there were generally three services on Holy Days and Sundays: MATTINS and MASS in the morning and EVENING PRAYER in the afternoon. But as the number of clergy, curates, chaplains and chantry priests increased, so did the frequency of daily services, which often included several celebrations of the mass. Medieval congregations took little part in the services, however, long passages of which were conducted in Latin, and there were no hymns and only occasional sermons. Nevertheless, the regular performance of elaborate ritual and the ordered sequence of PROCESSIONS and feast-days provided security in an otherwise wretched existence and created an intense attachment to the Church. Furthermore, the arrival of the FRIARS in the thirteenth century brought an entirely new perspective to public worship.
For post-Reformation services *see* REFORMATION.

SERVITOR Those brethren who undertook menial but important tasks such as serving in the community's FRATER, INFIRMARY and KITCHENS. They were appointed according to a weekly rota and were obliged to ensure that everything was prepared before handing over to the incoming servitor with whom they undertook the weekly washing of feet. The Benedictine rule acknowledged their value: 'Let the brethren serve one another and let no one be excused from the kitchen service, unless for sickness or because he is occupied in some business of importance, for this service brings increase of reward and of charity.'

SEVERY A compartment of VAULTING.

SEXT The monastic day office which took place at about noon ('the sixth hour') and usually followed High Mass. A simple office, similar to TERCE and NONE, it consisted of a hymn, the singing of part

of Psalm 119, a short chapter, and closing prayers, which included the lesser litany, the Collect and Lord's Prayer.
See also HOURS (CANONICAL) *and* HORARIUM

SEYNIES *see* PHLEBOTOMY

SHAFT That part of a COLUMN or PIER between the capital and base.

SHAVING *see* RASURA

SHEEP *see* WOOL

SHOES Although practice varied considerably among different houses, three types of footwear were usually provided, two for daytime use and one for the night. The CHAMBERLAIN issued pairs of heavy work boots at regular intervals of between one and five years, together with pairs of 'day shoes' for normal daytime wear. Initially, these would be made in a tannery and cobbler's workshop in the curia, but later they would be purchased or provided by a tenant in lieu of rent. Soft leather or felt 'slippers' were worn during the hours of darkness and as an indulgence for sick or recuperating brethren in the INFIRMARY. Not only were these more comfortable, they also allowed a monk to move about without disturbing others, especially during the night offices. New shoes were issued during Holy Week, the old pairs being distributed to the poor by the ALMONRY.
See also CLOTHING

SHRINE SCREEN A decorative stone screen that separates the HIGH ALTAR from a shrine (or shrines) to the east. The finest example in England is the late fourteenth-century Neville Screen at Durham Cathedral Priory which separates the High Altar from St Cuthbert's tomb (d. 687) (*see also* REREDOS).

SHRINES In AD 156 the author of *The Martyrdom of Polycarp* wrote that the martyr's bones had become 'more valuable than refined gold'. But by that time the mortal remains of saints and martyrs (*see* RELICS) had already acquired a broader potency that affected all objects which themselves had been in contact with the remains or, indeed, with the tomb in which they were preserved. Christians believed that reliquaries (*see* RELIQUARY) and shrines contained the living presence of the saints and that miracles could be performed through contact with the bones or the cloths (*brandae*) that had been touched by them (*see* Acts 19: 12). Such tombs were therefore places of healing, protection, forgiveness and spiritual guidance.

Palestine was perceived as one vast relic: it became the Holy Land of Christian imagination in which certain locations were particularly venerated for their associations with Christ. Thus, pilgrims immersed themselves in the Jordan as Christ had done and plucked leaves from the palm trees of Jericho and wore them in their hats, thereby acquiring the popular name of 'palmers'. Pilgrims to the Holy Land increased in number during the third and fourth centuries, many of them adding their own inventions to 'the steadily burning fire of their devotion' (Adair). Two monks, for example, claimed to have discovered the head of John the Baptist in the ruins of Herod's palace, and before long most churches in the Holy Land had acquired a 'relic' of some sort so that, by the beginning of the fifth century, pilgrimage was developing commercially, with the provision of lodgings and guided tours of the sacred sites (*see* ST JOHN OF JERUSALEM, ORDER OF and TEMPLAR, KNIGHTS).

The Cult of Relics

By this time, Europe had also established its own centres of pilgrimage, notably at Rome, where the relics of martyrs killed during the persecutions were venerated by thousands of pilgrims, including four Anglo-Saxon kings. Shrines of lesser saints and martyrs burgeoned throughout Europe and every church coveted a holy relic. In the sixth

century Pope Gregory the Great sent to Augustine and the missionaries in England 'all things necessary for the worship of the Church' including 'relics of the holy apostles and martyrs', and the second Council of Nicaea (787) ordered that no church should be consecrated without relics, which were to be placed in or upon an altar in a *reliquary*, or in a CRYPT beneath. Thus, it was not only the great abbeys and cathedrals that possessed relics: the parish church of St Denys at Stanford-in-the-Vale in Berkshire, for example, still has the reliquary which once contained one of St Denys's bones, St Wulfram's at Grantham in Lincolnshire possessed the relics of St Wulfram, while at St Edmund's, Salisbury, there was a piece of St Wolfride's skull.

Throughout Europe the market in relics expanded rapidly: not only those of native saints, but also imported items from Rome and Palestine, most of which were of extremely dubious provenance. This unsavoury trade flourished for several centuries, partly because it was believed that all relics possessed miraculous powers of self-multiplication. In Britain, Bede (d. 735) refers to shrines of native saints such as Alban, Oswald, Chad and Cuthbert that were visited from the fifth century. Not all saints were martyrs: some were *confessors* who had witnessed to the faith through suffering or by the impeccability of their lives. They were judged by the efficacy of their relics in working miracles, and many were thereby acclaimed saints. In medieval Norfolk, for example, there were some seventy places of pilgrimage associated with local saints or their relics. But very few shrines acquired truly international popularity. After Palestine and Rome came the shrine of St James at Santiago de Compostela in northern Spain and, in France, the shrines of St Martin at Tours and that of the reputed head of John the Baptist at Amiens. In Germany were the relics of the Three Kings at Cologne and the shrine of the Holy Coat (the seamless robe of Christ) at Trier. Italian shrines included the tomb of St Francis at Portiuncula near Assisi, that of St Anthony at Padua and the Holy House of Loreto, which had been miraculously transported from Nazareth to Italy in 1295. Of contemporary English shrines only those of St Thomas à Becket at Canterbury and Our Lady of Walsingham in Norfolk belonged to this first order, although Glastonbury in Somerset, with its mythical associations with Joseph of Arimathea and King Arthur, was also popular, as were the remote shrines of St Magnus on Orkney and Ynys Enlli (Bardsey), the 'island of innumerable saints', off the Lleyn peninsular, Gwynedd.

At Canterbury, the remains of Thomas à Becket (murdered 1170 and canonised 1173) were translated in 1220 to a new chapel, the Trinity Chapel to the east of the High Altar, where they remained until the Dissolution. Today, a simple candle marks where the magnificent, jewel-encrusted shrine once stood. Later, the delightful circular Corona Chapel was added at the east end of the cathedral, a unique feature in which was preserved a fragment of the saint's skull. The shrine space was deliberately planned, the walkway round the shrine illuminated by twelve magnificent windows that tell of Becket's miracles. To the twelfth-century pilgrim, these were events that had occurred within living memory – a kind of medieval journalism in stained glass.

The chapel of St Chad's Head survives to the south of the choir at Lichfield Cathedral. Pilgrims would have entered the chapel by a staircase, walked around the head and an arm bone displayed in a casket, and descended by means of a

Opposite: *The beautiful late fourteenth-century shrine screen at Durham Cathedral Priory. Given by John, Lord Neville in c. 1380, it separates the high altar from St Cuthbert's tomb and originally contained 107 gilded and painted statues.* (© John Crook/info@john-crook.com)

second staircase that still exists in the wall. However, so numerous were the pilgrims that the cathedral chapter decided to close one staircase and build, instead, an *exposition gallery* in which the precious relic could be displayed to the passing crowd below. The glorious, late thirteenth-century Angel Choir at Lincoln Cathedral was built to accommodate the translated remains (the head) of St Hugh of Avalon (*c.* 1135–1200), who was canonised in 1220. The space around the shrine contains a number of tombs and chantry chapels, deliberately erected in close proximity to the saint's remains, and was provided with entrances to the north and south for the benefit of pilgrims. The bronze canopy dates from 1986. The shrine of St Thomas Cantelupe (*c.* 1218–82) in the north transept of Hereford Cathedral was a remarkably popular place of pilgrimage and at one time rivalled even Becket's shrine at Canterbury. Bishop Cantelupe was Provincial Grand Master of the Knights Templar and the figures of fifteen knights of the order are carved in the lower section of the Purbeck marble tomb. The early fourteenth-century shrine of St Alban at the Benedictine abbey of St Albans (now the cathedral) was splendidly reconstructed from fragments in 1991–93 (there is a fourteenth-century WATCHING LOFT to the north), while at the heart of Westminster Abbey, to the east of the sanctuary, the shrine of St Edward the Confessor is surrounded by the tombs of five medieval kings of England and four queens, all of whom desired to be associated with the saint in death. Originally, the shrine comprised three elements: a stone base decorated with Cosmati work, a golden Feretory which contained the saint's coffin, and a wooden canopy that could be raised and lowered in order to protect the feretory. The shrine was dismantled during the Reformation and the feretory was removed. What is seen today is a rather battered stone base with remnants of the original decoration, on top of which rests the restored canopy. A blank space in the Cosmati floor shows that the shrine is no longer in its original position, and that it was raised on a platform and therefore visible beyond the western screen.

Penances and Indulgences

The popularity of pilgrimages in the Middle Ages owed much to the practice of prescribing them as *penances*. CONFESSION was followed by ABSOLUTION, which freed the repentant Christian from guilt but not from the punitive consequences of his sin. These could be commuted by performance of a penance, and many of those who were convicted of serious crimes by the ECCLESIASTICAL COURTS undertook long pilgrimages, clothed in sackcloth and ashes and with bare feet and fettered limbs. From the twelfth century, relief from purgatorial suffering could also be obtained by means of *indulgences*: certificates which stated that a period of PURGATORY had been remitted. Announcing the first crusade at Clermont in 1095, Pope Urban II offered a plenary INDULGENCE to all those who confessed their sins and 'took the cross', and in the thirteenth century the Franciscans claimed a papal plenary indulgence for all pilgrims to their shrine of the Portiuncula. Papal confirmation of this concession in 1294 established a precedent which was followed by the custodians of numerous other shrines, who sought partial indulgences from their bishops or from the pope himself. Inevitably, such privileges had to be paid for, but they must have represented a sound investment, for the price continued to increase throughout the fourteenth century. Many shrines acquired the right to offer indulgences associated with more famous shrines, thereby attracting pilgrims who could see little point in exposing themselves to the hazards of a long and expensive journey overseas. The sale of indulgences also enabled those who were too old or infirm to go on crusade to send a substitute and still claim the benefits of a plenary indulgence. Similarly, a substitute pilgrim could be engaged, even by a man's family after his death or as a result of a clause in a will which required prayers to be offered for the soul of the testator at a particular shrine (*see also* CHANTRY). Eventually, indulgences could be commuted to money payments, and in the late medieval period *pardoners* competed with each other, and with the local shrines, in the sale of certificates.

Curative Shrines

Not all those who set out on pilgrimage did so as a means of penance, however. In an age of rudimentary medical practice many travelled to shrines where the relics were associated with miracles of healing and the relief of suffering. The Fourth Lateran Council of 1215 had declared that illness was caused not by physical ailments but by sin, and it therefore followed that a visit to a shrine was likely to do more good than a visit to a physician. Others perceived the shrines as tangible evidence of the spiritual world of heaven, far removed from their own temporal existence but attainable through physical contact with the relics of saints and martyrs. Such places fed the medieval imagination and brought even the most sceptical of men into contact with the historical Jesus and the characters of a seemingly heroic age.

The healing powers of the seventh-century saint Melangell continue to attract pilgrims to her shrine at Pennant Melangell in Powys. Melangell came to the remote valley in 607, fleeing from a dynastic marriage arranged by her father who was a member of the ruling family in Strathclyde. Melangell (whose Latin name was Monacella) founded a nunnery in the valley and became associated with the cult of the hare which, in pagan Britain, was revered as a goddess of fertility. According to legend, she gave protection to a hare that was being hunted by Brochwel, prince of Powys. When the huntsman raised his horn to urge on the hounds, it stuck to his lips and the hounds were repulsed. Medieval pilgrims prostrated themselves beneath the RELIQUARY, sometimes remaining there all night in hope of a cure. The shrine, believed to be the oldest Romanesque reliquary in northern Europe, was removed from the church following the Reformation. But the saint's bones were preserved and placed in the restored shrine when it was reconstructed from broken fragments found in the lichgate and walls of the church.

Pilgrimage

The acquisition of potent and popular relics was, in medieval terms, a guarantee of financial security if not commercial success for many of the larger monastic houses, particularly those of Benedictine foundations. Hostelries such as the George and Pilgrim at Glastonbury were built to accommodate pilgrims in the fifteenth century, as were the Star and Cross Keys at Holywell and the New Inn at Gloucester. The body of the murdered Edward II (d. 1327) had been received for burial by the Abbot of St Peter's (now Gloucester Cathedral) in the previous century. Even though Edward was denied canonisation by the pope, his remains nevertheless attracted enormous numbers of pilgrims, whose patronage financed the rebuilding of the superb Perpendicular choir and presbytery in the abbey church (1337–50).

The George and Pilgrim at Glastonbury, Somerset. (Courtesy of Anthony Kersting)

Concerned that pilgrims should not invade their precincts, Cistercian houses tended to eschew relics, the abbeys of Rievaulx and Hailes being notable exceptions. The magnificent shrine containing the relics of Rievailx's founder, Abbot William (1132–45) was located in the cloister, near to the chapter house door, and is unlikely to have been accessible to the outside world. Hailes, it would appear, was an entirely different matter. We are told that in October 1242 Richard, Earl of Cornwall (1209–72) was in danger of drowning at sea. He vowed that if he lived he would found a religious house, and in 1245 his brother, King Henry III, gave him the manor of Hailes (Gloucestershire) in order that he could keep his pledge. In 1270 Richard's son Edmund presented the Cistercian monks of Hailes with a phial said to contain the blood of Christ. From then until the DISSOLUTION OF THE MONASTERIES Hailes attracted numerous pilgrims, their offerings paying for the construction of a magnificent CHEVET of chapels around the shrine. This arrangement allowed for a processional aisle and a suitably dignified space for the shrine behind the High Altar. The foundations of the shrine are still in evidence: a platform some 3m (10ft) in length and 2.6m (8ft) wide. It is unfortunate that nothing remains to indicate the form of the structure, although it may have been similar to the surviving shrine to Edward the Confessor at Westminster Abbey (*see above*).

Shrine offerings (rather than money gifts) included curiosities such as griffins' eggs, elephants' teeth and unicorns' heads, as well as the more usual precious stones and plate. Offerings belonged to the saints and were rarely converted into cash, even in times of crisis, and several monasteries were obliged to appoint a keeper (*tumbarius*) or Master of the FERETORY, who was responsible for security (*see also* WATCHING LOFT). But not all cults were successful, indeed the majority were surprisingly short-lived. Even at Canterbury, where in 1220 (the year of the translation of the relics) offerings at Thomas à Becket's tomb had totalled no less than £1,142, by the Dissolution of the Monasteries annual income from pilgrims had declined to £36.

Roads were rarely for the exclusive use of pilgrims, although causeways and bridges were often provided for their benefit, particularly where routes converged on a particular shrine. Along the more popular routes (many of which came to be known as *Pilgrims' Ways*), wayside inns, hostels, chapels and hospices developed, such as the infirmary at Castle Acre in Norfolk which was provided for ailing pilgrims on their way to Walsingham (*see also* SLIPPER CHAPEL). So numerous were the Walsingham pilgrims that in contemporary chronicles the Milky Way was sometimes referred to as 'the Walsingham Way'. The tower of St Catherine's chapel, high above the abbey at Abbotsbury, Dorset, and the even more prominent tower of St Michael's chapel on Glastonbury Tor in Somerset must have welcomed approaching pilgrims like beacons of hope (*see* CHAPELS). At Evesham Abbey there was a pilgrims' church within the precinct, while at Canterbury and Winchester special lodgings were provided. Arrangements were often made to supervise large numbers of pilgrims within the church itself: broad ambulatories (*see* AMBULATORY *and* RETRO-CHOIR), dedicated entrances and exits, and systems to control the direction and movement of queues, for example.

Not all shrines were located in major churches. Six miles from Hereford the church of the Nativity of the Blessed Virgin Mary at Madley was enormously popular in the Middle Ages because it housed a statue of the Virgin which (presumably) acquired a reputation for working wonders (*see* MARY, THE BLESSED VIRGIN). Chapels, a new chancel, additional naves and a crypt for the statue were all added to the original Norman church to accommodate the streams of pilgrims, whose offerings enabled the church to commission several treasures – notably a rare and beautiful early thirteenth-century east window of the trial of John the Baptist.

Pilgrimage was essentially a popular and spontaneous expression of emotion: one that was never admitted as an essential of Christian duty but which was generally tolerated and, in many cases, encouraged by the Church. As the cult grew, so it became necessary for the Church to exercise control, and in some cases even to prohibit certain practices, such as the veneration of holy wells, many of which were considered unsuitable for veneration because of their pagan origins. Despite the continuing success of several major shrines, the numbers of pilgrims on the roads of England declined during the fourteenth and fifteenth centuries and, as Chaucer's *Canterbury Pilgrims* suggests, many took the journey simply for the pleasures of travel and each others' company – a medieval package holiday. (Pilgrims to Canterbury carried small bells – hence the Canterbury Bell flower.)

For the majority of medieval society, to embark on a pilgrimage must have been the realisation of a lifetime's ambition: a unique opportunity to gain experience of the world beyond the confines of their town or village. Before leaving, it was necessary to obtain a priest's blessing, to make confession and, if the pilgrimage was to be a lengthy one, to make a will. Most pilgrims wore a long, coarse tunic known as a *sclavein* and a broad-brimmed hat turned up at the front. They travelled in bands for mutual protection, and usually on foot, although in later centuries more often on horseback. Twenty-five miles was considered to be a good distance to travel in a day and numerous settlements developed as commercial and religious centres once they became established as reliable stopping-places. Before returning, pilgrims purchased the distinctive badge of the shrine they had visited and this was worn on their tunic or hat as proof of their pilgrimage.

The Reformation and After

The English shrines were plundered in 1537–9 and most were dismantled (*see* REFORMATION, THE). At Canterbury, twenty-six wagonloads of treasures were removed from Thomas à Becket's shrine and taken to the royal mint, while the bones of the saint, who had opposed Henry Plantagenet, were scattered by order of Henry Tudor.

In October 1539 the Holy Blood of Hailes was confiscated and taken to London for examination. In the words of Bishop Latimer of Worcester, it was

> thought, deemed and judged [that] the substance of the matter of the supposed relic [was] an unctuous gum coloured, which, being in the glass, appeared to be a glistering red, resembling party the colour of blood; and after we did take out part of the said substance and matter out of the glass, then it was apparent glistering yellow colour, like amber or base gold and doth cleave to, as gum or bird-lime.

On 24 November the bishop of Rochester preached at St Paul's Cross. He displayed the relic and declared that it was 'honey clarified and coloured with saffron, as has been evidently proved before the King and his council'. The phial was then destroyed. As a postscript, it was claimed that the monks had contended that a man with mortal sin would be unable to see the Holy Blood and that the container had one side thicker than the other, which rendered it opaque. This, it was alleged, enabled the monks to show a penitent the opaque side and then, on payment of a sufficient sum, to turn it so that the relic was revealed.

Despite the suppression, pilgrimage in Britain survived the Reformation and remained a powerful image of the Christian tradition – although in a severely attenuated form. Indeed, in the nineteenth century it enjoyed a modest revival with the emergence of the Anglo-Catholic wing of the Church of England and today Walsingham and Lourdes are as popular as ever they were in the Middle Ages. Pilgrims still leave offerings in the niches of St Wite's tomb at Whitchurch Canonicorum in Dorset, one of the few medieval shrines in which the original relics have survived –

in this case the saint's bones. The thirteenth-century shrine is a simple stone chest with three large oval openings through which pilgrims placed their afflicted limbs in the hope that close contact with the relics would cure them.

SHRIVE To hear CONFESSION and give ABSOLUTION, or to disburden oneself by confession and then to receive absolution.

SHROUD BRASS (SHROUDED FIGURE) *see* CADAVER

SICKNESS *see* INFIRMARY

SIESTA From the Latin *sexta*, the sixth hour of the day, the monastic brethren were allowed to return to the DORTER in the afternoon until returning to the church for NONE.

SIGNATURES (ARCHBISHOPS AND BISHOPS) Archbishops and bishops of the Church of England and the Church in Wales sign, after a representation of the Cross, by their Christian name followed by the name of their PROVINCE or see (*see* DIOCESE). These are spelled normally, with the following exceptions:

Archbishops

Canterbury	Cantaur
York	Ebor
Wales	Cambrensis

Bishops

Carlisle	Carliol
Chester	Cestr
Chichester	Cicestr
Durham	Dunelm
Edinburgh	Edenburgen
Ely	Elien
Exeter	Exon
Gloucester	Gloucestr
London	Londin
Norwich	Norvic
Oxford	Oxon
Peterborough	Petriburg
Rochester	Roffen
Salisbury	Sarum
Truro	Truron
Winchester	Winton

Note: Ely and Truro now sign using the conventional spellings.

SILENCE An objective of both monastic and secular communities was *summa quies* – the absence of all excitement which might detract from contemplation. It was St Basil who wrote 'Quiet, then, is the first step in our sanctification'. The religious house was 'the home of silence', where voices were raised only in praise or prayer or in the reading of the scriptures in the CHAPTER and FRATER. According to the RULE, silence accompanied even those brethren who undertook a journey together.

> Let no-one think himself a well-ordered, religious or God-fearing canon, if he get into the habit of breaking silence without urgent reason . . . for this want of control of the tongue is an evident sign of a dissolute mind and a neglected conscience. Therefore, let Canons Regular regard silence as a precious treasure since through it a remedy against so many dangers is applied. (*Barnwell Observances*).

Noisy activities were located as far as possible from the CLOISTER and every person within the PRECINCT was required to be silent during the singing of the canonical hours: 'While any Hour save Compline is being sung in church, no brother shall talk to any officer of the monastery, nor within the bounds of the great court, nor even in the farmery, save for the sick who are so straitened as to be unable to keep silence for that space' (Lanfranc: *Constitutions*). But, inevitably, it became increasingly difficult to distance the cloister from the outside world. Many monastic houses became the administrative centres of vast estates, pilgrims were actively encouraged to visit SHRINES and the hospitality of the lords spiritual often eclipsed that of the lords temporal. Originally speech was permitted only in the PARLOUR, but restricted conversation was later allowed in the cloister, provided that permission had been obtained and the subject matter was of a religious nature: 'Let no one dare to ask about the gossip of the world, nor tell of it, nor speak of trifles or frivolous subjects apt to cause laughter.'

SILL The lower horizontal edge of a window.

SIMONIACAL ORDINATION Clerical office obtained by purchase.

SIMONY 'And when Simon [Magus] saw that through laying on of the apostles' hands the Holy Ghost was given, he offered them money, saying, give me also this power . . .' (Acts 8: 18–19). The term simony thereby denotes the purchase or sale of matters spiritual and, in particular, benefices and ecclesiastical offices. A simoniac is one who is guilty of simony and a simonist is one who defends the practice.

SINGING All the choir offices were sung (*see* DIVINE OFFICE), the singing of the monks or canons sometimes augmented by boys from a song school (*see* SCHOOLS). A portative organ (usually located on the PULPITUM) might sustain the singing, while PROCESSIONS were invariably accompanied by music.
See also CHURCH MUSIC, ORGANS, PLAIN-SONG *and* POLYPHONY

SINISTER *see* POINTS OF THE SHIELD

SISTERS *see* CANONESS REGULAR, BENEDICTINE NUNS, BRIGITTINES, CISTERCIANS, MAGDALENES, NUNS AND NUNNERIES, POOR CLARES (*see* MINORESS) *and* VOWESS.

SITES *see* MONASTIC BUILDINGS

SIX ARTICLES, THE Articles enacted by parliament in 1539 in response to the Ten Articles formulated by the Convocation of 1536 and the Bishops' Book of 1537. The Ten Articles and the Bishops' Book (entitled *The Institution of a Christian Man* and largely the work of Thomas Cranmer (1489–1556)) dealt with various doctrinal and other matters of dispute between the Roman Catholic and English Churches. The Six Articles were the first authoritative statement of the doctrine of the English Church, ostensibly enacted in the interests of moderation and uniformity but in practice savagely punitive measures intended to prevent the spread of Reformation practices and doctrines. They attempted to define those opinions which constituted heresy, defended auricular confessions and private masses, enforced clerical celibacy, confirmed monastic vows and maintained the doctrines of transubstantiation and communion in one kind. Denial of the real presence in the sacrament was to be punished by death by burning, and those who denied the efficacy of private confession and private mass were to be hanged. The Six Articles represented a severe blow to the aspirations of the English reformers and served to intensify existing divisions in the English Church. Nevertheless, Henry VIII achieved popularity from the Act, shrewdly sensing that his subjects were, for the most part, '. . . more inclined to the old religion than the new opinions'.
see REFORMATION, THE *and* THIRTY-NINE ARTICLES, THE

SIXTEENTH-CENTURY CHURCH *see* REFORMATION, THE

SKELETON BRASS *see* CADAVER

SLATES AND ROOFING TILES By the late thirteenth century the roofs of most major monastic and secular churches were covered with LEAD, while conventual buildings were generally roofed with stone slates, tiles, or shingles (oak tiles). Thatch was usually found only in the curia as roofing for mills, dovecotes and other agricultural buildings. It is not always possible to ascertain whether entries for 'tiles' in contemporary building accounts refer to roofing, paving or building tiles or, indeed, to stone slates, although roofing tiles are sometimes described as *thaktyles* or 'flat tiles'. In the Finchale Priory accounts for 1457 an entry 'carriage of 24 fothers of tiles from the quarry' clearly indicates that the 'tiles' were, in fact, stone slates (a *fother* of slates was sufficient to cover about 150sq ft).

The term 'slate' was originally applied to any kind of split stone (from the Old French *esclate* meaning 'something split') and this included not only slates for roofing but also *flags* for floors. (*For* floor and wall tiles *see* ENCAUSTIC TILES.)

Medieval slates were roughly hexagonal in shape, with a squared 'tail' and narrowing at one end, those used at the eaves of the roof being considerably larger. Tiles and stone slates were both hung in a similar manner, from the laths of the roof. In each case an oak peg was driven through a hole near the top edge of the tile so that it projected on the underside. The peg was then used to hang the tile from the lath, with each layer of tiles overlapping the row below it. Tiles were made with holes, ready for pegging, but slates had to be pierced: at Oakham in 1383 the 'boryng' of 2,500 slates cost 4*s*. In some districts, tiles were bedded on moss (*mosseying*), which prevented the wind and rain from penetrating between the tiles and provided protection against melting snow. Alternatively, the layers might be pointed or rendered with mortar.

Not all slates came from specialist quarries: most manors in the limestone belt which runs north-east from the Cotswolds, through Oxfordshire and Northamptonshire, had their own 'tile-pits' or *slat quarrs*. Stone for slates comes in thin layers which also provide *planks* or *pales* – fencing slates that were held together by iron clamps. A frosting process was probably first used at the Stonesfield quarries in Oxfordshire at the end of the sixteenth century. By this method *pendles* of fissile limestone are left exposed during the winter so that the moisture in the thin films of clay between the layers freezes and expands, causing the pendles to split easily into slates. Before this, quarries were chosen where the stone split naturally, so that the slater's only task was to shape and trim the slates, working with a *crapping stone* between his knees. This was a narrow stone set edgewise on the ground on which he trimmed three sides of each slate with a slat hammer until it was of the right shape and thickness. The edges were then trimmed by battering with the hammerhead, and a peg hole was made in the narrow end by boring or tapping lightly with the point of a slat pick. Piled 'ten flat and ten edgeways', 250 slates were considered a good day's work. Roofing slates varied in length and were measured against a slater's rule or *wippet stick*, which, in the Cotswolds, was marked with twenty-seven notches. Each size of slate had its own name and these varied, not only from one region to another, but among individual slaters. Workmanship was judged by the quality of swept valleys, which were always the weakest part of a stone-tiled roof. 'Valley stones' had to be cut in a triangular shape and arranged so that they left no cracks where the water could enter. Experts at *galetting*, as the craft was called, refused to use lead for this purpose.

Clay tiles, like bricks, were fired in kilns, although they needed to be harder and of finer quality. Roofing tiles varied considerably: the Romans favoured a combination of rounded tile (*imbrex*) and flat tile (*tegula*), the *imbrices* covering the joints between the *tegulae*. But, by the eleventh century, the craft of tile-making had degenerated and such niceties were no longer observed. During the fifteenth century complaints were made regarding the lack of uniformity in the size and quality of tiles. Indeed, it was said that many of the tiles produced at that time would last only four or five years. Consequently, an Act of Parliament was passed in 1477 regulating both the size of tiles and the manufacturing process itself. This required that flat tiles should measure 10½ by 6½ inches (27cm by 16cm), with a thickness of at least ⅝ of an inch (1.5cm). Ridge tiles (*crests*) should be 13½ inches by 6½ inches (34cm by 16cm), and gutter tiles 10½ inches (27cm) long. Ridge tiles (*crests*) were sometimes ornamented: 2*s* were paid at Banstead manor in 1373 'to John Pottere . . . for two crests made in the fashion of mounted knights, bought for the hall'.

SLEEP *see* DORTER

SLIPPER CHAPEL A chapel in which pilgrims removed their shoes before approaching a shrine (*see* SHRINES). The fourteenth-century 'Shoe House' or Slipper Chapel at Houghton St Giles in Norfolk is situated about 1.6km (1 mile) from the shrine of Our Lady at Walsingham. Here, the pilgrims would pause and meditate before embarking on the final stage of their journey – barefoot and penitent.

SLYPE A covered passage linking the CLOISTER with the INFIRMARY or the monastic cemetery. The slype was usually located at the north end of the east claustral range, between the south transept of the church and the chapter house. In Cistercian houses it was to the south of the chapter house. Closed by doors at each end, a slype was sometimes provided with seating and served as a common room where restrained conversation might be permitted. But as the regulations governing the use of the warming house (*see* CALEFACTORIUM) and inner PARLOUR were relaxed, so in some houses the slype was no longer needed for respite, and was used instead as a library or SACRISTY. In several Cistercian houses its length was divided to provide both library and sacristy with separate entrances from the cloister and church. In the fourteenth century, a gallery was constructed as an upper storey to the impressive slype (known as the Infirmary Passage) at Fountains Abbey. This led from the east cloister alley to the infirmary, with a right-angled extension (the Church Passage) to the Chapel of the Nine Altars at the east end of the church (*see* GALLERY). At Bury St Edmunds Abbey, the passage from the cloister to the cemetery was known as the 'Trayle'.

SOCLE A plinth at the foot of a wall.
See also HOLY WATER STOUP

SODOR AND MAN An Anglican diocese comprising the Isle of Man. The original diocese, which dates from the eleventh century, included the Hebrides and other islands off the west coast of Scotland, which were detached from it in 1334. It is believed that the words 'and Man' were added in error during the drafting of a legal document in the seventeenth century.

SOFFIT The underside of an architectural feature.

SOLAR From the Latin *solaris* meaning 'of the sun', the solar or *Great Chamber* was the principal private chamber of a SUPERIOR'S lodging. As the word suggests, the chamber was usually located to take advantage of the sunniest aspect of the building and was used as a quiet withdrawing room by an abbot and his guests. Typically, the solar would occupy the space at first-floor level, next to the hall with a vaulted UNDERCROFT beneath, large windows and a stair which ascended from the dais end of the hall.

SOLEAS A platform immediately in front of the screen which, in Byzantine churches, separates the SANCTUARY from the NAVE.

SONG SCHOOLS *see* SCHOOLS

SONGMEN *see* VICARS CHORAL

SORORUM Latinised place-name element meaning 'of the sisters' and suggesting that a manor was once held by a monastic foundation of nuns.
See also PLACE-NAMES (MONASTIC AND ECCLESIASTICAL)

SOUNDING BOARD (*also* TESTER) A flat, horizontal wooden canopy above a pulpit, intended to amplify and direct a preacher's voice for the benefit of the congregation. Most surviving sounding boards have six or eight sides and were erected in the late sixteenth, seventeenth or eighteenth centuries.
See also AMPLIFIERS

SOURCES *see* ARCHIVES

SOUTH RANGE Conventional description of the CLAUSTRAL range of buildings opposite the church, and that in which the FRATER was the principal room. However, there are several instances where the CLOISTER is located to the north of the church, and 'frater range' would therefore be a more accurate term. The frater was usually located on the ground floor or above an UNDERCROFT. In Cistercian houses it was generally at right angles to the cloister alley, although in some cases it was parallel to it. There was often a passage through the frater range, providing access to the outer court and to the undercroft beneath the adjacent DORTER in the east range.
See also EASTERN RANGE *and* WESTERN RANGE

SPANDREL (i) The surface between two arches in an ARCADE.
(ii) In a VAULT, the surface between two adjacent ribs.
(iii) The triangular area in (e.g.) an arched window or doorway framed by the horizontal and vertical lines of the DRIPSTONE and, on the third side, by the MOULDING of the arch. This type of spandrel is often decoratively carved.

SPEKE HOUSE *see* PARLOUR

SPIRELET *see* FLÈCHE

SPIRES *see* TOWERS

SPIRITUALITIES Sources of ecclesiastical income, such as TITHES, that were exempt from secular control. Conversely, temporalities were ecclesiastical holdings that were subject to such controls.

SPITAL Medieval form of the word 'hospital', its occurrence as a place-name element is usually indicative of the site of a former HOSPICE or LAZAR HOUSE (*see* HOSPITALS).

SPLAY A sloping edge or surface, as in the embrasures (*see* EMBRASURE) of windows that are set within thick walls.

SPRINGER *and* SPRINGING LINE *see* ARCH

SPUR (i) An ornamental protrusion between the circular base of a pier or column and the square plinth on which it stands.

A spandrel. (Tom Friar)

(ii) A sloping buttress.

SQUINCH An arch, or a series of concentric arches, constructed within the angle between two walls to support a superstructure e.g. a spire or dome.

SQUINT (HAGIOSCOPE) Squint is a term coined by Victorian ecclesiologists to describe rectangular openings cut obliquely through masonry to afford a limited view of the High Altar from a subsidiary altar. Hagioscopes were provided so that a priest could synchronise his celebration of the MASS with that at the High Altar, especially at the ELEVATION of the Host. At Buildwas Abbey, for example, a narrow opening was inserted just below the decorative STRING COURSE in the north wall of the presbytery. This provided an uninterrupted view of the High Altar from a small chamber over the north transept.

STABLES All religious houses had stables, and these were usually located in the CURIA. Working horses were needed for transport and for haulage on the monastic estates and superiors required horses for their carriages. In high-status houses, guests and their retinues would expect to be provided with stabling and the services of an ostler and blacksmith. At Cistercian Kirkstall Abbey, for example, the stables were ranged round the courtyard of the extensive guest hall which lay to the west of the church and claustral buildings. They were probably built when the hall was substantially enlarged, before the end of the thirteenth century.

STAINED GLASS Before the sixteenth century, window glass was made from a mixture of wood ash and river sand which was heated into molten form and either spun on the end of a rod into a circular sheet or blown into a long cylinder and cut longitudinally to produce a flat sheet. Although coloured glass was used in church windows from the seventh century, the earliest surviving examples in England are from the twelfth century. Most medieval coloured glass was manufactured in France and Germany and imported into England to be made into windows.

The term 'stained glass' is a misnomer. More accurately, it should be described as 'painted and stained glass'. There was, in fact, no stained glass until *c.* 1320, when silver stain was introduced (*see below*). Before that time powdered *pot metal* (glass which had been deeply coloured throughout) or coloured pigment mixed with *frit* (powdered glass) was painted on to a surface, using gum arabic as a binder. Pot metals were made by adding different metallic oxides to the molten clear glass: cobalt for blue, copper for ruby, manganese for violet, silver salts for yellow, iron for green or yellow, and small quantities of gold for a rose red. The colour produced also depended on the way the furnace was fired, and different results were achieved by varying the level of oxidation.

The ruby and blue glasses were very dark, and a technique called *flashing* was used to increase translucence, a necessary quality in England's relatively dull climate. In this process the blowpipe was first dipped into molten coloured glass and a cylindrical bubble was blown in the normal way. This was then dipped into white molten glass so that, after working, the final glass panel was coated on one side with a layer of colour.

The design (*cartoon*) of the window was drawn on a whitewashed table by draughtsmen (*tracers*) and the pieces of coloured glass were cut to the required shape. Before the introduction of the diamond cutter in the sixteenth century, this was done by drawing a hot iron across the glass and then applying cold water, causing the glass to crack along the incision. The pieces were then trimmed to a more precise shape with a *grozing iron*, and details such as faces, hair, limbs, linen folds and foliage were painted with a mixture of metallic oxide (iron or copper), powdered glass and gum. Finally, the glass sections were set out on an iron plate and covered with ash before being fired at *c.* 1,000°C (using beechwood) in a clay or dung kiln. This fused the paint onto the coloured glass.

The glass was then reassembled, adjacent pieces being held together by means of lead strips (*calms*) that were soldered at the joints, and a thick, black 'putty' was forced into the crevices between the lead and the glass. Lead was a most suitable material for the purpose because it was malleable when unheated and, having a low melting point, was easily cast into strips with grooves along the sides (known as H-sections) to accommodate the glass.

When completed, the window was fitted into the stonework opening by means of lead strips that were attached to iron saddle-bars or, in larger window openings, set within a decorative metal framework (*armature*). As tracery became more complex in the fourteenth century, so the upper lights of windows were used to accommodate separate sections of an overall design (*see* MEDIEVAL ARCHITECTURE).

As the craft developed, the calms were incorporated into the design itself and, from the fourteenth century, the flashed surface of coloured glass was often scraped away (*abraided*) to leave a pattern of clear glass which, when repainted with silver oxide and fired, turned to a dark yellow which passed for gold. This was particularly useful in heraldic designs when 'metal' charges (gold or silver) were depicted on a blue or red field, as in the ubiquitous royal arms of England.

Many heraldic devices were not of a convenient shape to be confined within strips of lead, and while large charges, such as beasts, could be built up using several pieces of glass leaded together, very small or repetitive charges were often difficult to reproduce. This problem was overcome by using small pieces of coloured glass and painting around

The arms of Edward III.

the outline of the charge with brown enamel to leave only the shape of the motif as the unpainted surface. Alternatively, a whole sheet was painted with brown enamel and the appropriate area then scraped away to form the desired shape. This technique may be seen in the ancient arms of France in which the small, diamond-shaped panels (*quarries* or *quarrels*) bearing fleurs-de-lis alternate with strips of blue glass for the field, producing a pattern of lozenges.

The lead that binds a stained-glass window responds to fluctuations of temperature by expanding or contracting. Thus, in a window's flexibility lies also its durability. Even so, a stained-glass window usually needs to be taken apart and reglazed in new lead approximately every two hundred years. While most stained glass remains in its original location many fragments (or even entire windows) may have been moved several times and may have been combined with glass of an entirely different period. For example, a series of twelfth-century biblical figures at Canterbury Cathedral is surmounted by heraldic figures of the fourteenth century, while at Salisbury Cathedral there are six thirteenth-century shields at the base of the west window which is composed, in part, of fifteenth-century glass. Of course, glass was particularly vulnerable to neglect and to vandalism by the iconoclasts and various Georgian and Victorian 'restorers'. Often, only fragments remain – either as solitary panels or in windows composed entirely of miscellaneous pieces. The wonderful 'Bishop's Eye' window in the southern gable of the Great Transept of Lincoln Cathedral is filled with fragments of glass of various ages and origins, reassembled from other locations in the cathedral – with dazzling effect (*see* ROSE WINDOW). In 1788 most of Salisbury Cathedral's ancient glass was removed by James Wyatt (1746–1813) as a consequence of the 'restorative improvements' that earned him the sobriquet 'Wyatt the Destroyer'. The Cathedral records tell us that 'Whole cartloads of glass, lead and other rubbish were removed from the nave and transepts and shot into the town ditch'. Similarly, at Durham Cathedral Priory in 1795 the fifteen windows of the Chapel of the Nine Altars were destroyed: 'The richly painted glass and mullions were swept away, and the present plain windows inserted in their place. The glass lay for a long time afterwards in baskets on the floor and when the greater part of it had been purloined the remainder was locked up in the Galilee.'
See also WINDOWS

STAIR TURRET A circular or polygonal turret attached to the outside of a church tower (often at a corner) and containing a spiral staircase from which the various levels within the tower may be reached.

STAIRCASES In the stair turrets of many medieval church TOWERS and monastic buildings, or sometimes within the thickness of stone walls, spiral staircases (*turnpike stairs*) were constructed within cylindrical shafts, each identical stone step (*winder*) cut to fit precisely within the shaft and held in place by the interlocking core of the steps immediately above and below. (In medieval castles turnpike stairs usually ascend in a clockwise direction, thereby facilitating the use of a weapon when facing down the stair in a defensive position, but impairing its use when attempting to ascend by force.) A turnpike stair may also be described as a *vice*.

Where there is no evidence of a stone staircase, a wooden 'open tread' ladder-type staircase would have provided access between the different levels of a building, usually by means of a single flight set against a wall or two flights at right angles to each other. These staircases were usually built of oak and were supported by a massive pillar.

STALLS Fixed seats in parallel rows on the north and south sides of the CHOIR to accommodate the monks or secular cannons during the DIVINE OFFICE. PLAINSONG was sung by two choirs alternately, with each choir (CANTORIS and DECANI) occupying the north and south stalls

The late twelfth-century choir at Rochester Cathedral has the oldest choir stalls in England, the back stalls dating from 1227. (© John Crook/info@john-crook.com)

respectively (*see* ANTIPHON *and* VERSICLES). Those stalls that have survived are usually separated by high projecting arm rests and have wooden screens behind them and elaborately carved canopies above, to minimise draughts. A ledge in front of each row of stalls supported service books and candles and, in some cases, AMPLIFIERS provided extra resonance and amplification during the singing of plainsong. Individual seats are usually hinged and may be lifted to reveal misericords (*see* MISERICORD), carved brackets which provided support and relief for the choir monks or canons, who were thus able to rest without sitting as they stood through interminable divine offices. Each monk or canon occupied a particular stall, the position reflecting his place in the community, the longest-serving members sitting furthest from the High Altar. In monastic churches, novices usually sat in the less elaborate, bench-like stalls at the front, which, in collegiate and cathedral choirs, are now occupied by the trebles. In an ABBEY the abbot and prior faced the east in the RETURNED STALLS, respectively south and north of the PULPITUM doorway. In a PRIORY these seats were occupied by the prior and sub-prior.

There are splendid sets of fourteenth-century stalls at Chester and Gloucester cathedrals. But in many cases, only the foundations of the medieval stalls have survived, the present structures being much-modified (usually Victorian) copies. Quite often the original seats and misericords have been incorporated into later stalls, as at Sherborne Abbey in Dorset (now the parish church). There are also several instances of stalls having been removed to parish churches, although these have invariably been reconstructed in a much-reduced form: the fifteenth-century stalls of Easby Abbey in Yorkshire, for example, which are now in the church of St Mary the Virgin at Richmond (the Easby canons were hanged for resisting Henry VIII's commissioners), and at Whalley in Lancashire, where the richly canopied stalls of the Cistercian abbey were removed to the parish church in order to avoid the iconoclasts' bonfires.

Some medieval parish churches were provided with single rows of stalls which were intended to accommodate unusually large numbers of chantry priests or the members of collegiate foundations (*see* CHANTRY COLLEGES *and* COLLEGIATE CHURCH). There are splendid examples of fourteenth-century canopied stalls at St Mary's church, Lancaster, at Nantwich in Cheshire, and at All Saints, Hereford, while there is a fine set of fifteenth-century stalls at St Laurence's church at Ludlow in Shropshire.

STATE PRAYERS In *The Book of Common Prayer*, prayers for the sovereign and royal family said toward the end of Mattins and Evensong.

STATIO Both the place where a community assembled prior to a procession and also the designated stopping-places (*stations*) where they halted to recite prayers during the procession. These were often indicated by markers, some of which have survived.

STATIONARIES Aged and infirm members of a community who were permitted partial retirement. They were lodged in the INFIRMARY, where there was a relaxation of the RULE – although they were still expected to attend DIVINE OFFICE (if not in the choir, then in the RETRO-CHOIR), to attend to their private devotions and to observe the vow of silence.

STATIONS OF THE CROSS The fourteen incidents which occurred on Christ's last journey from Pilate's house to his entombment. The Stations of the Cross may sometimes be found depicted in a series of paintings or carvings arranged round the walls of a church. During a devotion of the same name, each station is visited in turn.

STATUTE OF MORTMAIN (1279 *and* 1391) The 1279 statute forbade the gift of land to the

Church without the prior consent of the Crown. A later statute of 1391 required that in those parishes where the rectorial TITHES were held by an ecclesiastical institution, a proportion of the income should be used for poor relief (*see* MORTMAIN).

STELE A decorative motif consisting of a rectangular slab surmounted by a low, triangular pediment.
See also MONUMENTS *and* WALL MONUMENTS

STELLAR VAULT *see* VAULTING

STEW PONDS *see* FISHPONDS

STEWARD The chief agent of a manorial lord, with responsibility for the administration of a manor, for maintaining its records and presiding over its courts. The steward of a religious house was a layman employed by the community to act on its behalf in all civil matters and to exercise the delegated authority of the SUPERIOR in the manorial courts.

STIFF LEAF ORNAMENT A somewhat formal architectural ornament characteristic of the thirteenth century and especially evident in the treatment of capitals (*see* CAPITAL) and window and doorway mouldings. Unlike later NATURAL LEAF ORNAMENT, the carved foliage rises stiffly from the necking and falls in stylised, lobe-shaped clusters of leaves and flowers.
See also MEDIEVAL ARCHITECTURE

STILE (i) A vertical member in the framework of a panelled door.
See also BRACE, LEDGE, MUNTIN *and* RAIL
(ii) The vertical outer frame members of a wooden screen (also *style*).

STILTED ARCH *see* ARCH

STILTS The short, vertical sections at the base of a round arch which raise its height without increasing the span.

STONEWORK *see* BUILDING MATERIALS *and* MASONRY

STORE *see* CELLARIUM *and* UNDERCROFT

STOUP *see* HOLY WATER STOUP

STOVES

The bells of waiting Advent ring,
The Tortoise stove is lit again
And lamp-oil light across the night
Has caught the streaks of winter rain

Alas, most of John Betjeman's Tortoise stoves have disappeared from our churches, as have other makes, including those whose brass labels proudly proclaimed that they were manufactured under 'Gurney's Patent' by 'The London Warming & Ventilation Company' – there is a noble survivor at Hereford Cathedral. Installed in

Stove at Hereford Cathedral.

the nineteenth and early twentieth centuries, coke-fired stoves were, of course, intended to provide some respite from the chills of winter, although in such large spaces most were singularly ineffective. Old photographs of church interiors illustrate the range of stoves that was used for this purpose and the sometimes Heath-Robinson-like contraptions by which the fumes were removed.

STRAINER ARCH *see* ARCH

STRAP SCONCE A narrow, ornamental bracket, secured at each end and curving outwards from a wall, on the top of which are affixed a number of candleholders.

STRAPWORK A Renaissance form of decoration that originated in the Netherlands in *c.* 1540. Characteristic of the Elizabethan and Jacobean periods, strapwork consists of ornamental interlaced bands or straps, similar in appearance to fretwork or cut leather. In churches, it is usually executed in plaster, stone or wood in ceilings, friezes, screens, wood panelling, etc.

(Tom Friar)

STRING COURSE A continuous projecting horizontal band or moulding in the surface of a wall.

STUDY Special provision was made for study, which occupied about one-third of a monk's waking hours. In the cloister there were carrels (*see* CLOISTER) where the brethren could study without distraction, and time was set aside in both the INFIRMARY and the DORTER for that purpose (*see* SIESTA). But study in the monastic context was not academic: it consisted of reading from the scriptures and devotional works and was effectively a form of meditation that was intended to lead to a greater understanding of the MASS and the DIVINE OFFICE and to assist in the pursuit of personal impeccability.

STYLE *see* STILE

SUB-CELLARER Deputy to the CELLARER, the most important of the OBEDIENTIARIES. The sub-cellarer usually had specific duties relating to the provision of food and drink, and in some houses was responsible for the GUEST HOUSE. His assistant was the GRANATORIUS.

SUB-DEACON In the medieval Church, one of the three sacred ministers at High Mass whose responsibilities included that of chanting the Epistle. Until the thirteenth century, the office was considered to be one of the MINOR ORDERS.

SUB-PRIOR A prior's deputy, chiefly responsible for discipline and, in particular, for observance of the RULE (*see* DISCIPLINE, PRIORY *and* SECURITY). In a cathedral priory, the sub-prior exercised the same authority as a prior in a monastic community and was often assisted by a *third prior* in the administration of its daily affairs.

SUB-SACRIST (*also* MATRICULARIUS) The sacrist's deputy (*see* SACRIST), whose chief responsibilities included acting as the community's time-keeper, the regulating of any CLOCKS and the ringing of bells at the appropriate time. He was also expected to maintain a presence in the church when other brethren were engaged elsewhere. He slept and took his meals there and was usually provided with a chamber for that purpose.

SUBMISSION OF THE CLERGY (1532) The act whereby the English Convocations surrendered to the demands of HENRY VIII. Confirmed by parliament in 1534, its effect was to make the sovereign supreme in ecclesiastical causes.

SUCCENTOR (*also* SUB-CANTOR) In a monastic church, the succentor was deputy to the PRECENTOR and would sit opposite him in choir (*see* DECANI). In 1540 the succentor became a MINOR CANON in CATHEDRALS of the 'Old Foundation', where he is the deputy of the precentor.
See also CHURCH MUSIC *and* CLERGY (CHURCH OF ENGLAND)

SUFFRAGAN BISHOP *see* CLERGY (CHURCH OF ENGLAND)

SUPERIOR One who exercised authority over a religious community by election for life or by nomination of a mother house. In Benedictine, Cistercian and Premonstratensian communities the superior was an elected ABBOT or ABBESS and the deputy a prior or prioress (*see* PRIORY). Election was a matter for the convent, which usually chose one of its senior office-holders (*see* OBEDIENTIARIES), who was likely to be in his forties (although John Whetehamstede was elected abbot of St Albans at the age of 27). In those religious communities where the church served as a cathedral the bishop was the titular abbot, although in practice it was the prior who was head of the community, assisted by a SUB-PRIOR (*see* CATHEDRAL PRIORY). The superiors of houses of Augustinian Canons and of Dominican and Franciscan communities of FRIARS were also priors, as were the superiors of dependencies and alien priories (*see* ALIEN PRIORY), who were nominated by and subservient to a mother house and did not hold office for life.

A superior was the legal persona of a religious house and commanded the absolute obedience of the monks or canons. He set the tone for the whole community although he might often be resident for less than half the year. The reception of all but the humblest guests fell on the superior who, in a major house, would be expected to accommodate a constant stream of royal and aristocratic visitors, royal officials, justices and fellow ecclesiastical and monastic superiors. They would, of course, expect to be received in a manner appropriate to their status and the superior would of necessity maintain a substantial household of esquires, yeomen, grooms and servants. Inevitably his lodging had to be of sufficient size to accommodate large numbers of guests (together with the members of their households) and furnished to the highest standards of comfort and refinement (*see* SUPERIOR'S LODGINGS). Even the smaller houses found themselves offering hospitality, often prolonged and costly, to those who demanded it as a perquisite of their class. Technically, the manor houses on the abbey's estates were also for a superior's personal use, although they were often offered to lay stewards or tenant farmers or made available to the brethren for rest and recuperation (*see* GRANGE). A superior would employ his own steward, receiver and auditor to manage his affairs and would be advised on matters secular by a council of local gentry and lawyers.

The leading abbots and priors comprised a group of twenty-seven parliamentary prelates, many of whom were also royal councillors. Abbot Thomas Chillenden of Canterbury, for example, was a member of Richard II's council; Philip Repingdon, prior of Leicester, was a councillor to Henry IV; Abbot Thomas Spofford of York served Henry V and Reginald Boulers, abbot of Gloucester, was a councillor to Henry VI.
See also MITRED ABBOT

SUPERIOR'S LODGINGS Until the mid-twelfth century, superiors took their meals with the other monks and slept in the common DORTER. But as their feudal status and authority increased, so too did the need to meet with the secular world and to provide lodgings in order to fulfil their obligations as hosts (*see* GUEST HOUSE). Magnates, both noble and ecclesiastical, were the personal guests of the superior whose lodgings became increasingly opulent – with separate hall, chapel, parlour, and bed chambers that were often provided with individual latrines (*see* GARDEROBE). Of the magnificent abbot's quarters at Glastonbury Abbey, begun by John de Breynton (1334–42), only the south-west angle of the great hall and the splendid kitchens remain. Even so, of all the surviving monastic buildings in England, none is more redolent of the power and status of a religious superior (*see* KITCHENS). Such extravagance was not always welcomed, however. Many abbots and priors frequently protested that in meeting their social obligations they were also abdicating those of their PROFESSION. Indeed, in many cases a semblance of humility was maintained by providing a means of direct communication between the superior's chambers and the monks' dorter. Such palatial accommodation was sometimes forced on an unwilling superior: at Bridlington Priory the archbishop of York demanded that comfortable lodgings should be provided as a base for his visitations of eastern Yorkshire.

Where a superior occupied separate lodgings they were usually located between the inner PRECINCT and the CURIA or as an extension of the claustral buildings. At Cistercian Kirkstall Abbey, the remarkably substantial remains of the three-storied abbot's lodging have survived to the east of the REREDORTER. The staircase to the first floor may still be seen, while to the east were the kitchens and cellar and to the west the living rooms where the remains of several fireplaces have survived. The building running north of the abbot's lodging to the infirmary provided additional accommodation for monastic guests.

In common with other Cistercian houses, the west claustral range at Hailes Abbey was built to accommodate the *conversi* – the community's LAY BROTHERS. But from the mid-fourteenth century lay brethren began deserting the monasteries in large numbers, attracted by improved wages and working conditions as a result of a labour shortage following the Black Death (*see* PLAGUE). Consequently, abbots began appropriating increasing amounts of space in the west range for their own use, so that by the Dissolution of the Monasteries west ranges were often houses of considerable opulence. Hailes was no exception, and after the Dissolution the abbot's house became the private residence of the Tracy family.

In Augustinian houses it was the west claustral range that was usually provided specifically to accommodate the superior. At Lilleshall Abbey, for example, the abbot's lodgings occupied the entire upper floor, with the cellarer's UNDERCROFT beneath. Hall and chambers were converted to a private dwelling following the Dissolution, but were later destroyed, probably after a Civil War siege of the house, which had been fortified by the Royalist Sir Vincent Corbet. At the Cistercian abbey of Valle Crucis it was the monks' dormitory (in the east claustral range) that was purloined by the abbot in the late fifteenth century and converted into a comfortable hall and private chambers. By this time the few remaining choir monks would have found lodgings elsewhere within the claustral buildings.

Quite often, it would seem, proximity to the INFIRMARY and access to its kitchens dictated the position of the superior's lodging, while redundant buildings were frequently adapted for that purpose. In the last decades of the fifteenth century, Abbot John Burton converted the infirmary hall at (Cistercian) Rievaulx into one of the largest superior's lodgings in England and the GARTH of the infirmary cloister into a garden for the enjoyment of the abbot and his guests. At Furness Abbey (at the Dissolution the second richest Cistercian abbey in England), the infirmary was adapted for use as the abbot's lodgings and extended by cutting into the cliff on its east side and spanning arches between the existing building and the cliff face to support the extra rooms above. However, the extension overloaded the original structure and its vaults began to force the side walls outwards. To prevent collapse, three flying buttresses were constructed against the west wall. Similarly, at the Premonstratensian abbey of St Agatha at Easby a complex of ruined buildings to the north of the church included a hall and kitchen and may also have been an infirmary that was later converted to an abbot's lodging.

The abbot's lodging at (Cistercian) Byland Abbey was a detached building to the south of the infirmary range, its plan following the typical arrangement of a secular manor house of the period. At the west end a cross-wing formed the buttery and pantry (*see* LARDER), with doors to the thirteenth-century abbot's hall, which was entered by a doorway in the north-west corner. Towards the east end of the hall was an open hearth (presumably with a louvre in the roof above) and a dais. The hall was originally much longer, but was reduced in size in the fourteenth century by the insertion of a cross-wing at the east end. This contained two ground-floor chambers with large windows in the north wall and a chimney set into the dividing wall. To the east, above a twelfth-century vaulted undercroft, was the abbot's private chamber (*solar* or *camera*), and beyond this extended a further wing that may have included a small chapel on the first floor. The abbot's lodging at Roche Abbey (also Cistercian) was rebuilt in the fourteenth century and, again, is similar in plan to contemporary lay residences. It was built on two floors, and the upper storey was reached by means of a newel stair in the north wall. On the ground floor, the central room was the hall, which was heated by a fireplace in its east wall and entered from a porch in the south-west corner, which would have led into a SCREENS PASSAGE dividing the hall from the service rooms. To the east was a private chamber, and to the west a pantry and buttery were linked by a passageway to the detached abbot's kitchen and bakehouse.

By comparison with the lavish twelfth-century guests' houses and guests' hall at (Cistercian) Fountains Abbey (*see* GUEST HOUSE), the abbot's house was initially a modest affair. In *c.* 1160 it was decided that the abbot's duties had become so onerous that he should have lodgings of his own and a house was built for him at the east end of the monks' reredorter. This remained unaltered until Abbot Coxwold (1316–36) substantially enlarged the first-floor accommodation to provide a new hall 16.2m (54ft) long and 10m (33ft) wide and incorporated a series of prison cells on the ground floor (*see* PRISONS). A new 10m (33ft) square chamber was created within the eastern end of the monks' REREDORTER, with a latrine in its south-east corner. In the fourteenth century a

The abbot's lodgings at Muchelney Abbey, Somerset. Similar in size and comfort to many contemporary manor houses, the abbot's lodgings survived the Dissolution because they made a convenient and attractive home for the abbey's new owner. The openings of the south cloister alley were blocked to provide additional ground-floor accommodation. (Courtesy of John Mennell)

most unusual gallery was added, leading from the abbot's hall to a private chapel above the chapter house and to a seat within a window in the south gable of the Chapel of the Nine Altars from which services could be observed (*see* GALLERY). Abbot Marmaduke Huby (1495–1526) was responsible for the final remodelling of the house, and in particular the addition of a long gallery where the abbot and his guests could exercise indoors – an amenity that was becoming fashionable in contemporary country houses.

There are substantial remains of the fourteenth-century Prior's House at Finchale Priory: a first-floor suite of hall and rooms above a long undercroft. The chapel on the upper floor had a gallery or loft at its west end, similar to the chapels of many secular manor houses. Surviving features in the abbot's lodging at the Augustinian abbey of Haughmond, Shropshire, illustrate the former richness of the decoration. Shields, grapes, rosettes and roundels embellish the bay windows in the private chambers, while the raised dais and large, traceried gable window of the abbot's hall speak of his wealth and prestige.

SUPPORTERS (HERALDIC) Figures, usually beasts, chimerical creatures, or human forms, placed on either side the shield in a coat of arms to 'support' it.

SUPPRESSION *see* CHANTRY, CHANTRY COLLEGES, DISSOLUTION OF THE MONASTERIES, TEMPLAR, KNIGHTS *and* VALOR ECCLESIASTICUS

SUPPRESSION, ACT OF (1536) *see* DISSOLUTION OF THE MONASTERIES

SUPREMACY, ACTS OF (1534 *and* 1559) The Act confirming to HENRY VIII and his successors the 'style and title' of 'the only supreme head in earth of the Church of England' and all the prerogatives 'to the said dignity of supreme head of the same church belonging and appertaining'. It also declared the validity of the king's marriage with Queen Anne (Boleyn), together with the right of their lawful issue to succeed. Ironically, the third reading of the Act, on 23 March 1534, coincided with the pope's judgment in favour of Queen Catherine (of Aragon). Individuals were required to support the Act on oath, circumstances which presented partisans of the old order with a challenge that could not easily be resolved. Apparently, the furious Queen Catherine and her Spanish servants swore, in Spanish, that the king 'se ha hecho cabeza de Iglesia' ('has appointed himself head of the Church of England') instead of 'sea hecho . . .' ('the king may be made head . . .'). The Act of Supremacy was repealed by Queen Mary, only to be replaced under Elizabeth I in 1559 by a similar Act, which declared the Queen to be 'the only supreme governor . . . as well in all spiritual or ecclesiastical things or causes as temporal'.

SURPLICE A loose, white liturgical garment with wide sleeves, usually worn over a CASSOCK by the clergy, lay readers, servers and members of a choir. The surplice is a development of the alb, and from the twelfth century was worn by the lower clergy and by priests, except at the celebration of MASS. *See also* RUFF *and* TIPPET

T

TABERNACLE The tabernacle was a canopied structure used as a portable shrine by the Israelites during their wanderings in the wilderness. It contained the Ark of the Covenant, a wooden chest in which the writings of Jewish law were kept.

(i) From this, any architectural feature or decorative motif (*tabernacle work*) which resembles a canopied structure.

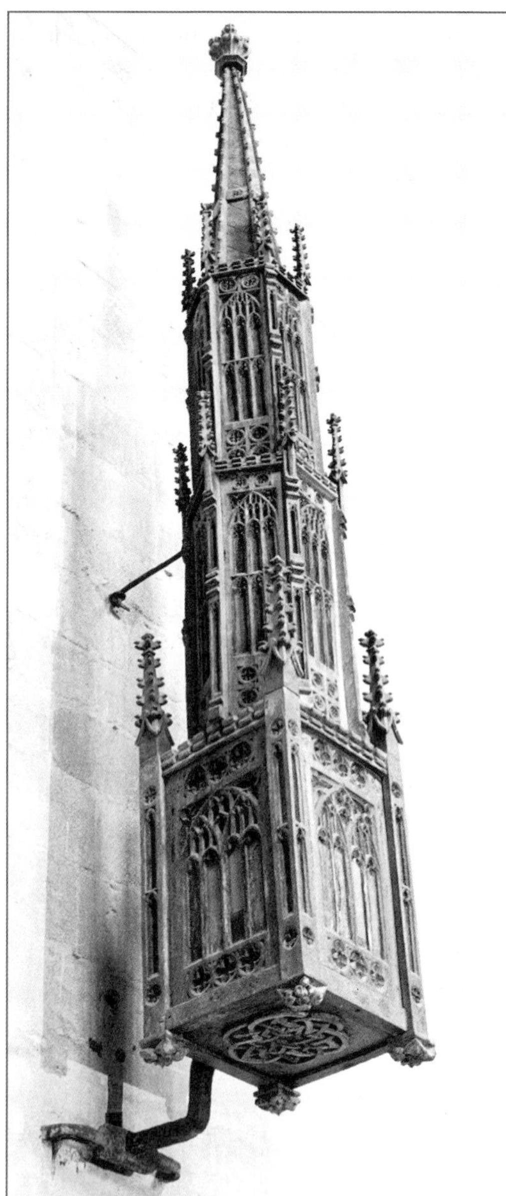

Medieval tabernacle at Milton Abbey, Dorset. (Courtesy of Florence Morris)

(ii) Specifically, a hanging *pyx-shrine* or *sacrament house*, shaped like a tapering ornamental tower or series of towers, in which the Blessed Sacrament was reserved (*see* PYX). Very few medieval tabernacles survived the Reformation. A superbly carved oak tabernacle at Milton Abbey in Dorset is fixed to north wall of the PRESBYTERY, while that from Hessett in Suffolk is now at the British Museum. In the Middle Ages tabernacles were suspended in front of the HIGH ALTAR and were raised and lowered by means of pulleys, as at West Grinstead in Sussex, where the pulley socket has survived.

(iii) From the sixteenth century the term has been used to describe the box of precious metal in which the Blessed Sacrament is reserved on a communion table or GRADINE (*see* RESERVATION).

TABLET A wall-mounted panel engraved with a commemorative inscription (*see* WALL MONUMENTS).

TABULA A monastic duty roster prepared by the PRECENTOR, read in CHAPTER on a Saturday and published on a board in the CLOISTER. The recess in which the tabula was placed may still be seen in the cloister of Fountains Abbey, Yorkshire.

TALKING *see* SILENCE

TAYLERY The monastic department responsible for the manufacture and repair of garments. The taylery was usually located in the CURIA and was often staffed by lay workers.

TE DEUM An ancient Latin hymn of praise to the Father and the Son beginning with the words *Te Deum laudamus* – 'We praise thee, O God' – sung at MATTINS or as a thanksgiving on special occasions. The inclusion of the *Te Deum* in the Office is mentioned in the RULE of St Benedict.

TEMPLAR, KNIGHTS (THE POOR KNIGHTS OF CHRIST AND OF THE TEMPLE OF SOLOMON) Together, the Hospitallers, the Teutonic Knights and the Knights Templar formed the three most powerful orders of chivalry to emanate from the Crusades. Within a few years of their foundation most of their brethren, while living under vows of religion, were conventual knights (their priests were known as *chaplains*) and the orders played an increasingly significant role in the defence of the Christian settlements in Palestine and Syria and in the administration of the Kingdom of Jerusalem. They constructed and garrisoned castles and fought alongside crusading forces in the perennial wars against the Egyptians and Turks.

Founded in 1118/19 by Hugues de Payns and Godeffroi de St Omer, the Order of the Poor Knights of Christ and of the Temple of Solomon was given a convent (headquarters) close to the Temple of Solomon by King Baldwin II of Jerusalem so that they should 'fight with a pure mind for the supreme and true king'. The knights, who lived according to the Rule of Bernard of Clairvaux under an elected Master of the Temple, dedicated themselves to the protection of pilgrims in the Holy Land and quickly achieved the sanction of the Church.

By the end of the thirteenth century the Templars had become established in almost every European kingdom and were in receipt of enormous grants of land. But their widespread influence attracted influential enemies. Strange stories circulated about their 'secret rites', and their failure to mobilise their considerable resources in 1291 following the fall of Acre (the last Christian stronghold in the Holy Land) caused universal resentment. Eventually, in 1308 Philip IV of France moved against them. Having obtained papal support for his campaign, Philip persuaded most European rulers to suppress the Templars. The order's officers were arrested, on the grounds of alleged heresy, sorcery, sodomy and corruption, and in France at least thirty-eight Templars are known to have died during 'examination'. In 1310, sixty-seven Templars were burned at the stake, in 1312 the pope transferred many of the order's holdings and possessions to the Hospitallers (*see* ST JOHN OF JERUSALEM, ORDER OF) and in 1314 the Grand Master of the order was burned alive in front of Notre Dame in Paris on the instructions of Philip the Fair. But by then, the Templars had created for themselves what was effectively a sovereign state in the Greek islands, notably at Rhodes, which they eventually lost to the Ottoman Turks in 1522. In 1530 the order's convent was re-established in Malta, where it remained until 1798.

Although in several countries the order survived, in England it was suppressed, but without undue severity. Its headquarters still stand at Temple Church in Fleet Street, London, a building the design of which was based on the Holy Sepulchre at Jerusalem. Both the Templars and the Hospitallers had about fifty preceptories or commanderies in the British Isles (*see* COMMANDERY), many commemorated by place-names such as St John's Jerusalem in Kent, St John's Wood in London, Temple Breuer in Lincolnshire, Templecombe in Somerset and Temple Guiting in the Gloucestershire Cotswolds. One of the most impressive Temple churches, St Michael's at Garway in Herefordshire, was originally a circular structure (of which no sign remains internally) with a detached, fortress-like tower to the north-west.

The habit of the order was white, with a red cross of eight points worn on the left shoulder, and its badges were the *Agnus dei* and a strange device consisting of two knights riding on one horse (presumably an allusion to the original poverty of the order) which was later translated into a pegasus.

TEMPLE PLACE-NAMES *see* TEMPLAR, KNIGHTS

TEMPORALE That section of a MISSAL or BREVIARY in which are set out the variable parts of the services for the ecclesiastical year.
See also SANCTORALE

TEN ARTICLES, THE *see* SIX ARTICLES, THE

TENEBRAE *see* HEARSE

TERCE The short office of the third hour (about nine in the morning). Similar in structure to SEXT

and NONE. Terce consisted of a hymn, three psalms (or a longer psalm divided into three parts) with antiphons, a chapter or reading, the lesser litany, Lord's prayer, versicles and collect.
See also HOURS (CANONICAL) *and* HORARIUM

TERTIARY A member of the Third Order of a mendicant order (*see* FRIARS *and* THIRD ORDERS). A secular tertiary is one who lives in the world, whereas a regular tertiary lives in a community.

TESTER *see* BALDACCHINO *and* SOUNDING BOARD

THIRD ORDERS Religious organisations associated with one of the mendicant orders (*see* FRIARS). Known as tertiaries, members of the Third Orders live either in the world (*Secular Tertiaries*) or in communities (*Regular Tertiaries*). They observe a RULE, recite an office (*see* DIVINE OFFICE) and may wear the habit of their order. All members of the Third Orders are under vows, as are their fully professed brothers and sisters in the First (male) and Second (female) Orders.

THIRD PRIOR *see* SUB-PRIOR

THIRTY-NINE ARTICLES, THE The doctrinal formulae issued by CONVOCATION in 1563 and finally adopted by the Church of England in 1571 as a statement of its dogmatic position. Since 1865 the Anglican clergy have been required to affirm only a general assent rather than to subscribe to the Articles in every particular.
See also REFORMATION, THE *and* SIX ARTICLES, THE

THURIBLE (*also* CENSER) A metal vessel in which INCENSE is burned. A thurible is usually suspended from chains by which it is swung during the incensation. The term *censer* is considered by some to be erroneous but is widely used.

THURIFER The person appointed to carry the THURIBLE.

TIERCERON RIBS *see* VAULTING

TILES (FLOOR) *see* ENCAUSTIC TILES

TILES (ROOFING) *see* SLATES AND ROOFING TILES

TIMBER Large quantities of timber from monastic estates were sold to secular factors or used in the construction of monastic buildings and for floors, screens, fittings and furniture. Most of the barns, workshops, mills and other buildings in the outer curia would have been timber-frame constructions. Indeed the claustral and administrative buildings of most early monasteries were originally built of wood. Most were replaced with stone, but not all: consequently they have decayed and are lost without trace.

Timber was also used as fuel for fires in the KITCHENS, INFIRMARY, GUEST HOUSE and CALEFACTORIUM (the monks' warming house). In some houses a *woodward* was employed to supervise the selection, collection and storage of timber and the replanting of the estate woodland.
See also WOODCARVING *and* WOODWORK

TIMETABLE *see* HORARIUM

TINCTURES *see* COLOURS (HERALDIC)

TIPPET A broad, black 'scarf' worn by Anglican clergy over the SURPLICE. The tippet evolved from the academic hood, the ends of which hung forward from the shoulders.

TIRONIANS Members of a reformed Benedictine CONGREGATION established in the diocese of Chartres in 1114. The name was derived from the apprentices (*tirones*), who were united by its founder to pursue their trades and skills in God's service. Of the five British priories, that at St

Dogmael, Ceredigion, was autonomous, as was its cell on Caldey, the 'Island of Saints' in Pembrokeshire. The parish church of St Dogmael may once have been the external chapel of the former priory.

TITHE BARNS *see* BARNS

TITHES (DECIMAE) Tithe was a tax of one tenth, specifically a tenth part of the annual produce of land or labour, levied in a parish to support its priest, to maintain the fabric of its church and to provide for the relief of the poor. There were three types of tithe: *praedial tithes* (calculated on income from produce), *mixed tithes* (calculated on income from stock and labour combined) and *personal tithes* (calculated on income derived entirely from labour). Income from customary sources, such as woodland and waste, was exempt. Produce raised as tithe was stored in *tithe barns* which, for the most part, were modest buildings far removed from the great monastic tithe barns that were constructed of more durable materials and have therefore survived in greater numbers (*see* BARNS).

In parishes where the rector was not the incumbent, the tithes were apportioned between the rector (which might be an institution such as a collegiate or monastic foundation) and the vicar (who was appointed as a deputy to take charge of the parish) and were known respectively as the Great or *Rectorial Tithes* and Small or *Vicarial Tithes*. In a wealthy parish, rectorial tithes could be a valuable form of endowment, and for this reason those who founded monasteries in the twelfth and thirteenth centuries often chose to provide income for their fledgling communities in the form of benefices rather than in the form of land. The new monastery would itself become the corporate rector and would thereby receive the rectorial tithes. From 1391, monastic rectors were required to set aside a proportion of their tithes for the benefit of the poor of their appropriated parishes.

With the DISSOLUTION OF THE MONASTERIES, many monastic holdings were conveyed by the Crown into private ownership, so that laymen could claim the rectorial tithes. The tithes of such impropriated parishes thereby became private property which could be freely purchased, sold or leased and were entirely divorced from the parish church and its incumbent.

TOMB CHEST The term is misleading because tomb chests do not contain mortal remains but are simply a form of monument. Stone tomb chests first appeared in the thirteenth century, inspired by the SHRINES of saints whose bodies were often enclosed in chest-like structures above ground level. Early tomb chests were surmounted by a coped top, but these were superseded by INCISED SLABS, BRASSES and EFFIGIES. Most tomb chests were free-standing, although many have subsequently been moved to a side wall. Where tomb chests were originally set against a wall they were usually placed within a low arch, the wall itself providing a CANOPY above. Alternatively, the tomb chest, its canopy, pillars and arch may be combined to form a screen between two parts of a church: the PRESBYTERY and AMBULATORY, for example.

In the thirteenth and fourteenth centuries the decoration of the sides and ends of a chest reflected contemporary architectural styles: panels containing carved quatrefoils (or, more rarely, trefoils, hexafoils or octofoils), or miniature blind arcading, often with WEEPERS carved within the recesses. From the mid-thirteenth century painted and gilded shields of arms were added, either within the quatrefoils or in the recesses of the arcading, or on the spandrels on either side of the figures. During the fifteenth century weepers were superseded by figures of angels, which sometimes carry shields, or the spaces in the arcading were filled entirely with heraldic devices.

There is sometimes a space beneath a tomb chest, and this may still contain the carved figure of a shrouded CADAVER to symbolise the transient nature of life on earth (*see* INTRANSI TOMB). Although difficult to see without prostrating one's self, the roofs of these compartments may be painted – with a depiction of the Annunciation or the figures of patron saints, for example.

Perhaps the finest of all medieval tomb chests, that of Richard Beauchamp, fifth earl of Warwick (d. 1439) at the collegiate church of St Mary, Warwick, was erected fifteen years after the earl's death and reflects a final flowering of several earlier styles. The Purbeck marble chest is surmounted by a magnificent, life-size, gilded bronze effigy and HEARSE, its head resting on a swan-crested helm, and the bear and griffin devices of the earldoms of Warwick and Salisbury at its feet. Fourteen weepers, located within canopied niches in the sides and ends of the chest, represent distinguished relatives or friends of the dead earl, each identified by its shield of arms, including that of Richard Nevill, the 'King-maker' (1428–71). There are also eighteen angels, each of which stands within a small, raised niche between the weepers, although for some reason these are not so finely carved.

Following the Reformation, religious motifs were replaced by heraldic ones and Renaissance influences are evident in the gradual introduction of classical forms, both in the decoration and in the structure of tomb chests. The sides of the chests were often divided into panels, using balusters, pilasters and colonettes. Figures were rarely used and heraldry, on both the tomb chest and its integral canopy, became increasingly elaborate (*see* CANOPY (MONU-MENTAL)). From the end of the sixteenth century, many tomb chests were constructed on two levels, to accommodate two or even three effigies. From the mid-seventeenth century, the tomb chest was superseded by the hanging wall monument (*see* WALL MONUMENTS) and it was not until the Gothic revival of the nineteenth century that tomb chests became fashionable once again.

For the Church Monuments Society *see* APPENDIX II.

TOMBS Strictly speaking, a tomb is a grave, vault or other place where human remains have been interred. However, the term is sometimes used erroneously to describe various forms of monument that are not necessarily erected over the place of interment.

See also BRASSES (MONUMENTAL), BURIALS (MONASTIC), CANOPY (MONUMENTAL), CEMETERIES, EFFIGIES, EPITAPHS, HEART BURIAL, INCISED SLABS, MONUMENTS, OSSUARIES, PLAGUE, SHRINES, TOMB CHESTS, VAULT, VISCERAL TOMBS *and* WALL MONUMENTS

TONSURE The formal shaving of the head which was introduced into the western Church in the seventh century as 'the outward and visible mark' of a monk or cleric. The difference between the Celtic and Roman tonsure was a matter of disputation at the Synod of Whitby in 664: the former was diamond-shaped while the latter was circular (to symbolise the Crown of Thorns) and, unlike the Celtic version, the hair was cut short above the nape. In the monasteries, the tonsure was normally renewed every three weeks (and before major FESTIVALS), barbers being engaged for the purpose by the CHAMBERLAIN, either from among the brethren or professionals brought in from a nearby town. The Winchester account rolls contain an entry 'for 36 shavings – 4*s* 6*d*' carried out in the cloister.

See also RASURA

TOUCH A black marble quarried near Tournai in Belgium (hence 'Tournai Marble') and, from the twelfth century, imported into Britain, notably in finished fonts and tomb slabs (*see* INCISED SLABS) and in decorative mouldings of the Tudor and Jacobean periods. Tournai marble is similar in appearance, although by no means identical, to PURBECK MARBLE and other cheaper 'marbles' by which it was later replaced.

See also MASONRY

TOURNAI MARBLE *see* TOUCH

TOWERS Cathedral and abbey towers were intended to demonstrate God's magnificence, and to declare the power and authority of the Church and of the men who financed their construction. They were designed, literally, to be awesome. In the medieval imagination they were immense 'lightning conductors', harnessing God's power and directing it into his Church on earth.

Describing Ely Cathedral Priory when approaching across the fens, Alec Clifton-Taylor wrote: 'When in medieval times this fenland was flooded, the cathedral would appear to be floating like a great ship at anchor'. Similarly, the triple towers of Lincoln Cathedral, high on its limestone ridge, dominate the surrounding levels, while Gloucester's sumptuous tower commands the Severn Vale like a beacon. (*see* colour plate 21) Even in this predominantly secular age, such towers remain potent symbols of historical continuity. Their BELLS marked the canonical hours and summoned the brethren to services – just as the bells of Sherborne and Tewkesbury, Great Malvern and Romsey call parishioners to mattins and evensong today. No two towers are alike, either in their construction or decoration, and there are considerable regional variations of style and materials (*see also* BELL-HATCH *and* BELL LOUVRES).

From the eleventh century, nearly all the great English Romanesque and Gothic churches were built to a cruciform plan, with additional TRANSEPT walls at right angles to those of the nave and choir to counteract the outward thrust of massive central towers (*axial towers*) daringly constructed above the void of the CROSSING. Ironically, the distinctive silhouettes of the English cathedrals – their towers and (sometimes) a spire providing a satisfying sense of equilibrium – are a consequence of their modest scale, the audaciously large French churches being structurally incapable of supporting the weight of a tower without the construction of massive (and intrusive) abutments (*see* VAULTING). Conversely, where a great English church has been deprived of its central tower, as at Westminster and Beverley, the visual effect can be devastating.

Late Norman towers are characterised by their square plan, massive masonry, shallow buttressing and flat or pyramidal roofs (*see* MEDIEVAL ARCHITECTURE). From *c.* 1130 the use of decoration increased, notably blind arcading (*see* ARCADE). Twin round-headed belfry openings are usually divided by a shaft and recessed within a large, round-headed containing arch. Despite their solidity (or, perhaps, because of it) many Norman towers collapsed. Of those which survived, that at Norwich Cathedral (*c.* 1145) is the tallest Norman tower in England and one of the finest with a graceful spire added in 1490 (*for* spires *see below*). Unfortunately, its original timber spire was blown down in 1362, taking part of the tower with it. Consequently, the stonework has been extensively renewed. The massive tower of Tewkesbury Abbey, completed in the latter half of the twelfth century, is equally impressive. Claimed by some to be the largest surviving Norman tower in the world, its walls are 14m (46ft) square and it rises to a height of 46m (148ft) – only the battlemented parapet and pinnacles are not original (they were added in 1600).

A number of larger churches have both axial and western towers, although these were rarely built at the same time. The west tower at Ely Cathedral Priory, for example, is spectacularly Romanesque (the octagonal belfry was added in 1392), while the fourteenth-century central octagon replaced an earlier AXIAL TOWER (*see below*). At Wimborne Minster the process was reversed: the axial tower is Norman (1120) while a new west tower had to be built in 1464 to carry a peal of five bells. Twin west towers, such as those at Durham Cathedral Priory and Southwell Minster, were a popular Romanesque feature that was later followed at other major medieval churches such as York and Beverley minsters and Lichfield, Lincoln and Canterbury cathedrals. (The twin towers in the west front of Westminster Abbey

At Wells Cathedral, the addition of a belfry storey in 1313 caused the tower to lean westward and cracks appeared in the masonry. Consequently, in 1338–48 the celebrated 'scissor arches' (strainer arches) were installed on three sides of the crossing. (Courtesy of Anthony Kersting)

are very much later. Designed by Sir Christopher Wren they were completed by Nicholas Hawksmoor in 1745.) Regrettably, many of these west towers have subsequently disappeared: at Ely the northern tower of a pair was lost in the fourteenth century, leaving the west front sadly asymmetrical, while Hereford's splendid west tower collapsed on Easter Monday 1786, destroying the entire west end of the cathedral. Neither tower was replaced. Uniquely in Britain, Exeter Cathedral has two fine Norman transeptal towers instead of an axial tower. These immense towers are all that remain of the earlier twelfth-century building and were once capped with low, pyramidal spires, the present pinnacles and crenellations dating from the late fifteenth century. Several screen façades have flanking turrets, another Romanesque feature, as in the thirteenth-century west fronts of Salisbury and Peterborough.

In the later medieval period, towers were often increased in height to provide more space for bells and to emphasise further the status of the abbey or cathedral. This was achieved either by demolishing and then rebuilding a tower or, more usually, by adding further storeys to an earlier one – easily recognised today by abrupt changes in architectural styles. When this was done, inadequate FOUNDATIONS, combined with the additional weight on the crossing piers, often led to structural problems. At Wells Cathedral, for example, the addition of a belfry storey in 1313 caused the tower to lean westward, and cracks appeared in the masonry. Consequently, in 1338–48 the celebrated 'scissor arches' (*strainer arches*) were installed on three sides of the crossing. Supplemented by hidden buttresses, these arches redistributed the stresses and braced the tower. Similarly, at Salisbury Cathedral the arches of the crossing were prevented from collapsing inwards by the introduction of broad, stone 'girders' in 1450. At Lincoln, the central tower (1200) collapsed after only forty years and was rebuilt in the Early English style in *c.* 1250 when it acquired a timber and lead spire. In 1306 the chapter decided to remove the spire and extend the tower upwards yet again, this time in a sumptuously Perpendicular style and with a prodigiously lofty spire that was destroyed in 1548 (*see below*). At 82.6m (271ft) Lincoln's axial tower is both the tallest and one of the most beautiful of English church towers, forming a composition of almost perfect proportions with the twin west towers, which themselves reach a height of 61m (200ft). It is also a *lantern tower*, one in which there is no vault immediately above the crossing, the space extending upwards and lit by windows.

The Octagon and Lantern Tower of Ely Cathedral Priory is a masterpiece of medieval architecture. Following the collapse, in 1322, of the original Norman crossing tower, responsibility for its replacement was given to the priory's SACRIST, Alan de Walsingham. Together with his (anonymous) master mason, and with advice from William Hurley, Edward III's master carpenter, de Walsingham designed and supervised the construction of the new structure – experiencing, it is said, 'a moment of supreme creative vision'. Rather than rebuilding the conventional tower, he decided to enlarge the crossing to form an octagonal space 23m (74ft) across. He achieved this by removing the remains of the four tower piers and incorporating one bay from each of the transepts, the nave and the choir into the central space. A stone vault was not feasible above such a vast space and so a timber roof was formed by a series of triangular frames attached to the crossing piers. Within this roof a second octagon (the octagon gallery) was inserted, formed around eight enormous vertical oak timbers, each nearly 1m (3ft) thick and 6m (20ft) high, together with a complex series of struts attached to the piers and walls of the lower octagon. These supported a ring beam on which stood the 12m (40ft) high posts of the lantern itself, the outer surface of which was encased in lead. This extraordinarily daring feat of engineering took over fourteen years to complete.

The triple towers of Lincoln Cathedral.

Weighing over two hundred tons, it appears almost to be suspended in mid-air. The lantern had to be wholly renewed in the nineteenth century by George Gilbert Scott (it is believed that it is a careful recreation of the original design) and restoration of the lantern windows was completed in 1991. (*See* colour plate 10)

The first Perpendicular cathedral tower, at Worcester Cathedral Priory, was completed in 1374 and, like Hereford, once carried a modest timber-framed spire. Its tall, crocketed pinnacles and almost perfect proportions were clearly a model for the tower at Gloucester Abbey, which was begun by Abbot Sebrok in 1450. However, Gloucester's sumptuous tower is loftier – 69m (225ft) against Worcester's 60m (196ft) – and, with its pierced parapet and corner turrets, its CORONAL is undoubtedly the most striking of any British cathedral. (*See* colour plate 21) It is likely that the architect also designed the tower of nearby Malvern Priory, which is almost identical and of a similar date but rises in two stages, rather than three, to a height of 38m (124ft). In 1365 work began on increasing the height of the western towers at Wells Cathedral (a task that took more than seventy years to complete) and in 1440 the axial tower underwent a Perpendicular transformation, the addition of traceried parapets and numerous pinnacles creating a tower of considerable refinement and loveliness.

The massive Romanesque west towers at Durham Cathedral Priory were remodelled in the thirteenth and fourteenth centuries and the corner pinnacles and parapets were added in 1801. Durham's thirteenth-century crossing tower was struck by lightning in 1429, causing the interior timbers to ignite and the structure to become unsafe. It was patched up but remained in a dangerous state until rebuilding began in *c.* 1465. Work was reaching completion when it was decided to add an upper stage so that the height of the new tower would complement that of the western towers. Regrettably, this squat extension sits uncomfortably within the crenellated parapet that was intended to complete the tower, although the decision to raise the height to 66m (218ft) was aesthetically a sound one. Bell Harry, the central tower at Canterbury Cathedral Priory, is considered by many to be the finest of Perpendicular towers. Built between 1494 and 1497, it was designed by the great late medieval architect John Wastell and reaches a height of 72m (235ft). Uniquely in England, it is lined with nearly half a million red bricks, the limestone facing having been imported from Normandy (*see* MASONRY).

The Cistercians

Initially, primitive Cistercian usage abjured the great tower as a symbol of pride, however, the GENERAL CHAPTER of 1157 seems to have relaxed its general prohibition, after which comparatively low 'lantern' towers were introduced at a number of English Cistercian abbeys, including Buildwas Abbey in Shropshire. But it was not until the late fifteenth and early sixteenth centuries that there was a general trend towards erecting great towers at Cistercian monasteries. Some abbeys succeeded in erecting axial towers (at Kirkstall, for example), but elsewhere this was found to be impracticable, indeed a number of towers collapsed during building. Consequently, in the early sixteenth century we find Abbot Marmaduke Huby of Fountains (1495–1526) adding a tower at the north end of the transept (*see* colour plate 2), while at Furness an additional tower was erected at the west end of the church. Both were of considerable height – that at Fountains was 48.7m (160ft) high – and were clearly intended to declare the abbeys' pre-eminence among Cistercian houses. (At the Dissolution of the Monasteries, Furness was the second richest Cistercian abbey in England after Fountains.)

Detached Belfries

Towers that contained belfries (*see* BELLS) were sometimes detached from the main body of the church. One of the earliest, at St Davids Cathedral, Pembrokeshire, is a thirteenth-century octagonal tower that was incorporated into the Porth y Tŵr, a fortified gateway to the close, in the fourteenth century (*see* FORTIFICATION). It now houses the cathedral bells. The splendid Perpendicular bell tower at Evesham Abbey is a rare survival. Measuring 33.5m (110ft) in height, it was built by Abbot Lichfield (the last of Evesham's abbots) in the early sixteenth century both as a detached belfry and as a focal point for pilgrims as they approached from the distant hills. The solid, four-square detached belfry at Chichester Cathedral is very different in appearance but no less effective. With its heavy, setback buttresses and (later) octagonal upper storey, it was built in *c.* 1400 to receive the bells (now eight in number) from the cathedral's central tower. There was an ugly, free-standing belfry in the close at Salisbury, but this was demolished by James Wyatt (1746–1813) in 1788, possibly the only benefit of the 'restorative improvements' to the cathedral that earned him the sobriquet 'Wyatt the Destroyer'.

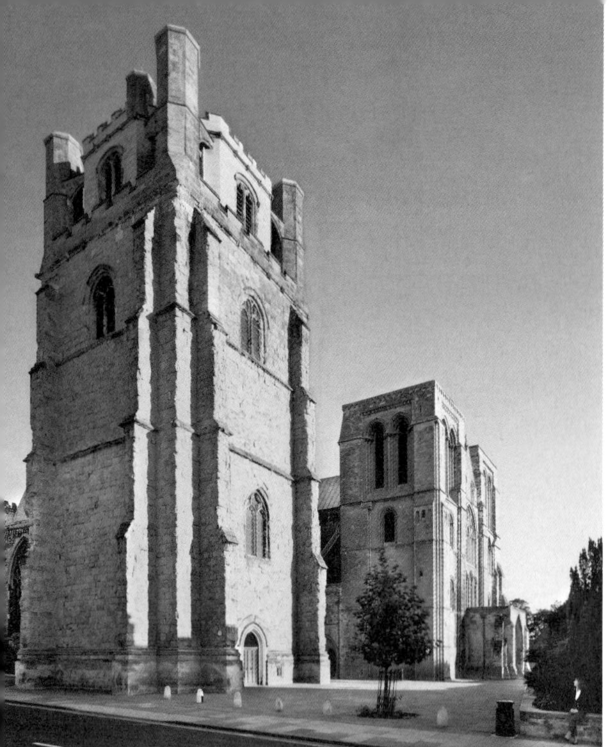

The detached bell tower at Chichester Cathedral, built in c. 1400 to receive the bells from the cathedral's central tower. (© John Crook/info@john-crook.com)

Spires

Most medieval spires are from the early Gothic period (*see* MEDIEVAL ARCHITECTURE), the builders of Perpendicular towers preferring to compete with one another in the architectural ornamentation of pinnacles, parapets and mouldings. Hereford Cathedral's timber and lead spire was one of the few early spires to have survived – but only until 1790. Although of no great height, the early fourteenth-century tower (*c.* 1325) is so massive and dignified that the loss of the spire seems hardly to matter (the corner pinnacles were added in 1830). The most elegant of all European spires, that of Salisbury Cathedral, was completed in 1380 and rises to 121m (404ft). It is by far the tallest in England, although that of Old St Paul's (destroyed by fire in 1561) was nearly 28m (93ft) taller. Salisbury's spire is embellished with three horizontal ornamental bands of carved stonework, but is otherwise plain. The difficulty of accommodating an octagonal spire within a square tower was cleverly overcome by adding a double tier of pinnacles at each corner of the tower and a gabled window (*lucarne*) at the base of each exposed face. Major restoration of the stonework was carried out in 1986–95 when, amazingly, the original timber framework inside the spire and the wrought-iron bars that strengthened the tower above the crossing vault were found to be in good condition (*see* colour plate 1).

Uniquely in England, Lichfield Cathedral has three spires (known as the 'Ladies of the Vale'), which have somehow survived numerous restorations, although the central spire has been rebuilt on two occasions – in the seventeenth and eighteenth centuries. The beautiful central tower of Lincoln Cathedral is 81m (271ft) tall and is the second highest in England. Amazingly, it was once crowned with a lead-covered timber spire which, rising 157m (524ft) above ground level, is believed to have been the tallest in Europe. On a clear day it would have been visible for nearly fifty miles across the fens. It was destroyed in a storm in 1548. As at Lichfield, there were also spires on the west towers, but these were taken down in the early nineteenth century. Next to Salisbury, the most celebrated English spire is that at Norwich Cathedral Priory, where the tall, Romanesque tower originally had a timber spire, lost in a storm in 1362. The graceful new spire, added in 1490, rises to 96m (315ft) and is the second tallest spire in England. The spire of Chichester Cathedral is a copy – but a very sympathetic one – of the original early fifteenth-century stone spire that collapsed in 1861 (in the words of a startled observer 'it telescoped into itself'). Designed by Sir George Gilbert Scott (1811–78), the rebuilt spire was completed on 28 June 1866, when the original weathercock was hoisted to the top.

Modern Cathedrals

Of the modern cathedrals (*see* POST-MEDIEVAL CATHEDRALS), J.L. Pearson's attractive triple towers and spires at Truro (1910) are essentially Early English in style, while Giles Gilbert Scott's enormous axial tower at Liverpool's Anglican cathedral (begun in 1904) reaches a height of

101m (331ft) and was only substituted for the twin towers of the original design after building had been in progress for several years. The brick tower of Edward Maufe's Guildford Cathedral (begun in 1936 but not completed until 1965) is a somewhat austere but dignified interpretation of Gothic, while Basil Spence's cathedral at Coventry (consecrated in 1962) incorporates the tower (1394) and spire (1433) of the former medieval cathedral, the bombed-out ruins of which remain as consecrated ground, a poignant reminder of the horrors of war. Rising to 90m (294ft), it is the third tallest spire in England (after Salisbury and Norwich), and with its delicate ornamentation and flying buttresses has been described (by John Harvey) as 'a work of genius fit to rank with the wonders of the world'. Together with the nave walls, crypt and south porch it miraculously remained unscathed after a devastating air raid in November 1940. The tower's twelve bells were rehung in 1987 to celebrate the new cathedral's silver jubilee and were rung for the first time when Coventry City won the FA Cup final.

TOWERS, DETACHED *see* TOWERS

TOWNS For the majority of brethren, monasteries were places of refuge from the stark and often brutal realities of the outside world. Consequently, many religious communities (notably the CISTERCIANS) welcomed the remoteness afforded by endowments of uncultivable and unproductive land, far removed from centres of population and the tribulations of urban life. However, despite monastic aspirations of self-sufficiency, it was inevitable that many of the more accessible monasteries should attract traders, craftsmen and itinerants to their gates, the proximity of the abbey affording a semblance of protection and the prospect of trade and employment. Several of these transitory communities developed into permanent settlements and, ultimately, into towns: at Burton upon Trent, Evesham, Eynsham, Glastonbury, Pershore, Romsey and Tavistock, for example, all of which were granted markets outside the abbey gates (*see* MARKETS, SHOPS AND FAIRS).

From the eleventh century, monastic superiors began to acknowledge the financial benefits of such an arrangement. Many towns were created on abbatial estates, promoted and protected by an abbey and subject to the overriding jurisdiction of the abbot who exercised authority over the construction and maintenance of roads and bridges, the appointment of civic officials, the control of markets and fairs and matters judicial. Settlers were attracted by land grants, low rents and other privileges and organised trading monopolies offered economic security and the right of controlling one's own property within a town. The chronicler of Battle Abbey records that, shortly after the monastery was founded by King William in *c.* 1070,

> A goodly number of men were brought hither out of neighbouring counties, some even from foreign countries. And to each of these the brethren who managed the building allotted a dwelling-place of certain dimensions around the circuit of the abbey; and these still remain as they were apportioned, with their customary rent or service.

The chronicler, who was writing a century after the event, lists 115 houses, most of them in the main street leading north from the abbey gate.

The ground in boroughs was rented out in standard *burgage plots* for which an annual rent was charged. However, if a town was economically successful, income from these rents could easily be exceeded by that from the tolls of markets and fairs and the proceeds of the borough courts. Over six hundred medieval boroughs have been identified in England of which about seventy-five were either created or inherited by monastic or canonical institutions. Of these, about forty were Benedictine, twelve were Augustinian and three were held by Cluniac priories. Some were ancient settlements adjoining monastic precincts, while others were

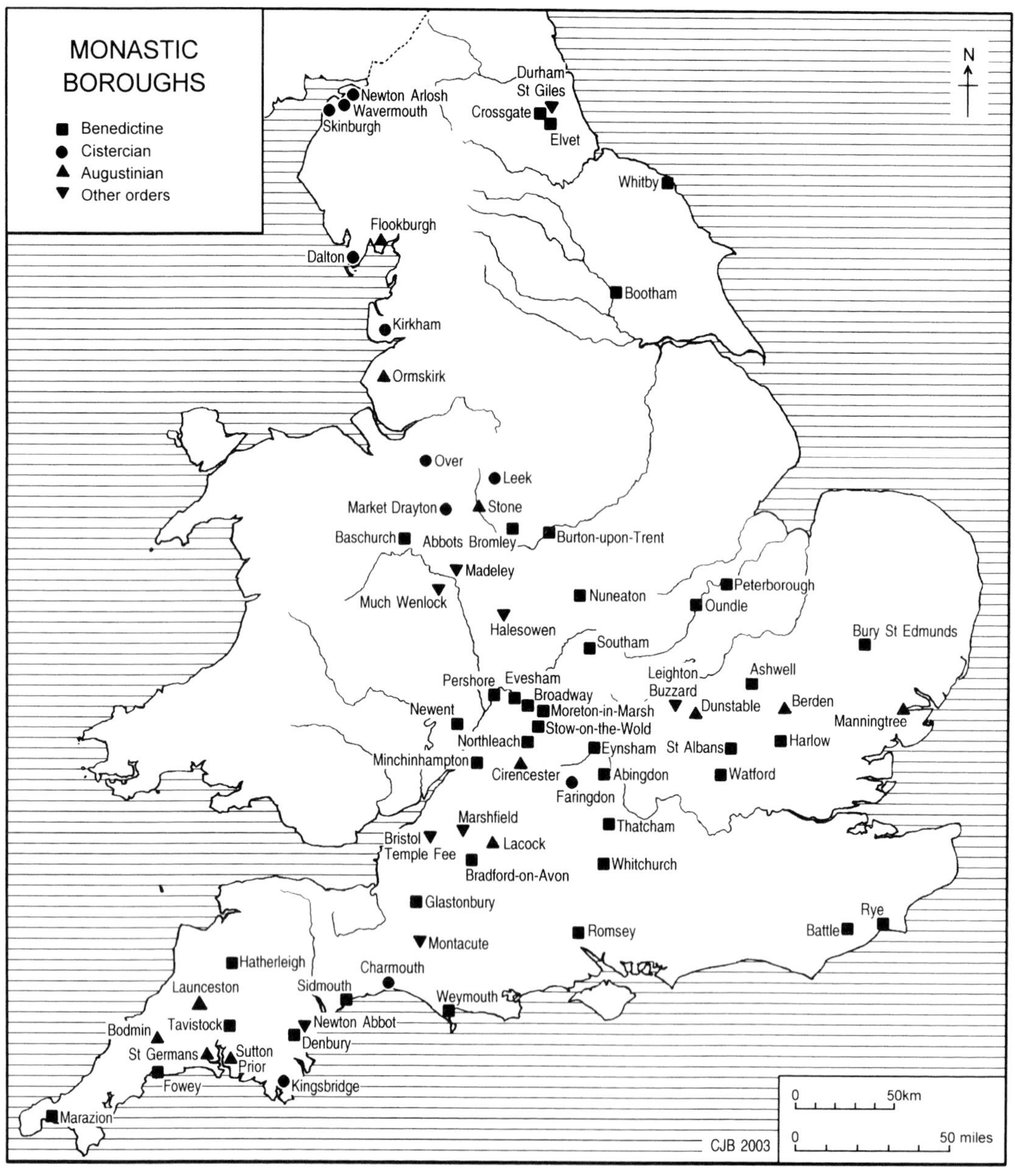

Boroughs founded or acquired by monastic houses. (By kind permission of James Bond)

planned new towns. A further nine boroughs were founded by the Cistercians and two by the Premonstratensians – all located on estates at some distance from their respective abbeys. Towns such as Abingdon, Bury, Peterborough and St Albans developed in this way, most eventually obtaining autonomy, although in some cases this was achieved only after protracted (and sometimes violent) conflict between the citizens and abbey officials (*see* FORTIFICATION).

The Augustinian abbey of Cirencester was founded within an existing town that already had an established wool market. But in 1190 the abbot purchased the entire borough and with it control of the huge profits from the flourishing Cotswold wool trade. By the thirteenth century the abbey's determination not to relinquish its hold on the town's commerce caused considerable resentment among the local merchants and townspeople. Similarly, at Bury St Edmunds numerous disputes between the abbey and the townspeople reached a climax in 1327 when the burgesses sought to obtain civic independence. Riots lasted throughout the summer and resulted in the burning of the abbey, the abduction of the abbot and the killing of several monks. In 1437 a minor dispute concerning the location of the parish font at Sherborne inflamed long-smouldering resentments and during the ensuing riot the parish priest shot a burning arrow into the (temporarily thatched) roof of the neighbouring abbey church, causing a devastating conflagration. The marks left by the flames can still be seen today, as can the wonderful fan vaulting to which the townspeople were compelled to contribute during the rebuilding of the abbey church in 1475 (*see* VAULTING). Of course, there are also many examples of religious houses living harmoniously alongside the boroughs. At Burton, for instance, the abbey provided the town with a school, market hall, paved streets and a water supply.

From the mid-thirteenth century there was a decline in the economic conditions that had previously encouraged the building of new towns. Even so, several prospered and expanded, either by ribbon development along existing streets or by the addition of new suburbs. Many 'Newland' place-names, as in towns such as Sherborne and Eynsham, originated at this time.

In the early fourteenth century London probably had a population of nearly 120,000 and cities such as York, Norwich, Lincoln and Bristol each had about 20,000 inhabitants. Of a total population of five million it is now believed that at least 700,000 lived in towns. Urban society was very well organised, with medieval old peoples' homes, orphanages, hospitals, social clubs and hotels. Large numbers of social institutions were provided by wealthy benefactors (*see* CHANTRY), by ecclesiastical foundations (*see* SHRINES) and by fraternities such as the Guild of Our Lady at Lavenham in Suffolk whose fifteenth-century meeting hall was built, in part, to ensure that masses were said for the souls of all paid-up members and as a social club for the town's élite, with its own resident cook and musician. The Black Death of 1348–69 (*see* PLAGUE) effectively curtailed the creation of new towns, Bewdley, built in 1477 on the banks of the River Severn in Worcestershire, being the last medieval planned town.

TRACERS *see* STAINED GLASS

TRACERY A decorative interlaced pattern, especially ornamental stone open-work at the head of a window (*see* MEDIEVAL ARCHITECTURE *and* WINDOWS).

TRACING FLOOR *see* MASTER MASONS AND ARCHITECTS

TRADE *see* MARKETS, SHOPS AND FAIRS

TRANSEPT From the Latin *transeptum* meaning 'cross-division', the transept is the transverse portion of a cruciform church, usually referred to as the north and south transept, with the CROSSING between. Confusingly, the two 'wings' of a transept are often described as though they are separate entities: Alec Clifton-Taylor, for example, defines the transept as 'an arm of the cross-piece of a cruciform church'. Even more confusingly, some larger churches (such as Canterbury, Lincoln and Salisbury cathedrals) have two transepts, the plan forming a patriarchal cross (an upright with two cross-members). Again, the four arms of these 'double' transepts are frequently referred to individually – at Lincoln, for example, the larger of the transepts is called the Great Transept while the two arms of the lesser transept are referred to as the 'north-east transept' and the 'south-east transept'. Although, strictly speaking, a transept is

The north transept of Peterborough Cathedral: a glorious example of twelfth-century Romanesque.

the single 'cross-member' of a cruciform church, it is difficult to argue with the practicality of defining each arm individually. Although there may be a commonality of architectural style (though by no means invariably so), no two wings of a transept are identical. As with the RETRO-CHOIR there remains a difference of opinion. The definition 'the transverse portion of a cruciform church, usually referred to as the north and south transept with the crossing between' would seem to be a satisfactory compromise.

The cruciform shape formed by the nave and transept was not merely symbolic. The two wings of the transept were, effectively, immense buttresses that assisted in counteracting the outward thrust of a central tower through the corner piers of the crossing. At Gloucester Cathedral, for example, enormous flying buttresses were constructed within the transept walls (and are visible where they pass through the triforium). The transept provided additional space for PROCESSIONS and for the subsidiary ALTARS of the ordained brethren, which were always set against the eastern wall or in chapels built out on the eastern side (there are examples of both at Lincoln). The NIGHT STAIR, usually in the south transept, led from the monks' dormitory (*see* DORTER) to the choir, the great clock in the transept marking the hours of the night office.

The end walls and gables of the transept are ideally suited to the insertion of magnificent ROSE WINDOWS (*see also* WINDOWS) and it is in the transept that many of the finest MONUMENTS are located, notably those from the post-Reformation period. The transept often enjoys greater architectural homogeneity than other parts of a building: at Peterborough Cathedral, for instance, where the transept is a glorious example of twelfth-century Romanesque (1140–55) with only minimal tracery added to the original Norman arches.

There are several instances of churches that comprise only a choir and transept. At Milton Abbey in Dorset, for example, the onset of PLAGUE brought building work to a halt and the nave was never built, while at Abbey Dore in Herefordshire the nave was demolished following the abbey's dissolution in 1536. Both of these truncated but splendid buildings remain in Anglican use.

See also MEDIEVAL ARCHITECTURE *and* PORTICUS

TRANSEPTAL Relating to a transept. Transeptal towers, for example, are towers that were constructed above the arms of a transept.

TRANSI TOMB *see* INTRANSI TOMB

TRANSLATION (i) Transferring a bishop from one see to another. Prior to the Reformation, this could only be achieved with the authority of the pope.
(ii) The removal of a saint's body or relics to a different place from that in which it originally came to rest.

TRANSOMS Horizontal bars of stone or wood across a panel or the opening of a window.
See also GLAZING BARS, MULLIONS *and* WINDOWS

TRAPPIST Popular name for the CISTERCIANS of the Strict Observance who follow reforms introduced to the mother house of La Trappe near Soligny by A.J. Le B. de Rancé in 1662.

TRAYLE *see* SLYPE

TREASURER The official responsible to the SACRIST for the security of a community's valuables – plate, vestments, rare books and documents and cash from donations, rents and trade. In smaller houses the treasurer was often also the SACRIST or sub-sacrist.

TREASURY In addition to the SACRISTY and MUNIMENT ROOM, several religious houses also had a strongroom in which a community's valuables were secured, together with those of corrodians (*see* CORRODY), guests and local landowners. The treasury was sometimes located in the vicinity of the DORTER, at the top of the NIGHT STAIR near to where the TREASURER had his bed or cubicle. However, this was not an invariable practice and treasuries were often located wherever there was a convenient space within the conventual buildings to construct a strongroom with a stone-vaulted ceiling (in case of fire), a secure means of access and a stout door. At Gloucester Abbey (now the cathedral) it was above the PARLOUR, between the TRANSEPT and the CHAPTER HOUSE, while at Fountains Abbey it was over the east bay of the chapter house and was accessed from a passageway that connected the dorter with the night stair. At Rievaulx Abbey, the treasury was in the east claustral range beneath the monks' DAY STAIR to the dorter. It was a narrow room with a barrel-vaulted ceiling and a tall, round-headed window in its east wall in which were both bars and shutters that could be secured from within. Originally, it was entered from the adjacent parlour, but this doorway was blocked in the fifteenth century and a new entrance made from the abbot's apartments. Small cupboards were provided within the walls, and coffers – each with three locks that could only be opened in the presence of three OBEDIENTIARIES, each of whom carried a different key. Other chests would have been allocated to different departments, each with a slot through which money could be deposited without having to release the lock. There are several examples of strongrooms constructed within a treasury chamber, as at Durham Cathedral Priory, where security was particularly rigorous. There, a strongroom was secured from an outer chamber by a reinforced door fitted with double locks and a lockable iron grille.

The reliquary arch and treasury above the north presbytery aisle at Norwich Cathedral Priory was designed to display the cathedral treasures to pilgrims passing below as they processed round the ambulatory. Today it contains cathedral artefacts and plate, together with silverware from other churches in the diocese. The treasury is approached by means of a spiral staircase and, as at most other cathedrals, it is open to the public (although not all cathedral treasuries are in their original location).

For the Royal Treasury at Westminster Abbey *see* PYX.

(Tom Friar)

TREE OF JESSE *see* JESSE TREE

TREE OF LIFE A decorative motif consisting of a stylised representation of 'the tree of life . . . in the midst of the garden' (Gen. 2: 9). In the western Church it is a symbol of salvation and is found, for example, in medieval WALL PAINTINGS. It can also be naturalistic in form, and as such was widely depicted in eastern art as a symbol of life and knowledge long before the time of Christ.

TREFOIL A figure having three radiating stylised 'petals', found both as an architectural motif and a heraldic device (*see* FOILS).

TRENDAL A circular candleholder suspended before a rood (*see* ROOD SCREEN).

TRIBUNE *see* GALLERY *and* TRIFORIUM

TRICK *see* COLOURS (HERALDIC)

TRIFORIUM The naves of large medieval churches usually consist of three storeys: an ARCADE of pillars separating the NAVE from the AISLES, a triforium or tribune, and a CLERESTORY which forms an upper level above the aisle roofs.

Many writers erroneously refer to the triforium and tribune as though they are synonymous. The *triforium* is an arcaded wall passage or area of blind arcading below the clerestory and above the arcade (*for* illustration *see* BAY). The *tribune* is an arcaded GALLERY which extends above the stone vault of an aisle and is generally found, in place of the triforium, in larger churches where the nave was constructed before the end of the thirteenth century. In most small churches, and in some larger ones of late Gothic date, this middle level is omitted.

See also MEDIEVAL ARCHITECTURE *and* MINSTRELS' GALLERY

TRINITARIANS *see* FRIARS

TRIODION *see* YEAR, LITURGICAL

TRIPTYCH A set of three painted and gilded panels forming an altarpiece. Triptychs originated in the portable altars of the medieval nobility and may be free-standing or placed against a wall – often behind an altar. The panels are hinged so that the outer leaves protect the centre when closed or support it when splayed. Like the DIPTYCH (which has two panels), a triptych usually depicts religious themes, although some also record genealogical and heraldic information.

One of the earliest surviving triptychs is a remarkable fifteenth-century depiction of five of the miracles of Christ, painted on oak panels in the chapel of the Almshouse of St John the Baptist and St John the Evangelist in Sherborne, Dorset. Described as of the school of Van der Weyden, its origin is unknown – it may be Dutch, French, or even Italian, and it was probably given to the brethren of the Alms House at the time of its foundation in 1437 (*see* ALMSHOUSES). A superb

The Van Aelst Triptych at Winchester Cathedral. (© John Crook/info@john-crook.com)

sixteenth-century triptych in Bishop Langton's Chapel at Winchester Cathedral depicts the holy family resting on the flight into Egypt. Attributed to Pieter Coecke van Aelst, it is on loan from St Michael's Church, Basingstoke. Among several more recent examples is a fine twentieth-century painted and gilded triptych in the Lady Chapel of Hereford Cathedral, while the chancel at Northampton Roman Catholic Cathedral is dominated by a splendid triptych made by Stephen Foster in 1998. Also at Hereford, in the south transept, is a charming German altarpiece (Hereford diocese has a twinning arrangement with Lutheran Christians in Nuremberg) on which is depicted the Adoration of the Magi.

TROPHY A sculptured assemblage of arms and armour, used as a memorial of military victory.

TRUMEAU A slender PIER dividing a large doorway.

TUDOR ARCH *see* ARCH

TUDOR ROSE A stylised five-lobed figure of a rose which combined, in a variety of forms, the red and white rose badges of York and Lancaster. Historically, the red rose has come to represent the concept of parliamentary sanction by which Henry VII acceded to the English throne. But in order that his descendants should enjoy an inalienable right of succession, he married Elizabeth of York – the heiress of the white rose. The rival roses were similarly combined in the beautiful Tudor rose, which was to become the universal symbol of the Tudor dynasty and of the new administration.

(Tom Friar)

TUNNEL VAULT *see* VAULTING

TURNING WINDOW *see* ROTA

TURNPIKE STAIR *see* STAIRCASES *and* VICE

TWENTIETH-CENTURY CATHEDRALS *see* POST-MEDIEVAL CATHEDRALS

TYMPANUM The space enclosed within a PEDIMENT or between a LINTEL and the arch above. The tympanum above the main entrance to a church is often ornately carved.

UMBRACULUM *see* BALDACCHINO

UNDERCROFT Not to be confused with a CRYPT, an undercroft is a stone-vaulted chamber beneath a building. It could be used for a variety of purposes, that beneath the monks' DORTER in the east claustral range might contain the DAY STAIR, SLYPE, PARLOUR and the vestibule of the CHAPTER HOUSE, for example. Where both the dorter and the undercroft extended beyond the cloister (typically, at Furness Abbey) the space may have been used for storage, or subdivided to provide offices for various monastic departments or to accommodate the novices. In most Cistercian abbeys, the undercroft beneath the LAY BROTHERS' dorter in the west claustral range was used by the CELLARER, both for storage and to accommodate his outer PARLOUR and CHECKER. The twelfth-century west claustral range at Fountains Abbey is the largest and best-preserved lay brothers' quarters in Europe. Measuring 91.5m (300ft) in length, the magnificent undercroft is

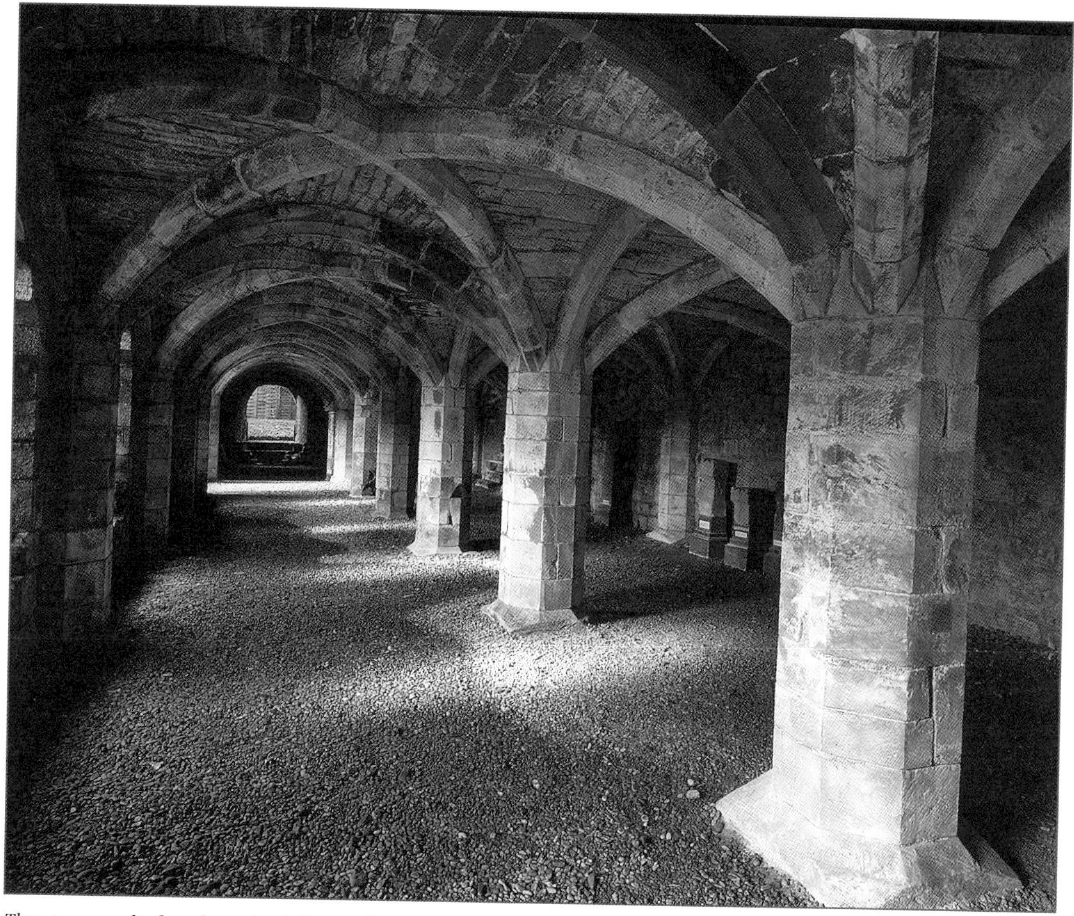

The stone-vaulted undercroft of the south cloister range at Lanercost Priory, Cumbria. (Bob Skingle/© English Heritage Photo Library)

vaulted in twenty-two double bays springing from a central line of piers. Originally, it was divided by cross-walls into a series of chambers. These included an outer parlour, with a wide door to the inner court (where the cellarer met with the outside world) and a small, round-headed door to the CLOISTER; six bays of storage space (*see* CELLARIUM), with an arched opening in the outer wall to admit wheeled vehicles; two bays comprising the cloister entry and the remaining twelve bays the lay brothers' refectory. A fine thirteenth-century ground-floor undercroft has survived in the south claustral range at (Augustinian) Lanercost Priory, although the canons' frater that once occupied the floor above was demolished following the Dissolution of the Monasteries. Three bays of the undercroft were used as a CALEFACTORIUM, with a fireplace in the south wall and 'board games' scratched into the sills of the window seats.

UNIVERSITIES, MEDIEVAL The ancient medieval universities of Oxford, Cambridge, St Andrews, Glasgow and Aberdeen (King's College) were ecclesiastical establishments subject to international papal authority. Admission to the early universities was not a perquisite of the medieval establishment, indeed a university education was one of the few means by which the sons of commoners, or even of aspiring peasants, could rise to eminence. Most students were aged between 15 and 19, and few teachers were over 30. Today's gowns and hoods originated in the academic dress of the medieval universities, where students were considered to be clerics and had their heads shaved in the style of a monk (*see* TONSURE). Oxford, the earliest university, is first mentioned in 1184, although it is likely that its foundation dates from the period 1164–9 when access to the university in Paris was disrupted during Henry II's conflict with Thomas à Becket. It was enlarged by the FRIARS in the 1220s (with the support of Parisian students), and the first colleges (Balliol, Merton and University) were founded in the second half of the century (*see* CHANTRY COLLEGES). The curriculum was based on the *Quadrivium* (arithmetic, geometry, astronomy and music) which, together with the lesser *Trivium* (rhetoric, grammar and logic), formed the 'seven liberal arts', all of which were taught in Latin. Medieval scholastic life was dominated by three apparently contradictory features: academic commitment and creativity, bureaucratic repression and sporadic lawlessness. The intellectual achievement of such Oxford scholars as Robert Grosseteste (b. *c.* 1175), Roger Bacon (1214–92) and John Wycliffe (*c.* 1330–84) was considerable, but all five universities earned a certain notoriety for petty regulation and were often viciously repressive. In the early fifteenth century a master of St Andrews who rejoiced in the office of Inquisitor of Heretical Depravity ordered one of his scholars to be burned alive for his heretical views. At Aberdeen, women were not admitted to the university precincts, the students themselves were not allowed to leave without permission, and all conversation had to be conducted in Latin. At Cambridge, students were forbidden from visiting the town's ale houses (and were so until 1940) and the university's regulations were enforced by Proctors' constables who, in the Middle Ages, were armed with pikes (*halberds*) – which still feature in university ceremonial. It is hardly surprising that such repressive measures provoked an excessive response from the students. In 1445, Godstow Nunnery near Oxford was apparently a favourite student brothel and rioting, usually between 'town and gown', was endemic throughout the Middle Ages.

USES Local modifications of the Roman rite (*see* LITURGY), most of which were abolished by the Council of Trent (1545–63). In England, the Use of Sarum (also the Sarum Rite or Use of Salisbury), and the fourteenth-century revision known as the New Use of Sarum, was used in many dioceses and provided material for the first *Book of Common Prayer* of 1549.
See also SARUM, USE OF

VAIR *see* COLOURS (HERALDIC)

VALOR ECCLESIASTICUS (1535) Popularly known as the 'King's books', the *Valor ecclesiasticus* was the official inventory of monastic and ecclesiastical properties compiled in 1534–5 as a consequence of Henry VIII's appropriation of ecclesiastical revenues (*see* DISSOLUTION OF THE MONASTERIES). In the *Valor ecclesiasticus* the landed income of the monasteries was recorded as £100,700. Twenty-eight houses each had a gross annual income of over £1,000, half of them in the range £1,700 to £4,000 – comparable with the income of a comital or ducal estate. Of these, all but six were Benedictine houses that had been founded in the tenth and eleventh centuries. At the other extreme, 168 houses received an annual income of less than £50, and 79 less than £20.
See also REFORMATION, THE

VAULT An arched roof (*see* VAULTING).

VAULTING Vaulting is the arched interior framework of a roof, usually constructed of stone or brick, although some vaults were built in wood (*see below*). Vaulted ceilings are a characteristic of MEDIEVAL ARCHITECTURE and of the nineteenth-century Gothic revival and are normally only found in cathedrals, major churches and in the smaller components of parish churches such as a chapel or porch. Begun in 1093, Durham Cathedral Priory was the first major church in England in which every element was vaulted in stone.

The shape of the vault follows the geometry of the ARCH and the simplest vault is, therefore, that which accompanies the semicircular arch. This is known as the *barrel vault* (also *tunnel vault* or *wagon vault*) and is commonly found in later Romanesque buildings. It is so named because of its semicircular section and barrel-like appearance. Where two barrel vaults intersect at right angles they form a *groined* or *cross vault*. Because of the enormous thrust exerted on supporting walls, the barrel vault was found to be singularly unsuited to wide spans, particularly in the monastic churches of western Europe, the components of which (nave, presbytery, transept and aisles) were usually of different heights and widths and could not be accommodated within a structure that was constrained by the geometry of the semicircular arch. Furthermore, the interior roofs of many early abbey churches were constructed of timber and were a considerable fire hazard. Consequently, it was the need for stone vaulting, combined with the structural limitations of the round arch, that led to the development in the early medieval period of the *ribbed vault* and pointed arch.

Ribs are raised bands of stone or brick that spring from the wall to support and strengthen the vault. The ribbed vault consisted of a quadripartite framework (bisected by diagonal ribs), supported during construction on a temporary timber structure (*centering*). Once the spaces between the ribs (*webs* or *cells*) had been infilled with cut stone pieces the vault became self-supporting and the centering was removed.

Vaults are divided into bays by *transverse arches* and, while bays created by semicircular arches were inevitably square, the diagonals of a ribbed vault were longer than the sides and it was therefore impossible for all the ribs to be semicircular (*see* BAY). This problem was overcome by adopting the pointed arch, which originated in the Middle East

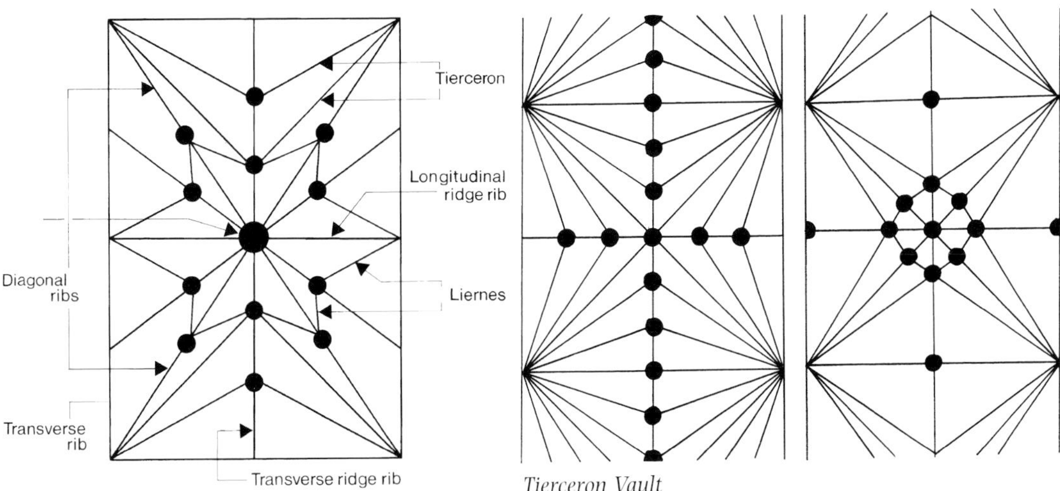

Tierceron Vault

(Courtesy of John Ferguson)

and, by the twelfth century, had already spread to countries such as Spain and Sicily where there was a strong north-African influence. The pointed arch was ideally suited to vaulting of various heights and spans and, during the four centuries of the Gothic period, it enabled buildings of increasing complexity and architectural audacity to be constructed throughout western Europe.

The early quadripartite ribbed vault, which consisted of four compartments within each bay, formed the basis for all future designs. Stone BOSSES were added at the intersections of the ribs, and these were often heavily carved with gilded and painted motifs. In the fourteenth century intermediate *tierceron ribs* were added which extended from the springing of the vault (the point at which it began to splay upwards) to the *ridge rib* (at the apex of the vault) and from this developed the *lierne vault* in which additional interlocking ribs (*liernes*) were introduced, forming elaborate patterns within the basic structural framework of ribs. A *stellar vault* is one in which the lierne ribs form a star-shaped pattern.

The final, Perpendicular phase of the Gothic period is characterised by *fan vaulting* which, as the name suggests, is an ornamental vaulting of inverted half-conoids (cones with concave sides). Each pair of half-conoids just meet at the centres of their curves, all the ribs are equidistant from each other and in many cases all have the same curvature. Each section of a fan vault was carved from a stone slab and the joints between the blocks may often be seen passing across the purely decorative tracery of the ribs. Fan vaulting was an English innovation, the earliest known example being in the chantry chapel of Edward, Lord Despenser at Tewkesbury Abbey in Gloucestershire. Despenser died in 1375 and it is likely that the same mason was responsible for the magnificent fan vaulting in the cloister at nearby Gloucester Cathedral which was completed not later than 1412. Fine examples of fan vaults are those at Sherborne Abbey in Dorset (1475–1500) and the chapel of King's College, Cambridge (1446–1515). However, it is the remarkable fan vault in the Chapel of Henry VII at Westminster Abbey (begun in 1503), with its extraordinarily flamboyant carved pendants, that is widely acknowledged to be 'the last great masterpiece of English medieval architecture' (see colour plate 7).

In England, only Westminster Abbey has a vault that that can begin to compare in height with those of European cathedrals: the vault of Notre Dame in Paris rises to a height of 33.5m (110ft), Rheims 38m (125ft), Amiens 42.7m (140ft) and Beauvais 47m (154ft). Westminster's vault, the loftiest in England, is 31m (102ft) above floor level, while the nave at Wells Cathedral rises to just 20m (67ft). In most great medieval churches, with the exception of those of the more austere monastic orders, vaulting would originally have been ablaze with brilliant colour and gilding. Although beyond the range of normal eyesight, the detail of carving and painting was faultlessly executed and was clearly intended for the greater glorification of God. It is only through the modern camera lens that we are privileged to approach such perfection for the first time.

There is a small number of wooden vaults (or, more correctly, ceilings) in major English churches, notably at Peterborough Cathedral, where the timber roof of the nave is decorated with remarkable paintings dating from *c.* 1220, and at Ely Cathedral Priory, where a timber panelled ceiling was added in the mid-nineteenth century by Sir George Gilbert Scott. This was designed and painted by Henry Styleman le Strange, an amateur artist who based his design on the painted ceiling at St Michael's church at Hildesheim, Germany. Le Strange died with only half the nave completed and the eastern bays were painted by his friend, Thomas Gambier Parry. Both men worked on their backs in appalling conditions and without ever being able to inspect their work from a distance. It would appear that in neither case did the original Norman builders intend to construct a stone vault – despite the massive dimensions of the nave arches.

(*See also* SCAFFOLDING AND CRANES)

Gothic vaulting: (top left) quadripartite ribs in the nave vault of Durham Cathedral, c. 1120; (top right) ribbed tierceron vault in the nave of Exeter Cathedral, 1353–69; (bottom left) lierne vault in the presbytery of Gloucester Cathedral, c. 1350; (bottom right) fan vaulting in the chapel of King's College, Cambridge, 1446–1515.

VEIL A headdress (*wimple*) worn by women at confirmation and marriage. Veils were worn by Roman matrons and from the third century were presented by bishops to consecrated virgins as a symbol of their spiritual marriage with Christ. Consequently, the veil became the most important element of a nun's habit – hence 'taking the veil' implied that a woman had obtained admission to a nunnery. Choir nuns, who were required to make a more solemn PROFESSION, were vested with a black veil, while lay sisters wore a white one.

VELLUM A superior form of PARCHMENT prepared by lime-washing and burnishing the skins of calves, kids or lambs. For the finest work, the skins of unborn or aborted animals were used.
See also MANUSCRIPT ILLUMINATION *and* SCRIPTORIUM

VENERABLE (i) In the medieval Church, a title bestowed on a deceased person during the process of beatification. Also used of those whose memory was considered to be worthy of veneration e.g. the Venerable Bede (*c.* 673–735).
(ii) The proper address of an archdeacon.

VENITE Psalm 95, so called from the first word of its Latin version: 'Venite, Exultemus Domino' ('O Come, let us sing unto the Lord . . .'). From the early sixth century the Venite was used in the first office of the day and from the BREVIARY it passed into Mattins in the *Book of Common Prayer*.

VERGER From the Latin *virga* meaning 'rod', an official responsible for carrying a *verge*, a mace or wand of office, before a dignitary. The term is now commonly applied to the person or persons who (in addition to their ceremonial duties) take care of the day-to-day management of a church.

VERSAL LETTER The embellished initial letter of a verse or paragraph of text (*see* LETTERING *and* MANUSCRIPT ILLUMINATION).

VERSICLES A versicle is a short sentence (e.g. from the psalms) which is said or sung antiphonally in a Roman Catholic or Anglican service, each half of a choir or congregation responding to the other (hence 'responses'). The two 'sides' of a choir are known as CANTORIS and DECANI. The traditional Anglican settings are the ancient PLAINSONG adapted by John Merbecke (1510–85) to the English words at the time of the Reformation. Various Elizabethan composers made 'harmonised' versions of the responses, a form now generally known as Festal Responses (*see* CHURCH MUSIC). In the absence of a choir, the responses are recited by the priest and congregation.
See also ANTIPHON, PRECES *and* STALLS

VERT *see* COLOURS (HERALDIC)

VESICA PISCIS In Christian art, a *vesica piscis* (literally, 'fish's bladder') is an almond-shaped halo, consisting of two arcs each passing through the other's centre, enclosing the body of Christ or that of the Blessed Virgin Mary.

VESPERALE (i) A cloth spread over the altar or communion table to protect the white linen altar cloths when not in use.
(ii) A liturgical book containing the psalms etc. used at VESPERS. Those of COMPLINE are usually appended.

VESPERS The Evening Office, which took place in the late afternoon between NONE and COMPLINE. It consisted of a hymn, two psalms, a New Testament CANTICLE, a short lesson, responsary, the Magnificat and prayers. With LAUDS, Vespers is the most important of the Day Offices and is of considerable antiquity. By the fifteenth century it was often attended by devout laity. The service of Evening prayer in the *Book of Common Prayer* was in part modelled on Vespers, with additions from COMPLINE.
See also DIVINE OFFICE, HOURS (CANONICAL), HORARIUM *and* VESPERALE

VESTIARIUM *see* VESTRY.

VESTIBULE An ante-chamber or entrance lobby next to the outer door of a church or monastic apartment. There was generally a vestibule to a CHAPTER HOUSE, and those that have survived are often of considerable architectural elaboration. The INFIRMARY usually had a vestibule and the head of the NIGHT STAIR may have been similarly enclosed.

VESTRY *or* REVESTRY The monastic vestry (*vestiarium*) contained the aumbries and chests for the storage of vestments which were the responsibility of the sacrist and his assistant, although in some larger houses there was also an official called a *vesterer*, who was charged with the care and maintenance of the vestments. It was here that ministers vested themselves according to their function (celebrant, deacon, priest, acolyte, etc.). The vestry was sometimes combined with the SACRISTY and was always located in close proximity to the church, to which it had direct access.

VICAR From the Latin *vicarius* meaning 'substitute' or 'deputy'. In the Middle Ages, many benefices were annexed by corporate bodies such as monastic or collegiate foundations which then received the Great (or Rectorial) Tithes, the Lesser (or Vicarial) Tithes going to a vicar who was appointed by them to administer the parish (*see* RECTOR). Following the DISSOLUTION OF THE MONASTERIES, many monastic estates became the impropriated property of laymen (lay rectors) who also acquired the right to nominate vicars (subject to a bishop's approval), together with responsibility for maintaining the chancel and vicarage.
See also APPROPRIATION *and* CLERGY (CHURCH OF ENGLAND)

VICAR GENERAL One who deputises for a bishop. In the early Church a bishop's authority could be delegated to an archdeacon but by the end of the thirteenth century the office of vicar general was established and its duties were defined. In the Church of England the office is usually committed to a diocesan chancellor.

VICARS CHORAL Today the vicars choral are adult male singers in the choirs of secular cathedrals of the 'old foundation' (*see* CATHEDRALS), although at York Minster they are traditionally known as *Song Men*. At other cathedrals the male members of choirs are usually described as *lay clerks*.

The word 'vicar' (which means 'deputy') indicates that the duties are those of a canon, exercised vicariously. Indeed, at one time, every canon could call upon the services of a vicar choral to act as his deputy. The office, as it now exists, originated in the Reformation, but in the medieval church all these various 'clerks' and 'vicars' were in holy orders.

Vicars choral were often provided with their own accommodation. To the south-east of the chapter house garden at Hereford Cathedral is the Cloister of the College of Vicars Choral, a quadrangle of fifteenth-century maisonettes that once housed the priests who sang in the cathedral choir. The vicars choral moved into their newly built college in 1472 for their own protection – apparently the streets of Hereford were overrun with brigands and the journey from their quarters outside the cathedral precinct was considered to be too dangerous (*see* CLOISTER).

The Vicars Close at Wells Cathedral is a delightful cul-de-sac of terraced lodgings, built in 1348 with its own chapel, refectory, exchequer and muniment room, to which a library was added in the fifteenth century. Originally there were forty-two small dwellings, but after the Reformation the gentlemen were permitted to marry and many of the houses were amalgamated to provide accommodation for their families. Apparently, the close was once a quadrangle which (it is claimed) provided a model for the university colleges at Oxford and Cambridge. The close is linked to the cathedral by a covered bridge, built in the mid-fifteenth century to provide protection at night and shelter during inclement weather (*see* colour plate 8).

The Vicars Close at Wells Cathedral. (Fred Musto/Mary Evans Picture Library)

The gate to the bridge is known as the Chain Gate, from the chains that at one time secured the entrance. The chapter of Wells, as originally constituted, consisted of fifty canon prebendaries (*see* PREBENDARY), a very large number, not all of whom were always present to undertake their cathedral duties. For this reason, a College of Vicars Choral was constituted to provide canonical deputies. The College was a corporate body with its own statutes and common seal and was granted estates, the income from which made it self-supporting. All vicars were required to be in choir daily for observance of the masses and the greater hours, six a side being the minimum required for the lesser hours (*see* HOURS (CANONICAL)). By the Cathedral Measures Act of 1931 all the corporate rights and freeholds were dissolved. The Vicars' chapel, hall and other possessions were transferred to the Dean and Chapter 'in particular for the use and benefit of the Vicars' and their houses passed to the Church Commissioners, although they remained the College of Vicars of the Cathedral Church of St Andrew in Wells, their number being fixed at no fewer than nine lay vicars and two priest vicars.
See also CHURCH MUSIC

VICE A small turning stair or 'turnpike' within the masonry of a wall or tower.

VICTORINES An order of canons regular founded in 1113 at the former abbey of St Victor at Paris. Their English houses included Wigmore in Herefordshire and the great abbey of St Augustine in Bristol which was reconstituted as a cathedral in 1542.

VIGIL A nocturnal act of prayer and devotion, either private or liturgical, often ending with the EUCHARIST. In the early Church, the Easter vigil lasted throughout the night while those which preceded Sundays and other festivals normally occupied only the beginning and end of the night. From these observances evolved the offices of VESPERS, MATTINS and LAUDS (mattins was originally called *vigils*). Eventually, fast, office and mass were anticipated and moved to the morning of the preceding day, the whole of which became a '*profestum*'. It is for this reason that Easter Eve, Christmas Eve, All Hallows Eve, etc. were of such importance in the medieval liturgical calendar.

VIKINGS, THE *see* ANGLO-SAXON CHURCH

VINEYARDS A favourable climate encouraged viticulture in southern England and the south Midlands from the eleventh century. Writing in *c.* 1123, William of Malmesbury stated that no other English shire had more vineyards than Gloucestershire and that wines from the Vale of Gloucester were hardly inferior to those of France. Most vineyards were on monastic estates, on well-drained south or south-east facing slopes, sheltered from cold north winds and from prevailing south-westerlies. Vines were grown further north, but for unripe grapes used for culinary purposes (*verjuice*) rather than for wine. The earliest English vineyards seem to date from a sustained period of clement weather in the eleventh and twelfth centuries and there is little evidence to support the popular notion that the Romans grew grapes during their occupation of Britain. Not much remains of the vineyards that once supplied the monastic communities with their wine: one of the four gates to the extensive precinct at Bury St Edmunds gave access to a vineyard and at Evesham the slopes may still be identified.

See also FARMING *and* WINE

VISCERAL TOMB A tomb containing the internal organs of the body. Eleanor of Castile, queen and wife of Edward I, died at Harby in Nottinghamshire on 29 November 1290. Her body was taken to London for burial at Westminster and her heart was interred at Blackfriars. However, her internal organs were buried in a visceral tomb at Lincoln Cathedral.

VISITATION (ECCLESIASTICAL) Episcopal visitations, periodic inspections of the temporal and spiritual affairs of dioceses, were first conducted in the sixth century and were regulated by ecclesiastical councils. From these a system of ecclesiastical visitations developed whereby bishops made three- or four-yearly inspections of their dioceses and archdeacons conducted annual inspections. The records of the visitations of bishops and archdeacons (or of their deputies), although not numerous until the mid-sixteenth century, are nevertheless an invaluable source of information. By the sixteenth century, the system of ecclesiastical visitations had become very much more complex and was used to enforce religious change and conformity.

Normally, religious houses were visited by the bishop in whose diocese they were situated. It was the bishop, therefore, who exercised the ultimate authority – subject always to appeal to the pope. However, many monasteries were exempted from diocesan control: the Benedictine houses of Bury St Edmunds, St Albans and Westminster, for example, all claimed exemption and were subject only to papal authority. The houses of the Cistercian, Cluniac, Gilbertine and Premonstratensian orders came under the jurisdiction of their mother houses, who appointed visitors to conduct regular inquiries (*see* CHAPTER HOUSE). Similarly, in the thirteenth century the houses of the international mendicant orders (*see* FRIARS) were inspected by visitors appointed by the governing councils of their orders.

VOTIVE CROSSES Small rudimentary crosses, scratched in stonework or on a church door, to commemorate the making of a vow.

VOTIVE LIGHT *see* CANDLES

VOUSSOIR *see* ARCH

VOWESS (*also* AVOWESS) A widow who has avowed to live a life of chastity and obedience to God's will but has not necessarily entered a religious community. Female figures in EFFIGIES and BRASSES are often dressed in the simple white widow's veil and wimple, sideless cotehardie and kirtle of a vowess, although many have also retained the symbols of their rank – the ducal coronet of a duchess, for example.

VOWS All religious were bound by vows of poverty, chastity and obedience. Poverty was not merely the abandonment of personal possessions, it involved also the renunciation of 'worldliness' and the individual will: all activities were undertaken communally, personal preferences were of no consequence and idiosyncrasies unsustainable. Chastity implied not only total sexual abstinence but also the diversion of energy away from 'licentious thoughts' and into God's work. Obedience was the opposite of egocentricity, an antidote to the temptations of the Devil, particularly the sin of pride, which was considered to be the most corrupting of the Seven Deadly Sins. The vows were made explicit by the RULE of a particular order and by the customaries of an individual house (*see* CUSTOMARY). They were symbolised by the three knots in a monk's girdle.

Once professed 'before the High Altar in the presence of all the community' (*see* NOVICE), the vows were irrevocable, although there were occasional dispensations (the PECULIUM and in the INFIRMARY, for example) and monastic superiors were often obliged to stretch the vow of poverty to its limit when fulfilling their responsibilities as ecclesiastical magnates (*see* SUPERIOR'S LODGINGS). St Benedict's original vows included a fourth, *stabilitas* ('stability' or, more accurately, 'perseverance'), by which a monk was obliged to remain for life in the house to which he was professed.

WAGES *see* PECULIUM

WAGON VAULT *see* VAULTING

WALES, THE MEDIEVAL CHURCH IN The ASCETICISM of St David who, according to his biographer Rhygyfarch, 'imitated the monks of Egypt and lived a life like theirs', was far removed from the self-indulgent hereditary canons of the twelfth-century Welsh *clasau* (*see* CLAS). Many of the monk-bishops of these ancient mother churches, once the instruments of Christian conversion, had become preoccupied with protecting their property and influence. To the Normans, the *clas* with its wooden huts, its married priests and hereditary offices was a singularly corrupt and archaic institution. Furthermore, although the Welsh had accepted the Roman Easter in 768, in almost all other matters they had remained faithful to the practices of the CELTIC CHURCH. To enthusiastic reformers, whose objective was uniformity of organisation, ritual and discipline throughout Christendom, the eccentricities of the Welsh Church were abhorrent. There were no stone churches (a particular cause of Norman contempt) and no monasteries following the RULE of St Benedict, the most powerful of the influences that united Latin Europe. What they found was a fossilised church, badly in need of rejuvenation, and they set about the task of reform with typical Norman insensitivity.

The Bishops

The reformers' first objective was to gain control of the dioceses and thereby to bring the Church in Wales within the jurisdiction of the archdiocese of Canterbury and subject it to Canon Law. Before the

Conquest, each of the early kingdoms probably had its own bishop (seven bishops' houses were recorded in Dyfed), but as the kingdoms united so the number of Welsh bishoprics decreased until only three remained: those of Gwynedd, Deheubarth and Glamorgan with *cathedra* at Bangor, St David's and Llandaf. The functions of the Welsh bishops were essentially those of their European fellows, but the organisation of their cathedrals was irregular and their diocesan boundaries indeterminate. In 1092 a Norman bishop was installed at Bangor, in 1107 at Llandaf, in 1115 at St David's and in 1143 at (the newly created) St Asaph.

In the twelfth century, diocesan and parochial boundaries began to be defined, a system of TITHES was introduced and, by the end of the thirteenth century, a judicial and administrative organisation had been established. The work was begun by Urban, bishop of Glamorgan from 1107 to 1134, the first of the Norman bishops of Wales to swear an oath of allegiance to the Archbishop of Canterbury. Anxious to keep Church property out of the hands of the rapacious Norman knights, Urban organised his diocese on the pattern of the Latin Church: he appointed a dean at his cathedral of Llandaf and divided the Vale of Glamorgan into small parishes.

At St David's there was a growing demand that the diocese should be elevated into an archbishopric with authority over all the dioceses of Wales. It was argued that St David himself had been an archbishop (although there is no evidence to suggest that the Celtic Church recognised such an office) and that the papacy had already endorsed the principle that every nation should have at least one archbishopric. Bishop Bernard's abortive struggle to promote St David's (and to elevate himself) occupied the last twenty years of his life. He died in 1148, but the issue did not die with him. It was raised again in 1176 and 1179 and at the end of the century Giraldus Cambrensis (1146–1223) campaigned vigorously (but without success) for the elevation of his beloved Church of St David.

The Benedictines

At the same time, the Norman establishment stripped most of the *clasau* of their revenues, transferring them to English monasteries or using the endowments to support new monastic communities, thereby securing control over the property of the Welsh Church. Sheltered by the invaders' fortresses, these Benedictine communities were often superior to those they replaced for Norman monasticism itself had only recently been reformed. But the imported French-speaking monks were distrustful of the 'shaggy and wild-eyed' Welsh and concerned themselves more with the spiritual welfare of the Norman garrisons than with that of the indigenous population. In 1141 Abbot Gilbert of Gloucester urged the Benedictine community of Ewenny to surround its house with 'a good ditch and an impregnable wall'. By 1150 there were seventeen Benedictine houses in Wales, dependent cells or priories of some of the foremost monasteries of France and England. Chepstow, for example, belonged to the abbey of Cormeilles and Brecon was a dependency of Battle Abbey in Sussex.

The Augustinian Canons

During the eleventh century papal reforms had hardly penetrated Wales, but the situation was very different after 1100. Initially, the issue had concerned the royal control of episcopal appointments, but once this had been resolved the reformers turned their attention to the localities and to the care of parish churches which, in many instances, continued to be treated by landowners as private properties. It was determined that these were best entrusted to the care of regular canons, communities of priests who lived by the rule of St Augustine (*see* AUGUSTINIANS). It was at Llanthony Priory, deep in the Black Mountains of Monmouthsire, that the first of these new communities was established between 1108 and 1118. Other Anglo-Norman Augustinian priories followed at Carmarthen (before 1127) and Haverfordwest (before 1200). In many respects, the

Augustinian houses were not so very different from the Celtic *clasau*; indeed, when the *clasau* of Penmon, Beddgelert and Aberdaron perceived a need for greater integration within the Latin Church they adopted the Augustinian Rule.

The Cistercians

The Benedictines were not the only monastic order in Wales. A Tironian house had been founded at St Dogmaels in 1115 (*see* TIRONIANS) and this was followed by Savigniac houses at Neath (1130) and Basingwerk (1131) and an early Cistercian community at Tintern (1131) (*see* SAVIGNIAC ORDER). The Savigniacs were later integrated into the Cistercian Order, the brethren of which lived a sequestered communal life: 'we will follow the rule in all that pertains to the common life so that we will eat, sleep, work and perform the services of God together . . . [but] we will live as hermits in all that concerns rigorous abstinence and the total renunciation of secular concerns' (*see* CISTERCIANS).

The next Cistercian communities to reach Wales were those of Whitland (1140) and Margam (1147), both daughter houses of the Abbey of Clairvaux. After initial failures, Whitland succeeded in founding a colony at Strata Florida (Powys) which, under the patronage of the Lord Rhys (d. 1197), became the mausoleum of the princes of Deheubarth. Whitland itself was the 'stem of a new tree' and its daughter houses included Aberconwy (Gwynedd), where Llywelyn I ('the Great') was buried in 1240, and Cwmhir (Powys), the resting place of Llywelyn II, the first and only native Prince of Wales (d. 1282). Although Whitland had been founded as the result of Norman patronage, all Cistercians houses were answerable to the head of the Order at Cîteaux in Burgundy and were therefore not directly influenced by the power of the English kings. Furthermore, to the Welsh, the Cistercian rule seemed almost a re-embodiment of the principles of the ancient (and uncorrupted) Celtic Church:

> For they showed forth the discipline of Clairvaux whence they came, and by works of piety they spread the sweet savour of their mother-abbey, as it were, a strong perfume from their own house. The story spread everywhere that men of outstanding holiness and perfect religion had come from a far land; that by their virtues they had glorified the monastic name. Many were therefore moved to emulate them by joining this company whose hearts had been touched by God. Thus very soon they grew into a great company . . .

Little wonder that every Welsh ruler sought to establish a Cistercian house within his territories and that the White Monks were held in such high regard by the Welsh people.

The Late Middle Ages

The half century that followed the Edwardian conquest of Wales (1282) is considered to be something of a golden age. In 1284 archbishop John Pecham, anxious to protect the interests of the Welsh Church and to foster the allegiance of the Welsh clergy, instituted a thorough investigation of the church in Wales. He visited the four bishoprics and published a series of edicts for their reform, he rebuked both the monks and the clergy for their dissolute way of life and castigated those who would seek to incite the populace by glorifying the ancestry of the Welsh. Despite the archbishop's admonitions, the Welsh Church was well served by its bishops, most of whom were Welshmen or men with Welsh connections. They

Opposite: *The Cistercian abbey of Valle Crucis, founded in 1201 by Madog ap Gruffudd Maelor, prince of northern Powys (Powys Fadog).* (Courtesy of Roy Morgan)

were also men of ability and energy who were chiefly responsible for consolidating the administrative and parochial framework of the Church, for promoting devotional prose and poetry in the Welsh language, and for the construction of a number of notable ecclesiastical buildings, including the choir of St David's cathedral and the completion of the magnificent Bishop's Palace.

There is very little evidence to suggest that at this time the Welsh clergy were critical of the system that had been imposed upon them. And yet, by the beginning of the fourteenth century, the Church in Wales was entirely under the control of the English crown. From 1294 it was taxed for the first time and there was a growing tendency for the king to reward his English officials with profitable benefices in Wales.

From 1350 there was a significant decline in the fortunes of the Welsh Church as a result of intellectual fatigue and economic depression. Indeed, the entire country was debilitated by recurring outbreaks of the PLAGUE and constant pressure from the English Crown for resources to finance the French wars. Throughout Europe, the Church was divided: the papacy had become little more than another state, greedy for power and wealth, and between 1379 and 1417 there were competing popes in Rome and Avignon. There was a dramatic fall in admissions to the monastic orders and no new orders were created which might have revitalised the spiritual life of the Church. As a consequence, clerics were preoccupied with safeguarding their incomes in the face of depression, while the monastic houses began leasing their lands and impropriating benefices in order to profit from parochial tithes. Ecclesiastical appointments were made for political reasons: most of the more lucrative Welsh benefices were filled by Englishmen and the Welsh bishoprics were used as pawns in the contest between the pope and the Prince of Wales, so that able Welsh clerics could no longer expect promotion in their own country. Although not as impoverished as some historians would have us believe, the ecclesiastical institutions of Wales were poor by comparison with those of England. The combined income of the three least-endowed Welsh dioceses was less than that of the poorest English diocese, while the total wealth of the Welsh religious houses could not equal that of Glastonbury Abbey in Somerset.

The Reformation

The Welsh had no representation in the English parliament and they were therefore denied an opportunity to express a view concerning the measures which terminated the link with Rome (*see* REFORMATION, THE). In 1534, Rowland Lee, the bishop of Lichfield, was appointed president of the Council of Wales and he initiated what has accurately been described as a reign of terror, intended to suppress lawlessness and to remind the Welsh of their subservience to the English Crown. His strategy appears to have succeeded because, unlike the men of Yorkshire and Cornwall, the Welsh showed no inclination to challenge the power of the Tudor reformers through armed insurrection. Nevertheless, Wales was a conservative country and it is unlikely that the legislation was welcome. It was not until 1549, when fundamental changes were imposed on the parish churches, that the implication of the religious changes had any real impact on the Welsh people.

As a consequence of the DISSOLUTION OF THE MONASTERIES all but three of the major Welsh religious houses were dissolved, an appalling loss, although by that time the intellectual climate had, for a century or more, become increasingly hostile to the monastic ideal. At the Dissolution, the thirteen Cistercian monasteries of Wales had a total establishment of only eighty-five monks and the Augustinian and Benedictine houses were even emptier. The monasteries were dissolved not because of their weakness, but because of their wealth. According to the *Valor ecclesiasticus*, the combined income of the Welsh houses was only £3,178, even though the Church owned as much as a quarter of the land in Wales. But, as has been

In 1648, parliamentary soldiers were dispatched to strip the roof of St David's Cathedral of lead. They burned what remained of the medieval library, destroyed the organ and bells, smashed the stained glass and tore up tomb brasses. As a consequence, the east end of the cathedral, stripped of its lead, fell into decay and remained without a roof for over two centuries.

seen, much of this land had already been leased by gentry families, often on long leases, which were confirmed at the time of the Dissolution. Thus the monastic lands passed not to the Crown, but into the absolute possession of the gentry. Similarly, in Wales a high proportion of the ecclesiastical benefices which had been appropriated by the monasteries passed into the ownership of lay rectors, where they remained impropriate until the disestablishment of the Welsh Church in 1920.

In 1563 the bishops of Wales and of Hereford were commanded to ensure that Welsh translations of the Bible and the *Book of Common Prayer* would be available in every parish church in Wales by St David's Day 1567 and that services were to be conducted in Welsh in those parishes where the language was in general use. At the close of the sixteenth century the notion that Protestantism was 'the English religion' had almost faded, thanks to a belief, widely disseminated at the time, that the Celtic church had been a truly Protestant church, the purity of which had been defiled by the Romish practices of Augustine and his successors. The Welsh were returning to the faith of their forefathers: a theory which served the English reformers admirably.

See also ANGLO-SAXON CHURCH *and* MEDIEVAL CHURCH

WALKING PLACE In the churches of the mendicant orders (*see* FRIARS), a passage formed by crosswalls between the nave and choir.

WALL MONUMENTS A mid-sixteenth-century development of the canopied TOMB CHEST, the wall monument was either secured to the wall (*hanging wall monument*) or supported at ground level (*standing wall monument*). Some wall monuments are quite bizarre: the seventeenth-century Allestry monument in Derby cathedral, for example, which contains a miniature coffin. Modest versions of the wall monument are often described as *wall tablets* or *memorial tablets*: small stone panels in a variety of shapes engraved with commemorative INSCRIPTIONS.

MONUMENTS, and the inscriptions engraved thereon, are an invaluable source of information concerning a church and its community (*see also* EPITAPHS). They can tell us about contemporary artistic styles and fashions and about local society: its fluctuating economic fortunes, its social conventions and its religious observances. They can tell us about individuals and their families: how they lived, what they looked like, how they died and how they wished to be remembered by later generations. And, by interpreting the HERALDRY in a memorial, we may trace a family's genealogy and establish its position in society.

Sixteenth Century

From *c.* 1550 the style and decoration of wall monuments followed that of the canopied tomb chest with rather stiff EFFIGIES in recumbent, kneeling or reclining postures or demi-figures. Renaissance forms and decoration superseded Gothic and were characterised by the use of STRAPWORK, ribbonwork, grotesques, allegorical figures, cherub-heads and so on. Heraldry is much in evidence and was usually concentrated in the CANOPY during the sixteenth and seventeenth centuries (in the eighteenth century the canopy was abandoned or reduced to an ornamental form rather than an architectural structure).

Seventeenth Century

In the early seventeenth century the Classical style was more refined, especially in the use of pediments on architectural canopies and frames. White and black MARBLE was popular, as was ALABASTER. Figures were more finely carved and were depicted in a variety of more natural poses, usually in contemporary dress, although Roman armour was popular from *c.* 1660. Pedestal busts were introduced at this time, as were medallion portraits, which were carved in relief. From *c.* 1660 marble replaced alabaster, especially in Baroque monuments, and recumbent or kneeling figures became increasingly rare. Allegorical figures, especially the Virtues, were common, as were symbols of mortality.

Cartouche tablets were particularly popular in the seventeenth and eighteenth centuries. These were usually made of marble and have the appearance of a sheet of paper with the sides curled up. Typically, the central section contains an inscription and, above it, a coat of arms or crest.

Eighteenth Century

By *c.* 1750 architectural canopies were no longer fashionable, and throughout the eighteenth century wall monuments varied considerably both in size and style. Indeed, some are so large and ostentatious that they appear grotesquely out of place in a medieval church. Figures are often dressed as Romans, either in armour or in loosely wrapped toga-like garments, and recline against an urn or on a sarcophagus. Recumbent and kneeling effigies are rare. Many monuments of the period are finely carved with rococo decoration, while small portrait medallions, busts, putti, urns, cartouches and symbols of mortality are ubiquitous. Heraldry remained an important although subdued element of design, with a shield or cartouche above or at the base, the arms being the only element of colour in the monument other than coloured marbles. When the deceased had enjoyed a military or naval career, or had been a prominent churchman, the monument was often flanked by guns, flags, a CROZIER or other appropriate devices.

Wall tablets in the north aisle of Bath Abbey, Somerset. (Courtesy of John Mennell)

Elegant, neo-classical black and white tablets characterised the period 1780 to 1840 and were a reaction against the flamboyance of earlier baroque and rococo monuments which recited the virtues of the deceased both in their architectural and sculptural ostentation and in the banality of their inscriptions. In these tablets a panel of white marble, usually a scroll or SARCOPHAGUS bearing a dignified inscription, is set against a background of black marble, with sculpture in shallow relief. The tablet may be oval, rectangular or shield-shaped, and surmounted by a draped urn, a broken column, a TREE OF LIFE or a figure of grief with a bowed head. The *stele* design, a rectangular slab surmounted by a low, triangular pediment, was particularly popular. Tablets were comparatively inexpensive and enabled all and sundry to elbow their way into posterity, often at the expense of architectural good taste: at Bath Abbey, for example, where the aisle walls are encrusted with tablets dating from the eighteenth and nineteenth centuries. During this period, heraldry in wall monuments was often restricted to a crest or was omitted entirely. Perversely, this coincided with the increasing popularity of funeral HATCHMENTS.

Nineteenth Century

The restrained neo-classicism of the late eighteenth century continued into the early nineteenth. Black and white marble was still popular (white increasingly so) and figures of mourning females, leaning over an urn or sarcophagus, were especially common. So too were angels, often depicted receiving the deceased, and symbolism such as opium poppies (the sleep of death) and a sickle cutting a rosebud (death taking a child). Costume is mostly contemporary, while military and naval figures may wear uniform. Inevitably, in the larger, standing wall monuments of the Victorian period there was a significant increase in the use of alabaster and a revival of Gothic features, such as canopies, tomb chests and recumbent effigies.

The Victorians were especially fond of brass wall plates, engraved and enamelled with 'Gothic' lettering, while the wall tablets of the late nineteenth and twentieth centuries are for the most part restrained and unobtrusive and may contain carved and painted coats of arms and finely carved inscriptions.

See also MEMORIAL

WALL PAINTINGS In the Middle Ages the interiors of churches would have been very different from the quiet, sober places they are today. Then, they were like immense picture books of painted plaster intended for the edification of the illiterate and designed to inspire fear and obedience. The walls of most pre-Reformation churches were covered with murals, depicting not only the lives of the saints and scenes from the scriptures, but also terrifying images of the inevitability of death and of divine judgment and retribution. Medieval wall paintings tell us much about popular theology and the basic teaching of the medieval Church.

In 604 St Gregory the Great declared that the walls of churches were to be the *biblia pauperum*, the Bible of the poor, and throughout the Middle Ages murals were considered to be the normal finish for church walls – except in the churches of the more austere monastic and secular orders, where the practice was strictly limited. Professional itinerant painters travelled from church to church working on newly plastered walls, wetted with limewater and smoothed with lime putty (stiff slaked lime), using inexpensive natural colours ground and tempered with limewater or skimmed milk. Delicate work often required the use of pigments and size. Pigments included iron oxides (which produced reds, browns, yellows and purple), lamp-black (candle soot), malachite (the green carbonate of copper), azurite (the blue carbonate of copper) and lime putty for white. For high quality work, such as the murals in the chapel of the Holy Sepulchre at Winchester (*see* below), more expensive materials were required: at that time a small quantity of imported ultramarine (obtained from lapis lazuli) was six times more expensive than gold. Squirrel hair (from the tail) was used for the finer brushes and hog's hair for others, and the pigment was often worked from scallop shells.

Most surviving paintings have been revealed in the past 150 years, although many others were unwittingly destroyed during Victorian restorations. Most lay forgotten beneath layers of whitewash (*albacio*), applied after 1547, when the government ordered the 'obliteration' of 'popish and superstitious' images, and in 1644, when, during the Civil War, the parliamentary authorities appointed a Commissioner for the Destruction of Images. Ironically, the coatings of whitewash may have assisted in the paintings' preservation. But it should not be forgotten that, in the late Middle Ages, as the number and size of windows increased, so available wall space was reduced; the insertion of new windows (and the enlarging of existing ones) resulted in the destruction of many earlier paintings. The later iconoclasts should not take all the blame.

In the cathedrals, there are substantial survivals at St Albans and fragments at Durham and Norwich, while the superb late twelfth-century paintings in the chapel of the Holy Sepulchre at Winchester Cathedral Priory were uncovered during conservation work in 1963. They depict Christ's body being taken down from the cross and his entombment, and a Byzantine influence is evident in the pathos of the imagery. The Winchester paintings provide an impressive illustration of the colour and decoration of twelfth-century church interiors and, of course, the considerable expense that could be incurred when a tour de force was required rather than a journeyman's painting.

An indication of how the Cistercian aversion to decoration had been relaxed by the late Middle Ages may be seen at Cleeve Abbey in Somerset, where a large, fifteenth-century wall painting depicts a scene from the *Gesta Romanorum*. This shows a double-arched bridge over a river, with fish and eels swimming in the water. At the centre of the bridge is a richly dressed old man at prayer. He is flanked by a lion and a horned dragon and accompanied by a pair of angels bearing the scourge and crown of thorns – instruments of Christ's Passion. On the left is a figure of St Catherine holding a wheel, the symbol of her martyrdom, and on the right is the figure of

Twelfth-century wall painting in the chapel of the Holy Sepulchre, Winchester Cathedral Priory, depicting the deposition and entombment of Christ. (© John Crook/info@john-crook.com)

St Margaret suppressing a dragon with her staff. Also at Cleeve is a charming example of medieval graffiti – the head of a tonsured monk and the name 'Thomas'.

WARD (i) A minor in the care of a guardian or court.
(ii) The notches of a key designed to prevent duplication.
(iii) An enclosed yard.

WARDEN (i) The superior of a collegiate or other quasi-monastic foundation such as an almshouse or hospital (*see* ALMSHOUSES *and* HOSPITALS). The warden of such an institution was usually a priest, but could be a layman. Other titles include custos, keeper, master, prior and rector. The vicar of the collegiate church of St Peter at Ruthin in Clwyd has been addressed as 'Warden' since the fourteenth century when a small community of priests first occupied the solid two-storey claustral buildings which still stand today. The warden lived in the cloister until 1954 – as did the church organist.
(ii) The superior responsible for a regional division (*custody*) of the Franciscan Order (*see* FRIARS).

WARMING HOUSE *see* CALEFACTORIUM

WASHING Washing was required at daybreak (before PRIME), before dinner (*see* FRATER) and after NONE. This usually took place in the LAVATORIUM or in the INFIRMARY, although there were also facilities for washing in the GUEST HOUSE and the SUPERIOR'S LODGINGS.
See also PLUMBING, WATER SUPPLY AND SANITATION

WATCHING LOFT An elevated observation post from which a SANCTUARY or shrine could be observed in order to prevent SACRILEGE or theft (*see* SHRINES). A rare example has survived at the former Benedictine church of St Albans, while at Worcester Cathedral there is an ORIEL above the choir which probably served a similar purpose. By the thirteenth century, the monks at the Cluniac priory of Thetford were able to rebuild the east end of their church to accommodate a statue of the Blessed Virgin Mary whose miraculous powers had enabled the priory to grow rich from the alms of pilgrims seeking cures. But rather than provide a LADY CHAPEL in its usual position to the east of the sanctuary, they built it to the north. This enabled them to control the flow of pilgrims who were observed from a watching loft entered by a spiral staircase at the west end of the chapel.

WATER *see* HOLY WATER *and* PLUMBING, WATER SUPPLY AND SANITATION

WEBS *see* VAULTING

WEEPERS Small stone or bronze figures set in the sides of tomb chests (*see* TOMB CHEST) and other MONUMENTS as symbols of perpetual mourning. Weepers first appeared on tombs towards the end of the thirteenth century and remained popular throughout the medieval, Tudor and Jacobean periods. They usually represent a dead man's grieving family and on medieval tombs may include members of eminent and magnate families with whom the deceased was related by inheritance or marriage. Individuals may sometimes be identified by small shields of arms placed beneath or between the niches in which they stand.

Medieval weepers were finely carved, dignified figures, cloaked and hooded, their heads bowed and their hands clasped in supplication. Figures of angels were also popular from the late fourteenth century and saints in the fifteenth. Angels may be winged or clothed in albs and they often hold shields painted with coats of arms or Christian symbols.

Elizabethan and Jacobean weepers are often crude by comparison (although there are some notable exceptions) and were sometimes painted in the form of a frieze on the front or sides of a monument. These weepers were usually separated

The shrine of St Alban and elevated watching loft at St Albans Abbey, Hertfordshire.

into two groups of figures, one of sons (kneeling in descending order of age behind their father) and the other of daughters (similarly kneeling behind their mother, who may hold an infant). Quite often there is a babe or two in swaddling-clothes (*chrisom-cloths*) bringing up the rear and it has been suggested that these represent children who died in infancy. However, the usual custom was for those who had predeceased their parents to carry a skull.

WELDON STONE A creamy, easily cut stone quarried in Northamptonshire.

WELLS *see* PLUMBING, WATER SUPPLY AND SANITATION

WELSH RECORDS The National Library of Wales at Aberystwyth contains court records, diocesan archives and other material relating to the Welsh Church. The Royal Commission on the Ancient and Historical Monuments of Wales has an extensive collection of plans, illustrations and photographs, while the National Museum of Wales has a substantial print and photographic archive. *For* addresses *see* APPENDIX II

WEST DOORWAY *see* DOORWAYS

WEST FRONT The western façades of Cistercian churches, and those of the other more ascetic orders, were usually comparatively austere in appearance, comprising a ceremonial doorway beneath a single large window or triple lancets and often a GALILEE porch (a characteristic Cistercian feature). Elsewhere, the west fronts of the great abbeys and cathedrals were less restrained. Where the west fronts of contemporary French churches combined large portals and tall TOWERS to emphasise their height, in England the emphasis was on width. West fronts were intended to emphasise the size and grandeur of a church by forming a broad decorative screen that extended beyond the nave and aisles within. The west façade was the public face of a major religious establishment, its architecture declaring both God's omnipotence and the power and authority of the Church. And while the laity was usually admitted through a north door at the western end of the NAVE (*see* PORCHES), it was through the great west door that PROCESSIONS entered the church, the architecture of the west front providing an often spectacular setting for the ceremonial that was enacted before it.

In its simplest form, this type of screen façade, with its central doorway and radiating wedge-shaped stones (*voussoirs*) forming an arch, originated in Aquitaine, which came under English control in the reign of Henry II (1154–89). Typical of the period, the ruined west front of the Norman church of St Botolph's Priory at Colchester comprises two tiers of blind arcading above three simple, semicircular arched doorways, the central one being higher than those at the sides. There is a similar, although more ornate and refined, arrangement in the west front of the twelfth-century church of the Cluniac priory at Castle Acre, Norfolk. Here there are four tiers of richly decorative blind arcading and, whereas Roman bricks were reused for the arches and doorways at Colchester, the ASHLAR used at Castle Acre allowed for more complex and accurately defined ornamentation (*see* colour plate 5).

The west front of Southwell Minster, Nottinghamshire, completed in 1140, is one of the best-preserved Romanesque façades. With its pair of plain but well-proportioned square towers flanking a fine ceremonial doorway, it is closer to its continental contemporaries than the broad west fronts that were favoured in Britain. Unfortunately, a tall Perpendicular window was inserted above the doorway in the fifteenth century, a somewhat incongruous element in an otherwise pleasing façade. Precisely what sort of windows it replaced is unclear, although it is likely that there would have been several tiers of small openings. The short, pyramidal, timber and lead spires on the towers were replaced in 1880. Of the same period, but of significantly greater ingenuity and beauty, the great, six-ordered arched recess above the west door of Tewkesbury Abbey rises to a height of 20m (65ft) and is flanked by a pair of turrets (it is likely that flanking towers were originally intended). Built in 1150, the arch was originally filled by a window, but this collapsed and was replaced by the present Perpendicular one in 1686. The west front of Hereford Cathedral was one of the finest Romanesque façades in England. However, on Easter Monday 1786 the large, fourteenth-century west tower collapsed, destroying the entire west end of the cathedral. James Wyatt (1746–1813) was commissioned to carry out the repairs and designed a new west front and in so doing shortened the nave by one bay. But Wyatt's plain west front was never popular and it was replaced in 1908 by the present, rather vulgar, Edwardian creation by John Oldrid Scott. To save money, no attempt was made to rebuild Hereford's west tower.

Although the west façade at Ely Cathedral Priory is incomplete and has later additions, in its original form it was extraordinarily ambitious, especially in its scale and the complexity of its blind arcading. A pair of transepts, with a single west tower rising between them, formed a west front of considerable width and architectural inventiveness. In the thirteenth century a large, three-storey galilee porch was added in front of the tower, while the north-west transept collapsed in the fifteenth century and, regrettably, was never rebuilt – giving the façade a disconcertingly lopsided appearance.

The elegant west front of Southwell Minster, Nottinghamshire, completed in 1140. (© John Crook/info@john-crook.com)

The early thirteenth-century west front at Wells Cathedral, the towers of which were extended upwards in the late fourteenth and early fifteenth centuries, was originally embellished with nearly four hundred statues in traceried niches. Of these, nearly three hundred have survived, 150 of them life size or larger. Measuring nearly 45m (147ft) in width, the west front extends far beyond the nave aisles and is one of the masterpieces of English Gothic architecture – an immense outdoor reredos containing one of the greatest collections of statuary anywhere in Europe. When the cathedral was dedicated in 1239 the entire surface of the west front would have been whitewashed and lined out in red to represent ashlar blocks, while the statues and architectural detail would have been brightly coloured and gilded. To those of us who admire worn and mellow stone, such a colourful display would appear singularly garish, but in the Middle Ages it served its purpose. Fortunately, at Wells the deep buttressing and arcades cast strong shadows so that it does not have the flat appearance of other west fronts, such as those at Southwell and Winchester. There are several clearly defined horizontal tiers that are carried round three faces of the towers. In the lowest of these are depicted the prophets and angels (of which few statues have survived) with the Blessed Virgin Mary immediately above the west door. Above them are biblical scenes, the Old Testament to the right and the New Testament to the left, while in the central tier are the figures of various martyrs – martyred monarchs and virgins to the left and saints and confessors, in the guise of

The great six-ordered arched recess above the west door of Tewkesbury Abbey, Gloucestershire.

bishops and abbots, to the right. Above them are depicted the Resurrection of the Dead and, in the central stepped gable, the nine Orders of Angels and the Apostles. Finally, at the top, is the figure of Christ in Majesty flanked by seraphim, dating from 1985 when it replaced a badly eroded medieval original. Thus, from the ground, there is an upward movement through time to eternity (*see* colour plate 17).

One of the most extraordinary features of the west front at Wells is its function as a backdrop and medieval sound-system for ceremonial occasions. Behind the façade are two hidden galleries, resonating passages in which a choir of men and boys responded through a series of megaphone-like openings with another choir gathered on the lawn in front of the cathedral. This was pure thirteenth-century liturgical theatre! In the outer façade the two rows of openings were disguised by painted angels which, when viewed by the crowd from below, appeared to be singing celestial antiphons in response to the earthly choir in the cathedral close.

Architecturally, the west front at Salisbury cathedral is rather similar in conception, although markedly inferior in execution. It incorporates a prominent doorway, and a number of windows that cut assertively across the horizontal arcading, detracting from the architectural unity of the façade. Furthermore, George Gilbert Scott's nineteenth-century restoration changed both the iconography and the style of many of the statues, all of which are distinctly mediocre when compared with those at Wells. As Alec Clifton-Taylor observed: 'It is a sad travesty of its great prototype'.

Another early thirteenth-century west front, at Peterborough Cathedral, has three gigantic, deeply recessed portals that rise 26m (85ft) to the full height of the walls, the central arch being narrower than the others. Each portal is topped by a triangular gable and the outer arches are flanked by square towers, each surmounted by a delicate, fourteenth-century spire. The elevation up to the level of the stringcourse forms a rectangle exactly twice as long as it is high – a double square. A Perpendicular two-storey porch, added in 1388, thrusts forward at the foot of the central arch and strikes a somewhat discordant note, although it is not in itself unattractive. Although not universally admired, Peterborough's west front is extraordinarily dramatic and entirely different from that at Wells, which was conceived at about the same time. It is also larger (47.5m (156ft) wide compared with 45m (147ft) at Wells) and depends for its effect on the audacity of its architecture rather than on its sculptural ornamentation. Whereas the west front at Wells is very much an integral part of the building, that at Peterborough is (literally) an afterthought (*see* colour plate 18).

The precursor to Peterborough was almost certainly the original eleventh-century west front at Lincoln Cathedral. Described by Alec Clifton-Taylor as an architectural 'hotch-potch', Lincoln's west façade is an immense, mid-twelfth-century stone screen with the original late Norman west front at its core. Three large, recessed Romanesque portals correspond with the nave and aisles within. However, the heightening and widening of the screen in the 1240s effectively created a western transept and extended the west front well beyond the body of the cathedral, its tiers of arcades, rows of (now empty) niches and octagonal angle turrets emphasising a horizontality that sits uneasily with the twin towers that thrust upwards behind it. The scale of Lincoln's west front is singularly impressive, although it possesses a fortress-like quality that some find disconcerting. However, it is in the quality of its sculpture that Lincoln exceeds most other cathedrals. It is likely that Bishop Alexander of Lincoln commissioned the west front's marvellous Romanesque frieze in the mid-twelfth century. Based on a number of contemporary continental examples, notably that at Modena Cathedral which the bishop visited in 1145 on his way to Rome, the decorative sculpture embraces the three doorways and a long frieze set in the wall above. Once brightly painted, it tells the sobering story of God's covenant with His people, its depiction of human frailty, divine punishment and a promise of salvation reading like a comic strip for the benefit of an illiterate and superstitious people. Unfortunately, many of the carvings have been lost, while others were recut in the nineteenth century. Today, many of the most delicate panels have been replaced with superbly carved 'free copies', the originals being preserved in the Cathedral's sculpture collection (*see* colour plate 19).

Undoubtedly the most impressive of late medieval west fronts is that at Beverley Minster. Its pair of lofty Perpendicular towers, elegant panelled tracery, and buttresses encrusted with statuary are beautifully composed and proportioned, and very much closer to the Romanesque ideal than the grandiose screen façades of Peterborough, Ely and Lincoln. This type of west front, which emphasises height rather than width, follows the continental pattern and is a very much more agreeable composition. There are other notable examples of this type of façade at Lichfield and Canterbury cathedrals and at York Minster, while the twin towers in the west front of Westminster Abbey were designed by Sir Christopher Wren and completed by Nicholas Hawksmoor in 1745.

The late fourteenth-century west front of Exeter Cathedral is a strange construction, having three planes, each of which intrudes rather clumsily on the window behind it. At ground level an *image screen* comprising tiers of sculpted figures (many of them sitting cross-legged) appears almost to have been added as an afterthought.

The carvings on the elegant early sixteenth-century west front of Bath Abbey are a quite extraordinary confection. They depict a dream in which Bishop Oliver King was exhorted to build a new abbey. Angels ascend ladders on the outer faces of the stair turrets to join an angelic host at the feet of Christ in majesty. On the flanking pinnacles are carved rebuses of an olive bush and crown, surmounted by a bishop's mitre for the bishop who is said to have heard a voice saying, 'Let an olive establish a crown and a king restore the church.' Whether or not the 'king' of his dream referred to the bishop or his monarch, he began building the new church in 1499 – the last major Perpendicular building in England. There are also sixteenth-century statues of St Peter and St Paul and a late nineteenth-century effigy of Henry VIII, Bishop King's patron (*see* colour plate 20).

WESTERN RANGE Sometimes known as the cellarer's range from the *cellarium*, the great monastic cellar or storeroom which was its principal feature, the western range of a CLOISTER consisted of a vaulted UNDERCROFT (which was originally sub-divided by partitions) above which was accommodation for the superior and his guests (*see* SUPERIOR'S LODGINGS) or, in Cistercian houses, the FRATER, DORTER, REREDORTER and common room of the *conversi* (*see* LAY BROTHERS).
See also EASTERN RANGE *and* SOUTH RANGE

WHEEL WINDOW *see* ROSE WINDOW

WHISPERING GALLERY *see* GALLERY

WHITE CANONS *see* PREMONSTRATENSIAN CANONS

WHITE FRIARS The Carmelite FRIARS.

WHITE LADIES A popular name for the MAGDALENES, for nuns of the Cistercian Order (*see* CISTERCIANS) and Augustinian canonesses.
See also NUNS AND NUNNERIES

WHITE MONKS Monks of the Cistercian Order (*see* CISTERCIANS).

WICKET A small gate within a larger one.

WIDOW'S VEIL *see* VOWESS

WINDOW GLASS *see* STAINED GLASS *and* WINDOWS

WINDOW MARKS *see* GLAZIERS' MARKS

WINDOW PLAN A plan of a church with the windows marked and numbered for identification. Church recorders usually mark the east window (behind the altar) '700' and work clockwise using Arabic numerals, with Roman numerals for clerestory windows and the suffix 'T' for tower windows.

WINDOW TRACERY *see* MEDIEVAL ARCHITECTURE, TRACERY *and* WINDOWS

WINDOWS Saxon and early medieval windows were generally small and narrow. In part this was because of the prohibitive cost of glazing, but of greater significance was the fact that contemporary builders, with a limited under-standing of constructional techniques, were concerned that walls should not be weakened by large openings (*see* ARCH). Window openings were fitted with wooden shutters, but although these helped to keep out the cold air in winter they also excluded the light so that semi-transparent materials, such as horn, were often used as cheap alternatives to glass.

As building techniques improved, so window openings became larger and wider. In churches, the 'seemingly ethereal fragility' of late Gothic architecture was arrived at only after centuries of experimentation and innovation. The narrow, pointed *lancet windows* of the Early English period evolved through the mullioned and transomed lights of the Decorated and the ornate tracery of the Perpendicular to the broad, square-headed windows of the late fifteenth century.

The style of the ornamental mouldings (*tracery*) in a medieval window can be an invaluable guide to the age of a building – or, rather, to that part of the building in which the window is located (*see* MEDIEVAL ARCHITECTURE *for* illustrations). But it should be remembered that windows were frequently replaced, openings enlarged and new ones inserted into earlier masonry.

The areas of glass (*lights*) in the lower section of a medieval (or Victorian Gothic) window may be divided (horizontally) by *transoms* and (vertically) by *mullions* which, in the upper part of the window (the *head*), branch into an ornate stone framework containing a geometrical pattern of small glass panels (*tracery lights*). The smallest of these tracery lights are called *eyelets*. Some sections of a window (usually the lower panels) may consist of *blind tracery*, which is filled not with glass, but with stone or other solid material. In larger churches, there may also be a circular ROSE WINDOW above the west door of the nave or, more usually, in the gable of a transept.

Medieval Windows

Gothic buildings were conceived from the inside, the heavenward thrust of glass and stone culminating in the ethereal fragility of the Perpendicular period. The 'realm of divine and saintly imagery' in the windows of the great abbey churches and cathedrals may indeed have educated and informed a largely illiterate population, but the complex themes contained therein could rarely have been discernable to the medieval congregation any more than they are today – without the benefit of binoculars. There can be little doubt that the principal function of these great windows was a spiritual one: they were created for the greater glorification of God. One has only to visit the ruined Cistercian abbey at Tintern to appreciate the effect that such enormous areas of glass were intended to create. Tintern's east window is 19.5m (64ft) tall and, even devoid of its glass, it never fails to stir the imagination.

Windows of the twelfth and thirteenth centuries (up to *c.* 1260) were predominantly ruby and blue, and created a homogeneous fabric of light that induced a sense of almost mystical contemplation. Unfortunately, little early glass remains intact in England and it is difficult for us to appreciate its overall effect without visiting European cathedrals such as Chartres. The finest medieval glass in England is to be found in the Trinity Chapel at Canterbury Cathedral Priory, where the twelve principal windows date from the late twelfth and early thirteenth century and depict various miracles attributed to St Thomas à Becket. Approximately half the original glass has survived, and it compares in quality (if not in quantity) with the best that Chartres has to offer (*see* colour plate 13). Several other early thirteenth-century windows, such as the circular 'Dean's Eye' in the north transept of Lincoln Cathedral, have the strong, deep tones of contemporary French glass, as they were made with coloured *pot metal* imported from the same sources (*see* ROSE WINDOWS *and* STAINED GLASS).

From the mid-twelfth century, most windows comprised a central pictorial motif contained within a medallion, or an arrangement of medallions set against a patterned background and within a plain or beaded border (*fillet*) next to the stonework frame. But from the late thirteenth century, larger openings and the consequential development of tracery with close-set mullions meant that glaziers were obliged to accommodate their designs within narrow vertical strips of glass rather than the uninterrupted spaces of earlier, round-headed windows (*see* ARMATURE). In order to produce an overall effect, they designed windows with horizontal rows of figures, often with *tabernacle work* (*see* TABERNACLE), as in the fourteenth-century west window at York Minster and the great Crécy window at Gloucester Cathedral (*see below*). Jesse windows were popular throughout the medieval period (*see* JESSE TREE),

The south façade of the ruined abbey church at Tintern, Monmouthshire, serves to demonstrate both the number and the size of window openings in a monastic church. (Courtesy of Roy Morgan)

but unfortunately none has survived intact in any English cathedral, although there are panels from thirteenth-century Jesse windows at Canterbury, Salisbury and York.

The years 1250 to 1325 are notable for *grisaille glass* (from the French *gris* meaning 'grey'): large areas of clear quarries surrounded by borders of monochrome foliage decoration and occasional medallions in colour. The best-known example is the Five Sisters window in the north transept of York Minster, which dates from the third quarter of the thirteenth century and possesses an almost three-dimensional quality. Despite its popular name it comprises five separate lancet windows, each measuring 16m (53ft) in height and only 1.5m (5ft) in width. Together they contain over 100,000 pieces of glass arranged in geometrical patterns set against a background of greyish foliage (there is one exception – a depiction of Daniel in the Lion's Den). However, the glass is not entirely devoid of iconography: the foliage is that of the plant *geum*, which, in the medieval period, was believed to possess powers of healing and was, therefore, associated with Christ. It has been said that over half the surviving medieval stained glass in England is to be found in York Minster.

At the beginning of the fourteenth century it was discovered that a yellow colour (known as *silver stain*) could be fired directly on to clear glass, so that features such as hair and drapery could be depicted without the need for cutting and leading separate pieces of glass. It also increased the use of clear and lighter coloured glass, exemplified in the windows of the Priory Church at Great Malvern – the most complete scheme of fifteenth-century glass to have survived in England. At Malvern, one can catch a glimpse of what an English monastic church would have looked like when builders fashioned their churches 'like lanterns of glass'. Indeed, the luminosity, delicate design and fine painting of early fifteenth-century English work is considered by many to have been superior to that of any other European country, although an apparent decline in the second half of the century caused Henry VI to engage Flemish artists to complete the great windows of his magnificent chapel at King's College, Cambridge.

At least half the surviving medieval church glass contains an element of HERALDRY. Many late medieval windows were *donor windows*, erected both as memorials and to commemorate the generosity of those who paid for their erection. These often contain coats of arms or kneeling figures wearing tabards emblazoned with the benefactor's arms. At York Minster, one Richard Tunnoc, a goldsmith and bellfounder, is actually depicted presenting his window to St William of York (*c.* 1325). But not all donors were individuals. Throughout the Middle Ages senior churchmen, magnates, guilds and fraternities endowed money for the repair of churches and, especially in the fourteenth century, groups of citizens would combine to pay for the refurbishing of their parish church. At Dorchester Abbey in Oxfordshire, for example, the south window of the chancel contains twenty-one heraldic shields recording for posterity the identity of those who financed the extension of the sanctuary in *c.* 1340. At this time, the practice of endowing chantries was particularly popular (*see* CHANTRY), and the shields or other heraldic devices in a chantry chapel window may include those of royal or magnate patrons for whom prayers were to be said, as well as those of the deceased armiger and his family.

Perhaps the greatest of all commemorative windows is the magnificent fourteenth-century east window in the presbytery of Gloucester Cathedral (*see* colour plate 6). Constructed between 1347 and 1350 it is 11.6m (38ft) wide and 22m (72ft) high: the area of a tennis court and the largest stone traceried window in England. In the lower lights are the shields of some of the commanders who fought at the battle of Crécy in 1346. It has been suggested that the window was commissioned by Thomas, Lord Bradeston in memory of his close friend and comrade in arms Sir Maurice Berkeley (Bradeston's arms are in the traditional 'donor position' at the bottom right-hand corner of the window). However, as Berkeley's feudal tenant, it is unlikely that Bradeston would have possessed the resources to undertake such a hugely expensive project and the window was almost certainly commissioned by more than one donor. Even so, the Hundred Years War made many magnates' fortunes and enabled England to emerge from the cultural shadow of France. The window is an early masterpiece of the new English Perpendicular style – 'a kind of symphony in which architecture, heraldry and religion all come together in a single hymn of praise to England's God, to England's king and to England itself' (David Starkey). Its centrepiece is the coronation of the Blessed Virgin Mary, who is surrounded by tier upon tier of apostles, saints and martyrs, together with figures of various abbots of Gloucester and bishops of Worcester. It has the appearance of a wall of glass – 'sparkling like icicles in the sunshine of a crisp winter's day' (Clifton-Taylor). In fact, the window is not all in one plane: ingeniously, the side sections are canted inward like a huge triptych.

The Great East Window at York Minster is exceeded in size only by that at Gloucester and, more recently, by Liverpool Anglican cathedral. Measuring 22.5m (74ft) high and 9.75m (32ft) wide, it comprises 117 panels arranged in thirteen rows of nine, each with 144 compartments in the tracery. Events from the Creation to the Apocalypse and scenes from the Book of Revelation are depicted, together with the Nine Orders of Angels, Patriarchs, Prophets, Israelite heroes and various saints ranged in the tracery lights. At the foot of the window are English kings, saints and archbishops of York – including Bishop Skirlaw of Durham, who donated the window. It was glazed by John Thornton of Coventry between 1405 and 1408 and contains one of the largest areas of medieval painted glass surviving anywhere in Europe. Clearly, Thornton would have engaged assistants in order to carry out such a huge work, but he contracted to paint all the histories and the main figures in his own hand. He received £56 for his labours and a bonus of £10 for completing the work on time.

The Post-Reformation

Following the REFORMATION countless medieval windows were destroyed and replaced with glass in which no religious or allegorical subjects were permitted. The duties of the iconoclast are vividly described by Richard Culmner in *Cathedrall Newes from Canterburie* (1644): 'on the top of the citie ladder, near sixty steps high, with a whole pike in the hand, rattling down Becket's glassy bones from the great idolatrous window'. Heraldry was an obvious and politically acceptable alternative and one which particularly appealed to the newly created Tudor aristocracy. Anxious to prove themselves equal in blood to the old magnate families, they erected MONUMENTS and commemorative windows that positively radiated heraldic splendour, their arms incorporating numerous acquired (or assumed) ancestral quarterings (*see* QUARTERING).

A fashion for secular Renaissance motifs, landscapes and classical figures, first apparent in the post-Reformation period, continued into the seventeenth, eighteenth and early nineteenth centuries and, from the late sixteenth century, transparent coloured enamels were widely used so that windows were treated as complete pictures and resembled transparent oil paintings.

The Victorians

The Gothic revival of the nineteenth century encouraged a return to medieval methods of glass manufacture that produced irregularities, variations in thickness and striations, all of which had given early medieval glass its richness. Augustus Pugin (1812–52) and others, following more or less closely the Gothic precedent, were influential until the 1860s. But despite the fact that coloured glass was being made to a standard unequalled since the Middle Ages, there would have been no Victorian renaissance had it not been for the work of William Morris (1834–96) and his circle. It was not Morris's intention simply to reproduce the forms of medieval art, indeed at first he refused to allow his firm, Morris & Co. (est. 1861), to supply glass to any medieval church. Rather, he wished to revive the spirit of the medieval craftsmen, championing a return to an ideal of beauty through utility and simplicity, while deploring the complacency of many of his contemporaries who not only overvalued their own work but undervalued, and sometimes destroyed, that of their predecessors. Morris's concern was entirely justified: the ubiquity of poor-quality Victorian glass, even in our cathedrals, is depressing. But, of course, there were exceptions. Hardman & Co. of Birmingham collaborated with Pugin to produce some stunning work: the magnificent south transept window (1847) at Milton Abbey, Dorset, for example, with its hieratic tiers of figures in brilliant colours. Henry Holiday (1839–1927) designed glass for Powell & Sons, and his Moses Window at Durham Cathedral Priory is wonderfully dramatic, with a strong use of colour. Pre-eminent among Morris's designers was Edward Burne-Jones (1833–98), whose richly coloured windows in the presbytery of St Philip's, Birmingham (now the cathedral) are particularly fine. The Ascension is depicted in the central window (1885) and on either side are the Crucifixion and the Nativity (both 1887). At the west end of the church is his amazing depiction of 'The Last Judgement', a window that is undoubtedly his greatest achievement and rightly claims its place among the masterpieces of stained glass (*see* colour plate 14). Burne-Jones's St Frideswide window at Christ Church, Oxford was executed in 1859 when he was only 26, while his windows at Waltham Abbey (1861) include both a Tree of Jesse and a rose window – described by June Osborne as 'the most revolutionary piece of design produced in nineteenth century stained glass'.

One consequence of the Gothic revival, and of the Victorians' enthusiasm for church restoration was a demand for stained glass that outstripped the capabilities of the best designers. Inevitably, there was a corresponding increase in the number of manufacturers who were more than willing to produce stock designs from catalogues, many of which were truly dreadful. Indeed, three-quarters of the glass in our churches belongs to this category, mass-produced, diamond-shaped panes decorated with monochrome motifs (*stamped quarries*) being particularly popular.

The Twentieth Century

Inspired by the writings of Morris and Ruskin, the Arts and Crafts Movement of the late nineteenth century reacted against the excesses of commercialism. Together with the Art-Workers' Guild, the Arts and Crafts Exhibition Society promoted the notion that designers should be fully conversant with the techniques and materials of their craft and, where possible, involved in the execution of their designs at each stage of the manufacturing process. The foremost advocate of this philosophy was Christopher Whall (1849–1924) who developed the use of a new material called *slab glass* (also *Early English* or *Norman* glass), which can be identified by examining the exterior of a window for its irregular 'lumpy' surface texture and the interior for its uneven density of colour. Slab glass became a key ingredient in the Arts and Crafts style, together with a variety of new painting techniques and the emphatic use of the lead-line as an integral element of the design rather than a functional necessity. And while commercial studios tended to use pseudo-Gothic architectural motifs in borders and canopies, Whall and his contemporaries preferred stylised natural forms such as boughs and foliage. His windows (1909) in the Lady Chapel at Gloucester Cathedral contain some of the finest post-medieval stained glass in England – vibrant both in colour and in line.

Described by Betjeman as 'Completely medieval minded . . . a great individualist', whose use of colour was 'dazzling yet subtle', the architect Sir Ninian Comper (1864–1960) was responsible for at least eight hundred windows which were singularly Gothic in character, containing much 'white space' and tabernacle work (turrets, battlements, etc.). Comper learned his craft under Charles Eamer Kempe (1834–1907), an eminent member of the Arts and Crafts Movement. And yet, contrary to Betjeman's view, much of his work is rigid and anaemic – exemplified by his Coronation window at Canterbury Cathedral.

Memorial windows were in great demand after 1918, but rarely rose above the banal – there is a particularly awful example in Winchester Cathedral. The end of the Second World War presented new opportunities for stained-glass artists. Much of the country's most valuable stained glass had been removed for safe-keeping, but windows of lesser importance had remained *in situ*, many of them to be destroyed in the blitz. At Canterbury Cathedral, the severely damaged glass in the south-east transept was replaced in 1960 by two great windows – 'Peace' and 'Salvation' – designed and executed by Hungarian-born Ervin Bossanyi. Each window measures 5.5m (18ft) by 2.6m (8.5ft) and demonstrates a brilliance of colour that is characteristic of central European art.

While Bossanyi believed in designing and constructing his windows, the majority of late twentieth-century windows are the result of collaboration between artist and craftsman. Marc Chagall (1889–1985) designed the window (illustrating Psalm 150) in the north ambulatory of Chichester Cathedral (1978), but it was made by Charles Marq of Reims. Similarly, John Piper's (1903–92) shimmering baptistery window at Coventry Cathedral was executed by Patrick Reyntiens in 1962. It contains 195 panels of brilliantly coloured glass, moving from darker reds, blues and greens at the periphery to a brilliant sunburst of white and gold at the centre. It is rightly considered by many to be one of the finest stained-glass windows in the country (*see* colour plate 15 and 16).

The Prisoners of Conscience window in the Trinity Chapel of Salisbury Cathedral, designed by Gabriel Loire and made in his workshop at

Chartres in 1980, is dedicated to prisoners who have suffered for their beliefs. Visible from the west end of the nave, the window, with its mysterious, deep, rich blues and pin-pricks of brilliant colour, is closer to early medieval glass than any other modern window in England. The magnificent west window of Sherborne Abbey in Dorset was designed and made in 1997 by John Hayward (who also designed the windows in the north transept at Norwich Cathedral). It replaced a Victorian window designed by Augustus Pugin, the workmanship of which was so poor that it came to be known as the 'Mr Blobby window' – a child's description of the degraded featureless faces of the figures. Hayward conceived the design as an immense tree at the end of an 'avenue' formed by the piers and intricate fan vaulting of the nave. Within its branches it was possible to develop a bold, theological statement about the Incarnation – the embodiment of God in human form. Like the best of their medieval predecessors, these wonderful modern windows induce a sense of almost mystical contemplation.
(*See also* ROSE WINDOW)

WINE Wine is one of the essential elements of the EUCHARIST. The words of administration imply that the consecrated wine conveys the Blood of Christ to the communicant, although in the medieval Church both the Body and Blood were considered to be present in each of the eucharistic species.

Although in monasteries beer was the usual beverage, wine was sometimes prescribed in the INFIRMARY and was occasionally allowed at mixtum (*see* FRATER) and COLLATION. It may also have been served to high-ranking guests in the GUEST HOUSE and SUPERIOR'S LODGINGS.
See also VINEYARDS

WOOD *see* TIMBER, WOODCARVING *and* WOODWORK

WOODCARVING There is a wealth of surviving woodcarving in the bench ends, BOSSES, misericords (*see* MISERICORD) and SCREENS of our medieval churches. These carvings include symbols, both religious and secular, hagiographical, mythological and even pagan, all of which would have been familiar to contemporary congregations. The introduction of wooden seating in churches provided opportunities for the carving of medieval imagery, although much of that which was religious was subsequently removed or defaced by the iconoclasts of the REFORMATION and Cromwell's commissioners. That which remains is, for the most part, secular and floreated in form, although there are several notable exceptions.

One consequence of the Black Death (*see* PLAGUE) was the creation of a new class of independent artisan. The late medieval woodcarver was a respected member of the community, highly skilled, well-versed in the iconography of his time and able to create his own own styles and designs. It is likely, therefore, that in matters of design he was his own master, and this may explain the ubiquity of pagan and mythological images which reflect the folklore that was so much a part of medieval life.

Birds were especially popular and are to be found in a variety of stylised forms, including a strange spoon-billed parrot at Stogursey in Somerset. So too are the implements of everyday life: ploughs, yokes, weavers' shuttles, teasels, hounds, horns, arrows and hawks' hoods. Even the medieval doctor is represented – as a chained monkey holding a bottle of urine. Surviving religious carvings include the symbols of the Passion, the Five Wounds, the Paschal Lamb and numerous devices associated with the saints and martyrs. Animals, both rural and heraldic, are common, although identification is sometimes difficult because medieval carvers were often asked to work from verbal descriptions of creatures they had never seen.

Inevitably, medieval motifs were imitated by the architects and designers of the Gothic revival but, with some notable exceptions, the carving is patently mechanical and lacks the vigour and animation of the original.

WOODWORK Timber is of two types: hardwood (from deciduous trees such as oak and walnut) and softwood (from coniferous trees such as cedar and yew). Neither term is necessarily indicative of the hardness or otherwise of a particular wood, although hardwoods tend to be more suitable for exterior use. Oak was used almost exclusively for the best-quality fittings and furniture up to 1660 and has continued in use to the present day. Walnut was fashionable from 1660 to 1770, mahogany from 1720 to 1770 and satinwood from 1770 to 1830. Inevitably, domestic furniture found its way into churches (often as bequests) and, from the late sixteenth century, exotic timbers such as ebony, lignum, and rosewood from South America and the East Indies were used to embellish larger pieces of furniture.

Before the fifteenth century, most woodwork and furniture was made by the same carpenters who constructed buildings using heavy beams and wooden planks, working with tools such as the axe, saw, adze, chisel and auger. Consequently, much medieval furniture (including that which was found in the domestic quarters of the poorer religious houses) was crude: hollowed-out logs for chests, planks supported on tripods for tables and pit-sawn boards for benches, all held together with wooden pegs or nails.

The mortice and tenon joint was introduced into English woodworking in the mid-fifteenth century and this enabled narrow strips of wood to be joined together to form a rigid framework, the intervening spaces filled with thin boards (*panels*). One consequence of the fourteenth-century Black Death had been the creation of a new class of independent artisan that included the joiner (as he came to be known) and woodcarver (*see* WOODCARVING). They used more sophisticated tools to make furniture which was lighter, stronger and more durable. Many chests, chairs, tables and cupboards were commissioned for churches at this time, and the lower sections of walls were often covered with panelling (*see also* LINENFOLD). Fittings such as SCREENS and bench ends, were embellished with chamfers and with mouldings derived from contemporary architectural motifs such as the ovolo, cavetto and ogee. These were either cut from solid wood or applied separately and, in furniture, geometrical patterns of light and dark-coloured woods were inlaid within the surface of surrounding timbers.

By the mid-sixteenth century the woodturner's craft was much in evidence. As the name suggests, the woodturner spins wood on a lathe and shapes it using a variety of gouges and chisels to produce chair and table legs, the balusters of STAIRCASES, communion rails and other items of 'turned' woodwork, including bowls and collection plates.

WOOL The great medieval monastic houses (notably those of the CISTERCIANS) were 'built on wool', having acquired (usually through endowment) vast tracts of dry, infertile land which, although unsuitable for arable farming, could be managed efficiently as sheep runs. Technically, the monasteries produced wool for their own needs (the Cistercian statutes of 1237 forbade their houses to trade in wool or hides) but as these were minimal there was a massive surplus, much of which was exported to the Continent. Wool from the north of England, from the south-east and from Dorset and Wiltshire was generally coarse and of relatively low value. Sheep from the Welsh border, Lincolnshire and the Cotswolds of Gloucestershire, on the other hand, were remarkable for the length and quality of their wool (in the thirteenth century the Tintern Abbey and Abbey Dore estates were reckoned to produce the finest wool). So valuable was the wool of the Cistercian monasteries that in 1193 the entire clip was seized as a contribution towards Richard I's ransom. In 1297–8 the Augustinian Canons of Leicester received £220 3*s* 10*d* from the sale of wool, more than one-third of its entire income.

English wool acquired an exceptional reputation and was much in demand by continental merchants, notably those of Flanders and northern France. But such a trade was wasteful of resources and successive medieval governments imposed strict controls on the export of wool through taxation and the staple system while encouraging the production of wool cloth by introducing advantageous trading tariffs for English merchants and the immigration to England of expert weavers from Flanders. Italian merchants such as the Frescobaldi and the Bardi regularly dealt with the monastic houses who often acted as middlemen in marketing their neighbours' wool as well as their own. In the thirteenth century some 10,000 sacks of wool were exported annually, representing the wool of about 3 million sheep with a value (at that time) of £60,000 to £100,000 a year. By the late thirteenth and early fourteenth centuries at least fifty-seven English and Welsh Cistercian houses had entered into contracts to supply wool to Florentine merchants. Of these, Fountains Abbey was the largest single exporter, selling seventy-six sacks a year (the product of over 15,000 sheep) closely followed by neighbouring Rievaulx (sixty sacks) and Jervaulx (fifty sacks). Even so, not all the wool from the monastic estates was exported: fleeces from the Benedictine and Augustinian flocks were usually sold into the home markets, unwashed and unsorted. By the fifteenth century exports had declined significantly, sales from Fountains Abbey being just seven sacks in 1457–8 and only four in the following year.

Sheep were usually housed in sheepcotes during the winter months, from Martinmas (11 November) to Easter. Sheepcotes are frequently mentioned in thirteenth- and fourteenth-century chronicles and accounts and were often of considerable size: that at Meaux Abbey, Yorkshire, was nearly 49m (160ft) long and 15m (50ft) wide, for example. Remote and isolated sheepcotes were usually surrounded by a hedged or walled enclosure used for marshalling the sheep: that attached to Rievaulx Abbey's sheepcote at Willerby occupied half an acre, while Fountains Abbey's sheepcotes at Baldersby in the Vale of York and at Allerston in the Vale of Pickering each had three acres attached.

Fleeces were usually carried by packhorse from shearing centres to a secure woolhouse where the wool was stored, washed, graded and packed and where it could be inspected by merchants. The Gilbertines were required to centralise the storage of wool within the precincts of their priories, while the larger Cistercian monasteries often established woolhouses at their granges (*see* GRANGE) and made them available to smaller monastic houses and lay proprietors. A late fourteenth-century woolhouse built by Beaulieu Abbey in Southampton has survived, while a mid-twelfth-century aisled woolhouse has been located south of the curia at Fountains Abbey. Once cleaned and sorted into woolsacks, the fleeces were carried to an agreed delivery point by cart or boat, Hull and London being by far the most important ports for this purpose.

See also BARNS

WORK *see* MANUAL LABOUR

WORKSHOPS *see* PRECINCT

YEAR, LITURGICAL The liturgical year of the western Church is based on the two great festivals of Easter and Christmas. The year begins on the first Sunday in Advent and, thereafter, Sundays are traditionally numbered through Advent, after Christmas and after Epiphany, through Lent, after Easter and after Whit Sunday or Trinity Sunday. In the Church of England the year is in three parts: the ten weeks before Easter (*triodion*), the paschal season (*pentecostarion*) and the remainder of the year (*octeochos*).

APPENDIX I

FURTHER READING

Abbeys: An Introduction to the Religious Houses of England and Wales, HMSO, 1978

Adair, J., *The Pilgrims' Way: Shrines and Saints in Britain and Ireland*, Thames & Hudson, 1978

Aston, M., *Monasteries*, B.T. Batsford, 1993

Baskerville, G., *English Monks and the Suppression of the Monasteries*, Weidenfeld & Nicolson, 2002

Bond, J., *Monastic Landscapes*, Tempus, 2004

Bottomley, F., *The Abbey Explorer's Guide*, Kaye & Ward, 1995

Brabbs, D., *Abbeys and Monasteries*, Weidenfeld & Nicolson, 1999

Brooke, C., *The Age of the Cloister: The Story of Monastic Life in the Middle Ages*, Sutton, 2003

Brooke, R., *The Coming of the Friars*, HarperCollins, 1975

Burton, J., *Monastic and Religious Orders in Britain*, Cambridge University Press, 1994

Butler, L. and Given-Wilson, C., *Medieval Monasteries of Great Britain*, Michael Joseph, 1979

Chadwick, N., *The Age of the Saints in the Early Celtic Church*, Llanerch Press, 1961

Chamberlin, R., *The English Cathedral*, Webb and Bower, 1988

Clifton-Taylor, A., *The Cathedrals of England*, Thames & Hudson, 2001

Cooke, H., *English Monasteries in the Middle Ages*, Phoenix House, 1961.

Coppack, G., *Abbeys and Priories*, B.T. Batsford / English Heritage, 1993

Cowen, P., *The Rose Window: Splendour and Symbol*, Thames & Hudson, 2005

Crossley, F.H., *The English Abbey*, B.T. Batsford, 1962

Day, P., *A Dictionary of Religious Orders*, Burnes & Oates, 2001

Deanesly, M., *A History of the Medieval Church*, Routledge, 2002

Dickens, A.G., *Late Monasticism and the Reformation*, Hambledon, 1994

Duffy, E., *The Stripping of the Altars: Traditional Religion in England 1400–1580*, Yale University Press, 1992

Forey, A., *The Military Orders from the Twelfth to the Early Fourteenth Centuries*, University of Toronto Press, 1992

Friar, S., *The Sutton Companion to Churches*, Sutton, 2003

Greene, J.P., *Medieval Monasteries*, Leicester University Press, 1995

Hall, R. and Stocker, D., *Vicars Choral and the English Cathedrals*, Oxbow, 2005

Harris, B.L., *Guide to Churches and Cathedrals*, Ebury, 2006

Harvey, J., *English Medieval Architects, a Biographical Dictionary down to 1550*, Palgrave Macmillan, 1972

Heale, M., *The Dependent Priories of Medieval English Monasteries*, Boydell Press, 2004

Knowles, D., *The Monastic Order in England*, 2nd edn, Cambridge University Press, 1966

—— *The Religious Orders in England*, 3 vols, Cambridge University Press, 1948, 1955, 1959

Knowles, D., *Bare Ruined Choirs: Dissolution of the English Monasteries*, Cambridge University Press, 1976
Knowles, D. and Hadcock, R.M., *Medieval Religious Houses in England and Wales*, Cambridge University Press, 1971
Knowles, D. and St Joseph, J.K., *Monastic Sites from the Air*, Cambridge University Press, 1952
Laing, L. and Laing, J., *Early English Art and Architecture*, Sutton, 1996
Lawrence, C.H., *The Friars: The Impact of the Early Mendicant Movement on Western Society*, Longman, 1994
Lehmberg, S., *English Cathedrals: A History*, Hambledon & London, 2004
Luxford, J., *The Arts and Architecture of English Benedictine Monasteries 1300–1540*, Boydell, 2005
Maud, T., *Guided by a Stone-Mason: The Cathedrals, Abbeys and Churches of Britain Unveiled*, I.B. Tauris, 1997
Mayr-Harting, H., *The Coming of Christianity to Anglo-Saxon England*, B.T. Batsford, 1991
Mead, R., *Walking the Cathedral Cities of England*, New Holland, 2003
Midner, R., *English Medieval Monasteries 1066–1540. A Summary*, Heinemann, 1979
Orme, N. and Webster, M., *The English Medieval Hospital*, Yale University Press, 1995
Platt, C., *The Abbeys and Priories of Medieval England*, Chancellor Press, 1995
—— *The Architecture of Medieval Britain*, Yale University Press, 1990
Prescott, E., *The English Medieval Hospital*, B.T. Batsford, 1992
Robinson, D., *The Cistercian Abbeys of Britain*, B.T. Batsford, 1998
Sackett, E. and Skinner, J., *Abbeys, Priories and Cathedrals: Photographs from the Francis Frith Collection*, Frith Collection, 2006
Tatton-Brown, T. and Crook, J., *The English Cathedral*, New Holland, 2002
Thompson, M., *Cloister, Abbot and Precinct*, Tempus, 2001
Thompson, S., *Women Religious*, Oxford University Press Reprints, 1992
Thorold, H., *Guide to the Ruined Abbeys of England, Scotland and Wales*, HarperCollins, 1993
Tobin, S., *The Cistercians*, Herbert Press, 1995
Venarde, B., *Women's Monasticism and Medieval Society*, Cornell University Press, 1999
Williams, D.H., *The Cistercians in the Early Middle Ages*, Gracewing, 1998
Woodward, G.W., *The Dissolution of the Monasteries*, Blandford, 1966

APPENDIX II

USEFUL ADDRESSES

Ancient Monuments Society, St Anne's Vestry Hall, 2 Church Entry, London EC4V 5HB. www.ancientmonumentssociety.org.uk

Anglican Church Music. www.churchmusic.org.uk

Architectural Heritage Fund, Clareville House, 26–7 Oxendon Street, London SW1Y 4EL. www.ahfund.org.uk

Arundel Roman Catholic Cathedral, Cathedral House, Parsons Hill, Arundel, West Sussex BN18 9AY. www.dabnet.org/arundel.htm

Ashmolean Museum, Beaumont Street, Oxford. www.ashmole.ox.ac.uk

Association for Studies in the Conservation of Historic Buildings, 201 Westway, London SW20 9LW. www.archaeology.co.uk/directory/viewsoc.asp?cat=z&soc=6

Association of Diocesan and Cathedral Archaeologists, 27 Grosvenor Street, Chester CH1 2DD. www.britarch.ac.uk/adca

Association of English Cathedrals. www.englishcathedrals.co.uk

Bath Abbey, The Abbey Office, 13 Kingston Buildings, Bath BA1 1LT. www.bathabbey.org

Birmingham Cathedral, Colmore Row, Birmingham B3 2QB. www.birminghamcathedral.com

Birmingham Roman Catholic Cathedral, St Chad's, Queensway, Birmingham B4 6EU. www.stchadscathedral.org.uk

Blackburn Cathedral, Church House, Cathedral Close, Blackburn BB1 5AA. www.blackburn.anglican.org/cathedral

Bodleian Library, Oxford OX1 3BG. www.bodley.ox.ac.uk

Borthwick Institute of Historical Research, University of York, Heslington, York YO10 5DD. www.york.ac.uk/inst/bihr

Bradford Cathedral, 1 Stott Hall, Bradford, West Yorkshire BD1 4EH. www.bradfordcathedral.co.uk

Bristol Cathedral, College Green, Bristol BS1 5TJ. www.bristol-cathedral.co.uk

British Archaeological Association, 1 Priory Gardens, Bedford Park, London W4 1TT. www.britarch.ac.uk/baa

British Architectural Library, 66 Portland Place, London W1N 4AD. www.riba-library.com

British Library, Great Russell Street, London WC1B 3DG. www.bl.uk

British Museum, Department of Medieval and Modern Europe, Great Russell Street, London WC1B 3DG. www.thebritishmuseum.ac.uk

British Society of Master Glass Painters, c/o Glaziers Yard, Lovers' Walk, Wells, Somerset BA5 2QL. www.bsmgp.org.uk

Bury St Edmunds Cathedral *see* St Edmundsbury Cathedral

Cambridge University Library, West Road, Cambridge, CB3 9DR. www.lib.cam.ac.uk

Camden Society *see* Ecclesiological Society

Canterbury Cathedral, Cathedral House, 11 The Precincts, Canterbury CT1 2EH. www.canterbury-cathedral.org

Carlisle Cathedral, 7 The Abbey, Carlisle, Cumbria CA3 8TZ. www.carlislecathedral.org.uk

Cathedral Architects Association, 46 St Mary's Street, Ely, Cambridgeshire CB7 4EY. www.buildingconservation.com/directory/ad262.htm

Cathedral Fabrics Commission for England, Church House, Great Smith Street, London SW1P 3NZ. www.buildingconservation.com/directory/ad073.htm

Central Council of Church Bell Ringers. www.cccbr.org.uk

Chelmsford Cathedral, Cathedral Office, New Street, Chelmsford, Essex CM1 1TY. www.cathedral.chelmsford.anglican.org

Chester Cathedral, 12 Abbey Square, Chester CH1 2HU. www.chestercathedral.org.uk

Chichester Cathedral, The Visitors' Office, The Royal Chantry, Cathedral Cloisters, Chichester, West Sussex PO19 1PX. www.fransnet.clara.net/chicath

Church Commissioners, 1 Millbank, Westminster SW1P 3JZ. www.cofe.anglican.org/about/churchcommissioners

Church Monuments Society, c/o Society of Antiquaries, Burlington House, Piccadilly, London W1J 0BE. www.churchmonuments society.org.uk

Church of England Record Centre, 15 Galleywall Road, South Bermondsey, London SE16 3PB. www.lambethpalacelibrary.org/holdings/CERC.html

Church Monuments Society, c/o Society of Antiquaries, Burlington House, Piccadilly, London W1J 0BE. www.churchmonumentssociety.org.uk

Church Recorders Committee of NADFAS, 8 Guilford Street, London WC1N 1DT (*see* National Association of Decorative and Fine Art Societies).

Clifton Roman Catholic Cathedral, Cathedral House, Clifton Park, Bristol BS8 3BX. www.cliftoncathedral.org.uk

Council for British Archaeology (CBA), Bowes Morrell House, 111 Walmgate, York YO1 9WA. www.britarch.ac.uk

Coventry Cathedral, 7 Priory Row, Coventry CV1 5ES. www.coventrycathedral.org

Department of the Environment, Transport and Regions, Bressenden Place, London SW1E 5DV. www.detr.gov.uk

Derby Cathedral, Cathedral Office, 1A College Place, Derby DE1 3DY. www.derbycathedral.org

Durham Cathedral, The Chapter Office, The College, Durham DH1 3EH. www.durhamcathedral.co.uk

Ecclesiastical Architects and Surveyors Association, c/o 453 Glossop Road, Sheffield S10 2PT. www.easanet.co.uk

Ecclesiastical History Society, Department of Medieval History, University of Glasgow, Glasgow G12 8QQ. www.ehsoc.org.uk

Ecclesiological Society, 3 Sycamore Close, Court Road, London SE9 4RD. www.ecclsoc.org

Ely Cathedral, Chapter House, The College, Ely, Cambridgeshire CB7 4DL. www.cathedral.ely.anglican.org

English Heritage, Fortress House, 25 Saville Row, London W1X 2BT. www.english-heritage.org.uk

Exeter Cathedral, 1 The Cloisters, Exeter, Devon EX1 1HS. www.exeter-cathedral.org.uk

Friends of Cathedral Music, 27 Old Gloucester Street, London WC1N 3XX. www.fcm.org.uk

Gloucester Cathedral, The Chapter Office, 2 College Green, Gloucester GL1 2LR. www.gloucestercathedral.org.uk
Greater Churches Group, c/o 12 Colston Parade, Bristol BS1 6RA. administrator@stmaryredcliffe.co.uk
Guildford Cathedral, Stag Hill, Guildford GU2 7UP. www.guildford-cathedral.org.uk
Guildhall Library, Aldermanbury, London EC2P 2EJ. www.cityoflondon.gov.uk/corporation
Guild of Church Musicians, St Katherine Cree, 86 Leadenhall Street, London EC3A 3DH. www.churchmusicians.org.uk

Heraldry Society, c/o P.O. Box 772, Guildford, Surrey GU3 3ZX. www.theheraldrysociety.com
Hereford Cathedral, The Visits Office, 5 College Cloisters, Cathedral Close, Hereford HR1 2NG. www.aph.org.uk/whattosee/page64.htm
Historic Buildings Council for Wales (Cadw), Cathays Park, Cardiff CF10 3NQ. www.cadw-wales.gov.uk
Historic Buildings and Monuments Commission for England *see* English Heritage
House of Lords Record Office (The Parliamentary Archives), Westminster, London SW1A 0PW. www.parliament.the-stationery-office.co.uk/pa/paarchiv.htm

Institute of Archaeology (Conservation of Historic Buildings), University College of London, 31–4 Gordon Sq., London WC1. www.ucl.ac.uk/archaeology
Institute of Heraldic and Genealogical Studies, Northgate, Canterbury, Kent CT1 1RB. www.ihgs.ac.uk
Institute of Historic Building Conservation, Jubilee House, High street, Tisbury, SP3 6HA. Website: www.lhbc.org.uk
Institute of Historical Research, University of London, Senate House, London WC1E 7HU. www.ihrinfo.ac.uk

Lambeth Palace Library, London SE1 7JU. www.lambethpalacelibrary.org
Leicester Cathedral, The Cathedral Centre, 21 St Martin's, Leicester LE1 5DE. www.cathedral.leicester.anglican.org
Lichfield Cathedral, 19A The Close, Lichfield, Staffordshire WS13 7LD. www.lichfield-cathedral.org
Lincoln Cathedral, Communications Office, Lincoln LN2 1PX. Website: www.lincolncathedral.com
Liverpool (Anglican) Cathedral, St James Mount, Liverpool L1 7AZ. www.liverpoolcathedral.org.uk
Liverpool Roman Catholic Cathedral, Mount Pleasant, Liverpool L3 5TQ. www.liverpool-rc-cathedral.org.uk

Manchester Cathedral, Manchester M3 1SX. www.dws.ndiect.co.uk/mc1.htm
Monumental Brass Society, Lowe Hill House, Stratford St Mary, Suffolk CO7 6JX. www.mbs-brasses.co.uk

National Archives, Kew, Richmond, Surrey TW9 4DU. www.nationalarchives.gov.uk
National Association of Decorative and Fine Art Societies (NADFAS), 8 Guilford Street, London WC1N 1DT (*see* Church Recorders Committee). www.nadfas.org.uk
National Library of Wales, Department of Manuscripts and Records, Aberystwyth SY23 3BU. www.llgc.org.uk
National Monuments Record Centre, Great Western Village, Kemble Drive, Swindon SN2 2GZ. www.english-heritage.org.uk/knowledge/nmr/index.asp
National Monuments Record of Wales, Crown Buildings, Plas Crug, Aberystwyth SY23 1NJ. www.rcahmw.gov.uk

National Register of Archives, Ruskin Avenue, Kew, Richmond, Surrey TW9 4DU. www.nationalarchives.gov.uk/nra

National Trust, 36 Queen Anne's Gate, London SW1. www.nationaltrust.org.uk

Newcastle upon Tyne Cathedral, Newcastle upon Tyne NE1 1PF. www.newcastle-ang-cathedral-stnicholas.org.uk

Newcastle upon Tyne Roman Catholic Cathedral, Clayton Street West, Newcastle upon Tyne NE1 5HH. www.stmaryscathedral.org.uk

Norwich Cathedral, 12 The Close, Norwich, Norfolk NR1 4DH. www.cathedral.org.uk

Norwich Roman Catholic Cathedral, Cathedral House, Unthank Road, Norwich, Norfolk NR2 2PA. www.stjohncathedral.co.uk

Nottingham Roman Catholic Cathedral, North Circus Street, Nottingham NG1 5AE. www.stbarnabasnottingham.org.uk

Order of St John Library and Museum, St John's Gate, Clerkenwell, London EC1M 4DA. www.sja.org.uk/museum

Ordnance Survey, Romsey Road, Maybush, Southampton SO9 4DH. www.ordsvy.gov.uk

Oxford Cathedral, Christ Church, Oxford OX1 1DP. www.chch.ox.ac.uk

Peterborough Cathedral, Little Prior's Gate, The Precincts, Peterborough PE1 1XS. www.peterborough-cathedral.org.uk

Pipe Roll Society. www.members.aol.com/piperollsoc/

Portsmouth Cathedral, Cathedral Office, St Thomas's Street, Old Portsmouth, Hampshire PO1 2HH. www.portsmouthcathedral.org.uk

Prayer Book Society, c/o Copyhold Farm, Lady Grove, Goring Heath, Reading RG8 7RT. www.prayerbook.org.uk

Prinknash Abbey, Cranham, Gloucestershire GL4 8EX. www.prinknashabbey.org.uk

Ripon Minster, Cathedral Office, Liberty Court House, Minster Road, Ripon, North Yorkshire HG4 1QS. www.riponcathedral.org.uk

Rochester Cathedral, Garth House, The Precinct, Rochester, Kent NE1 1SX. www.rochester.anglican.org/cathedral

Romsey Abbey, Romsey, Hampshire. www.romseyabbey.org.uk

Royal College of Organists, 7 St Andrew Street, London EC4V 3LQ. www.rco.org.uk

Royal Commission on the Ancient and Historical Monuments of Wales, Crown Building, Plas Crug, Aberystwyth SY23 1NJ. www.rcahmw.org.uk

Royal Commission on Historical Manuscripts. *See* National Archives.

Royal Commission on the Historical Monuments of England (RCHME), National Monuments Record Centre, Kemble Drive, Swindon, Wiltshire SN2 2GZ (NB: For London buildings: 55 Blandford Street, London). www.rchme.go.uk

Royal Institute of British Architecture, 66 Portland Place, London W1N 4AD. www.architecture.com

Royal School of Church Music, Cleveland Lodge, Westhumble, Dorking, Surrey RH5 6BW. www.rscm.com

St Albans Cathedral, St Albans, Hertfordshire AL1 1BY. www.stalbanscathedral.org.uk

St Edmundsbury Cathedral, Abbey House, Angel Hill, Bury St Edmunds, Suffolk IP33 1LS. www.stedcathedral.co.uk

St George's Chapel (and Library), Aerary, Dean's Close, Windsor Castle. www.stgeorges-windsor.org.uk

St Mary Redcliffe, Bristol. www.stmaryredcliffe.co.uk

St Paul's Cathedral, London EC4M 8AD. www.stpauls.co.uk

Salisbury Cathedral, 33 The Close, Salisbury, Wiltshire SP1 2EJ. www.salisburycathedral.org.uk
Sheffield Cathedral, Church Street, Sheffield S1 1HA. www.sheffield-cathedral.org.uk
Sherborne Abbey, Sherborne, Dorset DT9 3LQ. www.sherborneabbey.com
Shrewsbury Roman Catholic Cathedral, 11 Belmont, Shrewsbury, Shropshire SY1 1TE. www.dioceseofshrewsbury.org.uk
Society of Antiquaries, Burlington House, Piccadilly, London W1V 0HS. www.sal.org.uk
Society for Church Archaeology, St Mary's House, 66 Bootham, York YO30 7BZ. www.britarch.ac.uk/socchurcharchaeol
Society of Architectural Historians, Hon. Secretary, 6 Fitzroy Square, London. W1T 5DX www.sahgb.org.uk
Society of Archivists, Prioryfield House, 20 Canon Street, Taunton, Somerset, TA1 1SW. www.archives. org.uk
Society of Genealogists, 14 Charterhouse Buildings, London EC1M 7BA. www.sog.org.uk
Society for Medieval Archaeology, University College of London, 31–4 Gordon Square, London WC1H 0PY. www.medarchsoc.org.uk
Society for Post-medieval Archaeology, 267 Kells Lane, Low Fell, Gateshead NE9 5HU. www.britarch.ac.uk/spma
Society for the Protection of Ancient Buildings, 37 Spital Square, London E1 6DY. www.spab.org.uk
Society of Scribes and Illuminators, 6 Queen Square, London WC1N 3AR. www.calligraphyonline.org.uk
Southwark Cathedral, Montague Close, London SE1 9DA. www.dswark.org.uk
Southwark Roman Catholic Cathedral, Westminster Bridge Road, London SE1 7HY. www.southwark-rc-cathedral.org.uk
Southwell Minster, Bishops Drive, Southwell, Nottinghamshire NG25 0JP. www.southwellminster.org.uk

The Stationery Office (TSO). www.tso.co.uk
Tiles and Architectural Ceramics Society, c/o 37 Mosley Road, Timperley, Altringham WA15 7TF. www.tilesoc.org.uk
Truro Cathedral, Cathedral Office, 14 St Mary's Street, Truro, Cornwall TR1 2AF. www.trurocathedral.org.uk

Victoria and Albert Museum, Cromwell Road, South Kensington, London SW7 2RL. www.vam.ac.uk
Victorian Society, 1 Priory Gardens, Bedford Park, London W4 1TT. www.victorian-society.org.uk

Wakefield Cathedral, Northgate, Wakefield WF1 1HG. www.wakefield-cathedral.org.uk
Wells Cathedral, Chain Gate, Cathedral Green, Wells, Somerset BA5 2UE. www.wellscathedral.org.uk
Welsh Historic Monuments Office *see* Historic Buildings Council for Wales
Westminster Abbey, 20 Dean's Yard, London SW1P 3PA. www.westminster-abbey.org.uk
Westminster Roman Catholic Cathedral, 42 Francis Street, London SW1P 1QW. www.westminstercathedral.org.uk
Wimborne Minster, High Street, Wimborne Minster, Dorset BH21 1HT. www.wimborneminster.org.uk
Winchester Cathedral, 1 The Close, Winchester, Hampshire SO23 9LS. www.winchester-cathedral.org.uk
Worcester Cathedral, 10a College Green, Worcester WR1 2LH. www.cofe-worcester.org.uk/cathedral

York Minster, Visitors' Department, St Williams College, 4–5 College Street, York YO1 7JF. www.yorkminster.org

INDEX

Note: Bold page numbers refer to illustrations.